FOURTH EDITION

PSYCHOLOGY AND PERSONAL GROWTH

EDITED BY

Abe Arkoff

UNIVERSITY OF HAWAII AT MANOA

with

Sonja Jurick

Allyn and Bacon
BOSTON LONDON SYDNEY TORONTO

Editor in Chief, Social Sciences: Susan Badger
Senior Editor: Laura Pearson
Editorial Assistant: Marnie Greenhut
Cover Administrator: Linda Dickinson
Manufacturing Buyer: Louise Richardson
Editorial-Production Service: York Production Services

Cover Art: "Heart of Halley's". Original oil by George Sumner
A Division of Simon & Schuster, Inc.
160 Gould Street
Needham Heights, Massachusetts 02194

"Heart of Halley's"
© 1985, George Sumner.
Sumner Fine Arts,
Sausalito, CA 94965

Library of Congress Cataloging-in-Publication Data
Psychology and personal growth / edited by Abe Arkoff with Sonja
    Jurick. — 4th ed.
        p. cm.
    Includes bibliographical references.
    ISBN 0–205–13699—0
    1. Psychology. 2. Maturation (Psychology) 3. Self-actualization
(Psychology) I. Arkoff, Abe. II. Jurick, Sonja.
BF149.P835 1993
158—dc20   92–2434
                                                       CIP

Printed in the United States of America
10 9 8 7 6 5 4 3   98 97 96

For my fellow growers
Susan, Amy, and Ty

OVERVIEW

CONTENTS

THANKS

I am grateful to the following for writing so rousingly on psychology and personal growth and for allowing me to include their work in this book:

Robert E. Alberti and Michael L. Emmons. "Reaching Out." Excerpted from their book *Stand Up, Speak Out, Talk Back!* Copyright © 1975 by Robert E. Alberti and Michael L. Emmons. Reprinted by permission of Pocket Books, a division of Simon & Schuster, Inc.

Bem P. Allen. "Beautyism." Condensed from *Personality, Social and Biological Perspectives on Personal Adjustment*, pages 347–355. Copyright © 1990 by Bem P. Allen. Reprinted by permission of Brooks/Cole Publishing Co.

Clayton Barbeau. "Tough Guy, Little Boy or Person?" Condensed from *Delivering the Male* (San Francisco: Ikon Press, 1992). Used by permission of the author.

Karen Barrett. "Two-Career Couples: How They Do It." Reprinted by permission of the author from *Ms.* Magazine, June 1984.

Emanuel M. Berger. "Vocational Choices in College." Originally published in the *Personnel and Guidance Journal* 1967, 45, 888–894. Copyright © 1967 by the American Personnel and Guidance Association. Adapted and reprinted by permission.

Melinda Blau. "Adult Children—Tied to the Past." Reprinted by permission of *American Health* from its July/August 1990 issue. © 1990 by Melinda Blau.

Harold Bloomfield and Robert B. Kory. "Getting Unstuck: Joyfully Recreating Your Life" and "The Successful Life." Excerpted from their book *Inner Joy* and used by permission of Harold H. Bloomfield. Copyright © 1980 by Harold H. Bloomfield, M.D., and Robert B. Kory.

Harry Browne. "Freedom from Pretense." Reprinted with the permission of Macmillan Publishing Company from *How I Found Freedom in an Unfree World* by Harry Browne. Copyright © 1973 by Harry Browne.

Janice Castro. "The Simple Life." From "The Simple Life," *Time*, April 8, 1991. Copyright © 1991, The Time Inc. Magazine Co. Reprinted by permission.

James Lincoln Collier. "Winning over Worry." Reprinted with permission of the author and publisher from the April 1988 *Reader's Digest*.

Ken Dychtwald and Joe Flower. "The Cyclic Life." From *Age Wave* by Ken Dychtwald and Joe Flower. Copyright © 1989 by Ken Dychtwald. Reprinted by permission of Jeremy P. Tarcher, Inc., Los Angeles, California.

Wayne W. Dyer. "First Love." Excerpt from *Your Erroneous Zones* by Wayne W. Dyer. Copyright © 1976 by Wayne W. Dyer. Reprinted by permission of HarperCollins Publishers.

Kay Ebeling. "Casualties on the Road to Equality." Condensed from *Newsweek*, November 19, 1990, p. 9. Used by permission of the author.

Nora Ephron. "A Few Words about Breasts." From Nora Ephron, *Crazy Salad: Some Things about Women* (New York: Alfred A. Knopf, 1972). Reprinted by permission of International Creative Management, Inc. Copyright © 1972 by Nora Ephron.

Susan Faludi. "Backlash—the Undeclared War against American Women." From *Backlash* by Susan Faludi. Copyright © 1991 by Susan Faludi. Reprinted by permission of Crown Publishers, Inc.

Erich Fromm. "Self Love." Excerpt from *The Art of Loving* by Erich Fromm. Copyright © 1956 by Erich Fromm. Reprinted by permission of HarperCollins Publishers.

Nancy Gibbs. "The Road to Equality." From "The Dreams of Youth," *Time* (Fall 1990). Copyright 1990 The Time Inc. Magazine Company. Reprinted by permission.

Herb Goldberg. "The New Male: From Self-Destruction to Self-Care." Excerpted from his book of the same name by permission of William Morrow & Company, Inc. Copyright © 1979 by Herb Goldberg.

Daniel Goldstine, Katherine Larner, Shirley Zuckerman, and Hilary Goldstine. "The Three Stages of Love." A condensation of chapters 12, 14, and 17 in the authors' book *The Dance-Away Lover*, as it appeared in *New Woman*. Copyright © 1977 by Daniel Goldstine, Katherine Larner, Shirley Zuckerman, and Hilary Goldstine. Used by permission of William Morrow & Company, Inc.

Sol Gordon and Craig W. Snyder. "Coming to Terms with Your Own Sexuality" and "Cohabitation, Singlehood, and Gay Relationships." condensed from *Personal Issues in Human Sexuality* by Sol Gordon and Craig W. Snyder. Copyright © 1989, 1986 by Allyn and Bacon.

Lois Gould. "X: A Fabulous Child's Story." Copyright © 1972 by Lois Gould from a book with the same title published by Daughters Publishing Co., Inc. Permission for reprint here granted by Daughters Publishing Co., Inc.

Jerry Greenwald. "Loneliness-Inducing Games." Excerpted by permission from his book *Be the Person You Were Meant to Be* and an article, "Self-Induced Loneliness," in *Voices*, 1972, 8(1), 14–23. Used by permission of the author and publisher.

Amy Gross. "Small Terrors, Secret Heroics." Reprinted with permission of the author from *Mademoiselle*, June 1974. Copyright © 1974 by the Condé Nast Publications Inc.

Leonard H. Gross. "Short, Dark, and Almost Handsome." Reprinted by permission of author and publisher from *Ms.* Magazine, June 1975. Copyright © 1975 by Ms. Magazine Corporation.

printed by permission of the publisher from *College Is Only the Beginning: A Student Guide to Higher Education*, 2/e by John N. Gardner and A. Jerome Jewler. © 1989 by Wadsworth, Inc.

Robert Ornstein and David Sobel. "The Confidence Game." From *Healthy Pleasures*, © 1989, by Robert Ornstein and David Sobel. Reprinted with permission of Addison-Wesley Publishing Company.

M. Scott Peck. "Responsibility." Excerpted from *The Road Less Traveled*. Copyright © 1978 by M. Scott Peck, M.D. Reprinted by permission of Simon & Schuster, Inc.

Carin Rubenstein and Phillip Shaver. "Active Solitude." From *In Search of Intimacy* by Carin Rubenstein and Phillip Shaver. Copyright © 1982 by Carin Rubenstein and Phillip Shaver. Used by permission of Dell Books, a division of Bantam Doubleday Dell Publishing Group, Inc.

William A. Sadler, Jr. "The Causes of Loneliness." From *Science Digest* (July 1975). Used by permission of the author.

Lorna J. Sarrel and Philip M. Sarrel. "Sexual Unfolding—Ten Steps toward Adult Sexuality." Adapted with the permission of Macmillan Publishing Company from *Sexual Turning Points* by Lorna J. Sarrel, M.S.W., and Philip M. Sarrel, M.D. Copyright © 1984, 1992 by Philip and Lorna Sarrel, Ltd.

Martin Shepard. "Parents." Reprinted with permission of the author from his *The Do-it-Yourself Psychotherapy Book*. Copyright © 1976 by Martin Shepard.

Daniel A. Sugarman and Lucy Freeman. "The Positive Face of Anxiety." From their book *The Search for Serenity* (New York: Macmillan, 1970). Reprinted by permission of Curtis Brown, Ltd. Copyright © 1970 by Daniel A. Sugarman and Lucy Freeman.

Deborah Tannen. "You Just Don't Understand." Reprinted with permission from the December 1990 *Reader's Digest* with permission of Reader's Digest and William Morrow & Co., Inc. Adapted from *You Just Don't Understand* by Deborah Tannen. Copyright © 1990 by Deborah Tannen.

Carol Tavris. "No-Fault Psychology." Copyright © 1989 by Carol Tavris, Ph.D. Originally appeared in. *Vogue* (January 1989). And "Anger: The Misunderstood Emotion." From *Anger: The Misunderstood Emotion*. Copyright © 1982 by Carol Tavris, Reprinted by permission of Simon & Schuster, Inc.

J. William Worden and William Proctor. "What's Your PDA?" From *PDA: Personal Death Awareness* (New York: Prentice-Hall, 1976). Copyright © 1976 by J. William Worden, Ph.D., and William Proctor.

I am also grateful for permission to use the following special materials:

Letters to the Editor from Peter V. Fossel, Lois Demin Hedman, Robert Ingle, Crystal Jarek, Richard Levine, and Tina Porod, that were published in Time magazine in April 1991.

The poem "My dog is a plumber" by Dan Greenburg through the kindness of the Free to Be Foundation, Inc.

The poems "Beyond Perls" by Walter Tubbs and "Beyond Perls and Tubbs: A Chinese Viewpoint" by You-Yuh Kuo from *The Journal of Humanistic Psychology*, vol. 17, no. 3 (Summer 1977), pp. 77–79. Copyright © 1977 by Association of Humanistic Psychology. Reprinted by permission of Sage Publications, Inc.

The poem "Sex" by Arthur Guiterman through the kindness of his wife, Mrs. Arthur Guiterman.

A condensation of a case study from *The Silent Majority* by William A. Westley and Nathan B. Epstein through the kindness of the publisher, Jossey-Bass, and the authors.

An excerpt from a letter by Abraham Maslow through the kindness of his wife, Bertha G. Maslow.

The figure showing the relationship between appearance and the good things in life which is reprinted from Elaine Hatfield and Susan Sprecher, *Mirror, Mirror... The Importance of Looks in Everyday Life* by permission of the State University of New York Press. © 1986 the State University of New York.

An excerpt from Ann Landers's column, July 1, 1986. Permission granted by Ann Landers and Creators Syndicate.

The poem "To remember me" through the kindness of the poet, Robert Test. Copyright 1980 Robert Noel Test.

Excerpts from *Learned Optimism* by Martin Seligman. Copyright © 1991 by Martin Seligman. Reprinted by permission of Alfred A. Knopf, Inc.

The cover art, "Heart of Halley's" through the kindness of the painter George Sumner.

The readings entitled "The Basic Relationship," "Little Joys," "The Psychology of Optimism," "The Meaning of Personal Growth," "The Dying-Readiness/Freedom-to-Live Test," and "Myths about Love" are taken or adapted from *The Illuminated Life* by Abe Arkoff. Copyright © 1991, 1992 by Abe Arkoff. All rights reserved.

The reading entitled "Some Common Defenses" is revised from *Adjustment and Mental Health* by Abe Arkoff (New York: McGraw-Hill, 1968). Used by permission of the publisher.

Abe Arkoff

AND MORE THANKS

I am grateful to the many students and instructors who, over the years, have helped me select the readings for four editions of this book. My aim in producing a *readings text* rather than a conventional text has been to allow students to hear directly many provocative voices in the field of personal growth. My approach has been, first, to present my own students with readings that I have found rousing and important. Those readings that receive high student ratings go out to a panel of instructors for further evaluation. The readings that appear in each edition of this book are those that both students and instructors rate high.

Hundreds of students have helped in the selection of materials for this book—too many to acknowledge by name. The instructors who have assisted me in making selections for this edition are:

Andrew Barclay
Michigan State University

Roelof Bÿkerk
Grand Valley State University

James Calhoun
University of Georgia, Athens

Barbara Elicker
Sinclair Community College

Judith A. Farrell
Moorpark College

Wesley L. Fisher
Gloucester County College

Larry Fujinaka
Leeward Community College

Todd Gaffaney
Cerritos College

Kathryn Goddard
California State College, Long Beach

John Hartman
Southwestern Michigan College

Patricia L. Kranz
Millersville University

Arlin Mauer
Solano Community College

Suzanne Randolph
University of Maryland, College Park

Rick Risbrough
Diablo Valley College

Mark S. Warner
Louisiana State University

For their skilled and caring assistance, I am grateful to Sonja Jurick and to the following at Allyn and Bacon: Bill Barke, Editorial Director; Susan Badger, Editor-in-Chief, Social Sciences; Laura Pearson, Senior Editor; and Marnie Greenhut, Editorial Assistant. I am also grateful to York Production Services.

Abe Arkoff

TO THE READER

Who are you? You singly, not you together.
When did it start—that long day's journey into self?
When do you really begin to know what you believe
  and where you're going?
When do you know that you are unique—separate—alone?
                                        —Marya Mannes

Who in the world am I?
Oh, that's the great puzzle.
                    —Lewis Carroll

"Who Am I?"

This is a question we may seldom ask, at least in this form, but all through life we strive to find out who we are and to make some sense of our existence. Our search can be a happy exploration or a painful struggle. We seek to understand our many puzzling thoughts and feelings. We seek to assemble the many bits of our behavior to somehow make a whole. And, with encouragement, we may try to get behind the defenses we have so carefully erected to keep us from seeing ourselves and being ourselves.

"Who Am I Becoming?"

This is perhaps a more important question. One reason we have trouble knowing ourselves is that we are constantly changing. At the end of even the most uneventful day we are different from the person we were at the beginning. Some of us are eager to change and to cast off the old and try on the new. Others fear change and try to freeze themselves into what they already are. But eager or fearful, we are all caught up in a process of change—a journey of becoming that continues throughout life.

"Who Could I Be?"

This may be the most important question of the three. Within each of us are more powers than are ever tapped and developed, and within society today are more pathways to choose from than ever before. Who will we be 5 years, 10 years, 20 years from now? Who *could* we be if we are free to grow and know how to grow and know what to grow into?

The topics and readings in this book have been selected to help you in your search for answers to these questions and others like them. Taken together, the readings provide an introduction to the psychology of personhood or personal growth. I hope that these materials may help you gain a deeper insight into the processes, problems, and pleasures of becoming a person.

Abe Arkoff

PSYCHOLOGY AND PERSONAL GROWTH

PART

one

SHAPING
IDENTITY

There are over 5 billion people in the world today, and no two are exactly alike. You are unique. No one else looks exactly like you. No one else thinks or feels or acts the way you do. The qualities that distinguish you as a person and differentiate you from every other person make up your *identity*.

Sidney Jourard wrote that each of us, in a sense, is an invention. We are the persons we have been persuaded to be by our culture, our families, our teachers, and other "significant others." We have been taught how to think, how to feel, and how to act. Of course, we have a hand in the process, and if we don't like the way we are invented, we can get busy and re-invent ourselves.

Identity is a key concept or idea in the study of human beings. Once we humans gain some sense of our identity, we tend to behave in accordance with it. We think of ourselves as persons who can do certain things but who can't do certain other things. We think of ourselves as persons who should behave in this way and who must not behave in that way.

Generally speaking, we are most comfortable when we are being ourselves. We are upset when our thoughts and feelings and actions are not in harmony with the persons we think we are. And we are also upset when we are cast in situations or roles that demand behavior inconsistent with our concept of ourselves.

A strong—but not too strong—sense of identity is a highly valued attribute. With this sense, we know who we are, and we can relate this to who we have been and who we are becoming. There is change, but amid this change there is a core of sameness and continuity.

Erik Erikson, who has written extensively on the concept of identity, notes two problems especially prominent in adolescence and young adult-hood. The first problem, *identity diffusion*, describes those of us who are unable to define ourselves. We don't know who we are. We cannot hit upon a style of life, a way of relating to others, or a career direction.

The second problem, closely related to the first, is called *identity crisis.* This term can apply to a person who is in an acute stage of identity diffusion, but it is also an apt description of those of us whose concept of ourselves has become grossly unacceptable or out of keeping with the roles and goals we face. As a result, it becomes abruptly necessary for us to redefine ourselves to fit our lives or redesign our lives to fit ourselves.

Today's society is changing at a rapid pace and calling upon its members to change too. We are in for some interesting identity problems in the times ahead. Traditional ideas of what it means to be a male or a female, a student or a teacher, an employer or an employee, a child, a parent, or a spouse—the list could go on and on—are under assault. We may be continually called upon to re-invent or redefine ourselves or at least to arrive at a definition more open to change.

The three topics in Part I of this book relate closely to identity and have been selected to give the reader a fuller understanding of this important idea. The first topic, *self-image,* pertains to the picture or view we have of the total self. The second topic, *body image,* concerns our concept of the physical self, which is of course a salient part of the self-image. And the last topic in Part I is the *sex-role image,* which concerns our sense of maleness or femaleness that—from the moment of birth—is an inescapable aspect of who we are.

Self-Image

O wad some Power the giftie gie us
To see ourselves as others see us!
                    —Robert Burns

If we could see ourselves as others see us,
We might never speak to them again.
                    —Anonymous

Our *self-image* is the conception or picture we have of ourselves. It is the way we see ourselves. It is what we think ourselves to be.

Our self-image begins to form very early in life. In infancy, we constantly explore ourselves and the world around us. We learn what is "me" and what is "not me" and discover we are separate beings. We learn to respond to our own names and acquire a sense of our own identities.

As we grow, we develop an increasingly complex and sophisticated image of who we are. Our self-image is heavily influenced by certain "significant others"—the persons with whom we are in close interaction. In our earlier years, these influential persons almost certainly include our mothers, and fathers, our siblings, and perhaps other family members such as grandparents or uncles, aunts, and cousins. Later, neighborhood persons and teachers and schoolmates help shape our image of ourselves.

In our interaction with these significant others we come to a large extent to see ourselves as others see us. We learn from others' reactions what our qualities are and the value or worth attached to these qualities. We learn the areas of endeavor in which we do well and those in which we do poorly. We learn how competent, how attractive, how acceptable, how lovable we are.

With increasing age, we become less vulnerable to others and to the forces of our environment. We arrive at a firmer sense of self that is less open to challenge and change. But we also may become more adept at masking undesirable personal qualities—hiding them from ourselves as well as from others—until we become strangers to ourselves and scarcely know who we are.

Some psychologists believe that the basic human force or tendency is our striving to maintain and enhance our concept of ourselves. Other workers in this area do not assign the same preeminence to the self-image, but clinical and experimental evidence suggest that this image pervades each person's thoughts, attitudes, feelings, and actions. Once there is an understanding of who a person thinks he or she is, it becomes possible to better understand that individual's present behavior, relate the present to the past, and even make some predictions about the future.

Recently, educational programs designed to enhance self-esteem in various groups have gotten criticized. Critics worry that such programs may encourage us to feel better about ourselves without prompting us to become better, but the two go together; as we feel more worthy, we become more effective, and as we become more effective, we feel more worthy. Furthermore, it is important for us to feel good about certain indelible aspects of ourselves just as they are, for example, our race and ethnic background and gender.

KNOW YOURSELF

The first reading, written by Abe Arkoff,[1] suggests that the way we come to see and regard ourselves could be called "the basic relationship" because it becomes such a fundamental force in our lives. It is a force that affects our perceptions of our world, what we do in that world, and how we relate to our fellow human beings. This reading recommends that we improve the basic relationship by learning to know ourselves better and by accepting, prizing, and becoming the self each of us truly is.

LOVE YOURSELF

Wayne Dyer's advice in the second reading is to love ourselves first. If we care enough for ourselves, we can let those we care for be themselves. We don't need to manipulate them into shoring us up. Surprisingly, as Dyer shows, there are rewards to be gotten for not loving ourselves, but it's a costly business. A better bargain is Dyer's "easy-to-master self-love exercises."

---

1. My aim in producing a readings text rather than a conventional text is to allow students to hear many voices and viewpoints rather than just one. Still, as you will note, I manage to pipe up quite often. Whenever I couldn't find a reading that seemed necessary and appropriate, I sat down and wrote it.—THE EDITOR

CONTROL YOURSELF

In the last reading, Carol Tavris writes, "We are in the midst of an excuse epidemic in America." The authorities she cites note that we are increasingly led to define some of our common problems as "addictions" and ourselves as victims of life and biology. Our failure to accept responsibility and exercise control over our lives makes difficulties for others but even more for ourselves because it undermines our self-esteem.

To Explore Your Own Self-Image[2]

1. *Who am I? (twenty answers).* At the top of a sheet of paper write "Who am I?" Then quickly complete twenty answers to this question. Afterward analyze your answers. Also analyze your answering behavior—that is, the freedom with which your answers came, possible tendencies to self-censor your answers, and so on.
2. *Who am I? (essay answer).* At the top of a sheet of paper write "Who am I?" and then complete a brief essay to answer this question.
3. *Who am I? (dyad answers).* Pair with another person. "Who are you?" asks the first member of the pair. When the second member answers, the first member says "thank you" and without further comment asks the same question again and keeps asking it, pausing only for the response. When the second member runs out of answers (or when a prearranged time limit has been reached), the two members exchange roles and proceed as before. Afterward, the pair discusses what they have learned from this procedure.
4. *Who am I? Who would I like to be? (collage symbolization).* Construct two collages. The first collage is to represent your self-image or the way you see yourself. The second collage is to represent your desired self or the self you would like to be. To construct your collages, proceed in this way: Gather together some old magazines, and leaf through them without any preconceived notions of what you are looking for. Be passive and let the materials in each magazine nominate themselves. As something in a magazine suggests itself as an element of your self-image or desired self, cut it out and put it in the appropriate pile. When your search is complete, cull and synthesize the elements in each pile, and paste them onto the appropriate page. Don't put too much in each collage; include just what is strongest or most compelling. When you have completed the collages, write a description of each, indicating the meaning of the elements and insights you gained from this exploration.

---

2. These explorations or exercises—and those that are presented for each succeeding topic of this book—include some for groups of various sizes and some for pairs or for individuals.

5. *Who am I? Who would I like to be? (animal symbolization).* If you were to be reborn as an animal, what animal would you like to be? Write down the name of the animal and indicate why you find its qualities appealing. Also indicate the extent to which these qualities are present or absent in your present life.

6. *Who am I? Who do others think I am? (sack art).* Decorate the inside of a large grocery sack to represent your self-image or the way you see yourself. Decorate the outside to represent the self you think others see, the way you think you appear to others. Share the outside of your sack with others to see if they indeed see you as you think they do. Share the inside of your sack only if you wish to do so.

7. *Who am I? Who do others think I am? (small group validation).* Form a small group. Each member in turn serves as the focus. This person writes down the impression she or he thinks the group has of her or him. At the same time, the other members write down the impressions they have of the focal person. Then the focal person and other members read and discuss the congruence or incongruence of their separate images.

8. *Who am I? Who are all the I's of me? (situational selves).* You may have noted that you behave very differently in various kinds of situations, almost as if you were a different person in each. Some psychologists believe that we are so strongly affected by our environment that we should think of ourselves as relatively plastic and variable rather than fixed and stable. For example, we may be quite different when we are at home from when we are in the classroom or on the job. At the top of a piece of paper write down three situations or environments in which you commonly find yourself; then write a description of how you see yourself in each of these situations. Or write down the names of three of the most important persons in your life; then write descriptions of yourself as you see yourself interacting with each of these persons. Or, if you prefer, describe yourself as you think each of these persons would describe you.

9. *Who am I? Who are all the I's of me? (subselves).* You may have noted that your behavior varies considerably, almost as if you were different persons. Some psychologists believe it fitting to think of each person as a composite of a number of subpersonalities, all vying for expression. Think about your own subpersonalities and draw a flower with a petal of an appropriate size, shape, and color to represent each. Then label the petals and write an explanation of your flower.

10. *Who am I? What is the enduring core of me? (the core self).* You may have noted that you tend to be quite consistent in your behavior and relatively resistant to change. Some psychologists believe that the most important or central features of our self-image become stable and enduring; although less important, peripheral aspects may be easily acquired and changed. Draw a set of three concentric circles (a circle within a circle within a circle). In the innermost circle, list or describe those aspects of yourself (personal qualities, behaviors, values, goals, and so on) that are

most important and resistant to change. In the outermost circle, identify the least important and least stable aspects of yourself. The middle circle is for those aspects of intermediate importance and stability. As a last step, write an explanation of your circles.

11. *Who am I? What's good about me? (the positive self).* Research shows that the more positive you are in your view of yourself, the better off you are in many ways. A poor self-image can make you miserable and unable to function effectively. This exercise challenges you to think the utmost good about yourself. Pair with another person. Begin by telling something good about yourself. The other person responds by telling something good about herself or himself. Then it's your turn to tell something else that's good about you, and so on, back and forth. Continue until one of you is stuck for something to say; that means the other person wins!

12. *Who am I? What's good and not so good about me? (the positive and negative self).* At the top of a piece of paper, write "What I like about myself" and list—numbering as you go—all the things you like about yourself. Then make a list for "What I don't like about myself." Afterward, make sure that the first list is at least twice as long (or twice as important) as the second; keep working on it until it is.

To Read Further

Branden, N. (1983). *Honoring the self: The psychology of confidence and respect.* Los Angeles: J. P. Tarcher. (Bantam paperback, 1985)

Branden, N. (1987). *How to raise your self-esteem.* New York: Bantam. (Bantam paperback, 1988)

Mecca, A. M., Smelser, N. J., & Vasconcellos, J. (1989). *The social importance of self-esteem.* Berkeley: University of California Press. (paperback)

Pennebaker, J. W. (1990). *Opening up: The healing power of confiding in others.* New York: William Morrow.

Rowan, J. (1990). *Subpersonalities: The people inside us.* New York: Routledge.

Taylor, S. E. (1989). *Positive illusions: Creative self-deception and the healthy mind.* New York: Basic Books.

The Basic Relationship

Abe Arkoff

John Vasconcellos is a highly esteemed member of the California legislature, but he speaks candidly about his own early failure to value himself and of many later years of therapy to develop his self-esteem and personhood. Recently, recalling his own long trek to a better sense of self, he wrote,

> In school, I was a high-achiever, receiving awards and excellent grades. In adulthood, I became a prominent lawyer in a prestigious firm. My first campaign for a seat in the state legislature in 1966 was successful, and I have now been reelected eleven times.
>
> Yet, through it all, I had almost no sense of my self, no self-esteem. I worked for my successes only in a constant attempt to please others. My intellect functioned superbly, but the rest of my self barely functioned at all. I had been conditioned to know myself basically as a sinner, guilt-ridden and ashamed, constantly beating my breast and professing my unworthiness. I had so little self-esteem that I lost my first election (running for eighth-grade president) by one vote—my own. (Vasconcellos, 1989, pp. xiv–xv)

Vasconcellos notes that personal experience has taught him the importance of valuing oneself. He has increasingly focused on the issue of self-esteem both to help himself and others develop "a strong sense of self." He is the author of legislation creating the California Task Force to Promote Self-Esteem and Personal and Social Responsibility whose aim is to promote the well-being of the individual and society as a way of preventing rather than just reacting to serious social ills.

As a clinical psychologist, I have worked with many people who have come to me for help. Some were deeply troubled. Of these, I cannot recall a single one who had a good relationship with herself or himself. Not one was her or his own best friend. When they began to like themselves and trust themselves, I knew they were getting better. When they began to take some pride in themselves, I knew they were getting well.

Not long ago I heard a comedienne ask a group this question: "How many of you know how it feels to be the only person in a relationship?" This got a laugh, but thinking back on my clinical experience with human beings, it seems clear to me that the most important relationship we each have is the one with ourselves. How strange that most of us do not think of this as a relationship at all. How strange this is the relationship in which we sometimes appear least humane, treating ourselves in a way we would never treat somebody else.

Think about this with reference to your own self. You are always in your own presence, and just as you are aware of the world around you, you are aware of yourself. You think, you feel, you act. You also observe yourself thinking and feeling and acting. You reflect on yourself and come to know yourself. You have *reflective awareness*—the ability to consider your behavior as you observe it.

Because you have the power of reflective awareness, you are both actor and audience in your life. You perform and at the same time watch yourself perform. But you are not a passive audience. You, the audience, attend and consider. You weigh and evaluate. Sometimes you applaud, sometimes you hiss or jeer, sometimes rise and command. You (the actor) are influenced by you (the audience) just as you (the audience) are influenced by you (the actor).

Of course, there are other people in the audience too. In their response to you, they tell you who they think you are and what you can and can't do and should and shouldn't do. You observe these others and observe them observe you and observe yourself. Out of all these observations you shape and reshape the idea of who you are, and you shape and reshape your relationship to yourself. Your relationship to yourself could be called "the basic relationship" because how you come to see and regard yourself becomes such a fundamental force in your life.

THE DYNAMIC SELF-IMAGE

Our self-image is influenced by all that is happening in our life, and at the same time it is involved in making things happen—in guiding and controlling our behavior. It is dynamic, that is, active, changing, forceful (Markus & Wurf, 1987). Among its powers are those affecting the way we see our world, how we function in it, and how we relate to those with whom we come in contact.

The Self-Image and Perception

The way we perceive or view ourselves affects the way we view our world. We are the center of our universe. Perceptual psychologists Combs, Avila, and Purkey (1978) note that the self is the yardstick used to make judgments. They write, "Others are regarded as taller, shorter, smarter, more unscrupulous, older, or younger than ourself. As the self changes, the yardstick changes, and what we believe to be true changes with it. What is considered 'old' is likely to be quite differently defined at ages six, sixteen, thirty-six, or sixty" (p. 19).

In any situation the things possible for us to perceive are almost limitless. What we select to perceive and the meaning we attach to these perceptions relate closely to the picture we have of ourselves. By way of example, Don Hamachek (1978) writes, "Depending on one's concept of self, an exam is perceived as either something to avoid failing or something to pass with as high a grade as possible; a class discussion is viewed as either something to actively engage in or something to sit quietly through for fear of saying the wrong thing; front seats of classrooms are seen as either vantage points for better seeing or potentially dangerous spots where one could be more easily seen and, heaven forbid, called on!" (pp. 44–45).

The Self-Image and Behavior

Because of its influence on our perceptions, our self-image influences our behavior in many ways. Some psychologists believe that the basic human force is the striving to maintain and enhance our conception of ourselves (Combs, Richards, & Richards, 1976). We present ourselves to others in ways calculated to enhance our image in their eyes and in our own. We defend our image from attack, whether this be assault from without or doubts arising from within.

Our self-image serves us as a basic frame of reference—as a foundation or guide for our actions. We would be lost without it, and therefore we defend it against change. Some of us seem to be resistant to growth or positive movement in our lives, but this may be our way of being true to our picture of ourselves (Rosenberg, 1979).

Psychologists have suggested that when a person believes something to be so, he or she tends to behave in a way that makes it so; this is called a "self-fulfilling prophecy." If we see ourselves in a positive light, we are apt to try harder because we think our efforts will pay off, and we are more likely to succeed or define the outcome as successful. If we have a low opinion of ourselves, we may avoid a situation or approach it halfheartedly, and we are more likely to fail or to interpret the results as failure (Langer & Dweck, 1973).

The Self-Image and Relationships with Others

Our self-image influences our perceptions of others and our relationships with them. There is considerable evidence that we tend to see others as we see ourselves. Emerson wrote, "What we are, that only can we see." Hamachek (1978) adds, "When we think we are looking out a window, it could be that we are merely gazing into a looking-glass" (p. 47). He suggested that a good way to find out what a person is really like is to find out what this person thinks others are like. He writes, "The man who tells us that people are basically trustworthy and kind—ignoring the plain fact that they can also be devious and cruel—may be saying more about himself than about the world" (p. 47).

People who like and accept themselves tend to accept others (Berger, 1952; Pirot, 1986). Research shows that individuals who hold themselves in high esteem tend to take a favorable view of others and also expect more acceptance and less rejection (Baron, 1974; Walster, 1965). And, of course, when others are approached in this light, they are more likely to respond favorably.

If we dislike or reject ourselves, we are more likely to view and treat others in the same way, and consequently our relations with others will suffer. Oscar Wilder observed that "all criticism is a form of autobiography." Hamachek suggests some personal research that one can do on this point. He writes, "Pay particular attention to your feelings about yourself for the next three or four days and note how they influence your behavior toward others. It may be that it is not our friend or our loved one or our children we are mad at; it is ourselves. What we feel toward ourselves gets aimed at others, and we sometimes treat others not as persons, but as targets" (p. 46).

We tend to form relationships with persons who are similar to us, who see us as we see ourselves and who confirm our own positive self-impressions (Swann, 1984; Taylor & Brown, 1988). It's hard for us to rest easy in the company of those who don't see us as we wish to be seen (Laing, Phillipson, & Lee, 1966). Joseph Joubert understood this prime requisite of friendship when he wrote, "When my friends are one-eyed, I look at their profile."

THE MULTIPLE SELF

One of Shakespeare's most famous lines (part of the counsel that Polonius gives his son Laertes in *Hamlet*) reads, "This above all: to thine own self be true." Kenneth Gergen (1972), a psychologist who has made an extensive study of the self-concept, calls this advice "poor psychology." He believes we are unlikely to find a single self to be true to.

Gergen's research suggests that we are considerably affected by the situations in which we find ourselves—the self we are in one situation may be very different from the self we are in another. Different environments may prompt different thoughts and feelings about ourselves and therefore different behaviors. When we are talking to someone who is in a superior position, our self-relevant thoughts and feelings may be quite different from when we are with a subordinate. When we are standing up to a group, we may see ourselves differently from when we have reluctantly decided to go along with it (Markus & Kunda, 1986).

Gergen questions the assumption that many psychologists and laypersons make that it is

good—or even normal—to have a firm and coherent sense of self. In fact, he suggests that we should become concerned when we become too comfortable with a self or set in a particular identity. This may simply mean we have settled into a routine of the same situations ("a rut") that calls forth the same old responses.

Gergen concludes that "we are made of soft plastic and molded by social circumstances," but other research suggests that the self-concept is not all that malleable. Taken together, the evidence supports the conclusion that the self-concept is *both* stable and malleable. We have a certain core of ideas about ourselves, and we resist information that challenges this core. At the same time, we are influenced by the situations in which we find ourselves. How we see ourselves in a particular situation results from the reconciliation of self-conceptions prompted by this core and those called forth by that situation (Markus & Kunda, 1986). It can be trying when a core conception is challenged—for example, when we pride ourselves on our honesty but also see we are sorely tempted to lie or cheat to gain an important end.

Subpersonalities

Another psychologist, John Vargiu (1977), also believes that we may not be a single self, but he doesn't agree with Gergen that we shouldn't be. Where Gergen attributes our variability to the varying situations in which we find ourselves, Vargiu attributes it to a number of *subpersonalities*—semi-autonomous personages within us all striving for expression. He holds that we need to understand these subpersonalities better and bring them into harmony with each other; doing so, we become a single harmonized self.

St. Augustine eloquently described the struggle between two of his subpersonalities—the "animal man" and the "spiritual man." Recalling this struggle in his *Confessions*, he wrote, "My inner self was a house divided against itself." Ted Kennedy was described in a 1991 *Time* magazine profile as seemingly a person of several sets of selves. One set: statesman, serious lawmaker, family patriarch. The other set: over-age, drunken frat-house boor and party animal. The profiler suggested, "A man with Kennedy's temperament and past may need a sort of unofficial self that he can plunge back into now and then—

a rowdy, loutish oblivion where he feels easy, where he takes a woozy vacation from being a Kennedy" (Morrow, 1991, p. 27).

You may recall seeing an acquaintance behave in a quite uncharacteristic way. You wonder, what's got into him? Or you think, she's not herself today. Of course, she *is* herself—but a different one of her selves or subselves or subpersonalities.

Consider the inconsistencies or subpersonalities that may exist within yourself. Have you noted that you sometimes seem to get caught up in a particular way of being and behaving? You recognize it and could even give it a label since it is so salient and you have been caught up in it before. When you are under its spell, you see yourself and your world differently and behave differently, perhaps in a way you like or don't like. You may be able to identify a number of these subpersonalities in yourself, some in harmony and some in conflict with each other.

It may be useful to identify and study the subpersonalities in yourself. When I did so recently, these subselves were most salient: The Creative but Tiring Soul (a subself that enjoyed creating something new or different and watching it develop—for awhile), Dad (a caring, helpful subself), The Relentless Searcher (a subself that was always looking for something better but never quite finding it), and The Wise Old Man (an emerging subself, one with the ability to understand, accept and enjoy things as they are). I was pleased to note that The Examiner (a subself that was constantly scrutinizing things to see if they measured up) had been largely decommissioned.

It is important not to confuse the concept of "subpersonalities," which applies to normal behavior, with that of "multiple personality," which is a serious and disabling disorder (Rowan, 1990). This latter condition is quite rare and better known to Hollywood and television script writers than to psychiatrists or psychologists. The added personalities in multiple personality disorder are quite autonomous, even with differences in handedness (left or right dominance) and in patterns of handwriting and brain waves (Putnam, 1984) and usually operate without the awareness of the original personality.

Possible Selves

Markus and her colleagues (Markus & Kunda, 1986; Markus & Nurius, 1986) have been inter-ested in the concept of *possible selves*—the images we have concerning the persons we might be in the future. These include the selves we expect to be, the selves we hope to be, and also those we fear we might become. These images function as incentives and serve to guide us toward certain kinds of behaviors and away from others.

Markus (Possible selves, 1987) points out that our possible selves are influenced by our individual histories and also by developments in society. Social advances such as increased opportunities for women and blacks create new hoped-for possible selves among these groups. New or exacerbated social problems create new dreaded possible selves such as the AIDS-afflicted self, the drug-dependent self, the bag lady, and the street person.

The most striking finding of a study that compared possible selves in delinquent and nondelinquent boys (Oyserman & Markus, 1986) was the intensely negative set of feared selves among the delinquents (for example, being alone, poor, depressed, flunking out of school, junkie, drug pusher, criminal). Unwanted possible selves are not necessarily a negative influence because they can motivate the person to avoid them or to prepare to cope with them. However, for this process to be fully effective, the negative possible self must be countered by a positive possible self or direction that suggests what might be done. Not surprisingly, delinquent boys proved to have fewer matched pairs of negative and positive selves.

THE SELF-IMAGE, BODY IMAGE, AND GENDER

We live in a society in which looks are important. In many areas of our lives, attractive people fare better than those who are unattractive (Allen, 1990; Hatfield & Sprecher, 1986). One would expect good-looking persons to feel better about themselves than do those who are homely. But a review of pertinent research indicates that there is little connection between what we actually look like (as determined by objective judges) and our overall self-esteem (Hatfield & Sprecher, 1986).

While self-esteem is largely unrelated to what we *actually* look like, it is positively related to what we *think* we look like. Research indicates that persons who are satisfied with their bodies are likely to have a positive self-concept and to be satisfied with themselves generally. Persons dissatisfied with their bodies tend to have less favorable general impressions of themselves. This suggests that if we like our looks we like ourselves, or if we like ourselves, we like our looks (Hatfield & Sprecher, 1986).

"How can beautiful people end up with low self-esteem? How can physically unappealing men and women manage to maintain their self-regard?" These are questions posed by Hatfield and Sprecher. They found evidence that beautiful men and women were much more interested in appearance than were homely individuals; if beautiful folks bank their self-esteem on their looks, and surround themselves with or compare themselves to other beautiful people, they might feel a little less sure of themselves, for there is almost always someone superior somehow (and, of course, there is the awareness that beauty in time can be a depreciating asset). On the other hand, homelier folks may be less likely to move in beautiful circles or circles where beauty is highly valued or where unfavorable comparisons might be drawn, and they may be more likely to make more of their other attributes. These other attributes can be more enduring than physical beauty.

In much of the world, gender as well as beauty can grant status, and it can be a considerable advantage to be male. Males are generally more privileged and have more power. A study of stereotypes in 30 countries showed that in most countries, stereotypes of females are more negative than those of males (Williams & Best, 1982). It doesn't come as a surprise that a review of 29 studies between 1975 and 1985 showed that men generally have higher self-esteem than women (Skaalvik, 1986).

Research also indicates that women are less confident than men. Men and women interpret success differently: men tend to attribute their successes to internal factors—their own effort and ability—while women tend to attribute success to external factors—the ease of the task, luck, or fate. For failure, it's just the other way around: women who before sacrificed the credit suddenly turn internal and shoulder the blame (Tavris & Wade, 1984).

Several studies (Birnbaum, 1975; Coleman & Antonucci, 1982) found that married women who were employed outside the home had higher self-esteem than those who weren't. Outside employment apparently provides a sense of autonomy and mastery. Such employment can also provide women with more power in the family, and the greater the earnings the greater the power.

Tavris (McCarthy, 1990) believes that psychological research in this area is flawed because it assumes that the male is the norm and males are used as the basis of comparison. In this biased approach Tavris says, "Women have lower self-esteem than men do; women do not value their efforts as much as men do; women have more difficulty in developing a 'separate sense of self' " (p. 33). Tavris points out that if in the same studies the bias had been reversed and women had been used as the basis of comparison, these might have been the conclusions: "Men are more conceited than women; men are not as realistic as women in assessing abilities; men have more difficulty in forming and maintaining attachments" (p. 33).

IMPROVING OUR RELATIONSHIP TO OURSELVES

How can we improve our relationship to ourselves? We can take a big step forward by getting to know ourselves better and by allowing others to know us. Some further steps involve learning to accept, prize, and become ourselves. All of these steps are discussed more fully later in this reading.

Knowing Ourselves

"The unexamined life is not worth living," Socrates said. "Know thyself" has been the continuing advice of philosophers and poets through the centuries. It is fairly stock advice of clinical psychologists and psychiatrists today.

Not everyone agrees with this advice. In her recent book *What I Saw at the Revolution* (a memoir of the Reagan White House), presidential speechwriter Peggy Noonan called her boss the "least introspective of men . . . living proof that the unexamined life is worth living." The late actor Peter Sellers, known as "the great impersonator" and as someone who vanished into his roles, told an interviewer that he got to where he was by not following Socrates's advice. "To me," he said, "I'm a complete stranger" (Ansen, 1980, p. 43). In 1989, Donald Trump told an interviewer that he didn't want to be examined in any depth by anyone, including himself. "When you start studying yourself too deeply," he said, "you start seeing things that maybe you don't want to see" (Friedrich & McDowell, 1989, p. 54). Subsequent events suggest he might want to review this strategy.

Research suggests it's not so easy for us to see what we don't want to see. A prime reason for this is that, as psychologist Anthony Greenwald (1980) persuasively argues, our knowledge of ourselves is distorted by three self-serving biases. We operate like the propaganda ministries in totalitarian societies, and the truth may not be easily ascertained.

First, according to evidence mustered by Greenwald, we are *egocentric* and tend to see ourselves as more centrally involved in what is happening than we really are. We like to be important. As was noted earlier, we are at the center of our universe—we tend to overestimate our influence in a situation or the extent to which we are the target of attention. Second, we are subject to *beneffectance*, a word coined by Greenwald, to describe our tendency to take credit for what proves good but not the responsibility for what proves bad. We like to be well-regarded. For example, winners in almost any enterprise are more willing to accept the praise than losers are to accept the blame. Third, we tend to show *cognitive conservatism;* this describes our tendency to manage new information so that it accords with what we already know or think we do. We like to appear right. This may lead us to stick with old ideas about ourselves despite new facts or to revise our memories to make them agree with the new information.

There are various ways we filter incoming information and distort it to enhance ourselves. As noted earlier, we construct social relationships that facilitate positive or, at least, self-confirming self-impressions (Swann, 1984; Taylor & Brown, 1988). We select associates who see us as we see ourselves and indeed, are somewhat like ourselves; this reinforces our belief that we are correct in our beliefs, attitudes, and attributes. Incoming information is further distorted by the human tendency to give and receive mostly positive feedback; negative feedback is withheld or muted or put in euphemistic terms, making it ambiguous (Goffman, 1955).

The Pros and Cons of Self-Focus. How much of our attention should be focused externally on the world around us? How much should be *self-focused,* that is, concentrated internally on ourselves? Rick Ingram (1990) suggests "that a relatively even balance is optional for psychological functioning" (p. 168). Research shows a heightened degree of self-focused attention in various clinical disorders such as depression, anxiety, and alcohol abuse, but there is no conclusive evidence that one is the cause of the other. Ingram proposes that in pathological states of functioning, one is not just self-focused but *self-absorbed,* a condition in which internal attention is not only excessive but also sustained and rigid.

An important insight concerning self-focus is provided by the work of Ingram and Smith (1984). Among their subjects (university students in introductory psychology), those with higher scores on a depression inventory had self-focused thoughts that were equally positive and negative while similar thoughts in students with lower depression scores were largely positive. These findings were consistent with what has been called "the power of nonnegative thinking." They suggest that self-focused attention can have positive consequences when positively directed and employed in the service of constructive change.

The Pros and Cons of Self-Deception. A strong case for "creative self-deception" is made by Shelley Taylor in her book *Positive Illusions.* *Self-deception* refers to our efforts to hide the truth from ourselves while *creative self-deception* concerns our attempts to exaggerate the positive aspects of a situation. The considerable evidence Taylor assembles indicates that a perfectly accurate knowledge of oneself and one's world is neither usual nor even desirable. This evidence shows most persons possess unrealistically (but not outlandishly) positive self-impressions. For example, we are more aware of our strengths than our weaknesses. We see ourselves as better than average and better than others see us. We have exaggerated notions of our capacity to control the important events in our lives and are overly optimistic about the future.

Taylor holds that our positive illusions are generally kept modest and in check by feedback from the environment, and these illusions promote rather than sabotage our coping effort. Positive illusions foster a positive mood and promote happiness and contentment. This, in turn, enhances other aspects of mental health, including our ability to care for and care about others, and also our confidence in ourselves and in our capacity to engage in creative and productive work.

Taylor makes an important distinction between positive illusions, which are often operative in our daily lives, and mechanisms such as denial and repression, which come into play when we defend ourselves against threat.[1] The latter, in her estimation, cause us to distort or hide the facts while the former mute or blunt the facts (which are often ambiguous anyway) and lead us to interpret them in the best possible light. Positive illusions encourage an optimistic outlook and work to promote mental and physical health.

A major limitation of some self-deception is that it can keep us from owning our problems or deficiencies and working on them. Sheldon Kopp (1976) writes, "All evil is potential vitality in need of transformation. All of you is worth something, if you will only own it" (p. 223). He explains,

> We need to be in touch with and hopefully to own every part of ourselves so that we do not continue to be at war within ourselves. If a thief comes in the night, and we cry out and so scare him off, nothing is accomplished beyond the moment, and we must remain in fear. But if we do not alarm the thief, but let him draw near enough so that we may lay hold of him and bind him, then we have the chance of reforming him. So, too, our own willful impulses can become a rich source of renewal of imaginative powers. Our stubbornness can be transformed into determination, and our struggle with the other can surrender into intimacy. Each man must confront himself in order to accomplish

these transformations, this turning of the self. (1971, p. 41)

Self-deception is most likely to be useful when it is (1) temporary, (2) reserved for what otherwise might be an overwhelming situation, and (3) serves to maximize the positive and minimize the negative content of a situation without grossly distorting the facts or preventing actions essential to well-being. But an inflated notion of self can encourage persons to ignore risks that need to be considered, disregard steps that should be taken (as, for example, in matters of health), persevere at impossible tasks, pursue careers for which they are unsuited, and fail to prepare for likely catastrophic events. Furthermore, unquestioning faith in the absolute rightness of one's beliefs can lead a person to trample on the rights of others (Taylor & Brown, 1988).

Approaches to Self-Knowledge. A useful way to gain more self-knowledge is to make ourselves the object of study just as though we were a course in which we had enrolled. During one period of his life, Sigmund Freud spent the last half-hour of each working day analyzing himself. In one of my workshops, I share some things I have learned about myself from living with myself all these years and then ask my students to write a list of things they have learned about themselves. Some are a bit dumbfounded, but once they have set themselves to the task, most find they have quite a lot to write down.

One master at the art of self-reflection is Hugh Prather. In his notebooks, he carefully observes himself and candidly shares these observations with his readers. The following brief example from his book *Notes to Myself* shows him in his watchful but positive, nurturant pursuit of self-knowledge:

> One kind of lie that I tell pops out in conversation and takes me by surprise. Sometimes I like to correct these lies right on the spot, and when I do I find that most people don't think less of me. This kind of lie, when I notice it, usually helps me see where I feel inadequate—the areas where I could be more acceptant of myself.

Wilson Van Dusen (1972), a pioneer of inner space, notes that we are constantly generating fantasies, images, and feelings that tell us who we are. He writes that "we are almost overburdened with

---

1. For a discussion of denial, repression, and similar mechanisms, see "Some Common Defenses" on pages 250–264 of this book.

clues to our own nature" (p. 4). But he concludes that we scarcely make use of these clues and, therefore, remain strangers to ourselves.

Van Dusen pictures our inner life as a "mind-castle," but one that is lamentably underesteemed and unexamined. He writes, "If one were locked up in an ancient castle for one's whole life—a castle full of artifacts, dungeons, endless rooms, art, and books—one would spend much time exploring and recreating the lives of the inhabitants" (p. 1). Van Dusen maintains that indeed we are ensconced in such a mind-castle, but we don't avail ourself of the opportunity to explore. He continues, "Many know little more than a sitting room in the east wing and assume this is the whole. The size of the mind-castle is little appreciated. It includes all you have experienced, will experience, and in the remote corners, all you can experience" (p. 1).

Van Dusen recommends cultivation of the "lost art" of self-reflection, which he describes as "a gazing at one's life and circumstances as though it were a painting to be examined, felt, appreciated" (p. 49). To do this, he says, requires (1) some minutes of peaceful leisure, (2) the experiencing of what is, and (3) mulling this over or reflecting upon it. He also recommends that one does this regularly and writes it down afterward in a personal journal.

Disclosing Ourselves

Self-disclosure is the process of sharing our private thoughts and feelings with others (Jourard, 1971). In disclosing ourselves, we come to know ourselves better. By putting our thoughts and feelings into words, they become clearer to us and even take on new or fuller meaning. We receive feedback from others, and this helps us to refine and validate our own self-awareness (Johnson, 1986).

Psychologist Sidney Jourard (1971), who pioneered this area of research, held self-disclosure to be an important component of mental health. Mentally healthy persons, he concluded, have the ability to make themselves known to at least one significant other. By contrast, less healthy persons are unable or unwilling to drop their guard. They are thus alienated from others and from their own self as well. Jourard wrote, "Every maladjusted person is a person who has not made himself known to another human

being, and in consequence does not know himself. Nor can he be himself. More than that, *he struggles actively to avoid becoming known by another human being.* He *works* at it ceaselessly, 24 hours daily, and it is work!" (pp. 32–33).

None of us is completely transparent or completely opaque, nor should we be. Too much disclosure, like too little, can have negative effects. Disclosure requires the appropriate time and place and pace and person. In a comfortable setting, we tell someone we trust something from within ourselves. They listen without judging or giving advice—just being there with us. Then perhaps they share something from within themselves as we listen. In this way, we continue back and forth, learning about each other and at the same time learning about ourselves.

We can be uncomfortable with those who share too much too soon just as we may be with those who refuse or are unable to share themselves at all. Learning appropriate self-disclosure is an important social skill. Following are some guidelines for the use of self-disclosure (adapted from Johnson, 1986, p. 19). Self-disclosure is most appropriate or helpful when:

1. It involves persons who have a concern for each other
2. Its setting assures privacy
3. It is reciprocated
4. It takes into account the effect it has on each person
5. It deepens as trust and understanding deepens between the persons
6. It leads to greater insight and personal growth

As noted, in self-disclosure, each person must consider the effect of the disclosure on the other. Morton Hunt (1988) writes that the persons we pick to confide in should not be ones who might be wounded by what we reveal. For example, nagged by guilt concerning an affair, an unfaithful spouse may confess and ask forgiveness, but in doing so, the pain may be transferred to her or his mate. Hunt suggests that disclosures of this kind might better be made to professional counselors, along with certain confessions that tumble out and later are regretted. Concerning the latter, he gives this example:

Consider a woman with whom I had been friendly for years, who once wrote me a long and incredibly revealing letter when I was gathering data for a book on the problems of American women. Writing late at night when she was feeling sorry for herself, she told me that she often bitterly regretted having children.

They had brought her far less joy and far more emotional upset than she'd ever expected, and, while she often loved them, quite often she hated them. A day after I received the letter, she sent a telegram asking me to burn it. Though she and her husband were longtime friends of mine, I have not seen or heard from them since. Friendship, though it flourishes on the nutrients of sharing and intimacy, can be killed altogether by an overdose. (p. 325)

Research on self-disclosure indicates that it can serve to enhance interpersonal relationships (Berg, 1987; Berg & Derlega, 1987; Jourard, 1971). The more appropriately self-disclosing we are with others, the more they like us and the more they disclose themselves to us. Hiding ourselves from others can be not only hard work, as Jourard notes, but also a lonely business. Some of us equate silence with strength but it takes strength to risk revealing ourselves to another.

James Pennebaker and his colleagues (1986, 1988, 1990) have been studying the consequences of confiding versus not confiding traumatic events. Their results indicate that individuals who confront and work through previously inhibited experiences reap physiological, psychological, and social benefits. Physiologically, this disclosure leads to reduced stress-related autonomic activity and improved immune function and physical health. Socially, the disclosure usually strengthens the bond between disclosers and those they confide in. Psychologically, the disclosure promotes assimilation of the event and detachment from it. For example, in a study (Pennebaker, Kiecolt-Glaser, & Glaser, 1988) that asked the subjects to write on four consecutive days their deepest thoughts and feelings concerning the most upsetting experiences of their life, a gradual change in perspective was noted in several participants who concentrated on a single trauma:

One woman, who had been molested at the age of 9 years by a boy 3 years older, initially emphasized her feelings of embarrassment and guilt. By the third day of writing, she expressed anger at the boy who had victimized her. By the last day, she had begun to put it in perspective. On the follow-up

survey 6 weeks after the experiment, she reported, "Before, when I thought about it, I'd lie to myself. . . . Now, I don't feel like I even have to think about it because I got it off my chest. I finally admitted that it happened. . . . I really know the truth and won't have to lie to myself anymore." (p. 244)

Robert Ornstein and David Sobel (1989) write that although a case can be made for maximizing the positives and ignoring the negatives of life, there is a limit and a principle. The principle (which states the limit) is this: If the trauma is relatively small, it may be best to minimize, ignore, or deny it. But if the trauma is very upsetting, it will be better and healthier in the long run to face it and work it through.

People can learn to disclose themselves. In the warmth and security of certain relationships, we can dare to be who we are. We let down our guard and let others see us and we see ourselves more clearly. In the following material, a woman in psychotherapy describes her struggle to know herself and to let her therapist know her:

As I look at it now, I was peeling off layer after layer of defenses. I'd build them up, try them, and then discard them when you remained the same. I didn't know what was at the bottom and I was very much afraid to find out, but I had to keep on trying. At first I felt there was nothing within me—just a great emptiness where I needed and wanted a solid core. Then I began to feel that I was facing a solid brick wall, too high to get over and too thick to go through. One day the wall became translucent, rather than solid. After this, the wall seemed to disappear but beyond it I discovered a dam holding back violent, churning waters. I felt as if I were holding back the force of these waters and if I opened even a tiny hole I and all about me would be destroyed in the ensuing torrent of feelings represented by the water. Finally, I could stand the strain no longer and I let go. All I did, actually, was to succumb to complete and utter self pity, then hate, then love. After this experience, I felt as if I had leaped a brink and was safely on the other side, though still tottering a bit on the edge. I don't know what I was searching for or where I was going, but I felt then as I have always felt whenever I really lived, that I was moving forward. (Rogers, 1961, pp. 110–111)

Accepting Ourselves

Some of the dictionary's definitions of the word *accept* are "to be favorably disposed toward," "to believe in," and "to receive as adequate or satisfactory." If we accept ourselves or show *self-acceptance*, we are favorably disposed toward ourselves and believe we are okay. That doesn't mean we don't want to be better, but it does mean whatever we are right now, it's all right to be. If we reject ourselves or show *self-rejection*, we don't like or believe in ourselves, and we feel inadequate.

Before considering self-acceptance more fully, it may be helpful to look at self-rejection—all the things self-acceptance is not. Following is a checklist of behaviors seen in those who find themselves personally unacceptable, which is adapted from larger listings by Wayne Dyer (1976) and by Bloomfield and Kory (1980). The list is presented here just to get you thinking about yourself—it's not a deep and definitive device. As you think, answer each item "yes" or "no."

_____ 1. Do you feel embarrassed by your abilities or accomplishments?

_____ 2. Do you give credit to others when you really deserve it yourself?

_____ 3. Do you put others above you when you are really their equal or superior?

_____ 4. Do you fail to stand up for the things you really believe in?

_____ 5. Do you put yourself down when you have made a mistake?

_____ 6. Do you let others put you down?

_____ 7. Do you have a cute name for yourself that reduces you in some way?

_____ 8. Do you depend on others to bolster your opinions?

_____ 9. Do you believe that others cannot possibly find you attractive?

_____ 10. Do you believe that others are being kind out of charity or some ulterior motive?

_____ 11. Do you find it hard to say no to a request because of what the person might think of you?

_____ 12. Do you find it hard to complain about poor treatment because you are afraid of making a fuss?

Because the items in the preceeding list reflect self-rejection, each item that you answered "yes" suggests an area for you to work on to change the "yes" to "no." But don't put yourself down for your "yeses"—that would be another bit of self-rejecting behavior.

Following is a checklist describing self-accepting persons, those who have a healthy, positive self-image, adapted from a larger listing by Hamachek (1978). Such persons are at home with themselves and at home in the world because they see themselves and their world in an affirming way. This list, like the one on self-rejecting behavior (with which you might compare it), is presented to help you think about yourself—it's not intended to be a deep and definitive device. As you think, answer each item "yes" or "no."

_____ 1. Do you have certain values and principles that you are willing to stand up for even in the face of strong opposition?

_____ 2. Are you willing to modify your values and principles when you find them no longer tenable?

_____ 3. Can you act on your own best judgment without undue guilt or regret if you are mistaken or if others disapprove?

_____ 4. Do you retain confidence in your ability to deal with your problems even in the face of setbacks and failures?

_____ 5. Do you see yourself as equal to others as a person—regardless of differences in abilities, accomplishments or backgrounds—and with no need to devalue others or over-value yourself?

_____ 6. Do you take it rather for granted that your associates value you and consider you a person of worth?

_____ 7. Can you accept compliments without false modesty?

_____ 8. Do you resist the efforts of others to dominate you?

_____ 9. Are you able to enjoy yourself in a wide variety of activities involving loving, working, and playing?

_____ 10. Do you like and look for the best in yourself, like and look for the best in others, and feel that, all things considered, life is well worth living?

Because the items in the foregoing list reflect self-acceptance, each item you answered "yes" is evidence of a healthy, positive sense of self. Give yourself a pat on the back for your "yeses" and at the same time a little push to work on any item that wasn't answered in the affirmative.

Psychologist Nathaniel Branden (1985) often tells parents, "Be careful what you say to your children. They may agree with you" (p. 28). Children may be convinced that they are indeed "bad," "stupid," or whatever it was they were told over and over again. Worse yet, they may be convinced that whatever they are, they are not acceptable—they are not enough. Branden writes,

> In considering the many parental messages that may have a detrimental effect on a child's self-esteem, there is probably none I encounter more often in the course of my work than some version of "You are not enough." Unfortunately, early in life all too many of us receive this message from parents and teachers. You may have potential, but you are unacceptable as you are. You need to be fixed. ("Here, let me adjust your hair," "Your clothes aren't right," "Smile," "Let me rearrange your posture," "Stand straighter," "Lower your voice," "Don't be so excited," "Don't play with that toy, play with this toy," *"What's the matter with you!"*) One day you may be enough, but not now. You will be enough only if and when you live up to our expectations. (pp. 25–26)

If we accept the judgment that we are not enough, we may spend our lives in the exhausting pursuit of "the Holy Grail of enoughness." As Branden notes, this pursuit can take many pathways: "If I make a successful marriage, then I will be enough. If I make so many thousands of dollars a year, then I will be enough. One more promotion, and I will be enough. One more sexual conquest . . . one more person telling me I'm lovable . . . " (p. 26). Branden warns that the battle for acceptability or enoughness can never be won on these terms; in fact, the battle is lost the moment we concede that there is something that needs to be proved, and we can free ourselves of this endless pursuit only by rejecting this premise.

Not all professed self-rejection is what it appears to be. A psychologist who made a study of those of his clients who continually put themselves down found that they made their "I'm no good" statements not just because they felt inferior but also to accomplish something. Some constantly criticized themselves to pressure themselves to improve, to avoid responsibility, or to evoke sympathy (Driscoll, 1982).

As was indicated earlier, people who accept themselves are also more accepting of others. Those of us who accept and respect ourselves tend to respect others. Those of us who depreciate and reject ourselves reject and depreciate others as well.

It has been suggested that there may be an element of projection in the relationship between the acceptance of self and the acceptance of others. If we like ourselves, we assume others like us. If we depreciate ourselves, we may assume that others depreciate us, too. In retaliation, we reject and depreciate them in order to bolster our own feelings (Goldfriend, 1973).

Prizing Ourselves

To *accept* ourselves means we believe we are okay. That's a good beginning. To *prize* ourselves means we have a high regard for ourselves and even think we're special. That's even better, especially if it creates a quiet inner pride. I'm indebted to Carl Rogers for this use of the word *prize*, but in much the same way others have written about the importance of "self-esteem" or "honoring" oneself or "loving" oneself.

Strictly speaking, *self-esteem* is the evaluation we make ourselves. As the term is commonly used, to have self-esteem or, more exactly, to have high self-esteem means we place a high value on ourselves. We feel we are worthy. We take pride in ourselves.

Not one to hide pride under a bushel, Nathaniel Branden has written a book with the title (and on the subject of) *Honoring the Self*. "Honor thyself" might almost be an addition to the ten commandments. Logically it might precede the fifth commandment, "Honor thy father and mother," because, as Branden writes, the evidence is overwhelming that "the higher the level of an individual's self-esteem, the more likely that he or she will treat others with respect, kindness and generosity." There is also evidence that the higher the individual's self-esteem, the better her or his physical and psychological health (Coopersmith, 1967; Turner & Vanderlippe, 1958).

To take pride in oneself or to honor oneself will be for some a troubling notion. We may have been taught to be modest and humble. We may have been warned against the sin of pride. We may have been cautioned that excessive pride can result in arrogance or prejudice (Tavris, 1985), but pride can be either harmful or healthy. It can be arrogance toward others or a respect for self that makes arrogance unnecessary (Lynd, 1958; Rosenberg, 1979).

The efforts by some state and educational bodies to increase self-esteem in various groups have recently come in for some hard knocks and even attempts at ridicule (Adler, 1992). Some critics of these efforts seem worried that persons who are encouraged to feel good about themselves will become conceited ("I'm terrific!") and complacent and be in for some rude shocks in the real world. These critics maintain that effective functioning must precede a belief in oneself: First, you prove what you can do, and then you know you're good.

Research suggests there are several routes to follow to becoming more effective. Our opinion of ourselves indeed rises when we see what we can do. But when we are encouraged to raise our opinion of ourselves, we are willing to try more and become able to do more. Psychologist Andrew Sappington (1989) reviews the evidence and concludes, "Effective functioning can raise self-esteem, and high self-esteem can increase the chances of effective functioning" (p. 202).

Some critics of self-esteem movements believe in a kick in the pants (or the ego) to make us become more, but what about a pat on the back (and a sense of quiet pride) for who we are right now? Whoever we are, it helps to feel good about our race and ethnic origins, about our age and gender and sexual orientation, about our bodies. TV talk host Jenny Jones has had her original silicone implants replaced five times; her hardened breasts have no feeling, and the silicone leakage cannot be removed. "Learn to love yourself," she said in an interview. "If I could have learned that, I wouldn't have had to suffer these 11 years of torture" (Beck, 1992, p. A14).

To accept, to prize, to honor, to *love* oneself. In his classic essay, *The Art of Loving*, Erich Fromm speaks of "self-love," which he feels is closely related to love for others. He says, "The idea expressed in the Biblical 'Love thy neighbor as thyself!' implies that respect for one's own integrity and uniqueness, love for and understanding of one's own self, cannot be separated from respect and love and understanding for another individual. The love for my self is inseparably connected with the love for any other being" (p. 49).

For some of us, self-love may seem like selfishness, self-conceit, or self-infatuation. But these two sets of terms have little in common; they are poles apart in their implications. Fromm illustrates this point nicely in his contrast of selfishness and self-love. He writes,

Selfishness and self-love, far from being identical, are actually opposites. The selfish person does not love himself too much but too little; in fact he hates himself. This lack of fondness and care for himself, which is only one expression of his lack of productiveness, leaves him empty and frustrated. He is necessarily unhappy and anxiously concerned to snatch from life the satisfactions which he blocks himself from attaining. He seems to care too much for himself, but actually he only makes an unsuccessful attempt to cover up and compensate for his failure to care for his real self. Freud holds that the selfish person is narcissistic, as if he had withdrawn his love from others and turned it toward his own person. *It is true that selfish persons are incapable of loving others, but they are not capable of loving themselves either.* (p. 51)

Becoming Ourselves

We are each unique, and each of us has a life like no other life. There are general laws, but, as Danish theologian Sören Kierkegaard wrote, every person is an exception, and every person has something exceptional to offer. To quote the words of Nikos Kazantzakis, put in the mouth of his *Zorba the Greek:* "When I die, the whole zorbatic world dies with me."

The great philosopher Martin Buber (1951) held that for each of us to become ourself is not only our special opportunity but also our special responsibility. Quoting a Galician sage he wrote,

Every person born into this world represents something new, something that never existed before, something original and unique. "It is the duty of every person . . . to know and consider that he is unique in the world in his particular character and that there has never been anyone like him in the world, for if there had been someone like him, there would have been no need for him to be in the world. Every single man is a new thing in the world, and is called upon to fulfill his particularity in this world." Every man's foremost task is the actualization of his unique, unprecedented and never recurring potentialities, and not the repetition of something that another, and be it even the greatest, has already achieved. (p. 16)

Carl Rogers (1961) noted that each person coming to him for therapy appeared to be asking the same questions: "Who am I, *really*? How can I get in touch with this real self, underlying this surface behavior? How can I become myself?" (p. 108).

Rogers theorized that each of us is born with an inherent tendency to make the most of our own unique potential. We each have an inherent wisdom allowing us to distinguish those experiences or pathways that lead to fulfillment from those that lead to stagnation or destruction. Rogers wrote that each of us struggles (and here he quotes Kierkegaard) "to be that self which one truly is" (p. 110).

Alan Watts, in his beautiful book *Tao: The Watercourse Way*, explained the principles of "wu-wei" and "te." *Tao* is the flow of nature, *wu-wei* is the art of not forcing things, and *te* is the power that derives from this. Watts wrote that wu-wei is the life-style of one who follows the Tao; it is the style of swimming with the current and going with the grain.

There is a natural current or grain to our lives. When we are in harmony with it, we proceed with little effort. When we try to cross the current or go against the grain, we flounder and struggle. Finding our "natural current"—becoming ourselves—is not an easy task. E. E. Cummings wrote, "To be nobody but yourself in a world which is doing its best, night and day, to make you everybody else, means to fight the hardest battle which any human being can fight, and never stop fighting."

Some of us never make much progress toward becoming ourselves. We drift, never finding a sense of direction. This is well illustrated in the life of Biff in Arthur Miller's *Death of a Salesman*. At one point in the play, Biff sums up his failure when he says to his mother, "I just can't take hold, Mom. I can't take hold of some kind of life." It is also illustrated in Jessie Cates, the protagonist of Marsha Norman's drama *'night, Mother*. Jessie takes her own life, or it might be more accurate to say that she forfeits it. She explains that she has been waiting for herself, a self worth waiting for, a self that would make a difference, but that self wasn't going to show up, so there was no reason to live on.

Not everyone agrees that it is correct to speak about "finding" oneself. The process is hard work, and some believe that it would be more accurate to say we "create" ourselves, although it is a self compatible with our inner nature. The late novelist Mary McCarthy said, at a point fairly far along in her life, that she had given up the "quest" for self. She continued, "What you feel when you are older is that you really must *make* the self. You finally begin to make and choose the self you want" (McGuigan, 1989, p. 91).

Some of us need to remake or re-create ourselves. We may find that we are somebody else's invention, that we have been persuaded by our parents or teachers or other forces to be someone we're not and don't want to be (Jourard, 1975). We may have to rescue ourselves from our miscasting, assume our own character, and plot out our own life story (Kopp, 1987).

Psychotherapist Lawrence LeShan has worked with cancer patients for over 35 years. What he noted in long-term individual therapy with these patients is a chronic despair, but it is a despair that *predates* the appearance of cancer by many years and arises from a dilemma. Such patients had come to believe they could not be accepted for themselves, nor could they give up being the persons they were, in order to become persons loved only for what they did. More than that, in giving up on themselves, they felt they would be joining the rest of the world in the rejection of their real selves. The solution, LeShan advises those caught up in this despair, is to become "more and more the self you are." He continues,

> The more this becomes your path and goal, then the more those who approve of the person you really are can recognize you and move toward you. By and large, these will be the kind of people *you* like, although there will be exceptions. Only after people in despair have had the courage to show their true face can these others recognize and respond with liking and love. And it is only after

this—after finding and showing your true being—that love can be accepted and believed in. (p. 110)

Showing one's "true face" even to oneself can be a difficult task when it is a face one has somehow come to think is wrong or even evil. Some lesbians and gays have written of their confusion or consternation at discovering their sexual orientation and of their struggle to "come out of the closet" and be who they truly were. In one study (Jay & Young, 1979), a woman reported that she didn't realize she was a lesbian until she was 20, and her coming out was traumatic. "I used to look at myself in the mirror and cry. I couldn't believe what I was. How could a good girl like me be something as wicked as a lesbian? Once I found the gay bars and gay community I found that there were many 'good girl' lesbians" (pp. 55–56). She noted that since then, her self-image had improved each year, and now she wouldn't want to be anyone other than who she is.

We must constantly seek to understand ourselves if we are to become ourselves; but the understanding does not come once and for all. It comes little by little as we observe ourselves in every new situation. In every situation, we can learn to tell whether we are being genuine and true to ourselves, or phony and unauthentic (Friedman, 1952).

For ten years, I was a volunteer working with hospice patients and those with life-threatening illness. Being with a number of persons as they faced death, I've come to believe that dying has been hardest for those who never really lived their lives—those who were losing both life and their last chance to become themselves. I am reminded of the story told about Rabbi Zusya as he approached death. Rabbi Zusya said that when he met the Holy One, he would not be asked, "Why were you not like Moses?" No, he would be asked, "Why were you not like Zusya?" Zusya added, "It is for this reason that I tremble."

References

Adler, J. (1992, February 17). Hey, I'm terrific! *Newsweek*, pp. 46–51.

Allen, B. P. (1990). *Personality, social and biological perspectives on personal adjustment*. Pacific Grove, CA: Brooks/Cole.

Ansen, D. (1980, August 4). The great impersonator. *Newsweek*, pp. 43–44.

Baron, P. (1974). Self-esteem, ingratiation, and evaluation of unknown others. *Journal of Personality and Social Psychology, 30,* 104–109.

Beck, J. (1992, February 28). More self-esteem, fewer 'lifts.' *The Honolulu Advertiser,* p. A14.

Berg, J. H. (1987). Responsiveness and self-disclosure. In J. H. Berg & V. J. Derlega (Eds.), *Self-disclosure: Theory, research, and therapy* (pp. 101–130). New York: Plenum Press.

Berg, J. H., & Derlega, V. J. (1987). Themes in the study of self-disclosure. In J. H. Berg & V. J. Derlega (Eds.), *Self-disclosure: Theory, research, and therapy* (pp. 1–8). New York: Plenum Press.

Berger, E. (1952). The relation between expressed acceptance of self and expressed acceptance of others. *Journal of Abnormal and Social Psychology, 47,* 778–782.

Birnbaum, J. A. (1975). Life patterns and self-esteem in gifted family-oriented and career-committed women. In M. Mednick, S. Tangri, & L. Hoffman (Eds.), *Women and achievement* (pp. 396–419). New York: Halsted.

Bloomfield, H. H., & Kory, R. B. (1980). *Inner joy: New strategies to put more pleasure and satisfaction in your life*. New York: Wyden.

Branden, N. (1983). *Honoring the self: Personal integrity and the heroic potentials of human nature*. Los Angeles: Tarcher.

Buber, M. (1951). *The way of man*. Chicago: Wilcox and Follett.

Coleman, L. M., & Antonucci, T. (1983). Impact of work on women at midlife. *Developmental Psychology, 19*(2), 280–284.

Combs, A. W., Avila, D. L., & Purkey, W. W. (1978). *Helping relationships: Basic concepts for the helping professions* (2nd ed.). Boston: Allyn and Bacon.

Combs, A. W., Richards, A. C., & Richards, F. (1976). *Perceptual psychology: A humanistic approach to the study of persons.* New York: Harper & Row.

Coopersmith, S. (1967). *Antecedents of self-esteem.* San Francisco: W. H. Freeman.

Driscoll, R. (1982, July). Their own worst enemies. *Psychology Today,* pp. 45–49.

Dyer, W. W. (1976). *Your erroneous zones.* New York: Funk & Wagnalls.

Friedman, M. (1958). *To deny our nothingness: Contemporary images of man.* London: Macmillan.

Friedrich, O., & McDowell, J. (1989, January 16). Flashy symbol of acquisitive age. *Time,* pp. 48–54.

Fromm, E. (1963). *The art of loving.* New York: Bantam.

Gergen, K. J. (1972, May). The healthy, happy human wears many masks. *Psychology Today,* pp. 31–35, 64, 66.

Goffman, E. (1955). On face-work: An analysis of ritual elements in social interaction. *Psychiatry: Journal for the Study of Interpersonal Process, 18,* 213–231.

Goldfriend, M. R. (1973). Feelings of inferiority and the depreciation of others: A research review and theoretical reformulation. *Journal of Individual Psychology, 19,* 27–48.

Greenwald, A. G. (1980). The totalitarian ego: Fabrication and revision of personal history. *American Psychologist, 35*(7), 603–618.

Hamachek, D. E. (1978). *Encounters with the self* (2nd ed.). New York: Holt, Rinehart and Winston.

Hatfield, E., & Sprecher, S. (1986). *Mirror, mirror . . . The importance of looks in everyday life.* Albany: State University of New York Press.

Hunt, M. M. (1964, September). The limits of intimacy. *Reader's Digest,* pp. 69–71.

Ingram, R. E. (1990). Self-focused attention in clinical disorders: Review and a conceptual model. *Psychological Bulletin, 107*(2), 156–176.

Ingram, R. E., & Smith, T. W. (1984). Depression and internal versus external focus of attention. *Cognitive Therapy and Research, 8*(2), 139–152.

Jay, K., & Young, A. (1979). *The gay report.* New York: Summit Books.

Johnson, D. W. (1986). *Reaching out: Interpersonal effectiveness and self-actualization* (3rd ed.). Englewood Cliffs, NJ: Prentice-Hall.

Jourard, S. M. (1971). *The transparent self* (rev. ed.). New York: D. Van Nostrand.

Kazantzakis, N. (1952). *Zorba the Greek.* New York: Simon & Schuster.

Kopp, S. B. (1976). *If you meet the Buddha on the road, kill him!* New York: Bantam.

Kopp, S. B. (1971). *Guru.* Palo Alto, CA: Science and Behavior Books.

Lang, R. D., Phillipson, H., & Lee, A. R. (1966). *Interpersonal perception: A theory and method of research.* New York: Springer.

Langer, E. J., & Dweck, C. S. (1973). *Personal politics: The psychology of making it.* Englewood Cliffs, NJ: Prentice-Hall.

LeShan, L. (1989). *Cancer as a turning point: A handbook for people with cancer, their families, and health professionals.* New York: Plume.

Lynd, H. M. (1958). *On shame and the search for identity.* New York: Harcourt Brace.

Markus, H., & Kunda, Z. (1986). Stability and malleability of the self-concept. *Journal of Personality and Social Psychology, 51*(4), 858–866.

Markus, H., & Nurius, P. (1986). Possible selves. *American Psychologist, 41*(9), 954–969.

Markus, H., & Wurf, E. (1987). The dynamic self-concept: A social psychological perspective. *Annual Review of Psychology, 38,* 299–337.

McCarthy, K. (1990, October). People presume women and men differ; do they? *Monitor,* p. 33.

McGuigan, C. (1989, November 6). The company she kept. *Newsweek,* p. 91.

Miller, A. (1949). *Death of a salesman.* New York: Viking Press.

Morrow, L. (1991, April 29). The trouble with Teddy. *Time,* pp. 24–27.

Noonan, P. (1990). *What I saw at the revolution: A political life in the Reagan era.* New York: Random House.

Norman, M. (1983). *'night, Mother.* New York: Hill and Wang.

Ornstein, R., & Sobel, D. (1989). *Healthy pleasures.* Reading, MA: Addison-Wesley.

Oyserman, D., & Markus, H. (1986). *Possible selves, motivation, and delinquency.* Unpublished manuscript, University of Michigan.

Pennebaker, J. W. (1988). Confiding traumatic experiences and health. In S. Fisher & J. Reason (Eds.), *Handbook of life stress, cognition and health* (pp. 669–682). New York: Wiley.

Pennebaker, J. W. (1990). *Opening up: The healing power of confiding in others.* New York: Morrow.

Pennebaker, J. W., Kiecolt-Glaser, J. K., & Glaser, R. (1988). Disclosure of traumas and immune function: Health implications for psychotherapy. *Journal of Consulting and Clinical Psychology, 56*(2), 239–245.

Pirot, M. (1986). The pathological thought and dynamics of the perfectionist. *Journal of Individual Psychology, 42*(1), 51–58.

Possible selves. (1987, Spring/Summer). *ISR Newsletter,* pp. 5–7.

Prather, H. (1970). *Notes to myself.* Moab, UT: Real People Press.

Putnam, F. W. (1984). The psychophysiologic investigation of multiple personality disorder: A review. *Psychiatric Clinics of North America, 7*(1), 31–39.

Rogers, C. R. (1961). *On becoming a person.* Boston: Houghton Mifflin.

Roosevelt, T. (1946). *Theodore Roosevelt: An autobiography.* New York: Charles Scribner's Sons.

Rosenberg, M. (1979). *Conceiving the self.* New York: Basic Books.

Rowan, J. (1990). *Subpersonalities: The people inside us.* New York: Routledge.

Sappington, A. A. (1989). *Adjustment: Theory, research, and personal applications.* Pacific Grove, CA: Brooks/Cole.

Skaalvik, E. M. (1986). Sex differences in global self-esteem: A research review. *Scandinavian Journal of Educational Research, 30*(4), 167–179.

Swan, W. B., Jr. (1984). Quest for accuracy in person perception: A matter of pragmatics. *Psychological Review, 91,* 457–477.

Tavris, C. (1985, August). *Pride and prejudice.* Paper presented at annual convention of the American Psychological Association, Los Angeles, CA.

Tavris, C., & Wade, C. (1984). *The longest war: Sex differences in perspective* (2nd ed.). San Diego, CA: Harcourt Brace Jovanovich.

Taylor, S. E. (1989). *Positive illusions: Creative self-deception and the healthy mind.* New York: Basic Books.

Taylor, S. E., & Brown, J. D. (1988). Illusion and well-being: A social psychological perspective on mental health. *Psychological Bulletin, 103*(2), 193–210.

Turner, R. H., & Vanderlippe, R. H. (1958). Self-ideal congruence as an index of adjustment. *Journal of Abnormal and Social Psychology, 57,* 202–206.

Van Dusen, W. (1972). *The natural depth in man.* New York: Harper & Row.

Vargiu, J. G. (1975). Subpersonalities. In A. Arkoff (Ed.), *Psychology and personal growth* (2nd ed., pp. 22–27). Boston: Allyn and Bacon.

Vasconcellos, J. (1989). Preface. In A. M. Mecca, N. J. Smelser, & J. Vasconcellos (Eds.), *The social importance of self-esteem* (pp. xi–xxi). Berkeley: University of California Press.

Walster, E. (1965). The effect of self-esteem on romantic liking. *Journal of Experimental Social Psychology, 1,* 184–197.

Watson, D., & Clark, L. A. (1984). Negative affectivity: The disposition to experience aversive emotional states. *Psychological Bulletin, 96,* 465–490.

Watts, A. (1975). *Tao: The watercourse way.* New York: Pantheon.

Williams, J. E., & Best, D. L. (1982). *Measuring sex stereotypes: A thirty-nation study.* Beverly Hills, CA: Sage.

Zarin, C. (1990, July 30). A part in the play. *New Yorker,* pp. 37–45, 48–54.

To Apply This Reading to Yourself

1. *Do you have a good relationship with yourself? Describe this relationship as it seems to you.*

2. *What subpersonalities can you detect in yourself? Name and describe each one and its influence on you.*

3. *How does your self-image affect your behavior? Discuss this aspect of yourself. Give examples and be as specific as you can.*

4. *Discuss the relationship between your body image and your self-image and self-esteem.*

5. *Discuss the relationship between your gender and your self-image and self-esteem.*

6. *Do you tend to focus your attention on your own thoughts and feelings too much? Too little? Discuss this aspect of yourself.*

7. *Have you become aware of any of your own "positive illusions" or self-deceptions? If so, discuss this aspect of yourself.*

8. *How much insight into yourself do you have? How much of a puzzle are you? Discuss an important aspect of yourself that remains a mystery to you.*

9. *How much insight into yourself do you have? How much of an open or opening book are you? Discuss a recent situation or event that provided some important insight.*

10. *Do you tend to disclose too much? Too little? Appropriately? Inappropriately? And to whom? Discuss this aspect of yourself.*

11. *Do you have a confidant—a close friend to whom you disclose your deeper feelings and problems? Discuss the effect that having or not having such a person has on your life.*

12. *How accepting of yourself are you? How accepting of others are you? Discuss these two qualities and the relationship between them as you see them in yourself and your life.*

13. *How debilitating is your self-rejecting behavior? From the self-rejection checklist, pick out some items that seem important to you and to which you answered "yes." Discuss the effects of this behavior on you.*

14. *How enhancing is your self-accepting behavior? From the self-acceptance checklist, pick out some items that seem important to you and to which you answered "yes." Discuss the effects of this behavior on you.*

15. *Is your life right for you? Are you on the way to becoming yourself? As you answer, give your evidence.*

First Love

Wayne W. Dyer

You may have a social disease, one that will not go away with a simple injection. You are quite possibly infected with the sepsis of low-esteem, and the only known cure is a massive dose of self-love. But perhaps, like many in our society, you've grown up with the idea that loving yourself is wrong. Think of others, society tells us. Love thy neighbor, the church admonishes. What nobody seems to remember is love thyself, and yet that is precisely what you're going to have to learn to do if you are to achieve present-moment happiness.

You learned as a child that loving yourself, which was a natural thing for you then, was akin to being selfish or conceited. You learned to put others ahead of you, to think of others first because that showed you were a "good" person. You learned self-effacement and were nurtured on instructions like "share your things with your cousins." It didn't matter that they were your treasures, your prized possessions, or that mommy or daddy might not be sharing their big-people toys with others. You may even have been told that you were to "be seen and not heard" and that "you ought to know your place."

Children just naturally think of themselves as beautiful and terribly important, but by adolescence society's messages have taken root. Self-doubt is in full bloom. And the reinforcements continue as the years pass. After all, you're not supposed to go around loving yourself. What will others think of you!

The hints are subtle and not malicious in intent, but they do keep the individual in line. From parents and immediate family members to schools, churches and friends, the child learns all those fine social amenities that are the hallmarks of the adult world. Kids never acted that way with each other, except to please older folks. Always say please and thank you, curtsy, stand up when an adult enters, ask permission to leave the table, tolerate the endless cheek pinching and head patting. The message was clear: adults are important; kids don't count. Others are significant; you are insignificant. Don't trust your own judgment was corollary number one, and there was a full cargo of reinforcers that came under the subheading of "politeness." These rules, disguised under the word *manners*, helped you to internalize the judgments of others at the expense of your own values. It's not surprising that those same question marks and self-denying definitions persist into adulthood. And how do these self-doubts get in the way? In the important area of loving others you may be having a difficult time. Giving love to others is directly related to how much love you have for yourself.

LOVE: A SUGGESTED DEFINITION

Love is a word that has as many definitions as there are people to define it. Try this one on for size. *The ability and willingness to allow those that you care for to be what they choose for themselves, without any insistence that they satisfy you.* This may be a workable definition, but the fact remains that so few are able to adopt it for themselves. How can you reach the point of being able to let others be what they choose without insisting they meet your expectations? Very simple. By loving yourself. By feeling that you are important, worthy and beautiful. Once you recognize just how good you are, you won't have to have others reinforce your value or values by making their behavior conform to your dictates. If you're secure in yourself, you neither want nor need others to be like you. For one thing, you're unique. For another, that would rob them of their own uniqueness, and what you love in them are just those traits that make them special and separate. It begins to fit. You get good at loving yourself, and suddenly you're able to love others, to give to others, and do for others by giving and doing for yourself first. Then there are no gimmicks to your giving. You're not doing it for the thanks or the payoffs but because of the genuine pleasure you get from being a helper or a lover.

If the you is someone unworthy, or unloved by you, then giving becomes impossible. How can you give love if you're worthless? What would your love be worth? And if you can't give love, neither can you receive it. After all what can the love be worth if it's bestowed on a worthless person. The entire business of being in love, giving and receiving, starts with a self that is totally loved.

Take Noah, a middle-aged man who claimed to love his wife and children dearly. To show his affections he bought them expensive gifts, took them on luxurious holidays, and was always careful when away on business trips to sign his letters "love." Yet Noah could never bring himself to tell his wife or children that he loved them. He had the same problem with his parents of whom he was tremendously fond. Noah wanted to say the words; they ran through his head repeatedly, yet every time he tried to say "I love you," he got all choked up.

In Noah's head the words "I love you" meant he was putting himself on the line. If he said "I love you," someone must answer "I love you, too, Noah." His statement of love must be met with an affirmation of his own self-worth. Saying those words was taking too much of a chance for Noah, for they might not be answered and then his entire value would be in question. If, on the other hand, Noah could start with the premise that he was lovable, he would experience no difficulty in the "I love you." If he didn't get the desired, "I love you, too, Noah," then he would see that as having nothing to do with his own self-worth, since that was intact before he ever started. Whether or not he was loved in return would be his wife's problem, or whomever Noah was loving at the moment. He might *want* the other person's love, but it would not be essential to his self-worth.

You can challenge all of your self-feelings in terms of your ability to love yourself. Remember, at no time, under no circumstance is self-hate healthier than self-love. Even if you have behaved in a way that you dislike, loathing yourself will only lead to immobilization and damage. Instead of hating yourself, develop positive feelings. Learn from the error, and resolve not to repeat it but don't associate it with your self-worth.

Here is the guts of both self- and other-directed love. Never confuse your self-worth (which is a given) with your behavior, or the behavior of others toward you. Once again, it isn't easy. The messages of society are overpow-ering. "You're a bad boy," rather than "You've behaved badly." "Mommy doesn't like you when you behave that way" as opposed to "Mommy doesn't like the way you behave." The conclusions that you may have adopted from these messages are, "She doesn't like me, I must be a nerd" instead of, "She doesn't like me. That's her decision, and while I don't like it, I'm still important." R. D. Laing's Knots sums up the process of internalizing others' thoughts and equating them with one's self-worth.

> My mother loves me.
> I feel good.
> I feel good because she loves me.
>
> My mother does not love me.
> I feel bad.
> I feel bad because she does not love me.
> I am bad because I feel bad.
> I feel bad because I am bad.
> I am bad because she does not love me.
> She does not love me because I am bad.

The habits of thought of childhood are not easily outgrown. Your own self-image may still be based upon others' perceptions of you. While it is true that your original self-profiles were learned from the opinions of adults, it is not true that you must carry them around with you forever. Yes, it is tough to shed those old shackles and wipe clean those unhealed scars, but hanging on to them is even tougher when you consider the consequences. With mental practice you can make some self-loving choices that will amaze you.

ACCEPTING YOURSELF WITHOUT COMPLAINT

Self-love means accepting yourself as a worthy person because you choose to do so. Acceptance also means an absence of complaint. Fully functioning people never complain, and particularly they don't complain about the rocks being rough, or the sky being cloudy or the ice being too cold. Acceptance means no complaining, and happiness means no complaining about the things over which you can do nothing. Complaining is the refuge of those who have no self-reliance. Telling others about the things you dislike in yourself helps you to continue the dissatisfaction since they are almost always powerless to do anything about it except deny it and then you don't believe them. Just as complaining to others accomplishes nothing, so permitting others to abuse you with their own tote bags full of self-pity and misery helps no one. A simple question to ask will generally end this useless and unpleasant behavior. "Why are you telling me this?" or "Is there anything I can do to help you with this?" By asking yourself the same questions, you will begin to recognize your complaining behavior as ultimate folly. It is time spent in a wasteful manner, time which might be put to better use in practicing self-loving kinds of activities, such as silent self-praise, or helping someone else to achieve fulfillment.

There are two occasions when complaining is least appreciated in the world: (1) Whenever you tell someone else that you are tired. (2) Whenever you tell someone else that you don't feel well. If you are tired, you can exercise several options, but complaining to even one poor soul, let alone a loved one, is abusing that person. And it won't make you less tired. The same kind of logic applies to your "not feeling well."

Nothing is being said here about informing others of how you feel when they can help you in any small way. What is being challenged is complaining to others who can do nothing but endure the grumbling. Additionally, if you are truly working on self-love, and you are experiencing any pain or discomfort, you will want to work on this yourself, rather than choosing someone to lean on and have them share your burden.

Complaining about yourself is a useless activity, and one which keeps you from effectively living your life. It encourages self-pity and immobilizes you in your efforts at giving and receiving love. Moreover it reduces your opportunities for improved love relationships and increased social intercourse. While it may get you attention, the noticing will be done in a light that will clearly cast shadows on your own happiness.

Being able to accept yourself without complaint involves an understanding of both self-love and the complaining process, which are mutually exclusive terms. If you genuinely love you, then complaining to others who can do nothing for you becomes absurdly impossible to defend. And if you notice things in yourself (and others) that you dislike, rather than complaining you can actively set about taking the necessary corrective steps.

The next time you are at a social gathering of four or more couples, you can try this little exercise. Chronicle how much conversation is actually spent in complaining. From self to others, to events, prices, the weather, and on and on. Now, when the party is over and everyone has gone their separate ways, ask yourself, "How much of the complaining that went on tonight accomplished anything?" "Who really cares about all of the things that we bemoaned tonight?"Then, the next time you are about to complain keep the uselessness of that night in mind.

SELF-LOVE VS. CONCEIT

You may be thinking that all of this talk about self-love involves a form of obnoxious behavior akin to egomania. Nothing could be further from the truth. Self-love has nothing to do with the sort of behavior characterized by telling everyone how wonderful you are. That's not self-love, but rather an attempt to win the attention and approval of others by chest-thumping behavior. It is just as neurotic as the behavior of the individual who is overloaded with self-contempt. Boastful behavior is motivated by others, by an attempt to gain their favor. It means the individual is evaluating himself on the basis of how others see him. If he were not, he would not feel the need to convince them. Self-love means you love yourself; it doesn't demand the love of others. There is no need to convince others. An internal acceptance is sufficient. It has nothing to do with the viewpoints of others.

THE REWARDS FOR NOT LOVING YOURSELF

Why would anyone choose not to love himself? Where is the advantage? The dividends, while they may be unhealthy, are nevertheless there for you to examine. And this is the core of learning to be an effective person—understanding why you behave in self-defeating ways. All behavior is caused, and the road to eliminating any self-destructive behavior is strewn with the potholes of misunderstanding your own motives. Once you comprehend the *why* of your self-malice and the maintenance system for retaining it, you can begin to attack the behaviors. Without the understanding of self, the old actions will continue to recur.

Why have you chosen to engage in self-denouncing ways, however slight they may seem to you? It may be that it is just plain easier to buy the stuff that others tell you than to think for yourself. But there are other dividends as well. If you choose to not love yourself and treat yourself as unimportant by placing other heads higher than your own, you will . . .

- Have a built-in excuse for why you can't get any love in your life, that is, you simply are not worth being loved back. The excuse is the neurotic payoff.
- Be able to avoid any and all risks that go with establishing love relationships with others, and thereby eliminate any possibility of ever being rejected or disapproved.
- Find that it is easier to stay the way you are. As long as you're not worthy there is just no point in trying to grow or to be better and happier, and your payoff is remaining the same.
- Gain a lot of pity, attention and even approval from others, which substitutes nicely for the risky business of getting involved in a love relationship. Thus the pity and attention are your self-defeating rewards.
- Have many convenient scapegoats to blame for your own misery. You can complain and thus you don't have to do anything about it yourself.
- Be able to use up your present moments with mini-depressions, and avoid behavior that would help you to be different. Your self-pity will serve as your escape route.
- Regress to being a good little boy or girl, calling upon the leftover responses of a child and therefore pleasing those "big-people" that you learned to regard as superior to you. Your regression is safer than risk.
- Be able to reinforce your leaning-on-others behavior by making them more significant than you make yourself. A leaning post is a dividend even though you're hurt by it.

- Be unable to take charge of your own life and live it the way you choose, simply because you won't feel that you are worth the happiness you covet.

These are the components of your self-scorn maintenance system. They are the reasons you choose to hang on to the old thinking and behavior. It is just plain easier, that is, less risky, to put yourself down than to try to get up. But remember, the only evidence for life is growth, and so to refuse to grow into a self-loving person is a death-like choice. Armed with these insights into your own behavior, you can begin to practice some mental and physical exercises to encourage the growth of your own self-love.

SOME EASY-TO-MASTER SELF-LOVE EXERCISES

The practice of self-love begins with your mind. You must learn to control your thinking. This requires a lot of present-moment awareness at the times when you are behaving in self-condemnatory kinds of ways. If you can catch yourself as you are doing it, you can begin to challenge the thought in back of your behavior.

You find that you have just said something like, "I'm really not that smart, I guess I was just lucky to get an A on that paper." The bell should go off in your head. "I just did it. I behaved in a self-loathing way. But I'm aware of it now, and the next time I'll stop myself from saying those things I've been saying all my life." Your strategy is to correct yourself out loud with a statement such as, "I just said I was lucky, but luck really had nothing to do with it. I got the grade because I deserved it." One small step toward self-love, the step being a recognition of your present-moment put-down and a decision to act differently. Before you had a habit; now you have an awareness of wanting to be different, and you have made a choice to make it happen. It's just like learning to drive a stick shift. Eventually you'll have a new habit which will not require constant awareness. You'll soon be behaving in all kinds of self-adoring ways naturally.

With your mind now working for, rather than against you, exciting self-love activities are on the horizon. Here is a brief list of such behaviors to which you can add as you achieve a sense of self-esteem based upon your own worth.

- Select new responses to others' attempts to reach you with love or acceptance. Rather than instantly being skeptical of a loving gesture, accept them with a "thank-you" or "I'm happy that you feel that way."
- If there is someone that you feel genuine love toward, say it right out front "I love you" and while you check out the reactions you receive in return, pat yourself on the back for taking the risk.
- In a restaurant, order something you really enjoy no matter what it costs. Give yourself a treat because you are worth it. Begin to select items that you would prefer in all situations, including the grocery store. Indulge yourself with a favorite product because you are worth it. Outlaw self-denial unless it is absolutely necessary—and it rarely is.
- After a tiring day and a large meal take a brief nap or a jog in the park even if you have too many things to do. It will help you to feel one hundred percent better.
- Join an organization, or sign up for an activity that you will enjoy. Perhaps you've been putting this off because you have so many responsibilities that you just don't have the time. By choosing to love yourself, and partaking of the slices of life that you want, those others that you serve will begin to learn some self-reliance of their own. And you will find yourself with an absence of resentment toward them. You will be serving them out of *choice*, rather than obligation.
- Eliminate jealousy by recognizing it is a putdown of yourself. By comparing yourself to some other person and imagining you are loved less, you make others more important than you. You are measuring your own merit in comparison to another. Remind yourself that (1) Someone can always choose another without having it be a reflection on you, and (2) whether or not you are chosen by any significant other is not the way you validate your own self-worth. If you make it that way, you are doomed to eternal self-doubt, because of the uncertainty of how a particular someone out there is going to feel at any precise moment of any given day. Should he/she choose another, that choice reflects only the other, not you. With practice at self-love, any circumstances in which you've previously found yourself to be jealous will be reversed. You'll believe so much in you that you won't need the love or approval of others to give you value.
- Your self-love activity might also include new ways of treating your body, such as selecting good nutritional foods, eliminating excess weight (which can be a health risk as well as an indication of self-rejection), taking regular walks or bicycle rides, choosing plenty of healthy exercise, getting outdoors to enjoy fresh air because it feels good, and in general keeping your body healthy and attractive. Provided you want to be healthy. Why? Because you are important and are going to treat yourself that way. Any total day spent cooped up or inactive in boring routine activities is a vote for self-enmity. Unless you actually prefer being cooped up, in which case you make that choice.
- Sexually, you can practice greater self-love. You can stand naked in front of a mirror and tell yourself how attractive you are. You can get in touch with your body. Explore yourself sensually, give yourself goosebumps of shivery pleasure. With others, you can also choose sexual fulfillment for you, rather than making your partner's pleasure more important than your own. Only by choosing gratification for yourself can you give pleasure. If you aren't happy, generally your partner is disappointed. Moreover, when you choose yourself, others are more able to choose happiness for themselves. You can slow down the whole process of sex, teaching your lover what you like with words or actions. You can choose orgasm for yourself. You can make yourself achieve the ultimate physical experience by believing that you are worth it, and then getting lost in the excitement of verifying it for you. Why? Because you are worth it!
- You can stop equating your performance in anything with your own self-worth. You may lose your job, or fail a given project. You

may not like the way you performed this or that task. But that doesn't mean that you are without worth. You must know for yourself, that you are worth something regardless of your achievements. Without this knowledge, you will be persistently confusing yourself with your external activities. It is just as absurd to make your self-value depend upon some outside accomplishment as it is to tie it in with some external person's opinion of you. Once you eliminate this confusion, you will be able to set about all kinds of undertakings, and your final score—while it may be interesting to you—will in no way determine how valuable you are as a person.

To Apply This Reading to Yourself

1. *What messages did you receive as a child about loving or about not loving yourself? What has been their effect on you?*
2. *Compare your own definition of love with Dyer's. If you were to adopt his definition, how would your life be different?*
3. *Do you love yourself? Give some evidence to support your answer.*
4. *Have you ever gotten rewards for not loving yourself? Discuss yourself in this regard.*
5. *Try one or more of Dyer's "easy-to-master self-love" exercises, and discuss (1) your experience with them, and (2) the benefit that continuing such exercises would have for you.*

No-Fault Psychology

Carol Tavris

In California, a woman was accused of murdering her infant son. She killed him, the defense claimed, while suffering from postpartum depression. In San Antonio, Texas, a man confessed to raping a woman three times, but the jury agreed that *he* was the victim—of a high testosterone level. Michael Deaver excused his perjury by saying he was "forgetful" due to his drinking problem. We are in the midst of an excuse epidemic in America.

To William Wilbanks, professor of criminal justice at Florida International University in North Miami, these excuses are all variations on the same theme: "I can't help myself." Wilbanks calls this phrase the "new obscenity" because, he says, "it is offensive to the core concept of humanity": that human beings have free will and are capable of self-discipline and responsibility.

Across the country, clinicians are treating the "sexually compulsive" man who can't control his sexual desires, the "love-addicted" woman who can't break out of bad relationships, and millions of people addicted to drugs or alcohol—or who are allegedly addicted to those who are. "There is a growing tendency in the scientific community to view human beings as objects who are acted upon by internal and external forces over which they have no control," says Wilbanks. "We mistakenly infer that people *cannot* exercise self-control because they *do not* exercise self-control." We overlook the millions of men with high testosterone levels who do not rape, the depressed women who do not murder their children, and the great majority of addicts who decide to quit and do.

"The new obscenity of 'you can't help yourself' only convinces the person that her problem is hopeless and she might as well give up," says Wilbanks. "It thereby produces the very kind of problem behavior it attempts to explain. The problem with the medical model of misbehavior is that it completely ignores the idea of moral choice and resistance to temptation."

At the University of Kansas, C. R. Snyder, Ph.D., and Raymond L. Higgins, Ph.D., are also interested in the growing number of categories the public accepts as legitimate excuses for irresponsible, self-defeating, or criminal behavior. While Wilbanks is concerned about the effect of excuses on the legal system and society at large, Snyder is concerned about the effects of excuses on individual health and well-being.

Snyder has been studying the psychology of excuses for years. "Excuses—such as, 'It's not my fault,' 'The dog ate it,' 'I didn't *mean* to break her jaw'—soften the link between you and an unfortunate or negative action," says Snyder. "Of course, without excuses, we would be exposed and vulnerable; they protect our self-esteem. But sometimes, people also use excuses to rationalize the destructive things they do."

Excuses become self-defeating, says Snyder, when their costs outweigh their benefits. "A woman who blames unacceptable behavior on her depression or an 'addiction,' "he says, "finds that her future transgressions are automatically attributed to her problem—thus, her excuse becomes what's known as a self-handicapping strategy. It excuses her behavior in the short run, but in the long run it undermines her self-esteem and sense of personal control."

As a psychotherapist as well as a researcher, Snyder is particularly concerned about people who move from making the excuse to being the excuse. "With some people, the excuse becomes incorporated into their identities," says Snyder. "I couldn't help myself; I *am* an addict/rapist/abuser; I *am* depressed/shy/angry."

Snyder observes that it is particularly difficult to treat those with incorporated excuses. Once people define themselves as helpless slaves to a problem, they hand over control of the problem to others. Or they find an explanation for the problem that is out of their hands: "I can't help the way I am; my mother made me this way"— an ever-popular choice for blame. (As a client of one of Snyder's colleagues told him: "It's like this: if it's not my fault, it's her fault, and if it's not her fault, it's still not my fault.") For people whose excuses have become a problem, says Snyder, successful therapy depends on breaking down their self-deceptive, self-protective excuses and making them face the link between themselves and their actions.

Both Wilbanks and Snyder recognize that a humane legal system will consider some conditions—such as defending oneself or one's family, or having an organic brain disorder—to be legitimate excuses for a defendant's behavior. But they oppose the growing tendency in psychology and law to excuse behavior we don't like: to confuse moral judgments with scientific ones, and to confuse learned habits with organic deficiencies.

Furthermore, Wilbanks believes that for society's sake, as well as for the thousands of people who are being taught to think of themselves as helpless victims of life or biology, it is time to restore confidence in self-control and self-determination. "People can learn to respond to temptations by asking themselves, 'Is this behavior consistent with my self-image?'" says Wilbanks, "rather than, 'Can I get away with it?'"

To Apply This Reading to Yourself

1. *Discuss some undesirable behavior of your own over which you "have no control" (at least, sometimes) and include your response to the view taken by the author in the reading.*
2. *Discuss the extent to which your behavior and your life generally are dictated by forces over which you have no control.*
3. *Consider the excuses you have made for your behavior during the past year or some other period of your life, and compare their costs and benefits.*
4. *Have the excuses you have made for yourself or the excuses others have made for you been incorporated into your identity? Discuss this aspect of your life.*
5. *"My [parents, mother, father, disadvantaged background, unfortunate event, etc.] made me what I am." Do you now or have you ever thought this way? In your answer, discuss what both you and the reading have to say about this.*
6. *Do you now or have you ever considered yourself a helpless victim of life or biology? Discuss this aspect of yourself.*

Body Image

There is no more fascinating sight than your own image looking back at you in a mirror. You are drawn to it in a half-embarrassed way, excited and intensely involved. Do you remember the last time someone showed you a photograph of yourself? Wasn't there a surge of feeling and a deep curiosity about "How do I look?"

—Seymour Fisher

Our *body image* is our view or concept of our own bodies. This image includes what we see or think we see when we look at ourselves from the outside, so to speak, our reflection in a mirror perhaps or our impression on the bathroom scales. And this image is also based on how we sense or experience our bodies from the inside.

Our body image is a salient part of our self-image. Research has shown a close relationship between these two concepts. If we accept our bodies, we tend to accept or esteem ourselves generally. Those of us who reject our physical selves are likely to reject our psychological selves.

Conversely, if we generally dislike ourselves, we may dislike our bodies too. If we feel unloved and unlovable, we can see ourselves as ugly no matter what the mirror tells us. When we feel deeply anxious or guilty, we not infrequently displace our concern to our bodies and imagine we are ill or diseased in some way.

Our body image influences many of our thoughts, feelings, and actions. Seymour Fisher, a prominent researcher in this area, reminds us that our bodies intrude widely into our lives. The body is inescapable, and being an inevitable accompaniment of our awareness, it has great influence on us. By understanding body image, we can understand a good deal else about personality.

Our bodies constantly change throughout our lives, and our images of them change, too. However, perception may lag behind or outpace bodily change. The growth spurt during the adolescent years can be upsetting to the teenager (not to mention her or his parents), who in some ways seems to be a child in the body of an adult. Bodily changes occurring in middle and old age may be denied, resisted, or insistently camouflaged or, at the other extreme, they may be grossly overexaggerated into a one-foot-in-the-grave panic or depression.

The images we perceive and project are under our control to some extent. We all have a personal style, a way of dressing, adorning, grooming, and using our bodies, which relates to the person we are or want to be. Our style may have symbolic or even political significance, announcing a personal definition of ourselves and what we stand for. For example, a seemingly simple matter such as hair fashion can be an important emblem of one's identity.

Research suggests that body perceptions are frequently distorted or faulty. We may believe ourselves to be ugly, even though others see us as quite attractive (or it can be the other way around). Or we may think we are in precarious health, even seriously ill, although all medical findings are negative. Or, if we have been taught to focus on intellectual activities, we may be little aware of our bodies, and out of touch with ourselves below the neck or inside the skin.

TO A BODY, WITH RESERVATIONS

Poor body! Susceptible to disease, accident, and aging, and especially vulnerable to the criticism of its inhabitant. Many of us are not fully content with our bodies, and some are downright miserable. Research and common observation indicate that looks count, that there are definite advantages to being attractive, but also that looks aren't everything. Beauty fades and so does the happiness based on it. Our satisfaction with our bodies depends less on what we view than on the view we take. In the things of life that endure and count, what we do becomes more important than how we look.

In the first reading, Bem Allen takes a sharp look at *beautyism*—the tendency to treat beautiful people beautifully and less attractive folks less attractively. The research he musters supports the notion that "beautiful is good . . . but not always." Bem offers some suggestions for combating beautyism and urges us to "look beneath the skin" when we evaluate others—and ourselves.

In the rapid development of adolescence, we may feel wonder and agony as we watch our bodies grow up and fill out. Or not fill out—which is the personal agony of Nora Ephron who, in the second reading, writes of her failure to come to terms with her lack of "nice, big breasts" in a breast-worshipping age. She writes, "Well, what can I tell you? If I had them, I would have been a completely different person. I honestly believe that."

In adolescence, we watch our bodies fill out and grow up. Or not grow up—which is the personal experience of Leonard Gross who, in the third selection, describes his failure to grow tall in a culture that values and rewards height in males. Acutely aware of the handicap, he nevertheless carried on philosophically, even poetically. After all, although short, he was dark (at least summertimes), and handsome (almost). (The editor of the present book, 5 feet 4 1/2 inches tall at his long-past peak, found a lot to empathize with in this article.)

TO A BODY, WITH LOVE

Each of us is bodied, but not all of us love, accept, or even fully inhabit our flesh. We may camouflage our bodies or wrap them up to keep them out of sight. We may depreciate their importance or pledge our allegiance to intellect and to what lies above the neck. We may drive them like mad and fail to perform the factory-recommended maintenance.

In the last article on this topic, Abe Arkoff notes that many of us treat our bodies as the enemy. Although as a nation we are healthier than ever, we worry more about our bodies. We are not at home in them and not familiar with the way they work or content with the way they look. Arkoff gathers together some suggestions concerning the care and ownership of the body and also some ways we can come to know and even love our bodily selves.

To Explore Your Own Body Image

1. *Chronicling your body.* Your self-image is considerably affected by the image you have of your body. Your body image, in turn, is influenced by the salient events in your body's history. An in-depth history of the significant *body events* in your life can yield clues that are relevant to your current life. Body events include not only major illnesses and accidents but every significant happening including those of a positive nature (for example, becoming proficient in a sport or reaching puberty). In chronological order (earliest to most recent), number and list the most significant body events in your life. After each event, indicate its significance to the extent that you can do so. When you have completed your list, determine what relevance your body events, as a whole, have for your current life.
2. *Exploring your body.* Pick a place that offers privacy and as large a mirror as possible. Undress and carefully examine each part of your body. Then stand back a little and examine your body as a whole. Get in touch with your feelings as you do. Do you know your body? Do you like it? Is there a bodily part or aspect that you particularly like or dislike? If so, how does this affect you? What seems most salient about your body and your reactions to it? Think through your answers to these questions and write them down.
3. *Picturing your body.* How does your body appear to you? While standing, sitting, or lying down, eyes open or closed, focus your attention on the surface and inside of your body. Sense your body's

energy and shape, its strength and weaknesses, and its actuality and potentiality. When you are ready, imagine your body is constructed of circles, triangles, rectangles. If you like, visualize a shower of circles, triangles, and rectangles descending upon your body; some will harmonize and blend with and become your body while others will fall away. Then take a blank page of paper and draw a full-length representation of your body based on the image you visualized using only the circles, triangles, and rectangles. When your picture is complete, write a description of it, telling why you drew it as you did, and what you have learned from this exploration.

4. *Styling your body.* Each of us has a personal style that includes the way we dress and groom ourselves and also the way we speak and move our bodies. This style relates to the person each of us is or wishes to be. How important is your personal style to your self-definition? To explore this question, radically change your style for one day. Completely change the way you dress. Be utterly different. Record how you changed your style, how others reacted, how you felt, and what you learned from this exploration.

5. *Addressing your body.* Have you communicated with your body lately? Write your body a letter, setting down everything you have to say to it. Don't stop to plan your letter. Begin at once, starting with the salutation "Dear Body," and let the words flow out of your pen or pencil. When you have finished, write a reply (this will be your body's chance to express itself), setting down everything your body has to say to you. Again, don't stop to plan. Begin at once, letting the words flow out of your (body's) pen or pencil.

6. *Relaxing your body.* Pair with another person. One person is the relaxee, the other is the relaxer, and both are silent during this exploration. The relaxee assumes a relaxed posture. The relaxer tests and gently kneads, rubs, strokes, pats, taps, or slaps the relaxee wherever there appears to be tension. Then exchange roles. Afterward share your experiences with each other.

7. *Entrusting and awakening your body.* Pair with another person. One person is blindfolded, the other is sighted, and both are silent during this exploration. Avoiding all hazards and dangers no matter how minimal, the sighted person leads the blindfolded person in a 15-minute walk to explore the nearby environment. This walk should be made as rich a sensory experience as possible for the blindfolded person except, of course, that vision (which frequently overpowers the other senses) is not employed. When the time is up, silently exchange roles and proceed as before. Afterward, share your experiences and insights.

8. *Exalting the body.* Divide into small groups. Each group forms a circle. Every member of the group, in turn, silently and with eyes closed, sits or stands in the center. The others walk around the center person, carefully observing and then commenting on every favorable aspect of that person's face and body. After all members have had their turn in the center, they share their experiences.

9. *Body over mind.* Pair with another person, designating one partner the massager and the other the massagee. For a minute or so

each massager massages the face of the massagee into a frown, using a slow, gentle, and repetitive downward motion. Then each massager massages the face of the massagee into a smile, using a similar upward motion. Finally, the massagee is to think a happy thought while her or his face is massaged into a frown and a sad thought while her or his face is massaged into a smile. When all the above has been done, the massager and massagee exchange roles and proceed as before. Afterward, they share their experience with this exploration.

10. *Mind over body.* All members close their eyes except for one person who brings a stranger into the group. The person tells the group that "This stranger and I will chat for awhile. You are to listen and form an impression of this person's physical appearance." After the chat, the stranger leaves the room. Eyes are opened and an attempt is made to reach some group consensus as to the stranger's appearance. Then the stranger is brought back into the room for validation. Afterward, discuss the role that physical appearance plays in our impressions of and reactions to a person.

To Read Further

Barsky, A. J. (1988). *Worried sick: Our troubled quest for wellness.* Boston: Little, Brown.

Cousins, N. (1989). *Head first: The biology of hope.* New York: E. P. Dutton.

Hatfield, E., & Sprecher, S. (1986). *Mirror, mirror . . . The importance of looks in everyday life.* Albany: State University of New York Press. (paperback)

Justice, B. (1988). *Who gets sick: How beliefs, moods and thoughts affect your health.* Los Angeles: J. P. Tarcher.

Ornstein, R., & Sobel, D. (1989). *Healthy pleasures.* Reading, MA: Addison-Wesley.

Beautyism

Bem P. Allen

I learned the truth at seventeen
That love was meant for beauty queens
and high school girls with clear-skinned
  smiles
who married young, and then retired
To those of us who know the pain
of valentines that never came,
and those whose names were never called
when choosing sides for basketball
It was long ago, and far away
The world was younger than today
when dreams were all they gave for free
to ugly duckling girls like me.

     —Janis Ian, *At Seventeen*

People have been publicly concerned about racism and sexism for many decades. But only recently has there been concern about **beautyism**—the tendency to regard physically unattractive people unfavorably and to react more negatively to them compared to physically attractive people. Racism and sexism may be more serious problems, but we can learn much about the other "isms" by studying beautyism. Further, while most people acknowledge the harm done by racism and sexism, the extent of beautyism's harmful effects are unknown to most people.

 Social scientists seemed to have avoided studying beautyism until the mid-1960s when a group of researchers discovered more or less by accident that everyone wants an attractive date. Elaine Walster (now Hatfield) and her colleagues Aronson, Abrahams, & Rottman (1966) were actually investigating the matching hypothesis. They wanted to confirm that people would like dates whose attractiveness level was similar to their own.

 To test their hypothesis, the researchers offered first-year college students a chance for a "computer date" as they were signing up for classes. Date participants were assessed on level of self-esteem, degree of social skills, and level of intelligence. During these assessments, they were secretly rated on physical attractiveness.

 Although the student subjects were told they would be matched with someone who was similar to them, dates were randomly assigned. This procedure guaranteed that all possible combinations of characteristics would exist: attractive man who had high self-esteem, low social skills, and low intelligence matched with an unattractive woman who had low self-esteem, high social skills, and high intelligence; unattractive man who had low self-esteem, high social skills, and high intelligence matched with an attractive woman who had high self-esteem, low social skills, and high intelligence; and so forth.

 Subjects met at a dance and spent a couple of hours interacting. Then men and women were separated and asked "How much do you like your date?" and "How much would you like to date her (him) again?" A few months later, men were contacted to determine whether they had asked their "computer dates" out again. Results were very simple. There was no evidence for the matching hypothesis. Everyone preferred an attractive date. Such was true regardless of whether they were themselves homely or good-looking and regardless of whether the attractive date was socially clumsy, down on themselves and slow intellectually. Further, the follow-up a few months later revealed that men had been more likely to ask their computer dates out again if they were attractive. This study and others like it convinced social scientists that attractiveness was more than just important in determining date selection—it was all-important (Allen, 1978). Unattractive people were rejected in favor of attractive persons regardless of all other characteristics. Researchers then began to wonder in what other social realms might attractiveness play an important role.

BEAUTIFUL IS GOOD

Though exercise can change the body to a considerable extent, people with unattractive faces generally must resort to frequently painful surgery. But do ugly faces *cause* the negative reactions that their possessors habitually receive? If it could be shown that people are seen as more attractive and more socially desirable after surgery than before, a causal relationship between attractiveness and social reactions would be suggested. If increases in favorable reactions follow surgical enhancement of facial attractiveness, attractiveness may be seen as causing favorable social reactions. The other side of the causal coin—negative personal characteristics cause low attractiveness ratings—has received little support (Hatfield & Sprecher, 1986).

Kalick (1977; reported in Berscheid & Gangestad, 1982) had people rate patients before cosmetic facial surgery and again after surgery. Generally, he found that patients' attractiveness ratings became more favorable and so did reactions to their characteristics. After surgery, patients were rated as kinder, more sensitive, more likely to marry the person of their choice, higher in social and professional happiness, and more desirable. In a similar study, Cash and Horton (1983) had one set of raters do the "before" ratings and another set do the "after" ratings. Again attractiveness ratings became more favorable after surgery, as did ratings on a number of personality scales. Other work showed that reactions to patients on their own part and on the part of their parents improved after surgery, especially in the case of self-esteem (Arndt, Lefebvre, Travis, & Munro, 1986; Arndt, Travis, Lefebvre, & Munro, 1986; Jacobson, 1984).

Work on the effects of facial surgery suggests that becoming better looking makes people more desirable in many ways. In fact, much research indicates people *believe* that to be beautiful or handsome is to possess (almost) all the other characteristics valued in our society (Hatfield & Sprecher, 1986). That is, many stereotypes of attractive and unattractive people exist. The observation that most of the traits attributed to attractive people are very favorable and most of those ascribed to unattractive persons are decidedly negative has been dubbed "beautiful is good." The best-known study on this topic found that, compared with homely individuals, attractive people are believed to be more sexually responsive, warmer, more sensitive, kinder, more interesting, stronger, more poised, more sociable, more outgoing, more exciting as dates, of better character, and more likely to have happy marriages, better jobs, and fulfilling lives (Dion, Berscheid, & Walster, 1972). Compared with homely people, good-looking individuals are also expected to be more intelligent, more likely to succeed academically, more preferred as friends, more independent, less "scary," and more talented (Clifford & Walster, 1973; Dion, 1973; Dion & Berscheid, 1974; Landy & Sigall, 1974).

BEAUTIFUL IS GOOD . . . BUT NOT ALWAYS

However, all that glitters is not gold. Negative stereotypes of attractive people also exist. Dermer and Thiel (1975) did a study similar to that of Dion and colleagues' (1972) "beautiful is good" study but used more refined measures. Overall they found that beautiful people are more highly regarded than homely ones, but there were some notable exceptions. Attractive individuals were seen as more vain and egotistical, more likely to have an extramarital affair, and more likely to divorce. They were also viewed as less effective parents, more snobbish, more likely to link money with happiness, and less likely to be sympathetic to oppressed people. Some of these attributions may be due to jealousy, but not all of them (Krebs & Adinolfi, 1975). Basically, attractive people are seen as being self-centered.

Hatfield and Sprecher (1986) go so far as to suggest that beauty may sometimes be a serious handicap. Attractive people may find that paths to certain public service jobs are blocked because of their alleged self-centeredness (for example, social work). Beautiful people complain that others do not like them for their real selves, but rather for their looks. Attractive individuals may have trouble getting same-sex friends, because potential friends may be jealous. Some good-looking people even claim that they are handicapped with the opposite sex, because they may seem so unattainable that they are never approached.

There is another qualification to the "beautiful is good, ugly is bad" rule. Research sometimes "discovers" attributions that people do not make in real life. For instance, a study by Goldberg, Gottesdiener, and Abramson (1975) seemed to show that supporters of the women's movement are seen as unattractive relative to nonsupporters, but, according to Arthur Beaman and his colleagues, subsequent research did not support this conclusion (Beaman & Klentz, 1983). Apparently, only people who disagree with feminists see them as unattractive (Klentz, Beaman, Mapelli, & Ullrich, 1987).

"The ugly feminist fallacy" suggests that many people, even some researchers, link women's attractiveness to everything they do or believe. In turn, it is implied that being good-looking or not has greater implications for women than for men.

IS IT TRUE WHAT THEY SAY ABOUT ATTRACTIVE PEOPLE?

Though beautiful is not always "good," ugly is not always "bad," and attractiveness is more important for women than for men, both men and women are better off if they are attractive (Hatfield & Sprecher, 1986). So far, however, only what people *believe* about unattractive and attractive people has been considered. We still must discover whether attractive and unattractive individuals actually have the characteristics attributed to them.

If unattractive people are treated less well than attractive people beginning early in life, and if they are expected to be inferior to attractive individuals, one would predict that they will have less desirable characteristics and outcomes than attractive people (Allen, 1978). In fact, a great deal of research confirms that prediction. More favorable outcomes for attractive relative to unattractive people begin very early in life. Adams (1981) reports that attractive infants are looked at more often. When they grow to school age, they have higher-quality interactions with teachers. At the same time, unattractive children fare poorly in interactions with peers. At adulthood, males have more interactions with the opposite sex if they are attractive, and both sexes are more satisfied with all their interactions if they are attractive (Reis, Nezlek, & Wheeler, 1980). Other evidence related to interactions suggests that people receive more positive ratings when they are seen as friends with attractive people and when they are seen as unassociated with unattractive people (Kernis & Wheeler, 1981). Attractive people also have

higher self-esteem (Allen & Wroble, 1975; Mathis & Kahn, 1975).

Early positive attention, more frequent and more satisfying interactions, and higher self-esteem on the part of attractive individuals yield the prediction that they will have greater social skills. In a very impressive study, Goldman and Lewis (1977) made sure that results reflected actual differences between unattractive and attractive people in social skills, rather than just differences in attributions. Subjects conversed with targets over the telephone and then rated them on social skills *without having seen them.* The more unattractive were targets, the lower were their social skills ratings.

Several studies indicate that attractive people are more likely to get help when they need it (Harrell, 1978; West & Brown, 1975; Wilson, 1978). They are also more likely than unattractive people to fare well in court (Stephan & Tully, 1977). When the specific crime of rape is examined, it is found that rapists get longer sentences when the victim is attractive (Thornton, 1977) and that unattractive victims were judged to have provoked their own rapes more than attractive victims (Seligman, Brickman, & Koulack, 1977).

Attractiveness has some very practical effects at the polling place and in the job market. People tend to vote for more attractive candidates (Efran & Patterson, 1974; Madden & Martin, 1979). Cash, Gillen and Burns (1977) gave the same resumes to 60 actual personnel directors, except that some resumes had photos of attractive people attached and some had photos of unattractive people. Unattractive people were judged as less qualified for jobs. The fruits of one's labors may also be affected by attractiveness; Cash and Trimer (1984) found that attractive essay writers were given greater overall positive evaluations and received higher letter grades.

Attractiveness also relates to psychiatric problems. Farina, Fisher, Sherman, Smith, Groh, & Mermin (1977) took facial photos in such a way as to minimize any grooming differences between mental hospital patients and non-patients. Results showed that mental hospital patients were less attractive. Within the hospital setting, homely patients were less responsive, received more severe diagnoses, were visited less often and were hospitalized longer. In a careful replication, Napoleon, Chassin, and Young (1980) sought to confirm that unattractiveness may give rise to psychiatric problems, rather unattractiveness being the result of psychiatric problems. In their study, high school photos of patients were compared with those of their non-patient peers. Even before they developed mental illness, patients had been less attractive than others. Napoleon and colleagues also found that low-income people were less attractive than others. Other work suggests that mental health workers may be biased against unattractive people (Nordholm, 1980).

CAN BEAUTYISM BE OVERCOME?

In a number of surveys and interviews, people have seen attractiveness as superficial and suggested that it should not account for much in people's reactions to others (Allen, 1978; Hatfield & Sprecher, 1986). But people do not act according to these beliefs; attractiveness is terribly important. If it is terribly important, and we do not like that fact, we need to behave differently. The gap between how much we think attractiveness should be valued and how much we actually value it can be narrowed if we rear our children without indoctrinating them that "beautiful is good." We must alert them to the media bias in favor of attractive people (most TV characters are attractive). We must also stop showing our children affection by praising their looks. Just as people have become more tolerant of minorities and handicapped people once their plight is fully appreciated, people will be more tolerant of unattractive individuals when they recognize that the homely are also at a disadvantage. If we truly belief that beauty is skin deep, we should begin to look beneath the skin and attend to more internal, less superficial characteristics when we evaluate other people.

References

Adams, G. R. (1981). The effects of physical attractiveness on the socialization process. In G. W. Lucker, K. A. Ribbens, & J. A. McNamara, Jr. (Eds.), *Psychological Aspects of Facial Form.* (Monograph No. 11, Craniofacial Growth Series), Ann Arbor, MI: Center for Human Growth and Development, University of Michigan.

Allen, B. P. (1978). *Social behavior: Fact and falsehood.* Chicago: Nelson-Hall.

Allen, B. P., & Wroble, S. (1975, May). *Attractive people like themselves better than unattractive people . . . most of the time: Self-descriptions employing the AGT.* Paper presented at convention of the Midwestern Psychological Association, Chicago.

Arndt, E. M., Lefebvre, F., Travis, F., & Munro, I. R. (1986). Fact and fantasy: Psychosocial consequences of facial surgery in 24 Down syndrome children. *British Journal of Plastic Surgery, 39,* 498–504.

Arndt, E. M., Travis, A., Lefebvre, A., & Munro, I. R. (1986). Beauty and the eye of the beholder: Social consequences and personal adjustments for facial patients. *British Journal of Plastic Surgery, 39,* 81–84.

Beaman, A. L., & Klentz, B. (1983). The supposed physical attractiveness bias against supporters of the women's movement: A meta-analysis. *Personality and Social Psychology Bulletin, 9,* 544–550.

Berscheid, E., & Gangestad, S. (1982). The social psychological implications of facial physical attractiveness. *Clinics in Plastic Surgery, 9,* 289–296.

Cash, T. F., Gillen, B., & Burns, S. (1977). Sexism and "beautyism" in personnel consultant decision making. *Journal of Applied Psychology, 62,* 301–310.

Cash, T. F., & Horton, C. E. (1983). Aesthetic surgery: Effects of rhinoplasty on the social perception of patients by others. *Plastic and Reconstructive Surgery, 72*(4), 543–550.

Cash, T. F., & Trimer, C. A. (1984). Sexism and beautyism in women's evaluations of peer performance. *Sex Roles, 10,* 87–98.

Clifford, M., & Walster, E. (1973). The effects of physical attractiveness on teacher expectations. *Sociology of Education, 46,* 248–258.

Dermer, M., & Theil, D. (1975). When beauty fails. *Journal of Personality and Social Psychology, 31,* 1168–1176.

Dion, K. (1973). Young children's stereotyping of facial attractiveness. *Developmental Psychology, 9,* 183–188.

Dion, K., & Berscheid, E. (1974). Physical attractiveness and peer perception among children. *Sociometry, 37,* 1–12.

Dion, K., Berscheid, E., & Walster, E. (1972). What is beautiful is good. *Journal of Personality and Social Psychology, 24,* 285–290.

Efran, M. G., & Patterson, E. W. J. (1974). Voters vote beautiful: The effect of physical appearance on a national election. *Canadian Journal of Behavioral Science, 6,* 353–356.

Farina, A., Fischer, E. H., Sherman, S., Smith, W. T., Groh, T., & Mermin, P. (1977). Physical attractiveness and mental illness. *Journal of Abnormal Psychology, 86,* 510–517.

Goldberg, P. A., Gottesdiener, M., & Abramson, P. R. (1975). Another put-down of women? Perceived attractiveness as a function of support of the feminist movement. *Journal of Personality and Social Psychology, 32,* 113–115.

Goldman, W., & Lewis, P. (1977). Beautiful is good: Evidence that the physically attractive are more socially skilled. *Journal of Experimental Social Psychology, 13,* 125–130.

Harrel, W. A. (1978). Physical attractiveness, self-disclosure, and helping behavior. *The Journal of Social Psychology, 104,* 15–17.

Hatfield, E., & Sprecher, S. (1986). *Mirror, mirror . . . The importance of looks in everyday life.* New York: State University of New York Press.

Jacobson, A. (1984). Psychological aspects of dentofacial esthetics and orthognathic surgery. *The Angle Orthodontist, 54,* 18–35.

Kalick, S. M. (1977). *Plastic surgery, physical appearance, and person perception.* Unpublished doctoral dissertation, Harvard University.

Kernis, M. H., & Wheeler, L. (1981). Beautiful friends and ugly strangers: Radiation and contrast effects in perceptions of same-sex pairs. *Personality and Social Psychology Bulletin, 7,* 617–620.

Klentz, B., Beaman, A. L., Mapelli, S. D., & Ullrich, J. R. (1987). Perceived physical attractiveness of supporters and nonsupporters of the women's movement: An attitude-similarity-error (AS-ME). *Personality and Social Psychology Bulletin, 13,* 513–523.

Krebs, D., & Adinolfi, A. (1975). Physical attractiveness, social relations, and personal life-style. *Journal of Personality and Social Psychology, 31,* 245–253.

Landy, D., & Sigall, H. (1974). Beauty is talent. *Journal of Personality and Social Psychology, 29,* 299–304.

Madden, J. M., & Martin, E. J. (1979). An indirect method of attitude measurement. *Bulletin of the Psychonomic Society, 13,* 170–172.

Mathes, E., & Kahn, A. (1975). Physical attractiveness, happiness, neuroticism, and self-esteem. *Journal of Psychology, 90,* 27–30.

Napoleon, T., Chassin, L., & Young, R. D. (1980). A replication and extension of "physical attractiveness and mental illness." *Journal of Personality and Social Psychology, 89,* 250–253.

Nordholm, L. A. (1980). Beautiful patients are good patients: Evidence for the physical attractiveness stereotype in first impressions of patients. *Social Science and Medicine, 14A,* 81–83.

Reis, H. T., Nezlek, J., & Wheeler, L. (1980). Physical attractiveness in social interaction. *Journal of Personality and Social Psychology, 38,* 604–617.

Seligman, C., Brickman, K., & Koulack, D. (1977). Rape and physical attractiveness: Assigning responsibility to victims. *Journal of Personality, 45,* 554–563.

Stephan, C. W., & Tully, J. C. (1977). The influence of physical attractiveness of a plaintiff on the decisions of simulated jurors. *Journal of Social Psychology, 101,* 101–150.

Thornton, B. (1977). Effect of the victim's attractiveness in a jury simulation. *Personality and Social Psychology Bulletin, 3,* 666–669.

Walster, E., Aronson, V., Abrahams, D., & Rottmann, L. (1966). Importance of physical attractiveness in dating behavior. *Journal of Personality and Social Psychology, 4,* 508–516.

West, S. G., & Brown, T. J. (1975). Physical attractiveness, the severity of the emergency and helping: A field experiment and interpersonal simulation. *Journal of Experimental Social Psychology, 11,* 531–538.

Wilson, D. W. (1978). Helping behavior and physical attractiveness. *Journal of Social Psychology, 104,* 313–314.

To Apply This Reading to Yourself

1. *Discuss your own experience that either confirms or disconfirms the "beautiful is good, ugly is bad" rule.*
2. *What "beautiful is good, ugly is bad" messages did you receive as you were growing up, and what effect did they have on you?*
3. *How has your own degree of beauty or physical attractiveness been a help or a handicap for you?*
4. *Discuss the relationship you see between your degree of beauty or physical attractiveness and your self-esteem.*
5. *What role has physical attractiveness played in your own selection of employees, friends, dates, mates, and so on?*

A Few Words About Breasts

Nora Ephron

I have to begin with a few words about androgyny. In grammar school, in the fifth and sixth grades, we were all tyrannized by a rigid set of rules that supposedly determined whether we were boys or girls. The episode in *Huckleberry Finn* where Huck is disguised as a girl and gives himself away by the way he threads a needle and catches a ball—that kind of thing. We learned that the way you sat, crossed your legs, held a cigarette, looked at your nails—the way you did these things instinctively was absolute proof of your sex. Now obviously most children did not take this literally, but I did. I thought that just one slip, just one incorrect cross of my legs or flick of an imaginary cigarette ash would turn me from whatever I was into the other thing; that would be all it took, really. Even though I was outwardly a girl and had many of the trappings generally associated with girldom—a girl's name, for example, and dresses, my own telephone, an autograph book—I spent the early years of my adolescence absolutely certain that I might at any point gum it up. I did not feel at all like a girl. I was boyish. I was athletic, ambitious, outspoken, competitive, noisy, rambunctious. I had scabs on my knees and my socks slid into my loafers and I could throw a football. I wanted desperately not to be that way, not to be a mixture of both things, but instead just one, a girl, a definite indisputable girl. As soft and as pink as a nursery. And nothing would do that for me, I felt, but breasts.

I was about six months younger than everyone else in my class, and so for about six months after it began, for six months after my friends had begun to develop (that was the word we used, develop), I was not particularly worried. I would sit in the bathtub and look down at my breasts and know that any day now, any second now, they would start growing like everyone else's. They didn't. "I want to buy a bra," I said to my mother one night. "What for?" she said. My mother was really hateful about bras, and by the time my third sister had gotten to the point where she was ready to want one, my mother had worked the whole business into a comedy routine. "Why not use a Band-Aid instead?" she would say. It was a source of great pride to my mother that she had never even had to wear a brassiere until she had her fourth child, and then only because her gynecologist made her. It was incomprehensible to me that anyone could ever be proud of something like that. It was the 1950s, for God's sake. Jane Russell. Cashmere sweaters. Couldn't my mother see that? *I am too old to wear an undershirt.* Screaming. Weeping. Shouting. "Then don't wear an undershirt," said my mother. "But I want to buy a bra." "What for?"

I suppose that for most girls, breasts, brassieres, that entire thing, has more trauma, more to do with the coming of adolescence, with becoming a woman, than anything else. Certainly more than getting your period, although that, too, was traumatic, symbolic. But you could see breasts; they were there; they were visible. Whereas a girl could claim to have her period for months before she actually got it and nobody would even know the difference. Which is exactly what I did. All you had to do was make a great fuss over having enough nickels for the Kotex machine and walk around clutching your stomach and moaning for three to five days a month about The Curse and you could convince anybody. There is a school of thought somewhere in the women's lib/women's mag/gynecology establishment that claims that menstrual cramps are purely psychological, and I lean toward it. Not that I didn't have them finally. Agonizing cramps, heating-pad cramps, go-down-to-the-school-nurse-and-lie-on-the-cot cramps. But, unlike any pain I had ever suffered, I adored the pain of cramps, welcomed it, wallowed in it, bragged about it. "I can't go. I have cramps." "I can't do that. I have cramps." And most of all, gigglingly, blushingly: "I can't swim. I have cramps." Nobody ever used the hard-core word. Menstruation. God, what an awful word. Never that. "I have cramps."

The morning I first got my period, I went into my mother's bedroom to tell her. And my mother, my utterly-hateful-about-bras mother, burst into tears. It was really a lovely moment, and I remember it so clearly not just because it was one of the two times I ever saw my mother cry on my account (the other was when I was caught being a six-year-old kleptomaniac), but also because the incident did not mean to me what it meant to her. Her little girl, her firstborn, had finally become a woman. That was what she was crying about. My reaction to the event, however, was that I might well be a woman in some scientific, textbook sense (and could at least stop faking every month and stop wasting all those nickels). But in another sense—in a visible sense—I was as androgynous and as liable to tip over into boyhood as ever.

I started with a 28 AA bra. I don't think they made them any smaller in those days, although I gather that now you can buy bras for five-year-olds that don't have any cups whatsoever in them; trainer bras they are called. My first brassiere came from Robinson's Department Store in Beverly Hills. I went there alone, shaking, positive they would look me over and smile and tell me to come back next year. An actual fitter took me into the dressing room and stood over me while I took off my blouse and tried the first one on. The little puffs stood out on my chest. "Lean over," said the fitter. (To this day, I am not sure what fitters in bra departments do except to tell you to lean over.) I leaned over, with the fleeting hope that my breasts would miraculously fall out of my body and into the puffs. Nothing.

"Don't worry about it," said my friend Libby some months later, when things had not improved. "You'll get them after you're married."

"What are you talking about?" I said.

"When you get married," Libby explained, "your husband will touch your breasts and rub them and kiss them and they'll grow."

That was the killer. Necking I could deal with. Intercourse I could deal with. But it had never crossed my mind that a man was going to touch my breasts, that breasts had something to do with all that, petting, my God, they never mentioned petting in my little sex manual about the fertilization of the ovum. I became dizzy. For I knew instantly—as naive as I had been only a moment before—that only part of what she was saying was true: the touching, rubbing, kissing part, not the growing part. And I knew that no one would ever want to marry me. I had no breasts. I would never have breasts.

My best friend in school was Diana Raskob. She lived a block from me in a house full of wonders. English muffins, for instance. The Raskobs were the first people in Beverly Hills to have English muffins for breakfast. They also had an apricot tree in the back, and a badminton court, and a subscription to *Seventeen* magazine, and hundreds of games, like Sorry and Parcheesi and Treasure Hunt and Anagrams. Diana and I spent three or four afternoons a week in their den reading and playing and eating. Diana's mother's kitchen was full of the most colossal assortment of junk food I have ever been exposed to. My house was full of apples and peaches and milk and homemade chocolate-chip cookies—which were nice, and good for you, but-not-right-before-dinner-or-you'll-spoil-your-appetite. Diana's house had nothing in it that was good for you, and what's more, you could stuff it in right up until dinner and nobody cared. Bar-B-Q potato chips (they were the first in them, too), giant bottles of ginger ale, fresh popcorn with melted butter, hot fudge sauce on Baskin-Robbins jamoca ice cream, powdered-sugar doughnuts from Van de Kamp's. Diana and I had been best friends since we were seven; we were equally popular in school (which is to say, not particularly), we had the same success with boys (extremely intermittent), and we looked much the same. Dark. Tall. Gangly.

It is September, just before school begins. I am eleven years old, about to enter the seventh grade, and Diana and I have not seen each other all summer. I have been to camp and she has been somewhere like Banff with her parents. We are meeting, as we often do, on the street midway between our two houses, and we will walk back to Diana's and eat junk and talk about what has happened to each of us that summer. I am walking down Walden Drive in my jeans and my father's shirt hanging out and my old red loafers with the socks falling into them and coming toward me is . . . I take a deep breath . . . a young woman. Diana. Her hair is curled and she has a waist and hips and a bust and she is wearing a straight skirt, an article of clothing I have been repeatedly told I am unable to wear until I have the hips to hold it up. My jaw drops, and suddenly I am crying, crying hysterically, can't catch my breath sobbing. My best friend has betrayed me. She has gone ahead without me and done it. She has shaped up.

Here are some things I did to help:

Bought a Mark Eden Bust Developer.
Slept on my back for four years.
Splashed cold water on them every night because some French actress said in Life magazine that was what she did for her perfect bustline.

Ultimately, I resigned myself to a bad toss and began to wear padded bras. I think about them now, think about all those years in high school I went around in them, my three padded bras, every single one of them with different-sized breasts. Each time I changed bras I changed sizes: one week nice perky but not too obtrusive breasts, the next medium-sized slightly pointy ones, the next week knockers, true knockers; all the time, whatever size I was, carrying around this rubberized appendage on my chest that occasionally crashed into a wall and was poked inward and had to be poked outward—I think about all that and wonder how anyone kept a straight face through it. My parents, who normally had no restraints about needling me—why did they say nothing as they watched my chest go up and down? My friends, who would periodically inspect my breasts for signs of growth and reassure me—why didn't they at least counsel consistency?

And the bathing suits. I die when I think about the bathing suits. That was the era when you could lay an uninhabited bathing suit on the beach and someone would make a pass at it. I would put one on, an absurd swimsuit with its enormous bust built into it, the bones from the suit stabbing me in the rib cage and leaving little red welts on my body, and there I would be, my chest plunging straight downward absolutely vertically from my collarbone to the top of my suit and then suddenly, wham, out came all that padding and material and wiring absolutely horizontally.

Buster Klepper was the first boy who ever touched them. He was my boyfriend my senior year of high school. There is a picture of him in my high-school yearbook that makes him look quite attractive in a Jewish, horn-rimmed-glasses sort of way, but the picture does not show the pimples, which were air-brushed out, or the dumbness. Well, that isn't really fair. He wasn't dumb. He just wasn't terribly bright. His mother refused to accept it, refused to accept the relentlessly average report cards, refused to deal with her son's inevitable destiny. . . . "He was tested," she would say to me, apropos of nothing, "and it came out a hundred and forty-five. That's near-genius." Had the word "underachiever" been coined, she probably would have lobbed that one at me, too. Anyway, Buster was really very sweet—which is, I know, damning with faint praise, but there it is. I was the editor of the front page of the high-school newspaper and he was editor of the back page; we had to work together, side by side, in the print shop, and that was how it started. On our first date, we went to see *April Love*, starring Pat Boone. Then we started going together. Buster had a green coupe, a 1950 Ford with an engine he had hand-chromed until it shone, dazzled, reflected the image of anyone who looked into it, anyone usually being Buster polishing it or the gas-station attendants he constantly asked to check the oil in order for them to be overwhelmed by the sparkle on the valves. The car also had a boot stretched over the back seat for reasons I never understood; hanging from the rearview mirror, as was the custom, was a pair of angora dice. A previous girl friend named Solange, who was famous throughout Beverly Hills High School for having no pigment in her right eyebrow, had knitted them for him. Buster and I would ride around town, the two of us seated to the left of the steering wheel. I would shift gears. It was nice.

There was necking. Terrific necking. First in the car, overlooking Los Angeles from what is now the Trousdale Estates. Then on the bed of his parents' cabana at Ocean House. Incredibly wonderful, frustrating necking, I loved it, really, but no further than necking, please don't, please, because there I was absolutely terrified of the general implications of going-a-step-further with a near-dummy and also terrified of his finding out there was next to nothing there (which he knew, of course; he wasn't that dumb).

I broke up with him at one point. I think we were apart for about two weeks. At the end of that time, I drove down to see a friend at a boarding school in Palos Verdes Estates and a disc jockey played "April Love" on the radio four times during the trip. I took it as a sign. I drove straight back to Griffith Park to a golf tournament Buster was playing in (he was the sixth-seeded teen-age golf player in southern California) and presented myself back to him on the green of the 18th hole. It was all very dramatic. That night we went to a drive-in and I let him get his hand under my protuberances and onto my breasts. He really didn't seem to mind at all.

"Do you want to marry my son?" the woman asked me.

"Yes," I said.

I was nineteen years old, a virgin, going with this woman's son, this big strange woman who was married to a Lutheran minister in New Hampshire and pretended she was gentle and had this son, by her first husband, this total fool of a son who ran the hero-sandwich concession at Harvard Business School and whom for one moment in December in New Hampshire I said—as much out of politeness as anything else—that I wanted to marry.

"Fine," she said. "Now, here's what you do. Always make sure you're on top of him so you won't seem so small. My bust is very large, you see, so I always lie on my back to make it look smaller, but you'll have to be on top most of the time."

I nodded. "Thank you," I said.

"I have a book for you to read," she went on. "Take it with you when you leave. Keep it." She went to the bookshelf, found it, and gave it to me. It was a book on frigidity.

"Thank you," I said.

That is a true story. Everything in this article is a true story, but I feel I have to point out that that story in particular is true. It happened on December 30, 1960. I think about it often. When it first happened, I naturally assumed that the woman's son, my boyfriend, was responsible. I invented a scenario where he had had a little heart-to-heart with his mother and had confessed that his only objection to me was that my breasts were small; his mother then took it upon herself to help out. Now I think I was wrong about the incident. The mother was acting on her own, I think: that was her way of being cruel and competitive under the guise of being helpful and maternal. You have small breasts, she was

saying; therefore you will never make him as happy as I have. Or you have small breasts; therefore you will doubtless have sexual problems. Or you have small breasts; therefore you are less woman than I am. She was, as it happens, only the first of what seems to me to be a never-ending string of women who have made competitive remarks to me about breast size. "I would love to wear a dress like that," my friend Emily says to me, "but my bust is too big." Like that. Why do women say these things to me? Do I attract these remarks the way other women attract married men or alcoholics or homosexuals? This summer, for example. I am at a party in East Hampton and I am introduced to a woman from Washington. She is a minor celebrity, very pretty and Southern and blond and outspoken, and I am flattered because she has read something I have written. We are talking animatedly, we have been talking no more than five minutes, when a man comes up to join us. "Look at the two of us," the woman says to the man, indicating me and her. "The two of us together couldn't fill an A cup." Why does she say that? It isn't even true, dammit, so why? Is she even more addled than I am on this subject? Does she honestly believe there is something wrong with her size breasts, which, it seems to me, now that I look hard at them, are just right? Do I unconsciously bring out competitiveness in women? In what form? What did I do to deserve it?

As for men.

There were men who minded and let me know that they minded. There were men who did not mind. In any case, *I* always minded.

And even now, now that I have been countlessly reassured that my figure is a good one, now that I am grown-up enough to understand that most of my feelings have very little to do with the reality of my shape, I am nonetheless obsessed by breasts. I cannot help it. I grew up in the terrible fifties—with rigid stereotypical sex roles, the insistence that men be men and dress like men and women be women and dress like women, the intolerance of androgyny—and I cannot shake it, cannot shake feelings of inadequacy. Well, that time is gone, right? All those exaggerated examples of breast worship are gone, right? Those women were freaks, right? I know all that. And yet here I am, stuck with the psychological remains of it all, stuck with my own peculiar version of breast worship. You probably think I am crazy to go on like this: here I have set out to write a confession that is meant to hit you with the shock of recognition, and instead you are sitting there thinking I am thoroughly warped. Well, what can I tell you? If I had had them, I would have been a completely different person. I honestly believe that.

After I went into therapy, a process that made it possible for me to tell total strangers at cocktail parties that breasts were the hang-up of my life, I was often told that I was insane to have been bothered by my condition. I was also frequently told, by close friends, that I was extremely boring on the subject. And my girl friends, the ones with nice big breasts, would go on endlessly about how their lives had been far more miserable than mine. Their bra straps were snapped in class. They couldn't sleep on their stomachs. They were stared at whenever the word "mountain" cropped up in geography. And *Evangeline*, good God what they went through every time someone had to stand up and recite the Prologue to Longfellow's *Evangeline*: "... stands like druids of eld ... /With beards that rest on their bosoms." It was much worse for them, they tell me. They had a terrible time of it, they assure me. I don't know how lucky I was, they say.

I have thought about their remarks, tried to put myself in their place, considered their point of view. I think they are full of shit.

To Apply This Reading to Yourself

1. *What single feature or aspect of your body are you least satisfied with at present? How different might you and your life be if this aspect were as you would wish it to be? Write a brief paper incorporating your answers to these questions.*
2. *Recall and discuss your own feelings about your body as you watched its development during your adolescence.*
3. *What features or aspects of your body do you regard or value differently now than you did when you were an adolescent? What aspects might you value differently when you are considerably older than you are now? Why?*
4. *Allow an image of a woman with an ideal or perfect body to form in your mind's eye. If you are a woman, how different are you from this image and what meaning has the difference for you? If you are a man, how different is your wife/lover/girlfriend/current date from this image and what meaning does this difference have for you?*

Short, Dark, and Almost Handsome

Leonard H. Gross

I used to think it curious as I began to notice that the only men who stated their height on résumés I'd receive were those six feet or taller. Why, I puzzled, would these résumé writers think anyone could possibly care how tall an editor is—unless the dejected fellows were scraping the barrel of their assets for something to say about themselves.

One day I realized they weren't as off-base as I had thought. I chanced upon a sociological study, which found that when the starting salaries of graduates of the same business college were compared, the taller men's salaries were significantly higher. In addition, another social psychology experiment had 140 recruiters make a hypothetical choice between two equally qualified applicants, one man six feet, one inch, and the other five feet, five inches. Only one percent chose the short man.

These revelations stirred up some suppressed anxieties I guess I've never really shaken off. Being somewhat undersized all through childhood, I worried if I'd reach that critical five feet eight that enabled you to be a cop or a fireman (these occupations being symbols for the worrisome question—"Will I be a Real Man?"). Height can only be a factor insofar as it represents "Authority" and transmits a strong and dependable image, because a gun and penalties of law provide enough real power, and a hose will smother more flames than the foot of a fireman even as big as Wilt Chamberlain ever could.

Nonetheless, the smaller fellow is guided to a less "virile" occupation than that of a cop or fireman. But is this a sanctuary from insults about height? Absolutely not. Let the smaller man dare remind someone in his employ that she or he is spending too much time on the phone or is not performing as expected. You know what that makes him? A *Napoleon*. A midget getting even for his shortness by being mean and dicta-torial. Any other man discharging his duties in the exact same fashion would be judged secure in his authority. But the shorter man is a frightened, vengeful creep.

Another social psychology experiment shows how social importance is mingled in people's minds with height: when the same man was introduced to successive groups of students, each group was told he was of a different academic rank and was asked to estimate his height. The higher his rank, the taller the students judged him to be.

However, before we feel too much sympathy for the little guy, I should indicate that he has one grand consolation. *He is sure to have an even smaller wife!* Our culture's idolization of size, which is simply another facet of "might makes right," oppresses women even more powerfully. While some men may feel inadequate, our tendency to pair off couples where the husband is taller and the wife smaller makes every woman "less significant"—indeed the "weaker sex" or "the little woman."

True, men like Henry Kissinger—and the late Aristotle Onassis—have bucked this tide. But they have "social size," and may indeed still be considered "big" enough to have their "little woman" after all. For the rest of us, it's been an uphill battle all along.

In the Brownsville section of Brooklyn where I was raised, health was the paramount anxiety, and size the chief reassurance. Growth was the only achievement expected of a kid: "Drink your milk—ya wanna be a midget?" "Go to sleep . . . " (while it's still light out on summer evenings, and other kids are playing all over the streets) "that's when you *grow!*"

I recall being force-fed as a child, as if everything weighed in the balance. To get me to down hot cereal, my mother would go through a daily ritual: "Coming home from the store today I saw a dog, and do you know what that dog did?" "Wha . . . *(gulp)*." She'd shove the spoon down my throat. After 5,000 repetitions, I was still curious about that dog. It never occurred to me there was no story. Only a boy's undying trust in his mother could match her need to nourish and promote growth.

And, of course, Mom was under pressure, too. I remember the way my friend Izzy's mother used to pump me: "Your mother, she plays cards? She goes to movies? She works?" One day I asked Izzy what this constant probing was all about, and he let on, "You're smaller and skinnier than I am, so my mother thinks your mother runs around instead of feeding her family." By not growing, I betrayed my dear mother's devotion.

Well, I got mine in school when we had to line up in "size place" hundreds of times every day: "Time for gym. Class line up in size places!" "The class will now walk, double file, in size-order to the auditorium." To this day I can't fathom why teachers humiliated me and the other short kids this way. Couldn't we get to the damn auditorium simply on our feet, in any order? It followed only the mean Kafkaesque logic of tyranny: "You shouldn't kick a man when he's down." *"That's the best time to kick him!"* Why pick on short people?" *"They're perfect to pick on!"*

In each new grade the scramble was on to establish a pecking order. First, I'd eye the two or three kids in my size league to make certain they hadn't sprouted six inches over the summer the way all other kids did, then I'd affect a swagger to browbeat them into accepting my assertion of being taller. "No you're not," one might shriek . . . "Measure!" So back-to-back we'd be, a clenched fist warning the judge not to notice heels off the floor. Somehow I'd always psych out someone or other and be spared the ignominy of first in line, the class dwarf.

The other disgrace that rivaled school, though thankfully rarer, was family occasions—weddings, holidays, bar mitzvahs. There, aunts you didn't know, but who all looked alike, would exclaim, "Leonard. How are you? Oh, look how you've—Why aren't you as big as your cousins? Everyone in our family is so tall."

In my neighborhood, being "tough" was as important to us kids as our being well fed was to our mothers. "Hard guys" was the expression we used. We wore thick leather garrison belts outside the loops and around our hips like gunslingers. These were our chief weapons, and they were decorated with studs that could rake a face. We even wore them over our bathing suits. With the first chill, out came black leather motorcycle jackets. (Amazing how reputations for toughness grew around guys whom no one had ever seen in a single fight!)

And, of course, nothing symbolized toughness more than size. Bigness gave you Respect, in the Mafia sense. No one messed with you. You were secure. If you were small, you had to acquire devious defenses, such as being accommodating, sweet and self-effacing—like a girl. In fact, the words we had for those who were small and seemingly defenseless—who didn't compensate for their smallness with Edward G. Robinson snarls, or by giving off a fierce scent à la Jack Palance—were "sissy" and "fag"; in other words, girl-like.

So vital was our desire for power that the most compelling page of every comic was the Charles Atlas body-building ad. Generations have been responding to this story of a skinny kid—the 98-pound weakling—who gets sand kicked in his face by a bully at the beach. He suffers impotent fury as his date consoles him, "Don't let it bother you, *little boy*." A few frames later he is transformed by the Charles Atlas method and admired by all—women especially.

Which takes us to *sex*. Here's what sex was to me. Donald, my next-door neighbor and four years my senior, went through this hysteria at age 16 of courting anyone and everyone over the phone, while I eavesdropped. He spun fantastic images to information operators, wrong numbers, and mostly unknown girls whose phone numbers he received from friends. I could imagine the girls sitting in their steamy tenements gazing off into dreamy space while Donny teased their fantasies of a noble knight who would deliver them to the fairylands of Flatbush or, all things possible, Long Island. Even though I couldn't hear the girls' questions, Donny's answers made their wishes clear: "Almost twenty . . . about six feet—" Damn liar! I saw the sadness I had to look forward to.

Of course, I was endlessly reminded of my deficiency. Tarzan carrying away his Jane, bridegrooms carrying brides over the threshold. Would I be able to? Or the holy writ: "tall, dark, and handsome." Summertimes I was dark and almost handsome.

Even nature conspired against me by giving girls an earlier growth spurt. I didn't know then how miserable some girls were for being too tall. I had troubles of my own. For dances I could only invite the one or two girls who were shorter than I. (I could imagine their wretched deliberations: "Wear a prom dress with *flats!*") And of course there was "short" humor cascading everywhere, refreshing to all the world but scalding to me: "Confucius say, 'Small man who dance with big woman get bust in mouth.' " Or resonant with portents of sexual inadequacy: "When you're toes to toes, your nose is in It. When you're nose to nose, your toes are in It."

Psychologist Hugo Beigel has written: "Most men do not feel attracted to taller women; shorter males, as a rule, do not strike the female as true men." Has an aesthetic of sexual desirability emerged out of woman's desire to be kept childlike, and man's desire for an illusion of mastery? The convention of every man having his little woman perpetuates male superiority in that the woman of the couple is symbolically more childlike.

The irony of ironies for every boy youth who thinks he has to pose as fearless protector to get a girlfriend is that sensuality is the antithesis of *machismo*. In lovemaking, brutish pretenses evaporate into defenseless tenderness. But no Mister Softee could get to first base, at least in my time and clime. The psychoanalytic mystics, of course, tend to agree—with their endless lore of phallic aggressivity and passive female receptivity.

In answer to that myth and all the aspersions cast on my worth, I quote from the poem by Christopher Smart (1722–71), titled "The Author Apologizes to a Lady for His Being a Little Man":

Yes, contumelious fair, you scorn
The amorous dwarf that courts you to his arms,
But ere you leave him quite forlorn,
And to some youth gigantic yield your charms,
Hear him—oh hear him, if you will not try,
And let your judgment check th' ambition of your eye.

Say, is it carnage makes the man!
Is to be monstrous really to be great!
Say, is it wise or just to scan
Your lover's worth by quality or weight! . . .
Does thy young bosom pant for fame:
Would'st thou be of posterity the toast!
The poets shall ensure thy name,
Who magnitude of mind not body boast.
Laurels on bulky bards as rarely grow,
As on the sturdy oak the virtuous mistletoe.

Look in the glass, survey that cheek—
Where Flora has with all her roses blushed;
The shape so tender—look so meek—
The breasts made to be pressed, not to be crushed—
Then turn to me—turn with obliging eyes.
Nor longer nature's works, in miniature, despise.

Young Ammon did the world subdue,
Yet had not more external man than I;
Ah, charmer, should I conquer you,
With him in fame, as well as size, I'll vie.
Then, scornful nymph, come forth to yonder grove,
Where I defy, and challenge, all thy utmost love.

To Apply This Reading to Yourself

1. *Consider your height. Would you want to be taller or shorter! How different would you and your life be if you were six inches shorter or taller! Write a brief paper incorporating your answers to these questions.*
2. *What concerned you most about your body during your growing-up days! Why! Write a brief paper incorporating your answers to these questions.*

3. *What social importance do you attach to height! To weight! To attractiveness! Why!*
4. *Allow an image of a male with an ideal or perfect body to form in your mind's eye. If you are a man, how different are you from this image and what meaning has this difference for you! If you are a woman, how different is your husband/lover/boyfriend/current date from this image and what meaning does this difference have for you!*

To a Body, With Love

Abe Arkoff

At midnight on October 22, 1780, Benjamin Franklin was in agony with the gout. He decided to have a written conversation with this old enemy, and this is how the interchange began:

> **Franklin:** *Eh! Oh! Eh! What have I done to merit these cruel sufferings?*
>
> **Gout:** *Many things; you have ate and drank too freely, and too much indulged those legs of yours in their indolence.*
>
> **Franklin:** *Who is it that accuses me?*
>
> **Gout:** *It is I, even I, the Gout.*
>
> **Franklin:** *What! My enemy in person!*
>
> **Gout:** *No, not your enemy.*[1]

The gout is quite eloquent and goes on to make its case that it is not the enemy, but a friend trying to get Franklin to abandon his dissolute habits. Franklin promises to mend his ways, but the gout takes its leave with the uneasy feeling that prudence would not long prevail.

To some observers, it appears that many of us treat our bodies as the enemy. A tidal wave of recent books and articles suggests that we are not at home or at ease with our bodies. Although as a nation we are healthier than ever, we worry more about our health. Furthermore, the body is to us an unknown continent—we scarcely know our esophagus from our elbow. To make matters worse, we don't like what we see in our mirrors. Surveys show that a lot of us aren't content with the way we look.

A lack of knowledge about the body can be a serious matter. This lack can cause us to neglect needed medical attention and to waste time and money on attention that either is not needed or can even harm us. Similarly, a lack of satisfaction concerning the body must be taken seriously. Body-image researcher Thomas Cash[2] writes, "Obviously, if one dislikes the body one 'lives in,' it's difficult to be satisfied with 'the self who lives therein' " (p. 61). Research shows that body satisfaction and self-esteem are strongly related to each other.[3-6] More is said about this later in this reading.

Actually—after 3 million years of evolution—the human body is quite remarkable. It has developed its own considerable defenses against disease, as well as powerful mechanisms for regeneration and healing. How sad that, like Rodney Dangerfield, our bodies frequently seem to "get no respect." Following are some simple suggestions on how we can take responsibility for and come to know, care for, and even love them.

OWN YOUR BODY

Your body belongs to you. It doesn't belong to any disease process. It doesn't belong to your doctor. It doesn't belong to the advertising or fashion industries. It is not the property of the state or national government. Your body is yours, but have you taken ownership of it and accepted full responsibility for it?

Each of us is a psychobiological unit integrated with the external environment, and a disturbance in any part of this system affects all of it. Much of this system is or can be brought under our own control. Speaking of an illness, we say, "I got sick." But often it might be as accurate to say, "I made myself sick; I've eaten/drunk/smoked too much." Or "I've driven myself too hard." Or "I've done nothing to deal with my physical/emotional/spiritual/vocational/etc. problems that are grinding me down."

Some of us ignore the condition of our bodies until we are laid low in some way. Then, accepting little responsibility for our bodies' disrepair and not much for their rehabilitation, we deliver them into the hands of physicians. "My body is sick; make it well," is what our actions say.

The notion that we need take no responsibility for our health or our illnesses increasingly has come under attack. A related and equally changeworthy notion is that we need take no responsibility for our lives, for frequently, the pain and suffering we ask our physicians to relieve or to tranquilize out of existence are integral parts of living that call for some courage and effort rather than medication.[7]

Norman Cousins is a classic example of a person who took responsibility for his own body and health. Suffering from a crippling collagen (connective tissue) disorder, which physicians believed to be irreversible, he personally devised, with the support of his doctor, a new regimen, which included large doses of vitamin C and laughter (the latter provided by such things as *Candid Camera* video classics and humor books). He returned himself to health and in his account of his experience wrote, "I have learned never to underestimate the capacity of the human mind and body to regenerate—even when the prospects seem so wretched."[8]

In response to his article, Cousins received some 3000 letters from physicians. Many of these letters reflected the view that no medication a doctor prescribes is as potent as the state of mind in which the patients address their own illness. These doctors felt that their most valuable service was to help each patient mobilize her or his own physical and psychological recuperative powers.[9]

When we take ownership of our bodies, we put ourselves in charge of their welfare. That doesn't mean we should not seek professional advice and assistance. But it does mean that whether we are in the pink or near the pale, we take full responsibility for what we do to our bodies and what we allow others to do to them.

KNOW YOUR BODY

Most of us know very little about our bodies. Seymour Fisher[10] writes that although our bodies are our dearest possessions and confront us everywhere, they remain a mystery. Why should this be so?

One reason suggested by Fisher is that our bodies are frequently concealed from sight by clothing. Even with our clothes off, it would be difficult to get a view of many bodily parts without some ingenious arrangement of mirrors. Then too, our bodies are constantly changing, and there may be a considerable time lag before we bring our body images up to date.

Even when we seek to scrutinize our bodies, we may have trouble in doing so. Fisher writes that when we look at our bodies, we do so through "an elaborate set of selective filters and screens." We may feel shamed by the appearance

of certain parts and worried by the fragility of others. We see only what we want to see or what we will allow ourselves to see.

Sometimes we see what we are afraid we'll see. Of a group of nearly 500 children, more than half the girls considered themselves overweight although only 15% were.[11] In a survey of college students, it was found that of those who were actually normal in weight, 58% of the women and 20% of the men classified themselves as overweight.[12] Misbeliefs about weight can have an important bearing on eating habits and disturbances, as well as on general well-being.

Although we are one of the most health-conscious people ever to inhabit the earth, we are also medical illiterates. Few schools have comprehensive health-education programs. In a study conducted by the National Research Council in 1990, 40% of the American high school students completing a year-long biology class did no better when tested than half of a companion group who never had such a course, and some did even worse. Equally dismal was the performance of a cross-section of more than a thousand U.S. adults on a body-knowledge quiz; half of the questions (which were assumed to be at the seventh-grade level) were missed by half of those surveyed.[13]

For most of us, the interior of the body is a mystery in itself. It has been found that when people are asked to sketch in the main organs of their bodies, many have only a vague notion of what these organs are and where they are located. In one study involving 87 adults, the stomach was omitted by 16, the lungs by 19, the intestines by 19, the liver by 26, the brain by 34, the kidneys by 40, and the sex organs by 41. The drawings were generally crude, and those organs not missing were often misplaced. Despite the stomachaches and upsets that are common to us all, only half the respondents put the stomach in the right place. The investigator concluded that the results were "just plain shocking."[14]

Essential health information seems similarly lacking. Some years ago, Blue Cross commissioned a Harris Poll in which those surveyed were asked whether they could recognize the symptoms of major illness. The 65% who said they could were then asked to name the seven danger signs of cancer. Although these signs have been publicized for years, 30%

could not name a single one, and only 13% named four or more.[15]

Because we know so little about the body and about scientific methods, we are easily swayed and misled. It has been estimated that medical quackery costs Americans a whopping $2.7 billion each year. Questionable therapies for cancer, heart disease, and arthritis add up to $10 or $11 billion. Almost as much goes down the drain for unnecessary vitamins, food supplements, potions, and pills. In a recent Food and Drug Administration survey, more than 25% of the respondents admitted to using unproven remedies such as chemical rubs for arthritis and herbal teas for hypertension.[16]

Our lack of health knowledge contributes to our worry. The more we focus on our bodies, the more we find to focus on. Psychiatrist Arthur Barsky[17] writes, "Lots of insignificant, benign illness comes and goes from day to day: a sore inside the cheek, a rash, a poor appetite, diarrhea" (p. 23). When healthy people are asked to keep track of all their symptoms, they find something to record one day out of every four.[18] In a two-week period, only 15% of us are symptom-free.[19] Barsky notes, "In 30 to 60 percent of all visits made to primary-care and general practitioners today, no serious medical cause can be found for the patient's symptoms." He adds, "And if we focus not on symptoms but on patients, we find that 25 to 40 percent of those who are being cared for in general medical outpatient settings have no serious diseases whatsoever" (p. 108).

When we feel sick, often it is not because our bodies aren't right, it's because our lives aren't right, and we somaticize our problems. It's easier to blame our bodies and seek a potion than to evaluate our lives and work to make them better. Barsky points out that how we feel about our bodies may symbolize how we feel about ourselves and our lives. If we don't like our bodies or if we feel they are weak, inadequate or sick, it can be a comment on our larger self. We may not need a better body, we may need to get ourselves a life. Barsky writes that no amount of medication or surgery can cure a person who "needs to be sick." Illness may be a way of asking for help or attention, or of seeking a way out of a difficult life situation. Illness can confer power by entitling the person to special consideration.

Paradoxically, we expect both too much of our bodies and too little. We expect to be symptom free and to have all our sufferings remedied. At the same time, we give too little credit to our bodies' ability to protect and repair themselves. Barsky writes, "The human body is actually a remarkably rugged and hardy biological system, one that is extraordinarily resistant to disease and injury" (p. 17). In his book, *Lives of a Cell*, Lewis Thomas[20] writes, "The great secret . . . is that most things get better by themselves. Most things, in fact, are better by morning" (p. 100).

We need information about bodies in general and our own bodies in particular. For those of us who lack this information, some excellent books are available at almost every bookstore. An example is *Core Concepts in Health* (brief sixth edition) by Paul Insel et al.,[21] which is used as a text in the "Modern Health" course at my university. One of the authors' goals is to instill in the reader a sense of personal power in health matters. They write, "Everyone has the ability to monitor, understand, and affect his or her own health."

Each body, of course, is like no other body and has its own special requirement, aversions, and eccentricities—its own way of making itself known. By paying attention to our bodily signs, signals, and symptoms, we can learn a lot about ourselves.

One of the most important sets of symptoms relates to anxiety. *Anxiety* is a state of arousal caused by threat or challenge, but in a particular situation, we may be aware only of a subjective feeling of dread and/or physical upset but not of the causes. With medical assurance that our symptoms are those of anxiety, we gain some important information about ourselves that we can put to use in future situations. We learn that sudden difficulty in breathing, heart palpitations, overwhelming weariness, or other idiosyncratic symptoms or patternings represent signs of threat or challenge. We then can pursue and deal with these threats or challenges (if we resist the urge to run from the situation or to deaden ourselves with tranquilizers).

One rather fascinating and ingenious way of getting to know your body better involves opening a new channel of communication. Ira Progoff[22] recommends that you have a dialogue with your body. (Benjamin Franklin's conversation with his gout is an example of this approach.) You can start by writing down all the salient memories you have of your body, such as the time you broke your leg, learned to swim, were first aware of your sexual feelings, and so on. Next, drawing upon these memories, write a brief summary of your relationship to your body. Then relax, sense the presence of your body as though it were a person, speak to it, allow it to speak to you, and write down your dialogue.

A similar but somewhat simpler method is one called "Body Letters." You simply sit down and without stopping to think, write a letter to your body, saying everything you wish to say to it. Then you become your body (you are anyway, of course) and without pausing, write a reply.

Dr. Robert Blau,[23] a physician, describes a patient's use of a related method in the following report:

> Joyce R., a forty-four year old nurse, had a chronic sore throat following a tonsillectomy three years ago. She was a shy, intense woman, new to the area and far from home. She greatly missed her family and wrote to them every week. Joyce seemed to be more comfortable writing than speaking. She felt awkward with strangers and ill-at-ease when making conversation.
>
> She had consulted several physicians who, despite many tests, were unable to find any organic reason for her pain. A friend suggested to Joyce that she "write a letter" to her painful throat. This excited her, as she had previously had this idea, but had dismissed her thought as "crazy." As her family doctor, I doubted that such an activity could have much effect other than catharsis. Yet since no other treatment was helping, I agreed to have her try it. She began a daily correspondence with her throat. Her first letter said simply, "Dear Throat, I am very sorry that you are hurting. I'm doing the best I can to make you well. Please be patient. Love, Joyce."
>
> The next day she wrote her throat a note of appreciation for giving her a morning without pain. She sent encouragement by saying that she was going to see another doctor—a throat specialist. After this consultation, she sent her throat a note of sympathy because the doctor, after many diagnostic procedures, was unable to suggest anything. After several weeks of writing, Joyce began to notice that her throat became most painful when she was upset or felt imposed upon. She then wrote and told her throat, "I have not been dealing with my present problems in an intelligent, mature way.

> I think your pain is trying to tell me that. I will take more time for myself, think more carefully about planning my time, and try to deal more directly with my responsibilities."
>
> After a month, Joyce found that her throat began giving her messages and explanations in return. By writing the other side of the dialogue, she learned that she put all her hurts and upsets in her throat when she was unable to tell others what she wanted. They were "stuck in her throat," as it were. She began writing to her throat when she was upset, and explaining what her difficulties were. Giving her throat this information seemed to alleviate her pain. She found that if she didn't acknowledge what troubled her in this clear, direct way, the pain would recur.
>
> After several more months, she found it was no longer necessary to write to her throat. She could speak directly to it and the pain would relent. Now when her throat begins to feel uncomfortable, she accepts this as a signal to look at whatever is bothering her. Vocalizing feelings and resentments usually helps to relieve her pain.
>
> Joyce sees this letter-writing process as a way of becoming conscious of her inner and outer functioning. The discovery that her pain had its own purpose and wisdom enabled her to learn what she was doing that caused her pain, and what she could do to remedy the situation. For her, pain became a creative focus through which personal change could occur. Her pain had persisted until she had learned its lesson, its meaning. Her gradual return to health seemed to be a result of this new self awareness and her willingness to change her ways of responding to stress. (pp. 45–47)

CARE FOR YOUR BODY

Marvelous and complicated though the body is, the care it needs is ordinarily quite simple. Even the extraordinary care it sometimes requires may not be very sophisticated. In his book *A Surgeon's World*, Dr. William Nolen declares that in 6 months, the average person could learn to recognize and treat most problems the physician sees during an average day.[24]

The causes of illness and wellness generally reside in everyday living habits.[25, 26] Dr. Lester Breslow surveyed 7000 adults and found that seven simple and unsurprising habits were crucial to good health:

1. No smoking
2. Moderate drinking

3. Seven or eight hours of sleep nightly
4. Regular meals with no snacking
5. Breakfast every day
6. Normal weight
7. Moderate, regular exercise

Breslow found the people with all seven habits to be healthier than those with six, those with six to be healthier than those with five, and so on. Also, the health difference made a difference: with six or seven of these habits, a 45-year-old man could anticipate another 33.1 years of life; with none, one, two, or three of these habits, he could expect 21.6 more years. The difference in habits made for an estimated difference of 11.5 years in longevity.[27]

It isn't necessary to kill yourself to save your life. For example, a little exercise—not a lot—is all the exertion the body requires for health. Robert Ornstein and David Sobel[28] write, "It takes very little physical activity to achieve many health benefits. Even the most dedicated sloth can make great gains in health and well-being by increasing activity from none to some. Beyond that there may be diminishing returns" (p. 106).

A relevant study involved a large group of men at risk for developing heart disease. Those who burned 500 calories per week in leisure-time activity had considerably more fatal heart attacks than those who expended 1600 calories. However, increasing activity to 4500 calories per week did not result in a further reduction of fatalities. Only 30 to 69 minutes per day of light to moderate activity (walking, bicycling, bowling, dancing, swimming, gardening) could make a crucial difference.[29] A further study included a large group of men and women who were followed for 8 years. Those who were initially more fit, as judged by a treadmill exercise test, had considerably lower rates of cardiovascular disease, cancer, and mortality. What was most striking was that the greatest reduction in risk occurred between the lowest level of fitness and the next lowest level. Moderate exercise, such as a daily brisk walk of at least 30 minutes would be enough to raise the fitness level and to confer substantial health benefits.[30] Most persons could easily incorporate this into the routine of their daily lives.

Although "no pain, no gain" is the battle cry of some exercise freaks, Ornstein and Sobel relegate it to the slogan graveyard. They write, "Human beings did not evolve to run 26 miles at a time, but to walk; we didn't evolve to bench press 200 pounds, but to carry 20 or 30 pounds long distances" (p. 104). They point out the high rate of injury in those joggers and others who exercise vigorously every day and suggest a pace and especially a level of persistence closer to the tortoise than the hare.

Not only health habits but also broader patterns of living or personality have been found to be related to long life. Robert Samp made a study of 2000 long-lived people and found results similar to Breslow, indicating a relationship between good health and good habits. In addition, Samp discovered a relationship between good health and such traits as moderation, optimism, serenity, interest in others, and interest in the future.[31]

In their book *Human Life Styling*, John McCamy and James Presley suggest we have a "natural knowledge" of what is best for us.[32] The following exercise, modified from one of theirs, is a way to get in touch with that knowledge or intuition:

Find a comfortable posture, close your eyes, and relax. Breathe slowly and deeply. As you inhale, be aware of the outside air coming into your body to become part of you. As you exhale, visualize your breath going out to become part of everything around you. Knowing this, see yourself at one with your environment.

Next, visualize yourself as a natural human being at your best in a natural environment that is best for you. See what you are eating, drinking, and doing. Take time to observe yourself as you spend a day under these circumstances.

Then, when you are ready, open your eyes. Compare the care you gave your body in your visualization with the care you usually give it. Although your real life and environment may be far from "natural," how could you improve your patterns of diet and exercise and take better care of yourself?

A small change in daily habits can make a big difference in your level of wellness. To get started, you might draw up what Emily Coleman and Betty Edwards[33] have called a "body contract," which is simply a written pledge to your body to treat it better in some carefully specified way. If you are a little uncertain of your commitment, you might promise yourself something good if you succeed (for example, to purchase cassettes or CDs with the money you don't spend on cigarettes) and/or something bad if you fail (to purchase no cassettes at all for a specified penalty period or to pay a forfeit to a cause you dislike intensely).

LOVE YOUR BODY

In 1972 and again in 1985, *Psychology Today* asked its readers to complete a questionnaire concerning their body attitudes. Both sets of respondents showed considerable concern about their body appearance, but the later group reported more body dissatisfaction than the earlier one.[34,35] A national survey conducted in 1990 found only 30% of the adult respondents happy with their looks.[36]

In his book *Bodies: Why We Look the Way We Do (And How We Feel About It)*, sociologist Barry Glassner[37] faults American society for making us dissatisfied with how we look. We work harder to look better but with little sense of success. Glassner writes, "All our efforts to beautify and condition our bodies have not made us, as a nation, any happier with the way we look."

Investigations involving adolescents and women have shown these groups to have a particularly unhappy or anxious body preoccupation. Iris Litt and Marvin Gersch,[38] two physicians in adolescent medicine write, "In our experience, it is unusual to find a teenager who doesn't regard himself (or herself) as too fat or too thin, too tall or too short, regardless of reality. In one way or another, young people are concerned about their acceptability, their lovability as human beings. They most naturally express this feeling through worrying about their rapidly changing appearance."

When it comes to "body loathing" instead of body love, women are especially vulnerable, says psychologist Rita Freedman[39] in her book, *Bodylove. Body loathing* is a preoccupation and dissatisfaction with appearance, which causes anxiety, guilt, and shame over real or imagined flaws. Of the women she surveyed (a varied but not random sample), 84% reported they sometimes, often, or constantly were self-conscious about their appearance.

"Thou shalt be thin" has, in effect, become the Eleventh Commandment in this country. There is a national abhorrence of fat. That's the conclusion of historian Roberta Seid[40] in her book, *Never Too Thin: Why Women Are at War with Their Bodies.* She writes, "On any day, 25 percent of us are on diets, with another 50 percent just finishing, breaking, or resolving to start one."

One consequence of what has been called "the tyranny of slenderness" is an epidemic of eating disorders. It has been estimated that 5–10% of adolescent girls and young women suffer from *anorexia nervosa,* a disease in which those afflicted (almost always females) starve themselves, sometimes literally to death. Many more suffer from the gorge–purge syndrome of *bulimia;*[40] these are persons who eat gluttonously and then purge themselves through self-induced vomiting or the use of laxatives.

Elaine Hatfield and Susan Sprecher[41] point out that it is good to be beautiful—research shows good things come to those who are—but it is really not much worse to be average in looks. They summarize the data they have gathered in the graph in Figure 1. This shows the relationship between appearance and a number of other variables: happiness, self-esteem, job opportunities, dating opportunities. As the graph indicates, it can be a definite disadvantage to be ugly or terribly disfigured. If one is either, it can be

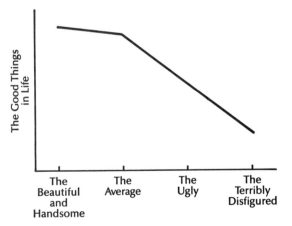

Figure 1. The relationship between appearance and the good things in life (from Hatfield & Sprecher, 1986).

worth the effort to improve ones appearance, but the rewards of going from average to spectacular are meager.

According to Hatfield and Sprecher, beautiful people are assumed to be good whether they are or not. But the confusion of beauty with goodness works both ways. If we are good, liked, appreciated, or respected, research indicates we will be seen as better looking than we really are.

Research by Hatfield and her colleagues[42,43] with dating couples, newlyweds, and couples married up to 70 years showed physical appearance to be just 1 of 25 traits considered critically important in lovers, friends, and coworkers. Therefore, we can decide whether to work on our appearance, our personality, or our behavior. Hatfield and Sprecher conclude that as far as appearance is concerned, "while one must pay some attention to the physical, it is more critical to nurture the mind and the spirit" (p. 375).

In nurturing the mind and spirit, it is interesting to note that there is little relationship between our actual physical attractiveness (as judged by others) and our self-esteem. There is, however, a strong relationship between our own judgment or view of our body and our self-esteem. The more kindly we regard our bodies, the more kindly we regard ourselves.[44]

For example, Helen, a 49-year-old woman interviewed by Mary MacVean,[45] weighs 280 pounds and feels good about herself. Helen has successfully separated her weight from her worth. Her weight goes up and down, and she says she likes herself whether she's fat or thin. However, when she's heavy, she attracts nicer men. Helen is a member of the National Association for the Advancement of Fat Acceptance. The association does not advocate dieting but rather the right of all persons to dignity and happiness regardless of weight.

To *accept* a body means simply to take a positive attitude toward it. We accept our bodies as we would our children, not for any reason except for the fact that they exist and they are ours. They are as they are, and that is all right.

A positive body attitude is facilitated by accentuating positive thoughts and *self-talk* (statements to ourselves) about it and by eliminating negative thoughts and statements. We find things about our bodies to admire or be grateful for and tell ourselves about them. When we catch ourselves dwelling on a negative aspect, we stop immediately and occupy ourselves with a positive one.

How can we accept something that is less than what we want it to be? If you stop to consider the matter, you'll find that acceptance is easier than rejection. It's difficult to reject something that's always present. To do so takes a lot of *wishing work*—wishing this were so or weren't so— and a lot of *ignoring work*—ignoring something that won't go away. When we accept something, we embrace it, allow it to be, make the most of it, and also get on with other things.

Psychotherapist Martin Shepard[46] believes that if we are truly ourselves, we will eventually find people who will love and respect us. He writes, "I believe there is a buyer for every human characteristic under the sun. Some of us like aggressive people, others passive ones. Some like them fat and some like them thin." His message is that if we allow ourselves to be ourselves, we accept ourselves sooner, and sooner or later, others will accept us, too.

TO A BODY, WITH LOVE

One way to evaluate your relationship to your body is to make use of the dialogue or letter techniques that were described earlier. If you want to check your love for your body, you might sit down now and write it a love letter. In your letter, tell your body all you like and appreciate about it, any regrets you have about your treatment of it in the past, and any promises you plan to keep concerning it in the future.

You and your body should be able to tell from your letter how loving you are and plan to be. Then, become your body and write a reply (it's always nice to hear from a loved one). Here, as an example for those who don't mind reading the mail of others, is an exchange of letters:

Dear Body,

Well, I've resisted writing to you, just as I've sometimes resisted living in you these past many years. I haven't thought too much of you as a body (at least, what met the eye below the neck)—you were too short, too unmuscled, too nearsighted, too allergy-prone, too this, too that. I've put you down and largely abandoned you to take up residence in my (or is it "your" or "our") head. Now, I'm back in some surprise to say: I think I like you, and what was all the fuss about!

I stand in front of the mirror and look at you. There you are—a bit dilapidated after many years of wear, tear and deferred maintenance—but still all in one piece and functioning well enough for my purposes. You have passion. You almost never catch a cold or get the flu. You don't need much sleep. You only bulge a little despite our sweet tooth. You're content with long walks and hardly cast an envious glance at the joggers and runners zipping by.

Sometimes I wonder what I would have become had you developed in accordance with my boyhood dream. Instead, I spent my adolescence in the library and a lot of the rest of my life as well. My life has worked out well for me: I have a family that's dear, good friends, and enjoyable work in a beautiful place. We've been companions on an increasingly pleasant journey.

So this is an apology, thank-you, and let's-get-better-acquainted letter. I know I've made you promises, and I hereby promise to come down out of my head and start keeping them. Now that I think you're okay—well, even better than okay—I'm looking forward to a happier and happier association.

With love,
Abe

Dear Abe,

After all these years, it was good to get your letter showing (if you will permit a body metaphor) some change of heart. You know, having you for an inhabitant hasn't been the easiest thing in the world for me. There are moments and even days when you seem to care, but you are (oops, here comes another one) something of a backslider.

But give credit where it's due, I always say. You're a faithful walker. You watch your diet (except for, ah yes, that tooth and midnight raids on the refrigerator). You don't smoke, and there's only an occasional vodka martini (well, make that a double). The results of our last physical were okay, considering the mileage. It's only that we could be so much more to each other (notice how I'm trying to put this in a positive and cooperative way). Remember that series of massages so long ago—how good they felt! Why did we stop! Let's get some more. The "chi" class was nice, but you said it might be followed by some more. What happened! And, since we're walkers, how about some serious hiking and even backpacking (notice that no mention has been made of the north face of Mount Everest).

I think there is more in me than you suspect. You seem so concerned these days with your spiritual growth, and you proceed almost as if you want to rise above your body—me, that is. But don't forget that body, mind, and spirit proceed together, and body discipline can be an avenue to what's above.

Now that we have some communication started, let's try to (brace yourself) stay in touch. We've got some good years ahead, and I'll be with you every step of the way.

Faithfully,
Your Body

References

1. Franklin, B. (1945). *A Benjamin Franklin reader* (N. G. Goodman, Ed.). New York: Thomas Y. Crowell Company.
2. Cash, T. F. (1990). The psychology of physical appearance: Aesthetics, attributes, and image. In T. F. Cash & T. Pruzinsky (Eds.), *Body images: Development, deviance, and change* (pp. 51–79). New York: Guilford Press.
3. Berscheid, E., & Walster, E. (1974). Physical attractiveness. In L. Berkowitz (Ed.), *Advances in experimental social psychology* (Vol. 7, pp. 158–216). New York: Academic Press.
4. Cash, T. F., Winstead, B. W., & Janda, L. H. (1986, April). The great American shape up: Body image survey report. *Psychology Today*, pp. 30–37.

5. Franzoi, S. L., & Shields, S. A. (1984). The body esteem scale: Multidimensional structure and sex differences in a college population. *Journal of Personality Assessment, 48,* 173–178.

6. Striegel-Moore, R. H., Silberstein, L. R., & Rodin, J. (1986). Toward an understanding of risk factors for bulimia. *American Psychologist, 41,* 246–263.

7. Paton, A. (1974, December 7). "Medicalization" of health. *British Medical Journal,* 573–574.

8. Cousins, N. (1977, May 28). Anatomy of an illness (as perceived by the patient). *Saturday Review,* pp, 4–6: 48–51.

9. Cousins, N. (1978, February 18). What I learned from 3,000 doctors. *Saturday Review,* pp. 12–16.

10. Fisher, S. (1973). *Body consciousness: You are what you feel.* Englewood Cliffs, NJ: Prentice-Hall.

11. Seligman, J., Joseph, N., Donovan, J., & Gosnell, M. (1987, July). The littlest dieters. *Newsweek,* p. 48.

12. Klesges, R. C. (1983). An analysis of body-image distortions in a nonpatient population. *International Journal of Eating Disorders, 2,* 35–41.

13. Frank, J. D. (1975). Mind-body relationships in illness and healing. *Journal of the International Academy of Preventative Medicine, 2*(3), 46–59.

14. Blum, L. H. (1977). Health information via mass media: Study of the individual's concept of the body and its parts (Pt. 1). *Psychological Reports, 40*(3), 991–999.

15. Mark, N. (1976, January). How television tries to close the health information gap. *Today's Health,* pp. 331–33; 52.

16. Michelmore, P. (1989, January). Beware of the health hucksters. *Reader's Digest,* pp. 114–118.

17. Barsky, A. J. (1988). *Worried sick: Our troubled quest for wellness.* Boston: Little, Brown.

18. Dunnell, K., & Cartwright, A. (1972). *Medicine takers, prescribers, and hoarders.* London: Routledge and Kegan Paul.

19. Hanney, D. R. (1979). *The symptom iceberg: A study of community health.* London: Routledge and Kegan Paul.

20. Thomas, L. (1975). *The lives of a cell.* New York: Bantam Books.

21. Insel, P., Roth, W. T., Collins, L. M., Petersen, R. A, & Stone, T. (1990). *Core concepts in health* (brief 6th ed.). Palo Alto, CA: Mayfield.

22. Progoff, I. (1975). *At a journal workshop: The basic text and guide for using the Intensive Journal.* New York: Dialogue House.

23. Belknap, M. M., Blau, R. A., & Grossman, R. N. (1975). *Case studies and methods in humanistic medical care,* (pp. 45–47). San Francisco: Institute for the Study of Humanistic Medicine.

24. Nolen, W. A. (1972). *A. surgeon's world.* New York: Random House.

25. Leonard, G. (1976, May 10). The holistic health revolution. *New West,* pp. 40–49.

26. Bloomfield, H. H., & Kory, R. B. (1978). *The holistic way to health & happiness: A new approach to complete lifetime wellness.* New York: Simon and Schuster.

27. Breslow, L. A. (1972). A quantitative approach to the World Health Organization definition of health: Physical, mental and social well-being. *International Journal of Epidemiology, 1*(4), 347–355.

28. Ornstein, R., & Sobel, D. (1989). *Healthy pleasures.* Reading, MA: Addison-Wesley.

29. Leon, A. S., Connett, J., Jacobs, D. R., Jr., & Raurama, R. (1987). Leisure-time activity levels and risk of coronary heart disease and death. *Journal of the American Medical Association, 258* (17), 2388–2395.

30. Blair, S. N., Kohl, H. W., III, Paffenbarger, R. S., Clark, D. G., Cooper, K. H., & Gibbons, L. W. (1989). Physical fitness and all-cause mortality: A prospective study of healthy men and women. *Journal of the American Medical Association, 262* (17), 2395–2401.

31. Bloomfield, H. H., & Kory, R. B. (1978). *The holistic way to health & happiness: A new approach to complete lifetime wellness.* New York: Simon and Schuster.

32. McCamy, J. C., & Presley, J. (1975) *Human life styling*. New York: Harper & Row.
33. Coleman, E., & Edwards, B. (1977). *Body liberation: Freeing your body for greater self-acceptance, health, and sexual satisfaction*. Los Angeles: J. P. Tarcher.
34. Berscheid, E., Walster, E., & Bohrnstedt, G. (1973, November). The happy American body. A survey report. *Psychology Today*, pp. 119–123, 126, 128–131.
35. Cash, T. F., Winstead, B. A., & Janda, L. M. (1986, April). The great American shape-up. *Psychology Today*, pp. 30–34, 36–37.
36. Cimons, M. (1990, August 19). Most Americans don't like their looks, poll discovers. *The Sunday Star-Bulletin & Advertiser*, p. A20.
37. Glassner, B. (1988). *Bodies: Why we look the way we do (and how we feel about it)*. New York: Putnam.
38. Litt, I. F., & Gersh, M. (1972, September). Body image problems in the teens. *PTA Magazine*, pp. 12–13, 30.
39. Freedman, R. (1989). *Bodylove: Learning to like our looks—and ourselves*. New York: Harper & Row.
40. Seid, R. P. (1989). *Never too thin: Why women are at war with their bodies*. New York: Prentice-Hall.
41. Hatfield, E., & Sprecher, S. (1986). *Mirror, mirror . . . The importance of looks in everyday life*. Albany: State University of New York Press.
42. Hatfield, E., Nerenz, D., Greenberger, D., Lambert, P., & Sprecher, S. (1982). *Passionate and companionate love in newlywed couples* (unpublished manuscript). Department of Psychology, University of Hawaii at Manoa, Honolulu.
43. Traupmann, J., & Hatfield, E. (1981). Love and its effect on mental and physical health. In R. Foge, E. Hatfield, S. Kiesler, & E. Shanas (Eds.), *Aging: Stability and change in the family* (pp. 253–274). New York: Academic Press.
44. MacVean, M. (1990, October 10). Self-esteem is the scale a lot of people live by. *Star-Bulletin*, pp. D1–D6.
45. Shepard, M. (1976). *The do-it-yourself psychotherapy book*. New York: E. P. Dutton.

To Apply This Reading to Yourself

1. *Do you own your body? To answer this question, discuss how responsible you have made yourself for what you and others do to your body.*
2. *How much do you know about your body—its outsides and insides, its requirements, aversions, and eccentricities, and its signs, signals, and symptoms? Answer this question, and cite your evidence.*
3. *Do you care for your body? To answer this question, discuss the extent to which you observe each of Breslow's seven health habits.*
4. *Do you accept your body? And what relationship do you see between your acceptance or rejection of your body and your overall self-esteem?*
5. *How much do you love your body? To answer this question, write a love letter to your body. Then, as your body, write a reply.*

Sex-Role Image

My dog is a plumber, he must be a boy.
Although I must tell you his favorite toy
Is a little play stove with pans and with pots
Which he really must like, 'cause he plays with it lots.
So perhaps he's a girl, which kind of makes sense,
Since he can't throw a ball and he can't climb a fence.
But neither can Dad, and I know he's a man,
And Mom is a woman, and she drives a van.
Maybe the problem is in trying to tell
Just what someone is by what he does well.

—Dan Greenburg

One's *sex-role image* is one's view or concept of oneself as a male or female. It is the sense of masculinity or femininity, of being a boy or a girl, a man or a woman. This image is based on our perceptions of sex-role standards, that is, of culturally approved male and female behaviors, and the extent to which we value, accept, and are able to fulfill these behaviors.

The most salient feature of our self-image or identity is our gender. Probably the first question asked about a new baby is, "Is it a boy or a girl?" And an early question in guessing the identity of a person in the game "Twenty Questions" is, "Is it male or female?" Once we know a person's sex, we can make some educated guesses about who the person is and also who he or she will become.

Gender is so important in society's ordering of things that there is not a neuter pronoun in the English language appropriate to describe the individual beyond his or her first few days of life. We can call a newborn baby "it," but "it" soon becomes a he or a she. If we write "yes" or "undecided" in response to "Sex" on a computerized survey, the machine is not amused. The computer, like society at large, needs to know how to classify us so we can be dealt with in proper fashion.

Each of us learns her or his gender very early, and the importance of this distinction is impressed on us all throughout life. Jerome Kagan, a prominent developmental psychologist, notes that "The child as young as four has dichotomized the world into male and female people and is concerned with boy–girl differences." By the time we are 7 years old, according to Kagan, we are intensely committed to molding our behavior to that prescribed for our own sex, and we become anxious and even angry when we are in danger of behaving in ways reserved for the opposite sex.

All during our formative years, we are taught to behave in sex-appropriate ways. We are rewarded for doing so, and we are rejected or punished when we are less masculine or less feminine than society prefers. We also learn sex-appropriate behavior by identifying ourselves with our same-sex parents or other appropriate persons and modeling ourselves after them.

This process of matching behavior to biology is a more ambivalent one for girls than for boys. The male sex role is generally more privileged and more favorably regarded. *Sex-role stereotypes*—that is, widely shared beliefs concerning males and females in our society—favor the former at the expense of the latter. The job market, the business world, the law, and other components of our society show the same unfortunate favoritism.

The struggle for equality has been long and difficult. Modem American women have been told that they "can have it all" (full career, spouse, and children), but the obstacles can be formidable. In the job market, some encounter the antagonism of males as they compete for scarce and privileged jobs. On the home scene, some find their husbands resistant to sharing familial burdens (but not so adverse to the additional income). Women who delay marriage and family until their careers are established often find eligible males less attracted to (even threatened by) females who have "made it."

Some observers have concluded that equality does not work; they call for a renewal of conventional roles and more emphasis on traditional masculinity and femininity. But others insist that this would not be a renewal but rather a retreat to a dull, constricted past; they say that the only way for both men and women to have full, satisfying lives is to enhance women's access to full careers and to increase men's involvement in the home and family.

BECOMING MALE

Some observers on today's scene are wondering whether male privilege isn't just an illusion for most men. Sam Keen and poet Robert Bly, at the forefront of a new men's movement, find men unsure of themselves and isolated; they have grown up with largely absent fathers and have no close male friends. Men's lives are filled with physical, psychological, and social problems. Their lives are shorter than those of women and more often end in accidents, homicide, or suicide. Males are more likely to have a speech, learning, or behavior disorder.

More males are caught up in alcohol or other drugs, and more are chronically homeless or in prison.

In the first selection, psychotherapist Clayton Barbeau laments that many American men have been taught to "tough it out" and as a consequence are out of touch with their feelings and hampered in forming meaningful relationships. By contrast, there is another and smaller group of men ("boys") who have never outgrown their dependent status. Barbeau writes, "I would define men as those persons who, whatever their experiences of the masculine mystique, have chosen to avoid the stereotypical male role *as well as that of the boy.*"

Barbeau laments the American tough-guy mystique—but Herb Goldberg uses stronger language. To Goldberg, "the blueprint for masculinity is the blueprint for destruction." In the second selection, he offers some guideposts for those who would like to join him in becoming "new males" and thus avoid paying the price extracted from most men.

BECOMING FEMALE

Researchers Judith Bardwick and Elizabeth Douvan note that in establishing identity, girls have an easier time than boys in early childhood but a more difficult time later on. Some early patterns such as dependency are considered feminine, and boys are soon under pressure to abandon this behavior and establish their masculinity and identity. Girls grow to puberty with bisexual identity. This identity is partly based on such feminine traits as dependency and conformity and partly on what later comes to be seen as a more masculine pattern of mastery and achievement. In adolescence and early adulthood, achievement traditionally has not been as highly valued in females as in males, and at this time, young women may redefine themselves and emphasize an identity based on interpersonal relationships.

Joni Mitchell, as some of us may remember, sang about "a woman of heart and mind," and psychologist Laura Brown has taken this as a metaphor for women's adult development. Recently, speaking for her gender before the American Psychological Association, Brown said, "We must find ways to become both creatures of heart and mind—both instinct and intellect—to be our bodies but not defined by them, to use our abilities to think and analyze in a manner that respects our experiences of femaleness in a male-dominated culture." That's a tall order, but one that many women are seeking to fill.

In the third selection, Nancy Gibbs celebrates the waning of tradition and the waxing of the women's movement. She believes the fight for equality has "largely been won." Today's young women, she writes, dismiss gender stereotypes and limitations, although they are aware of the greater burdens borne by women. The young college women Gibbs surveys plan to have it all—good careers, good husbands, and two or three children.

That the fight for equality has been largely won will come as news to many women. If so, asks feminist Susan Faludi in the fourth reading, why do American women make up two thirds of the poor adults? Why is battering the chief cause of injury to women and sexual violence greater than ever? Why do wives come home from their jobs to take up most of the family and household burdens?

Faludi musters considerable evidence that the feminist movement has suffered a "backlash" from forces determined to keep women in their traditional place, but to Kay Ebeling, who tells her story in the fifth reading, it is the movement that has "backfired," freeing men but leaving women as its casualties. Ebeling faults the movement for encouraging women to abandon biologically determined roles for visions that can't be lived. To Ebeling, biology *is* destiny, and she is nostalgic for the prefeminist days with Dad at work and Mom at home with the kids. (Interestingly enough, in a poll reported by Gibbs, two thirds of the women respondents and nearly half of the men said they would be interested in staying home and raising children—if they had the opportunity.)[1]

BECOMING ANDROGYNOUS

Sex-role differences are becoming less pronounced, and there is controversy as to whether this process should be speeded up, slowed down, or reversed. Many feminists and other individuals feel that differences in roles should be minimized, and some have called for changes in society to produce more psychological *androgyny* (a word of Greek origin from *andro*, male, and *gyn*, female). The new, androgynous person they describe would integrate the most valued qualities of both sexes or, to say it another way, this person would be free of gender constraints to arrive at her or his own unique personality.

Other observers find androgynous notions incompatible with their idea of our primal nature. Some, like Ebeling, call upon women to stop competing with men and fulfill their own "child-bearing biology." Some, like Bly, call upon men to stop being "soft males" and assert their "primitive masculinity," which includes decisiveness, fierceness, and—somehow—sensitivity. Some make the case that the sex role is the very cornerstone of identity, and we must learn this role before we can know who we are. In this view, boys and girls get support and assistance in self-definition by interacting with members of their own sex and by taking stances in relation to the opposite sex.

What would happen to a person who was not locked into a sex role at birth? In the last reading, Lois Gould presents a fable concerning a child who was raised not as a boy and not as a girl, but as an X. What happened? Well, society's computers—set for cards punched M or F but not X—boggled a bit. But as for X, X did Xcellently, and so did everyone else once they got used to the notion.

---

1. For further support of women's traditional role, see Patricia Kroken's "I'm a housewife—and I have a right to be proud" on pages 376–377 of this book. For support for the feminist vision of full careers for married women, see Karen Barrett's "Two-career couples: How they do it" on pages 378–383.

To Explore Your Sex-Role Images

1. *Defining sex roles (five answers).* What is a man? What is a woman? At the top of a sheet of paper write this incomplete sentence: "A man is..." Quickly complete the sentence five times. Then write this incomplete sentence: "A woman is..." And quickly complete this sentence five times. Afterward, study your answers and consider all your attitudes and assumptions regarding men and women. Then summarize and write down your findings and conclusions.

2. *Defining sex roles (group answers).* What is a man? What is a woman? In some prescribed order (around a circle, if you are seated in one, or back and forth across rows or up and down columns), each member of the group in turn recites this incomplete sentence and quickly completes it: "A man is..." Keep going until the members run out of responses. Then each member of the group in turn says this sentence fragment and completes it: "A woman is..." Again, keep going until the responses run out. Afterward, discuss the qualities that have been associated with each sex.

3. *Defining ideal sex roles (collage symbolization).* What is an ideal female? What is an ideal male? Construct two collages. The first collage is to represent or symbolize the ideal female as our society defines her. The second collage is to represent or symbolize the ideal male as defined by society. When you have completed the collages, write a description of each, indicating the meaning of the elements and any insights you gained from this exercise.

4. *Criticizing sex roles.* What's good and bad about the opposite sex? Divide into female and male subgroups. Each subgroup meets separately and arrives at a list of three praiseworthy (positive, good) qualities and three changeworthy (negative, bad) qualities associated with the opposite sex. Then the entire group reassembles for a discussion of the lists.

5. *Weighing sex roles.* What is there in each sex role that might cheer or chaff you? Write down each of the following incomplete sentences in turn and quickly complete it: (1) "Some reasons that I like being a member of my sex are..." (2) "Some reasons that I don't like being a member of my sex are..." (3) "Some reasons that I would like to be a member of the opposite sex are..." (4) "Some reasons I would not like to be a member of the opposite sex are..." Afterward, discuss the privileges and limitations of each sex role as you see them.

6. *Learning sex roles.* How did you become a male or female? How did you learn your sex role? Think back on the experiences you had as you were taught or as you learned your sex role. Weave some of the most salient or memorable of these experiences together into a brief essay or sex-role autobiography. A possible title for your essay/autobiography might be "How I became a (man, woman)." Or "Growing up (female, male)."

7. *Cartooning sex roles.* How did you become a male or a female? In his cartoon strip "The Road to Manhood" (see p. 68), Matt Groen-

ing presents his version of the steps to becoming a man. Draw your own cartoon strip showing the more salient events on your road to manhood or womanhood. (You may censor some of the panels.)

8. *Debating sex roles.* Arrange for a debate among group members on this proposition: "Resolved that in our society males and females should be treated alike." Or "Resolved that classical female and male roles should be upheld."

THE ROAD TO MANHOOD

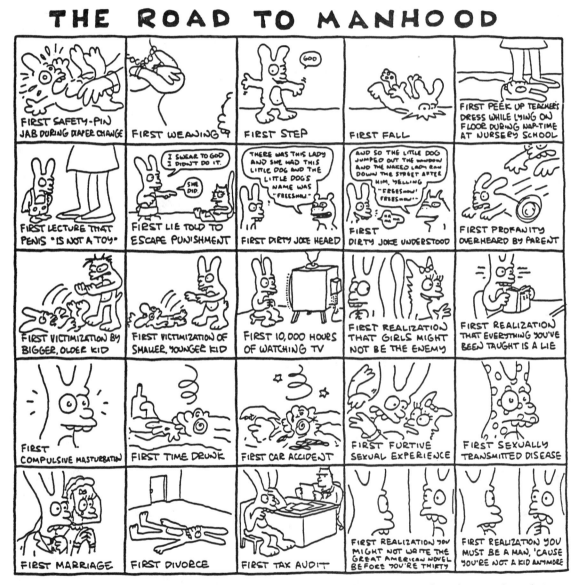

© 1986 *Life in Hell* by Matt Groening. All Rights Reserved. Reprinted by permission of Pantheon Books, a division of Random House, NY.

9. *Exploring androgyny.* Make a list of your own psychological characteristics that in our culture are considered to be stereotypically or primarily masculine and another list of those that are regarded as stereotypically or primarily feminine. Afterward write a brief paper that includes the two lists as well as discussion of yourself as an androgynous or non-androgynous person.

10. *Promoting androgyny.* A number of authorities have called for societal changes to fashion a more androgynous individual, especially one who integrates the most-valued psychological qualities currently associated with each sex. Choosing among the qualities that are stereotypically masculine or feminine or neither, draw up a list of those that might be desirable in this new, androgynous person. Afterward write a brief paper that includes your list and indicates your feelings about the movement toward androgyny.

To Read Further

Baker, M. (1991). *Women: American women in their own words.* New York: Pocket Star Books. (paperback)

Baraff, A. (1991). *Men talk: How men really feel about women, sex, relationships and themselves.* New York: Dutton.

Bly, R. (1990). *Iron John: A book about men.* Reading, MA: Addison-Wesley.

Cook, E. P. (1985). *Psychological androgyny.* Elmsford, NY: Pergamon. (paperback)

Cosell, H. (1985). *Woman on a seesaw: The ups and down of making it.* New York: Putnam.

Faludi, S. (1991). *Backlash, the undeclared war on American women.* New York: Crown.

Farrell, W. (1986). *Why men are the way they are: The male–female dynamic.* New York: McGraw-Hill. (Berkley paperback, 1988)

Fezler, W., & Field, E. S. (1985). *The good girl syndrome: How women are programmed to fail in a man's world—and how to stop it.* New York: G. P. Putnam & Sons. (Berkley paperback, 1987)

Gilmore, D. D. (1990). *Manhood in the making: Cultural concepts of masculinity.* New Haven, CT: Yale University Press.

Kamen, P. (1991). *Feminist fatale: Voices from the "twentysomething" generation explore the future of the "women's movement."* New York: Donald I. Fine. (paperback)

Keen, S. (1991). *Fire in the belly: On being a man.* New York: Bantam.

Kimmel, M. S., & Messner, M. A. (1989). *Men's lives.* New York: Macmillan.

Levine-Shneidman, C., & Levine, K. (1985). *Too smart for her own good? The impact of success on the intimate lives of women.* Garden City, NY: Doubleday. (Bantam paperback, 1986)

Shreve, A. (1991). *Women together, women alone: The legacy of the consciousness-raising movement.* New York: Fawcett Columbine.

Tannen, D. (1990). *You just don't understand: Women and men in conversation.* New York: Ballantine. (paperback)

Thompson, K. (Ed.). (1991). *To be a man: In search of the deep masculine.* Los Angeles: J. P. Tarcher. (paperback)

Zweig, C. (1990). *To be a woman: The birth of the conscious feminine.* Los Angeles: J. P. Tarcher. (paperback)

Tough Guy, Little Boy, or Person?

Clayton C. Barbeau

Most "male" and "female" traits are not biologically determined at all but are the result of early conditioning. All the stereotypes of the culture may be brought into play by the surrounding adults. Grandfather buys the little boy a toy gun or boxing gloves for Christmas and gives the little girl a cuddly doll.

The little girl finds herself cooed over at being so delicate, "just a doll," and the little boy is called "toughy" and rough-housed as a little "he-man." Very soon the "little man" is told to be "brave" because "big boys don't cry." He is taught that crying is for "sissies," i.e., for his sister or other females, but not for males. He will actively be discouraged from playing with dolls unless they are "GI Joe" or other comic-book heroes. Should he come home seeking sympathy because Joey down the block has punched him, he will likely be told that he has to "fight his own battles" and, perhaps, to "punch Joey back" if he gets hit again. The message is very clear: "A man doesn't ask for sympathy or help. A man takes care of himself."

Despite some evidence that younger children are socializing with the opposite sex at an earlier age than previously, the young boy generally finds himself still being discouraged from playing at "girls' games" such as "house" or "cooking." If he does have a particular friend who is a girl, he will become aware of sly winks overhead and the adult smirk surrounding the comment: "John has a little girl friend." The implication, of course, is that having a friend of the opposite sex implies more than mere friendship. The genital difference rather than the personal relationship is given prominence. Very rapidly he learns to "go play with the boys."

In playing with the boys he gets his cruelest lessons in growing up male. He learns rapidly that if he is to have the esteem of his male friends, he must not express any fears, he must not cry nor betray any such "sissy behavior." He learns to look down on girls as weaker than himself. Certain manifestations of creativity may also be taboo. "I loved helping my mother in the kitchen," one client said, "preparing food with her, even cleaning up. But I learned very early never to mention this to my chums. Eventually, I felt I was 'odd' in liking kitchen work and so quit helping out." He is not alone. In one family I recently worked with, the boy children were not expected to do the dishes or help with any housecleaning but their own rooms. The girls, however, were expected to help their mother with the "women's work." Through such conditioning processes the boy child learns to avoid expressing sensitivity and to remain ignorant of various domestic and child-care skills.

By the time he enters school, the young boy finds himself in an ambivalent position regarding the opposite sex. He has been told repeatedly that he mustn't hit a girl (though, apparently, it is all right to hit a boy); that girls are weaker than he is; girls are not to have things thrown at them; girls can't play football. In short, girls are fragile, delicate, weak beings in need of a boy's protection and care. At the same time, his life is governed, for the most part, by his mother. Whether his father is absent because of divorce or death or is simply away at his job, or whether (as is often the case) the father simply chooses to spend little time interacting with him, the young boy sees his mother as the one who controls the quality of his life. She is the powerful being who gives or withholds approval, who provides lunch and love. He leaves the authority figure of his mother to go to school, where, despite the increasing frequency of male teachers at the grammar-school level, his first authority figure in the outside, larger society is usually another woman. Competent, grown-up, she likewise has power over his daily happiness or unhappiness. If most principals are still men, such administrators, like his father, are most often distant figures. Direct, daily authority over him is most often exercised by a woman.

The contradictions inherent in this conditioning of the young boy are evident and not easily solved. For some males the dichotomy continues to be a source of ambivalence even into adulthood. As adults, such males vacillate between patronizing the "little woman," insisting on her dependency or childlike status and yet, at the same time, living in secret fear of her power to make their life miserable. These are the males whose sense of masculine strength is bought only by the superficial or real dependency evidenced by their wives.

A clear example of this was brought to my attention by a woman who, when the youngest child entered school, decided to take some courses herself. Her husband gave verbal approval, but as the weeks went by she realized a pattern of sabotage was at work. "He invited his supervisor to dinner on one of my class evenings. On another, he needed the car. On another, he notified me at the last minute that he was staying on at the office, leaving me no time to find a baby-sitter and a way to class. Of course, I missed those evenings. When I realized what was happening, I simply no longer fell for his tricks. Then he withdrew. He stopped any lovemaking. He grew sullen. He hasn't touched me physically in three months. When I touch him, he shies away. Last week I confronted him on this and he said, 'Divorce me. You don't need me any more. Divorce me and do your own thing. I'll keep the kids. They need me. You don't need me anymore. Go on, be independent, if you want to. . . . ' "

Many mates who panic at any show of their wife's financial or social independence don't manifest it so clearly. Some merely insist on total control of the purse strings, keeping their wives in the dark about the family's financial status. Others vacillate between attempts to live out the role of "he-man" proffered by the male mystique and the passive dependency of the little boy.

At some point in his growing up, nearly every male has had to cope with the competition of the playing field. If not in impromptu games arranged among the boys themselves, then in Little League or, inevitably, in school, they find themselves tested. I was a very small boy for my age. I did not begin to grow tall until late adolescence. I recall the agony of those childhood days when I was always the last, or second to last, chosen to play on any team. Sometimes I went, as it were, by default, as the last kid standing there: "Well, if we gotta take him, we gotta." In baseball I was inevitably sent to right field,

where not too many balls were hit and where, ostensibly, I wouldn't cost the team too many runs. Because I was so short I wasn't very good at basketball either. And because I was skinny I wasn't much help in football. Since sports are where male toughness is best displayed, where prestige is won among peers and the school heroes created—idols of cheerleaders and prize dates for school dances—I learned early on that I was neither prize hero nor prize date. I doubt that mine was an isolated experience of boyhood. After all, what percentage of boys can make the team?

I personally compensated by vicariously participating in the exploits of fictional heroes, reading everything I could get my hands on. This led to a certain verbal proficiency and psychological acumen that came in handy for a small kid. More than once some bruiser's desire to exercise his masculine prowess on my obviously puny form was sidetracked by my skillful use of language. Certainly as time went on I discovered that girls liked talking with me, and since they were more scholastically inclined than most boys were, I got along well with them. However, when the chips were down they dated the athletes. The most memorable example of this was the lovely girl who was the light of my life for a few months. We walked and talked together, did our homework together. Our idyll ended when she abruptly dropped out of school because she had gotten pregnant as a result of backseat gymnastics with one of the school's athletes.

A retired military man came to me seeking counsel for a most painful marital situation. One aspect of the problem was his wife's alcoholism and her bizarre behavior while intoxicated. The other was her increasing paranoia when sober and her demand that they move to another apartment or house—demands he had been meeting about three times a year before coming to see me. He was a career military man, having gone to military academies even in his earliest youth. He had earned more than one man's share of decorations and medals. His initial minutes with me were spent in embarrassed apologies for being there: "You must think I'm a failure. God, I never thought I'd have to ask anyone for help."

I reassured him I didn't think him a failure at all. Quite the contrary, in overcoming the most stringent conditioning in male toughness that the culture has to offer, he had shown great courage. Out of love for himself and his wife he had taken a step that went against all his training. That was heroism. As he told his tale of this domestic combat that had taken a more drastic toll on him than any wartime ordeal, I was studying him intently. When he finished, I asked, "And how do you feel about that?"

His chin firmed, his eyes flashed, his teeth seemed to bite off the words. "I'm mad. I'm goddam angry."

I looked at him and shook my head. "I don't believe you, Colonel. I accept the fact that you believe you at the moment, but I don't. Until I asked that question, your body posture, your eyes, your pulse rate, the way you were breathing, your tone of voice—everything about you said you were really sad, terribly unhappy."

All the tension went out of him, and tears welled into his eyes. "I'm so unhappy I could cry." And then, suddenly aware of the tears, he hurriedly swabbed them away despite my suggestion that he might want to give himself permission to let them flow a bit. He was embarrassed, however, and our final minutes of working together were marred by his constant references to his tears: "I must apologize . . . God . . . this never happened to me before."

As it turned out, he didn't keep his second appointment. Nor was I surprised, for the emotions touched in him during that first session were, from his point of view, signs of weakness. The male mystique of toughing it out, of never showing vulnerability or sensitivity to pain, of never admitting a mistake, is still very much the code among American (and many other) males. With precisely those attitudes most men assuredly oppress themselves.

In the boy child, such attitudes are motivated by the desire to avoid at any cost that awful insult of "sissy." In the grown mate, these attitudes are motivated by the horror of being thought a homosexual. I see before me now the tear-streaked face of a high-school classmate whose father, upon learning of his son's ambition, absolutely derided and successfully thwarted the boy's dream of becoming a ballet dancer. No son of his was going to shame him by getting into a "fairy profession." I recall the number of epithets, particularly in college days and in the military, that were used to keep young

men part of the male herd, epithets that always implied that deviation from the male code of toughness was a sign of one's being a "queer," a "faggot," or a "fairy." These were the ultimate insults. They were especially favored by drill instructors who wanted to inspire greater enthusiasm during bayonet practice.

The competitive spirit coupled with the fear of homosexuality proves a strong double lock on the male's inner self, especially in his dealings with males. In such dealings he either fears that the other male will use it against him if he reveals himself and his feelings (especially his fears or weaknesses), or else he fears that his very desire for such sharing may be some hidden homosexual prompting. This pattern is changing with the younger generation to some degree, but few males have intimate male friends. The large majority of men remain trapped in their own self-built prisons. In a discussion of this topic at the home of a Stanford University student, a young woman contended she did not think this was as valid for men now in their twenties. Significantly, two men, one a medical resident, disagreed with her. Equally significant, no other men disagreed with their comments.

If the majority of men do not have true friendships with other men, there seem to be just as many who do not share their feelings with their wives. I draw not only upon my own counseling experience but upon the comments of hundreds of women I have met during my lecture tours when I say that one of the most common complaints I hear from wives is that their husbands won't share with them on the emotional level. In counseling I find this silence flows from the husband's fear that his wife will think him weak or unmanly if he voices some self-doubt or gives evidence of some sensitivity of feeling. After all, as protector of the "weaker sex" he must show himself strong, ready to meet any situation, prepared to "tough it out."

The tragedy in this, of course, is that the male is often quite out of touch with his own feelings, has had little, if any, experience in articulating his inner states to himself or to others. His whole upbringing has worked to disconnect him from the tender, sensitive, caring, suffering, needing aspects of his being. If the male mystique has taken firm hold of him, he not only merely hides these things from his fellows, he has great difficulty acknowledging them even to himself. One does not have to be a psychotherapist to know that men have all the capacity for feeling, for laughter and tears, for tenderness and love, all the yearnings for warmth and emotional closeness, all the capacity for spiritual experience and aesthetic delight that women do. But so many men have become wary of disclosing these aspects of their being to anyone else for fear of being thought weak and unmasculine that they have actually lost touch with their own inner life.

Precisely because they have lost touch with themselves, having played the male role so long they believe the mask to be their true face, these males tend to give "objective" responses to emotional situations, to withdraw, get "uptight," become more impersonal even as their wives demand or request or plead for more emotional rapport. Often, in the counseling situation to which they have been brought by the wife threatening divorce, they will counter her statements of emotional neediness by reciting a list of the material things they have worked so hard to get for her.

It is my personal experience that we have altogether too many males in our society (that is, masculine gender human beings) who are still imprisoned in the male mystique, who are oppressing themselves and trying to live up to a code that is dehumanizing to them and to women and is injurious to our whole society.

We have another, though smaller, group of "boys" (that is, human beings of masculine gender) who have never outgrown their passive dependency status and who married Mommy or who, if single, assume a passive attitude toward their own lives. One woman who read this book in its early draft insisted, "I like the distinction you make between men and boys. However, I believe that *all* men marry their mothers, and nearly all married men I know are passive in their relationships with their wives." Another wrote: "All that space devoted to the 'male' and so little to the 'boy,' when it is the multitude of boys in our midst who are in the majority! Surely most wives seem to be trying, though it is not their responsibility, to get their husband/boys to become men. Some would even welcome a 'male' instead of a 'boy,' if that were the choice."

The "boy" is the husband who says "I don't care," or "Whatever you want, honey" to the

wife seeking some help in decision-making. He may be ridiculously insistent that his children agree with him in inconsequential things, saying "They have no respect" if they don't do so. He is usually, though not always, sexually less active than his wife wishes. At work he is considered "a good guy" because he is "one of the gang," but he is not a leader and envies the freedom and "devil-may-care" attitude he sees, however mistakenly, in the others. Married or single, he sees himself as a victim of circumstances, a person whose life is made up of "good breaks" or "bad breaks." If married, he is constantly worried about pleasing his wife/mother but feels unappreciated by her and by the children and unknown by anyone on earth.

It was not always thus. His mother loved him, he knows. And when he met his wife-to-be he saw in her all the qualities of his mother's nurturing and tender self. His earliest months in the marriage were, typically, quite delightful, and he felt he was the luckiest man on earth to have found so much tenderness, caring, and attention. The change began when the first child arrived. Usually at this point the seeds of the male's discontent begin to germinate. His wife is now obviously somebody else's mother, and she shows this new person the tenderness and love once entirely his. A new demand for growth is also made upon him now: that he assume new responsibilities, parental ones. He may resent this, consciously or unconsciously. It is not uncommon for him to feel like a "motherless child," deserted, misunderstood, orphaned. He may turn increasingly to his own natural mother for consolation. At his core, often enough, is a ball of anger that he finds frightening and that he suppresses most of the time. This anger finds expression, when it does, in the sort of behavior his wife has seen in the children when they are going through the "terrible twos," i.e., being contrary, yelling, breaking things, sulking. He smiles a lot when he is with people outside the family circle.

I would define men as those persons who, whatever their experiences of the masculine mystique, have chosen to avoid the stereotypical male role *as well as that of the boy.* Having seen fit to take charge of their own lives, they assume responsibility for themselves, their feelings, their personals goals and desires. They seek clarity with themselves, first of all. They tend to be in touch with their own needs and wants. They are willing to express their feelings, will risk themselves in encounters with those around them. Men confront the woman they've married or have just met not as inferior, nor as servant to their needs nor as a potential validation of their manhood or a replacement for mother, but as a unique human being whose mystery is inexhaustible.

The male world has for too long been structured as a world without tenderness, without sensibility, without caring, without tears, without the freedom to express honest emotions spontaneously. In short, the male world has been a world without love.

The boy's world, by contrast, is structured around the passive dependency of someone unwilling to enter the adult world of accepting responsibility for the creation of his own life, of someone seeking only to be cared for and nourished by the mother figure he married or by anyone else who is willing to assume responsibility (and blame) for his life.

The times demand that our boys grow up to be men. The day has come for males to quit playing the old roles and to take off their masks. The world is crying out for more men willing to take on the responsibilities of men and to engage in the work of men: building up the community of love.

To Apply This Reading to Yourself

1. *Discuss your experience in learning the behaviors appropriate or inappropriate to your sex role.*
2. *Discuss the gender taboos (behaviors considered inappropriate to your sex) you have personally encountered.*
3. *Discuss any shortcomings you have felt in trying to fill the role of a boy or girl or a man or woman.*
4. *If you are a male, discuss your ability to express your feelings and share them with others. If you are a female, discuss the emotional expressivity of the males to whom you are closest.*
5. *If you are a male, have you been raised to "tough it out"? Discuss this aspect of your socialization. If you are a female, discuss this quality in the males to whom you are closest.*
6. *Discuss any personal observations you may have concerning males who remain "boys"—passive, dependent, and/or seeking to be cared for by mother figures.*
7. *If you are a male, what is your reaction to the suggestion that you and other males generally put aside your armor and toughness? If you are a female, how would you benefit and what might you lose if the males closest to you and males generally put aside their armor and toughness?*

The New Male: From Self-Destruction to Self-Care

Herb Goldberg

THE CARDBOARD GOLIATH

Women bend and men break. The blueprint for masculinity is a blueprint for self-destruction. It is a process so deeply embedded in the male consiousness, however, that awareness of its course and its end has been lost. . . .

The brittle male conducts his life by his *ideas* about masculinity. Living up to the *image* is the important thing. Though the moment-to-moment experience may be painful and generally unsatisfying for him, his mind is continually telling him *what he is supposed to be.* As long as he is able to be that way, he can fend off the inner demons that threaten him with accusations of not being "a man." . . .

Traditional masculinity is largely a psychologically defensive operation rather than an authentic and organic process. A man's psychological energy is used to defend *against,* rather than to express, what he really is. His efforts are directed at proving to himself and others what *he is not:* feminine, dependent, emotional, passive, afraid, helpless, a loser, a failure, impotent and so on. He burns himself out in this never-ending need to prove, because he can *never* sufficiently prove it. To his final day he is driven to project himself as "a man," whether on the battlefield, behind the desk, in lovemaking, on the hospital operating table, in a barroom or even on his deathbed. . . .

The nature of masculinity is such that the male is unable even to recognize that he is in hazard. His life seems to him to be totally within his control. Unaccustomed to self-examination, he blocks out awareness of the way he lives and the conditioning that created it. He stoically accepts his lot as given, or at best, a challenge that the "real man" will accept and cope with and only the "sissy" will not.

Some men do escape this process of constriction and live a more expressive existence. . . . These are men who have found it impossible to conform, because they have never lost touch with the person inside and are therefore not able to regiment themselves into a style that will require them to suppress their individual humanness. . . .

Others who sometimes escape the process of constriction are those who experience a shattering crisis early in life and are able to learn and benefit from it and reorganize their lives in a new and more authentic way. These are men who perhaps had some personal problems and also possessed the openness to reach out for professional help. They opted to stay with their own self-discovery long enough to break through and undo harmful attitudes and reaction patterns that would have otherwise suffocated them.

THE NEW MALE: GUIDEPOSTS

In this age of gender redefinition we are all psychological pioneers. The new directions are uncharted and fraught with the anxieties and pain involved in cutting loose from familiar rituals and predictable responses. . . .

When I am asked about my own motivations for changing, my response is that the alternative of *not* changing seems far worse and more frightening. Mine is not idealistic rebellion or personal sacrifice. From my point of view it is a matter of survival. I do not want to pay the price I see extracted from most men around me.

I offer the following basic directions as tone setters and guideposts for men to help them develop a process and rhythm that will break through and beyond their embedded patterns and reflexes. They are, I believe, to be approached in slow motion and with constant questioning and examination. It is not just a matter of the simple development of some cognitive solutions. Intelligent awareness can help define a vision, but the movement toward it will require his total person.

1. Recognize and Resist Responding to Words of Sexist Masculine Intimidation.

Over the years, the vocabulary of masculinity has become laden with words that menace the male and have the symbolic power to trigger reactions that are self-destructive, because of a deeply rooted tendency in the man to do whatever will allow him to avoid their implications.

These words are often used in wholesale fashion. They are intimidating partially because they cover, in loose and general ways, a wide variety of responses that are actually quite different from each other. Under the spell of masculine intimidation, these labels get reduced to a similar narrow meaning which blocks the man's capacity to see and come to grips with his inner experience: something which would allow him to act on the basis of long-range better sense and the instinct for survival rather than immediate compulsion. To avoid these labels, he settles for the momentary reduction of anxiety. Among these words of sexist intimidation, the following are some of the most powerful motivators.

"Coward." How many men have needlessly placed themselves in jeopardy, been injured or killed because they responded to challenges or threats to their masculinity when little or nothing was at stake except to avoid the label "coward"? In many of these instances, the healthy response would have been to *flee* rather than to *fight*, or simply to refuse to participate.

So too have the words "afraid of" bullied him and made it difficult for him to take the long view. He would assume a responsibility, accept a challenge, put up with an onerous situation, endure an unsatisfactory relationship just to prove that he wasn't *afraid* to do it; that he didn't "chicken out." This made it impossible for him to understand and learn from the important messages his acknowledged fear would have provided.

"Failure." Men are living in an era when they are confronting proliferating and hazardous double-binds. On the one hand, it is suggested to them that success and winning are not the all-important things in life. At the same time, words such as "loser" and "failure" are still applied in derogatory fashion to men who do not effectively compete in the prescribed ways.

Even among the seemingly enlightened segments of the population, subtle evaluations that categorize men in this way are constantly being made. The message is usually indirect—for ex-

ample, when a successful and powerful man is viewed as charismatic, dynamic, interesting, exciting and so on, while the man who is not is described as "boring," "negative," "drab," "uninteresting," and the like.

Even the question "What does he do?" when asked as the source of primary interest in discussing a man has that same undertone. Certain kinds of work imply a positive image and give a man allure. Others immediately fix him with a negative stereotype.

The insidious and pervasive power of such labeling forces men into narrow, repetitive ruts and channels so that they can preserve their image of being a "success" and avoid the alternative negative labels. . . .

"Latent Homosexual." These words have had a particularly devastating impact on men in terms of blocking the development of affectionate, warm, caring experiences between them. A man who finds himself responding to another man with loving and sensual feelings, unless he has a strongly rooted sexual identity and equally strong self-esteem, tends to be flooded with anxiety and self-doubt. "Maybe I'm a latent homosexual," he tells himself.

Most men, to ensure that they will not be suspect, therefore keep a deliberate and self-protective distance from other men and do so with a defensive, isolating rigidity that loudly signals the message "Don't touch me."

If the words "latent homosexual" imply the potential for an affectionate and sensual response toward a man, practically all men could be considered "latent homosexuals." It is only that most men have rigid and powerful defenses against this tendency that allows them to masquerade as being "totally masculine."

Very simply, all males who have been raised in our culture and who have had women as their primary nurturing and identification figures are "latent homosexuals," in that they have a strong feminine imprint and potential. Their powerful reaction against closeness with men is psychologically defensive; a phobia protecting them against this very threatening interest and desire.

Except in limited instances, the label "latent homosexual," as it is so loosely applied, is a term of sexist intimidation. Warmth, affection, physical touching in a gentle, caring way and attention paid to the needs and feelings of a man all fall under the hostile, intimidating rubric of this label. This is particularly unfortunate and destructive because it sets up such powerful barriers to supportive, loving friendships among men, which are absolutely imperative if he is ever to free himself from this dangerous emotional isolation and his inordinate and debilitating dependency on "his" woman. . . .

2. Cultivate Buddyships.

It is my belief that well-founded and self-caring meaningful change and growth for men can only happen if they develop same-sex support systems that would lighten their dependency on women and would also allow them to go through whatever changes they need to go through without fear of alienating their sole source of intimacy.

The one factor more than any other that has facilitated the changes in women's consciousness in fairly rapid and smooth fashion is their ability to take and give support and comfort to each other and to get enough satisfaction from these relationships to compensate for the periods when their relationships with men were in crisis or entirely absent. Because of a sense of mutual support, women did not feel the need to ask for men's permission to change, nor did they fear alienating the man or incurring his disapproval if they risked change.

Likewise, unless men go through their changes without the terror of losing their woman's love, any change will be contingent on and limited by her approval. In addition, a caring, loving buddyship relationship in a time of unpredictable and volatile heterosexual relationships can provide roots and sources of pleasure, warmth and comfort. The most exciting and dramatic potential in the cultivation of a buddyship orientation is the reduction and softening of the defensive, guarded, detached and competitive posture most men have toward each other. . . .

3. Reintegrate Your Feminine Side and Revel in the Pleasure of Experiencing and Giving Expression to These Denied Parts of Your Personality.

A counterpart to assertion training for women ought to be passivity training for men. As women have been integrating their masculine side, men need to integrate their feminine side in

order to move beyond the present liberation crunch. In other words, men must take the benefits of women's growth and not just stretch their capacities thin to handle more stress and responsibility.

Specifically, as women integrate their previously repressed assertiveness, autonomy, sexuality, anger and aggression, men need to reclaim emotions, dependency needs, passivity, fluidity, playfulness, sensuality, vulnerability, and resistance to always assuming responsibility. Men too need to become balanced people.

If all that the growth and change in women's consciousness will mean for men is an adaptation to her expanded identity, he will be locking himself into an unbearable position. Women's liberation must not be allowed to mean for men accommodation to her new image. Rather, it must herald the opportunity for men to become fully human themselves, and in the process, like her, reconstruct or even abandon relationships where their changes and growth are not accepted, nurtured and cherished.

4. Postpone Binding Commitments.

The powerful external pressures on the man as a young, growing person, I believe, make it necessary for him to take a number of adult years to establish and develop an autonomous, inner-directed focus on who he is and what he wants.

The traditional male harness has meant the early and often premature establishment of career, marriage and family, which gave the man the appearance of maturity but actually made genuine self-development very difficult, because he was constantly struggling to deal with external pressures. Just as women are realizing and rebelling against their traditional role harness, men need now to recognize and alter their self-damaging orientation of assuming and striving to live up to the inordinate demands and pressures laid on them in early life.

5. Recognize and Acknowledge Emotions as Critical Guides to Reality.

The masculine orientation to emotions has characteristically been to perceive them as an interference, threat or challenge which he needed to learn to control and transcend. Consequently, men have given up one of the truest indices for self-understanding and the accurate perception of their relationships. It is perhaps the most harmful aspect of male conditioning that emotions have been made synonymous with femininity and that men have thus been deprived of access to their humannness. Identification and acceptance of fear, affection, resentment, boredom, resistance, longing, sadness, hurt, frustration and so on are crucial to men's development as full people. . . .

6. Ask for Help.

It is the masculine orientation not to ask for help, to go it alone, to seek quick, unambiguous answers and to reject any approach that is not clear-cut and obvious in its logic.

In matters of the emotions and psychological processes, only charlatans hold out the promise of rapid, dramatic change. Defenses cause a person to see himself and reality as he wishes. Change is difficult because it requires bringing back into awareness and integration disowned and threatening parts of oneself. The ability to ask for help is important in allowing oneself to accept support. It is equally important as a symbol of one's capacity to recognize that the problems and issues are often too complex and overwhelming to negotiate by oneself.

Help can come from many sources, not necessarily professional. The important part is being able to acknowledge one's confusion enough to say, "I need help."

7. Custom-Make Your Life.

Look around and ask yourself if on a personal and interpersonal level it still makes sense to live up to old models. Technologically we are living in a highly sophisticated space age, while on the level of human interaction most of our expectations and value systems are ages old and anachronistic.

We are all pioneers in this era of loosening and changing gender definitions to fit human needs rather than to reinforce masculine and feminine stereotypes. It is both an exciting and a threatening time. There will be periods when the changes seem to be too painful, even impossible. The solace I choose in those moments is to ask myself, "Do I want to repeat the cycles, fit the patterns and play the games that seem to have been played by others from time immemorial? Do they feel good, and do they yield what they're supposed to?" That, I believe, is enough of a spur to maintain momentum in those threatening moments when wresting oneself free from very powerful, very established and very debilitating sexual role models seems like an impossible challenge.

To Apply This Reading to Yourself

1. *Goldberg writes, "Women bend and men break." Do you agree? Why or why not?*
2. *Consider a traditional male you know. Is he a "cardboard Goliath"? Give your evidence for your answer.*
3. *Whether you are a man or a woman, consider your present role behavior. Does it result from questioning and examination or from pressured and unthinking acceptance? Give your evidence for your answer.*
4. *Goldberg maintains that to become balanced persons, women must integrate their masculine side and men their feminine side. How well have you done this? Give your evidence for your answer.*
5. *Goldberg's suggestion that men "custom-make" their lives rather than fitting themselves into old patterns would seem to apply to women as well. Is your life custom-made, or are you living a model right off the rack? Give your evidence for your answer.*

The Road to Equality

Nancy Gibbs

Young Americans inherit a revolution that has largely been won. One measure of the success of the women's movement is the ease with which it is taken for granted. Few daughters remember the barriers their mothers faced when applying for scholarships, jobs and loans—even for a divorce. Today's young adults dismiss old gender stereotypes and limitations. They expect equal opportunities but want more than mere equality. It is their dream that they will be the ones to strike a healthy balance at last between their public and private lives: between the lure of fame and glory, and a love of home and hearth.

If there is a theme among those coming of age today, it is that gender differences are often better celebrated than suppressed. Young women do not want to slip unnoticed into a man's world; they want that world to change and benefit from what women bring to it. The changes are spreading. Eager to achieve their goals without sacrificing their natures, women in business are junking the boxy suits and one-of-the-boys manner that always seemed less a style than a disguise. In psychology the old view that autonomy is the hallmark of mental health is being revamped. A sense of "connectedness" to others is now being viewed as a healthy trait rather than a symptom of "dependent personality disorder." In politics women candidates are finding that issues they emphasize may carry more weight than ever with voters tired of the guns-not-butter budgets of the 1980s.

In many ways the 16 million or so women between the ages of 16 and 22 are the generation that social scientists have been waiting for. They were born between 1968 and 1974, a tiny but explosive glimpse of history in which the women's movement took hold. Studies of women's changing expectations have found that during those years the proportion of young women who planned to be housewives plunged from two-thirds to less than a quarter—an astounding shift in attitude in the flick of an apron.

Child rearing became less a preoccupation than an improvisation, housework less an obsession than a chore. Young daughters watched as their mothers learned new roles, while their fathers all too often clung to old ones. They were the first generation to see almost half of all marriages end in divorce.

Disheartened by their mothers' guilt during the '70s and their older sisters' exhaustion hauling baby and briefcase through the career traffic of the '80s, today's young women have their own ideas about redefining the feminine mystique. When asked to sketch their futures, college students say they want good careers, good marriages and two or three kids, and they don't want their children to be raised by strangers. Young people don't want to lie, as their mothers did, when a baby's illness keeps them from work: they expect the boss to understand. Mommy tracks, daddy tracks, dropping out, slowing down, starting over, going private—all are options entertained by a generation that views its yuppie predecessors with alarm. The next generation of parents may be less likely to argue over who has to leave work early to pick up the kids and more likely to clash over who gets to take parental leave.

Wild optimism is youth's prerogative, but older women shudder slightly at the giddy expectations of today's high school and college students. At times their hope borders on hubris, with its assumption that the secrets that eluded their predecessors will be revealed to them. "In the 1950s women were family oriented," says Sheryl Hatch, 20, a broadcasting major at the American University in Washington. "In the '70s they were career oriented. In the '90s we want balance. I think I can do both."

It is not that older women begrudge the young their hopes; rather they recognize how many choices will still be dictated not by social convention but by economic realities. The earning power of young families fell steadily during the '80s, so that two incomes are a necessity, not a luxury, and a precarious economy promises only more pain. When factories cut back, women are often the first to be laid off. As Washington battles its deficits, cutting away at food, health and child-care programs, it is poor women who will feel the hardest pinch.

These prospects are not all lost on young people: there is plenty of room for realism between their dreams and their fears. A TIME poll of 505 men and women ages 18 to 24 by Yankelovich Clancy Shulman found that 4 out of 5 believed it was difficult to juggle work and family, and that too much pressure was placed on women to bear the burdens. But among those with the education to enter the professions, the response often comes in the form of demands. "What's different between these women and my generation," says Leslie Wolfe, 46, executive director of the Center for Women Policy Studies in Washington, "is that they say, 'I don't want to work 70 hours a week, but I want to be vice president, and *you* have to change.' We kept our mouths shut and followed the rules. They want different rules."

And if the economy cooperates, they may just pull it off, with some help from demographics. This baby-bust generation is about one-third smaller than the baby boomers who came before, which means that employers competing for skilled workers will be drawing from a smaller pool. Today's young people hope that that fact, combined with some corporate consciousness raising about the importance of families, will give them bargaining power for longer vacations, more generous parental leaves and more flexible working conditions.

Employers who listen carefully will hear the shift of priorities. Many college students, while nervous about their economic prospects, are equally wary of the fast lane. "We have a fear of being like the generation before us, which lost itself," says Julia Parsons, 24, a second-year law student at Georgetown University Law Center. "I don't want to find myself at 35 with no family. It's a big fear." Big enough, it seems, to account for a marked shift away from 1980s-style workaholism. The TIME poll found that 51% put having a long and happy marriage and raising well-adjusted children ahead of career success (29%).

The men are often just as eager as women to escape the pressure of traditional roles. "The women's movement has been a positive force," says Scott Mabry, a 22-year-old Kenyon College graduate. "Men have a new appreciation of women as people, more than just sex objects, wives, mothers." TIME's poll found that 86% of

Table 1. TIME Poll

WHAT YOUTH THINK
LOVE & MARRIAGE

Which of the following is an essential requirement for a spouse?	Females	Males
Physically attractive	19%	41%
Masculine/feminine traits	41%	72%
Well-paying job	77%	25%
Intelligent	95%	88%
Ambitious and hardworking	99%	86%
Faithful	100%	97%

How difficult is it to have a good marriage today?	Very difficult	Difficult	Easy	Very easy
Females	18%	56%	23%	3%
Males	22%	55%	18%	4%

Will couples in your generation be more or less likely than those in your parents' generation to get divorced?

More likely 85%   Less likely 14%

BRINGING UP BABY

If you had the opportunity, would you be interested in staying at home and raising children?	Females	Males
Yes	66%	48%
No	33%	51%

Would you raise your own children the same way you were raised?	
Yes, the same	56%
No, very differently	43%

THE MORE THINGS CHANGE

Do you think it is easier to be a man or a woman?	Females	Males
To be a woman	30%	21%
To be a man	59%	65%

Which of the following is your single most important goal?	Females	Males
A successful career	27%	32%
A happy marriage	39%	30%
Well-adjusted children	23%	9%
Contributing to society	6%	16%

From a telephone poll of 505 Americans aged 18 to 24 taken for TIME by Yankelovich Clancy Shulman. Sampling error is plus or minus 4.5%.

young men were looking for a spouse who was ambitious and hardworking; an astonishing 48% expressed an interest in staying home with their children. "I don't mind being the first one to stay home," says Ernesto Fuentes, a high school student in Los Angeles' working-class Echo Park district. "The girl can succeed. It's cool with me."

For their part, many women fully expect to do their share as breadwinners, though not necessarily out of personal choice so much as financial need. "Of course we will work," says Kimberly Heimert, 21, of Germantown, Tenn., a senior at American University. "What are we going to do? Stay at home? When I get married, I expect to contribute 50% of my family's income."

When asked how family life will fit into their ambitious plans, young people wax creative. Many want to be independent contractors, working at home at their own hours. Some talk of "sequencing": rather than interrupting a career to stay home with children, they plan to marry early, have children quickly and think about work later. "I'll get into my career afterward," says Sheri Davis, 21, a senior at the University of Southern California. "I'm not willing to have children and put them in day care. I've baby-sat for years and taken kids to day-care centers. They just hang on my legs and cry. I can't do that." Other women claim to be searching for the perfect equal-opportunity mate. Melissa Zipnick, 26, a kindergarten teacher in Los Angeles, saw her own working mom wear herself out "catering" to her father and brother. "I intend to be married to someone who will share all the responsibilities," she vows.

But such demands and expectations are accompanied by a nagging sense of the obstacles. The fear of divorce, for instance, hangs heavily over young men and women. Nearly three-quarters of those in the TIME poll said that having a good marriage today is difficult or very difficult. More than half would not choose a marriage like their parents', and 85% think they are even more likely to see their marriages end in divorce than did their parents' generation. "A lot of my friends' parents are divorced," says Georgetown's Parsons. "In most cases it happened when the mother was trying to decide whether to stay home or go to work. And the women were left so vulnerable." Careers become a form of insurance. "I don't want to depend on anybody," says Kellie Moore, 19, a U.S.C. junior who plans to get a business degree. "I have friends who have already set up their own credit structure because they watched their mothers try to set one up after a divorce."

Given this combination of goals and fears, young women would appear to be disciples of feminism, embracing the movement as a means of sorting out social change. But while the goals are applauded by three-quarters of young people, the feminist label is viewed with disdain and alarm; the name Gloria Steinem is uttered as an epithet. Some young people reject the movement on principle: "The whole women's movement is pushing the career women," says Kathy Smith, 19, a sophomore at Vanderbilt, "and making light of being a homemaker."

Others feel that the battle belonged to a different generation, without realizing that the very existence of a debate about family leave, abortion, flextime and affirmative action is the fruit of an ongoing revolution. Minority women seem to be the group least likely to abandon the feminist label, perhaps because they are most aware of how many critical battles remain to be fought. In fact, argues Stephanie Batiste, 18, a black freshman at Princeton, "minority women are almost a separate women's movement . . . You're very alone. You get a lot less support."

Here, then, is a goal for the women's movement: the education of the next generation of daughters in a better understanding of their inheritance, their opportunities and their obligations. And there are lessons to learn in return. Speaking of the new generation, Leslie Wolfe of the Women Policy Studies Center says, "I think they are more savvy than we were, about sexism, about discrimination, about balancing work and family, about sex." They may be wiser, too, about seizing fresh opportunities without losing sight of tradition. Historian Doris Kearns Goodwin once wrote of a woman's dream: "The special heritage of values and priorities that have been traditionally associated with women as wives and mothers can be seen as sources of strength to create an enlarged vision of society." A society so enlarged and strengthened will make more room for everyone's dreams.

To Apply This Reading to Yourself

1. *What mix of career, marriage, and childrearing would be best for you? Why? What compromises or adjustments would you be prepared to make or have you made?*
2. *Describe your parents' mix of career, marriage, and childrearing, and also indicate how well it served them and you.*
3. *Do you think it is generally easier today to be a man or to be a woman? Why? In your own case, would your life be easier if you were a member of the opposite sex? Why or why not?*
4. *Indicate which of the following is your single most important goal, and give your reasons: (a) a successful career, (b) a happy marriage, (c) well-adjusted children, or (d) contributing to society.*
5. *If you had the opportunity, would you be interested in staying at home and raising children? Why or why not?*

Backlash—The Undeclared War Against American Women

Susan Faludi

To be a woman in America at the close of the 20th century—what good fortune. That's what we keep hearing, anyway. The barricades have fallen, politicians assure us. Women have "made it," Madison Avenue cheers. Women's fight for equality has "largely been won," *Time* magazine announces. Enroll at any university, join any law firm, apply for credit at any bank. Women have so many opportunities now, corporate leaders say, that we don't really need equal opportunity policies. Women are so equal now, lawmakers say, that we no longer need an Equal Rights Amendment. Women have "so much," former President Ronald Reagan says, that the White House no longer needs to appoint them to higher office. Even American Express ads are saluting a woman's freedom to charge it. At last, women have received their full citizenship papers.

But what "equality" are all these authorities talking about?

If American women are so equal, why do they represent two-thirds of all poor adults? Why are they still far more likely than men to live in poor housing and receive no health insurance, and twice as likely to draw no pension? Why does the average working woman's salary still lag as far behind the average man's as it did twenty years ago? Why does the average female college graduate today earn less than a man with no more than a high school diploma (just as she did in the '50s)—and why does the average female high school graduate today earn less than a male high school dropout?

If women "have it all," then why don't they have the most basic requirements to achieve equality in the work force? Unlike virtually all other industrialized nations, the U.S. govern-ment still has no family-leave and child care programs—and more than 99 percent of American private employers don't offer child care either.

If women are so "free," why are their reproductive freedoms in greater jeopardy today than a decade earlier? Why do they still shoulder 70 percent of the household duties—and the only major change in the last fifteen years is that now middle-class men *think* they do more around the house. Furthermore, in thirty states, it is still generally legal for husbands to rape their wives; and only ten states have laws mandating arrest for domestic violence—even though battering is the leading cause of injury to women.

Seen against this background, the much ballyhooed claim that feminism is responsible for making women miserable becomes absurd—and irrelevant.

Women themselves don't single out the women's movement as the source of their misery. To the contrary, in national surveys 75 to 95 percent of women credit the feminist campaign with *improving* their lives, and a similar proportion say that the women's movement should keep pushing for change. Less than 8 percent think the women's movement might have actually made their lot worse.

What actually is troubling the American female population, then? If the many ponderers of the Woman Question really wanted to know, they might have asked their subjects. In public opinion surveys, women consistently rank their own *inequality*, at work and at home, among their most urgent concerns. Over and over, women complain to pollsters about a lack of economic, not marital, opportunities; they protest that working men, not working women, fail to spend time in the nursery and the kitchen. The Roper Organization's survey analysts find that men's opposition to equality is "a major cause of resentment and stress" and "a major irritant for most women today." It is justice for their gender, not wedding rings and bassinets, that women believe to be in desperately short supply.

Some social observers may well ask whether the current pressures on women actually consti-tute a backlash—or just a continuation of American society's long-standing resistance to women's rights. Certainly hostility to female independence has always been with us. But if fear and loathing of feminism is a sort of perpetual viral condition in our culture, it is not always in an acute stage; its symptoms subside and resurface periodically. And it is these episodes of resurgence, such as the one we face now, that can accurately be termed "backlashes" to women's advancement. If we trace these occurrences in American history, we find such flare-ups are hardly random; they have always been triggered by the perception—accurate or not—that women are making great strides. These outbreaks are backlashes because they have always arisen in reaction to women's "progress," caused not simply by a bedrock of misogyny but by the specific efforts of contemporary women to improve their status, efforts that have been interpreted time and again by men—especially men grappling with real threats to their economic and social well-being on other fronts—as spelling their own masculine doom.

The force and furor of the backlash churn beneath the surface, largely invisible to the public eye. On occasion in the last decade, they have burst into view. We have seen New Right politicians condemn women's independence, antiabortion protesters firebomb women's clinics, fundamentalist preachers damn feminists as "whores" and "witches." Other signs of the backlash's wrath, by their sheer brutality, can push their way into public consciousness for a time—the sharp increase in rape, for example, or the rise in pornography that depicts extreme violence against women.

More subtle indicators in popular culture may receive momentary, and often bemused, media notice, then quickly slip from social awareness: A report, for instance, that the image of women on prime-time TV shows has suddenly degenerated. A survey of mystery fiction finding the numbers of female characters tortured and mutilated mysteriously multiplying. The puzzling news that, as one commentator put it, "So many hit songs have the B-word [bitch] to refer to women that some rap music seems to be veering toward rape music." The ascendancy of virulently misogynist comics like Andrew Dice Clay—who called women "pigs" and "sluts" and strutted in films in which women were beaten, tortured, and blown up—or radio hosts like Rush Limbaugh, whose broadsides against "femi-Nazi" feminists made his syndicated program the most popular radio talk show in the nation.

Backlash happens to be the title of a Hollywood movie in which a man frames his wife for a murder he's committed. The backlash against women's rights works in much the same way: its rhetoric charges feminist with all the crimes it perpetrates. The backlash line blames the women's movement for the "feminization of poverty"—while the backlash's own instigators in Washington pushed through the budget cuts that helped impoverish millions of women, fought pay equity proposals, and undermined equal opportunity laws. The backlash line claims the women's movement cares nothing for children's rights—while its own representatives in the capital and state legislatures have blocked one bill after another to improve child care, slashed billions of dollars in federal aid for children, and relaxed state licensing standards for day care centers. The backlash line accuses the women's movement of creating a generation of unhappy single and childless women—but its purveyors in the media are the ones guilty of making single and childless women feel like circus freaks.

To blame feminism for women's "lesser life" is to miss entirely the point of feminism, which is to win women a wider range of experience. Feminism remains a pretty simple concept, despite repeated—and enormously effective—efforts to dress it up in greasepaint and turn its proponents into gargoyles. As Rebecca West wrote sardonically in 1913, "I myself have never been able to find out precisely what feminism is: I only know that people call me a feminist whenever I express sentiments that differentiate me from a doormat."

The meaning of the word "feminist" has not really changed since it first appeared in a book review in the *Athenaeum* of April 27, 1895, describing a woman who "has in her the capacity of fighting her way back to independence." It is the basic proposition that, as Nora put it in Ibsen's *A Doll's House* a century ago, "Before everything else I'm a human being." It is the simply worded sign hoisted by a little girl in the 1970 Women's Strike for Equality: I AM NOT A BARBIE DOLL. Feminism asks the world to recognize at long last that women aren't decorative ornaments, worthy vessels, members of a "special-interest group." They are half (in fact, now more than half) of the national population, and just as deserving of rights and opportunities, just as capable of participating in the world's events, as the other half. Feminism's agenda is basic: It asks that women not be forced to "choose" between public justice and private happiness. It asks that women be free to define themselves—instead of having their identity defined for them, time and again, by their culture and their men.

The fact that these are still such incendiary notions should tell us that American women have way to go before they enter the promised land of equality.

To Apply This Reading to Yourself

1. *Are you content with the status of women relative to men in America? Why or why not?*
2. *Do you agree with Faludi that there is an "undeclared war against American women"? Why or why not?*
3. *Do you agree with Faludi that "fear and loathing of feminism is a sort of perpetual condition in our culture"? Why or why not?*
4. *Do you agree with Faludi that the image of women on TV and in general has degenerated? Why or why not?*
5. *Faludi writes that feminism simply asks that "women be free to define themselves—instead of having their identity defined for them, time and again, by their culture and their men." Are you in sympathy with this goal? Why or why not? What would you do or what are you doing to further or frustrate this goal?*

Casualties on the Road to Equality

Kay Ebeling

The other day I had the world's fastest blind date. A Yuppie from Eureka penciled me in for 50 minutes on a Friday and met me at a watering hole in the rural northern California town of Arcata. He breezed in, threw his jammed daily planner on the table and shot questions at me, watching my reactions as if it were a job interview. He eyed how much I drank. Then he breezed out to his next appointment. He had given us 50 minutes to size each other up and see if there was any chance for romance. His exit was so fast that as we left he let the door slam back in my face. It was an interesting slam.

Most of our 50-minute conversation had covered the changing state of male–female relationships. My blind date was 40 years old, from the Experimental Generation. He is "actively pursuing new ways for men and women to interact now that old traditions no longer exist." That's a real quote. He really did say that, when I asked him what he liked to do. This was a man who'd read *Ms. Magazine* and believed every word of it. He'd been single for 16 years but had lived with a few women during that time. He was off that evening for a ski weekend, meeting someone who was paying her own way for the trip.

I too am from the Experimental Generation, but I couldn't even pay for my own drink. To me, feminism has backfired against women. In 1973 I left what could have been a perfectly good marriage, taking with me a child in diapers, a 10-year-old Plymouth and Volume 1, Number One of *Ms. Magazine*. I was convinced I could make it on my own. In the last 15 years my ex has married or lived with a succession of women. As he gets older, his women stay in their 20s. Meanwhile, I've stayed unattached. He drives a BMW. I ride buses.

Today I see feminism as the Great Experiment That Failed, and women in my generation,

its perpetrators, are the casualties. Many of us, myself included, are saddled with raising children alone. The resulting poverty makes us experts at cornmeal recipes and ways to find free recreation on weekends. At the same time, single men from our generation amass fortunes in CDs and real-estate ventures so they can breeze off on ski weekends. Feminism freed men, not women. Now men are spared the nuisance of a wife and family to support. After childbirth, if his wife's waist doesn't return to 20 inches, the husband can go out and get a more petite woman. It's far more difficult for the wife, now tied down with a baby, to find a new man. My blind date that Friday waved goodbye as he drove off in his RV, I walked home and paid the sitter with laundry quarters.

The main message of feminism was: woman, you don't need a man; remember, those of you around 40, the phrase: "A woman without a man is like a fish without a bicycle"? That joke circulated through "consciousness raising" groups across the country in the '70s. It was a philosophy that made divorce and cohabitation casual and routine. Feminism made women disposable. So today a lot of females are around 40 and single with a couple of kids to raise on their own. Child-support payments might pay for a few pairs of shoes, but in general, feminism gave men all the financial and personal advantages over women.

What's worse, we asked for it. Many women decided: you don't need a family structure to raise your children. We packed them off to day-care centers where they could get their nurturing from professionals. Then we put on our suits and ties, packed our briefcases and took off on this Great Experiment, convinced that there was no difference between ourselves and the guys in the other offices.

'BIOLOGICAL THING'

How wrong we were. Because like it or not, women have babies. It's this biological thing that's just there, these organs we're born with. The truth is, a woman can't live the true feminist life unless she denies her childbearing biology. She has to live on the pill, or have her tubes tied at an early age. Then she can keep up with the guys with an uninterrupted career and then, when she's 30, she'll be paying her own way on ski weekends too.

The reality of feminism is a lot of frenzied and overworked women dropping kids off at day-care centers. If the child is sick, they just send along some children's Tylenol and then rush off to underpaid jobs that they don't even like. Two of my working-mother friends told me they were mopping floors and folding laundry after midnight last week. They live on five hours of sleep, and it shows in their faces. And they've got husbands!

Women should get educations so they can be brainy in the way they raise their children. Women can start small businesses, do consulting, write freelance out of the home. But women don't belong in 12-hour-a-day executive office positions, and I can't figure out today what ever made us think we would want to be there in the first place. As long as that biology is there, women can't compete equally with men. A ratio cannot be made using disproportionate parts. Women and men are not equal, we're different. The economy might even improve if women came home, opening up jobs for unemployed men, who could then support a wife and children, the way it was, pre-feminism.

Sometimes on Saturday nights I'll get dressed up and go out club-hopping or to the theater, but the sight of all those other women my age, dressed a little too young, made up to hide encroaching wrinkles, looking hopefully into the crowds, usually depresses me. I end up coming home, to spend my Saturday night with my daughter asleep in her room nearby. At least the NBC Saturday-night lineup is geared demographically to women at home alone.

To Apply This Reading to Yourself

1. *What is your view of the feminist movement? Why?*
2. *Ebeling sees women as the casualties of feminism. She writes, "Feminism freed men, not women." Do you agree? Why or why not?*
3. *Ebeling writes, "As long as biology is there, women can't compete equally with men." Do you agree? Why or why not?*
4. *Ebeling appears nostalgic for the traditional pattern of Dad at work and Mom and kids at home. Would this patterning suit you? Why or why not?*

X: A Fabulous Child's Story

Lois Gould

Once upon a time, a baby named X was born. This baby was named X so that nobody could tell whether it was a boy or girl. Its parents could tell, of course, but they couldn't tell anybody else. They couldn't even tell Baby X, at first.

You see, it was all part of a very important Secret Scientific Xperiment, known officially as Project Baby X. The smartest scientists had set up this Xperiment at a cost of Xactly 23 billion dollars and 72 cents, which might seem like a lot for just one baby, even a very important Xperimental baby. But when you remember the prices of things like strained carrots and stuffed bunnies, and popcorn for the movies and booster shots for camp, let alone 28 shiny quarters from the tooth fairy, you begin to see how it adds up.

Also, long before Baby X was born, all those scientists had to be paid to work out the details of the Xperiment, and to write the *Official Instruction Manual* for Baby X's parents and, most important of all, to find the right set of parents to bring up Baby X. These parents had to be selected very carefully. Thousands of volunteers had to take thousands of tests and answer thousands of tricky questions. Almost everybody failed because, it turned out, almost everybody really wanted either a baby boy or a baby girl, and not Baby X at all. Also, almost everybody was afraid that Baby X would be a lot more trouble than a boy or a girl. (They were probably right, the scientists admitted, but Baby X needed parents who wouldn't *mind* the Xtra trouble.)

There were families with grandparents named Milton and Agatha, who didn't see why the baby couldn't be named Milton or Agatha instead of X, even if it *was* an X. There were families with aunts who insisted on sending tiny baseball mitts. Worst of all, these were families that already had other children who couldn't be trusted to keep the secret. Certainly not if they knew the secret was worth 23 billion dollars and 72 cents—and all you had to do was take one little peek at Baby X in the bathtub to know if it was a boy or a girl.

But, finally, the scientists found the Joneses, who really wanted to raise an X more than any other kind of baby—no matter how much trouble it would be. Ms. and Mr. Jones had to promise they would take equal turns caring for X, and feeding it, and singing lullabies. And they had to promise never to hire any baby-sitters. The government scientists knew perfectly well that the baby-sitter would probably peek at X in the bathtub, too.

The day the Joneses brought their baby home, lots of friends and relatives came over to see it. None of them knew about the secret Xperiment, though. So the first thing they asked was what kind of baby X was. When the Joneses smiled and said, "It's an X!" nobody knew what to say. They couldn't say, "Look at her cute little dimples!" And they couldn't say, "Look at his husky little biceps!" And they couldn't even say just plain "kitchy-coo." In fact, they all thought the Joneses were playing some kind of rude joke.

But, of course, the Joneses were not joking. "It's an X" was absolutely all they would say. And that made the friends and relatives very angry. The relatives felt embarrassed about having an X in the family. "People will think there's something wrong with it!" some of them whispered. "There is something wrong with it!" others whispered back.

"Nonsense!" the Joneses told them all cheerfully. "What could possibly be wrong with this perfectly adorable X?"

Nobody could answer that, except Baby X, who had just finished its bottle. Baby X's answer was a loud, satisfied burp.

Clearly, nothing at all was wrong. Nevertheless, none of the relatives felt comfortable about buying a present for a Baby X. The cousins who sent the baby a tiny football helmet would not come and visit any more. And the neighbors who sent a pink-flowered romper suit pulled their shades down when the Joneses passed their house.

The *Official Instruction Manual* had warned the new parents that this would happen, so they didn't fret about it. Besides, they were too busy with Baby X and the hundreds of different Xercises for treating it properly.

Ms. and Mr. Jones had to be Xtra careful about how they played with little X. They knew that if they kept bouncing it up in the air and saying how *strong* and *active* it was, they'd be treating it more like a boy than an X. But if all they did was cuddle it and kiss it and tell it how *sweet* and *dainty* it was, they'd be treating it more like a girl than an X.

On page 1,654 of the *Official Instruction Manual*, the scientists prescribed: "plenty of bouncing and plenty of cuddling, *both*. X ought to be strong and sweet and active. Forget about *dainty* altogether."

Meanwhile, the Joneses were worrying about other problems. Toys, for instance. And clothes. On his first shopping trip, Mr. Jones told the store clerk, "I need some clothes and toys for my new baby." The clerk smiled and said, "Well, now, is it for a boy or a girl?" "It's an X," Mr. Jones said, smiling back. But the clerk got all red in the face and said huffily, "In *that* case, I'm afraid I can't help you, sir." So, Mr. Jones wandered helplessly up and down the aisles trying to find what X needed. But everything in the store was piled up in sections marked "Boys" or "Girls." There were "Boys' Pajamas" and "Girls' Underwear" and "Boys' Fire Engines" and "Girls' Housekeeping Sets." Mr. Jones went home without buying anything for X. That night he and Ms. Jones consulted page 2,326 of the *Official Instruction Manual*. "Buy plenty of everything!" it said firmly.

So they brought plenty of sturdy blue pajamas in the Boys' Department and cheerful flowered underwear in the Girls' Department. And they bought all kinds of toys. A boy doll that made pee-pee and cried, "Pa-pa." And a girl doll that talked in three languages and said, "I am the Pres-i-dent of Gen-er-al Motors." They also bought a storybook about a brave princess who rescued a handsome prince from his ivory tower, and another one about a sister and brother who grew up to be a baseball and a ballet star, and you had to guess which was which.

The head scientist of Project Baby X checked all their purchases and told them to keep up the good work. They also reminded the Joneses to see page 4,629 of the *Manual*, where it said, "Never make Baby X feel *embarrassed* or

ashamed about what it wants to play with. And if X gets dirty climbing rocks, never say 'Nice little Xes don't get dirty climbing rocks'."

Likewise, it said, "If X falls down and cries, never say 'Brave little Xes don't cry.' Because, of course, nice little Xes *do* get dirty, and brave little Xes *do* cry. No matter how dirty X gets, or how hard it cries, don't worry. It's all part of the Xperiment."

Whenever the Joneses pushed Baby X's stroller in the park, smiling strangers would come over and coo: "Is that a boy or girl?" The Joneses would smile back and say, "It's an X." The strangers would stop smiling then, and often snarl something nasty—as if the Joneses had snarled at *them*.

By the time X grew big enough to play with other children, the Joneses' troubles had grown bigger, too. Once a little girl grabbed X's shovel in the sandbox, and zonked X on the head with it. "Now, now, Tracy," the little girl's mother began to scold, "little girls mustn't hit little—" and she turned to ask X, "Are you a little boy or a little girl, dear?"

Mr. Jones, who was sitting near the sandbox, held his breath and crossed his fingers.

X smiled politely at the lady, even though X's head had never been zonked so hard in its life. "I'm a little X," X replied.

"You're a *what*?" the lady exclaimed angrily. "You're a little b-r-a-t, you mean!"

"But little girls mustn't hit little Xes, either!" said X, retrieving the shovel with another polite smile. "What good does hitting do, anyway?"

X's father, who was still holding his breath, finally let it out, uncrossed his fingers, and grinned back at X.

And at their next secret Project Baby X meeting, the scientists grinned, too. Baby X was doing fine.

But then it was time for X to start school. The Joneses were really worried about this, because school was even more full of rules for boys and girls, and there were no rules for Xes. The teacher would tell boys to form one line, and girls to form another line. There would be boys' games and girls' games, and boys' secrets and girls' secrets. The school library would have a list of recommended books for boys. There would even be a bathroom marked BOYS and another one marked GIRLS. Pretty soon boys and girls would hardly talk to each other. What would happen to poor little X?

The Joneses spent weeks consulting their *Instruction Manual* (there were 249½ pages of advice under "First Day of School"), and attending urgent special conferences with the smart scientists of Project Baby X.

The scientists had to make sure that X's mother had taught X how to throw and catch a ball properly, and that X's father had been sure to teach X what to serve at a doll's tea party. X had to know how to shoot marbles and how to jump rope and, most of all, what to say when the Other Children asked whether X was a Boy or a Girl.

Finally, X was ready. The Joneses helped X button on a nice new pair of red-and-white checked overalls, and sharpened six pencils for X's nice new pencilbox, and marked X's name clearly on all the books in the nice new bookbag. X brushed its teeth and combed its hair, which just about covered its ears, and remembered to put a napkin in its lunchbox.

The Joneses had asked X's teacher if the class could line up alphabetically, instead of forming separate lines for boys and girls. And they had asked if X could use the principal's bathroom, because it wasn't marked anything except BATH-ROOM. X's teacher promised to take care of all those problems. But nobody could help X with the biggest problem of all—Other Children.

Nobody in X's class had ever known an X before. What would they think? How would X make friends?

You couldn't tell what X was by studying its clothes—overalls don't even button right-to-left, like girls' clothes, or left-to-right, like boys' clothes. And you couldn't guess whether X had a girl's haircut or a boy's long haircut. And it was very hard to tell by the games X liked to play. Either X played ball very well for a girl, or else X played house very well for a boy.

Some of the children tried to find out by asking X tricky questions, like "Who's your favorite sports star?" That was easy. X had two favorite sports stars: a girl jockey named Robyn Smith and a boy archery champion named Robin Hood. Then they asked, "What's your favorite TV program?" And that was even easier. X's favorite TV program was "Lassie," which stars a girl dog played by a boy dog.

When X decided that its favorite toy was a doll, everyone decided that X must be a girl. But then X said that the doll was really a robot, and that X had computerized it, and that it was programmed to bake fudge brownies and then to clean up the kitchen. After X told them that, the other children gave up guessing what X was. All they knew was they'd sure like to see X's doll.

After school, X wanted to play with the other children. "How about shooting some baskets in the gym?" X asked the girls. But all they did was make faces and giggle behind X's back.

"How about weaving some baskets in the arts and crafts room?" X asked the boys. But they all made faces and giggled behind X's back, too.

That night, Ms. and Mr. Jones asked X how things had gone at school. X told them sadly that the lessons were okay, but otherwise school was a terrible place for an X. It seemed as if Other Children would never want an X for a friend.

Once more, the Joneses reached for their *Instruction Manual.* Under "Other Children," they found the following message: "What did you Xpect? *Other Children* have to obey all the silly boy-girl rules, because their parents taught them to. Lucky X—you don't have to stick to the rules at all! All you have to do is be yourself. P.S. We're not saying it'll be easy."

X liked being itself. But X cried a lot that night, partly because it felt afraid. So X's father held X tight, and cuddled it, and couldn't help crying a little, too. And X's mother cheered them both by reading an Xciting story about an enchanted prince called Sleeping Handsome, who woke up when Princess Charming kissed him.

The next morning, they all felt better, and little X went back to school with a brave smile and a clean pair of red-and-white checked overalls.

There was a seven-letter-word spelling bee in class that day. And a seven-lap boys' relay race in the gym. And a seven-layer-cake baking contest in the girls' kitchen corner. X won the spelling bee. X also won the relay race. And X almost won the baking contest, except it forgot to light the oven. Which only proves that nobody's perfect. Other Children noticed something else, too. He said: "Winning or losing doesn't seem to count to X. X seems to have fun being good at boys' skills *and* girls' skills."

"Come to think of it," said another one of the Other Children, "maybe X is having twice as much fun as we are!"

So after school that day, the girl who beat X at the baking contest gave X a big slice of her prize-winning cake. And the boy X beat in the relay race asked X to race him home.

From then on, some really funny things began to happen. Susie, who sat next to X in class, suddenly refused to wear pink dresses to school any more. She insisted on wearing red-and-white checked overalls—just like X's. Overalls, she told her parents, were much better for climbing monkey bars.

Then Jim, the class football nut, started wheeling his little sister's doll carriage around the football field. He'd put on his entire football uniform, except for the helmet. Then he'd put the helmet in the carriage, lovingly tucked under an old set of shoulder pads. Then he'd start jogging around the field, pushing the carriage and singing "Rockabye Baby" to his football helmet. He told his family that X did the same thing, so it must be okay. After all, X was now the team's star quarterback.

Susie's parents were horrified by her behavior, and Jim's parents were worried sick about his. But the worst came when the twins, Joe and Peggy, decided to share everything with each other. Peggy used Joe's hockey skates, and his microscope, and took half his newspaper route. Joe used Peggy's needlepoint kit, and her cookbooks, and took two of her three baby-sitting jobs. Peggy started running the lawn mower, and Joe started running the vacuum cleaner.

Their parents weren't one bit pleased with Peggy's wonderful biology experiments, or with Joe's terrific needlepoint pillows. They didn't care that Peggy mowed the lawn better, and that Joe vacuumed the carpet better. In fact, they were furious. It's all that little X's fault, they agreed. Just because X doesn't know what it is, or what it's supposed to be, it wants to get everybody *else* mixed up, too!

Peggy and Joe were forbidden to play with X any more. So was Susie, and then Jim, and then *all* the Other Children. But it was too late; the Other Children stayed mixed up and happy and free, and refused to go back to the way they'd been before X.

Finally, Joe and Peggy's parents decided to call an emergency meeting of the school's Parents' Association, to discuss "The X Problem." They sent a report to the principal stating that X was a "disruptive influence." They demanded immediate action. The Joneses, they said, should be *forced* to tell whether X was a boy or a girl. And then X should be *forced* to behave like whichever it was. If the Joneses refused to tell, the Parents' Association said, then X must take an Xamination. The school psychiatrist must Xamine it physically and mentally, and issue a full report. If X's test showed it was a boy, it would have to obey all the boys' rules. If it proved to be a girl, X would have to obey all the girls' rules.

And if X turned out to be some kind of mixed-up misfit, then X should be Xpelled from the school. Immediately.

The principal was very upset. Disruptive influence? Mixed-up misfit? But X was an Xcellent student. All the teachers said it was a delight to have X in their classes. X was president of the student council. X had won first prize in the talent show, and second prize in the art show, and honorable mention in the science fair, and six athletic events on field day, including the potato race.

Nevertheless, insisted the Parents' Association, X is a Problem Child. X is the Biggest Problem Child we have ever seen!

So the principal reluctantly notified X's parents that numerous complaints about X's behavior had come to the school's attention. And that after the psychiatrist's Xamination, the school would decide what to do about X.

The Joneses reported this at once to the scientists, who referred them to page 85,759 of the *Instruction Manual.* "Sooner or later," it said, "X will have to be Xamined by a psychiatrist. This may be the only way any of us will know for sure whether X is mixed up—or whether everyone else is."

The night before X was to be Xamined, the Joneses tried not to let X see how worried they were. "What if—?" Mr. Jones would say. And Ms. Jones would reply, "No use worrying." Then a few minutes later, Ms. Jones would say, "What if—?" and Mr. Jones would reply, "No use worrying."

X just smiled at them both, and hugged them hard and didn't say much of anything. X was thinking, What if—? And then X thought: No use worrying.

At Xactly 9 o'clock the next day, X reported to the school psychiatrist's office. The principal, along with a committee from the Parents' Association, X's teachers, X's classmates, and Ms. and Mr. Jones, waited in the hall outside. Nobody knew the details of the tests X was to be given, but everybody knew they'd be *very* hard, and they'd reveal Xactly what everyone wanted to know about X, but were afraid to ask.

It was terribly quiet in the hall. Almost spooky. Once in a while, they could hear a strange noise inside the room. There were buzzes. And a beep or two. And several bells. An occasional light would flash under the door. The Joneses thought it was a white light, but the principal thought it was blue. Two or three children swore it was either yellow or green. And the Parents' Association missed it completely.

Through it all, you could hear the psychiatrist's low voice, asking hundreds of questions, and X's higher voice, answering hundreds of answers.

The whole thing took so long that everyone knew it must be the most complete Xamination anyone had ever had to take. Poor X, the Joneses thought. Serves X right, the Parents' Committee thought. I wouldn't like to be in X's overalls right now, the children thought.

At last, the door opened. Everyone crowded around to hear the results. X didn't look any different; in fact, X was smiling. But the psychiatrist looked terrible. He looked as if he was crying! "What happened?" everyone was shouting. Had X done something disgraceful? "I wouldn't be a bit surprised!" muttered Peggy and Joe's parents. "Did X flunk the *whole* test?" cried Susie's parents. "Or just the most important part?" yelled Jim's parents.

"Oh, dear," sighed Mr. Jones.

"Oh, dear," sighed Ms. Jones.

"*Sssh*," ssshed the principal. "The psychiatrist is trying to speak."

Wiping his eyes and clearing his throat, the psychiatrist began, in a hoarse whisper. "In my opinion," he whispered—you could tell he must be very upset—"in my opinion, young X here—"

"Yes? Yes?" shouted a parent impatiently.

"*Ssshh!*" ssshed the principal.

"Young *Sssh* here, I mean young X," said the doctor, frowning, "is just about—"

"Just about *what*? Let's have it!" shouted another parent.

". . . just about the *least* mixed-up child I've ever Xamined!" said the psychiatrist.

"Yah for X!" yelled one of the children. And then the others began yelling, too. Clapping and cheering and jumping up and down.

"*SSSH!*" SSShed the principal, but nobody did.

The Parents' Committee was angry and bewildered. How *could* X have passed the whole Xamination? Didn't X have an *identity* problem? Wasn't X mixed up at *all*? Wasn't X *any* kind of a misfit? How could it *not* be, when it didn't even *know* what it was? And why was the psychiatrist crying?

Actually, he had stopped crying and was smiling politely through his tears. "Don't you see?" he said. "I'm crying because it's wonderful! X has absolutely no identity problem! X isn't one bit mixed up! As for being a misfit—ridiculous! X knows perfectly well what it is! Don't you, X?" The doctor winked. X winked back.

"But what *is* X? " shrieked Peggy and Joe's parents. "We still want to know what X is!"

"Ah, yes," said the doctor, winking again. "Well, don't worry. You'll all know one of these days. And you won't need me to tell you."

"What? What does he mean?" some of the parents grumbled suspiciously.

Susie and Peggy and Joe all answered at once. "He means that by the time X's sex matters, it won't be a secret any more!"

With that, the doctor began to push through the crowd toward X's parents. "How do you do," he said, somewhat stiffly. And then he reached out to hug them both. "If I ever have an X of my own," he whispered, "I sure hope you'll lend me your instruction manual."

Needless to say, the Joneses were very happy. The Project Baby X scientists were rather pleased, too. So were Susie, Jim, Peggy, Joe, and all the Other Children. The Parents' Association wasn't, but they promised to accept the psychiatrist's report, and not make any more trouble. They even invited Ms. and Mr. Jones to become honorary members, which they did.

Later that day, all X's friends put on their red-and-white checked overalls and went over to see X. They found X in the back yard, playing with a very tiny baby that none of them had ever seen before. The baby was wearing very tiny red-and-white checked overalls.

"How do you like our new baby?" X asked the Other Children proudly.

"It's got cute dimples," said Jim.

"It's got husky biceps, too," said Susie.

"What kind of baby is it? " asked Joe and Peggy.

X frowned at them. "Can't you tell?" Then X broke into a big, mischievous grin. *"It's a Y!"*

To Apply This Reading to Yourself

1. *What insight or perspective does this reading give you concerning your own life?*
2. *Discuss the pressure you felt in growing up—whether imposed by others or yourself—to make your behavior conform to that prescribed for your gender.*
3. *Discuss the pressure you currently feel—whether imposed by others or yourself—to make your behavior conform to that prescribed for your gender.*
4. *What do you find positive and negative about your own sex role?*
5. *Write a brief description of a person who possesses and integrates the most valued qualities of each sex. How different are you from this person? How like this person would you care to be? Why?*
6. *What qualities would you like each of your children (present or future, and regardless of sex) to have? Why? Are there any qualities you would value only in a son or only in a daughter? Why or why not?*

PART
two

REACHING OUT

Our lives are interwoven with the lives of others. We humans are social creatures (but not necessarily sociable ones). In the average day we may find ourselves awash in a sea of strangers, in closer interaction with a dozen acquaintances, and in intimate communication with a handful of friends, relatives, or loved ones.

Some years ago Barbra Streisand presented a song about "people who need people" who, she sang on, "are the luckiest people in the world." But probably all of us need people. We need them for the best of reasons, for example, to love and nurture and to be loved and nurtured by in return. And we need them for the worst of reasons, perhaps for purposes of domination, control, or aggression.

In our society, there is considerable emphasis on doing things with others and on getting along with them. We start life in a group—our family—and we soon belong to a number of other neighborhood, school, and community organizations. Even at elementary school age, we may be a member of four or five groups which include perhaps a gang, a playground, a scouting organization, and a hobby club. As we grow older, we may continue to join, moving to groups appropriate to our age and interests.

With all our exposure to interpersonal living, we should be experts at it, but this does not appear to be the case. Halfway through this century, David Reisman in his widely acclaimed book *The Lonely Crowd* noted how isolated many people were even though they were constantly surrounded by others. Since that time a number of authorities have made similar observations, and Gerald Phillips and Nancy Metzger in their book *Intimate Communication* declare, "Our society is filled with people who are ineffective in the way they deal with others. We have not even begun to assess the human impact of ineffectuality, and the related problems of loneliness and boredom, but we discover a great many people hurt because they are not capable of managing their relationships."

Although many of us are inexpert at reaching out to others, there is no end of experts who want to tell us how to do so. Popular magazines and the best-seller lists are filled with writing on this subject. Over the years there has been a constant flow of books on how not to be shy, how to influence, dominate, or get the best of others, how to prevent others from getting the best of us, how to win friends, find lovers, love, make love, and even how to say good-bye.

While many authorities have been lamenting our inability to be with others, some have deplored our lack of ability to be alone. They hold that the most basic relationship—the one on which all others build—is to oneself, and to find out who we are, we sometimes need to distance ourselves from others. They encourage us to lose ourselves—and find ourselves—in solitude.

The three topics presented in part two of this book relate to the problem of reaching out, and later topics will extend this discussion in other contexts. The first topic discusses *aloneness* and makes considerable distinction between loneliness and solitude. The second topic concerns *assertiveness* and how we can affirm ourselves while also affirming others. The last of these topics deals with *sexuality*—a way of relating that has so much potential for pain and pleasure.

Aloneness

I asked a man to sleep with me last night. He was my friend—affectionate, handsome, and, most important, available. After I asked him, he sat very quietly on the footstool near my chair for several minutes and then he said no. I felt rejected, hurt, and when he left, I asked myself why I needed affection and closeness so desperately that I had to use sex to get it. I have felt this kind of loneliness all my life.

—Terri Schultz

I find it wholesome to be alone the greater part of the time. To be in company, even with the best, is soon wearisome and dissipating. I love to be alone. I never found the companion that was so companionable as solitude.

—Henry David Thoreau

What we need . . . are classes on how to be alone: Aloneness 1A, Intermediary Aloneness, Advanced Aloneness. The great joy of these new classes is that attendance would not only not be required, it would be forbidden.

—Anne Taylor Fleming

Aloneness refers to our separation from others. To be alone is to be separate, to be apart, to be by oneself. From birth to death, much of life is spent alone.

Each of us appears to need some separation from others and also some union with them. Both privacy and contact are essential. In a private space or with a certain psychological distance, we can renew our sense of self, our uniqueness and integrity. But life is a series of relationships, and we also need to be at home in our world, to interact with, nourish, and be nourished by others.

It is fortunate when our contact boundaries—those imaginary membranes between us and our social environment—are relatively fluid. Sure of our own identity, we can move forward to contact others. But not captured by others, we can move back to be with and affirm ourselves.

Some of us have trouble with our contact boundaries. Unsure of our identity, we may erect a wall to keep from being overwhelmed or engulfed. Or we rush about to find others to complete us and make us whole. Some may be stuck at the boundary, venturing little into themselves or out to their social milieu.

Aloneness, as the concept is used here, is without any connotation of value. To be alone is neither bad nor good in itself. "Loneliness" and "solitude" are terms that are frequently used to connote negative and positive aloneness, respectively.

Loneliness subsumes a number of negative separation experiences. When we are lonely, we suffer because of our longing for a relationship. This longing may be for another person or group, or it may be for a way of life or for a part of ourselves that has no opportunity for expression.

Solitude subsumes various kinds of positive aloneness. This kind of separation is self-chosen and comfortable, and it may be enriching. Dwelling within oneself can be like being in an oasis, refuge, or retreat. We can let down our guard and gain some perspective. Solitude can bring a sense of centeredness and serenity that Walt Whitman aptly described when he wrote, "I exist as I am, that is enough/If no other in the world be aware/I sit content/and if each and all be aware/I sit content."

Cultures vary in the amounts of privacy and contact they provide and foster, and individuals within a culture vary even more in their contact needs. I know a person who visited for awhile in an intimate Indonesian household where, except at the front, there were no doors to shut; curtains hung in the archways. He hungered sometimes to be by himself, to retire to a room and slam the door shut. "Have you ever tried to slam a curtain?" he asked me.

Recently, there has been considerable emphasis in the American culture on "popularity," "fitting in," and "getting along." As children, we are taught the importance of being likeable and sociable. We are sent alone to a corner or to our room for punishment while, by contrast, happy events are typically shared. We can come to consider aloneness an undesirable experience and go to great lengths to avoid it.

Both privacy and contact can be enriching. We need to learn the value of each and arrive at a balance that is right for us. In reviewing her own balance of privacy and contact, Joan Mills writes, " 'I cannot bear to be lonely,' I say, and it is true. My heart thrives upon the talk—and silences—by which we communicate with a near but always separate and different other. I like to close the distance with a touch of the hand; it reassures me. But I was a solitary child, and the habit of solitude is in me, too . . . It's separateness that sweetens togetherness—or is it the other way around?"

THE PAIN OF LONELINESS

In the first reading, William Sadler identifies five dimensions of loneliness, each with its own source and remedy. He emphasizes that the causes of loneliness are often beyond the individual's control and that a particular instance of loneliness can be dealt with effectively only if its specific origin is addressed. Sadler's five dimensions of loneliness (and their associated origins) are (1) interpersonal (longing for or missing another); (2) social (feeling cut off from or shut out of a particular group or social unit); (3) cultural (feeling severed from a customary or traditional way of life); (4) cosmic (feeling "out of touch with an ultimate source of life and meaning"); and (5) psychological (feeling alienated from an important part of oneself).

While Sadler holds that the sources of loneliness are often external to the individual, in the second selection, Jerry Greenwald insists that each of us is the primary cause of our own loneliness. He describes a number of "loneliness-inducing" games—ways we go about making ourselves lonely. Greenwald writes that in our loneliness we may seek from others what we should provide for ourselves. We should stop our games, nourish ourselves, and then reach out to nourish others. "A genuinely nourishing person," Greenwald concludes, "will not be lonely."

THE PLEASURE OF SOLITUDE

Some of us avoid being alone, but in the last reading, Carin Rubenstein and Phillip Shaver encourage us to give solitude a chance. They point out the essential link between solitude and intimacy; in solitude, we come to know ourselves better, and this enhances intimacy with others. If we are not comfortable with ourselves, our relations with others may not be much better. Solitude for some can be an unhealthy escape, but used properly, it soothes, strengthens, and brings us closer to others.

To Explore Your Aloneness

1. *Diagramming aloneness and relatedness (the personal sociogram).* Each of us is, existentialist James Bugental reminds us, at once *a part of* and yet *apart from* all others. We are separate but related. Social scientists have called the most important persons in an individual's life "significant others." Consider the significant others in your life. Who are they? How close do you feel to each? To answer these questions, construct a diagram, figure, or drawing to show how you experience your relationship to each of your significant others. You might begin by listing the names of those to be included. When you have done this, relax, and in your mind's eye allow the names to arrange themselves in some diagrammatic or symbolic way, which you can then set down on paper.

2. *Sharing interpersonal loneliness.*[1] Interpersonal loneliness is that in which you long for or miss someone. It may be a family member who has died or withdrawn affection or a friend who has moved away or a lover who has become estranged. Or it may be simply the lack of a companion to whom you could relate and share life. Sometimes the person is not missing but is closed off or cannot be contacted or communicated with in a meaningful way. Write down your experience of interpersonal loneliness, and share it with the larger group or in smaller groups or dyads.

3. *Sharing social loneliness.* Social loneliness is that in which you are cut off from or shut out of a particular group or social unit. Perhaps you are excluded from or unable to form meaningful contact with your peer group or those with whom you live or study or work. Because of relocation, illness, retirement, or change in values, you may lose touch with groups that have been important sources of contact. Write down your experience of social loneliness, and share it with the larger group or in smaller groups or dyads.

4. *Sharing cultural loneliness.* Cultural loneliness is that in which you are cut off from a customary or traditional way of life. If you move to a new country or from one region to another with quite different cultural patterns, you may experience this loneliness. Other kinds of cultural loneliness are homesickness, and, in periods of rapid change, nostalgia and longing for old cultural ways and patterns. Write down your experience of cultural loneliness, and share it with the larger group or in smaller groups or dyads.

5. *Sharing cosmic loneliness.* Cosmic loneliness is that in which you find yourself, as William Sadler puts it, "out of touch with an ultimate source of life and meaning." You feel this loneliness when life seems senseless or purposeless, or when you have no relationship to anything that transcends yourself. This dimension has also been called "spiritual loneliness," and some persons have found their cosmic and spiritual longings fulfilled through religious, mystical, and humanitarian pursuits. Write down your experience of cosmic loneliness, and share it with the larger group or in smaller groups or dyads.

6. *Sharing psychological loneliness.* Psychological loneliness is that in which you are separated from or out of touch with an important part of yourself. You can suffer this kind of loneliness when you are caught up in a lifestyle that is wrong for you or out of keeping with your inner nature. Or it may be that important parts of yourself are unexpressed or buried. When this happens, you feel unfulfilled, inauthentic, or phony. Write down an experience of psychological loneliness that you have had, and then share it with the larger group or in smaller groups or dyads.

7. *Exploring solitude (the private time).* Social contact has been highly regarded in our society; the value of solitude has been

1. The definitions of interpersonal, social, cultural, cosmic, and psychological loneliness presented here are taken from the work of William A. Sadler, Jr.

much less emphasized or understood. To explore solitude, set aside a period of time for at least three consecutive days to simply be by yourself. Try to reserve the same time and the same length of time each day. During this time be by yourself (no other persons or pets) and listen to yourself (no music, radios, or TV). Sit with yourself or walk with yourself (as long as the walk is not directed toward getting you someplace). Stay in the present; if you catch yourself ruminating about yesterday or planning tomorrow, let these thoughts slip away and bring yourself back to now. After each period or, if you like, only after the last period, write down what you have learned from your solitude.

8. *Exploring solitude (the captive place).* Imagine that for one week you were quarantined in a room by yourself, or locked into solitary confinement, or snowbound in a cabin in the mountains. Supply your own details to complete your fantasy. How difficult would this situation be for you? How rewarding could you make it by relying upon your inner resources? Think through and write down your answers.

9. *Exploring solitude (the chosen place).* Construct in your imagination a private sanctuary or refuge for yourself. It may be in a clearing in the woods by a pond or stream, or a serene overlook at the end of a hidden trail, or a place with impenetrable walls and massive, bolted doors. Work on your sanctuary in your mind's eye until you can see it clearly and it is just the way you want it. Then, for one week, whenever you feel jostled, harassed, or overwhelmed, imagine yourself in your private sanctuary. At the week's end, write down a description of your sanctuary and your experience with it.

10. *Valuing aloneness (the poet's corner).* Fritz Perls, who originated a technique called "Gestalt therapy," wrote a poem titled "The Gestalt Prayer." As a philosophy for living, it provoked some controversy and a number of poetic rejoinders.[2] Perls' poem is below and is followed on page 102 by two contrary ones (the last expresses a Chinese viewpoint). Which poem do you prefer as a personal philosophy? Why? As an alternative, write a poem that expresses your philosophy exactly.

I do my thing and you do your thing.
I am not in this world to live up to your
  expectations,
And you are not in this world to live up to
  mine.
You are you and I am I;
If by chance we find each other, it's beautiful.
If not, it can't be helped.

　　　　　　　　　　　　　　　　—Fritz Perls

2. Greening, T. C. (1977). Gestalt prayer: Final version? *Journal of Humanistic Psychology, 17*(3), 77–79.

If I just do my thing and you do yours,
We stand in danger of losing each other
And ourselves.

I am not in this world to live up to your
expectations;
But I am in this world to confirm you
As a unique human being,
And to be confirmed by you.

We are fully ourselves only in relation to each
other;
The I detached from a Thou
Disintegrates.

I do not find you by chance;
I find you by an active life
Of reaching out.

Rather than passively letting things happen
to me,
I can act intentionally to make them happen.

I must begin with myself, true;
But I must not end with myself.
The truth begins with two.

—Walter Tubbs

If I just do my thing and you do yours,
We stand in danger of losing our society
And eventually ourselves.

We owe our present to our past
And ourselves to previous generations.
How much can we call ours?

Wild geese fly easier as a group.
Tulips look more beautiful in clusters.
We do not find each other by chance,
Nor join together only by twos.
Don't think too much about yourself.
There are many things we can do together.

We must begin with ourselves, true.
But why not lose ourselves, too,
In communal spirit,
For all, not for one or two?

—You-Yuh Kuo

To Read Further

Burns, D. D. (1985). *Intimate connections*. New York: New American Library.
(paperback)
Greenwald, J. (1980). *Breaking out of loneliness*. New York: Rawson, Wade.

Lindbergh, A. M. (1955, 1975). *The gift from the sea.* New York: Pantheon.

Lynch, J. J. (1977). *The broken heart: The medical consequences of loneliness.* New York: Basic Books.

Moustakas, C. E. (1990). *Loneliness.* New York: Prentice-Hall. (paperback)

Moustakas, C. E. (1990). *Loneliness and love.* New York: Prentice-Hall. (paperback)

Rubenstein, C. & Shaver, P. (1982). *In search of intimacy.* New York: Delacorte Press.

Schultz, T. (1976). *Bittersweet: Surviving and growing from loneliness.* New York: Crowell.

Storr, A. (1988). *Solitude: A return to the self.* New York: Free Press.

Zimbardo, P. G. (1987). *Shyness.* New York: Jove.

The Causes of Loneliness

William A. Sadler, Jr.

About a year ago, I had an interview with a reporter that illustrates one of the paradoxes associated with loneliness. She called to ask about my work on the subject, hoping to get help with an article. After giving her some information, I suggested she get in touch with the department of urban studies at a university in the city where she worked. I felt certain that its in-depth, long-range study of a large urban area would yield some insights into loneliness that would be relevant to her article and her newspaper's readers.

Several weeks later, the reporter called back to say that she had been turned away at the university. She was told by the department's assistant director that loneliness was not a social problem worth studying, that no data on loneliness were available, and that none was expected from their study program. Yet during the reporter's visits to mental health clinics and counselors in that area she was told that breakdowns, divorces, alcohol and drug addiction, and suicide were markedly increasing, and that problems such as these were related to chronic loneliness.

That's the paradox. Loneliness is so often dismissed by experts studying modern life, while at the same time it is reported to be an increasingly significant problem in individual and social being.

How can we account for the fact that loneliness, which I find to be a serious problem for many persons in modern America, is virtually ignored by the social sciences? I think there are two basic reasons. The first is theoretical. Until recently we lacked the clear concepts that would allow investigators and counselors to define loneliness and to understand it in a reliable way. The second reason is personal and has to do with the general attitude of the public toward loneliness, which sees it merely as a symptom of a weak character. The result is that one tends to downplay the impact it has in one's life, or even to deny that it has any significance at all. A common response given to persons who admit being lonely is: "Well, what's wrong with you? You don't need to be lonely. Go out and get busy. Join a club. Do something." Frequently through workshops, interviews, and articles I have found the response to be given more negative than this.

Investigations done in the last few years have permitted us to be more precise in defining loneliness. The conceptual understanding of loneliness, which will be presented in this article, shows why the accusatory response misses the mark. Many people in our society are lonely, not because of personality defects, but because there are factors "out there" that cause them to be lonely. Hopefully, this attitude will do more than resolve the paradox. It will help us all understand loneliness more intelligently and sympathetically, and provide a few realistic ideas about how to cope with it productively.

What is meant by *loneliness?* People use the term in different ways. Often loneliness is confused with merely being alone or with isolation. Your own experience should tell you that these are not identical. You can be alone and not lonely. People locked in solitary confinement do not always experience loneliness, at least not to any severe degree. To concentrate on isolation as much as social science has done when it has tried to get at loneliness is to miss the obvious. Some of the most painful, lonely feelings arise in the midst of a relationship or a group. Dr. Carl Jung suggested that "loneliness does not come from having no people about one, but from holding certain views that others find inadmissible." Adolescents, for example, frequently complain of the loneliness they experience in their homes, when they sense a generation gap. Adults they love simply do not understand them.

For this reason I suggest that loneliness is not just a physical condition. It is primarily an *experience.* Furthermore, it is probably unique to mankind. In his study on "the biology of loneliness" the late Dr. Ralph Audy Ph.D., M.D., of the U.C.L.A. Medical Center in San Francisco came to the conclusion that although there are analogies to it in the animal world, only human beings really know loneliness. Animals certainly manifest discomfort from prolonged separation. Ethologists and animal psychologists suggest that there is a basic animal need for attachment and that problems arise when that need is frustrated. It seems likely that humans have a similar need. But the kind of loneliness that I think is particularly troublesome in modern society is more complicated than mere frustration of this need for attachment.

In studying countless expressions of loneliness, both of modern Americans and from other times and places, I have found some common elements. The first and most outstanding feature of loneliness is a painful feeling, sometimes experienced as a sharp ache, as in moments of grief or separation; but it can also be a dull lingering form of stress that seems to tear a person down. Sometimes lonely feelings produce the "blues" of depression; but again, there is a difference between loneliness and depression. In the latter case, when a person is really "feeling down," he does not want to do anything. Depression corrodes motivational resources. Loneliness, by contrast, has a driving power. It sets people in motion—to go out, turn on TV, write a letter, make a phone call, or even get married.

There is another important aspect to this feeling. It is a significant signal coming from within ourselves that something is missing from our lives. Isolation does not imply any special type of awareness; loneliness does. A chief element of loneliness is a painful feeling that tells us something unpleasantly important about ourselves. All types of loneliness that I have studied have this element of painful self-awareness.

Loneliness also speaks of relationship, or rather, the absence or weakness of relationship. There are many different forms of relationship that can produce loneliness. One can be lonely for another person, a group, a home, a homeland, a tradition, a type of activity, and even a sense of meaning, or God.

A notable factor in much modern American loneliness is the quality of surprise. Loneliness so often strikes us unexpectedly. If you plan a trip by yourself, you prepare for lonely moments along the way. When they occur, you can handle them. When loneliness happens where you least expect it, such as in the home, at work, or among friends, it has a tremendous impact. We often do not know how to cope. It can make us confused, distraught, depressed, frightened, and even outraged.

Loneliness that frustrates our expectations is particularly hard to manage. It is this kind that so frequently disturbs people today. In nomadic and hunting societies persons were reared to expect long periods of aloneness. Facing loneliness was once a mark of manhood in American civilization. In an earlier era, Americans were reared to face life on their own in the struggle to achieve success through work. In that sense, being alone was part of the definition of successful living.

In this century the emphasis has been different. "Making it" has come to include "getting along with others." Learning to "fit in" is stressed at home, in school, in churches, and even in sports. Growing up in America often means developing expectations of involvement, popularity, and numerous attachments. Today, as we tend to evaluate our personal success in terms of being liked, loneliness strikes with a force that is hard to handle. It suggests failure or at least a frightening vulnerability.

One reason loneliness hangs on is because people are either not fully aware of it or not prepared for it. They push it out of their consciousness. They try to find some remedy in drugs, in "busyness," in overly dependent relationships, or by increasing their memberships. I am convinced that much of the fear associated with loneliness, as well as many behavioral problems that arise from too much of it, are unnecessary. We will continue to misunderstand the pain and the problem associated with loneliness until we recognize how complex its multiple causes or sources can be.

I have chosen to refer to these different sources and types of loneliness in terms of *dimensions*. After studying a variety of expressions of lonely people in different contexts, I now classify these expressions according to the object that a person feels is missing or from which he or she feels separated. The dimension aspect refers to the area of relationship a person perceives to be the source of his suffering. There seem to be *five* fairly distinct dimensions. I have labeled them: *interpersonal, social, cultural, cosmic,* and *psychological*. The term dimension suggests that the loneliness has a particular source and also constitutes a distinct type. However, there are few pure types. Sometimes people may experience several of these dimensions at once, often without being fully aware of it. More importantly, they indicate the extent of distress that lonely people may experience. For example, when individuals experience loneliness in four or five dimensions simultaneously and over a long period of time, they can find the stress intolerable and eventually break down.

Of the five the *interpersonal dimension* is generally the most familiar type. In this situation one person misses another. Often it is most intense when a very special person is missed. For example, one English study done by the Women's Group on Public Welfare, a social action organization, suggested that in this context the worst loneliness is a communication gap, such as one preceding the dissolution of a marriage:

"Perhaps there is no greater loneliness than that suffered when a marriage breaks down, particularly in a situation where partnership has so far foundered that communications between the two have become impossible," the study stated. "The divorced and widowed are often more lonely than those who have never been married. This deeper loneliness could be due not only to the loss of a close companion but also where, having married young, they have never learned to live with or face up to loneliness in earlier life."

The *social dimension* of loneliness is another familiar type. Here the individual feels cut off from a group that he or she considers important. Here it is a social relationship rather than an interpersonal one that is felt to be ruptured or lacking. Terms such as *ostracism, exile, rejection, blackballed, fired, discrimination,* and *expelled,* to mention only a few, resonate with the sense of this particular kind of loneliness. Often one gets an important sense of self-worth through membership and participation in a particular social environment. Once that membership is denied and participation is no longer possible, a person feels not just cut off but lacking in self-esteem. Not surprisingly a person who feels this social isolation often develops a low self-image and feels impotent to change this unsatisfactory relationship. Literature of minority groups, deviants, and more recently both the youth and the elderly is filled with lamentation and outrage at this kind of loneliness that is unwittingly imposed by society.

When these two forms of loneliness occur in the same individual simultaneously over a prolonged period of time, the result can be unfortunate in growth as well as behavior. Dr. Gisela Konopka, professor of social work at the University of Minnesota, found, for example, that complex, chronic loneliness was a primary factor contributing to the delinquency of adolescent girls. They were unwanted at home, often had no close friends, and were rejected at school and by clubs. Without any meaningful social role in which to demonstrate their worth and have it approved, as well as being without intimate communication, they acted out their feelings of lonely worthlessness in destructive acts of crime. The same applies to boys. The black Puerto Rican author, Piri Thomas, in his autobiography *Down These Mean Streets,* traces back the violent behavior, which led to his imprisonment, to an agonizing loneliness that stemmed from two sources: a lack of communication in his family, and ostracism by a white society because of his dark skin.

Retired persons may also experience an unexpected frustration associated with job severance. These people feel cut off, not merely from work, but from a network of relationships that had provided them with companionship and meaningful support. Housewives, too, have complained of similar combinations of lonely feelings, especially after several moves which leave them cut off from old friends, neighborhoods, and favorite groups.

My own research suggests that there may be a connection between rage and unmitigated complex loneliness. I have found that as you press people with questions on their loneliness they get very violent. In one group I had there was a divorced woman who felt extremely hostile toward her husband. She had lost her father at an early age and looked to her husband as a kind of father figure. He was a failure in every conceivable way and as a result she had bottled up this frustrated rage toward him. One day I threw a pillow down on the floor and said "There's your husband. Do to it what you would do to him." She killed him. Stomped him to death.

I believe that further investigation will bear out this tentative conclusion: very lonely people, who get angry rather than get depressed, will be prone to express their lonely frustration in destructive ways. I do not think it is mere coincidence that we are witnessing an unequalled rise in violence at the same time loneliness is so pervasive and intense. Personal accounts like that of Piri Thomas and studies of the Watts riots have shown that loneliness can be linked with violence when it is combined with a deep sense of frustration, especially in the economic and political realms.

The *cultural dimension* of loneliness refers to an experience some people have who feel themselves separated from a traditional system of meanings and a way of life. Immigrants and people who are continually mobile often experience this in the form of homesickness. People in America can sense this kind of loneliness if they feel the American heritage to be disintegrating. The term alienation may point to this form of loneliness, when it refers to a particular perception. Alienated people often feel that they are strangers in their own land. Members of American minority groups are particularly prone to this kind of loneliness. Even with close family relations they sometimes suffer from lingering loneliness, of being unable to identify with the American cultural heritage.

The feelings linked with cultural dislocation and culture shock likewise indicate a distinct form of loneliness, a sense of being uprooted and out of place. The nostalgia for those "good old days" when there was predictable order and cohesiveness also suggests this form of loneliness. In some cases loneliness may merely be a part of alienation; but in others, where there is a definite awareness of being separated from a meaningful tradition, I think the term loneliness is more accurate.

The *cosmic dimension* of loneliness may take a variety of forms, but essentially it refers to an experience in which a person feels out of touch with an ultimate source of life and meaning. Often it takes a religious form. Religious persons sometimes lament a felt absence of God. The Bible is filled with expressions of lonely persons longing for God. Much contemporary religion also answers to this need of loneliness, promising people a sense of presence and communion in their condition of existential estrangement or loneliness.

In workshops I have had persons express this cosmic loneliness in various ways. One middle-aged man confessed that a constant source of frustration came in the form of "missing God." Earlier he had been a strong believer, but now was an agnostic. He missed the sense of relatedness his youthful faith had given him. Religious persons who have been divorced have found themselves excluded from their religious community and they too have felt the anguish of this kind of loneliness. Some people have expressed a cosmic loneliness in their perception of the apparent absurdity of life. Erich Fromm suggested in *Escape from Freedom* that the experience of being morally and cosmically lonely is characteristic of persons who have realized the implications of autonomy in the modern world. Flight into conformity, becoming overly dependent on others, obsessive concern with others, a compulsive drive for achievement and recognition are some of the unproductive attempts of people to escape this dimension of loneliness.

The *psychological dimension* refers both to the experience a person has of being separate from himself as well as to the personal impact of the other four causes. A student who was in one of my courses made an observation that I have found many respond to: "I am loneliest when I am out of touch with myself." William James and C. J. Jung suggested the experience of a divided self is the root of modern man's search for a deeply personal religion or self-actualization or both. Much success of the Human Potential movement is related to the resolving of loneliness within one's self as well as that which comes from the lack of any intimate relationships with others. The perception of one's self as divided is a distinct form of "suffering self-recognition of separateness." Here again one usually stumbles into this perception unawares so that this loneliness is aggravated by a clash of expectations.

The psychological dimension indicates a distinctly internal source of loneliness, whereas the other four dimensions specifically refer to external sources. Some aspects of loneliness can be traced to personality features that possibly stand in the way of self-actualization. Shyness, fear of loving and being loved, self-pity, and the development of a schizoid personality are examples of traits that can contribute to loneliness. But one point I emphasize as a sociologist is that *personal troubles often come from outside,* even though the individual experiences them as very private and intimately his own. This sociological analysis helps to get us beyond a narrow psychological and everyday notion that somehow an individual is at fault when he is feeling lonely. On the contrary, if an individual has lost a parent, a friend, or child in death, has moved from home, has changed or lost his job, is rejected by his group, and has lost his religious faith, is confused by his ambiguous American heritage, and does not feel deep, abiding loneliness, then I suspect that something drastic is lacking within him. Much loneliness that I have examined is a normal response to breaks in an individual's important relationships.

In all five dimensions there is the element of a suffering self-recognition of separateness from something, though each general type can be distinguished from the others. In each situation there are different kinds of relationships lacking. Consequently, there are different needs to be met. Recognizing specific needs proper to different dimensions is extremely important when someone is trying to cope with loneliness. For example, a person who sorely misses a special other person will not have the need satisfied by joining a group. Yet in spite of an impressive history of failure, we continue to encourage widows to compensate by joining organizations. That is, we tell them to look to the social dimension to satisfy an interpersonal need. We offer hand-holding to members of minority groups who suffer from a sense of exclusion, instead of creating a place for them to experience participation. Many attempts to cope with loneliness are unsuccessful because the need of a particular type of loneliness has not been met. The conventional wisdom that recommends lonely people keep busy does not confront the problem of loneliness. It dodges it and instead applies compul-

sive activity like a narcotic. I have been told by countless widows that they have tried this formula only to find that they return home to an empty house exhausted and all the more vulnerable to the painful void of their lives.

If we recognize loneliness as a significant form of self-perception, consider its context, and identify the dimensions involved, then we will be better prepared to face it realistically and positively. We need to get away from the simplistic notion that for loneliness "all you need is love." Love is often not enough. Social action is sometimes necessary and individual preparation for loneliness is essential.

If more than just an interpersonal dimension is present, then a more complex form of response will be needed. For example, persons suffering from both interpersonal and social loneliness are more prone to low self-esteem. The latter can jeopardize close, interpersonal relationships and discourage persons from taking an active role in a group. Meaningful participation in a group and developing some social role of importance can help combat the troubles stemming from the social dimension of loneliness. It also can improve self-esteem, and prepare a person to become more ready for mature friendships and love.

If we are to meet the needs of lonely people effectively, we must get at the sources of their loneliness. Too often we treat loneliness merely as a symptom; that's one reason it keeps recurring. To confront loneliness in the modern world, our response will have to be a multi-level one. This concept of the five dimensions of loneliness can be helpful to social scientists, counselors, and anyone in detecting intelligently the types of loneliness we may encounter in the course of our lives. It also suggests the various sources from which it arises, and the multi-dimensional approach needed to cope adequately with the complex problem of loneliness.

To Apply This Reading to Yourself

1. *What importance has* interpersonal loneliness *had in your life? Describe your experience with this dimension of loneliness and its effects on you.*
2. *What importance has* social loneliness *had in your life? Describe your experience with this dimension of loneliness and its effects on you.*

3. *What importance has* cultural loneliness *had in your life? Describe your experience with this dimension of loneliness and its effects on you.*
4. *What importance has* cosmic loneliness *had in your life? Describe your experience with this dimension of loneliness and its effect on you.*
5. *What importance has* psychological loneliness *had in your life? Describe your experience with this dimension of loneliness and its effects on you.*
6. *What dimension or combination of dimensions of loneliness affect you most deeply at present? How do you experience and deal with this loneliness? Write a brief paper incorporating your answers to these questions.*

Loneliness-Inducing Games

Jerry A. Greenwald

A human being is responsible to himself for everything he does. A person in a state of loneliness is responsible for his loneliness. How does the lonely person actively go about making himself lonely? How does he go about preserving and enhancing his loneliness? He may know exactly how he does it. More frequently, he is unaware of his attitudes and behavior patterns which drive others away, or how he makes himself unapproachable and unavailable for nourishing interaction.

The descriptive patterns that follow illustrate some of the ways people create their loneliness. These games not only create loneliness; they also produce other toxic reactions to the person himself and to others.

SOMEBODY FILL ME UP

The lonely person often feels unable to initiate any effective solution to his emptiness and passively looks to the world to hand him what he needs. His helpless attitude places the burden on others. His cry is "Here I am! Somebody please love me! I need it desperately!" The nourishing person will back away from this kind of relating because of the insatiable demands being imposed. The lonely person rarely is aware of this toxic attitude and continues to experience his loneliness as a mystifying puzzle.

June could be described only as a self-adoring person who expected the world to do her bidding. She was a beautiful child and clearly her parents' favorite. She had four older brothers, and her arrival was the fulfillment of a dream for both her father ("I always wanted a little girl I could spoil rotten") and her mother ("Now I can share things with her I never had when I was growing up"). Her four brothers had been repeatedly admonished by both parents to "take care of little sister." She was voted the most popular girl in school, was chosen prom queen in her senior year, and had been considered by a talent scout for a movie contract. Her exceptional beauty only enhanced her expectation that the world would be happy to do her bidding. During her college years and later, men clamored to win her favor. Her husband too adored her and took constant delight in pleasing her with gifts, exotic vacations, and other surprises.

June had continuously postponed having children, offering a variety of excuses to her husband, who wanted a large family. Their marriage reached a crisis when, at thirty-three, she still wanted to postpone having a family. Her husband's patience was at an end, and he decided to leave, assuring her that he would come back when she was ready to have children. He never returned home, and she never asked him to. A year later he asked her for a divorce, informing her that he had met someone else. June was outraged, as were her parents, at his "lack of consideration."

Her parents, of course, were quick to assure her that she would find another husband who would really appreciate her. Various men did show a genuine interest in her. However, when they did not respond with the adoration and solicitude she had come to expect, she became indignant and would stop seeing them. She continued this dating pattern for several years, becoming aware of an increasing loneliness which the love and admiration of her family no longer alleviated. She was honestly baffled that men were not delighted to do her bidding for the sheer joy of winning her favor. She concluded, quite erroneously, that they were simply interested in her sexually and decided that she would "wait until the right one comes along."

She moved in with her parents shortly after her divorce. Gradually she stopped dating and became increasingly withdrawn and irritable, particularly toward her parents, whose continuing solicitude seemed to be increasingly frustrating to her. She honestly had no awareness of how she had alienated herself and created her lonely existence.

Often the lonely person proclaims to the world that he has "a lot to give" if only he could find the right person to appreciate him. Intimacy is an attitude and a way of being; it is not some kind of prize package one can hope to find or to work hard enough to deserve. The lonely person's attitude of withholding his love is often a facade with which he deceives himself. Actually, he is constantly evaluating others like a personnel manager screening people for a job. The "job" goes unfilled and the person remains lonely—*and* safe from his fear of intimacy and his dread of choosing the "wrong" person.

This pattern occurs in some unusually attractive women who have many relationships with men and yet remain unmarried, and in men who fear that all women are "just looking for security." In each instance, no one meets their expectations, so they continue to remain isolated (and safeguarded) from intimate relating.

HOLIER THAN THOU

This brand of self-induced loneliness is popular among the "psychologically sophisticated." The message they send to others is "If you have hang-ups, you're not for me," or "Get yourself straightened out first, and then we'll see." The implication of holier-than-thou people is "I have hang-ups too [thus demonstrating their liberal, enlightened attitude], but they are minor, especially in the light of my far greater assets. If you have any real hang-ups, you are automatically ineligible for an intimate relationship with me."

LOSER-ORIENTED PATTERNS

Picking "losers" means selecting people who cannot really satisfy what the person knows he wants in a relationship. Loneliness is often sustained by the person's continually selecting "losers" and investing his time and energy in them. For some men, the last woman they will approach is exactly the one they would most like to meet. Instead, they select those women who present less of a challenge. Attractive women sometimes complain that many interesting men seem afraid to approach them. Instead, such men choose to become involved with women they find less exciting and less interesting but who are also less threatening.

Single women who repeatedly involve themselves with married men insure themselves against long-lasting relationships and increase the likelihood of perpetual loneliness. They use a variety of rationalizations to justify beginning a relationship with a man who is obviously unavailable ("I'll keep it light." "Why not?" "I know just where I stand."). They avoid their anxiety and suffer the loneliness of a sporadic, unstable relationship. In all likelihood, despite the woman's best intentions, she becomes increasingly emotionally involved, while continuing to live on the fringes of the man's life. As time passes, she becomes emotionally unavailable to other men. They bore her; they are uninteresting; she keeps thinking of her lover. This may continue for years until eventually there is a breakup which is apt to be unusually devastating. The woman experiences the despair and loss of a love relationship without ever having the intimacy of a mutually sharing full relationship.

WHAT IF PEOPLE KNEW

Self-induced loneliness may be deliberately initiated by the person who is convinced that if others really knew him they would have nothing to do with him. He hides what he considers to be unacceptable in himself, although frequently he doesn't even know what this is. On this basis, he is convinced that he is unlovable and unacceptable. To the degree to which he remains too fearful to risk expressing himself, he remains fragmented and isolated from full intimacy with others.

Men in particular often consider their "weaknesses" to be so intolerable that they must be forever hidden. Particularly in the presence of others, but even in solitude, they totally reject their need to cry. They may consider any fear to be a fault that would disillusion others about their manliness. They believe that to express emotions, particularly anxieties, constitutes failure as a man and must be avoided at all costs. The effect, of course, is to create barriers even against the women they love, marry, and live with. Since such men never reveal their true responses, the degree of possible intimacy in any relationship is permanently limited.

Other forms of "unacceptable impulses" with which a person may isolate himself include fantasies that he is strange, perverted, or "crazy."

These fantasies maintain their power to destroy primarily by remaining hidden. The person is convinced that he would be labeled weird, perverted, or insane. He chooses to go through life fragmenting his self unnecessarily and sustaining his barrier against deeper intimacy.

Culturally unacceptable impulses include feelings and actions that in childhood were loaded with guilt and shame and therefore represent whole areas of the person that are unacceptable and must be hidden.

Stanley grew up in a home in which his parents were constantly fighting and arguing. While their fights never led to physical violence, his father repeatedly threatened physical attack and would at times pound his fists vehemently against a table or wall. His mother's characteristic response was "You might just as well hit me; you're killing me anyway." When these arguments were particularly intense, Stanley would become frightened to the point of panic. He was aware of vague feelings that, somehow, it was his fault that his parents argued so much. As far back as he could remember, he had become frightened when anyone got angry. On rare occasions, he would become irritable or upset about something. His mother's reaction of "You're turning out just like your father" terrorized him, and he would literally beg his mother's forgiveness.

By the time Stanley entered high school, he needed to act out a ritual with his mother in which he would insist that she tell him exactly three times that she had no anger toward him and that she loved him. When his mother balked at doing this or called it nonsense, he would become so anxious that she eventually went along with his obsessive need for absolution. His father would accuse his mother of ruining their son—"Look what you've done: he's afraid to open his mouth." This would frequently result in another fight, which only added to Stanley's already intolerable guilt feelings.

In his junior year in high school, the counselor recommended family therapy. This helped to alleviate the friction in the home, and Stanley seemed to settle down to a more stable adjustment. He became a quiet, introverted man with a very passive, withdrawn life style. He dated infrequently throughout his twenties and early

thirties. He related to people by passively complying with what they wanted, while continuing to suppress the growing pressure of his unexpressed anger. He never broke off a relationship (he was absolutely unwilling to be angry or to reject anyone), but became increasingly noncommunicative. When he wanted to end a relationship, he would become so malleable and compliant that the woman would eventually become exasperated and break off with him.

Stanley had a job with a large accounting firm, where he was an exemplary employee. As he grew older, he refused more and more social invitations. His increasing withdrawal reflected his overwhelming fear: "I would rather continue to suffer my longing for intimate involvement than risk anyone's getting angry with me, or take the chance that anyone might see my anger and resentments."

As a child, he had learned that his resentment toward his parents was totally unacceptable. Such impulses continued to dominate him in adult life, and he continued to see them as intolerable parts of himself which would cause him to be shunned by everyone—if people ever found out.

THE "BEING HURT" FANTASY

Loneliness can be self-induced by a belief that if one is rebuffed, the pain will be catastrophic. In response to this fear, many lonely people have insulated themselves emotionally by building psychic barriers to prevent anyone from getting close to them. Their fear of rejection is such that they greatly exaggerate the pain of being rejected. In essence, they are phobic about life and choose the protection of casual, superficial relationships. When they feel growing intimacy with another person, they invariably end the relationship. In the most obvious sense, they choose their loneliness.

THE STORM TROOPER

Some lonely people are puzzled by their lack of intimacy because they feel they have a genuine interest in others. They consider themselves extraverted, and indeed they are. Their "fascination" with others may take the form of intense, wide-eyed attention to the other person's every comment and a barrage of questions, which the victim is likely to experience as an invasion rather than an inviting gesture toward contact. Or the "blitzkrieg" comes in the form of a heated argument which the storm trooper insists is only a "stimulating discussion." Sometimes, after listening closely to show how interested he is, he decides to "share himself" and then proceeds to monopolize the conversation, oblivious to the boredom of his listener. He is unable to perceive others as individuals, much less appreciate them as people. Instead, his preoccupation is with doing his own thing, and he leaves little or no room for the needs of other people for self-expression.

PSYCHIC ANESTHESIA

The use of alcohol and drugs is frequently an effective way of inducing psychic isolation. Many people drink or use tranquilizers and other drugs to be more open and outgoing, and superficially this goal is accomplished; conversation flows more easily, tension is reduced, and the person may be more able to enjoy himself. However, anesthetizing one's inhibitions does not lessen the underlying withdrawal pattern. Rather, the opposite occurs, since avoidance of anxiety and fear increases their threatening quality. In addition, the person's potential for learning to cope more effectively with his fears is also anesthetized. The effect is usually a psychological dependency on alcohol or drugs in social settings. Over a period of time, the person's openness without his artificial "relating aids" diminishes while his withdrawal tendencies increase.

It is paradoxical that the more successful a person is in concealing his anxiety, the more empty he is apt to feel inside. Over a period of years people become very skillful at concealing characteristics that they feel are unacceptable. Yet inwardly they are tormented with feelings of inadequacy and self-contempt. Because their inner pain is so intense, it is difficult for them to believe that it does not show. Conversely, the more aware they become of how effectively they have fooled others, the more they come to be-

lieve that they would be rejected were they to drop their pretenses.

THE JOKER

The joker must be the life of the party at all times. He must be clever, amusing, and witty whenever others are present. He is also a subtle saboteur. Serious or intimate conversations sometimes do occur, but they are apt to be short-lived. At the point at which the other person may feel some real closeness, he is undercut by the joker's ubiquitous humor, which wipes out the previous intimacy. Inappropriate joking and laughter can be extremely poisonous to the growing depth of a relationship. The joker's acquaintances—and that's the extent of his relationships—learn never to take him seriously, and they count on him for only one thing: a lot of laughs. Frequently, the joker himself is the victim of deep depression and loneliness—about which he will also try to joke.

SEXUALITY AS AN AVOIDANCE OF INTIMACY

The acceptance of sex education and the availability of material on sex techniques is a two-edged sword. Knowledge about sex can enhance the intimacy between two people. It can also become an end in itself that short-circuits the growth of deeper feelings, and this is how the lonely person often uses his own sexuality. A man may use sex largely to display his talents and impress his partner. It is not infrequent that this is his primary gratification in the sex act. In a nourishing relationship, sex is an expression of emotional union and intimate sharing. For the "sex technician," sex is essentially manipulation, an end in itself, and rarely evolves into deeper feelings of love. This is the pattern of many young adults, heterosexual or homosexual, who find themselves confronted with increasing loneliness and feelings of emptiness despite constant sexual activity.

Sexual promiscuity is a not-so-subtle way of avoiding intimate relationships. "One-nighters" of both sexes are willing to engage in physical intimacy as long as they feel no threat of becoming emotionally involved. Promiscuous people are usually lonely. While sometimes promiscuity is an expression of desperate longing for contact, it nevertheless tends to prevent one from finding longer-lasting relationships.

WELL, WHY NOT?

Lonely people often refuse to be discriminating even when they are aware that a particular relationship is poisonous to them. A woman may date a man she doesn't particularly enjoy only because he takes her out. She refuses to consider that this makes her less available for a more meaningful relationship while she is settling for minor gratifications. A man may date a woman purely for sex and feel he is outmaneuvering her by getting her into bed without making any commitment himself. Such patterns of manipulation lead to counter manipulations and only create the emptiness and frustration of pseudo-intimacy. Any pattern in which a person settles solely for secondary gratifications is a detour away from nourishment and toward loneliness.

ALONENESS PHOBIA

For some lonely people there is no such thing as pleasurable solitude. The need of such a person to avoid being alone is often compulsive. He may have schedules of activities to fill any void, even a single evening, and a priority list of people he can call should some free time occur. He may even keep track of exactly how many names he has and fanatically maintain his list at a reassuring number. What is important to him is the quantity of contacts, rather than caring for those people or appreciating their individuality or uniqueness. He fills his time but perpetuates his loneliness, since he is interested in others as a means to an end. Because he is so preoccupied with escaping loneliness, he does not have time to form real relationships.

His list of casual friends usually consists of others who are also lonely and readily available. They too have developed toxic ways of relating and have little nourishment to give. Their mutual emptiness is often revealed in their expectant expressions when a new member enters their group; perhaps he can provide some healthy excitement. Their disappointments are contin-

ual and inevitable, yet they persist in sustaining their "contacts" and schedules in order to avoid being alone.

HOW COULD YOU DO THIS TO ME?

Some chronically lonely people insist that they are willing to go "more than halfway" with others. At the same time, they complain that somehow they have been undeservedly abused and manipulated. They project their self-induced loneliness onto the rest of the world. They insist that their expectations are reasonable—even meager.

For example, the domineering mother who cries to her child that "All I want is for you to be happy!" really means "All I want is to make the major decisions in your life." When, in adulthood, the child finally takes his stand and refuses to be poisoned further, the bewildered mother cannot believe "that my own child would desert me after all I've done for him."

WALLS OF AVOIDANCE

An experienced waiter can walk the length of a restaurant without catching the eye of a single customer. Similarly, the lonely person feeds his loneliness by avoiding contact. His eyes are usually looking either down or away, and he seldom looks at anyone for more than an instant—least of all if the other person should look back. He rarely smiles and often has a stony expression that makes him difficult to approach. In this way he may have developed such an effective mask of self-containment that in actuality his life is largely limited to his inner world.

Making contact with such a person requires unusual persistence and tenacity. It is possible that an aware person can develop a relationship with a person who seems aloof. However, those who hide themselves increase the odds against getting what they want in this world. Instead, they tend to ensure that they will remain lonely.

BEING PRESENT IN BODY ONLY

Talking to a person who is uninterested in contact is like talking to a well-trained yes-man. His attention floats everywhere as he shows only sporadic interest in anyone while inwardly daydreaming, fantasizing, or thinking about other things. His responses are polite, but indicate his lack of attention. Since he's not really there, no nourishment emanates from him, nor is he available to receive any. In relating, he leaves the other person hanging in a frustrated, unfinished situation. Typically, the other person senses that he is not fully interested. Nourishing people will abandon this fruitless process in short order and leave the person to himself. Those who usually seem detached and uninterested in other people bring that loneliness on themselves by their constant avoidance. Being blinded and out of contact, they fail to "see" others who are available and interested.

BUSYWORK

This popular brand of self-induced loneliness is subtle, since the person's overt behavior appears to be the opposite of a withdrawing, isolating pattern.

Jeffrey remembered his childhood as having been lonely. He grew up in an exclusive suburb in the hills overlooking a large metropolitan area. He rarely saw other children in his neighborhood, since the winding streets were dangerous for play, and there were no sidewalks. The remoteness of his home made it even more difficult to find playmates his own age. Even the maid had to be picked up by car from the nearest bus line, three miles away. His brother was six years older and had always been totally uninterested in Jeffrey. He considered his sister, who was only two years younger, a nuisance or, at best, someone to tease. He was starved for human contact. "Both my parents always seemed to be away or rushing around doing one thing or another. I felt that when they did pay attention to me, it was mainly because they didn't want to hurt my feelings. I knew they loved me, but I didn't feel they understood what I needed."

Jeffrey graduated from medical school with top honors and rapidly gained a reputation as an outstanding cardiovascular surgeon. In addition to his busy practice, he participated in medical-association activities and made frequent lecture tours. He often flew to various parts of the country when called in as consultant by his medical colleagues. For years he had instructed his wife to keep a suitcase packed and ready at all times for such emergency trips.

Jeffrey was perplexed by recurring periods of depression which seemed to increase over the years. "This is absolutely absurd. I know this is some functional [psychological] disorder. I'm increasingly irritated with these moods of mine, which really distract from my work" was his statement to the therapist in his initial consultation. Jeffrey's wife was also very active and seemed to flourish on social activities and organizational work. She too suffered from these periodic depressions. Her solution was constant use of tranquilizers. Obviously, the family life was remarkably similar to that in which Jeffrey grew up. They too lived in a remote suburb, with their two daughters.

Jeffrey's first severe depression occurred when his second daughter left home for college. "They grew up so fast! I never really got to know them!" His self-prescribed solution for his depression was more activity, and he accepted a faculty position at a local medical school in addition to his other activities. His colleagues sometimes kidded him about being "the busiest doctor in town" and jokingly warned him that he might not be immune to cardiovascular disease himself. His response was always "I flourish on work. I don't know what I would do without it."

He was totally unaware of exactly how true his statement was. His day-to-day activities were dictated by his appointment book. When he and his wife were alone, they found they had long since forgotten how to simply enjoy each other and share any intimate relating. Their sex life was perfunctory and their dialogues superficial and focused on events and happenings. Each night his wife took her sleeping pills and went to bed. It was then that Jeffrey felt the gnawing feeling in his stomach most intensely. (He had no idea that it was loneliness gnawing at him.) His life was meaningful primarily because of his professional activities, through which he could escape his loneliness.

When he suffered a mild coronary, his whole life style crumbled. He knew he could survive and live a normal life, but only if he were willing to cut his strenuous schedule drastically. This he did—only to find that his leisure time now cre-

ated a new stress. He didn't know what to do with himself and began to show signs of irritability, restlessness, and emotional strain. He developed what was diagnosed as a "severe anxiety neurosis with strong depressive features."

Reluctantly, Jeffrey began intensive psychotherapy. He initially flew into a rage when the therapist suggested that he was essentially a very lonely man. His rage melted into a flood of tears (the first time he had cried since he was a small boy). He then verbalized the fleeting awareness that he had had, over the years, of feeling lonely and frightened. He suddenly realized that he had buried these feelings in a frenzy of activities.

THE EMBARRASSMENT OF LONELINESS

For some people, the most painful part of their loneliness is the shame of other people's knowing about it. Their main effort, then, is not to discover ways of overcoming the real problem, but to create a facade of "happiness and belongingness" that will successfully hide the truth from others. Such people may radiate an air of indifference, snobbishness, or aloofness as if to emphasize that they don't need anyone. As they learn to play this deceptive game more skillfully, their mask tends to guarantee their isolation. They succeed only in avoiding the embarrassment of being "caught" in their loneliness, which, they believe, would be far worse than the loneliness itself.

In a joint consultation, the following dialogue took place between LaVerne, a thirty-six-year-old divorcée with no children, and Harry, who was forty-two, had been divorced for three years, and had two children. They had gone together for more than a year, and Harry wanted to marry her. She had consistently rejected marriage, at the same time acknowledging that she cared for him. The appointment with the therapist was made by Harry, who was increasingly angry at LaVerne's refusal to make a commitment. His growing irritation was beginning to disrupt their relationship.

Harry: I just don't understand why you don't want to get married.

LaVerne: That's an old-fashioned sentimental trip. Who needs it!

Harry: I thought you loved me. You certainly said it enough times when we were close or making love.

LaVerne: That's a dirty trick. You catch me when I'm off guard and then throw it back in my face that I said I loved you.

H: Well, if you don't love me, I'd like you to tell me.

L: (Her face reddening in obvious embarrassment) Well, uh—uh—not in front of the doctor . . . Harry, I care for you—you know that . . .

H: This is how you frustrate me. Just tell me whether you love me or not. If you don't, I'll go away. I won't bother you any more.

L: You're crowding me. I'm happy the way things are. I don't want to get trapped into marriage.

H: Seeing you a couple of times a week and knowing you're dating other men is too hard for me. I miss you and feel lonely even when I try to date other women. It's you I want to be with. Don't you ever feel lonely?

L: (Now really blushing, one foot wiggling up and down) Jesus, Harry, you ask such dumb questions. What's this lonely business? (Sounding contemptuous) Me, lonely . . . that's silly. I've got people calling me all the time. (Obviously angry) How could you even ask such a dumb question?

H: You see what I'm up against, Doctor. We've had this argument many times. Yet when I start to walk out, she stops me and tells me not to go—that she needs me.

L: Dammit, Harry, you're embarrassing me.

H: Well, it's true, isn't it?

L: (Now very frustrated) You really embarrass me. What do you want me to do, crawl to you?

H: (Quite surprised) Now, that's really weird. I asked you if you love me and you say I'm asking you to crawl to me. I guess there's no hope for us. I guess you are happy with all your friends. You don't need me. I'm the one who needs a more intimate relationship.

L: Sometimes I think you're a sentimental fool, Harry. You're too old-fashioned.

Finally, several weeks later, Harry gave up and walked out in the middle of the hour. LaVerne, at last, burst into tears and, as if confessing something she felt deeply ashamed of, admitted her intense loneliness and her equally intense fear of anyone's knowing of it.

THE EXPERT RELATER

A new breed of loneliness has arisen as a manifestation of the "age of psychology." Its victims make a fetish of their "psychological enlightenment" and act as if they were the in-group (one-upmanship) simply because they have undergone analysis and therapy. They claim to have learned to "let it all hang out" and in other ways play games of false openness, self-reliance, and even intimacy. Their "warmth" is readily demonstrated by their willingness to hug, kiss, and "relate" without fanfare or hesitancy. They may consider participation in a nude group as final evidence of their maturity.

Any endeavor, however great its nourishing potential, can be distorted into a toxic experience by those who are interested primarily in becoming more successful manipulators. In their hands, the potential for human growth through the psychotherapeutic arts becomes simply another tool of poisonous manipulation—of themselves or others. Growth and maturity are the legitimate goal of a genuine therapeutic experience. Instead, some people only learn more gimmicks which look like intimate relating but turn out to be games. As a result, the loneliness remains as intense as ever and is only briefly relieved by these experiences. Their daily lives remain empty, reflecting an absence of real integration and growth from their therapeutic experiences.

WHY NOT ASK?

Self-initiating behavior can create loneliness when carried to extremes so that it becomes a manifestation of greediness or a spoiled-child pattern. Some people insist that they are justified in asking others for anything they want. Often, people who have been in psychotherapy justify this attitude under the guise of "self-expression." This attitude reflects a lack of sensitivity about the poisonous effect it may have on others. An intimate relationship between two people begins to develop from their initial contact and is gradually shaped by their continuing pattern of relating. Regardless of how present-oriented a person may be, he is influenced by his past experiences in the relationship. The more a nourishing person experiences the other as always asking for something, the more apt he is to withdraw or develop a "no" response as a prevailing counterattitude. The why-not-ask person is responsible for his greediness and its toxic effect on the relationship.

The caring person is aware of other people's limitations and avoids asking the impossible. Without such awareness, a partner in a meaningful relationship may bring about its destruction by greedily ignoring the limits of the other.

June and Jim met, fell in love, and decided to live together. June was more extraverted and full of energy. Jim was a graduate student who enjoyed solitude and preferred a few close friends. His parents were both dead and had left him with sufficient income for both of them to live on. He considered their living together a "trial marriage" and hoped it was the beginning of a lasting intimate relationship. June's attitude was essentially "Why not!" They moved into an apartment building complete with swimming pool and social-activities center.

Jim's studies were a full-time job, which he took quite seriously. June enjoyed dabbling in all kinds of activities and experiences. She was bright, she had a college degree, and her interests included pottery making, painting, and writing poetry. She also enjoyed sports, all kinds of outdoor activities, and travel. She had no hesitation in approaching strangers and quickly made friends wherever she went. She seemed to enjoy picking a person's brain for knowledge and information. Her barrage of questions was limited only by the willingness of the other to answer. She never seemed to have enough. For her, people were like books: she would open them with curiosity, possibly find them of interest, finish with them, and go on to the next one. At first, Jim enjoyed the accounts of her daily experiences and admired her ability to relate to peo-

ple. She was quite free in asking him for money, showing him travel brochures, and talking about all the things they could do together.

These activities were exciting to Jim also, but June's continual requests began to burden him. She would usually ask for something with the phrase "Would it be possible for you to . . ." Since almost anything June asked for was possible, Jim would usually find himself nodding his head in agreement, though often without any real enthusiasm.

About nine months after they had moved in together, a crisis developed. June, because of her frenzy of activities, was coming home later and later. Gradually, Jim began preparing more meals for himself. At times he would prepare something for the two of them and wait until she arrived. June seemed to appreciate this. One day June had another one of her "bright ideas." "Jim," she said, "since I'm so busy with all my activities that keep me away from the house and you're usually here studying, how would you feel about preparing all the meals?—so that you'll know just what you're going to have to eat, and it will be ready when you like it." Jim's outburst surprised both of them. "Goddammit, what are you contributing to this relationship? All I hear is 'Gimme, gimme, this is trippy and that's trippy.' I'm working for my degree and supporting you while you flit around doing what you damn please. And now you want me to cook for you."

June concluded that he was simply in a bad mood, shrugged her shoulders, and left for the evening. However, Jim had decided that henceforth when June approached him, he would deliberately focus on saying "no" even before he heard her request. At first she would walk away with an "Okay," as if he were in another grouchy mood and would soon get over it. When Jim, however, continued his stand against June's constant demands, she responded by going out with other men. She had told Jim of her intention, and he had no objection. For him, their relationship was already at an end. He had been drained by her "honest requests," and he asked her to move out. June was surprised and deeply hurt. Telling Jim that she was thinking of dating other men was simply one of her maneuvers which she thought would bring back his accept-

ing, pliant attitude toward her. She still loved him deeply, but failed to understand that her asking had drained him and had become such a burden that it had suffocated his love.

After June moved out, she felt a deep longing and loneliness for Jim. Still perplexed about what had happened, she decided that she had been fooled and readily told everyone that Jim was really a bastard who "just got tired of me and kicked me out."

While intimate human relationships are an essential source of nourishment, relating itself can be a way of generating loneliness when it has a poisonous effect on the self-nourishing capabilities within the person or on his partner.

CONCLUSION

The prime source of loneliness is within the person. He will be lonely to the degree to which he is fragmented and alienated from himself. He cannot substitute relations with other people for his own fragmented self, and this is exactly what the lonely person is most apt to spend his life trying to do. No matter how rich and gratifying a relationship may be, when a person seeks from others that which he needs to find within himself, he only creates a lonely, alienated existence. It is absurd to ask one person to take responsibility for another's loneliness, no matter how caring and loving that person might be. Further, this is the kind of manipulation that can ultimately destroy any relationship, however nourishing. When the responsibility for seeking one's own nourishment *and being* nourishing is neglected by one or both people, the deadly games of manipulation inevitably follow.

As long as a person insists on feeling victimized, he creates a stalemate for himself from which no change is possible. When he is willing to accept responsibility for what he does to himself, he opens himself to experimentation, risk-taking, and discovering more gratifying ways of being. Self-induced poisoning processes are based on fears and lack of confidence in one's own ability to do better. There is no guarantee of a painless antidote for loneliness. A person needs to discover how to activate his own capabilities.

When a person's behavior becomes authentic and his actions are in good faith, he knows others are responding to him. His lifelong anxiety about being "found out" and his fears of rejection lessen as he gives up his false fronts. He becomes a more nourishing person.

A genuinely nourishing person will not be lonely.

To Apply This Reading to Yourself

1. Would you agree that you are primarily responsible for any loneliness that you have had—that your loneliness is largely self-induced? Why or why not?
2. Describe your use of a "loneliness-inducing" game.
3. Greenwald writes about people and relationships that are "toxic." Describe a toxic relationship you have had or have observed.
4. Greenwald writes about people and relationships that are "nourishing." Describe a nourishing relationship you have had or have observed.
5. How toxic or nourishing are you and your current relationships? Write a brief paper giving your answer to this question.

Active Solitude

Carin Rubenstein and Phillip Shaver

For some people, being alone automatically implies loneliness; for them, the word *solitude* evokes images of isolation, panic, fear, inability to concentrate, numbness, or boredom. For others—poets and artists, for example—solitude carries almost the opposite meaning: bliss, relaxation, personal integration, a feeling of warm connectedness with the world and other people, creativity, and reflection. What are the differences between these people—or between times in the life of a particular person when one rather than another reaction predominates?

The difference is partly one of perspective. Sometimes, because of past or recent experiences, we conceive of aloneness as being cut off, bereft, alienated from others, the way a child feels after being sent to his or her room for punishment. (As the poet Coleridge put it in "The Rime of the Ancient Mariner": "Alone, alone, all, all alone, / Alone on a wide wide sea! / And never a saint took pity on / My soul in agony.") In this state of mind, we feel a keen sense of loss and powerlessness—loss of other people's approval and company, and powerlessness to do anything about it. The loss calls attention to deficiencies in ourselves; we are "bad," unworthy of love, deserving of rejection, vulnerable and helpless. In this state, self-esteem is diminished; we become frightened and defensive. We can't relax or be creative.

In contrast, the orientation we call active solitude emphasizes the positive side of being alone. In solitude, you are together with yourself, physically but not psychologically cut off from other people; free to explore thoughts and feelings without regard for anyone else's immediate reactions. You can hear your own mental voice and react to your own subtle desires and moods. Oddly enough, the result is often a deeper affection for other people. One of our respondents in Billings, Montana, wrote us, for example, that she spends ten days in total solitude each year—causing rumors among her neighbors that her marriage is on the rocks. Leaving husband, children, dog, and three canaries back home, she retreats to a mountain cabin by herself—to think, read, and write. "I have a ball—no obligations and no distractions. No radio, no TV, no screaming kids or pesky husband. For ten days I have just me. I love being away from it all for those days. Funny thing is though, I appreciate them a whole lot more when I get back—a year's worth of appreciation builds up in just ten days."

One of the people we interviewed told us: "Odd as it sounds, I'm more able to be by myself when I feel most in tune with my lover. It's easier to concentrate on work, to be creative. I know when we're apart that we'll soon be together, that she's there if I need her. And we're more valuable to ourselves and get along better when we've spent time alone."

Although the words "alone" and "lonely" come from the same middle English root—meaning "all one" (or only one)—they are not psychological synonyms. Many people—for example, those trapped in unhappy marriages or forced to live with relatives who "don't understand"—are much lonelier living with others than are the hundreds of thousands who live alone but have close ties with friends and family. It's clearly possible to be lonely without being alone and alone without being lonely.

Many people find that the first few minutes or hours of solitude are unsettling. While working individually on this book, for example, having set aside time for reflection and writing, we often spent the first half hour (at least) with unnecessary phone calls, irrelevant reading, and distracting, time-wasting trips to the bathroom or refrigerator. The urge to avoid self-confrontation, to escape the feeling of aloneness that solitary thought requires, is powerful indeed. In the first few moments of solitude, many people make a hasty decision to go shopping or turn on the television set, and they immediately lose the opportunity for creativity and self-renewal. If this pattern becomes habitual, their sense of identity and personal strength is eroded and they become chronically afraid of solitude.

The writings of religious hermits throughout history reveal that they too suffered an initial period of doubt, agitation, and panic when they first got out into the wilderness by themselves. Most of them, however, like most of us in our successful attempts at creative solitude, waited out this temporary anxiety and found themselves moved and enriched by the rewards of solitude.

In extreme forms, solitude has often been used in *rites de passage* to transform boys into men. In many primitive societies, pubertal boys were sent off into the forest, jungle, or plains, and ordered to remain alone for periods ranging from overnight to several months. The boys were thought to die a symbolic death and become transformed: when they returned to the world of the living as men, their boyhood ignorance and dependence were gone forever. If this sounds barbaric, consider that Outward Bound, a popular American recreation group for men and women of all ages, requires its participants to take solo wilderness trips; the experience of solitary survival is assumed to foster independence and self-sufficiency.

Some researchers have tested the idea that solitude can be strengthening. During the sixties and seventies, John Lilly experimented with "restricted environmental stimulation" by placing people in immersion tanks full of warm salt water, asking them to remain inside for hours, even days, at a time. Psychologist Peter Suedfeld claimed more recently that REST, or *Restricted Environmental Stimulation Therapy*, calms mental patients, helps overweight people lose weight, smokers quit smoking, alcoholics reduce their drinking, and stutterers speak more clearly. REST simply places patients in dark, soundproofed rooms for about eight hours without radios, books, or other diversions.

Strangely enough, meditation and reflection—although usually solitary activities—are almost the opposite of what we normally think of as self-consciousness or self-preoccupation. When properly pursued, they aren't at all narcissistic. When we are self-conscious in the usual sense (anxious or embarrassed), the self that occupies our attention is, meditation experts say, a figment of our social imagination; it is the self of the adolescent conformist wondering nervously if he is accepted by the group. Surprisingly, when we are alone and allow ourselves to pass through the initial period of agitated discomfort, this social pseudoself eventually evaporates, revealing a more relaxed and substantial self underneath.

This genuine self needs no outside approval and is not simply a social creation. People who make contact with this deeper self find that their subsequent social relations are less superficial, less greedy, less tense. They have less need to defend their everyday social selves, their social masks.

Our first piece of advice, then: *When you are alone, give solitude a chance. Don't run away at the first sign of anxiety, and don't imagine yourself abandoned, cut off, or rejected.* Think of yourself as *with yourself*, not *without* someone else. Allow yourself to relax, listen to music that suits your feelings, work on something that you've been neglecting, write to a friend or for yourself in a journal, or just lie back and be at peace. If you are religious, your solitude may take the form of conversations with God or meditation on religious ideas. Whatever the content of your solitude, if you allow the first burst of anxiety to fade, you will open a door to many rewarding hours: of quiet prayer or contemplation; full enjoyment of music, sketching, or painting; total involvement in a novel or book of poetry; recording your own thoughts, feelings, songs, or poems. This solitude is a far cry from loneliness.

If you think about this, you can begin to see why active solitude and intimacy are related. In solitude, we experience our most genuine needs, perceptions, and feelings. We listen to our deepest selves. Intimacy involves the disclosure of this deeper self to trusted friends or lovers, and really listening, in turn, to their needs, thoughts, and feelings. In other words, in solitude we are intimate with ourselves in a way that enhances our intimacy with other people.

If you find that you can't be comfortable with yourself, you are probably a dissatisfying friend and lover as well. Perhaps you fear there is really nothing very interesting about you; your value is assured only when you are with and approved by someone else. This idea was taken to a supernatural extreme by Henry James, in a story called "The Private Life." Lord Mellifont completely vanishes when he is left alone. "He's there from the moment he knows someone else is." Mellifont is "so essentially, so conspicuously and uniformly the public character" that he is simply "all public" and has "no corresponding private life." Discovering this horrible fact, the narrator of the story feels great sympathy for Mellifont. "I had secretly pitied him for the perfection of his performance, had wondered what blank face such a mask had to cover, what was left to him for the immitigable hours in which a man sits down with himself, or, more serious still, with that intenser self his lawful wife."

We know from our research that adults who have suffered painful losses or rejections in the past are more likely to feel this way and to panic when they are alone; we also know that such people tend to have self-esteem problems. But as long as they cling desperately to others rather than confronting and overcoming their fears and feelings of inadequacy, they are unlikely to become confident and independent. For these people, spending time alone is an essential part of overcoming loneliness.

We don't want to oversell solitude. In fact, for some people solitude replaces normal social life, causing them to become self-contained, fussy, and rigid. Psychiatrist George Vaillant described such a man, in his late forties at the time they talked: "During college he had dealt with his very real fear of people by being a solitary drinker. He enjoyed listening to the radio by himself and found math and philosophy his most interesting courses. Although afraid to go out with girls, he was very particular about his appearance. . . . Thirty years later, [he] was less interested in clothes, but had become terribly preoccupied with keeping fit. He admitted that in his life 'things had taken the place of people' and that he loved to retreat into the 'peace and quiet of a weekend alone.' Approaching old age with no family of his own, he daydreamed of

leaving his rare book collection to a favorite young cousin; but he had made only a small effort to get to know this cousin personally." Vaillant went on: "Not only had he never married, but he never admitted to being in love. Unduly shy with women in adolescence, at forty-seven [he] was still put off by 'eager women' and still found 'sex distasteful and frightening.' He had gone through life without close friends of any kind, male or female, and . . . still found it difficult to say good-bye to his mother."

How can you tell if solitude is leading you toward or away from other people? In general, if you find yourself soothed and strengthened by solitude, *more aware of your love for other people*, and less frightened or angry in your dealings with them, then solitude is a healthy part of your social balance. If you find, on the other hand, that you use solitude as a chronic escape from other people, and if people generally seem to you to be scary, selfish, cruel, or too messy, then you are retreating into a shell of solitude. We say this not because we wish to impose some superficial standard of sociability on everyone, but because studies like Vaillant's indicate that long-term defensive withdrawal from other people leads to unhappiness, alcohol and [other] drug abuse, underachievement, and vulnerability to illness.

Practice active solitude, then, *but not to the detriment of intimacy, friendship, or community*. Let active solitude be the ground from which your feelings of intimacy and community grow.

To Apply This Reading To Yourself

1. *Discuss the use you have made of solitude and its effects on you.*
2. *Discuss the use you have made of meditation and its effects on you.*
3. *Discuss any use you have made of solitude as an unhealthy escape or defensive withdrawal.*
4. *Rubenstein and Shaver note their own maneuvers in delaying entrance to a period of solitude or solitary effort. Discuss your own maneuvers in this regard.*
5. *Rubenstein and Shaver note we are more likely to resist being alone if we have suffered painful losses or rejections, but alone time is essential to overcoming the resulting loneliness. Discuss your own loneliness after a painful loss or rejection, and indicate how you dealt with it.*

Assertiveness

*Ready now? Stand up! Speak out! Talk back! You'll
like yourself better for it.*
— Robert E. Alberti and Michael L. Emmons

*If I am not for myself, who will be for me? But if I am
for myself only, who am I?*
— The Talmud

What is *assertiveness?* *Assertiveness* (or *assertion*) refers to the expression of one's own rights without infringing on the rights of others. When we are assertive, we stand up for ourselves and express our thoughts and feelings directly, honestly, and appropriately. We show respect for ourselves, but at the same time we demonstrate respect for those with whom we are involved.

By contrast, *nonassertiveness* (or *nonassertion*) refers to the failure to express one's rights. When we are nonassertive, we hold back and fail to present our thoughts and feelings. Or we express ourselves in such half-hearted, roundabout, or self-effacing ways that we can be misperceived or disregarded. In being nonassertive, we do not show respect for ourselves, and although we sometimes rationalize that we hold ourselves back for altruistic reasons, there may be an implicit disrespect for others and for their ability to stick up for themselves and deal with their own problems and disappointments.

Aggression is frequently confused with assertive behavior but is very different in its manifestations and effects. *Aggression*, broadly defined, is hurtful behavior; it can be used to express one's rights but at the expense of another person. When we are aggressive, we lash out verbally or physically, directly or indirectly, in the attempt to belittle or to overpower others or to put them down. When we use aggression, we do not show respect for others, and we may show a simultaneous lack of respect for our own capacities, in that we have found it necessary to resort to such tactics.

Consider, for example, this situation. You are attending a lecture with a number of other people who fill the room. The lecturer speaks so softly that you and those around you can barely hear. What would you do? An assertive way of dealing with the situation would be to raise your hand, tell the lecturer that you are having difficulty hearing, and ask her or him to please speak a little louder. A nonassertive way would be to do nothing or to try to find a place closer to the speaker. An aggressive response might be to yell out, "Louder! We can't hear you!" Or, in aggressive retaliation, you might abandon listening and hold your own loud conversation or upbraid the lecturer for a lack of sensitivity to the audience.

We can be assertive in nonverbal as well as in verbal ways. It's not just what we say, but also how we say it. Vocal tone, inflection, and volume are all important factors. So are facial expression, eye contact, gestures, and body posture, and in a particular situation we may be able to express and assert ourselves eloquently without saying a word.

In being assertive, our general behavior lends support and emphasis to what we are saying. Our body postures and gestures typically convey strength, eye contact is firm, and speech is fluent, expressive, and clear.

In being nonassertive, our general behavior frequently suggests weakness, uncertainty, and anxiety. We may not look directly at other persons; perhaps we shift back and forth from foot to foot or move nervously around. Speech may be hesitant, too soft, or muffled, and we may laugh nervously.

In being aggressive, verbal and nonverbal behavior may combine to threaten, dominate, or put someone down. Perhaps we move in very close, point a finger, or raise a fist. Or we attempt to stare or talk other persons down. Our voices may be loud, biting, sarcastic, or condescending.

How assertive are we? A number of recent observers and experimenters have concluded that many of us are not as assertive as we should be. As an illustration, imagine yourself in this situation: You have just completed a call in a public phone booth when someone approaches and says that he has just left his ring there. "Did you find it?" he asks. You haven't seen the ring and say so. "Are you sure?" he continues. "Sometimes people pick things up without thinking about it. Would you empty your pockets?" In a situation like this, how would you respond?

When this procedure was actually carried out as an experiment on 20 unsuspecting subjects, 16 of them (80 percent) emptied their pockets. One cannot infer too much from this modest investigation except that its results were consistent with those of a number of other investigations conducted by psychologist Thomas Moriarty and his students. Moriarty discovered, to cite some further findings, that college students at work on a difficult test generally were reluctant to ask another student to refrain from playing loud and heavy rock music, and other students who were observed in the university library or in a local cinema were hesitant to hush up noisy conversationalists.

Our many daily affronts and insults have been called "little murders," and Moriarty noted that subjects in his experiments behaved like "good victims." Moriarty writes, "I believe that many of us have accepted the idea that few things are worth getting into a hassle about, especially with strangers. And I believe that this is particularly true of younger people." Many of us apparently maintain a passive no-hassle attitude even when very basic rights are infringed upon or openly violated.

Is assertiveness important? People who complete assertiveness training generally report some personal gains. For one thing, skill in assertion improves our relationships with ourselves. Typically, we gain respect for ourselves, and we have more confidence in and control over our behavior. We are better able to express ourselves, pursue our goals, and meet our needs.

A second area of gain comes in our relationships with others. Asserting ourselves and sharing our thoughts and feelings seem vital to true intimacy. Our assertions and disclosures can encourage others to respond similarly and to open themselves to us. By contrast, non-assertion can lead others to disrespect us or look upon us with pity or disgust, while aggression can disrupt a relationship and encourage others to retaliate or withdraw.

This does not mean, of course, that all assertiveness leads to improved relationships, especially when it disrupts what another feels is a desirable status quo. However, when relationships are disrupted, they sometimes can be reconstructed in a way that allows all parties to grow. An assertive person can be a fuller person and can lead a richer life, and those with whom he or she interacts can similarly benefit.

Assertiveness, as the above discussion implies, includes both "standing up" and "reaching out" behaviors. The former is concerned with the maintenance of rights and the latter with the expression of regard and caring. More has been written about the former, but both are necessary if we are to affirm ourselves and also to help others find affirmation.

In recent years, an increasing amount of attention has been given to the topic of assertiveness by scientists, feminists, and workers in the field of personal growth. There have been many articles and books on this subject, and training workshops are offered in many parts of the country. We appear to be entering a more assertive age.

COOL DOWN!

Is it better to express or to suppress anger? As Carol Tavris indicates in the first reading, no answer is right for every situation. Suppressing anger can be a poor tactic if this perpetuates a stressful situation. Expressing anger is counterproductive if it makes a stressful situation worse. Says Tavris, "If you want your anger to dissipate and the association in question to remain congenial, keep quiet. But if you want to *stay* angry, if you want to use your anger, keep talking." As a rule, she suggests that we cool down and let life's small indignities pass but that we stand and fight against the larger ones. She adds, "And, most important, learn the difference."

STAND UP!

A case for standing up and fighting back *respectfully* is made by Arthur Lange and Patricia Jakubowski in the second selection as they examine assertive, nonassertive, and aggressive behavior. Assertion involves respect for both one's own rights and those of others, while nonassertion violates the former, and aggression violates the latter. Lange and Jakubowski review some of the reasons why people act in each of these three ways and some of the consequences of those actions. A chief reason for behaving assertively is that by doing so, we increase our own "sense of self-respect and personal control."

REACH OUT!

Expressing a positive, caring feeling is as much an assertive act as standing up for a personal right but, as Robert Alberti and Michael Emmons note in the last reading, "reaching out" may be more difficult for some than "standing up." Our culture does not encourage great freedom in positive expression, and, for our part, we may see it as an unnecessary or even hazardous business. Alberti and Emmons feel that the risk is well worth taking. They invite us to take the initiative in saying hello, offering compliments, and showing we care.

To Explore Your Own Assertiveness

1. *Identifying human rights.* On more than one occasion, you've probably said something like, "I believe that I had a perfect right to do what I did." And you also may have had occasion to protest that someone had no right to treat you in a particular way. What *are* your human rights? Think through and list on a sheet of paper all the rights you believe are yours as a human being. If you have trouble putting these rights into words, you might begin by recalling times when you felt badly treated; these may have been times when your rights were violated. And you might also recall those times when your treatment of another person left something to be desired. When your list is complete, you might compare it with the lists of others or form small groups to discuss and arrive at a common list.

2. *Identifying role rights.* Think through and list on a sheet of paper the rights that belong to all persons who occupy a particular role. You might, for example, consider the rights of one of the following: children, parents, lovers, spouses, students, instructors, employees, or employers. When your list is complete, check to see whether you have included any rights that might belong to all groups or all human beings. Or you may pair or form small groups

with others who have worked on different sets of rights to see how many rights appear on more than one list and seem to transcend roles.

3. *Differentiating nonassertiveness, assertiveness, and aggressiveness.* Recall three situations in which you were frustrated or badly treated or in which your rights were violated in some way. Then describe your response in each situation and classify it as nonassertive, assertive, or aggressive. If your response was not sufficiently assertive, indicate a more assertive alternative. As an optional step, share your descriptions (but not your classifications or alternatives) with others, and ask them to classify each response and suggest alternative ways of dealing with the situation. Then compare your classifications and alternatives with theirs.

4. *Role-playing assertiveness.* Recall a recent incident in which your behavior was less assertive than it might have been. Perhaps you complied with an unfair request, submitted to an imposition, or failed to express your thoughts, feelings, or beliefs in an honest or appropriate way. Write this incident down, indicating your response and how you would like to respond should a similar situation arise in the future. Then form groups of three. Each member, in turn, reads her or his incident and practices a more assertive response by enacting it with a second member; the third observes and offers suggestions and reinforcement.

5. *Practicing assertiveness.* Make up a list of simple practice assignments in assertiveness that are appropriate to your own situation and life. Then proceed to carry them out, and observe and later record your experience. Sample assignments are (1) go to a restaurant, ask for a particular table, order a particular item but then change the item, and, if appropriate, compliment the waiter or chef or manager as you leave for anything you particularly enjoyed or appreciated; (2) buy an item in a store and later return it; (3) borrow something from a friend or neighbor; (4) make a point of telling each person you know and interact with during the course of a day something you like about her or him.

6. *Reaching out.* Observe yourself on two fairly typical days. On the first, behave as you usually do. On the second, take every appropriate occasion to reach out to others—to nod, say "hello," strike up a conversation, pay a compliment, offer help, or say and show you care. Afterward, write down your experience and any insights or conclusions you formed.

7. *Seeing, touching.* An important method of reaching out to others is through eye contact or touch, but many of us are uncomfortable in doing so. Contact of this kind is a learnable skill and frequently taught in assertiveness training. As a simple exercise, begin by having everyone move freely around the room. As any two meet, they establish eye contact and hold it for a little while, shake hands firmly (putting their hands as far forward into each other's as possible) or touch in any appropriate way, and then move on to contact another. Afterward, assemble to share reactions.

8. *Stroking.* A *stroke* is any sign of recognition or approval that one person gives to another. Many people are starved for strokes, and

many have trouble in giving, receiving, and believing strokes. Stroking is a learnable skill and is frequently taught in assertiveness training. As a simple exercise, begin by forming small groups, and designate one person as the focus. Members of the group take turns in complimenting the person or in contacting the person in some appropriate verbal or physical way. After each stroke, pause to allow time for it to "soak in." Then the focus person nods, smiles, or says "Thank you" and is ready for the next stroke. After each member has had a turn as the focus person, the group shares its experiences.

9. *Seeing, touching, stroking.* Seeing (eye contact), touching (body contact), and stroking (signs of approval and recognition) are important ways of reaching out to others. As a simple exercise, begin by having everyone move freely around the room. As any two meet, they establish eye contact, shake hands firmly or embrace, and then exchange simple strokes. (Examples: "I like your smile." "That's a nice shirt you're wearing." "I really appreciate the experiences you share in this class.") Take time with each contact; don't rush it; let the strokes "soak in." After everyone has made contact with all others at least once, assemble to share reactions.

10. *The "I can't because" list.* Draw a vertical line down the middle of a sheet of paper. At the top of the left side, write "I can't." At the top of the right side, write "Because." On the left, list all the situations in which you can't be as assertive as you would like to be. On the other side, for each item, indicate the reasons why you can't. Examples:

I can't	*Because*
I can't speak up in class	because I might make a fool of myself.
I can't tell my neighbors to turn their stereo down	because I want to stay on good terms with them.
I can't tell my parents I love them	because it would embarrass them and me too.

Afterward, select from the list one situation that is particularly bothersome, and challenge your reason for not trying to change the situation. Is your reason for not being assertive good, sufficient, or valid? How do you know? How could you assert yourself in a way that would be acceptable and effective?

To Read Further

Alberti, R. E., & Emmons, M. L. (1990). *Your perfect right: A guide to assertive living* (6th ed.). San Luis Obispo, CA: Impact. (paperback)

Bower, S. A., & Bower, G. H. (1991). *Asserting yourself: A practical guide for positive change* (updated ed.). Reading, MA: Addison-Wesley. (paperback)

Phelps, S., & Austin, N. (1987). *The assertive woman: A new look.* San Luis Obispo, CA: Impact. (paperback)

Tavris, C. (1989). *Anger: The misunderstood emotion* (rev. ed.). New York: Touchstone. (paperback)

Anger: The Misunderstood Emotion

Carol Tavris

Woman A: *"You'll feel better if you get your anger out."*

Woman B: *"Anger! Why should I be angry!"*

Woman A: *"Because your father left you. Underneath, you're blaming him for not keeping his obligation to protect you forever."*

Woman B: *"Left me! What are you talking about! He died. I don't feel angry. I feel sad."*

Woman A: *"Why are you denying your true feelings!"*

Woman B: *"Margaret, you're going to drive me crazy. I don't feel angry, damn it!"*

Woman A (smiling): *"So why are you shouting!"*

That exchange, overheard in a New York City restaurant, illustrates one of today's most accepted myths of popular psychology: that expressing anger is crucial to health and happiness. Social psychologist Leonard Berkowitz of the University of Wisconsin calls advocates of this view "ventilationists," because they believe it's unhealthy to bottle up feelings. "Many go further," he writes, "and argue that by showing our emotions we eliminate tensions, conquer aches and pains, and promote 'more meaningful' relationships with others."

"There is a widespread belief that to discharge one's feelings is beneficial," writes psychiatrist John R. Marshall of the University of Wisconsin department of psychiatry. "People feel that there's some value in hitting, throwing or breaking something when frustrated."

But is there? In the aftermath of the abrupt transition from Puritan restraint to liberated self-expression, many people are uncertain how to behave: some overreact angrily at every thwarted wish; others suffer injustice in silence. Who's right?

In one experiment, psychologist Jack Hokanson of Florida State University found that aggression *was* cathartic: the blood pressure of angry male students would return to baseline more quickly when they could retaliate against the man who had angered them. But this was true only when the man who angered them was a fellow student; when he was a teacher, retaliation had no cathartic effect. Expressing anger to a superior is *itself* an arousing, anxiety-producing action. Far from reducing anger, it complicates it.

Then Hokanson noticed that women were not behaving the same as men. When insulted, women didn't get belligerent; instead, they said something friendly to try to calm the woman who angered them. For women, any aggression, even toward a classmate, was as arousing and upsetting as aggression toward authority was for men.

Further research gave Hokanson the idea that aggressive catharsis is a learned reaction to anger, not an instinctive one. The learned aspect of catharsis works like this: someone irritates you and provokes you over the edge of self-control. Now you do something—you swear, or hit, or pound out Stravinsky on the piano. All these reactions lessen your physiological arousal and its corresponding sensation that your blood is boiling. At the same time, you're acquiring a cathartic habit.

This habit doesn't mean you'll be less angry in the future. It means that when you *are* angry, you're apt to do whatever worked for you before, whether it was swearing, writing a letter, having a drink, or hitting the person who aroused you.

Thus most ventilationist theories today concentrate on what a person should do to bring down anger. But *any* emotional arousal will eventually simmer down if you just wait long enough. This is why the classic advice for anger control—count to ten—has survived for centuries.

Berkowitz, who has studied the social causes of aggression, finds that ventilation-by-yelling does not reduce anger. "Frequently, when we tell someone off, we stimulate ourselves to continued aggression," he observed. This is why a minor annoyance, when expressed in hostile language or behavior, can flare into a major argument.

Anger and its expression do not exist in a vacuum. In all areas of our lives we make choices about how to behave, when to speak, whether to reveal anger. Suppressed anger can be "bad" if, because we do not reveal our feelings, a stressful situation continues; expressed anger can likewise be "bad" if, in revealing our feelings, we make the stressful situation worse.

Actress Lynn Fontanne once said that the secret of her successful marriage and acting partnership with Alfred Lunt was that they were never impolite to each other. Civility is not, mind you, the same as silence. Couples who aren't defeated by rage know two things: when to keep quiet about trivial angers, for the sake of civility, and how to discuss important ones, for the sake of personal autonomy and change. As the catharsis studies show, sometimes the best thing you can do about anger is nothing. Let it go, and it will often turn out to be unimportant and quickly forgotten. Keeping quiet also gives you time to cool down and decide if the matter is worth discussing.

The most successful therapeutic methods for helping people who are quick to rage take mind and body into consideration. Practitioners of yoga learn techniques to calm distracting or infuriating thoughts. Western psychologists are catching on. Ray Novaco of the University of California at Irvine, for example, works with people who have problems with chronic anger, teaching them three things: how to think about their anger; how to control arousal; how to behave constructively. Anger is often inflamed by the statements we make when we are provoked: "Who does he think he is to treat me like that?" "What a vile and thoughtless woman she is!" Novaco teaches people to empathize with the provocateur's behavior, trying to find justification for it and ways to deal with it: "Maybe he's having a rough day" or "She must be very unhappy if she would do such a thing."

On the ground that you can't laugh and frown at the same time, some psychologists use "humor therapy" with clients who have anger problems. When I was a child, my father often used this tactic on me. Once, when I was enjoying an angry mood, he insisted I accompany him to an afternoon of Charlie Chaplin movies. There I learned that you cannot maintain a sullen mood when you are laughing out loud.

Many believe that talking out anger gets rid of it—or at least makes you feel less angry. But several studies show that talking out an emotion often doesn't reduce it and may, in fact, merely *rehearse* it. As you recite your grievances, your emotional arousal builds again, making you feel as angry as you did when the infuriating event first happened. Anger only feeds on itself. And, sure as the sunrise, it makes for a grumpy life.

Now, none of this is to make a case for *always* keeping quiet when you're angry. The point is to understand what happens when you *do* decide to express anger. Each of us must find his own compromise between expressing every little thing that irritates, and passively accepting the injustices we feel. Discussing anger can lead to practical solutions; it can also become obsessive and useless.

Thus the decision about whether or not to express anger rests on what you want to communicate and what you hope to accomplish. If you want your anger to dissipate and the association in question to remain congenial, keep quiet. But if you want to *stay* angry, if you want to use your anger, keep talking.

The moral use of anger requires an awareness of choice and an embrace of reason. For the small indignities of life, the best remedy is almost always a Charlie Chaplin movie. For the larger ones, fight back. And, most important, learn the difference.

To Apply This Reading to Yourself

1. *Describe a situation in which you* suppressed *your anger with* unfortunate *results.*
2. *Describe a situation in which you* suppressed *your anger with* fortunate *results.*

3. *Describe a situation in which you expressed your anger with* unfortunate *results.*
4. *Describe a situation in which you expressed your anger with* fortunate *results.*
5. *How do you typically deal with your anger! What effect has this had on you and your relationships!*

Assertive, Nonassertive, and Aggressive Behavior

Arthur J. Lange and Patricia Jakubowski

Assertion involves standing up for personal rights and expressing thoughts, feelings, and beliefs in *direct, honest,* and *appropriate* ways which do not violate another person's rights.[1] The basic message in assertion is: This is what I think. This is what I feel. This is how I see the situation. This message expresses "who the person is" and is said without dominating, humiliating, or degrading the other person.

Assertion involves respect—not deference. Deference is acting in a subservient manner as though the other person is right, or better, simply because the other person is older, more powerful, experienced, or knowledgeable or is of a different sex or race. Deference is present when people express themselves in ways that are self-effacing, appeasing, or overly apologetic.

Two types of respect are involved in assertion: respect for oneself, that is, expressing one's needs and defending one's rights, as well as respect for the other person's needs and rights. An example will help clarify the kind of respect involved in assertive behavior.

A woman was desperately trying to get a flight to Kansas City to see her mother who was sick in the hospital. Weather conditions were bad and the lines were long. Having been rejected from three standby flights, she again found herself in the middle of a long line for the fourth and last flight to Kansas City. This time she approached a man who was standing near the beginning of the line and said, pointing to her place, "Would you mind exchanging places with me? I ordinarily wouldn't ask, but it's extremely important that I get to Kansas City tonight." The man nodded yes, and as it turned out, both of them were able to get on the flight.

When asked what her reaction would have been if the man had refused, she replied, "It would have been OK. I hoped he would say yes, but after all he was there first."[1]

In this example the woman showed self-respect for her own needs by asking whether the man would be willing to help her. Also, she respected the man's right to refuse her request and not fulfill her need.

How is respect shown when refusing another's request? It depends on how that request is refused. A request may be refused aggressively: "What do you mean you want to borrow my car! I don't know where you get your nerve!" Such aggressive refusals involve only one-way respect; that is, respect for one's right to refuse but not for the other person's right to ask. A request may also be refused nonassertively: "What can I say . . . I feel just awful saying this, really bad . . . I can't loan you my car. Oh gee, what a terrible thing to say!" Here the person refused the request, but did it in a way that showed lack of self-respect: It suggested that the refuser was a bad person who should not have denied the request. In addition, the nonassertive refusal did not respect the other person's right to be treated as a capable person who can handle a disappointment. In contrast, an assertive refusal would be: "I'd like to help you out, but I feel uncomfortable loaning my car." The assertive refusal shows the two-fold respect: self-respect in the self-confident way the request is refused and respect for the other person's right to ask.

In our view, the goal of assertion is communication and "mutuality"; that is, to get and give respect, to ask for fair play, and to leave room for compromise when the needs and rights of two people conflict. In such compromises neither person sacrifices basic integrity and both get some of their needs satisfied. The compromise may be one in which one person gets her needs taken care of immediately while the other party gets taken care of a little later. For example, one weekend the friends see a movie and the next weekend they bowl. Or the compromise may involve both parties giving up a little. They attend *part* of an outdoor concert and then take a short *walk* and talk. When personal integrity is at stake, a compromise is inappropriate and non-assertive.

We are opposed to viewing assertion as simply a way "to get what one wants" for three reasons. First, this view emphasizes success in attaining goals. Thus it can cause people to become passive when they believe that acting assertively will not get them what they want. Second, this view concentrates only on the asserter's right and not on the personal rights of both parties. Such an attitude increases the chances of people using aggressive or manipulative methods to get what they want. Third, it may lead to irresponsible behavior in which assertion is used to take advantage of other people. We have frequently heard people say that they can assertively ask for favors and it's just too bad that the other person is not strong enough to refuse their requests. In contrast, we advocate *responsible* asserting which involves mutuality, asking for fair play, and using one's greater assertive power to help others become more able to stand up for themselves. Interestingly, a by-product of responsible assertion is that people often do get what they want. Why? Because most people become cooperative when they are approached in a way which is both respectful of self and respectful of others.

Nonassertion involves violating one's own rights by failing to express honest feelings, thoughts, and beliefs and consequently permitting others to violate oneself, or expressing one's thoughts and feelings in such an apologetic, diffident, self-effacing manner that others can easily disregard them.[1] In the latter type of nonassertion, the total message which is communicated is: I don't count—you can take advantage of me. My feelings don't matter—only yours do. My thoughts aren't important—yours are the only ones worth listening to. I'm nothing—you are superior.

Nonassertion shows a lack of respect for one's own needs. It also sometimes shows a subtle lack of respect for the other person's ability to take disappointments, to shoulder some responsibility, to handle his own problems, etc. The goal of nonassertion is to appease others and to avoid conflict at any cost.

Aggression involves directly standing up for personal rights and expressing thoughts, feelings, and beliefs in a way which is often dishonest, usually inappropriate, and always violates the rights of the other person. An example of "emotionally dishonest" aggression is a situation where individuals who feel saddened by another person's mourning for the death of a loved one sarcastically degrade the mourner ("That's just what I like to see—a grown person sniveling like a two-year-old brat"), instead of revealing their own sad and helpless feelings.

The usual goal of aggression is domination and winning, forcing the other person to lose. Winning is insured by humiliating, degrading, belittling, or overpowering other people so that they become weaker and less able to express and defend their needs and rights. The basic message is: That is what I think—you're stupid for believing differently. This is what I want—what you want isn't important. This is what I feel—your feelings don't count.

Nonverbal Components of Assertive, Nonassertive, and Aggressive Behavior

So far we've discussed the verbal components of assertive, nonassertive, and aggressive behavior. The nonverbal components of these behaviors are equally important, if not more so. Research has shown that the vast majority of our communication is carried out nonverbally.[2] Take a moment to consider how the statement "I like you" can be said as a sincere statement, a question, or a sarcastic remark, by simply changing voice inflection, facial expression, and hand gestures. Likewise, an otherwise verbal assertive statement can become nonassertive or aggressive depending on the nonverbal behaviors which accompany the verbal statement.

Eisler, Miller, and Hersen[3] have pinpointed some of the nonverbal behaviors which may be important in assertion: duration of looking at the other person, duration of speech, loudness of speech, and affect in speech. Research has generally supported the importance of these nonverbal behaviors[3] with the exception of the length of time it takes the person to respond to the other individual.[4] Other nonverbal behaviors which may be important in assertion, nonassertion, and aggression are described below.

In assertive behavior, the nonverbals are congruent with the verbal messages and add support, strength, and emphasis to what is being said verbally. The voice is appropriately loud to the situation; eye contact is firm but not a staredown; body gestures which denote strength are used; and the speech pattern is fluent—without awkward hesitancies—expressive, clear, and emphasizes key words.

In nonassertive behavior, the nonverbal behaviors include evasive eye contact, body gestures such as hand wringing, clutching the other person, stepping back from the other person as the assertive remark is made, hunching the shoulders, covering the mouth with the hand, nervous gestures which distract the listener from what the speaker is saying, and wooden body posture. The voice tone may be singsong or overly soft. The speech pattern is hesitant and filled with pauses and the throat may be cleared frequently. Facial gestures may include raising the eyebrows, laughs, and winks when expressing anger.

In general, the nonassertive gestures are ones which convey weakness, anxiety, pleading, or self-effacement. They reduce the impact of what is being said verbally, which is precisely why people who are scared of acting assertively use them. Their goal is to "soften" what they're saying so that the other person will not be offended.

In aggressive behavior, the nonverbal behaviors are ones which dominate or demean the other person. These include eye contact that tries to stare down and dominate the other person, a strident voice that does not fit the situation, sarcastic or condescending tone of voice, and parental body gestures such as excessive finger pointing.

Examples of Assertive, Nonassertive, and Aggressive Behavior
In each example, the first response is aggressive, the second, nonassertive, and the third is assertive.

Confronting a Professor Who Gives Inappropriate and Excessive Amounts of Work—
1 Dr. Jones, you have some nerve giving me this kind of work. I know you have control over me, but I don't have to take this stuff. You professors think you can use grad students for anything you please—Well not this time!
2 OK, Dr. Jones, I'll do it. I guess you must have a reason for asking me to do this

stuff . . . even if it isn't related to my assistantship. I don't suppose you'd consider letting me off the hook this time? Huh?
3 Dr. Jones, when you give me work that's not related to your class, I'd have to put in extra hours beyond what's appropriate for my assistantship. For those reasons I need to say no on this extra work.

Talking with Someone Who Has Just Made a Sexist Remark—
1 Who the hell do you think you are? God's gift to women?
2 Oh come on (ha ha). You know how much that irritates me when you say things like that (ha ha).
3 Frankly, I think that remark demeans both of us.

Refusing an Extra Helping of Food at a Dinner Party—
1 You'd just love me to put on a few pounds of fat!
2 Gee . . . ah . . . Well, since you insist . . . I'll change my mind. Yeah, give me another piece.
3 That food does look good but I don't want any more.

Trying to Get a Group on the Subject After They've Wandered into Tangential Areas—
1 Can't you people get back to work and stop this goofing off?
2 I guess it's just my hang-up. Do you think it'd be OK if we got back to the original subject? I've forgotten it myself (ha ha).
3 What we're talking about is interesting; however, I'm feeling the need to get back to the original subject.

ASSERTIVE BEHAVIOR

Reasons for Acting Assertively
Assertion Rather Than Nonassertion. Losing other people's approval is usually a major issue for people who are often nonassertive. In a way it's like believing "I will only survive if I have other people's approval." However, nonassertion does not guarantee approval. People may pity rather than approve of nonassertion; often this

pity eventually turns into irritation and finally disgust.[5]

A major reason for acting assertively is that it increases *one's own self-respect*. Indeed, an unpublished study by Judy Demplewolff showed that group members' self-concepts significantly changed after assertion training. A second reason is that assertion eventually results in greater self-confidence which can then reduce the need for others' approval. Third, while it is true that people will sometimes disapprove of assertion, usually other people respect and admire those who are responsibly assertive, show respect for self and others, have the courage to take stands, and deal with conflict openly and fairly. Lastly, assertion—more frequently than nonassertion—results in individuals getting their needs satisfied and preferences respected.

Assertion Rather Than Aggression. A major fear of people who are frequently aggressive is that they will become more vulnerable and lose control over other people. It's like believing "I can only survive if I'm invulnerable and able to control people." That aggression does not guarantee successful control over other people is usually overlooked. When people apparently acquiesce under aggression, often they simply have gone "underground" and subtly sabotage the aggressor's control. (This sabotage process is described more fully later in this chapter.)

A major reason for acting assertively is that it increases *one's control over oneself*, which feels good. Second, assertion eventually results in greater feelings of self-confidence which reduces insecurity and vulnerability. Third and very importantly, assertion rather than aggression results in closer, more emotionally satisfying relationships with others. Fourth, while it is true that assertion will mean that sometimes individuals will not achieve their objectives and "win," assertion maximizes the likelihood that both parties can at least partially achieve their goals and get their needs met.

There are many different ways of acting assertively. It is important that the trainer know the various types of assertion so that group members can be helped to find better alternatives when one type of assertion is inappropriate or does not meet a member's needs. The different types of assertion are more accurately thought of

as principles to help guide the person's assertion instead of as techniques to use *on* other people.

TYPES OF ASSERTION

Basic Assertion
Basic assertion refers to a simple expression of standing up for personal rights, beliefs, feelings, or opinions. It does not involve other social skills, such as empathy, confrontation, persuasion, etc. Examples of basic assertions are:

When being interrupted—
Excuse me, I'd like to finish what I'm saying.
When being asked an important question for which you are unprepared—
I'd like to have a few minutes to think that over.
When returning an item to a store—
I'd like my money back on this saw.
When refusing a request—
No, this afternoon is not a good time for me to visit with you.
When telling a parent you don't want advice—
I don't want any more advice.

Basic assertion also involves expressing affection and appreciation toward other people:

I like you.
I care for you a lot.
Having a friend like you makes me feel happy.
You're someone special to me.

The following is a particularly touching example of assertively expressing affection:

A father overheard his five-year-old child saying to a playmate: "Are you having a good time!" When the playmate replied "Yes," the child continued, "I am too. I'm so glad that I invited you to come over and play!"

Empathic Assertion
Often people want to do more than simply express their feelings or needs. They may also want to convey some sensitivity to the other person. When this is the goal, the empathic assertion can be used. This type of assertion involves making a statement that conveys recognition of the other person's situ-

ation or feelings and is followed by another statement which stands up for the speaker's rights.[1] Examples of empathic assertions are:

> *When two people are chatting loudly while a meeting is going on—*
> You may not realize it, but your talking is starting to make it hard for me to hear what's going on in the meeting. Would you keep it down?
> *When having some furniture delivered—*
> I know it's hard to say exactly when the truck will come, but I'd like a ball park estimate of the arrival time.
> *When telling a parent that you don't want advice—*
> I know that you give me advice because you don't want me to get hurt by mistakes I might make. At this point in my life, I need to learn how to make my own decisions and rely on myself, even if I do make some mistakes. I appreciate the help you've given me in the past and you can help me now by not giving me advice.[1]

There is considerable personal power in the empathic assertion because other people more easily respond to assertion when they have been recognized first. This power, however, should not be used as a manipulation to merely gain one's own ends, without genuine respect for the other person. Repeatedly saying, "I understand how you feel but . . . " can be just "mouthing" understanding and conning other people into believing that their feelings are being taken into account when in fact their feelings are really being discounted. Such behavior does not involve empathic assertion.

Another important benefit of the empathic assertion is that it causes the speaker to take a moment to try to understand the other person's feelings before the speaker reacts. This can help the speaker keep perspective on the situation and thus reduces the likelihood of the speaker's aggressively overreacting when irritated.

Escalating Assertion

According to Rimm and Masters,[6] escalating assertion involves starting with a "minimal" assertive response that can usually accomplish the speaker's goal with a minimum of effort and negative emotion and a small possibility of negative consequences. When the other person fails to respond to the minimal assertion and continues to violate one's rights, the speaker gradually escalates the assertion and becomes increasingly firm. We have observed that often it is not necessary to go beyond the initial minimal assertion; but if it is necessary, the person can become increasingly firm without becoming aggressive. The escalating assertion can occur from a request to a demand, from a preference to an outright refusal, or, as the following example illustrates, from an empathic assertion to a firm basic assertion.

> *The speaker is in a bar with a woman friend, and a man repeatedly offers to buy them drinks—*
> That's very nice of you to offer, but we came here to catch up on some news. Thanks, anyway!
> No, thank you. We really would rather talk just to each other.
> This is the third and last time I am going to tell you that we don't want your company. Please leave![7]

In this example, the final blunt refusal was appropriate because the earlier escalating assertions were ignored. If the woman had started with the highly escalated assertion the first time the man had approached, her response would have been inappropriate. Since assertion involves direct, honest, and *appropriate* expressions of thoughts and feelings, her reaction would be aggressive, rather than assertive. Likewise when a person has not objected to taking the minutes of a meeting, but one day suddenly says, "I'm getting sick and tired of being the secretary just because I'm the only woman in the group," her response would be aggressive, rather than assertive. Only if her comment had been preceded by successively escalated assertions which had been ignored would her comment be appropriate and assertive.

A final point about the escalating assertion is that just before making the final escalated assertion, we suggest that one consider offering a "contract option," in which the other person is informed what the final assertion will be and is given a chance to change behavior before it occurs. For example, when a repair shop repeatedly refuses to settle an unreasonable bill, one may say, "I'm being left with no other alternative than to complain to the Better Business Bureau and your distributor. I'd prefer not to do that but I will if this is the only alternative I'm left with." Often people only recognize that one means business at the contract option point.

Whether the contract option is simply a threat depends on how it is said. If it is said in a menacing tone of voice which relies on emotionality to carry the argument, it is a threat. When the contract option is carried out assertively, it is said in a matter-of-fact tone of voice which simply gives information about the consequences which will occur if the situation is not equitably resolved.

Confrontive Assertion

Confrontive assertion is used when the other person's words contradict his deeds. This type of assertion involves objectively describing what the other person said would be done and what the other actually did do, after which the speaker expresses what he wants.[1] The entire assertion is said in a matter-of-fact, nonevaluative way, as the examples below show:

I was supposed to be consulted before the final proposal was typed. But I see the secretary is typing it right now. Before he finishes it, I want to review the proposal and make whatever corrections I think are needed. In the future, I want to get a chance to review any proposals before they're sent to the secretary.

I thought we'd agreed that you were going to be more considerate towards students. Yet I noticed today that when two students asked for some information you said that you had better things to do than babysit for kids. As we discussed earlier, I see showing more consideration as an important part of your job. I'd like to figure out what seems to be the problem.

I said it was OK to borrow my records as long as you checked with me first. Now you're playing my classical records without asking. I'd like to know why you did that.

The above are examples of initial confrontive assertive statements. In most cases the ensuing conversation would be an extended interaction between the two people. This is particularly true in the last two examples in which the speaker wanted additional information and the resulting discussions would be problem-solving ones.

In contrast to assertive confrontation, aggressive confrontation involves judging other people—rather than describing their behavior—and trying to make others feel guilty. For example:

Hey, those are my records! Evidently your word means absolutely nothing to you! Just for that I want my records right now and in the future you're going to find them locked up. Then you'll have to ask me first.

I-Language Assertion

I-language is particularly useful as a guide for helping people to assertively express difficult negative feelings. In addition, the principles in I-language can help individuals learn how to determine when their feelings stem from some violation of their rights and feelings, or whether their negative feelings are due to their trying to impose their own values and expectations on other people.

I-language assertion is based on the work of Thomas Gordon[8] and involves a four-part statement:

> When . . . (speaker objectively describes the other person's behavior).
>
> The effects are . . . (speaker describes how the other person's behavior concretely affects his life or feelings).
>
> I feel . . . (speaker describes feelings).
>
> I'd prefer . . . (speaker describes what he wants).

Three points merit further comment. First, we believe that the "I feel . . . " part of the statement is optional. Saying, "I feel . . . " does clarify for oneself and for others just precisely what one's feelings are and thus it may reduce misunderstandings about the nature of one's feelings. However, describing one's feelings may be inappropriate in some situations, e.g., business. Second, we believe that the "I'd prefer . . . . "part of the statement is also optional. As Gordon cogently notes, excluding it gives the other person maximum opportunity to offer his own ideas for dealing with a situation. However, including it gives the other person some information as to what the speaker, at least, would like to see happen. Third, I-language assertion is initially presented as a formula. After individuals feel comfortable using the formula, they may wish to intermix the four components so that it matches their own natural style of speaking.

The following example illustrates I-language assertion in which one expresses irritation and describes the concrete effect of the other person's behavior. A desk is shared by two people, one of whom is disorganized and the other is neat.

Today I saw Ms. Van Buren to give her my report and I didn't have all of it because my papers got mixed up with yours. The disorganization on this desk has gotten to be a real problem for me and I'm getting upset. I'd like to hear your suggestions so that this problem doesn't come up again.

Depending on the speaker's wants, alternative ending assertions could be:

I'd like to talk to Ms. Van Buren about our getting separate desks, or *Would you be willing to keep your side of the desk more organized?*

The example below illustrates how the I-language assertion could be done when the effect of the other person's behavior is less concrete:

When your half of the desk is so disorganized, I find it hard to think and concentrate on my work because I'm worried that my papers may be mixed with yours. This is really bothering me. Do you think we could work something out to help me?

Does the following statement identify a concrete effect?

When your half of the desk is so messy, I start feeling angry and that upsets me. I'd like you to be more neat and organized.

No. The speaker has not specified a concrete effect but rather has attempted to impose the speaker's own idiosyncratic values on the other person—all under the guise of being assertive.

In contrast to assertively expressing irritation in terms of I-language, aggressively expressing irritation tries to make the other person responsible for having caused the bad feelings and uses You-language instead of I-language. In the following example, the first statement is aggressive and the second statement is assertive.

You make me mad when you always butt in! What's wrong with you anyway!

When I'm constantly interrupted, I lose my train of thought and begin to feel that my ideas aren't important to you. I start feeling hurt and angry. I'd like you to make a point of waiting until I'm finished speaking.

NONASSERTIVE BEHAVIOR

Reasons Why People Act Nonassertively
There are at least five major reasons for nonassertive behavior. The first of these concerns the failure to distinguish assertion from aggression and nonassertion from politeness.

Mistaking Firm Assertion for Aggression. To many individuals, firm assertive behavior sounds like aggression. Their own unique learning backgrounds have caused them to equate any show of assertive firmness or anger with aggression. Furthermore, the culture at large has not sufficiently distinguished between assertion and aggression—indeed, neither have some prominent behaviorists.[9] Thus, individuals mislabel their own natural assertive impulses as dangerous urges which are to be severely controlled. Women in particular may be told that their natural assertive behavior is aggressive and masculine.

Mistaking Nonassertion for Politeness. Many people act nonassertively under the mistaken notion that such behavior is really just being polite and considerate. They may have been taught that it is not polite to end a telephone call when the other person called first, to use the word "I" to interrupt someone even if the other person talks ad nauseam, to disagree with someone who's older, disabled, or has higher status, to refuse food at someone's home, to ask guests to leave when the evening has worn thin, to agree with a compliment, or to compliment oneself, etc.

Failure to Accept Personal Rights. A second major reason why people act nonassertively is that they do not fully accept their personal rights; in other words, they do not believe they have the right to express their reactions, to stand up for themselves, to take care of their own emotional needs. Often they do not believe that they are entitled to express certain kinds of feelings, e.g., hurt, anger, disappointment, affection. Frequently they not only believe that they should not express these feelings but that *they should not have these feelings in the first place!*

Anxiety about Negative Consequences. A third major reason why people act nonassertively concerns their anxiety about what would happen as a result of any assertive behavior. Common fears are that they will lose other people's affection or approval, that other people will think they are foolish, stupid, or selfish, that they will hurt other people's feelings or badly damage other's lives, and that other people will become angry or rejecting.

Mistaking Nonassertion for Being Helpful. A fourth cause of nonassertion is the belief that one's nonassertion actually helps the other person. In reality such behavior involves "rescuing" the other person. Rescuing is giving help the other person actually does not need and sacrificing one's own needs. Unhealthy rescuing can be distinguished from genuine helping. In genuine helping, the receiver's behavior changes in positive ways, and at some point, the receiver no longer needs the help.[10]

Deficient Skills. A last major reason for nonassertion is that people may simply not know how to act otherwise. They may not have the learned assertive skills because they lacked opportunities to vicariously acquire such skills by watching how other people have handled similar situations. For example, adults who as children rarely went to restaurants may simply not have learned how to request service or return badly cooked food.

Consequences of Acting Nonassertively

The usual goal of nonassertion is to appease others and to avoid conflict at any cost. Even where the nonassertion *costs people their own integrity*, the immediate consequence of allowing individuals to avoid or escape from anxiety-producing conflicts is very reinforcing. For example, even when a man's nonassertion is viewed as feminine, such punishment is usually not strong enough to counter the more immediate tension reduction which occurs when he successfully avoids a potential conflict by acting nonassertively.

In addition, people may be encouraged to be nonassertive by others who praise them for their selflessness, femininity, for being a good friend, child or student, and for being quiet, subservient, and generally agreeable and not causing problems for other people.

In the long run, however, a person who is frequently nonassertive feels a growing loss of self-esteem and an increasing sense of hurt and anger. Even more internal tension may then result. When this tension is constantly suppressed, somatic problems may develop, such as headaches, stomach aches, backaches,[5] and sometimes even general depression.[1] Other people who are interested in close relationships which are characterized by the honest expression of thoughts and feelings may withdraw or not even start a relationship with a nonassertive person. People who feel guilty about inadvertently taking advantage of another person's nonassertiveness may withdraw from that person. Finally, although other people may initially feel sorry for the nonassertive person, their pity often turns into irritation, and finally disgust and lack of respect.[5]

AGGRESSIVE BEHAVIOR

Reasons Why People Act Aggressively

There are many kinds of cognitive, affective, and behavioral patterns which lead to aggressive behavior. Five patterns which are primarily behavioral will be described here.

Powerlessness and Threat. A general cause of aggression is the feeling of being vulnerable to an anticipated or actual attack by another person. The resulting aggressive overreaction is instigated by threat and a sense of powerlessness.

Prior Nonassertion. It may seem surprising that a second chief cause of much aggression is due to the person's prior nonassertion. The subtle ways in which aggression can result from nonassertion deserve some consideration.

Aggression can occur when a person has been nonassertive for a period of time, allowing rights and feelings to be violated, with the result that hurt and anger build to the point that the person finally feels justified in expressing these feelings and aggressively standing up for rights. In other cases, individuals may nonassertively allow their rights to be abused and misunderstandings grow as part of a game. After their aggressive outburst of feelings, they expect the other person to feel guilty and become more affectionate. Thus, their aggression is a kind of game to manipulate emotional closeness, rather than to directly ask for affection or act in ways that openly show their vulnerability, thus increasing closer personal relationships.

At other times people act aggressively as a way to prevent themselves from becoming nonassertive. For example, when individuals have been assertive in repeatedly refusing someone's request, they may be afraid that they will back down and accede to the request if asked once more. As a way of preventing themselves from becoming nonassertive, they may start to make themselves feel self-righteous anger and blame the other person: "Who does he think he is anyway? I've already said no three times!" These feelings then erupt into aggressive behavior.

Aggression and nonassertion are related in another subtle way in which individuals are nonassertive towards people who have greater power and they inhibit their hurt and angry feelings. Then they aggressively express these feelings with those people over whom they have power. The classic example of this type of aggressive–nonassertive pattern are employees who acquiesce to an employer's unreasonable requests, and then finding themselves overburdened with work, personally blame subordinates for their failure to work even harder.

Finally, aggression is related to nonassertion in that *both* involve denying certain personal rights. For example, in order to justify asking for help when individuals do not feel they have the right to be weak and need help, they may start seeing the other person as bad and selfish for not volunteering to help ("All you ever do is think of yourself! Can't you see that I need help getting the house ready for company!").

In other cases when individuals mistakenly believe that the other person had "no right" to act in a certain way, there is a strong tendency for individuals to exaggerate the supposed misdeed and to overreact in a punitive manner. For example, a person who believes that a friend does not have the right to request to borrow the car typically becomes aggressive when such a request is made. The aggressor reasons that the absurdity of such a request is so obvious that the other person should not even have had to ask! Interestingly, these aggressors almost invariably also believe that they do not have the right to make a comparable request and would never do so, regardless of how great their need was. Often persons who deny themselves the right to ask for personal favors from others deny others the same right.

Overreaction due to Past Emotional Experiences. Thirdly, aggression may be due to a person's overreacting to a current situation because of some past unresolved emotional experience. The person reacts to the present with the emotions that are actually linked to some past experience or significant person, as the following case example illustrates:

Sitting with her husband and woman friend, a wife was trying to explain the need for the Equal Rights Amendment. Her husband casually asked why it was needed since the issues were already covered by the other amendments in the Constitution. The wife overreacted and started to berate the husband for his ridiculous position. After the tirade, her woman friend calmly asked the husband whether the wife always reacted so strongly. He responded, "Yeah, when we start talking about issues like this, Kathy gets pretty uptight." The calm way in which both her friend and husband reacted caused Kathy to realize that she had acted as though she had been personally attacked; in reality her husband had only asked for additional information. In thinking about her own overreaction, she realized that the feelings of powerlessness and personal attack she experienced were the same that she had felt as an adolescent, arguing to no avail with her unyielding father about religion and other issues. Discussing an emotionally charged issue produced feelings of powerlessness and thus triggered aggression, even though her husband did not respond like her father. In subsequent disputes she deliberately reminded herself that the other person was not her father, that she was no longer a child, etc. This self-talk helped her to maintain her perspective, composure, and assertion when presenting her opinions to potentially rejecting individuals.

Beliefs about Aggression. Fourthly, aggression may result from the belief that aggression is the only way to get through to the other person. In the 1960s, for example, when college students challenged the administration and met with an unyielding stance and a complete discount of their complaints, many students became extremely aggressive upon hitting that "brick wall." A related cause of aggression is the belief that the world is hostile and one must be aggressive in order to survive.

Reinforcement and Skill Deficits. The fifth cause of aggression is that individuals may simply have received positive reinforcement for this behavior in their home or subculture. Also, individuals may react aggressively because they have not acquired the needed assertive skills which would be appropriate for a particular situation.

Consequences of Aggression

Since behavior is more easily influenced by immediate consequences, it is unfortunate that the most immediate consequences of aggression are usually positive, while the long-run consequences are negative. Immediate positive results include emotional release, a sense of power, and getting goals and needs met without experiencing direct negative reactions from others.

The long-term negative consequences include losing or failing to establish close relationships and feeling one has to be constantly vigilant against attack from others. Highly aggressive behavior may eventually cause individuals to lose jobs and promotions, get high blood pressure, become alienated from their children and mates, get into fights, or have trouble with the law. Because of these negative consequences, persons who are frequently aggressive eventually may feel deeply misunderstood, unloved, and unlovable.

In addition, when one is aggressive, other people may retaliate in direct or indirect ways by causing work slowdowns, property damage, by making deliberate mistakes, backbiting, through doing things that are subtly irritating, or by becoming self-destructive in an attempt to make the aggressor feel guilty.

People who are frequently nonassertive and who become aggressive only sporadically may feel immediate guilt, shame, and embarrassment after their aggression. Usually these bad feelings just make the individuals resolve to say nothing in the future because they feel they easily "get out of control" when they finally do express themselves. Unfortunately, this resolution does not solve the problem and merely sets in motion the vicious cycle of long periods of nonassertion which eventually explode in aggressive behavior.

People who are the target of aggression may experience various negative effects such as lowered morale in the family or a loss of initiative and creativity at work. The children of aggressive parents may suffer in many different ways. A son of an aggressive father who sees the most important male model in his life hurt other people, may feel ambivalent about his own masculinity, believing that "being a man" means hurting other people. An aggressive mother may cause a son to be suspicious, fearful, or hostile towards women. Similarly, the daughter of an aggressive mother may become alienated from herself as she tries to deny those parts of herself which are like her mother. When the father is aggressive, the daughter may avoid or fear men, may develop a subservient, masochistic relationship with other men, or may become hostile and rebellious towards men.

SUMMARY

Assertion involves standing up for personal rights and expressing thoughts, feelings, and beliefs in direct, honest, and appropriate ways which respect the rights of other people. In contrast, aggression involves self-expression which is characterized by violating others' rights and demeaning others in an attempt to achieve one's own objectives. Nonassertion involves behavior which violates one's own self by failing to express honest feelings or thoughts. It may also involve diffident, overly apologetic, or effacing expression of personal rights and preferences.

It is important that assertive skills be used responsibly, that is, used in ways which treat others fairly and help facilitate others becoming more assertive.

Losing others' approval is a major fear which prompts many individuals to act nonassertively. For those who are frequently aggressive, a typical fear concerns their losing control and power over other people. A major reason for acting assertively rather than unassertively is that assertion increases one's own sense of self-respect and personal control.

References

1. Jakubowski, P. (1977). Assertive behavior and clinical problems of women. In E. Rawlings & D. Carter (Eds.), *Psychotherapy for women: Treatment towards equality.* Springfield, IL: Charles C. Thomas.
2. Mehrabian, A. (1972). *Nonverbal communication.* Chicago: Aldine/Atherton.
3. Eisler, R. M., Miller, P. M., & Hersen, M. (1973). Components of assertive behavior. *Journal of Clinical Psychology, 29,* 295–299.
4. Galassi, J. P., Galassi, M. D., & Litz, M. C. (1974). Assertive training in groups using video feedback. *Journal of Counseling Psychology, 21,* 390–394.
5. Jakubowski-Spector, P. (1973). Facilitating the growth of women through assertive training. *The Counseling Psychologist, 4,* 75–86.
6. Rimm, D. C., & Masters, J. C. (1974). *Behavior therapy: Techniques and empirical findings.* New York: Academic Press.
7. Jakubowski, P. (1977). Self-assertion training procedures for women. In E. Rawlings & D. Carter (Eds.), *Psychotherapy for women: Treatment towards equality.* Springfield, IL: Charles C. Thomas.
8. Gordon, T. (1970). *Parent effectiveness training.* New York: Peter H. Wyden.
9. Salter, A. (1949). *Conditioned reflex therapy.* New York: Farrar, Straus & Giroux.
10. James, M., & Jongeward, D. (1971). *Born to win.* Reading, MA: Addison-Wesley.

To Apply This Reading to Yourself

1. *Describe a kind of situation in which you are typically nonassertive or aggressive but in which* basic assertion, *as Lange and Jakubowski define it, might be preferable. Then indicate why you haven't been assertive in this situation and how you might be.*
2. *Describe a kind of situation in which you have been typically nonassertive or aggressive but in which* empathic assertion, *as Lange and Jakubowski define it, might be preferable. Then indicate why you haven't been assertive in this situation and how you might be.*
3. *Describe a kind of situation in which you are typically nonassertive or aggressive but in which* escalating assertion or confrontive assertion or I-language assertion, *as Lange and Jakubowski describe them, might be preferable. Then indicate why you haven't been assertive in this situation and how you might be.*
4. *Describe a recent difficult situation in which you were properly assertive. Indicate why you were assertive and the consequences of this assertiveness.*
5. *Discuss the reasons for and the consequences of any recent nonassertive behavior you have exhibited.*
6. *Discuss the reasons for and the consequences of any recent aggressive behavior you have exhibited.*

Reaching Out

*Robert E. Alberti
and Michael L. Emmons*

We have found that expressing *positive, caring* feelings is often more difficult for non-assertive and aggressive persons (and for many otherwise assertive persons) than "standing up" behavior. Particularly for adults, positive expressions are often inhibited. Embarrassment, fear of rejection or ridicule, the "superiority of reason over emotion" are all excuses given to explain the inhibition of spontaneous expressions of warmth, caring, and love.

Freedom of positive expression has not been encouraged in our culture. Polite restraint is the accepted order of things. Nevertheless, the new lifestyles and youth subcultures, which have been most obvious among potent forces for change, encourage greater spontaneity. We heartily endorse greater openness in the communication of genuine positive feeling toward other persons.

The difficulty some persons have in saying "thank you" is at once amazing and very sad. Wayne, an acquaintance of ours who heads a multi-million-dollar giant organization, is noted for almost never expressing appreciation to the people who work for him. A job well done is seldom rewarded in any overt manner. Wayne is evidently afraid to act in a warm positive fashion—perhaps because he might appear "soft," or maybe because others might come to *expect* some sort of praise for their efforts. Needless to say, morale in the organization is not particularly high.

Why are we so afraid of caring? What makes it so difficult for me to say to you I really enjoy your friendship? Why is reaching out to another person—even to say "hello"—such an onerous chore?

We seem to have a really mixed-up view of "love" in Western culture. It gets all tangled up with sex and becomes a source of embarrassment, fear, and taboo. If somehow another person's company is genuinely satisfying, enjoyable, or exciting, society suggests that we'd better look for something wrong, be careful, hold back. "Don't take a risk, you might get hurt."

Surely it is possible to genuinely care for—love—another person without "romantic" involvement! What a narrow view of love that allows only for romantic/sexual relationships! An important public official in California has been the object of scorn and ridicule for signing letters to other public officers with the closing "Love, . . . " How sad for us that we cannot tolerate the concept of love between persons outside of the romantic context.

SAY IT OUT LOUD!

Expressing your positive feelings for another person is a highly assertive act. And, as with other assertions we have noted, the act itself—that is, *doing it*—is more important by far than the words you use or your own style of communication. This is even more true for expressions of caring. Nothing represents a more personal, individual expression than that which says, "You mean a great deal to me at this moment."

Consider some ways of communicating that message:

A warm, firm, and extended handshake. (Ever notice the duration and feeling of a "brotherhood" hand clasp—e.g., fraternity members?)

A hug, the squeeze of an arm, an arm around the shoulders, an affectionate pat on the back, the squeeze of a hand held affectionately.

"Thank you."

"You're great!"

"I really understand what you mean."

A warm smile.

Extended eye contact.

"I'm here."

A gift of love (made by the giver, or uniquely special to the recipient, etc.).

"I believe you."

"I trust you." (Better yet, an *act* of trust.)

"I love you."

"I believe in you."

"I'm glad to see you."
"I've been thinking of you."
"You've been on my mind."

Probably none of these messages is a new thought to you. Yet you may find it difficult to allow yourself to say or do them. It is too easy to be hung up on embarrassment, or to assume: "She knows how I feel," or "He doesn't care to hear that." But *who* doesn't care to hear that? All of us need to know we are cared about and admired and needed. If those around us are *too* subtle in the expressions of positive regard, we can too easily begin to doubt, and perhaps look elsewhere for what the Transactional Analysis people call our "strokes"—positive feedback from others.

We recently asked a group of university students to identify for us some of the experiences which were rewarding for them—what made each of them feel especially good. Here are some of their favorite "strokes" (notice how many involve someone else expressing a caring thought!):

Praise	Request to repeat a
Payoff	job previously
Assurance	done
Encouragement	Making new friends
Independence	Positive comment
Security	Touch
Recognition	Satisfaction
Appreciation	Approval
Affection	Reward
Friendliness	Jobs completed
Achievement	Recognition when
Getting an *A* on an	speaking
exam	Greeting someone
Having someone say	else
"hello"	Singing
Receiving a compli-	Keeping my plants
ment	alive
Giving a compli-	Good grades
ment	Compliments from
Having a friend	the opposite sex
Helping others	Personal satisfac-
Laughter	tion with myself
Spoken affirmation	My boyfriend's/girl-
Implementation of	friend's actions of
ideas	love toward me
Expressed interest of	Acceptance of an
others	invitation

Despite the obvious importance to each of us of *hearing* positive feedback from others, so many people who enter therapy are found to be unhappy precisely because they lack such response from someone who cares.

In very intimate relationships, between lovers for example, it is often assumed that each partner "knows" the feelings of the other. Such assumptions often lead to the marriage counselor's office, with complaints such as, "I never know how he feels"; "She never tells me she loves me"; "We just don't communicate any more." Frequently it is necessary only to reestablish a communication pattern in which each partner is expressing *overtly* his/her feelings—particularly those of caring. The expression of caring is seldom a panacea for all the ills of an ailing marriage, but can shore up the foundation by helping each partner to remember what was good about the relationship in the first place!

Ellen and Doug are a good example—maybe we should say a *bad* example—of a couple who built their relationship primarily upon assumptions. During the courtship and honeymoon days, of course, each wanted to make a good impression on the other. Their style was to say very little, or to be very positive and enthusiastic about *anything* suggested by the other. The result was a double facade—neither knew what the partner was *really* thinking or feeling.

Doug had been raised in a family where few emotions were displayed. Ellen, on the other hand, was fairly insecure and needed constant reassurance of Doug's caring for her. When he failed to tell her of his love—which was common, since he had never learned such expressiveness—she felt he did *not* love her. Doug, for his part, resented Ellen's demands of attention. Love can be a problem, even for those who are experiencing it!

GOOD SHOW!

Compliments are a frequent source of discomfort for non-assertive and aggressive persons. To offer to someone else kind words about him/herself as a person or about something done for you may be a difficult thing for you. Again, we encourage *practice* of that which causes you some anxiety.

Go out of your way to praise others—not dishonestly or insincerely, but whenever a genuine opportunity presents itself. Don't concern yourself with waiting for the "right words" either. Your thoughtfulness—the honest expression of what you are feeling—will convey itself with almost any vehicle *if you act!* Try simply, "I like what you did," or "Neat!" or a big smile.

Accepting compliments—to hear someone else direct a very positive statement to you, or about you to a third person—is perhaps an even more challenging task, particularly difficult if you are not feeling good about yourself. Nevertheless, it is an assertive act—a mutually enhancing response—to accept praise from another person.

Consider first that you really have no right to deny that person his/her perception of you. If you say, "Oh, you just caught me on a good day!" or "It wasn't anything special," or "It was an accident that it turned out well," you have, in effect, told the complimenter that she/he has poor judgment, that she/he *is wrong.* That person, too, has a right to feelings, and if he/she is positive toward you, do him/her—and yourself—the service of accepting.

We are not suggesting that you go about praising yourself, or accepting credit for achievements which are not your own. We do feel, however, that when another person sincerely wishes to convey a positive comment about you, you allow the expression of that feeling without rejection or qualification. Try saying at the least, "It's hard for me to accept that, but thank you"; or better yet simply, "That feels good," or "I like to hear that."

If you can begin to give and receive genuine affection for other persons, if you can allow yourself to hear positive things about you, if you can share your own joy with another, and glow with one who is joyous, you will experience a quality of life which makes all other assertive acts pale by comparison.

And the paradox is, all you have to do to achieve *this* is to relax and let it happen!

REACHING OUT

At a large gathering of people, you find no familiar faces. Suddenly a stranger comes up to you and begins a conversation, relieving your anxiety and "lost" feeling.

Two days after you move into a new neighborhood, the couple next door appear at your house with a loaf of freshly baked bread and a pot of coffee.

As you look in vain for a street sign in a foreign land, a native approaches you and says: "May I help you find your way?"

Such thoughtful acts can produce a warm feeling for the person who was assertive enough to reach out. We often hesitate to initiate contact in these ways, for much of the same reason we fail to assert ourselves in other circumstances—we are afraid of being rejected. Perhaps, you may say to yourself, that stranger at the party is looking for someone in particular, and I would just get in the way. So you both remain alone.

The new neighbors, you and your spouse decide, would rather become acquainted "gradually"—"when we meet by accident while putting out the garbage cans." As a result of your hesitation, they see the community as distant and not very friendly.

And the foreign visitor returns home convinced that people in this country are indeed aloof and do not help travelers from other lands.

Taking the initiative in these and similar situations is a difficult assertive act, one that requires both a degree of concern for the other person and some courage on your own. Yet, when you reach a point at which you are able to be the initiator of conversation, the one who does reach out to others, you are at a high level of assertiveness.

We ask members of our assertive behavior groups to perform several acts requiring initiative. It is strange how at once easy and difficult it is to begin a conversation with a stranger. How easy, for example, to approach someone who is sitting on a bus, plane, or in a theater, and ask, "Is this seat vacant?" Yet you may not recognize that having asked the question *you have started a conversation!* The ice is broken, the barrier crossed, and one need merely keep the ball rolling at that point ("Where are you headed?" "Where is your home?" "How long have you been waiting?" "My name is Joe Doe/Mary Roe.").

Yet we make these circumstances difficult by *assuming*. (She doesn't want to talk to me. I don't have anything to say. He'll tell me to go to hell. My voice will sound funny. An earthquake will swallow us both up if I dare speak.) Such assumptions are almost never valid, but they can be checked out merely by asking! Don't depend on reading the other person's mind. Find out for yourself by taking the risk and reaching out! It's another important way to care about yourself and others.

To Apply This Reading to Yourself

1. *Are you satisfied with the way you reach out and express your positive, caring feelings toward others? Why or why not?*
2. *Are you satisfied with the ways others (especially significant others) reach out and express their positive, caring feelings toward you? Why or why not?*
3. *Is your "stroke economy" (signs of recognition, approval, and caring) flourishing (lots of incoming and outgoing strokes), languishing (few strokes either way), in deficit (more going out than coming in), or in surplus (more coming in than going out)? Discuss the state of your "stroke economy" as it has appeared in the past few weeks or month.*
4. *Discuss your ability to express and receive love. Or practice this ability and record your experience.*
5. *Discuss your ability to express and receive compliments. Or practice this ability and record your experience.*
6. *Discuss your ability to initiate contact with strangers. Or practice this ability and record your experience.*

Sexuality

Amoebas at the start
 Were not complex;
They tore themselves apart
 And started Sex.
                        —Arthur Guiterman

Sex as fun
Sex as play
Sex as duty
Sex as proof
Sex as deceit
Sex as reward
Sex as release
Sex as revenge
Sex as pleasure
Sex as rebellion
Sex as affection
Sex as adventure
Sex as livelihood
Sex as aggression
Sex as abasement
Sex as acceptance
Sex as dominance
Sex as submission
Sex as experiment
Sex as procreation
Sex as punishment
Sex as togetherness
Sex as achievement
Sex as transcendence
—after J. L. Mafetti and E. M. Eidlitz

There are many remarkable things about sex. First, there are its many possibilities for pleasure and renewal. Sex can be great, and "great sex," writes Alexandra Penney (in her book *Great Sex*), "is *intense, passionate, magical*" (her italics, but I agree).

To be fair, sex also has possibilities for fear, frustration, and boredom. Sir Thomas Beecham once wrote, "No woman is worth the loss of a night's sleep." On this side of the Atlantic, great sex is apparently not rampant either; for example, "sexperts" William Masters and Virginia Johnson have estimated that half of the marriages in this country are currently or imminently "sexually dysfunctional."

A third remarkable thing about sex is the range of importance attached to it. Shere Hite, in her nationwide study of female sexuality, found some women who never desired sex and others who wanted it more than once a day. Alfred Kinsey discovered among his 5,000 male subjects a quite healthy man who had had only 1 ejaculation in 30 years and another who in the same period had averaged 30 per week! A national survey of male sexuality by Anthony Pietropinto and Jacqueline Simenauer revealed that 6 out of 10 men felt that sex was a "very important" pleasure, but only 2 out of 10 felt it was the "most important" pleasure. (One man, a flier, put sex second to his job because, as he said, "I can spend a hell of a lot more of my time flying than I can screwing.")

Fourth, it is remarkable how absolutely simple sex can be and how amazingly complex. At the simple end are the first innocent rubbings of the young child and also the more experienced rubbings of a young woman who reported: "When I desire erotic excitement, nothing comes close to masturbation—especially with a vibrator. I know how to trigger orgasm after orgasm." At the complex end, sex can become linked with love or hate, aggression or abasement, dominance or submission, affiliation, achievement, or a number of other motives. Sol Gordon put it well when he said that an adolescent boy might not have orgasm until several days after his first coitus—not until he announced it to his buddies.

Still, considering the many motives with which sex becomes linked and the many purposes that sex serves, it's remarkable how many things that we take to bed with us—and how many things that we look for in bed. Here's the way one woman described her feelings to interviewer Wendy Sanford: "Sometimes I make love to get care and cuddling. Sometimes I am so absorbed in the sensations of touch and taste and smell and sight and sound that I feel I've returned to that childhood time when feeling good was all that mattered. Sometimes we tumble and tease. Sometimes sex is spiritual—High Mass could not be more sacred. Sometimes I make love to get away from the tightness and seriousness in myself. Sometimes I want to come and feel the ripples of orgasm through my body. Sometimes tears mix with juices mix with sweat, and I am one with another. Sometimes through sex I unite with the stream of love that flows among us all." And she added to sum it up: "Sex can be most anything and everything for me. How good that feels!"

Let's consider one more remarkable fact before this introduction ends. It's remarkable how sex can change for us over our life cycle.

There are seasons to our sexuality. We may have less animated sex as we move along in years, but not necessarily less great sex. One woman put this well as she described to Sanford her marital relationship: "We have been married for fifteen years. For several years we were passionate lovers. There was a lot of romance in our lives. Now there is less romance and very deep love and friendship. Sex is no longer the most important thing in our lives. We have sex less frequently and yet our lovemaking feels good in different ways than in those early years. We feel very warm, intimate and deeply trusting of each other."

BECOMING SEXUAL

How do we become sexual adults? An answer to this question can be found in the first reading, written by Lorna and Philip Sarrel, who are a social worker and a gynecologist, respectively. Drawing upon their wide clinical experience—much of it at a university clinic—they discuss ten developmental "tasks" that must be dealt with on the way to maturity. As they show, the process of "sexual unfolding" is not just one of excitement and pleasure; there is also considerable confusion, anxiety, and pain.

How can we put sex into perspective? The answer given in the second selection, by Sol Gordon (a distinguished clinical psychologist and sex educator) and Craig Snyder (a prominent marriage–family–sex counselor), is to downrate sex and to divest it of the false assumptions, myths, and hang-ups with which it abounds. On their list of the 10 most important characteristics of a relationship, sex is only number 9. They set forth their ideas concerning sexual conduct, which they admit are biased but only "toward common sense and respect for individual differences." Gordon and Snyder are aware that certain of their ideas will not coincide with those of their readers but relish bringing a bit of debate to this controversial area.

BECOMING CAUTIOUS

How can we fulfill ourselves sexually in this sexually hazardous age? In the last reading, health-nurse specialist Linda Morphis charts a safe passage through the sexual shoals. She shows the reader how to prevent unwanted pregnancy and sexual disease and how to minimize the risk of sexual exploitation. Wishing won't make it so; responsible effort is required. She writes, "Only through awareness, understanding, and responsible sexual behavior can you establish your sexual self-confidence and experience the joy of sex."

To Explore Your Own Sex Attitudes and Behavior

1. *Sex words.* Sex words can provoke anxiety, and we may be surprisingly unable to define, spell, or pronounce them or use them

matter-of-factly in everyday conversations. See whether this is so for the members of your class. Form small groups, and sit in a circle. Have someone begin by picking a word from the following list, and saying it, face-to-face, to the person on her or his left. This second person repeats the process. Keep the word going until there is a complete round in which everyone has said the word correctly and matter-of-factly. Then start another word around. *Note:* The point is not to try to say the word in a matter-of-fact way, but to keep saying it until it becomes matter-of-fact. Take a break at any time to discuss the feelings and reactions of the group members.

vagina	scrotum	menstruation
penis	testicles	erection
vulva	sexual intercourse	orgasm
clitoris	coitus	cunnilingus
nipple	masturbation	fellatio

2. *Sex terms.* Someone prepares a number of packs of cards, each card with a sex term on one side and its definition on the other. Form small groups and have the members of each sit in a circle. In the center of the circle display the cards, term sides up and definition sides down. Someone volunteers to define one term and others in the group may add or modify the volunteer's definition. When this is done, the volunteer turns over the card, reads the given definition, and leads any further discussion there may be concerning the term. Then go on to the next volunteer and card and continue as before.

3. *Sex attitudes.* Select a sex-related practice or behavior toward which you have a strong and definite attitude, then prepare a statement giving your attitude and your reasons for it. As an option, these statements might be shared in the larger group, in small groups, or in dyads. In making your selection of a practice or behavior to write about, you might consider the following: abortion, anal sex, birth control, bisexuality, cohabitation, extramarital sex, homosexuality, masturbation, nudity, oral sex, pornography, premarital sex, promiscuity, prostitution, sex education, and sex without love.

4. *Sex problems.* Consider the sex problems, or difficulties, or worries that you have now, have had in the past, or anticipate in the future. Write one of these problems on a 3×5 card or slip of paper without identifying yourself in any way, and put this into a box to be provided for this purpose. Then the instructor or a designated person or panel selects and reads some of the problems, commenting on them and/or leading a discussion concerning them. As an alternative, form small groups; each member can be given one problem at random from the box, which he or she can read and seek discussion on in the group.

5. *Sex fantasies.* Most of us have sexual fantasies, although we seldom reveal them to others. These fantasies may be satisfying in themselves, or they may be used to create, augment, or maintain

excitement during masturbation or intercourse. In our fantasies, we may indulge in sex behavior that in real life would be impossible or improbable, or even harmful or repugnant. Write one of your sex fantasies on a 3 × 5 card or slip of paper without identifying yourself in any way, and deposit this into a box to be provided for this purpose. Then the instructor or designated person or panel selects and reads some of these fantasies, commenting on them and/or leading a discussion on them. As an alternative, form small groups, and give each member one fantasy at random from the box, which he or she can read and seek discussion on in the group.

6. *Sex information (family planning).* Invite a qualified counselor to talk to your group about contraceptive methods and family planning. Afterward, share your reactions with each other.

7. *Sex information (STDs and sexual dysfunctions).* Invite a qualified person (possibly someone from your student health service) to talk to your group about sexually transmitted diseases (STDs), which have reached epidemic proportions in this country and raised considerable concern. As an alternative, have a representative of the Life Foundation or some other group working with AIDS talk to your group, or invite a qualified sex therapist to discuss sexual dysfunctions and therapy programs.

8. *Sex understanding.* Invite a representative from an organization with a particular sexual orientation or advocacy to your group for an exchange of viewpoints and insights. For example, to discuss homosexuality, invite representatives of gay and lesbian groups, or to discuss pornography, invite representatives from anti-pornography and civil-libertarian groups. Afterward, share your reactions with each other.

9. *Sex counsel.* Consider some sex advice that you were given. Or consider some sex advice that you have read, perhaps in a newspaper column or book. As you think back on this advice, does it seem appropriate and wise? Why or why not? If you needed advice or assistance concerning a sexual problem, would you seek help? If so, from whom? Write your answers to these questions, and, as an option, share them in the larger group, in small groups, or dyads.

10. *Sex education.* There are few areas that touch our life as much as sex, and few that are as neglected or as poorly taught in schools, colleges, and the home. Herant Katchadourian, an authority in this area, points out that sex has not generally been considered a fit topic for either academic or familial pursuit. He notes, "Opposition to sex education is rarely absolute; some recognition is given to the need for instruction, while controversy centers upon the question of where, when, and by whom." Consider your own sex education. Where, when, and by whom did it occur? How adequate was it? And, based on your experience, what kind of sex education, if any, would you recommend? Write your answers to these questions, and, as an option, discuss them in the larger group, in small groups, or in dyads.

To Read Further

Comfort, A. (1991). *The joy of sex: The gourmet guide to lovemaking in the '90s*. New York: Crown.

Gordon, S., & Snyder, C. W. (1989). *Personal issues in human sexuality: A guidebook for sexual health* (2nd ed.). Boston: Allyn and Bacon. (paperback)

Masters, W. H., Johnson, V. E., & Kolodny, R. C. (1986). *Masters and Johnson on sex and human loving*. Boston: Little, Brown.

Olds, S. W. (1985). *The eternal garden: Seasons of our sexuality*. New York: Times.

Reinisch, J. M., with Beasley, R. (1990). *The Kinsey Institute new report on sex: What you must know to be sexually literate*. New York: St. Martin's Press.

Sarrel, L. J., & Sarrel, P. M. (1984). *Sexual turning points: The seven stages of adult sexuality*. New York: Macmillan.

Sexual Unfolding—Ten Steps toward Adult Sexuality

Lorna J. Sarrel and
Philip M. Sarrel

We often begin a sexuality discussion group by asking the participants to think back to their own childhood and adolescent experiences with sex; how they learned about sex and how they felt about it. After allowing for a few minutes of silent recollecting, we say to the group, "Now that you've had a chance to think about your own experiences, ask yourselves, 'What would I want my kids to experience?' "

This is how we'd like you to read this article—backward first, into your own memories, and then forward, thinking how you can use what you read to help your teenage sons and daughters have a smoother, less anxious and confused transition into adult sexuality than you had.

Did you notice that we immediately assume that your memories of adolescent sexual learning aren't just memories of excitement and pleasure but include memories of confusion and pain? Because that is what most—not all, but most—people tell us; and not just the patients who come to us with sex problems, but the parents and teachers who attend discussion groups about sex education in the schools, the college and medical students we teach, and the professionals we train.

Certain developmental "tasks" must be tackled, questions answered, and life experiences assimilated if one is to function as a sexual adult. Working with students over a span of four or more years, the nature of this process of becoming a sexual adult became clear to us. As a way of understanding and communicating, we have divided sexual unfolding into ten steps or categories. We'll tell you what they are and then discuss each one in turn.

First, a few definitions:

puberty. The period of biological change in which the transition from boy to man and from girl to woman occurs.

pubarche. The beginning of puberty.

menarche. The time of the first menstrual flow.

semenarche. The time of the first seminal emission.

sexual unfolding. This is a term coined by us that refers to the process, set in motion by puberty, of learning whom you will become as an adult sexual being.

1. ADAPTING TO THE BODILY CHANGES OF PUBERTY

When our daughter was ten, she needed a ladies' size 8 shoe. This was a problem. Little-girl shoes aren't made in that size, and women's shoes look ridiculous on a ten-year-old. She was not unusually tall or physically precocious. What had happened to her happens to many girls at that age: Their hands and feet have a growth spurt. It is one of the earliest physical changes of puberty, and it usually happens to girls a year or more before it happens to boys.

Even this innocuous event has sexual implications. For girls, it ushers in an awkward few years when they are neither here nor there; they are *preteen*. The discrepancy between the earlier-growing girls and their littler boy friends makes some girls feel "unfeminine" and some boys feel inferior and intimidated.

Boys experience the changes of puberty at widely differing ages. Some boys have gone through all the stages—hand and foot growth, skeletal and muscle-mass growth, hair development, penile and testicular development, and ejaculation and voice change—before others have even begun. Thus some seventh graders are starting to shave when some of their classmates have not even entered the earliest stages of puberty.

Joe S., a thirty-three year old man who consulted us, didn't regard his physical self in any positive way whatsoever. Most important, he always felt he had a small penis, and when he developed an erection, it always curved slightly to one side until fully erect. He felt the size and curvature of his penis were abnormal.

It turned out that Joe's feelings of inadequacy had been established around the time of puberty. "What did you look like then?" we asked him. He had been a little on the chubby side, and at times his penis had seemed so small, he could hardly see it. He had also been very embarrassed about having some breast enlargement—which occurs temporarily in about 75 percent of boys at puberty and is usually normal. He remembers looking like a little boy until his late teens, when he finally reached his present height, hair developed on his chest, and the breasts seemed to disappear. Although he then realized his penis wasn't terribly small, he still felt it was smaller than other men's, and he did connect it to his former wife's nonorgasmic response. "If I were bigger, maybe she would have had orgasms."

Many men have feelings similar to Joe's, which are rooted in their feelings about their bodies during adolescence. If a boy doesn't know, for example, that some breast enlargement is normal, imagine the psychological impact of such a phenomenon just when a boy is feeling a strong need to be different from girls and to be like other boys, and social roles are starting to demand "masculinity."

All boys develop a pubic fat pad. This pad of tissue surrounding the base of the penis has the effect of making the penile shaft appear smaller, especially if one is looking down at it. If the penis is observed in a mirror or from the side, it doesn't appear as small as when viewed from above.

Another source of misunderstanding about penis size stems from the fact that boys don't often have an opportunity to see other boys' erect penises. In the nonerect condition, there can be major differences in penile length, but as Masters and Johnson have found, when fully erect, there isn't much difference. Still, boys and men learn about themselves, vis-à-vis others, in the nonerect state.

Another factor in judging comparative penis size is that, in showers or locker rooms, where males are naked together, it is not unusual for some to experience a low level of sexual arousal, with accompanying partial engorgement of the penis. A full erection does not usually develop, but there can be an increase in the size of a boy's or young man's penis compared with those of others who do not experience the scene as sexually stimulating. Since about 40 percent of boys have adolescent homosexual experiences, size comparisons at such times may also be a source of later insecurities about having a small penis. Whatever their origins, feelings about penis size are often an important part of a man's image of his sexuality.

Eric Berne, the father of transactional analysis, wrote in *Sex in Human Loving* a chapter entitled "Sex is Wet." Wetness introduces both boys and girls to their own "adult" sexuality: boys through ejaculation (more about that in a moment), girls *not* through menstrual blood, as most people would think, but through vaginal discharge. One or even two years before menarche (the onset of menses), as the level of circulating estrogen increases, the vaginal walls change and normal vaginal secretion is produced rather copiously, sometimes more copiously than it will ever again be in that young woman's lifetime. Since the average age of menarche in the United States is twelve and a half, the average girl will be discharging white or clear vaginal fluid from the age of ten, and many will begin at eight or nine. This is one of the best-kept secrets about puberty. The average pediatrician is only dimly aware of it, if at all. Hardly any eight-year-old girls are taught about it.

Why is it important? Often it's not. The girl either accepts the new wetness in her underpants or she asks her mother, who provides a vague but reassuring response. Sometimes, however, it is confusing, repulsive, or frightening. Women recollecting the experience may say, "I thought I must have had some kind of infection and I kept waiting for it to get worse or better," or, "I thought I'd made it happen from touching myself," or, "The only white discharge I'd ever heard of was semen, so I assumed I must have a penis inside me and they'd eventually find out I was a freak—a boy/girl." One patient of ours was taken to a doctor at age ten or eleven because her mother thought the girl had vaginitis (a vaginal infection). The examination by her mother's gynecologist was embarrassing and scary. The doctor prescribed some medication to be inserted into the vagina, but the girl couldn't bring herself to stick anything inside herself, so the mother inserted the medication. Her memory focuses on the messiness. To this day, she is repulsed by her own vaginal secretions and by seminal fluid leaking out after intercourse.

This case may sound extreme, but it isn't an unusual story. The point of the story, and the point of learning about vaginal discharge, is to normalize it—to help women recall their experiences and to understand both that the discharge is normal and that an early negative reaction is typical. It is also important to stress the need for girls to be taught about their bodies and to know that curiosity about one's own sexuality is healthy. If we really want to encourage a girl to feel good about her awakening sexuality, perhaps we should tell her that this discharge is important and valuable because later on in life, when she has sexual intercourse, her wetness will help make it more pleasurable.

Not too long after the vaginal discharge begins, breasts start to grow. No one has captured the emotional agony of being a late developer, or the flattest girl in the eighth grade, better than Nora Ephron in her personal memoir "A few words about breasts."[1] Breasts, apparently, have an enduring symbolic value in our society. They are equated with femininity, attractiveness, sexiness. Girls lacking in breast tissue fear they will lack the associated attributes.

Girls with larger-than-average breasts can also suffer embarrassment, but of a different kind. "In high school, I always wore big sweaters or layers of clothing to hide my big breasts. They seemed to call attention—not to me as a person, but to my sexuality. I wasn't ready to be seen as sexual." Boys often read large breasts as a sign of sexual readiness, and some women tell us they actually got the reputation of being "fast" simply on the basis of their anatomy.

One of our patients was particularly bitter about always being a sex object. "From the time I was eleven and, it seemed overnight, developed huge tits, men would whistle and comment; boys wanted to date me and get their hands on me. I got so I hated my breasts and I hated men. I really didn't trust guys. They just wanted to be seen out with the biggest pair in the school. I think to this day I don't really trust men, and I know I don't like my body."

1. This memoir appears on pages 44–48 of this book.

Breast growth alerts the world that a girl is approaching menarche. It's the eleventh hour, but still not too late to tell her about menstruation. "But don't all girls today know about that by fourth grade?" people ask. Shockingly, the answer is no. A study sponsored by Tampax in the early 1980s found that one-third of the girls in America didn't know what was happening to them when they got their first period.

Retrospectively, the first period stands out as a developmental marker. In spite of the other signs of transformation into a woman, menstruation is still *the* event. Girls who experience it early feel pushed into adulthood and are shy about it. Girls who experience it later than their friends feel left out. Sociological studies indicate that girls whose developmental timetable is about average are more self-confident and popular. As women recall these years, no one ever seems to feel that she was this happy average. There was always something not quite right. Where have all the happy average developing girls disappeared to?

Of the women college students we surveyed, almost 80 percent were using tampons one year after menarche, 90 percent by two years after. Inserting a tampon is usually a girl's first experience with vaginal penetration. It is an important moment, because her feelings about vaginal penetration will color her sexual experiences for the rest of her life.

There appears to be a natural reluctance to let something penetrate our body boundaries and enter our interior space. We cross these boundaries regularly when we eat, less regularly when we clean our ears or stick a finger up a nostril. Experiences with needles or with having a doctor take a throat culture usually reinforce the reluctance. But in order to have intercourse, the female has to allow a fairly large object to penetrate inside her, and using tampons can be an excellent psychological preparation for that experience—that is, if there is no difficulty using the tampons. The women we counsel who, as adults, have a fear of vaginal penetration and whose vaginal muscles tense often have tales to tell of troubles using tampons. Not infrequently, they have never been able to insert one.

Most girls can learn to use tampons, although it may require coaching from outside the bathroom door by a mother, sister, or two or three best friends. Those who can't learn are usually very scared, and so their muscles tense and make the opening small; or they may have a physical problem, such as a strand of hymenal tissue partially blocking the way.

It is ironic—and mildly disturbing—to realize that the girl's first period (menarche) is the biological counterpart of first ejaculation (semenarche) in the boy. We have coined the term *semenarche* because there is no word for first ejaculation. Both menarche and semenarche are the result of maturation in the central nervous system, the hypothalamus (part of the brain), and the pituitary gland, which stimulates gonadal function and sex hormone production. Some women become irritated when they hear this analogy because they associate menstruation with pain and nuisance, while they imagine first ejaculation to be a pleasurable experience. They think it's unfair. It may be cold comfort, but the fact is that first ejaculation is not an entirely pleasurable experience for about 50 percent of boys. It occurs, typically, between age twelve and age fifteen. Our data show that only 31 percent of the boys knew exactly what was happening to them. A full 42 percent say that the experience left them confused, embarrassed, or fearful, and not solely with a feeling of pleasure.

Menarche is not usually a totally private event. Girls are likely to tell their mothers and/or close friends. Boys, on the other hand, are intensely private about semenarche. According to our findings, only 12 percent tell another living soul. We know from a study of sexual learning done a few years ago in Cleveland that 99 out of 100 parents never discuss ejaculation or wet dreams with their sons.

As with menarche, semenarche is a symbolic milestone, *the* turning point in adolescent male sexuality. Kinsey, whose researchers had personally interviewed 291 boys and young men, said the first ejaculation is the single most important psychosexual event of male adolescence. It sets a stamp upon the boy's feeling about ejaculation and about his sexuality. From Kinsey, we know that it almost always leads to a fairly regular pattern of masturbation and/or wet dreams within just a few months.

In a questionnaire study conducted by us, and in our clinical practice, 15 percent of men could not recall their semenarche. However, in the course of therapy, when psychological defenses were lowered and the men started to feel more comfortable with their sexuality, only about 3 percent could not recall the details of what had happened. Sometimes the story is of a mostly negative experience. "I thought I was having a heart attack"; "I thought I had wet the bed and couldn't control myself"; or, "I couldn't urinate afterward and was sure I had damaged myself"; or, "I was the youngest and the baby-sitter manipulated me. She knew what was happening, but I didn't. I was just scared"; "The game was to hit the cookie in the middle of a circle and to see who came fastest"; or, "I was in the bathtub and saw the sperm floating on the water. I thought, 'I'm too young to be a father.'"

Menarche and semenarche have this in common, then: Both mark a special moment in time when, biologically, we change from girl to woman and from boy to man; and both are complex psychosocial events, which may leave a permanent stamp on our sexuality. As for adequately preparing our children for this step in sexual unfolding, we have barely begun.

2. OVERCOMING GUILT, SHAME, FEAR, AND CHILDHOOD INHIBITIONS ABOUT SEX

In some societies, erotic feelings and overt sexual behavior are permitted and are expressed throughout childhood. By contrast, American children have a dozen or more years of learning during which, typically, sex is shrouded in shameful mists; hands are removed from genitals with outraged glares, and information is withheld or parceled out grudgingly. Perhaps one reason we need a prolonged adolescent-youth phase in our culture is to allow enough time to rid ourselves of all the negative messages we have received over the years concerning sex.

A large share of guilt and shame about sex comes from childhood learning about masturbation. In spite of direct threats or subtle injunctions, children do masturbate. In examining the sexual histories of adults, we hear how wide a range of experience this can be. Some people say they have always masturbated since their earliest, dim recollections of early childhood. This was often a casual sort of self-pleasuring and play, but tinged with a sense of the furtive and kept secret. Many men and women tell us they knew the word *masturbation* for a long time before they connected it with their own self-pleasuring. Others remember masturbating until they were discovered and scolded or until they stopped for unknown reasons. Still others have no memory of masturbation.

At puberty there are hormonal, anatomical, and physiological changes—not to mention psychosocial changes—that affect masturbation behavior. As we have already stated, boys begin to ejaculate and are likely, soon afterward, to start a pattern of regular masturbation. In girls, the clitoris enlarges from its prepubertal size and may focus a girl's attention. Even with pubertal changes, though, not all adolescents masturbate. At the time they enter college, about five out of six males are masturbating. The freshman year apparently provides a strong impetus, so that half of those who had never masturbated before will begin to do so in that year. Eventually only one male in twenty does not masturbate.

In 1969 and the early 1970s, the data we collected on the sexual knowledge, attitudes, and behavior of women students showed that about one-third of them masturbated—a statistic that exactly agreed with the Kinsey findings for this age group. Starting in 1973, there was a sudden and steep rise in the number of women students who said they masturbated. To some degree, the change may simply have reflected a greater willingness to admit to masturbating, but there has undoubtedly been a marked change in young women's actual behavior. From 1976 on, the statistic has been fairly consistent, and now about 85 percent of college women say they are masturbating.

What role does masturbation play in a young person's sexual unfolding? The answer will obviously vary from one person to the next. It can be a very important, positive force when there is not a great deal of guilt or conflict. Masturbation can provide important lessons for each of us about our own sexuality. When we masturbate, we experience the physiological changes of sexual response and these become familiar. We learn what kinds of stimulation are pleasurable. At orgasm, we discover that we can let go and lose control without any terrible consequences. We learn to integrate fantasies with arousal from touching. All of this can be important preparation for sharing sex with another person.

Ironically, the liberation of masturbation from irrational fears and the modern attitude of acceptance have generated a new set of problems for some young men and women. They now feel that they should or must masturbate. A thirteen-year-old had this experience. His Boy-Scout troop heard a lecture on sex in which they were repeatedly reassured about the normality of boys masturbating. He had never masturbated and, in fact, the idea wasn't very appealing to him. He went home and talked to his father, who told him, "Of course, all boys do." Five years later, this boy came for help because he was unable to masturbate to the point of ejaculation. Most of his problem was simply his goal orientation. He was trying so hard to do the thing "all normal boys do" that he was anxious every time he stimulated himself. The anxiety interfered with his sex response. (This anxious self-observation is called *spectatoring*. It is a concept we will refer to often because it is a major factor in all sexual dysfunctions.)

Young (and not so young) women also come under some pressure to masturbate. There must be thousands of women across the United States who have read something in a magazine or book or seen something in a movie that encourages them to try masturbation. Unfortunately, they also get the idea that it should "work" immediately, or at least very quickly. When there isn't some readily observable result, these women feel they have failed, and their sexual self-image goes down a few notches. Of course, once they begin trying to force a "result," they are likely to become anxious self-observers and then erotic response is almost impossible. For many women, learning to experience sexual arousal and orgasm is a very slow process that can't be rushed. Patient but persistent exploration is the most helpful attitude. It is also important to understand that a person doesn't *have* to masturbate in order to be fully sexual.

We have stressed conflict about masturbation because that is an important, almost universal theme, but there are many other sources of guilt, shame, and inhibition young people struggle to outgrow. There are painful memories of being caught playing doctor or reading *Playboy*; of an adult grabbing a towel when you entered unexpectedly; of Daddy's anger the time you asked what *fuck* meant. There is the less specific but still powerful sense that sex was a burden for your mother and a painful, unapproachable topic. There is the lingering shame over the erection that happened in front of the class and the sound of everyone giggling. There are all the *don'ts* ever said to you: Don't let a boy touch you there. Don't get carried away. Don't let a boy use you. Don't be a tramp. Don't disappoint us. Don't get a girl pregnant.

Painful memories fade and, often, negative attitudes are replaced. Unfortunately, negative attitudes toward sex tend to persist even when new ideas have been accepted intellectually. A young woman patient who described herself as "emancipated from my sexually repressive background" found that her mother's injunctions about not letting anyone touch you "down there" would suddenly come into her mind when she was in bed with her boyfriend. She said it was like having her mother sitting on her shoulder. In the course of sex therapy, she had a dream in which "a little person, looking a lot like you, Lorna, was sitting on my shoulder, telling me it was okay." After this dream, she found that she could enjoy sex without nagging guilt. Her "emancipated" ideas had gotten through from her head to her gut.

Another woman was amazed to realize, during the course of therapy, that she had negative feelings about her genitals. She couldn't really relax when her husband touched her clitoris or stimulated her genitals with his mouth (cunnilingus). One day, as we talked about her early experiences with that part of her body, she remembered something she had forgotten—that as a child she always had two towels, one for her face and body and one for "down there." Remembering this helped her recognize the extent to which she had been conditioned to think of her genitals as a dirty and shameful part of her.

There are tremendous pressures on young people today to be sexually sophisticated and experienced—whether they want to be or not. Some plunge into sex with the idea that once they do it, all their fears and ambivalence will magically melt away. A few months later, they appear in our office in a state of confusion. The fears and ambivalence are worse than ever.

One sophomore woman, Susan, had been a virgin and, in fact, had never done more than kiss and hug in a car until she met a twenty-four-year-old medical student, Michael, and fell for him in a big way. He seemed to assume that there would be an immediate full sexual relationship between them. She thought she would seem hopelessly childish or hung up if she refused. In the one month they were together, she had her first experiences with mutual nudity, genital touching, intercourse, cunnilingus, and fellatio. Then Michael left for medical school two thousand miles away. She started to have difficulty concentrating. Images would flood her mind—images of an ax mutilating her breasts or a razor slashing at her genitals. When Susan first came to see Lorna about these disturbing images, she had no conscious guilt or conflict about what she had done sexually. It took several weeks for her to recognize that she had suppressed all the doubts and fears she had had about sex because she wanted so desperately to hold onto this man. I (Lorna) urged her to tell him her real feelings. She finally did, in a letter. He wrote back a sympathetic response. After this her images stopped appearing. When Michael came to visit for a week, they had a pact—nothing beyond kissing and hugging until she felt *really* comfortable with the next step. She needed to go slowly and to respect her own feelings—all her feelings, not just the ones she thought would please Michael.

Most young people are like Susan in their need to take things gradually. The slightly out-of-date courtship rituals of times past served the purpose of pacing: they called for one month at the good-night-kiss stage, one month of breast touching outside clothing, one month of bare-breast touching but nothing below the waist, and so on, until you reached "third base" or maybe "went all the way." You had a chance to become comfortable with each step before you went on to the next. You even had a chance to get to know each other! Is it the distortion of nostalgia that makes that sound so good?

About 80 percent of college students have intercourse before they graduate, and most have gone a long way toward putting their sexual inhibitions and fears behind them. It is very upsetting to see how years of psychological growth can be wiped out overnight by one trauma. The kinds of trauma we are talking about are a pregnancy scare, an unwanted pregnancy, an abortion, being raped, or getting a sexually transmitted disease. Any of these can be experienced as a punishment for sexual behavior, and the guilt, fear, and shame associated with sex can come flooding back.

The adolescents and young adults who have the greatest burden of shame and fear are those who have been the victims of incest or other sexual abuse. Whether or not they consciously recall the abuse, they often avoid sexual interaction or may engage in sex while emotionally dissociating from the experience. They usually need extensive and specialized therapy to resolve the trauma of abuse.

3. SHIFTING PRIMARY EMOTIONAL ATTACHMENT FROM PARENTS TO PEERS

This process can best be illustrated by a brief case history. A young woman named Sheila, who had transferred from a local community college to Yale University in her junior year, came to us at the Sex Counseling Service because she had been having recurrent nightmares about forgetting to take her birth-control pills. She had been taking the pill for about four months, ever since she had become serious about a fellow student named Gary, and she had never actually forgotten to take it. The nightmares were upsetting and led her to wonder what was going on inside her to cause them. Was it an omen?

This was not Sheila's first sexual relationship. She and a boyfriend had had intercourse for almost her entire sophomore year. She had taken birth-control pills then, too, but had never had the nightmares. She said she had never felt guilty about having intercourse. In fact, she had told her parents about it. This was not contrary to their values and had not been a source of conflict or tension.

The obvious question seemed to be: what was different now? What in Sheila's current life experience could account for the conflict symbolized by the dreams? There seemed to be two important things in her life that were new: (1) she was living away from home for the first time; and (2) she realized that this was the first time she was really in love.

Sheila was very close to both parents and to a younger sister, who was extremely dependent on her. Since she had fallen in love with Gary, about two months into her junior year, she had not been writing or calling her family as often as she thought she should. In addition, although her parents had met Gary, she couldn't bring herself to tell them how deeply she cared for him. She realized that she felt guilty about possibly loving Gary more than she loved her parents or her sister. Once Sheila recognized the source of her conflict, she was able to tell her parents about her feelings for Gary. She began to feel better about her relationship both with her family and with Gary. The nightmares gradually faded and then disappeared.

The primary emotional attachment being displaced is not necessarily an attachment to a parent. During his first year in college, Bill had intercourse for the first time without any difficulties. His girlfriend at that time was sexually experienced. She and Bill were good friends, but at all times it was understood that they were not "lovers." Toward the end of one year, they stopped having sex with each other and remained friendly classmates.

During the summer, Bill returned home. Home was a ghetto area of a large East Coast city. Bill spent the summer doing church work and renewing his close friendship with his parish priest. Bill's priest was a man who had recognized Bill's potential for academic excellence when Bill was a preteen. Throughout those years and his teenage years, the priest nurtured and encouraged Bill to reach for and attain goals in school and in sports. "Father" became a father substitute and was, indeed, the most important person in Bill's life. His influence was the major factor in Bill's going on to a prestigious academic career.

On returning to college for his sophomore year, Bill met Linda. They were in the same math class. Gradually over the course of the first semester, they became close friends and then began experimenting with sex together. Linda had no previous experience with intercourse. Bill's earlier experience faded and seemed to disappear. This was an entirely new kind of relationship for both of them. They were in love. After several months of petting and sleeping together, they decided to have intercourse. Linda came to see us with Bill. She was fitted with a diaphragm. Talking about their relationship indicated, to us at least, that they were a couple for whom sexual intercourse seemed very right and very appropriate.

We had not heard about Bill's relationship with his priest. Only when Bill was unable to have an erection did his feelings about abandoning his priest come to the surface. Fortunately, Bill and Linda had a return appointment scheduled with us. (Whenever we prescribe any contraceptive method, we ask our patients to return within a month to six weeks for a follow-up visit, just to let us know how they are doing and to see if there are any further questions.) They did not seem too upset by the failure to have intercourse. An appointment was made for Bill to speak alone with Phil.

At the appointment, Bill was able to talk about his relationship with his priest. The subject came up in response to my (Phil's) question: "Is there anyone else with whom you have a deep emotional attachment whom you have not told about your relationship with Linda?" Bill had told his mother. He hadn't said anything to his father, as he felt he really didn't have much of a relationship with him. He had avoided the subject with his priest.

After hearing more about Bill's priest and the man's values and concerns, I encouraged Bill to go home and tell the man about Linda. He did that, and the priest was fully accepting of Bill's falling in love and having a significant relationship with a female peer. "Father" was also accepting of Bill's sexuality—somewhat to Bill's amazement. For the next two years, when we periodically had opportunities to talk with Bill and Linda, there were no sexual difficulties.

4. ANSWERING QUESTIONS ABOUT ONE'S SEXUAL ORIENTATION

Throughout adolescence and into our twenties, we are all seeking an identity, making choices, and labeling ourselves. In the area of sexuality, one of the major identity issues is, Am I homosexual, heterosexual, or perhaps bisexual? Some people seem to feel sure about their answer to this question even from preadolescence, but some young people have a degree of uncertainty.

There is agreement among most authorities today that all of us incorporate elements of masculinity and femininity in our personalities, and also a degree of bisexual potential. Early adoles-

cent sexual experiences with friends of the same sex are not uncommon. And even when there is no overt sexual activity, there is likely to be the awareness of attraction and perhaps fantasies. In their book *Homosexuality in Perspective*, sex researchers William H. Masters and Virginia E. Johnson state that people who are basically heterosexual often have homosexual fantasies and that people who are basically homosexual often have heterosexual fantasies. Learning to accept the complexities of our own sexual nature can help us in the process of sexual unfolding. We can be more comfortable with our heterosexuality or our homosexuality if we are not constantly trying to prove to ourselves and to the world that we are 120 percent one or the other.

Just as women like to look at women's bodies, we have found that many men admire other men's bodies. Because men don't talk about this, it is not unusual for a man to feel there is something peculiar about himself if he is interested in the way other men look. The sexual issue raised is usually one of sexual orientation, that is, If I like to look at other men, doesn't that mean I'm homosexual?

TR is nineteen years old. He saw us because he felt shy and had not been dating women at all since entering college. A tall, attractive, athletic young man, he "confessed" that he occasionally liked to look at other men's bodies and, although he had had no homosexual experience, was worried that this was a sign of "being gay." In high school, he had had a girlfriend and found sex with her exciting and satisfying, but he had not had sexual feelings for other girls and wondered if his lack of interest might be yet another sign of being gay.

We talked for several hours over the course of about a month. During that time, he began to open up about his feelings toward his roommate and some other friends. To his surprise, he found that most of them shared his feelings, although none of them was gay. He said he also began to notice that in a museum, "almost every man stopped to look at the statues of men as much as the statues of women." Over the summer vacation he saw his former girlfriend and realized that not having sexual feelings for other women had more to do with his feelings toward her than with his sexual orientation.

The need to be 120 percent heterosexual is something men seem to worry about much more than women. In our counseling work, we frequently see young men who are in a panic about possibly being homosexual. Almost any sexual experience that seems peculiar or below par can raise the specter of confused sexual preference. Experiences that have led predominantly heterosexual men to wonder about their sexual orientation include:

1. Early adolescent or preadolescent same-sex sex-play experiences. We have seen a carry-over impact in college students, especially when the early homosexual play led to the first ejaculatory experience. Homosexual imagery from the experience may persist in fantasy, and subsequent heterosexual experiences may not be as physiologically intense. An extra heterosexual performance pressure may develop in an attempt to dispel homosexuality, which in turn may lead to sexual dysfunction.
2. Delayed sexual maturation and onset of sexual behavior. Not being average is often equated, particularly by males, with homosexuality. "I didn't start pubertal changes until I was almost sixteen. I knew I wasn't a girl. But then I also knew I wasn't a man. I concluded I must be homosexual." Students who don't masturbate and discover that "all" the others do have seen us, thinking their lack of masturbation was a sign of homosexuality.
3. Being turned off by particular kinds of behavior, e.g., cunnilingus.
4. A more intense sexual response from self-stimulation as compared with intercourse.
5. Being a virgin at an age when he thinks everyone else has had intercourse.
6. Sexual inadequacy. Many male students who have consulted us about a sexual dysfunction have at some time expressed the idea that the root of the problem might be homosexuality.

Young women seem to be less troubled than young men by homosexual feelings. Statistics show that they probably have distinctly homoerotic feelings less often than young men. When they are attracted to another female, have homosexual fantasies, or "fall in love" with a female friend, they often accept their feelings as natural. They are much less likely to walk into a professional's office panicked about being homosexual.

This is not to say that some young women don't feel confused by their sexual attraction to women—just that they tend to be calmer about it. We have talked with quite a few students who wonder if they should act on their homosexual feelings. Sometimes it has been hard to sort out how much is spontaneous attraction and how much is feminist ideology.

We have been impressed by the apparently effortless transition some young women have made from heterosexual relationships into homosexual relationships and occasionally back to heterosexuality. Such easy shifts of sexual orientation would have been much more difficult in the past. A wider acceptance of the concept of bisexuality probably allows for more experimentation. We think no one yet knows what, if any, long-term effect this might have on an individual's sexuality. Perhaps, in fact, this is not as new a phenomenon as it appears. Kinsey noticed in his studies that sexual orientation did shift in some people as they moved through life, through shades of homosexuality, bisexuality, and heterosexuality.

For either sex, the process of sexual unfolding toward a primarily homosexual orientation can present some special problems. The homosexual world has its own sexual myths, its own codes and expectations. Until very recently, each individual had to find his or her own path without much guidance. Now that there are gay alliances, gay support groups, gay magazines and newspapers, and books about the gay world, information is much easier to come by. There are still, of course, the sexual, interpersonal, and social issues to be grappled with.

In our homophobic society, recognizing one's own gayness and moving toward accepting it can be very difficult. Of course the AIDS epidemic among gay men has added a frightening new dimension to the question of a man's sexual orientation. Young people should have sensitive, nonjudgmental counseling available to them if they are struggling with questions about their own sexual orientation. On our campus, in addition to mental health professionals, there are student counselors and gay discussion groups available.

5. LEARNING AND COMMUNICATING WHAT WE LIKE AND DISLIKE

A friend and fellow sex therapist told us this story. Her six-year-old daughter had just finished looking through a sex education book (which to our minds is distinctly too detailed and graphic for young children). She looked up and asked, "Mommy, does everyone do all the things they show in here?" What she was really asking, we think, was, "Do you and Daddy do those things?" but never mind that; we want to focus on the question she verbalized.

Her mother, being well schooled in these matters and also a wise person, said, "People do what they like—what feels nice. People don't do things if they'd rather not." The daughter breathed a small sigh of relief. Her mother (remember she *is* a therapist) said, "You sound relieved." The girl responded, "Well, I don't think I want to do what they show on page 36!"

This six-year-old is way ahead of the thousands of high school and college students who seem to think they *must* do everything sexual there is to do. Not only that, they must like it. We think they mistakenly interpret the concept that sex is normal and natural as meaning that sex is automatic and simple. It isn't. For most people, it takes some getting used to and practice. What happens to each person along the way to discovering what she or he likes and doesn't like is very important.

Rather than discuss it in the abstract, let's take one young woman, Barbara, and follow her through this process in her sexual unfolding. At fifteen, Barbara had her first experience with genital petting. She found the erect penis startling at first but then learned to enjoy giving her boyfriend pleasure by stimulating him to orgasm with her hand. She became very excited by his touching her clitoris and usually had an orgasm when he kept up the touching long enough. When he stopped before her orgasm, she was too shy to ask him to continue.

Her next boyfriend, Zachary, seemed obsessed with fellatio, so she tried it. She didn't enjoy it, but it was all right since it pleased him

so much. On a few occasions he "slipped" and ejaculated in her mouth. She didn't like the taste of the semen and gagged. But she continued fellatio with him for another three years. She did have orgasms with Zachary by his stimulating her with his hand.

When the relationship broke up, she met Tim (later to be her husband). They had intercourse on the third night they were together. Barbara found that intercourse was nice, but she never had an orgasm. Tim tried stimulating her clitoris with his hand "but it just didn't work." She absolutely refused even to try fellatio.

When Lorna saw her, Barbara was upset about her sexual relationship with Tim. A further relevant fact emerged. Barbara had been masturbating since she was four. Her pattern had always been the same. She would lie facedown on the bed with her hand between her thighs, one finger touching her clitoris. She always had an orgasm.

If we step back and analyze Barbara's story, we see that one problem had been her reluctance to say "I like it when you touch me this way," or "Please keep doing what you're doing." Another problem had been her inability to say no when she found she disliked something, particularly fellatio. She had thus built up an aversion to fellatio.

The main goal of therapy with Barbara was to help her identify what, specifically, she did and did not like and to get her to be completely open and honest about her preferences with Tim. In discussing the fellatio experiences she had had with Zachary, it became clear that the real problem had been the fear that he would ejaculate in her mouth. She didn't trust him. When Barbara and Tim talked it over, she realized that she could trust him. She was able to try orally stimulating him—very cautiously at first, and then without reservation. Barbara also identified the type of stimulation she needed. She gave Tim more guidelines and was able to have an orgasm from his manual stimulation.

Finally, Barbara learned that the man-above position she and Tim always used wasn't really the best for her. Through the years of masturbating lying facedown, that position had become eroticized. They found that using a rear-entry position with either one of them touching her clitoris, Barbara could have an orgasm easily.

Barbara's story doesn't cover one final point we want to make about learning to communicate with a partner. We all too often see young women who have not learned to say *stop* even when sex actually hurts. They seem to think that once a man is aroused, they dare not interrupt, so they continue with intercourse in spite of burning and stinging and a total lack of pleasure. If you put up with pain or discomfort once in a rare while, that is probably not so bad. But if you put up with pain all the time or with any regularity, sex becomes paired in your mind with pain. This will almost inevitably lead to serious problems—to involuntary muscle spasms at the vaginal opening (your vagina will say no for you) or to a fear of all sexual interaction.

Young men may be more automatic with regard to orgasm than are young women, but they do have lessons to learn about their own preferences. Often they are so focused on arousing the female, on pushing all the right buttons, that they pay no attention to how they themselves like to be touched. The most typical response made by young men (and older ones, too) to the request, "Tell me what you'd like me to do" is, "Oh, everything you do feels good." This is usually frustrating to the young woman who is trying to learn about both men in general and this young man in particular, and it doesn't set a good example. She may then find herself too shy to tell him how she would like to be touched.

Some young men have always masturbated in a particular way and have very distinct needs, perhaps for very vigorous stimulation or concentration on one part of the penis such as the frenulum or (less common) the base of the shaft. Unless a man can explain his needs or show his partner how to stimulate him, he may lose his erection or be unable to ejaculate. Young women often feel not just shy about stimulating the penis but actually frightened about causing pain or injury. They need to be shown, usually by having the young man's hand over hers, just how firmly the penis can be manipulated.

Some young men who like touching and/or being touched very softly resist their own inclinations because it seems unmanly. We have been struck by the number of athletes who express this conflict. Could it be that behind all the macho rough-and-tumble they have yearnings for tenderness that they have been denying for years?

When it comes to oral sex, both men and women tend to worry that they may be imposing something unpleasant on their partner. Among the students we surveyed, we found that women underestimated the percentage of men who like cunnilingus. Likewise, the male students underestimated the percentage of women who enjoy fellatio. Since oral sex is now so prevalent among young people (among students we studied, 60% of the virgin females had had oral sex experience, and virtually every nonvirgin had), it is particularly important that young couples be able to communicate openly about it.

6. FIRST INTERCOURSE (A STEP? A HURDLE? A STUMBLING BLOCK?)

Half of American young women now have intercourse before they graduate from high school. By contrast, in the 1950s, Kinsey found that by age twenty, "only" 23 percent of women had lost their virginity. When we were in college, in the Eisenhower—togetherness—gray-flannel-suit 1950s, hardly a female admitted to non-virgin status, not even to her best friends.

Now not only is a female's first intercourse likely to occur between her sixteenth and nineteenth birthdays, but she is likely to feel proud about it and tell her best, and not-so-best, friends. The cultural script calls for a coolness—a kind of low-key enthusiasm that, unfortunately, is not what many girls who experience intercourse for the first time actually feel. Almost all studies agree: The majority have very mixed emotions. A recent study by David Weis at Rutgers University found that one-third of young women felt exploited during their first intercourse. Although about two-thirds of the women said they had experienced sexual pleasure, half of this group also experienced high levels of guilt and anxiety. One-third of the total experienced no pleasure at all but only guilt and anxiety.

The rest of the findings in this study sound like what every mother knows and wishes her daughter knew. If you are older (at least 17), if you haven't rushed into intercourse but have built up to it gradually, and if your partner is loving, tender, and considerate, you are more likely to enjoy it and less likely to feel anxious and guilty.

Conversations with students we teach tend to confirm Weis's results and add more food for thought. Following are some excerpts from one such conversation with a group of students.

"I was the most uptight girl in my high school. I had hardly dated because I was known as 'too serious.' When I met Jeff the summer after my junior year, I was totally naive about sex. No, it was worse than that—I thought sex was bad and I was scared of the whole thing, from kissing onward. I don't know how Jeff put up with me. He was three years older and experienced. The thing is, I guess, he was experienced enough not to push. But the main thing that helped me to change was his attitude toward sex. He was so easy with it. I don't mean casual, just relaxed. In fact, I would say he's reverential toward sex. He helped me to see that it could be beautiful. The first time we were naked together, he got tears in his eyes. When I asked him why, he said, 'Because it's so lovely and because it shows you trust me.' We knew each other two years before we had intercourse. The first time I expected problems, but there were none. His penis fit inside easily and it felt great. I know that if it hadn't happened with someone like Jeff, who I loved and trusted, I would have been tense and it wouldn't have been a good experience. As it was, well, it was great—really great."

After hearing this story, another woman student said, "I envy you. My first time was lousy. He was seventeen and I was fifteen. We were both virgins and both insecure as hell. He was too short and unathletic and I was too tall and brainy. We did it at his house when his parents were away. We thought we would feel more sure of ourselves afterward. I'd say it was the opposite. I know I felt it was a lousy disappointment. It didn't hurt—not much—but I kept waiting for it to be like in the movies. When I didn't feel anything, I decided I was probably genetically frigid or something. If I could do it over, I'd erase the whole event. As a matter of fact, I've never had sex since that time."

First intercourse is a special emotional event, and it also involves new "technical" steps. Unless pregnancy is desired, it should involve contraception. It involves the penis entering the vagina or, preferably (because it tends to work better), the woman moving her vagina so that it surrounds the penis. Lots of things can get in the way of insertion: a hymenal strand, a thick hymen with a small opening (rare), tight vaginal muscles, the wrong angle, not being able to locate the vaginal opening, the man's loss of erection, or his ejaculating before insertion.

There is the question of position. This seems to be mostly determined by the culture. We understand that in northern Sweden, 97 percent of couples say they virtually always use the "missionary" position. In Africa and India, of course, the native population thought that was a laughable position. We advise the female-above position for starters because the woman can be in control of the matter and is therefore less likely to feel frightened. She should go slowly and give her muscles a chance to relax and allow the hymen to stretch rather than tear. By the way, the majority of women today report little or no bleeding and little or minimal pain.

Intercourse can be a truly complicated behavior, involving thoughts and concerns that distract from the pleasure. For the young man: "Am I hard enough yet? We'd better hurry because I'm close to coming. Is she ready? Am I hurting her? Can anyone hear us? If I come, will she know? If she comes, will I know? My arms are tired (missionary position). It's too dry. It's too slippery. Maybe she isn't enjoying it."

For the young woman: "How can I tell if he's ready? Am I lubricated? Who should decide when we actually go ahead and do it? Can anyone hear us? Will I come? If I don't, will he be upset? How should I move? Should I make noises? What would my mother think?"

Immediately after the very first intercourse experience, people may be surprised by their own feelings, which can range from vague disappointment, shame, and disgust to exaltation, contentment, and overwhelming feelings of love. It isn't unusual to cry—not so much from sadness as from intensity of feeling.

The sessions in which we have discussed first intercourse with students have been searching, revealing, and thought-provoking experiences. These discussions, combined with the histories told to us by individuals, have given us much to think about in trying to understand the potential meaning of first intercourse. It can be a symbol of independence and of assertion, or just the opposite—of dependence and submission. It can be the discovery of a new dimension of shared pleasure and satisfaction or it can be a time of pain and fear and a sense of loneliness. It is a step in the process of separation from mother and father—"like being four and going on five."

We have to conclude that in reality, the experience is rarely all of the positives and none of the negatives. Many of the young people who have told us their story experienced a mixture of feelings. However, it is encouraging to us to see that an increasing number have a positive experience—a step in the right direction for the development of adult sexuality.

7. COPING WITH SEXUAL DYSFUNCTION OR "COMPULSION"

Some dysfunction is a normal (although not universal) part of sexual unfolding in adolescence. Many young women don't experience orgasm with a partner for months or even years after beginning sexual relations. *Most* young men experience premature ejaculation, and many have transitory problems with erection. A few have trouble having an orgasm.

The impact of a sexual dysfunction on a young person in the midst of sexual unfolding will vary with the person and the situation. Often it passes without any repercussions, but sometimes it can create serious problems.

Penny, a twenty-year-old, talked with us about her lack of social and sexual relationships. For the past year and a half, she had more or less deliberately avoided contact with men, although there were two men she counted among her friends. Penny felt that her unwillingness to date centered on her worry that she was sexually inadequate and always would be. She had had a relationship with a boy when she was seventeen that had included petting but not intercourse. She had enjoyed the relationship and the sex, although she had begun to wonder when the wonderful experience she had heard about—orgasm—would happen to her.

She had no other sexual experiences until she met Dan through her work. He was older and very sexually experienced, and he prided himself on being a good lover. From the beginning of their relationship, he set out to give Penny an orgasm. One of the reasons she decided to say yes to intercourse was her hope that at last she would have an orgasm. Not surprisingly (to us),

Penny never could have an orgasm with Dan, no matter what techniques they tried. We say this was not surprising to us because we had heard this kind of story many times before and know that trying so hard to "achieve" orgasm is almost guaranteed to block it.

When the relationship with Dan ended, Penny's self-esteem was badly shaken. She was convinced that if she couldn't respond to Dan's "expert" attempts, she'd never be able to have an orgasm. She thought of herself as sexually abnormal and inhibited. She concentrated on her work, gained fifteen pounds, and withdrew from any relationship that might have involved sex.

If Penny hadn't sought professional help, she might have spent many years, perhaps even her lifetime, with a negative sexual image. In the course of therapy, she was able to come to appreciate her self as a sexual female. This gave her enough self-confidence to risk a relationship with a new young man, and, we are pleased to say, the story had a happy ending.

Sexual compulsion is another matter. We use the word *compulsion* in the heading of this section to refer to sexual behavior that is out of control, repetitive, self-destructive, and usually not sexually satisfying. One example would be a young man who had an endless series of one-night-stands that were not pleasurable, although he usually did ejaculate. After intercourse, he was always cold and nasty. Therapy revealed a deep-seated rage against women. He entered psychoanalysis.

Another example would be a young woman whose father deserted the family when she was six to lead a hippie life-style, including drug experimentation. From age fourteen onward, she was attracted to men who were socially inappropriate and sometimes frankly dangerous. Her sexual experiences were never pleasurable, but she couldn't stop the pattern of behavior.

Compulsion in sexual behavior usually derives from a desperate need to find love and acceptance through any means, and sex is perhaps the easiest way to feel popular and liked and to get some cuddling and touching. When sexual behavior is engaged in for these reasons, the sex itself is usually unsatisfying and often downright unpleasant. The person rarely satisfies the deep need for love and acceptance and comes to associate sex with displeasure. Some people spend years, from their teens into their twenties, in this kind of compulsive sexual behavior. In spite of multiple sexual experiences, they do not mature psychosexually; they do not go through the growing process of sexual unfolding. They usually end up seeking professional help and must, in a sense, go back to work through the stage of sexual development they skipped.

8. UNDERSTANDING THE PLACE AND VALUE OF SEX IN OUR LIVES

In their initial year on campus, many students begin to question the values they grew up with. The sheer multiplicity of sexual values they see around them makes moral absolutes seem impossible or irrelevant. It is hard to find any students who are willing to state general principles of sexual morality. They say, for example, "I won't have intercourse until I'm in love and in a really committed relationship, but I don't think it's necessarily wrong to have casual sex."

In the early 1970s, there was one very widely held but unspoken value—to be a virgin was embarrassing and probably meant that you were hung up (heaven forbid). If you were sexually inexperienced, you didn't talk about it, and you hoped to change your status as quickly as possible. Thank goodness, that pressure has eased. Since about the mid-1970s, along with the generally conservative shift on campuses has come a healthier acceptance of diverse sexual values. Some students became outspoken in their support of virginity as an ideal, and people didn't snicker.

What to do about parents and sex is a moral–ethical–emotional dilemma faced by most students. Should I tell them I'm going on the pill? Should I be honest about the fact that we're sharing an apartment next term? What would my father think if he knew I'd gotten her pregnant, just like he did when he was nineteen? Sometimes, at nineteen, it seems morally necessary to be absolutely truthful. Depending on the family and the truth to be shared, this can be fine or it can be a disaster, causing a serious, sometimes permanent rift in the family. It often goes back to a question of the unfolding process—the need to separate emotionally from parents. Some young people need to wrench away; others can make the separation more gently.

It helps to have a person or persons to talk to when you are struggling with questions of sexual values. Peer influence on sexual behavior and judgments is extremely important. In fact, the sociologist Ira Reiss has found that a student's perception of his or her peers' sexual behavior is *the* single most important factor influencing the student's sexual behavior. Notice, we said the student's *perception*—not what the peers are actually doing. The opportunity, then, to receive a more accurate picture of peer sexual behavior is crucial. Virtually all students overestimate the extent of their peers' sexual experience. One student enrolled in a course on human sexual development put it very simply. He said, "The value of this course to me was in learning I'm not the only virgin on campus and not the only one who *wants* to be." Another student summed her experience in the sexuality course and its impact on her values this way: "This course has been an eye-opener. I'm very inexperienced sexually and always thought sex would just happen to me at some point. Now I see that it's complicated and a serious matter—something to think about, not just do. I wonder what would have happened to me if I'd had to learn the lesson the hard way."

9. BECOMING RESPONSIBLE ABOUT SEX

Think back to your adolescence. If you had intercourse during that period of your life, the chances are very great that you frequently used no contraceptive device whatsoever. If you were lucky, you managed to avoid an unwanted pregnancy. You may marvel now at your own lack of forethought and perhaps imagine that today's adolescents would never be so foolish. But statistics show that although there is some improvement in adolescents' use of birth control measures, a majority of sexually active adolescents still have intercourse without protection.

What makes bright, capable young people act so foolishly? A certain percentage are deliberately omitting birth control. They want to become pregnant or at least wouldn't mind if it happened. But most of the time it's a matter of ignorance (everyone knows you can't get pregnant the first time you do it), magical thinking (it can't happen to me), an unconscious desire for pregnancy (for example, a wish to punish Mother or to hold onto a boyfriend), or the failure to accept that you are—you really *are*—having intercourse.

This last point may sound farfetched, but it isn't. It may be one of the most common reasons for failure to use birth control. In 1967, when we were new to the field of sex education and sex counseling, we saw an eighteen-year-old, who telephoned us late one evening, crying. "I think I may be pregnant, but I don't want to go to the college medical service, I don't trust them. If I'm pregnant, I think they'll tell my parents." We arranged for her to have a pregnancy test, which, to the relief of everyone, was negative. We then talked to her about birth control. She answered, "Oh, I don't need birth control. We're never going to do it again. Besides, both of us are Roman Catholic and don't believe in using contraception." This isn't the end of the story. Several months later, the same girl called and we went through the same sequence, including her statement, "We're never going to do it again." The most remarkable part was her belief that she wouldn't do it again. She was much too guilty about it to admit to herself: "I am having intercourse."

A graduate student recently said to us, rather wistfully, "Oh, for the good old days when all you had to worry about from sex was getting knocked-up." Nowadays, sex is fraught with possible consequences and every few years, there seems to be a new sexually transmitted disease. Herpes was the worry of the late 1970s and early 1980s. Then we all learned that we could get a deadly, incurable HIV infection from sex. And in the late 1980s and early 90s, we learned about an epidemic of human papilloma virus (HPV or "genital warts").

On June 18, 1991, the *New York Times* reported the good news that 52% of single 18- to 44-year-olds have changed their sexual habits because of the fear of AIDS. This is good news because it is a large increase in responsible behavior compared with earlier surveys, but, of course, it leaves us wondering how to reach those who apparently are not changing their behaviors to avoid AIDS.

On our campus, there is a curious dichotomy of attitudes. There are still too many students who feel that they are safe from AIDS because they have sex only with fellow students—a dangerously facile assumption. By contrast, an increasing number of students are insisting on mutual HIV testing before starting a sexual relationship. And many students are taking birth-control pills for contraception and using condoms to avoid STDs.

AIDS and other STDs have altered the social and psychic map of adolescent sexuality. For decades, the age of sexual initiation got younger and younger. Now, we have the cruel irony of young teens taking on a behavior that requires adult judgment and restraint, sophisticated medical knowledge, and a cautiousness that few teens possess.

Studies of teen pregnancy have consistently shown that young people who are in conflict about sex—who feel guilty, ashamed, and furtive—are less likely to use contraception when they have intercourse. Those who feel comfortable with their own sexuality and right about their behavior are better contraceptors. It is clear that sexual responsibility—whether to avoid unwanted pregnancy or STDs, is not promoted by withholding information or by lecturing about abstinence. If we want young people to behave with adultlike responsibility, we must treat them like adults.

10. INTIMACY—COMBINING LOVE AND SEX

The yearning to fall in love is almost universal in our culture. Love is extolled as the greatest human experience. Even if it is unrequited and anguished, we all know it is "Better to have loved and lost, Than never to have loved at all." Freud told us there are only two hallmarks of the healthy, mature person—the capacity to work productively and the capacity to love.

We are still basically Victorian in our beliefs about love. Although we hear rumblings from time to time of alternative ideals such as open marriage, hardly anyone today questions the assumption that love is some combination of sex and personal intimacy. The definitions of love offered by a group of students confirm this.

You should care deeply about each other as people, respect each other, enjoy being together and be sexually attracted.

Passionate liking.

Love is trust, concern, commitment, and sexual fulfillment.

I don't know yet, but I expect to recognize it by how I feel—yearning to be with him, I guess, and wanting to make love.

I've had some real "crushes" on girls, but I don't think it's real love unless it's mutual. When two people love each other, they naturally want a long-term, exclusive relationship. My image of love is old-fashioned. I want to be a virgin until I marry and hope my wife would also be a virgin. I see marriage as a sacred commitment.

Knowing each other completely—emotionally and physically—without defenses or barriers.

All these definitions assume that love and sex will be inseparable. That's interesting because all of us, including these students, know that love or intimacy can exist without sex and sex can be experienced without any intimacy at all ("By the way, what did you say your name was?"). Intimacy usually evolves over time, although we have heard people describe brief encounters that are intensely close and moving—a moment of mutual openness that is an incapsulated intimacy. We have also heard, sadly, about decades of marriage in which there is no openness or sharing beyond "Where should we go on vacation this year?" and perhaps pro forma sexual intercourse.

Although all humans yearn to connect with others we don't seem to have an instinct for how to go about doing it. It's something we learn. We learn first of all from being held, cuddled, touched, fed, and loved as infants. Throughout childhood, we learn the "rules" that govern contact between persons. We learn that it's all right to kiss and hug certain people under certain circumstances. If we're lucky, we learn mostly about trust and tenderness. If we're not so lucky, we learn mostly about pain, mistrust, and how to hide and protect ourselves. Boys learn one set of rules; girls learn another. Boys are more likely to learn how to hide their feelings and to make less affectionate physical contact. Girls learn the language of emotional expressiveness, are cuddled more, and may even be accomplished flirts by age three.

When it comes to learning how to integrate love and sex, sociologists tell us that boys and girls once again travel different paths. Boys know about sex but must learn about love from girls, whereas girls know how to love but must learn how to enjoy sex from boys. This was always a rather weak generalization and becomes weaker all the time as the power of the sexual double standard fades. Yet it is consistent with what many people still tell us in their sexual histories.

Males are much more likely than females to describe an early and intense genital focus. Sexual awareness begins with experiences of erection and is tremendously intensified by semenarche (first ejaculation). As we mentioned earlier, in the young boy, the stimulus for genital excitement may be almost anything. Gradually he learns to respond to what the culture tells him is appropriately sexy for a male. For some years, ejaculations are likely to be achieved entirely through masturbation or wet dreams and, for about one third of all boys, in occasional sex play with other boys. The boy's subculture promotes a focus on ejaculation as *the* fact of sex through jokes and teasing about how many times in a row you can "jerk off," how far you can spurt, and so on. When boys begin to interact with girls, they often have one overriding aim—to see how much they can "get." Girls are experienced primarily as objects of desire, and peer approval is given for "scoring."

Females tend to describe their experiences differently. Little girls certainly have erotic feelings, and some masturbate with vivid fantasies similar to boys', but the majority—at least as recalled in adulthood—remember romantic fantasies and intense crushes on particular people—boys, men, girls, women. The daydreams are of walking and talking with and pleasing the "loved" one. A little later, the daydreams include a hug or a kiss.

When our son was in the ninth grade (fourteen years old), he did a study of his fellow ninth-graders' sexual knowledge as a biology project. He found that both girls and boys were reasonably well informed about their own sex. Girls knew about menstruation and female orgasm. Boys knew about wet dreams, erection, and ejaculation. But both sexes were startlingly ignorant about the other sex.

Most boys and girls put the pieces of the puzzle together during mid- and late adolescence. They talk to friends, read books, see movies, attend a sex education course. They have experiences that teach them not only the facts and the techniques but also the feelings generated by having sex with another person.

One of our culture's injunctions to the male begins to come into play usually by mid-adolescence: Thou shalt care for the female and be concerned with her pleasure. At age sixteen or seventeen, then, touching a girl's genitals has many levels of meaning. The heart beats faster, the erection becomes harder while he thinks, "Wow, she's letting me do it; wait till I tell Mike and Paul." At the same time, he observes her response. He wants her to like it because he's scared and tentative and he needs her pleasure and reassurance. He may also think that if she's aroused, they could end up having intercourse (often a mistaken assumption). Part of his role as a male in this situation is to give his partner pleasure. If he thinks that she is aroused and enjoying his touches, he is likely to feel good about himself—and about her.

By the college years, there is usually another significant shift for the young man. He is less focused on sex as a means of gaining prestige points with his friends and more concerned about what sex *means* between himself and the young woman. He is more interested in an ongoing relationship and wants to be liked by the person he chooses. If he really cares about her, he will want to do everything he can to keep her attached to him, and good sex (we all seem to know this instinctively) can be a powerful cement. Our culture still gives the male 90 percent of the responsibility for how things go sexually, so he will tend to take the blame if it isn't "good." He can also begin to take very real pleasure in his partner's sexual responses. Now that he feels a bit of security, he notices and feels her arousal; it turns him on. He can enjoy this kind of giving.

Of course, it isn't only sex that promotes male-female intimacy. In fact, sex, in the absence of other forms of contact, can be alienating. The trends toward coeducation, mixed dorms, and male-female equality are vital elements in the story of intimate relations between the sexes today. Boys and girls, young men and young women are getting to know one another intellectually and socially in informal settings, working together, each respecting the other. Some of the mystique is gone, but in its place there can be—and increasingly there is—real understanding and real caring. Sex, in this context, can be integral to a larger relationship, another way for two people to know one another. Whether you call that intimacy or love, it is one of the best experiences life has to offer.

To Apply This Reading to Yourself

1. *Discuss your experience in adapting to your bodily changes at puberty.*
2. *Discuss the negative messages about sex that you received as you grew up and their effects upon you.*
3. *Discuss your experience in shifting your primary emotional attachment from your parents to your peers.*
4. *Discuss your experience as you raised questions and sought answers concerning your sexual orientation.*
5. *Discuss any of your sexual experiences that played an important part in your sexual unfolding.*
6. *Discuss the place and value of sex in your own life.*
7. *Contrast the sexual guidance that you received as a child with the guidance that you intend to provide (or have provided) for your own children.*

Coming to Terms with Your Own Sexuality

Sol Gordon and Craig W. Snyder

Sexual intercourse, as an aspect of our sexuality, is greatly overrated. If some people's public personas were to be believed, however, it would often appear that only nuclear war is a more important issue in their lives.

Sexual intercourse is, at best, number nine on our list of the ten most important characteristics of a relationship. This is our sense, in order of importance, of what it's all about:

1. Loving, caring, and intimacy together
2. A sense of humor and playfulness
3. Honest communication and interesting conversation
4. A passionate sense of mission or purpose
5. Friends together and separately
6. Commitment to one's own identity and ideals
7. Tolerance for occasional craziness, irritableness, conflict, error
8. Acceptance of each other's style
9. Sexual fulfillment
10. Sharing household tasks

Occasionally, when this list is presented to an audience, an outraged male will suggest that it is nonsense (no female ever has); how could sex be number nine? The reply is always, Because there are eight things more important. And besides, of the 3243 really important aspects of a relationship, sex is one of the top ten. Not bad.

A strange alliance of forces in our society has conspired to debase the meaning, intent, and value of sexuality. Some well-intentioned ministers claim that if you have sex before marriage, you'll have nothing to look forward to in marriage, or there will be no surprises after you marry. This might be countered with the claim that if you are expecting sexual intercourse to be the only surprise in marriage, don't marry. It's not worth it. There are also supersophisticated researchers who would have us believe that sex is something you can qualify, all of which contributes to the disastrous illusion that sex is akin to a gymnastic performance. Some researchers actually want us to take seriously the absurd notion that men reach their sexual peak at age 19 and women at 29. Where did they get data like this, from a random sample of 85-year-old men and women? A distraught young man once came to me (Sol Gordon) and sadly revealed his fate: "I'm 20 years old and already past my prime, and I haven't even started yet."

Nevertheless, the fact that human sexuality has become an area of scholarly research in a wide variety of disciplines is a sign of progress. A great deal of knowledge has been generated through research efforts, which collectively have established sexuality as a legitimate academic discipline. At times, however, an overly scientific approach to sexuality has depersonalized the essence of sexuality and fueled a conceptualization of sex that is performance- and competition-oriented. Thus, we encourage readers not to develop an antiresearch bias, but rather to question the validity of the procedures and findings of the research they encounter.

What has all this to do with coming to terms with one's own sexuality? It's the introduction. A way of putting sex into a perspective along with other aspects of your existence.

Sexual intercourse is one aspect but not the overwhelmingly important part of a relationship. This is not to say that in some families sex isn't number one. It is often number one when there is a problem or hangup. It is number one when couples are more preoccupied with performance or orgasms than they are with the relationship. It assumes enormous proportions if a couple believes that If we really love each other, we will have great sex or simultaneous orgasms. The fact is that some couples really love each other, yet have sexual relations that appear less than adequate, even dysfunctional. On the other hand, there are couples who hate each other and have great sex together. Sex is neither a test nor a proof of love. Sexual intercourse can be and often is an enjoyable aspect of a relationship for well-adjusted couples—well-adjusted being operationally defined as people who like each other and who enjoy being married to each other (and includes those living together in committed relationships).

It is in this context that some crucial aspects of sexuality are elaborated on the following pages as an aid in exploring and evaluating your own sexual behavior, knowledge, and feelings. As will be evident, certain ideas and biases will not coincide with your own. The process of disagreement and debate in our pluralistic society is an excellent medium for personal growth and education. Our bias is toward common sense and respect for individual differences. This is preferable to "hard data," or rigid moralistic imperatives. Nevertheless, consider this quote from Virginia Woolf: "At any rate, when a subject is highly controversial—and any question about sex is that—one cannot hope to tell the truth. One can only show how one came to hold the opinion one does hold. One can only give one's audience the chance of drawing their own conclusions as they observe the limitations, the idiosyncrasies of the speaker."

APPRECIATING OUR SEXUALITY: SOME CONCEPTS

These concepts are particularly important in appreciating our own sexuality:

Normal and Abnormal. Normal sexual behavior *among adults* is defined as being voluntary, nonexploitative, and consensual. Generally, this behavior is not only pleasurable and guilt-free, but also enhances self-esteem and protects the health of each partner. Abnormal sexual behavior is often characterized by being compulsive (involuntary), exploitative, (often) nonconsensual, guilt-ridden, and rarely pleasurable. It generally lowers self-esteem. Provided sex meets these general criteria and does not seriously conflict with the participants' values, it does not matter how and where it takes place.

Select, Don't Settle. Human beings are not like animals. Animal sex is biologically programmed, but even animals "make do" with their own if the opposite sex is not available. It appears that no sensible person need worry that heterosexuality, as a primary lifestyle, will disappear. The real concern in most of the world is overpopulation,

not whether more people are bi-, auto-, or homosexual, or simply don't want to have children.

It also seems evident that one's sexuality is not rigidly fixed even though there is evidence to believe that what is termed *constitutional homosexuality* is a sexual orientation and not readily subject to change (the same is true of *constitutional heterosexuality*). People do go through stages, make mistakes, and experience different feelings at varying times of their lives. Those cycles can include long or short periods of fidelity or infidelity, homosexual incidents, a brief encounter, a weird indiscretion or a "perversion" here and there. People can grow and profit from both good and bad experiences.

It's even okay to feel that you are naturally attracted only to members of the opposite sex, for whatever reason, and not care how open or modern you are supposed to be. Other possibilities and attractions are boundless, but it's not okay to exploit people and abuse them for your own pleasure.

This does not mean, select one thing and that's it. What makes sense in one period of your life makes no sense in another period. Nor does it mean that people don't have to work for and toward what they want most from their lives. Furthermore, not every meal has to be a gourmet feast.

All Thoughts Are Normal. Sexual thoughts, wishes, dreams, and daydreams and turn-ons are normal, no matter how "far out." Behavior can be wrong, but ideas cannot be. Thoughts, image, and fantasies cannot, in themselves, hurt you. Guilt is the energy for the repetition of fantasies that are unacceptable to you.

Anybody with some degree of imagination has, from time to time, a range of thoughts, from murderous, sadistic, incestuous, or rape fantasies, to heroic escapades and undying love. That does not mean that they are going to come true, or that people are going to act them out. As a matter of fact, accepting as normal one's "unacceptable" thoughts is the best way of keeping them under voluntary control. People who constantly repress their fantasies or become preoccupied with them, because of guilt, are the ones most likely to be harmful to themselves and others.

Guilt is a good thing to feel if you've done something wrong. There are, however, two types of guilt: mature and immature. The former type helps you organize yourself and enables you to respond in a more rational manner to a similar situation or temptation in the future. Mature guilt can enhance your self-image provided you don't overdue it and let it degenerate into immature guilt, which disorganizes and overwhelms a person. You can usually tell if your guilt is immature because it is an overreaction to something you did wrong, or more commonly, to something you didn't do but just thought about. More often than not it is a way of expressing hostility toward yourself and results in feelings of depression. Almost everyone at one time or other suffers from immature guilt. This is not to be confused with normal bad/upset feelings or with grieving and mourning in response to real events in a person's life.

Sexual Arousal. The popular culture, especially its mass media, creates the notion that there are standard stimuli for getting aroused. Men, for example, are supposed to be aroused by the pretty girl selling automobiles or by *Playboy* bunnies. That's all right except that men who aren't aroused by the current fashion often feel compelled to fake it. The fact is that human beings are sexually aroused by a variety of stimuli. *Not* knowing that *all* forms of arousal are all right is what causes trouble.

Some people feel guilty if they are sexually aroused when playing with children, roughing it with dogs, being attracted to their parents, sitting in moving vehicles, having sadistic fantasies, or looking at pornography. If you can accept the arousal experience without guilt, no harm is done. And why not enjoy some of it? A problem exists if you act out the sexual arousal, or if you can get excited only or mainly by thoughts or acts you or your partner find unacceptable and exploitative.

Masturbation. Nearly all professionals these days say that masturbation is all right and that it is a normal developmental stage. Then there is a pause: It's all right if you don't do it too much. And nearly everyone is asking, How much is too much?

A lot of men and women don't often admit it, but they achieve their best orgasms by masturbating. Married people with satisfactory sex lives masturbate. Some people masturbate rarely or not at all. That's all right, too. Guilt about masturbation is about the only thing that's not desirable.

Telling the Truth About Your Sexual Past. This may be a good thing, but you should make sure that you are telling the truth for the right reasons. Sometimes people reveal their past to hurt or express hostility toward their partner. Others want to know the past for abusive purposes. Don't let it all hang out. There is a great need for privacy in some aspects of our lives.

Coitus. Many myths are perpetuated by some "sexperts" who write sensuality and sex manuals. There is no special amount of time a man's penis is supposed to stay in a woman's vagina to guarantee satisfaction. For some, it's seconds; for others, a couple of minutes. As a matter of fact, it can vary from time to time and each time. There just are no standards for everyone. Find out by experimenting with what is most enjoyable for the two of you. Intercourse is not essential for sexual pleasure, nor is having an orgasm each time or even most of the time, and certainly not having simultaneous orgasms.

Female Orgasms. More nonsense has been written about this subject than any other area of sexuality. Women have been made to feel so insecure that some need a *Good Housekeeping* seal to certify their orgasms. Often they pose the question in a serious way to a professional: How can I tell if I have an orgasm? And just as often the professional will respond with an uninformed answer. If you had one, you'd know it. This response only reinforces the insecurity.

Orgasm is mainly a psychological phenomenon—with associated physical sensations. We define orgasm as a very brief, intensely pleasurable sensual experience accompanied by a series of contractions. Orgasm is not always necessary to enjoy sexual intimacy and a mature relationship with another human being. It's just another dimension of pleasure that is good to experience.

Most women who enjoy their bodies, have good feelings about themselves, and like the idea of sexual intimacy have orgasms:

- If they are not intent on having one each time.
- If their partner doesn't ask each time, Did you have one? (What kind of conversation is that, anyway?)
- If they don't take seriously some of the research, especially that which suggests the type of father you should have had to achieve orgasm.
- If they feel comfortable about masturbating.

Male Orgasms. The best-kept secret is that when a man ejaculates he doesn't always have an orgasm. Any man who denies it either is not telling the truth or can't be trusted. Sometimes a man will ejaculate and feel nothing at all. At times there is a little pleasure and at times a great deal. Orgasms vary in strength and pleasure, during masturbation, intercourse, and all sexual acts. Men sometimes fake orgasms. Men are better programmed to experience orgasm than women, but this is changing.

Size. An all-American hangup! Men worry whether their penis is *big* enough. Freud got it wrong. It's men who have penis envy. Size has nothing to do with giving or receiving sexual pleasure. Besides, one cannot tell the size of a penis by looking at it when it is not erect. Some hang long; some appear quite small but erect to sizes larger than those that appear huge.

Women needlessly worry that their partner's penis is either too small for satisfaction or too big (painful) for their vagina. When we recall that the vagina accommodates the birth of a baby, it is difficult to believe genital size is a factor in pleasure or pain. On the other hand, tension and an inability to relax can be related to both pleasure and pain.

Breast size or shape has nothing to do with sexual or personal adequacy. In the early stages of puberty, girls often worry because of uneven or late breast development compared to their friends. This is sad, because there is a wide range of perfectly healthy, normal stages of growth. Many females with large breasts are as self-conscious as those with small ones. The most current style is: the larger the better. At other times, preferences dictated: the smaller the better.

Sublimation. People used to think (and some still do) that sex could be sublimated or propelled into "higher channels" without direct expression by being creative, athletic, doing charitable work, or becoming a priest or a nun. Adult sexuality can only be: expressed, repressed, but it cannot be sublimated.

The individuals with the greatest potential for problems are those who repress significant aspects of their sexuality. Repressed sexuality is often revealed by means of: physical disorders, immaturity, revulsion in response to natural bodily functions, meanness, obsessive-compulsive neurosis, fears of homosexuality, and failure to achieve orgasm, among others. Some people who are emotionally mature never have had sexual intercourse. They are usually able to acknowledge, but suppress, impulses toward sexual relations or masturbation. Many people are emotionally immature but have highly satisfactory sexual experiences. Many people are emotionally mature who enjoy an active, vigorous sex life. The range of sexual expressions in its relationship to maturity is infinite.

Normal Sex Problems. Just about everybody is sexually dysfunctional sometimes. In other words, they are unable to "perform" despite wishing they could. An occasional experience of erectile dysfunction, having premature ejaculation, not reaching orgasm, or being turned off from sex altogether is not uncommon. If you don't panic or become fixated into what could be merely a temporary out-of-sorts state of mind, the situation will improve. If you attach too much importance to what could be a temporary problem, it can get worse.

Role Playing (Positions and Techniques). Every sexual relationship can by enhanced by varying roles during encounters. One can be active or passive, both can be active or both passive. One can care for and be taken care of, bathe someone or be bathed, massage or be massaged, and relate similarly in bed.

When you get down to it, no one need be frozen in an assigned role. Traditional concepts of what is supposed to be maleness and femaleness (or active and passive) no longer apply, if they ever really did. What counts is communication and intimacy, which translate into sexual rapport. Roles, positions, and techniques are only the mechanical "how-tos" in a mutually responsive relationship.

On Being Horny. Feeling horny is not mainly physiological, biological, constitutional, or hereditary. It is primarily a psychological phenomenon. If you feel horny and your spouse or lover has a "headache," masturbate. If you have a mature (not guilt-ridden) attitude toward masturbation, you will feel better afterward. In any case, don't go around telling everybody you feel this way since it is terribly boring and sometimes burdensome to be with a person who is complaining that he or she is horny.

Homosexuality. It is no longer believed that homosexuality is caused by any one thing or a special combination of factors. Homosexuals exist in every culture and society. Ancient Greek culture found homosexuality acceptable. Our culture has frowned upon it.

It is a false assumption that a person who has homosexual thoughts or dreams must be a homosexual. Mature people are aware of the fact that they have both homosexual and heterosexual feelings, even though the majority of them prefer sexual activities with members of the opposite sex. In this connection, it might be helpful to point out that it is not easy to judge a person's sexual orientation by appearance. Some feminine-looking men or masculine-looking women are heterosexual; and some highly masculine, so-called macho all-American, types are gay.

The gay liberation movement together with notable research, such as that conducted by Bell and Weinberg (1978), has made it abundantly clear that homosexuals are just as healthy or unhealthy as heterosexuals. Sexual orientation does not determine whether a person is mature or normal. Saying a person is a homosexual tells us as much about a person as saying a person is heterosexual. If we're going to sex-identify each other, let's start out with the idea that we are all *human sexuals.*

People have the right, without stigma or coercion, to be what they are. If some 90 percent of the population are heterosexual, that's their business. If perhaps 10 percent express themselves as homosexual, bisexual, or by no overt sexual be-

havior, that's their business as well. Certainly it is cruel and immoral for government to have anything to say about sexual relations between two consenting adults. It is hoped a time will come when people's sexual orientation will be of little or no legislative interest and certainly none of anybody's business (unless that body is an unwilling partner).

Perversion. This is an old-fashioned word used to describe what some people find revolting. For example, there are still some people who consider anal or oral sex perverted. Fancy names for perversions are exhibitionism, masochism, sadism, fetishism, voyeurism, necrophilia, and bestiality. There is nothing wrong with any kind of sex between consenting adults in private, if each partner is nonexploitative and the act is voluntary. Anal and oral sex are enjoyable for many people and are also ways for those who don't want, or can't have, sexual intercourse to have sexual pleasure. Due to the risk of contracting AIDS, both these practices are considered unsafe except when they occur in strictly monogamous relationships whose partners know they're not infected.

The more accepted term is sexual deviation. Perversion probably should be restricted to sexual arousal behaviors that are harmful to another person or animal. This refers to sexual activity that is usually compulsive and guilt-ridden. Examples might be a male who gets his kicks from displaying his penis to a woman in a public place or a woman who enjoys intercourse only when she causes physical pain to her partner. We all have "perverted" feelings at times. They are neurotic if they are one's main way of getting sexually satisfied.

Fear of Other People's Preferences. It's all right to have sexual preferences. It is not necessary to enjoy or "be into" anal, oral, auto-, homo-, or group sexuality to be "with it." But having fixed powerful emotions, such as feeling that something is revolting, disgusting, perverse, obscene, or unnatural, in response to behavior that is enjoyable *to others,* usually means that you have a problem. Males are occasionally heard to say, If any faggot so much as comes near me, I'll kill him. This may mean that the person who makes the threat is immensely threatened by his own homosexual impulses, which, of course, we all have. It does not necessarily suggest that the person is, in fact, a homosexual.

Sexual Addictions. Compulsive masturbation means you do it not because you like it but because you can't help it. (However troublesome, it is still "safer" than compulsive eating or drinking.) Compulsive heterosexual or homosexual behavior (even if not forced on the other person) takes place outside an interest in a relationship. It does not enhance or enrich the person, and it rarely provides gratification beyond momentary relief. A person who is always "on the make" is rarely capable of a sustained relationship, and despite boasting to the contrary, usually does not enjoy sex. Sexual molestation of children is always pathological. Obsessive-compulsive involvement in sadomasochism or pornography also can represent a sexual addiction. When you seldom or never become sexually aroused without involving the compulsive behavior or object, most likely an addictive process is present. Addictions are often found in behaviors that inflict themselves in exploitative ways on others, such as exhibitionism, voyeurism, or making obscene phone calls.

First Experiences of Sexual Intercourse. Many first experiences of sex are not pleasurable despite stories to the contrary. This is especially true if they occur when you are too young, too immature, or on your honeymoon. It is especially important not to diagnose yourself on the basis of these experiences. Men sometimes think they are sexual freaks if they have erectile dys-

function or ejaculate prematurely on their first encounters. Women may feel that they are not sexual or feminine if they don't have an orgasm the first time around.

It is surprising how many people have acknowledged that their first sexual experiences were empty, flat, repulsive, and even painful. Yet, sex can become a beautiful experience if two people care about each other and give priority to their relationship. On the other hand, sex can become a nightmare if the two don't care about each other or concentrate on position games and simultaneous orgasms, or if they have to sneak, hide, and hurry.

On Being Sexually Attractive. People who are self-accepting are sexually attractive to *some* other individuals! It doesn't matter what the cosmetics and toothpaste industries have to say about it.

As the above list illustrates, people experience pressures to be healthy and well adjusted in many areas of their lives. We are not suggesting that we have to be completely comfortable with our sexuality, only that we not be hung up or pervasively preoccupied with it. We are suggesting that once we put our own sexuality into perspective, we will be making fewer mistakes as we relate to our friends, family, and children.

There exists no such thing as complete comfort or self-actualization with regard to one's sexuality. Such mythical comfort represents a self-defeating goal for people who might otherwise be content with their own level of growth.

Reference
Bell, A. P., & Weinberg, M. S. (1978). *Homosexualities: A study of diversity among men and women.* New York: Simon & Schuster.

To Apply This Reading to Yourself

1. *For Gordon and Snyder, sexual fulfillment is number 9 on the list of the 10 most important characteristics of a relationship. Where would you place it on the list? Why?*
2. *Concerning sexuality, Gordon and Snyder state, "Our bias is toward common sense and respect for individual differences. This is preferable to 'hard data,' or rigid moral imperatives." Discuss*

your own bias on sexuality, indicating the extent of your agreement or disagreement with the authors.

3. Pick out one of Gordon and Snyder's sexual ideas with which you strongly agree, and indicate why.

4. Pick out one of Gordon and Snyder's sexual ideas with which you strongly disagree, and indicate why.

5. Pick out one of Gordon and Snyder's sexual ideas with which your own position has changed, and indicate how this change has come about.

6. Pick out one of Gordon and Snyder's sexual ideas with which you and some significant other (parent, child, spouse, lover, etc.) take very different positions, and discuss this difference and its effects.

Sexual Shoals

Linda Morphis

Few things in life are as intensely pleasurable as sex, and few things are fraught with so much frustration and danger. Becoming clear on sexual issues is vital to healthy growth and development. Expressing yourself sexually with another can be either positive and enriching or destructive to yourself and to others. Only through awareness, understanding, and responsible sexual behavior can you establish your sexual self-confidence and experience the joy of sex. Sex does not establish who you are—it expresses who you are.

Read that again. Sex does not establish who you are. While sex itself is perfectly natural, bragging about it is always undesirable. All too often, college students find themselves listening to all sorts of fanciful stories about the sexual experiences of other students. It may seem as if everyone in college were a walking encyclopedia of sex! But while talk about sex certainly has become more open in recent years, the act of sex needs to remain a private matter between two individuals. While sex can be a joyous experience, it's not a prerequisite for success and happiness in life. In fact, contrary to popular belief, many college students choose to remain sexually inactive until marriage.

Peer pressure can transform sex from expression into obsession, and that can take most or all of the pleasure out of it. No book can tell you what your choices should be, and you should not listen to your friends just because their ideas seem right for them. Sexual feelings and desires are natural aspects of being human, and engaging in sexual intercourse is a personal, moral decision. Before you determine the degree of intimacy appropriate in a relationship, you should examine your values and clarify your feelings. College students frequently have "serial monogamous" relationships. Typically, they do not have multiple partners at any given time, but a series of monogamous relationships lasting any-

where from several weeks or months to several years.

Discrimination in how you express yourself sexually can ward off the guilt, worry, and remorse that too often limit the beauty of sharing oneself sexually with another individual. Sexual expression, therefore, can be part of an enduring and intimate relationship and requires the characteristics of self-knowledge, courage, communication, trust, and awareness.

For more information about sex, find out whether your college or university offers a course in human sexuality, and if so, take it. You may also want to visit your campus counseling center or peer advisement center. Like other important things in life, sex can be more rewarding if you first do your homework.

SEXUAL RESPONSIBILITY: BIRTH CONTROL

Although responsibility is a common thread running through all aspects of a healthy relationship, sexual intimacy makes special demands for responsible behavior. Unwanted pregnancies and sexually transmitted diseases are potential consequences of sexual activity that you must deal with in a mature and responsible manner. Although most birth-control methods were developed for use by women, both partners should share the responsibility for preventing unwanted pregnancy. Resources for further information on contraceptive methods are available on most college campuses. It is important to understand the mechanics, benefits, and risks of all types of birth-control methods, so that you may select a method that best suits your needs and sexual behavior pattern. Here is a brief summary of current contraceptive methods. Contact your health center on campus for more detailed information.

Oral Contraceptives ("the pill"). Oral contraceptives, which must be prescribed, are tablets that contain hormonal substances. Pills that contain estrogen and a progestogen, work by preventing ovulation. They are a very effective method of contraception. Certain restriction to their usage exists, but by and large, they are safe for 85 percent of the total female population and 95 percent of college-age females.

Norplant System. Norplant is a long-acting, reversible, hormonal contraceptive that has recently been approved for use in this country. It consists of six small plasticlike capsules that are inserted under the skin of a woman's upper arm. These hormone-containing capsules provide effective contraception for up to 5 years.

Intrauterine Device (IUD). An IUD is a small plastic or plastic-and-metal device that sometimes also contains synthetic hormones. It is inserted into the uterine cavity and probably prevents pregnancy by physically disturbing the uterine lining. It carries the chance of unrecognized expulsion, as well as a marked increased risk of deep pelvic infection with secondary infertility. These problems have caused most manufacturers to stop making IUDs, and the majority of practitioners no longer recommend them; however they are still available and are effective contraception under the right circumstances.

Surgical Sterilization. With surgical sterilization, a woman's fallopian tubes are cut, tied, blocked, or have a portion removed to prevent the egg from reaching the uterus (*tubal ligation*). For a man, a portion of the vas deferens is removed to prevent sperm from traveling from the testes to the prostate (*vasectomy*). A physician must perform these operations, which have no known side effects and are intended to be permanent. Such procedures are seldom recommended until a couple has had children or is absolutely certain they don't want any. Obviously, it is seldom the technique of choice for college students.

Barrier Techniques. With barrier techniques, we come to a place for male participation. In fact, to achieve maximum effectiveness, the male must participate! Additionally, here for the first time we have a pregnancy-prevention technique that also provides some degree of protection against the spread of sexually transmitted infections, especially when the male partner gets into the act. There are four major types of barrier contraceptives. Each is mentioned separately, but it is only when both partners accept mutual responsibility and each uses a barrier simultaneously that maximum protection is attained. This level of effectiveness still falls somewhat short of that provided by oral contraceptives, but consistent use leads to a reasonably close approximation, especially when combining two methods (e.g., condom and spermicide).

1. Condom (prophylactic, "rubber"): A condom—a sheath of latex or animal membrane—may be purchased without a prescription and is placed over the erect penis before intercourse. Its purpose is to prevent semen from escaping, but it must be applied with a little "slack" at the end to prevent rupture with ejaculation, and careful removal of the penis from the vagina is essential to prevent spillage. Initiation of intercourse before applying a condom decreases its effectiveness to the level of the withdrawal technique.

2. Spermicides: Spermicides include foams, creams, gels, and suppositories that can be purchased without a prescription. They are inserted into the vagina shortly before intercourse in order to kill sperm. As previously mentioned, these products are most effective when used with condoms.

3. Vaginal Sponge: The vaginal sponge is the newest (and most expensive) of the nonprescription barriers. Made of polyurethane foam shaped to fit closely to the cervix, the spermicide is incorporated into the sponge and is activated by wetting prior to insertion into the vagina.

4. Diaphragm and Cervical Cap: Both the diaphragm and the cervical cap must be fitted individually by a practitioner who will supply the unit or provide a prescription for it. Although they are classified together, these should not be confused with one another. The diaphragm has been around for years, is larger than the cervical cap, and fits into the vaginal canal. The cervical cap is a more recent option. Shaped somewhat like a thimble, it is fitted to cover the cervix. Both require the accompanying use of a spermicidal cream or gel to achieve adequate contraceptive protection. Regular inspection for even the smallest of holes and replacement at rea-

sonable intervals are essential. Moreover, an intervening pregnancy or a weight gain or loss of 15 to 20 pounds warrants a reevaluation because of a possible size change.

Withdrawal. As the name implies, withdrawal is accomplished by the male withdrawing the penis from the vagina prior to ejaculation. Unfortunately, occasional leakage of semen may occur without either participant being aware of it, and at other times, the emotions of the moment overwhelm one's best intentions. Either event will result in the presence of sperm in the vagina; hence, this method is only slightly more reliable than hope!

Rhythm. The theory of the rhythm technique is that certainty of the time of ovulation (release of an egg) allows a couple to avoid intercourse when conception is most likely. In reality, the practice is more complex and requires knowledge, consistency, and commitment. It is, however, an excellent adjunct to barrier methods.

Douching. Douching involves washing the semen out of the vagina immediately after intercourse and provides the poorest results of any method mentioned. No self-respecting sperm will wait around long enough for this sort of nonsense.

Morning-After Pill. This is treatment with a high dosage of the female hormone estrogen. If used shortly after unprotected intercourse (a maximum of 72 hours), the hormone prevents implantation of an egg by altering the uterine lining tissue. While not meant to be used as a contraceptive per se, it is an alternative that is available in an emergency situation (such as following a rape or breakage of a condom).

SEXUAL RESPONSIBILITY: SEXUALLY TRANSMITTED DISEASES

The newer term for venereal disease (VD) is sexually transmitted infection or sexually transmitted disease (STD). No matter what we call them, the meaning is the same—infections that are spread by sexual contact. Whenever and wher-

ever sexual activity increases, so does the incidence of STDs.

There is no such thing as "safe sex" except for that between uninfected partners. In the absence of proper testing, the problem is knowing who's infected and with what. No current protection against STDs is 100% safe, effective, or fail proof. However, there are ways to have "safer sex" and reduce the risk of becoming infected.

The best possible protection against STDs is, of course, not being sexually active. Otherwise, knowing your partner and limiting the number of partners should both be high-priority precautions. If you have decided to become sexually intimate with an individual, decide beforehand to be verbally intimate with that person. This means establishing a relationship that can include clear, open dialogue concerning STDs. You might say something like this: "Look, I feel like we're headed for a sexual relationship and I have some concerns about sexually transmitted infections. I do care for you, and I also care for myself. I need to know if you have been treated for, or have any infections—anything I need to know about. You can ask the same of me."

A further important precaution is the use of barrier contraception. In addition to providing contraception as was previously mentioned, these methods offer protection against STDs. Even if you or your partner is already using the pill, use condoms and a spermicide as well. Evidence shows that spermicides that contain nonoxynol-9 kill some STD organisms, and condoms protect against a variety of STDs, including AIDS. Research is continuing in this area; consult your physician to take advantage of the latest findings.

Often, negative attitudes about condoms are related to beliefs that condom use is unsatisfying, uncomfortable, and unnatural, to feelings of embarrassment, and to the idea that condoms can interfere with sexual sensation. Discuss the use of condoms and spermicide with your partner. Be assertive—your well-being is reason enough to insist they be used.

It is sometimes easier to have thought of possible responses before bringing up the subject of condoms. It can be very helpful to role-play situations with a trusted friend prior to bringing up the subject with your partner. Think of possible objections he/she might have and how you can best respond, and remember, if all else fails, the bottom line should be—no condom, no sex.

Partner Says:	You Say:
Hey, don't you trust me?	Don't *you* trust *me!* I really believe this is the best thing for us.
It just doesn't feel as good with a rubber on.	Well, that may be, but I think we can figure out other ways to feel loving and satisfied.
I hate stopping everything to put that thing on—I get out of the mood.	I think I can change your mind—let me show you . . .
I didn't bring one with me.	I did.
We didn't use one last time.	I know, and I realize that was a mistake we don't have to keep making.
Oh come on, it'll be okay without it—I love you.	I love you too, and I want both of us to be safe.
I don't even want to do it if we have to use that.	(Take a deep, determined breath) I'm sorry you feel that way, but that's the way it has to be.

A brief discussion of the major STDs affecting college students today follows. Remember that campus or local health clinics are readily available and are excellent sources for further information and/or treatment. All STDs require medical attention, and all partners must be treated.

Chlamydia or NGU. Chlamydial infection or NGU (nongonococcal urethritis) is a potentially serious and very prevalent disease. It has become more common than gonorrhea. The symptoms may include a puslike discharge from the tip of the penis or from the vagina and a tingling sensation upon urination, but frequently—especially in women—there are no obvious symptoms. Some men may have such a slight discharge that they will hardly notice it. Treatment is with an antibiotic. Symptoms, if they appear, usually do so about 1 to 3 weeks after

contact with the infected partner. Pelvic inflammatory disease (PID), a consequence of untreated chlamydial infection in women, is the leading cause of infertility.

Gonorrhea. This bacterial infection usually causes symptoms 2 to 10 days after exposure. Men may notice a discharge from the penis, as well as pain when urinating. Women may have an unusual discharge also, although as with chlamydia, women frequently have no symptoms. Examination and culture can verify whether you have a gonococcal infection. An untreated infection can lead to PID, sterility, and arthritis, as well as to problems in the newborns of an infected mother. Treatment is with an antibiotic.

Genital Herpes. This is a disease caused by a virus (herpes simplex virus—HSV I or HSV II), and there is presently no known cure. The disease causes painful, fluid-filled blisters that form on the genitals. These will rupture and eventually heal without scars. The disease recurs in most people infected with herpes, most often during times of physical or emotional stress. Treatment can prolong time between outbreaks and soothe the symptoms; however, it will not make the disease go away. Even so, if you suspect you may have genital herpes, seek medical assistance because several other diseases may cause similar sores in the genitals. You must avoid sexual contact when sores are present. Herpes is thought to be associated with an increased risk of cervical cancer in women and can have serious effects on an infant delivered through the infected vagina. Symptoms of herpes usually appear 2 to 20 days after you have been exposed to the infection. You can get genital herpes from HSV I, which causes cold sores or fever blisters in the mouth. Oral–genital sex and kissing should always be avoided if mouth sores are present.

Genital Warts. Genital warts (condyloma) first appear as small pink or red cauliflower-like growths on the vaginal lips, penis shaft, urinary opening, or rectum. They are usually painless, but some people may have itching, burning, or slight bleeding from these areas. In some cases, warts may extend into the vagina up to the cer-

vix. These warts may become so large in pregnant women as to make a vaginal delivery impossible. In males, they may spread up to the urethra and cause blockage. Genital warts may also increase a woman's risk of developing cervical cancer. The average incubation period of condyloma is 1 to 3 months but may extend to several years before symptoms develop. Removal methods include acids, blistering agents, laser treatments, freezing, and even surgical excision. Treatment depends on the size and location of the wart.

AIDS. AIDS stands for acquired (not inherited) immune deficiency (a breakdown of the body's defense system, producing susceptibility to certain diseases) syndrome (a spectrum of disorders and symptoms). People with AIDS suffer from unusual life-threatening infections and/or rare forms of cancer. Information on AIDS changes almost daily as we learn more about the syndrome. To date, we know that AIDS is caused by a retrovirus, called human immunodeficiency virus (HIV). This virus is extremely fragile and does not survive outside of body cells. It is present in the body fluids (notably in blood, semen, and saliva) of people who have been infected; these people may or may not have symptoms. Although it is certainly transmitted by blood and semen, there is no evidence that AIDS is transmitted by saliva because the virus is present there in very small amounts.

Anyone can get AIDS. While high-risk groups such as homosexual or bisexual men and IV drug users have been identified, it is vital to understand that AIDS is not a disease striking only these groups. People who don't belong to any of the established risk groups, women as well as men, have contracted AIDS; most have been sexual partners of those in one of the risk groups. AIDS can be transmitted sexually between men and women; some prostitutes carry the virus because they have multiple sexual partners and are commonly intravenous drug abusers. AIDS is also transmitted from mother to infant before or during birth. And make no mistake—college students are prime targets for AIDS, possibly because they do not view themselves as being "at risk." Because other STDs occur at an alarming rate on college campuses (10 percent of visits to college health services are for STD diagnosis and treatment), it is not unrealistic to think that the same sexual behaviors also put students in a high-risk category.

All people with positive blood tests for the antibody to the AIDS virus must regard themselves as carriers of the virus; whether or not they have symptoms, they are contagious and can transmit the infection to others. At this time, there is no cure or vaccine for AIDS, and none is likely in the foreseeable future. It is a killer—educate and protect yourself!

SEXUAL EXPLOITATION

Unfortunately, not all sexual interactions occur between two consenting adults. All too often, both women and men are victimized by unscrupulous individuals. While not an easy subject to discuss, it is nevertheless one that demands awareness and positive action to avoid.

Rape. There are many myths and misconceptions concerning sexual assault. Knowing the facts and understanding some of these common myths can help to change the "blame the victim" attitude:

- Women "ask" to be raped by the way they dress or act.
- Rape only happens to a certain type of woman.
- Men deserve to have sex with their date after spending a bundle of money on her.
- Most rapists are strangers.
- Rape occurs when a man gets so turned on for sex he can't control himself.
- A man can't be raped.
- When a woman says "no," it's a man's job to show her she means "yes."
- Rape rarely occurs on college campuses.
- When a woman does a stupid thing, such as going off with a man she hardly knows or getting stoned at a party, she deserves to be raped.

Rape is clearly and legally defined as sexual intercourse without consent, using force, the threat of force, or deception. It is an act of violence and aggression. Rape, rather than being an expression of sexual desire or gratification, is instead the use of sex to express issues of power, revenge, or anger. It can happen to anyone—male or female—and at any age. Reported cases have ranged from a 92-year-old woman to a 6-month-old child.

While men can be and are raped (almost always by other men), most rape victims are women between the ages of 16 and 24. Statistics vary, but all estimates indicate that rape is a very serious problem. Probably one out of every four college women will be a victim of rape or attempted rape, and in the majority of such cases, they will be acquainted with the assailant. If the rapist and the victim are acquainted, the assault is called "date rape" or "acquaintance rape."

Date rapes most frequently occur when a woman is alone with a man but can happen when others are relatively close by—it can take place in an upstairs bedroom with many people present at a party downstairs. Any time that a woman is alone with a man, whether in his room, his apartment, or his car, she is vulnerable.

There are many factors at play in a date/acquaintance rape situation. These may include the use of alcohol and/or other drugs, miscommunication, societal roles, and a disregard for a woman's rights.

Alcohol and/or other drugs very frequently play an important role in date rape. It may become a problem if the woman has had too much to drink or has taken too many other drugs to actually realize what situation she is in until it is too late. She may pass out only to awaken and find a man having sex with her totally without her consent. On the other hand, it may also be that the woman has had little to no alcohol but the man has been drinking excessively and becomes sexually aggressive and demanding.

Poor communication can result in date or acquaintance rape. Both men and women need to be aware of the nonverbal messages they send that may contradict the words they are saying. It is important that two people communicate and be aware of the signals sent with posture, voice tone, gestures, and eye contact. Mixed signals may be interpreted in a totally different manner than was intended. The woman acts in a friendly manner; the man interprets this friendliness as an invitation to have sex. "No" is heard as "maybe," and even a strong protest can be ignored under the delusion that women say "no" when they mean "yes." If a woman protests only

mildly, the man may think he is merely "persuading" her, not forcing her to have sex. (He may also think this, however, even if she protests vigorously.) Sometimes, a woman is not clear in her own mind what she wants or she may think that she will make up her mind as she goes along, while her male partner is interpreting her nonverbal messages, such as her enjoyment of kissing and caressing, as meaning that she wants to have sex with him. If she subsequently changes her mind and feels that she does not want to have sex, the man can feel cheated, rejected, and angry and may decide he has been teased or misled and "deserves" to get some satisfaction, regardless. The result can be, and often is, rape.

This lack of communication also plays into societal roles, for both for male and female. Men are generally taught and encouraged to be the aggressor, to be competitive, to not take "no" for an answer, and to keep on trying. Masculinity involves experimentation with sexual satisfaction and strong sexual feelings. Women, on the other hand, are socialized to be more passive, dependent, submissive, and placating. They are discouraged from experimenting with their sexuality. In this context, a woman is allowed to have sex if she "is swept away" with emotion, but along with this is the idea that she cannot agree to sex too readily, for fear of being labeled as "easy." And from somewhere within all the societal expectations and miscommunications between individuals emerges the concept of the "no actually means yes" dilemma, both for men and for women.

In the final analysis, however, date/acquaintance rape is not simply the product of miscommunication or disrespect for the rights of others; nor is it merely the result of interpreting societal roles and stereotypes in a negative way. While these issues are most certainly contributing factors—it remains foremost a violent act of aggression, one of misdirected anger and assertion of power. It is a problem that threatens the essence of intimate relationships between men and women—that being trust—and thus goes far beyond individual and personal concern. It concerns all men and women and must be approached by both with insight, awareness, and a desire to take positive corrective action.

Guidelines for women:

Date/acquaintance rape may not always be avoidable, but there are some things you can do to reduce risks and stay in control of the situation.

1. Avoid situations that isolate you from others. Cars, dorm rooms, and off-campus apartments are the types of places where you may be vulnerable.
2. Stay sober, and be able to get yourself home. Have your own transportation or taxi fare.
3. Be independent and aware of your dates. Have opinions on what you will do, and pay your own way.
4. Be aware of specific situations in which you feel uncomfortable or not in charge. Trust your gut instinct; if you are uncomfortable and want to leave early, do it without fear of seeming rude.
5. Do not give mixed messages—say "yes" when you mean "yes" and "no" when you mean "no." Passivity may be interpreted as permission, and if a woman ignores sexual overtones she does not like, it may be viewed as tacit approval to continue—men are not mind readers.
6. Refuse verbally, clearly, and with determination, to participate in sexual activities that are against your will. Do not worry about being "impolite." Accepting the myth that women should not act forcefully—or that anger is unfeminine—makes women more vulnerable.
7. Watch out for men who ignore your personal space boundaries, ignore what you have to say, hold stereotypical beliefs about women, do what they want regardless of your wishes, or accuse you of being "uptight" if you resist their sexual advances.
8. Remember—if you are raped, it was not your fault. No one asks to be raped or deserves it. Tell someone—this may be your first step to recovery. Contact your university health service for help, or look in the phone book for local support organizations.

Guidelines for men:

Take responsibility for your actions, and avoid getting involved in an acquaintance-rape situation.

1. It is never okay to force yourself on someone. Even if you feel you've been "led on"; you've paid for an expensive evening; she is dressed in a sexy way; she's had sex with you before—repeat—it is **never** okay.
2. If you are getting an unclear message from your partner about having sex, do not assume that you want what your partner wants—ASK!
3. If your partner is unsure about what she wants, be sensitive, and suggest talking about it. Do not try to pressure her into having sex.
4. Your desires and your actions are two different things. You are responsible for your actions even if you are sexually excited or if you are intoxicated.
5. No one asks to be raped or enjoys having sex forced on them. No matter how a woman behaves, she does not deserve to have her body used in ways she does not want.
6. In order to consent, your partner must have the ability to make a decision. If that person is physically or mentally incapable of making a decision, the act of sexual intercourse is considered rape.
7. Remember, rape is a crime of violence. It is illegal.

Sexual Harassment. Webster defines *harassment* as "to annoy persistently." Add the word *sexual*, and the term *sexual harassment* takes on a new, very disturbing meaning. It is a widespread problem on college campuses and while harassment can be directed at a person of the same or the opposite sex, studies indicate that as many as 30 to 40 percent of women experience some form of harassment. It can be seen in an abuse-of-power situation involving exploitation of the relationship between faculty or administrators and students, or between students themselves.

Sexual harassment, in general, involves *unwanted* sexual attention. The elements of choice, mutual attraction, caring, and a reciprocal interest in pursuing a relationship are absent in sexual harassment. It is coerced, unethical, and unwanted intimacy, and may primarily be divided into two categories—verbal and physical. Verbal harassment may include:

- Suggestive or insulting sounds
- Jokes about sex
- Sexual comments and remarks about clothing, body, or intimate activities
- Sexual propositions or invitations
- Demeaning sexist remarks

Physical harassment may include:

- Staring, leering, or ogling in a sexual way
- Any inappropriate touching, patting, or pinching
- Purposely brushing against the body
- Attempted or actual fondling or kissing
- Making obscene gestures
- Coerced sexual intercourse, assault

Such inappropriate behaviors are particularly offensive when the harasser is in a position of relatively greater power, such as when suggested as a condition of a student's grade or employment, or when the behaviors create an atmosphere that interferes with or prevents an individual's academic or work success. Other things such as the display of obscene photography or insults about women in general are considered by some to be a form of sexual harassment. The key element in any of these situations is that when an individual makes it clear that the behavior is unwanted, the behavior continues.

Not only is sexual harassment obnoxious and deplorable, it is also illegal. Title IX of the Educational Amendment of 1972 prohibits sex discrimination in institutions receiving federal funds. Title IX requires an institution to provide an environment free of discrimination and clearly prohibits sexual harassment of students by faculty and staff, as well as harassment of students by students. It is also prohibited by both Title IX and Title VII of the Civil Rights Act of 1964, as amended in 1980. Although varying from state to state, the state laws concerning sexual assault and abuse may offer protection to harassed students. Local laws prohibiting disorderly conduct or obscene or lascivious behaviors may be applicable to peer harassment.

While standards of these laws may still be evolving, the majority of colleges and universities take the situation very seriously and have formed clear and explicit guidelines prohibiting sexual harassment, as well as appropriate channels for reporting harassment incidents. If such policies are not in place, immediate action should be taken by university administration to make them so. Some experts contend that universities may indeed be liable if acts of harassment by either university employees or fellow students are not dealt with swiftly and effectively.

Do not assume that by remaining silent the harassing behavior will stop. In the vast majority of instances, silence is perceived as agreement, and the offensive behavior continues and will probably escalate. If you encounter sexual harassment or are unsure that what you are experiencing is sexual harassment, seek the advice of an appropriate official. Show your disapproval by letting the individual know that the behavior is offensive to you and must be stopped. Keep a record of each incident in as much detail as possible, include dates, places, times, and witnesses, as well as describing the situation.

Other ways in which students may actively work to eliminate sexual harassment include the following:

- Contact experts on sexual harassment, and have them present workshops and talks on the subject. This not only educates people as to what sexual harassment is and what to do about it, but can also stimulate action on campus to get policies adopted and grievance procedures instituted if none exist.
- Develop pamphlets, posters, and fliers on sexual harassment, and include these in student-orientation packets. This may help prevent sexual harassment from occurring and also informs people about it before it occurs. It may also help in dealing with the situation more effectively, should sexual harassment occur.
- Gather information on your campus concerning sexual harassment, and publicize this information in student newspapers.

You have the right—legally, morally, and ethically—to expect freedom from sexual harassment. Creating an environment that promotes academic success, as well as individual freedom and development, is the responsibility of university administration, faculty, staff, and each individual student.

To Apply This Reading to Yourself

1. Discuss any peer pressure you have observed or experienced concerning sexual conduct.
2. Discuss the degree of responsibility that you and/or your peers show concerning sexual conduct.
3. Discuss the principles that you believe should govern the degree of sexual intimacy in a relationship.
4. Discuss any sexual exploitation you have observed or experienced.
5. Morphis writes that some sexual exploitation is due to faulty communication. Discuss your own observations, conclusions, and/or experience in this regard.
6. Discuss the relative risk of sexual exploitation in the various environments in which you move (college, work, leisure activities, etc.) indicating what is being done or could be done to minimize this risk.

PART
three

EXPLORING
FEELINGS

Humans are emotional beings. We feel love and hate. We feel delight and sorrow. We feel shame, guilt, and pride. We feel anger, rage, and jealousy. Sometimes we even feel calm and at peace.

Emotion can be defined as a feeling state that stems from and influences the individual's behavior. Our behavior affects our feelings. When our goal-seeking behavior is going well, our emotional tone is generally positive; we are in good spirits and may feel cheerful or elated. When goals are blocked and needs go unmet, our tone is negative, and we may feel angry or depressed.

Our behavior affects our feelings, and our feelings affect our behavior. Research has shown that when we are happy, we tend to be more generous and benevolent. When we are angry, we may be tempted to strike out, and when we are fearful, we tend to withdraw. When we are very relaxed or content or sometimes when we are very anxious or depressed, we may be nearly immobilized, and it may be difficult for anyone to get us to do anything.

Strong and persistent emotions can make us ill. We may refer to a trying situation as "sickening" and mean this in both a figurative and a literal sense. In strong feeling states, the body is mobilized for action, and changes take place in the internal organs. With unremitting mobilization, certain physiological dysfunctions or psychosomatic illnesses may occur.

Emotions can make us ill, but they are also important to our well-being and even our survival. Our emotions motivate and enliven us. They color and enrich our lives. The ability to express one's feelings with honesty and grace is a highly valued skill and important in human relationships.

Many different states of emotion have been described by psychologists, writers, poets, and others who have been interested in human feelings. Interestingly, surveys of textbooks and professional journals indicate that psychologists have for many years been preoccupied with the study of unpleasant emotions. By contrast, a survey of literary sources shows a greater emphasis on pleasant states of feeling.

In Part Three of this book, the focus is on two exceedingly important emotions: *anxiety* and *happiness.* Of all the emotions, anxiety has been one of the most studied by psychologists. Our times have been lamented as the "age of anxiety," although not everyone agrees that we human beings are too anxious. It has been pointed out, for example, that our society requires anxiety to make it work, just as each individual requires a certain amount to act as a signal, rouser, and moving force. Anxiety can be either a positive or a negative force in our life. The readings on anxiety have been chosen to highlight both its positive and its negative aspects and to show us how to value the positive and minimize the negative.

Unlike anxiety, happiness has been subjected to little scientific study until recently. For example, many psychology textbooks do not have a single listing for happiness in the index. Yet the pursuit of happiness has been a persistent quest even though not everyone agrees that happiness is a worthy or even achievable state. The readings on this topic suggest how we can pursue happiness and also catch its cousin, optimism.

Anxiety

It is clear that we have developed a society which depends on having the right amount of anxiety to make it work.

—Margaret Mead

I think I've got a secret. It's keep your bloody eyes open, all your senses open. You never know what might be useful. It's like a disease with me. Learning to fly in the navy during the war, you had to develop a technique, a certain feeling, a poise—it was fatal to be too relaxed, fatal to be too tense.

—Laurence Olivier

Anxiety is a state of arousal caused by a threat to well-being. When we are anxious, we feel endangered or challenged in some way, and we are tense or uneasy and ready to act or respond. To be anxious is, of course, a common human experience. For some of us who are particularly vulnerable, feelings of this kind may be more salient than any other emotion.

Anthropologist Margaret Mead wrote that our society needs a certain amount of anxiety to function properly, and psychological research suggests that stress, up to a certain point, is helpful in learning and performing certain tasks. Too much anxiety can disorganize our efforts or even paralyze us. With too little anxiety, we may not rouse ourselves and do the things that need to be done.

Although our era has been called "the age of anxiety," Mead found modern stress preferable to the terror, fright, and hunger of simpler societies. With some "megafrightening" crises as possibilities, we may wonder how well off any of us are in this Spaceship Earth. For starters (although "enders" might be a better word), there are the threats of nuclear Armageddon, massive changes in climate and in ocean level because of the warming of the planet, a serious global water shortage, and an international financial crisis. Our world has become riskier, and in such a world, it has been said, you're crazy if you're not frightened. The choice between these two options is not appealing.

Our era might also be called "the age of the tranquilizer." Enormous quantities of pills have been consumed by individuals who are seeking relief from their anxieties, fears, and worries. In recent years, many people have sought other ways of combating anxiety or finding peace of mind through relaxation techniques, meditation, individual and group therapies, and related experiences of various kinds.

Many persons believe that somehow they should be free of anxiety. They consider anxiety a sign of abnormality because to be normal means (they think) that one is relaxed, happy, and has peace of mind. But meaningful living necessarily involves anxiety—a small amount much of the time, and perhaps great bursts or waves upon occasion. A moderation of anxiety, a tolerance for it, and an understanding of it—not a completely stress-free life—is as much as we should want and aspire to achieve.

APPRECIATING ANXIETY

In the first reading, Daniel Sugarman and Lucy Freeman focus on the merits of anxiety. Anxiety alerts us, rouses us, and prompts us to do what we should do. Anxiety is both a sign and a price of growth; we become anxious when we leave comfortable plateaus and begin the ascent to higher reaches. Some of us so fear fear—become so anxious about being anxious—that we become worse off than before. Anxiety, these writers point out, is not necessarily the enemy; it can be a good—though sometimes painful—friend and helper.

Anxiety can be a sign of growth, but it also can be a sign that we need to grow. The latter may be true if our anxiety is especially severe or persistent or if we are going to considerable lengths to avoid it or defend ourselves against it. In such cases, we may need to do a better job of facing up to our fears or outwitting our worries or redesigning our lives. For some ideas on how to do this, read on.

FACING FEARS

Fear is a term that has been used almost interchangeably with anxiety, but a useful distinction can be made between the two. Anxiety is an emotion, while fear is an ideation; that is, fear is the idea that a particular stimulus or set of conditions will produce the emotion of anxiety. The term phobia, rather than fear, is used when the aversive stimulus has the potential for causing very strong anxiety. One could have a fear or a phobia but avoid anxiety by avoiding the stimulus that triggers it; for example, one could fear heights but have no anxiety as long as one remained at low elevations.

Where do our needless or exaggerated fears come from? Some appear to be fixated—they are childish fears we have never outgrown, possibly because our parents never challenged them or never helped us deal with them. Some may be fears our parents taught us through excessive warnings or by their own example.

Some of our fears are traumatic in origin—they result from shocking experiences that sensitize us to particular stimuli. After a wildly turbulent flight, we may dread the return trip home. Through *generalization*, not only the original stimulus but others associated with it can evoke some degree of anxiety; the connection may be so subtle that a particular fear may seem senseless. For example, after the turbulent flight, we may become anxious at the sight of the return ticket there on the dining room table or our hostess's chicken a la king (which, come to think of it, was what flew off the tray when the plane went into a seemingly endless free fall).

Many of our fears involve errors in appraisal. We make too much of little dangers—overestimating the possibility that something will occur or overestimating the consequences if it did. At the same time, we may underestimate our ability to cope with the situation.

The most common strategy for dealing with fear is avoidance. We stay away from what we fear. If we fear flying, we travel by car or by train, or we simply stay home. If we fear speaking in public, we sit in the back row, where we won't be called on to speak. If we fear the water, we stay high and dry. Of course, such maneuvers may prove inconvenient and may make our lives more narrow or less rich than they otherwise would be.

According to folk wisdom, the thing to do if you are thrown from a horse is to get right back on. Or if you nearly drown, get back in the water. One reason for fear to persist is that we assiduously avoid the feared situation and never learn to deal with it. It's generally true that we overcome fear best by facing up to it.

Clinicians have devised various procedures to help their clients face and master their fears. One approach, which might be called "head-first-into-the-deep-end," brings the person back into the feared situation to demonstrate that there is no danger or that the danger can be managed. A second, more gentle approach is the "feet-first-into-the-shallow-end" technique; in one variation, the client is taught deep relaxation and then proceeds to visualize aspects of the feared situation, arranged in a hierarchy according to their power to provoke anxiety (least to most); as one aspect is accommodated without disrupting the relaxation, the situation at the next higher level of anxiety provocation is visualized, and so slowly all the way to the top of the hierarchy and finally out to the actual situation itself.

In the next two readings, two laypersons demonstrate their personal use of head-first and feet-first tactics (and all done without paying a cent to a psychologist). In the second selection, head-firster Amy Gross suggests that we overcome our fears by heroically facing them. She points out that everyday life is filled with small terrors and monsters, and we need to confront them and stare them down. Her path to growth leads us into and through our fears. "The alternative," she writes, "is flight, constant flight."

Morton Hunt suggests a less heroic approach in the third reading. His own life has taught him to cope with frightening prospects by taking one step at a time and focusing only on that one step. Then he moves on to the next step, feeling a sense of accomplishment with each move. We, too, can move single step by single step, until we have gotten to where we want to go and can look back amazed and proud of the distance we have come.

OUTWITTING WORRY

A *worry* is a fear concerning an anticipated event. Worrying is a common kind of human suffering. Many events that we worry about never happen, but as we fret and stew about them we foresee and foretaste and experience them in some degree. Although inveterate worriers may feel themselves to be passive victims of their condition, some authorities have noted that worry is self-instigated and self-maintained and not without its rewards or payoffs.

One reason for worry's popularity is that worry works; at least, most things we worry about don't happen, so worry appears to be a good control device. (Who knows what would have happened if we had left the flight entirely up to the crew?) Some of us expect life to be exacting, and worry is a way of paying our dues; it's a kind of self-punishment so that we don't get worse. Also, occupying ourselves with worry over things we can't control can excuse us from attending to more painful problems. One last set of reasons: Worry proves to others we care (we worry so) and is a way of controlling them (you can't do that because it would worry me too much).

A number of psychologists have been busily researching worry, and in the last reading, James Lincoln Collier reviews their insights and recommendations. These workers point out the considerable difference between *worry* (a fretting over what could go wrong) and *problem solving* (a focus on what can be made to go right). They recommend we set aside regular periods for worry and confine our worry to these periods. When worries occur out of bounds, we quickly interrupt them and relax ourselves or substitute positive thoughts and images. Such tactics won't eliminate all worries but can help many of us to worry much less.

To Explore Your Own Anxiety, Fear, and Worry

1. *Exploring fear.* Consider one of your present fears. Write a description of it and indicate what you think its causes or meanings are, how it affects your life or how you deal with it, and how you might ameliorate or get rid of it.
2. *Sharing fears.* Form small groups or dyads. In turn, each member describes a present fear, its causes or meanings, and its effects or influence. Then the other members of the group respond to this person and suggest ways of dealing with, ameliorating, or eliminating this fear.

3. *Empathizing with fear (individual approach)*. Everyone anonymously writes a personal fear on a 3 × 5 card or slip of paper and places it in a box. Each draws a card and accepts the fear described on it as her or his own. Then, in the larger group or in a small group or dyad, each describes the fear he or she has drawn and elaborates on it, suggesting its causes or meanings, its effects or influence, and ways that it might be dealt with, ameliorated, or eliminated.

4. *Empathizing with fear (group approach)*. Everyone anonymously writes a personal fear on a 3 × 5 card or slip of paper and places it in a box. After forming small groups, each group draws out as many cards as it will have time for. One member of the group reads the fear on the card, and the entire group accepts the fear as its own, elaborating on it, suggesting its causes or meanings, its effects or influence, and ways it might be dealt with, ameliorated, or eliminated.

5. *The worry list*. On a sheet of paper, list everything you are worried about. Then cross off all those items that would have very little chance of happening or would not be particularly terrible or catastrophic if they did. Afterward, write a brief paper justifying the remaining worries. As an option, form dyads, and try to talk each other out of the remaining worries.

6. *The payoff sheet*. It is sometimes said that it is useless to worry, but worrying has been shown to have many uses or payoffs. Worrying may serve as a diversion to draw our attention away from more vexing problems, and it may give us an excuse for not acting (because we are too worried) or for acting in the wrong way (because worry drives us to it). Worrying, too, can attract the commiseration and assistance of others or announce to the world that we are caring and concerned. And worrying sometimes seems to serve as self-imposed suffering, a price we pay to rid ourselves of guilt or to keep something worse from happening. Why do *you* worry? Take a sheet of paper, and list all the uses and payoffs you can for your worrying behavior. Afterward, as an option, share your list in the larger group, in smaller groups, or in dyads.

7. *The fear of growth*. We desire to grow, but we also fear growth. We may cling to the comfort and safety of staying where (or who) we are and avoid the uncertainty, risk, and responsibility of becoming something more. Why do you *fear* growth? What fears do you have about changing or becoming more than you are? Write at the top of a sheet of paper: "I fear growth because . . . ." Then brainstorm (uncritically conjure up) and write down as many reasons as you can why you might fear growth. Then go back and underline any reasons that seem more real or important to you and discuss these in a brief paper or share them in the larger group, in small groups, or in dyads.

8. *The anxiety and conflict of growth*. We can fear growth just as we can fear not growing, and sometimes we are caught in a conflict between growth and antigrowth forces in ourselves. Our anxiety may stem from this conflict and be a signal of it. If we understand this anxiety and refuse to run from it, we may break through to a

new period of growth. Draw a vertical line down the middle of a sheet of paper. Over the left column, write the title "Growth Forces." Over the right column write the title "Antigrowth Forces." Now write a dialogue or argument between the two, taking each side in turn.

First identify with your growth forces and speak or write in your "growth-forces voice," arguing for moving forward and growing. ("I am bored silly; I've got to get moving.") Then identify with your antigrowth side, speak or write in your "antigrowth voice" and argue for drawing back and standing pat. ("Better stay just where I am. Things aren't so bad. Why take risks?") Keep the dialogue/argument going until one side seems to come out on top. As an alternative, have a volunteer (or a number of volunteers in turn) conduct the dialogue/argument out loud before the larger group or in small groups. For this purpose, use two chairs, one for the volunteer to sit on while enacting the growth role and the other while enacting the antigrowth role.

9. *Debilitating and facilitating anxiety.* Anxiety can be a negative or positive force, but we more often think of it as the former than the latter. Think through your own life and find two examples of anxiety-laden experiences, one in which anxiety proved negative and debilitating and the other in which it was positive or facilitating. Write these down, and, as an option, share them in the larger group, in small groups, or in dyads.

10. *Exploring existential anxiety.* Existential anxiety is that which surrounds our attempts to find meaningful and fulfilling lives for ourselves. Write a brief essay on your own existential anxiety. You might title it: "What I find frightening (and/or challenging) about this time of my life."

To Read Further

Burns, D. D. (1990). *The feeling good handbook: Using the new mood therapy in everyday life.* New York: Plume. (paperback)

Davis, M., Eshelman, E. R., & McKay, M. (1988). *The relaxation & stress reduction workbook* (3rd ed.). Oakland, CA: New Harbinger. (paperback)

Kopp, S. (1988). *Raise your right hand against fear. Extend the other in compassion.* New York: Ballantine. (paperback)

Mason, L. J. (1986). *Guide to stress reduction* (rev. ed.). Berkeley, CA: Celestial Arts.

McCullough, C. J. (1990). *Always at ease: Overcoming shyness and anxiety in every social situation.* Los Angeles: J. P. Tarcher.

Wolpe, J. M., & Wolpe, D. (1988). *Life without fear: Anxiety and its cure.* Oakland, CA: New Harbinger. (paperback)

The Positive Face of Anxiety

Daniel A. Sugarman and Lucy Freeman

Anxiety is the most painful of all emotions, and many people will do anything to avoid direct confrontation with it. Like a child terrified of going to the dentist, they permit anxiety to fester and cause psychic decay. They refuse to submit to the direct confrontation which removes the decay and the chronic pain. Some use so much energy defending themselves against anxiety that there is little left for the enjoyment of living.

We are learning that it is not anxiety itself, but the way we handle anxiety, that makes the difference between emotional sickness and health. A refusal to acknowledge the anxiety within us prevents the possibility of greater personality growth.

The widespread use of tranquilizers has helped—and hindered. On one hand, millions have obtained sufficient relief from anxiety to cope with daily difficulties; but the indiscriminate use of these powerful medications has prevented many from coming to terms with their conflicts. If they were just a little more desperate, they might seek psychological help and get at the source of the anxiety.

THE GIFT OF ANXIETY

In our hedonistic society, it is difficult for many to believe that anything which stings a bit can be of value. Nevertheless, in spite of our love of the sun, rainy days are important in the total scheme of things. Without any anxiety, we would become like vegetables, unable to sense the passing danger that threatens us from every side. The hyper-vigilance anxiety brings makes it easier for us to detect danger and take appropriate measures against it.

One mother described to me how, in putting her eight-month-old baby to bed one night, she felt suddenly anxious about his health. It seemed he did not look healthy, as though he were coming down with a cold; nor did she like the way he sounded when he cried. With these thoughts in mind, when she went to bed, she had difficulty sleeping. About two in the morning, she became aware of wheezing noises from the child's bedroom. Dashing to his side, she found him in the midst of a severe attack of the croup. Hardly breathing, the child was rushed to the emergency room of a hospital where his life was saved. In this case, as in others, without anxiety on the part of the mother, there might have been a tragedy.

A patient of mine, made anxious one evening by a television program warning against breast cancer, decided to examine her breasts. To her horror, she noted a small lump. Prompt biopsy, performed forty-eight hours later, revealed the lump to be malignant. Although she lost a breast, she is now, five years later, very much alive and well. Without her anxiety, the outcome probably would have been different.

Too often we are ashamed to admit anxiety. Nourished by an emotional diet of heros, we inflict unreasonable expectations upon ourselves. A deer or rabbit, unencumbered by the pretense of courage, will take to its heels at the first sign of danger and, by doing so, ensure its survival.

An adolescent patient told me that several other teen-agers had tried to tempt him into a drag race on a busy highway. When he refused to take part because he felt that to race on that particular highway was too dangerous, the others called him chicken. He replied, "I'd rather be a chicken than a dead duck."

Often those willing to acknowledge their anxiety turn out to be stronger than those who equate anxiety with cowardice. I have seen patients delay treatment because they were "going to work it out by myself," only to crack under the burden of unbearable anxiety.

One woman developed a severe anxiety condition during the early 1940s. Sent to a state mental hospital, she was given shock treatments, insulin therapy, and medication. In spite of all attempts to help her, her anxiety remained at a painfully high level. After five years of unsuccessful attempts to cure her, her family signed a permission form for a lobotomy (an experimental operation in which certain sections of the brain are destroyed, causing the person to become unable to experience anxiety in any depth).

After the lobotomy, she seemed considerably improved. She began to sleep and gained over fifty pounds. She no longer was agitated or anxious, and it was decided she could be sent home. Once home, however, she had to be cared for almost constantly by her family because she had lost all sense of possible danger. She could not emotionally comprehend that cars traveling at a rapid speed could pose a threat, and she would cross the street on a red light. One day, while no one was watching, she blindly walked into a speeding car. Although she survived the accident, she paid a terrible price for her lack of fear.

The more psychologists learn about the child, the more they learn about the role anxiety plays in helping us to grow into human beings. Some feel that without anxiety the child would never learn the social skills required to live among other people. It is probably the anxiety over losing the approval and love of parents that propels us to higher marks in school and control of our aggressive and sexual impulses.

Anxiety is the force behind much learning. A student under the pressure of a final examination in physics may be motivated to pick up the book, burn the midnight oil, and cram. As a result, he may find that, not only has he passed the test, but learned a bit of physics. His more carefree classmate, not anxious enough to study, may find his academic career prematurely terminated as a result of flunking the exam.

In many ways, anxiety can force us to learn something that will increase our security. Psychoanalysts point out that one of the greatest motivations for a child to learn to walk is that once he learns, he can overcome to some extent the anxiety he feels when separated from his mother. Being able to walk permits him to reach his mother more readily, and he no longer feels so helpless.

Anxiety can also be a sign that we have violated some moral code. One woman, although in love with her husband, started an affair in a childish attempt to get revenge because she felt he had neglected her. As the affair progressed, she developed many symptoms of anxiety. She felt shaky and light-headed and very depressed. During the course of psychotherapy, she became aware of the underlying motives for her affair and gave up the destructive relationship with her lover. She was able to tell her husband how she felt about him. Although there was a period of strife, their problems were out in the open, and her anxiety diminished. In this case, as in others, anxiety had mounted to the point that the person finally did something about an unhappy life.

Anxiety may also prepare us for a stressful future situation. A man who has to give an important speech can be goaded by anxiety to rehearse not only his speech but the fear he may feel on the podium. As he faces this fear in anticipation of the event, there is a better chance that on the day of the speech he will be less afraid.

Dr. Irving Janis, a psychologist, studied the relationship between anxiety in patients about to undergo surgery and their recovery. He reported that those patients completely without anxiety before an impending major surgical operation had a more difficult postoperative period. He concluded that patients who expressed reasonable anxiety before surgery had fewer reactions of fear and anger after surgery.[1]

THE SIGN OF GROWTH

One young man in his middle twenties came to me for psychological consultation and testing. He drank excessively and was separated from his wife, whom he had beaten rather cruelly on several occasions. He had a severe psychosomatic skin condition which had persisted for seven years. Repeated consultations with dermatologists produced little change, and every dermatologist he saw suggested that he receive psychotherapy. Although not painful, the skin condition was disfiguring and marred what otherwise would have been a handsome appearance.

After looking over his psychological test and the interview material, I felt the prognosis for the change in this man was dim. In both his interview and the projective testing, it seemed that he rarely experienced even a twinge of overt anxiety. It was evident his symptom was bound up with whatever anxiety he felt and that he had little conscious awareness of being anxious.

The appearance of anxiety in psychological testing or clinical interview is a favorable prognostic sign. Psychotherapists know that when a patient complains of anxiety and tension and anxiety-related symptoms, his chances of recovery are usually good; but when a patient has all his anxiety bound up in a particular symptom and feels little overt discomfort, the path of therapy is likely to be extremely difficult. The more anxious a patient, the greater his motivation to change and to explore his unconscious conflicts. As he becomes more comfortable, this motivation may diminish, so that he loses interest in further exploration.

When I was interning in clinical psychology, I worked at a large Veterans Administration neuro-psychiatric hospital, which held several thousand patients. At that time, the hospital was divided into two units. One was an acute intensive treatment unit for recent admissions and patients readmitted after having made a good adjustment for a time outside the hospital. In general, the treatment facilities were aimed at this particular group, thought to have the best prognosis for recovery and discharge. The second unit was for continued care. On this service were placed patients who had either been hospitalized for many years or whose prognosis was poor.

I was impressed with the fact that, for the most part, those patients in the second unit made the best hospital adjustment and were relatively free from anxiety. Many, having lived in the hospital for years, were allowed grounds privileges, went home weekends, and in general were model patients. They slept well, ate well, and required little tranquilizing. The staff referred to them as burnt out. This meant there was little evidence of anxiety or conflict, that they had adjusted to a marginal level of existence.

On the acute intensive treatment unit, however, the situation was very different. These patients were agitated, anxious, fearful, and confused. When you walked into one of these wards you could sense the suffering and turmoil, signs that the patients were still fighting to resolve their conflicts rather than giving in to the regressive illness.

THE PRICE OF GROWTH

As we move through life, the stability of our personality is not always the same. There are times our defenses work well and life proceeds with little anxiety; but there are other times when defenses fail and we feel less stable or more anxious. Sometimes we experience anxiety when underlying growth is taking place. There has been little awareness that hardly any personality growth occurs without some anxiety.

Even the ancients recognized that anxiety and growth were associated. In the Bible a state of fear and anxiety is closely connected with impending revelation. When Moses came down from the mountain after his encounter with God, he frightened the people of Israel; it is written that, "When Aaron and all the people of Israel saw Moses, behold, the skin of his face shone, and they were afraid to come near him."[2]

The study of history and social psychology suggests that, in many situations, a state of national panic is the prelude to increased awareness of national goals and to legislation that may create a period of greater calm and stability.

Many positive steps in our life are accompanied by anxiety. Each time we extend ourselves further, accept new responsibility, or affirm our independence, we may also feel a measure of anxiety.

Once while traveling on a train in September, I sat next to a young girl who, pale and tense, sat with her teeth clenched, obviously very anxious. We began to talk; she told me she was on her way to college and that this was the first time she had ever been away from her family. As she spoke of leaving home, she plainly revealed both the anxiety she felt and her determination to become independent.

She described how she had always been overprotected by her mother and three older brothers and said that although it was hard for her to do, she had decided it would be the best thing for her to go to college in a distant city.

After she got off at her destination, I thought about her and the fact that she would have been relatively free of anxiety had she decided to remain at home. She was not going to let a little anxiety stop her from developing into an independent young woman. Some others, afraid of the anxiety of separation, have remained home, tied to mother and hearth forever.

In children the relationship between anxiety and growth is emphasized. I observed my son at the local swimming pool. Barely knowing how to swim at the beginning of the summer, he made tremendous advances under the tutelage of a good instructor. Towards the middle of the summer, he was able to navigate anyplace in the pool. Not content with this, he began to eye the diving board. With some trepidation, he first dived from the side of the pool. He then tried the low board. After a time, he looked up at the high board. After some encouragement, he mounted to the top of the high board, a pathetic sight to see. He was pale, tense, and very anxious. Finally, he jumped. When he emerged from the depths, he had on his face that smile of pure joy that comes from having conquered anxiety.

Observation of children shows that they will attack again and again a fear situation until it no longer causes anxiety. Once they have mastered it, they are ready to move on to the next fearful situation. Almost every sign of growth and independence contains some seeds of anxiety. The first day at kindergarten, the first night of sleeping at a friend's house, the first time on a bicycle—all produce anxiety. The child who has learned early not to shrink in the face of anxiety, but to move through it, will have that sense of increasing mastery which sets the foundation for a healthy personality.

Adults, too, may experience anxiety when they are about to grow or undertake some new responsibility. One man described the anxiety he felt at his house-closing. He had always had difficulty in accepting responsibility or long-term commitments. He had been living in a small, overcrowded apartment with his wife and two children. Although wanting to own a house, he had previously rejected this idea as bearing with it too much responsibility. Intellectually, he knew that living in a house was the only sensible thing to do, but his emotional difficulties prevented him from taking the step. After some therapy which helped him gain confidence in himself, he bought a house. His anxiety at the closing could be seen only as a prelude to growth and a rejection of his old neurotic patterns of behavior. After a short spell of discomfort, he began to feel good about what he had done.

Often we feel anxiety when we violate some childish, no longer appropriate, taboo. I worked with a young lady who was in acute conflict over her wish to remain home with her aged father and her love for a young man who wanted to marry her. She had been raised in a home where she had been controlled by a guilt-inducing father. After her mother had died, five years prior to treatment, her father in subtle, and not-so-subtle, ways had made it clear that he "probably couldn't live if she left him." After work, she would come home to care for this tyrant. She felt chronically depressed, but did not realize the cause of the depression.

The situation came to a crisis when she fell in love. When the young man proposed, she was thrown into acute anxiety, and sought help. After a short period of treatment, she decided she would accept the proposal of marriage, but still became anxious each time her father made her feel guilt for leaving him. Shortly after the wedding, however, she felt happier than she had been in her entire life. Her father, now thrown on his own, became more active socially and even resumed working. She reported he was faring better than at any time since his wife had died.

Almost every milestone in our life may be a source of anxiety—the first day of school, graduation, the first job, marriage, the birth of a child, the sending of a child to camp. Sometimes, too, anxiety will arise when we assert ourselves to others, going against the dreams they may have for us. A young adolescent I saw was rather introverted, preferring to spend time either by herself or with one or two close friends. She had literary ability and in one afternoon might produce a poem or short story, many of which were published by the school magazine. Her English teacher, recognizing her talent, encouraged her to send her work to other magazines. When writing, or with one or two of her friends, she felt at peace with herself and the world.

Her mother, however, had different ideas about the proper activities for her daughter. When she sat down to write, her mother would disparage her efforts, asking why she was not out with the group.

After a period of therapy, armed with a greater sense of self-respect and self-understanding, this girl was able to take a stronger stand against her mother's demands. As she did so, she began to experience anxiety. Although more uncomfortable, she was now accepting a sense of her own identity.

Sometimes anxiety will flash to warn us that something is amiss. One man, a patient of mine, for several years had held a particular job that was well below his potential. This man was bright, sensitive, and alert, but because he had a low sense of self-esteem, his level of aspiration was far below his ability. In treatment, it became evident he was bored by his job—the boredom that comes from doing something for which one is highly unsuited. After a while, he resolved to give up the job and go back to school. Not unexpectedly, his anxiety decreased. Boredom is a way of denying anxious feelings.

In essence, anxiety warns us that our relationship with ourselves is not all it should be. Seen in this light, anxiety no longer is a frightening enemy which must be tranquilized out of sight.

AT TIMES OF CRISIS

At the time of a psychic crisis, anxiety mounts just the way our temperature rises as our body defenses rally to fight an infection.

Anxiety, viewed correctly, can be seen as an indicator of a possible threat to our integrity and personality. If we can affirm ourselves by moving through rather than fleeing from anxiety, healthy growth can be the result.

Once I served as head counselor in a girls' camp situated in a rural, secluded area. The counselors were young and insecure, hardly much older than the girls they were hired to supervise. Most of the young counselors felt homesick during the week of orientation that preceded the arrival of the campers. Observation of two preceding years in this camp had taught me that if the counselors could endure the first week of indoctrination, their homesickness would end as soon as they became busy with responsibilities. Life in camp would then settle down into pleasant routine.

One morning, about three days before the girls were to arrive, two tearful seventeen-year-old junior counselors came to see me and said they were so homesick that they wanted to leave. I allowed them to express their feelings, gave them Kleenex to wipe away the tears, and pointed out that for them to remain in camp and follow through on a commitment they had made

would be a sign of growth. I suggested that before they made any decision about leaving, they wait and see how they felt when camp swung into full operation in a few days.

One of the young counselors, unable to tolerate her separation anxiety for one more day, decided she wanted to leave immediately, and arrangements were made for her to depart the next morning. The other one clenched her teeth and said she would give it a try for one week more. When the campers arrived and a full program went into operation, she became involved in camp activities and was visibly more content. There was no more talk of going home. One day towards the end of the summer, she spontaneously came over to me and said, "I want to thank you! I feel more grown-up than ever before."

Although hardly a controlled experiment, this illustrates the point that whenever we feel in conflict, with heightened anxiety, the way is open either to growth or regression. If we can learn to use anxiety as a mandate to growth, we will be far happier.

It is precisely at times of crisis and acute anxiety that old patterns begin to break down and there comes the chance to build new ones. During heightened anxiety, we become inordinately suggestible and seek new solutions to problems. This is why someone in a crisis very often needs prompt, understanding, professional help.

When a patient is in therapy, one often sees an increase in his anxiety as the herald of improvement. Sometimes a patient finds this alarming. At such times, it is necessary for him to be aware that the anxiety indicates something within is stirring and does not necessarily mean he is getting worse.

Dr. Karen Horney wrote: "Any anxiety that does arise during analytic therapy is usually alarming to the patient because he tends to regard it as impairment. But more often than not this is not so . . . emerging anxiety may also have an eminently positive meaning. For it may indicate that the patient now feels strong enough to take the risk of facing his problems more squarely. . . ."[3]

When a patient begins to *feel* his suffering for the first time in his life, anxiety may result. I worked with a young, unmarried, professional woman who, at the beginning of therapy, had many symptoms of, although she experienced little, overt anxiety. As she began to get more in touch with her feelings, her anxiety increased, for she confronted her own emptiness, yearnings, and unfulfilled desires.

During this difficult time in her therapy, I received a letter in which she said that she could not sleep, that she had a million conflicting thoughts, that she felt depressed and lonely, and that anything could start her crying. She said that she was ashamed of her feelings and almost wished she had never gone into therapy because before it, she had felt that she could never love anyone or anything and could accept not getting married or having anybody, but that now she felt capable of loving deeply and wanted a family.

In many ways she *was* more comfortable before therapy. Although she had symptoms, she was protected behind the barricade of not feeling. As her feelings were released, she felt at first as if she would be swept away by their intensity. But after a short while, she was able to live more comfortably with herself in a manner she never before believed possible.

Sometimes patients avoid anxiety in the early stages of therapy by blaming all their difficulties upon their mother or father or society. After a while, if therapy is successful, the patient realizes that while all these may have contributed to his emotional distress, his own strong desires and imagination were partially responsible. He also knows that what he does about his life now is solely up to him. This may create new anxiety for a time.

Dr. Thayer A. Greene[4] wrote:

> How much easier and less anxiety-producing it is to perceive the problem as social and collective rather than individual and personal. Yet whatever social forces operate upon our lives, it is we who must make an individual response. No single lesson makes itself more clear to those who have gone through extensive psychotherapy than that to blame it all on God, society, mother and father, rarely if ever brings healing and change. When all the accounts have been added up, the individual must still pay the bill if he is to be freed from the negative and confining power of the past—not only his own but that of his family and culture.

Whether or not the particular dilemma in which an individual finds himself is his "fault" is usually quite beside the point. The handicap, the crippling anxiety, the behavioral compulsion, may not be his fault at all and yet be his *fact*, i.e., the reality of his life situation. He must engage himself personally with this fact in order to grow.

With patients who do well in psychotherapy, I have noted that although in the early part of treatment, they handle severe anxiety by saying, "Isn't it awful?" Or "Aren't I terrible?" they gradually accept anxiety as an *opportunity* to learn more about themselves. When anxiety can be regarded as a teacher, the patient often becomes an apt pupil. To use anxiety constructively, as a valuable tool in learning about ourselves and what threatens us, is not an easy task. But if we can learn to do this, we will be rewarded with the prize of increased self-knowledge.

Sometimes psychotherapy allows a patient to become *too* comfortable; his anxiety has been tranquilized. Then the job of the therapist is to mobilize a bit of anxiety so that the healing process may once again take place.

THE WILLINGNESS TO BE HUMAN

To some extent I have stressed the anxiety that results from conflict and from crisis. There is, however, the anxiety that comes from being alive, for, to be human is to be finite and limited, and to be finite and limited is to be anxious.

In some dark, deep recess of our minds, in spite of the din of music and noise and friends and work and travel and sports and food, we never lose the awareness that some day we will die. When we feel alive, we are using our full potential and the thought of death drifts into the shadows.

The knowledge of our finiteness can help us to savor the moments we live, to help us use our limited time in a useful, enjoyable manner. That knowledge can also help keep us appropriately humble in the face of the forces of nature, can make us give pause and consider our little vanities. The knowledge that we are temporary visitors on this planet can put petty quarrels into proper perspective. Temporary frustrations can be seen as part of reality. We can live more in the present and stop pursuing a vain, relentless search for security. Once we accept a certain basic anxiety, we can begin to live more fully.

The willingness to recognize the reality of anxiety indicates an ability to recognize all of reality. Most of us are all too eager to deny that we are anxious. When we do, we gain momentary relief, but pay a high price. We keep out of touch with our real feelings. Our chances of facing our conflicts and easing our anxiety are lessened. We find that we are more alienated than ever, both from our feelings and other people.

If one is able to acknowledge anxiety and battle it, healing forces are frequently set in motion. Dr. Paul Tillich once spoke of the necessity of having the "courage to be," which includes the acceptance and facing of anxiety.

Paradoxically, true courage seems to begin with the admission of anxiety, just as the possibility of true living begins when we do not deny the possibility of death.

THE FEAR OF FEAR

In our society which, sometimes subtly, sometimes not so subtly, suggests that we should be happy all the time, anxiety is too often hidden; unhappiness, uncertainty, conflict, and doubt are all denied. I have seen a large number of patients who practically considered it un-American to be anxious. They feel guilty because they have moments of panic in spite of having accumulated all the necessary material possessions they wish. Often the first step with such patients is to help them feel less guilty about the fact that they *are* anxious.

Anxiety is as normal a part of the life process as teething. Like teething, it can be unpleasant and, if severe, cause pain. Too often, the fear of anxiety makes the anxious person avoid anything that might possibly cause it. Then a growing fear of anxiety results which may create more discomfort than the original fear.

If you ski, you know that the ability to ski increases by taking the risk of feeling frightened on the new high slope that looks possible but difficult. As soon as you master this slope, skiing down it without anxiety, you are ready to move to the next mountain, one that offers still more challenge.

If someone looks on anxiety as an enemy, a "disease," the therapeutic way is likely to be rougher and longer. But if he views anxiety as an opportunity to look within, as a mandate for further development, not only will the psychic way be easier, but his anxiety will also lessen that more swiftly. Anxiety is a feeling to become aware of, to be faced, to be understood, and then, almost automatically, it is present only when we realistically need it.

References
1. Janis, I. L. (1958). *Psychological stress.* New York: Wiley.
2. Exodus 34:30
3. Horney, K. (1950). *Neurosis and human growth* (p. 340). New York: W. W. Norton.
4. Greene, T. (1967). *Modern man in search of manhood* (p. 12). New York: Association Press.

To Apply This Reading to Yourself

1. *Sugarman and Freeman write that anxiety is a "gift." Consider your own life, and write a brief paper specifically indicating how you have benefited from anxiety.*
2. *Sugarman and Freeman note that anxiety is a "sign of growth." Consider your own life, and write a brief paper indicating how this has been true for you.*

3. *Sugarman and Freeman state that anxiety is a "price of growth." Consider your own life, and write a brief paper indicating how this has been true for you.*

4. *Sugarman and Freeman write of the anxiety that comes from recognizing that we are finite and limited and subject to the workings of fate and death. Some writers have called this "existential anxiety." Write a brief paper on your own existential anxiety or your lack of it.*

5. *Sugarman and Freeman write that many of us suffer from "the fear of fear." Consider your own feelings of this kind, and write a brief paper describing them and their influence on you.*

Small Terrors, Secret Heroics

Amy Gross

People think adventure is to be found outside the usual course of life. They set aside vacations for the pursuit of danger, they travel to it, buy equipment for it, and after their wrestle with the elements, or the rapids, or the mountain side, they return to hohum life. And they regard as heroes those who have made danger their way of life. It's not hard to understand the call of that sort of heroism, the seduction of the big dare. Entering that space between life and death, you taste perfect freedom.

People theorize that modern life is so tame, the opportunities for raw bravery and aggression so rare, that only through vigorous sports and dangerous play can we detonate our pent-up energies and remember our animalhood. That physical putting-to-the-test is the great escape from the predominantly mental lives we live. For many, work is an abstraction and its reward, money, is another abstraction, an essentially arbitrary gauge of achievement except for a gambler whose work is collecting money. The bodily tests of one's powers—win or lose, survive or not—is nothing if not concrete.

But it seems to me that these sports, these physical challenges are really only exercises. When you think of the adventures, the terrors, the possible leaps, the opportunities in everyday life to choose between heroism and cowardice, you know that you don't have to travel to danger. In fact, the stakes are higher at home. It is easier to risk death scaling a mountain than to risk being old and alone, or unloved and unneeded, or being thought stupid or insane. It is easier to die than to live as a failure. And so, every day, there are risks we refuse, possible terrors we avoid. We do what other people expect from us, so they'll love and want us; we perform according to the rules of success and sanity; we remain silent when we should speak up and speak though we have nothing to say; and our lives stay small. We don't recognize as adventures the challenges that come to us, and we shrink from designing our own. Only in a somewhat extraneous experiment like riding the rapids or skydiving do we dash out of the tameness enforced on us by our own fears. I'm not saying that someone who lives courageously every day wouldn't want or need to spend a week in the wilderness; only that attention should be paid to the opportunities for wildness at home.

These more subtle heroics are seemingly small acts. The fact that they require enormous courage is usually known only to the protagonist. For one man, speaking in public is so terrifying, he gratefully allows others in his work-group to talk for him. It would be a very small act if he were once to present his own work, a very private victory. For him, afraid of appearing afraid, certain he was about to make a fool of himself, the experience would be a free-fall. He would be risking everything. In anyone else's eyes, he would only have stopped being silly. These small acts have to do, often, with overcoming the terrors other people tell you are silly. The reason to overcome is not to please these other people. The reason is the one offered by the man who climbs the mountain—because it's there. The at-home fears block one's way more resolutely than any mountain.

For many people, silly as it sounds, going to a party is a small act of courage. Initiating a conversation with that stranger across the room, for some people, can be an act no less noble than facing a bull in a ring. I'm not being facetious here. I've stood at a party a step away from an author whose work awes me, mentally testing and rejecting opening lines, choking when one or another began to rise out of my throat. Getting back on a horse after you've been thrown is simple (and practical—how else are you going to get back to the stables?). To venture a conversation with a superior stranger is to risk everything—being seen as an ant. Your specialness is at stake. Will the superior being recognize your own superiority? Will you come off as just another face? Are you just another face? Dragons test only your strength. Strangers test your wit, or your face, or whatever it is you rely on to barter your way through the open market. If I ever approach that author and survive, I'll feel as though I'd vanquished dragons.

Daring to make a soufflé, to argue a grade, to tell the truth, to say yes or to say no, to admit "I want," or "I deserve," these can all be moments of heroism, invisible leaps that free you, if only from the fear of accepting the dare. I read that someone is going to motorcycle-jump a string of 17 trucks, a large and remarkably useless act. A woman who has been painting for years, who one day picks herself up and brings her work to a gallery, is leaping further than that. Risking being told she's no good, risking her hope that she is saying something unique with her paints, that *she* is unique—that's a very great risk. If she avoids the gallery judge's criticism, she can continue to cherish what are possibly fantasies of talent and success. To bring in her work is to subject her fantasies to the test of reality. There are all kinds of ways to deal with the rejection that might be her reward. Would she have the wisdom to apply those ways? Should she protect herself from such a challenge to her wisdom? Sure. Why not? It's not noticeable cowardice to play life safe, it's the way we all play it, one way or another. But to risk, to leap, to throw one's fantasies into the ring is to pursue danger. Mighty exciting. The truth, we've been told, will set us free, one way or another.

There's a woman I know, a social worker who has to commute an hour and a half every day to the hospital where she's on staff. She hears about a job opening at a better hospital, only ten minutes from home; the job is bigger than hers and so is the salary. This is terribly upsetting news. She asks everyone what she should do, apply or not. Of course, everyone tells her to apply. But, she argues, what if she got the job and then couldn't do the work? A challenge like hers, when unmet, is obsessing. She talks and talks about applying. Finally, the decision is made for her—she hears the job is taken.

When people asked her, "What do you have to lose?" she thought they didn't understand what was at stake. Her definition of herself, her "ego" as she put it. She has a bank of negative judgments and if she were to apply and not get the job, or get the job and then be fired, all those judgments would be confirmed. Once and for all she would know herself—and the world would know her—to be a failure. The underlying prem-

ise is that her success to date is due to luck and the gullibility of her supervisors. By not applying for the bigger job, she protects herself from the confirmation of that premise, and retains the right to think she might have been able to do the job. It's a common bargain, but a bad one. Not risking defeat is always defeat. The fact is, she did have nothing to lose—by not applying she's already lost. Once a dare, the opportunity to leap presents itself, you can't escape a sense of failure until or unless you abandon yourself to the leap. And the defeat following a risk taken must be, at the least, a peaceful one. The defeat of not even trying is acidified by the anger of impotence.

Another woman has been living with a man for several months. The basis of her attachment is in its alternative—being alone, having to look for a new man. Now, nothing is ever so clear-cut that rationalization is impossible. She argues that she has some feeling for the man, she has not met anyone better, the man is easy, undemanding. In her mind, leaving him would be like cutting herself off from an anchor. She would be adrift. She doesn't see how she could take care of herself, what would happen to her . . . she might be alone forever. Her fear is the expectation of total catastrophe. Ignoring all the laws of probability, she is positing only one alternative and that one is unacceptable.

For her to break out would be a feat more astonishing, if less flamboyant, than any escape performed by a Houdini. She would be setting off on an adventure comparable to Robinson Crusoe's, as true a test of individual resources as his. No ferreting for berries, but could she nourish herself?

Her refusal to try—to leap into the fear—is not blatant cowardice. Her dread of aloneness is ubiquitous and natural. How many of us ever leave a bad setup without the towrope of The Other Man or The Other Woman? I never have. If she were to let go of her man—cleanly and crisply—it would be an ostensibly small act. In my eyes, at least, it would be heroic.

I remember a friend of mine telling a man who had just swallowed his first tab of LSD (remember LSD?), "If you see anything frightening, walk towards it." Afterwards, the man described what happened when he hallucinated grotesque faces. At first, he had shuddered and pulled back, and the faces continued to menace. Then he tried staring them down, moving towards them. The faces turned into fantastic Thai dancers, costumed in spangles, and apparently arranged just for his delight. It meant something to the man that he could defend himself against his own monsters. You could shrug off his adventure by saying that his fears were only hallucinations, but so are most fears hallucinations.

Staring down monsters is the essence of adventure, and the monster is never the mountain or the bull or the string of 17 trucks or the stranger. The monster is always your own self-doubts. And whether you're daring to explore a dark cave or daring to dial a certain telephone number, the aftereffects are the same. You've called on your own power and it's been there for you; you've learned, once again, that you have nothing to fear from yourself and so it seems there's really nothing at all to fear; and, for a while, anyway, you know you are larger than your fears. And when you feel the snap of that fear-band breaking—when you submit the piece of work, or close the oven door on the soufflé, that moment of letting go, falling free, taking your chances—what a rush that is. I don't know what residue is left by adrenaline after its surge has powered you through a crisis. But whatever the residue is, someone ought to bottle it. The high doesn't last long, but it's what makes the pursuit of danger so addictive.

I got hooked on fear four years ago. I was spending a week at Big Sur, taking a seminar at Esalen, a so-called "growth center," famous primarily for its hot-springs baths where men and women bathed in the nude. The place was on a cliff above the Pacific and the bathhouse was pronged into the side of the cliff, cantilevered out over the ocean. Idyllic setting. Tainted only by the fact that I was there with a man and between us, something had gone very wrong. Some poisonous combination of fear and rage had made us each other's enemies. So there we were, in this paradise, on teeth-edge with each other, and the second day, he said he was going to the baths and was I coming? I was not, in no way. He was impatient—no, disgusted is more accurate—with my uptightness. Okay, he said, and slapped a towel over his shoulder and walked away, down the thin rocky path to the bathhouse.

The grounds were deserted. I figured everyone was at the baths, or resting between semi-

nars, and I started towards our room. And then I thought about never having been in a hot-springs bath, and from what I'd read, it must be luxurious, and my friend's sneer kept stabbing at me, and I knew that the only reason I wasn't going to the baths, and was instead going to spend a gorgeous afternoon hiding away in a dark room, was that I was afraid to take off my clothes in front of strangers. All the rage I'd been secretly storing suddenly turned itself on me. Coward. Idiot.

I remember clearly what it felt like to turn my body back towards the baths. Like an unoiled robot, commanded by a distant brain. It is not an exaggeration to say I was trembling. My throat felt strangled, my stomach was clamped in a spasm, and various loud throbbings in my body distracted me from seeing or hearing as I went down that path. At the bathhouse, there were a few stone steps and two signs, "Men" and "Women." I turned left towards "Women" and immediately knew the signs were vestigial. Half the bodies were male. There were four square cement tubs—shallow, about three feet deep—and one was empty of people. That's all I was looking for and all I saw. Mechanically, I ripped off my clothes and aimed the body towards my tub. I sank into a corner, immobile, and stared and saw nothing.

When I came to, sometime later, I noted that the bathhouse was three-sided, and I was facing the fourth side, open onto the sky and the ocean. Between the railing and the tubs were massage tables. On one was a naked young woman sitting in lotus position and playing a recorder. On the next, was a young man in an inverted lotus— head and shoulders on the mat, legs folded in air, also very naked. They were beautiful, those two, with their background of sky, and the music was perfect, and I decided I would come to Esalen and live, I would be a waitress.

Later I found my friend sitting on the steps of the lodge with his towel. Where were you? he asked.

I was at the baths.

He looked surprised, pleased. Oh, you must have been on the other side. I thought you weren't going.

I started to explain and then I started to cry, and then I noticed that my eyes were focusing peculiarly. Objects—trees, rocks, a porch railing—were startlingly three dimensional. I was seeing their spaces and the depth of space between them, and there seemed to be a fresh space in my own head. And looking at him, I saw just my old friend. Not the monster I'd been living with. I could see his kindness and his concern. He was just my friend. My usual eyes had slipped an evil mask over his face.

We had a good time together for the next few days. We had fun, I was light and playful. No self-consciousness, no need for it. Who was watching me? Whose judgment could I fear? What did a judgment have to do with me? I, anyone, was as impossible to judge as a stone. One can, of course, judge a stone, but does that judgment worry the stone?

In those few days, I was fearless. Fearless, as I remember it, feels like innocence. As though I didn't know what it was to be hurt, or to inflict hurt. No second thoughts. That automatic and unconscious rating of myself against other people was unnecessary—every person was my peer. Laughter was different too, sweeter.

The fog came down again, but those few days of superclarity were a taste of a possible state, a place I want to return to. The price of passage there was self-defiance, overruling powerful habits of defense. And the only route there was through the fear. There's always the chance now that another fear walked into might take me back.

It's pretty funny to talk about stripping as the way to Nirvana, but silly as it sounds, taking off my clothes was as much a plunge into terror, and the unknown, and freedom, as skydiving would be for me. My point is not to denigrate skydiving. It is, rather, to say that you don't have to rent a plane to fall free. Life is so playfully arranged, we can trust it to supply us with endless opportunities to turn our bodies around, and walk into terror. Why we are, most of us anyway, so afraid, I don't know. Maybe we're trained in fear, by people who are fortunate enough to have a lot to lose. But hoarding security, like hoarding money, leaves us nothing to show. A miser lives in destitution. Risking it all, pursuing danger, whether in the air or in the living room, seems to be the better way to play this game. The alternative is flight, constant flight.

To Apply This Reading to Yourself

1. *Amy Gross writes, "When you think of the adventures, the terrors, the possible leaps, the opportunities in everyday life to choose between heroism and cowardice, you know that you don't have to travel to danger." Write a brief paper describing the challenges you find in your own everyday life, along with your heroic or cowardly responses.*
2. *Write a brief paper about the "secret heroics" you have shown in the face of one of your "small terrors."*
3. *Write a brief paper about the "blatant cowardice" you have shown in the face of one of your "small terrors."*
4. *Write a brief paper about some "small terror" or fear in your current life, indicating what it is, how it affects you, and how you deal with it.*
5. *Write a brief paper describing a "small terror" in your current life that you might, as Amy Gross suggests, stare down or walk into.*

The Lesson of the Cliff

Morton Hunt

It was a sweltering July day in Philadelphia—I can feel it still, 56 years later. The five boys I was with had grown tired of playing marbles and burning holes in dry leaves with a lens and were casting about for something else.

"Hey!" said freckle-faced little Ned. "I got an idea. We haven't climbed the cliff for a long while."

"Let's go!" said someone else. And off they went, trotting and panting like a pack of stray dogs.

I hesitated. I longed to be brave and active, like them, but I'd been a sickly child most of my eight years and had taken to heart my mother's admonitions to remember that I wasn't as strong as other boys and not to take chances.

"Come on!" called Jerry, my best friend. "Just because you've been sick is no reason to be a sissy." "I'm *coming!*" I yelled, and ran along after them.

Through the park and into the woods we went, finally emerging in a clearing. At the far side, 40 to 50 feet away, loomed the cliff, a bristling, near-vertical wall of jutting rocks, earth slides, scraggly bushes and ailanthus saplings. From the tumbled rocks at its base to the fringe of sod at its top, it was only about 60 feet high, but to me it looked like the very embodiment of the Forbidden and Impossible.

One by one, the other boys scrabbled upward, finding handholds and toeholds on rocky outcrops and earthen ledges. I hung back until the others were partway up; then, trembling and sweating, I began to climb. A hand here, a foot there, my heart thumping in my skinny chest, I made my way up and up.

At some point, I looked back—and was horrified. The ground at the base of the cliff seemed very far below; one slip and I would fall, bouncing off the cliff face and ending on the rocks. There, shattered and strangling on my own blood, I would gurgle, twitch a few times, and then expire, like the cat I had seen run over a few days earlier.

But the boys were chattering above me on an earthen ledge two-thirds of the way to the top. It was 5 to 6 feet deep and some 15 feet long. I clawed my way up to them; then I crawled as far back on the ledge as I could, huddling against the rock face. The other boys stood close to the edge and boldly urinated into space; the sight made me so queasy that I surreptitiously clutched at the rocks behind me.

In a few minutes, they started up to the top.

"Hey, wait," I croaked.

"So long! See you in the funny papers," one of them said, and the others laughed.

"But I can't . . . I . . . " That spurred them on: jeering and catcalling back to me, they wriggled their way to the top, from where they would walk home by a roundabout route. Before they left, they peered down at me.

"You can stay if you want to," mocked Ned. "It's all yours." Jerry looked concerned, but he went with the others.

I looked down and was overcome by dizziness; a nameless force seemed to be impelling me to fall off. I lay clinging to a rock as the world spun around. I could never climb back down. It was much too far to go, too hazardous; partway, I would grow feeble or faint, lose my grip, fall and die. But the way up to the top was even worse—higher, steeper, more treacherous; I would never make it. I heard someone sobbing and moaning; I wondered who it was and realized that it was I.

Time passed. The shadows gradually lengthened, the sun disappeared from the treetops beyond the clearing below, dusk began to gather. Silent now, I lay on my stomach as if in a trance, stupefied by fear and fatigue, unable to move or even to think of how to get back down to safety and home.

January 1945, Watton Air Base, East Anglia. This morning I found my name posted on the blackboard: Tomorrow I fly another weather reconnaissance mission over enemy territory. All day my mind was whirling; at dinner I felt as if I might throw up at any moment.

I knew that I needed a good night's sleep, so I took a pill and went to bed early, but I could not make myself stop imagining the endless flight in which I, as pilot, and my navigator would venture in our unarmed twin-engine Mosquito far into German-held territory.

Hour after hour I thrashed around in bed; from time to time I would drift off, only to wake with a dreadful start, gasping for breath, my heart flopping like a beached fish as I imagined the shellburst in the cockpit, the blood and the sickening white-hot pain, the fire, smoke and spurting oil, the Mozzie winging over into a spin while I, shattered and half-conscious, am too weak either to fight the controls or pull myself up and out the escape hatch as the plane screams down and down.

Next morning, in the locker room, as I get into my flight outfit, it is clear to me that I simply can't do it. The mission is a 1000-mile trip, three hours of it over German-held territory and Germany itself—too deep in to go unnoticed. I can't possibly strap myself into that defenseless little plane and, with my own hands and feet, make it climb 5 miles high, guide it out over the winter sea and into a Europe bristling with Nazi anti-aircraft batteries, radar stations and fighter planes, and finally make it back to safety.

Even as I zip up my boots and pull on my helmet, I know I can't. I will get in the plane, warm up and check out the engines, but at the runway my hands will freeze on the controls, and I will be unable to make the plane move.

January 1957, New York. I'm delirious with joy.

I've always felt that if I didn't write a book by the time I was 40, I'd never do so. With only three years to go, I've been offered a book contract—by the most distinguished of American publishers. Alfred Knopf himself, after reading an article of mine, had written to invite me to submit a proposal. After months of hard work, I had turned in an outline and sample chapter. Now Knopf and his editors have said yes.

But, later in the day, I begin to fear that I have made a terrible mistake. I've suggested a history of love, tracing its evolution from the time of the early Greeks to the present—a vast project, but fun to think about and to sketch in outline form. Yet now that the moment of truth has come, I see how rash I've been. Having spent months researching and writing the sample chapter, I can look ahead—and what I see is frightening.

How could I have imagined I'd ever be able to learn what love meant to the ancient Greeks, to the imperial Romans, to the ascetic early Christians, to the knights and ladies of the Middle Ages, to—? Enough! It's hopeless, impossible, more than any one person can do.

Or, at least, more than I can do. Even if I found everything I needed in the library and took reams of notes, how could I ever make sense of it all? Or organize it? Or write about it entertainingly, sentence after sentence, page after page, chapter after chapter? Only now, when a contract is being offered me, can I see clearly what I will have to do—and realize that I cannot.

June 1963, New York. I am lying in bed, sleepless, although it is 2 A.M.; I suspect that she, quiet in the dark next to me, is awake too. Tonight we agreed that it was useless to go on and that I should move out as soon as I can.

But I feel as if the ground is giving way beneath me, as if I am falling through space. How can we ever decide how to divide our possessions and our savings? How will we work out my rights as an absentee father? Will I be able to find a place for myself and, without help, make it homelike? I have never lived alone; how will I feel when I close the door at night and am imprisoned in my solitude?

What will I tell my family, and how will they take it? Will my married friends shun me? What can I say to my 8-year-old son, and what will happen to his feelings about me? Where will I meet single friends? Whom will I talk to, eat with, share my life with? I haven't the least idea how to start; I haven't been single since my 20s.

Yet what if, somehow, after a while, I were to meet the right woman and feel desire stirring in me? But here my mind goes blank. I haven't been to bed with another woman in over 17 years; how should I behave, what should I do? What if my hesitant actions are scorned? What if I seem clumsy, gross, nervous, foolish?

And even if all goes well, how will I know whether what I feel is love or only lust? Can I trust myself to love again—or trust anyone else to love me? Will anyone, could anyone, ever do so? Will I ever want to marry again? There is so much to be said, learned, worked out first; so many hints, allusions, promises, bargains, plans; so many beliefs and tastes to be exchanged and harmonized—no, it is too hard a road to travel, too remote a goal. I can't do it.

Twilight, a first star in the sky, the ground below the cliff growing dim. But now in the woods the beam of a flashlight dances about and I hear the voices of Jerry and my father. My father! But what can he do? Middle-aged and portly, he cannot climb up here. Even if he could, what good would that do?

Staying well back from the foot of the cliff so that he can see me, he points the beam up and calls to me. "Come on down, now," he says in a perfectly normal, comforting tone. "Dinner's ready."

"I can't!" I wail. "I'll fall, I'll die!"

"You got up," he says. "You can get down the same way. I'll light the way."

"No, I can't!" I howl. "It's too far, it's too hard, I can't do it."

"Listen to me," my father says. "Don't think about how far it is, how hard it is. All you have to think about is taking one little step. You can do that. Look where I'm shining the light. Do you see that rock?" The beam bounces around on a jutting outcrop just below the ledge. "See it?" he calls up.

I inch over. "Yes," I say.

"Good," he says. "Now just turn around so you can put your left foot on that rock. That's all you have to do. It's just a little way below you. You can do that. Don't worry about what comes next, and don't look down any farther than that first step. Trust me."

It seems possible. I inch backward, gingerly feel for the rock with my left foot and find it. "That's good," my father calls. "Now, a little bit to the right and a few inches lower, there's another foothold. Move your right foot down there very slowly—that's all you have to do. Just think about that next step, nothing else." I do so. "Good," he says. "Now let go of whatever you're holding onto with your left hand and reach back and grab that skinny tree just at the edge, where my light is. That's all you have to do." Again, I do so.

That's how it goes. One step at a time, one handhold at a time, he talks me down the cliff, stressing that I have only to make one simple move each time, never letting me stop to think of the long way down, always telling me that the next thing I have to do is something I *can* do.

Suddenly I take the last step down onto the tumbled rocks at the bottom and into my father's strong arms, sobbing a little, and then, surprisingly, feeling a sense of immense accomplishment and something like pride.

January 1945. I taxi out onto the runway and firmly shove the throttles forward. I remember at last that I *know* how to do what I must. All I have to do is take off and climb to 25,000 feet, heading eastward over East Anglia; that's all I need think about right now. I can do that.

Later: The North Sea is just ahead. All I have to do, I tell myself, is stay on this heading for about 20 minutes, until we have crossed over Schouwen Island in the Netherlands. That's all; I can do it.

Over Schouwen Island, my navigator tells me to turn to a heading of 125 degrees and hold it for 10 minutes, until we reach our next checkpoint. Good; that's not so hard; I can do that.

That's how it goes. I drive the roaring little plane across Holland and Germany, high over fields and woods, cities, rivers and mountain ranges, never envisioning the whole trip but only the leg we are flying, never thinking of the hours ahead but concentrating on getting through each brief segment of time, each measured span of miles, until at last sunlight dazzles off the wrinkled sea ahead of us and in a few minutes we are out of enemy territory, safe and still alive.

January 1957. After tossing about much of the night, thinking about the impossibly ambitious book I had said I could write, I remember the old lesson once again: Though I know what the goal is, I can avoid panic and vertigo if I look only at the next step.

I'll keep my gaze on the first chapter: All I have to do is read whatever I can find in the library about love among the Greeks; that isn't impossibly hard. Then I'll tell myself that all I have to do is sort out my notes, dividing the chapter into a number of sections; I can do that. Then I'll make myself look no further ahead than writing the first section. And with that thought, I heave a great sigh and fall asleep.

And that's the way I spend more than 2 1/2 years. Then, one exhilarating afternoon, the last of 653 pages emerges from my typewriter and, like a boy, I turn somersaults on the living room floor in sheer joy. Some months later, I hold in my hands the first copy of my book, *The Natural History of Love*—already chosen by the Book of the Month Club—and a few weeks after that I read my first major review, praising the book, in *The New York Times Book Review*. For a while, I occasionally leaf through the book, marveling that I could ever have done all this—and knowing that I learned how, long ago, in the dusk on the face of a small cliff.

September 1963. I unlock the door of my tiny apartment, carry my bags in and close the door behind me. I have taken one step; it wasn't so hard. I had remembered the lesson that I have applied again and again throughout my life; one step at a time, one step that I can manage.

The first was to find an apartment; I looked no further into the future until I had done that. Then I went about furnishing my two rooms; I looked no further ahead until that was done. Today, I am moving in; I have made my own little nest, and it looks pleasant. I unpack, make

a few phone calls, fix lunch, feel at home. Good; I've taken that step.

By the next year, I have constructed a new life, gotten my final divorce decree, acquired the social and emotional skills that I need as a middle-aged single man (I would remain one for five years), and even have become a passable bachelor cook. And discovered once more, to my surprise, that I do know how to make my way toward a distant, difficult goal.

I have realized with the same surprise, time and again throughout my life, that, having looked at a far and frightening prospect and been dismayed, I can cope with it after all by remembering the simple lesson I learned so long ago. I remind myself to look not at the rocks far below but at the first small and relatively easy step and, having taken it, to take the next one, feeling a sense of accomplishment with each move, until I have done what I wanted to do, gotten where I wanted to be, and can look back, amazed and proud of the distance I have come.

To Apply This Reading to Yourself

1. *Describe a problem that overwhelmed you, but which you might have dealt with successfully by working on it one step at a time.*
2. *Describe a problem that you dealt with successfully by working on it one step at a time.*
3. *Describe a formidable problem or task that you now face in your life. What is the first step that you might take toward its mastery?*

Winning over Worry

James Lincoln Collier

"I've been a chronic worrier all my life. I'd sit there at my desk worrying about a problem in my business, and then I'd begin to worry about how I was going to support myself, about what I would do in my old age. It would just spiral up."

In his mid-30s, wealthy, chairman of a national insurance company, this man would seem to be someone who has nothing to worry about. Yet worry he did, until recently. "If I didn't have business problems, I'd find something else to worry about," he says. "I guess I was spending half my day worrying, and half the night too. I was losing so much sleep that I was tired all the time, and my productivity was falling off."

Everybody worries, but a handful of social scientists who came to focus on this topic while studying insomnia are now saying that most of the worrying we do serves no purpose. More than that, they are telling us that we can learn to worry less.

These researchers have found that worriers like the insurance executive experience the phenomenon of the "racing mind." "The flow of worrisome thoughts is relentless and seems unstoppable," says Thomas Borkovec, a psychologist at Pennsylvania State University and one of the pioneers in worry research. Typically, a person might begin by worrying whether his car needs new brakes. Next he sees the brakes failing and the car knocking down a child. This leads to a vision of himself in court, in financial ruin, with his family on welfare.

Put this way it sounds amusing, but to the worrier it is far from funny. With ever-increasing worries come muscle tension, upset stomach, anxiety and depression, which can eventually lead to more serious health problems. "Worrying is circular," says Elwood Robinson, a young psychologist who heads the Worry Treatment Program at North Carolina Central University in Durham. "It builds, so you feel worse and worse." And, according to a recent study of Americans' mental health, worry is one of the few emotional problems that are on the increase in this country—for reasons that are not altogether clear.

Consider the case of a mother of two adolescent sons. Age 42, she looks 25 and has a relaxed manner—hardly someone who would seem to be a chronic worrier. She began to worry some in college. As she went on to graduate, get married, then begin teaching and having children, her worries increased. So did her physical symptoms: stomach problems, insomnia. At night she would lie in bed worrying about her children, about the students she was teaching, about whether she was doing a good job. (Low self-esteem is characteristic of worriers.) About four years ago she was feeling so much stress that she had to give up her teaching position.

Rowland Folensbee, a psychologist who heads a Houston worry clinic, says that this pattern is common. "Some people are not worriers at first, but *become* worriers. They find that their worry incubates. It is fired off by more and more distant triggers." Where they might once have worried about paying a bill, they'll eventually worry about paying for things they haven't even bought yet. Folensbee has had patients so prone to worry that they decide not to undergo treatment because the prospect "worries" them too much.

Worry, as these researchers define it, is what the mind does while the body is feeling anxious or tense. Says Folensbee, "It's very difficult to have an empty mind—not to think about anything at all." Worrying seems to give the tense person "something to do." According to Borkovec, such a person feels that the worry is "part of me, what I do all the time. Not to be doing that makes me uncomfortable because it's not myself."

Everybody worries at one time or another, but there are what Folensbee calls "grades of tendency to worry." According to Borkovec's estimates, 30 percent of us are nonworriers, 15 percent are chronic worriers, and the rest of us fall somewhere in between. All of the researchers feel that it isn't so much a question of how much you worry, but whether it is causing problems—costing you sleep, distracting you at work or school, or often making you feel bad.

The first task in reducing worry is to recognize when you are worrying. The second step is to interrupt this worry before it can build.

Folensbee asks clients who suddenly realize they're worrying to focus on an object—something positive—and carefully describe it to themselves. The theory is that the mind cannot hang on to two thought processes at once.

"Imaging" can help stop the worry spiral. A person worrying about a plane trip might see himself getting airsick or the plane crashing; instead, he should work up images of a smiling flight attendant and the interesting people he'll meet—replacing negative thoughts with positive ones. "We're trying to get people to think more realistically about the things that worry them," Robinson says. "We have people who worry endlessly about their schoolwork, yet they have always done well. We say to them, 'Look, have you ever flunked a course before?'"

Another technique that Robinson suggests is "relaxation training"—going over each muscle group one by one, tensing and releasing them, helping them to relax. Whatever the technique, the point is to halt the worry cycle. People learn to do this surprisingly quickly. Usually within a week or so they have reduced markedly the time they spend worrying. "Worry is a habit," Borkovec says. "To counteract that habit we need substitute habits."

Finding substitutes is half the plan. The second half is a concept not unlike the religious tradition of prayer. Put aside a period each day when you sit down and deliberately worry about things on your mind. It is easier for most people to stop worrying during the day and concentrate on productive thoughts if they tell themselves that they'll have a chance to get back to the worry later.

The period of deliberate worry also seems to burn away the worry. Exactly how this works isn't understood, but psychologists have long known about the phenomenon of "habituation" with regard to stimuli: if you smell corned beef and cabbage for a while, you stop smelling it. In the same way, worry tends to decrease during this period of enforced worry.

Researchers agree that the worry period ought to be 30 minutes long. Don't use your favorite living-room chair, because the associa-tions might make you start worrying every time you sit there. Nor should you have your worry period just before bed. Folensbee has his clients write down their worries to help them concentrate. The chairman of the insurance company does his worrying between 5 and 5:30 in the afternoon. He shuts his door, turns on a low light, and lies down with pad and pencil.

Some people insist that worry is useful, but there is an important difference, the researchers say, between worrying and problem-solving. "Instead of fretting endlessly over negative outcomes, we should look for positive solutions," Robinson says.

The new worry programs are able to reduce worry in many clients by nearly 50 percent. Some benefit a great deal, others less so. Such a program can be followed at home, without formal training in a clinic, using the three basic steps:

1. Learn to recognize immediately when you've started on a worry cycle.
2. Interrupt the worry cycle by imaging, concentrating on another, positive object, or relaxing. Tell yourself you'll have a chance to worry later.
3. Set aside a 30-minute worry period each day, and stick to it.

Chances of success are better if someone checks to see whether you're following the techniques and reminds you to keep at it. Folensbee says, "People start coming up with excuses—'My child has been sick, and I couldn't find time for my worry period,' and so forth. This program is effective when applied for several weeks, but the basis for it is continued application." Another caution: the worry period *must* be 30 minutes long. The researchers have discovered that a shorter worry period might actually *increase* the amount you worry. (Researchers can't explain this phenomenon yet, but it shows up clearly in their studies.)

Nobody will ever stop worrying completely, but many people can learn to worry much less. The insurance-company executive has. Last year he worried about everything. Now, he says, "When I get into my worry session, half the time I can't even come up with something to worry about."

To Apply This Reading to Yourself

1. *Make up a list of all the things you worried about this past year, and indicate how your worrying helped you in each instance. Then add a note telling what you learned from this exercise.*
2. *Make up a list of all the things you are worried about right now in your life, and indicate how your worrying helps you in each instance. Then add a note telling what you learned from this exercise.*
3. *Make up a list of all the things you are concerned about right now in your life, and in each instance indicate the extent to which your concern is expressed in worry (fretting about what could go wrong) or problem solving (a focus on what could be made to go right).*
4. *Describe the use you have made of worry in your own life, and indicate how it has helped or hurt you.*
5. *Try out the three-step worry-control program described in the reading, and describe your experience with it.*

Happiness

We hold these truths to be self-evident, that all men
are created equal, that they are endowed by their
Creator with certain unalienable Rights, that among
these are Life, Liberty and the pursuit of Happiness.
—from the Declaration of Independence

In the Declaration of Independence, the Founding Fathers of this country proclaimed our right to pursue happiness, and many of us are busily engaged in this pursuit. It may come as a surprise that a number of writers on happiness have concluded that it is an unimportant emotion and some that it is a rather impossible one. There are also those who believe that we can never find happiness (whatever its worth) by pursuing it—in fact, they claim that it is how we make ourselves unhappy.

Is happiness important? This question may seem needless because so many of us are committed to its pursuit. Happiness achieved a rank of fifth in a list of eighteen values or goals that were appraised for importance by a national cross-section of adult Americans some years ago. In a similar appraisal with midwestern college students as subjects, happiness was found to rank second, and students from three community colleges in California ranked happiness first. "Becoming happy and content" was also among the highest rated life goals in a nationwide survey of freshmen.

Political scientist John H. Schaar, critic George Jean Nathan, and physicist Albert Einstein are representative of those who have discounted the importance of happiness. Schaar wrote that happiness may be a goal unworthy of a great nation or a great person and that the persons we admire most are not necessarily the happiest ones. Some support for this view is provided by Nathan, who held that "no happy man ever produced a first rate piece of painting, sculpture, music, or literature." And Einstein seemingly dismissed the whole subject when he wrote, "Well-being and happiness are such trivial goals in life that I can imagine them being entertained only by pigs."

Alden Wessman and David Ricks, who studied mood and personality in a group of college men and women, arrived at what may be a happy compromise concerning the importance of happiness. They wrote, "We think it desirable that people be happy—we hold happiness generally superior to misery. But happiness is not everything." These two investigators found much to respect and admire in the lives of their less happy subjects and summing up, they wrote, "In short, while we do not depreciate—and in fact rather admire—happiness in many of its features, we also hold that it is not the sole criterion for judging the worth of human life."

Is happiness possible? Some philosophers have concluded that unhappiness is our more natural state. Nietzsche brooded and wrote, "I fear we are not born to be happy." In the same vein, but with a lighter spirit, psychoanalyst Thomas Szasz aphorized, "Happiness is an imaginary condition, formerly often attributed by the living to the dead, now usually attributed by adults to children, and by children to adults." Schaar concluded that a temporary and qualified happiness is the most we can hope to achieve. The same conclusion was reached by George Bernard Shaw, and he was immensely relieved by it. He wrote, "A lifetime of happiness! No man alive could bear it; it would be hell on earth."

A number of psychologists have cautioned us not to seek—as some of us apparently do—perfect happiness or even almost perfect happiness. Albert Ellis and Robert Harper announce, "Anyone who tries to give you a rule by which you can always be happy is either a fool or a knave." Robert Peck studied a group of fairly typical adults and concluded that for most people, life is never "brilliantly happy." He wrote, "Unalloyed joy is an unknown or forgotten sensation." And he adds that the most we can ask for is "good health, mental and physical, with which to meet each day."

By contrast, voices within humanistic psychology and especially in the human potential movement have been raised to affirm the individual's great capacity for happiness. Abraham Maslow, one of the chief optimists concerning the possibility of happiness, lamented his fellow psychologists' obsession with negative emotions and pointed out that there are more moments of happiness in our lives than are generally acknowledged. Herbert Otto agreed and wrote, "Perhaps the natural state of the human organism is one of joyful communion with others, with itself, and with the universe." Other representatives of this more optimistic group include William Schutz and Alexander Lowen; their respective (and aptly titled) books *Joy* and *Pleasure* present their prescriptions for maximizing happiness and well-being, mostly through awakening and enlivening the body.

Can happiness be pursued? And, if so, how? First of all, there is some controversy between those who suggest roundabout and those who urge direct paths to happiness. The former believe that we find happiness when we stop looking for it or that happiness comes secondarily or incidentally as we occupy ourselves in other pursuits. In his book *The Meaning of Happiness*, Alan Watts wrote that "happiness cannot be had by any form of direct striving. Like your shadow, the more you chase it, the more it runs away." And fellow philosopher Aldous Huxley compared happiness to coke (he meant a form of coal, not cola or cocaine), saying it was "something you get as a by-product in the process of making something else."

By contrast, there are those who advocate pursuing happiness head-on. Implicit in some indirect notions is that happiness has to be earned somehow, and you get it for doing good or doing well. The direct approach holds that happiness need not be merited as much as it must be willed or practiced, which requires us to focus on it in a straightforward and even businesslike way.

A second controversy concerning the pursuit of happiness pits the environmentalists against the personalists. The utopians and the Skinnerians are examples of environmentalists who advocate the creation of better societies to produce happier people. Bertrand Russell, in his book *The Conquest of Happiness*, wrote that in judging the society of the future the question will be "whether those who have grown up in it will be happier than those who have grown up in our society or those of the past." In B. F. Skinner's utopian novel *Walden Two*, society's master planner—Frazier—announces that in addition to making a science of human nature possible, his goals are to "make men happy" and "to assure the continuation of that happiness."

Unlike the environmentalists, the personalists believe that the well-spring of happiness (or joy or tranquility) is within the individual. Each of us can create her or his own happiness, independent—or somewhat so—of environmental conditions. And, in the same way, each of us creates her or his own unhappiness. John Milton expressed this view over 300 years ago when he wrote, "The mind is its own place, and in itself/Can make a heaven of hell, a hell of heaven." Even more to the point are Samuel Johnson's lines, "How small of all that human hearts endure,/That part which laws or kings can cause or cure!/Still to ourselves in every place consigned,/Our own felicity we make or find." Several of the selections that follow have more to say about this.

THE PURSUIT OF HAPPINESS

Make the most of little joys. That's the recommendation of Abe Arkoff in the first reading. He notes that it is frequent little joys rather than the occasional big joy that make for a general sense of well-being; there is much in our daily rounds that can bring us moments of pleasure. As a start, Arkoff suggests that the reader make up a list of such enjoyments and then get busy and make the most of them.

Be receptive to peak experiences. This is one of a number of lessons that Abraham Maslow shares in the second selection (a classic paper in psychology). Maslow writes that *peak experiences*, those moments of awesome or intense happiness—are common and precipitated by many things. Some of us reject or fail to make the most of such experiences because we fear emotion and the loss of control. Maslow notes that if we open ourselves to them, peaks can be highly therapeutic and can even change our lives.

Change your view of the world; the cause of happiness or, at least, unhappiness is in your head and not in external events. This is the insight that Arnold Lazarus and Allen Fay present in the third reading. They hold that we create our own unhappiness by the view we take of external events; by changing our perceptions, we can change the way we react and feel. Lazarus and Fay present a simple three-point plan to get us started on the path to greater happiness.

THE POWER OF OPTIMISM

Optimism and happiness go together. The happier we are or the better our mood, the more optimistic we are about the future. Most of us are happy most of the time, and most of us are optimistic, in fact more so than circumstance might seem to warrant, according to psychologist Shelley Taylor. However, in her book, *Positive Illusions*, she makes the case that our optimism serves us well by helping us to cope with and confront adversity.

In the fourth reading, Abe Arkoff (is that guy here again?) writes that we can learn to be optimistic. He takes note of Martin Seligman's finding that optimists and pessimists have different ways of accounting for the events in their lives. Pessimists hold themselves responsible for adverse events and believe that these events or their effects will persist and affect everything they do. Optimists are less likely to see such events as their fault or as permanent or pervasive in effect. We can increase our optimism by monitoring our thoughts and by disputing and replacing those that bring us down.

Optimism and happiness are associated, and so are optimism and health. Bernie Siegel, a medical doctor whose books *Love, Medicine, and Miracles* and *Peace, Love, and Healing* have caused a stir, suggests we should not rely on modern medicine alone. The effects of the mind on the body are considerable, and in his view, anything that offers hope or creates optimism has the potential to heal. In Siegel's experience, almost all the persons who recover from so-called incurable illnesses have acted positively and thought optimistically—they made significant changes in their lives prior to the healing and looked upon their disease as an opportunity to make a new beginning rather than as a death sentence.

In the last reading, Robert Ornstein and David Sobel highlight the connections among optimism, control, and well-being. They write, "The optimistic belief that we are in control, capable and competent to make changes, is critical to health." What we expect is what we tend to get, and pessimists expect and get more illness than optimists. Ornstein and Sobel suggest that to bolster our optimism and self-confidence, we set ourselves up for success by taking small, achievable steps in the direction in which we want to go.

1. *The mood scale.*[1] Draw seven ladders standing side by side. Each ladder is to have nine rungs. Number the rungs from 1 (bottom rung) to 9 (top rung). Let the top rung represent the happiest state you can possibly imagine for yourself and the bottom rung the most depressed state you can imagine. Just before retiring one night, put an "h" on a rung of the first ladder to represent your highest mood for the day (even if it was experienced for only a few moments), an "l" to represent your lowest mood, and an "o" to represent your overall summary for the day. Do the same the next day, using the second ladder, and so on until you have ratings for one week. Then study your ratings and write a report on what you have learned about yourself and your moods (especially your highest moods).

2. *The mood elevator.* We can elevate our moods by looking for the good in ourselves and others. For this exploration, each member receives an envelope and as many slips of paper as there are persons in the group minus one. Members write their names on their envelopes and send them circulating around the group. As each envelope comes to you, anonymously write a compliment for that person on a slip and insert it in the envelope. When all envelopes have made the rounds, take turns reading your compliments aloud to the group.

3. *The peak experience.* "Peak experience" is used to describe our best and most positive moments—instances of great happiness, ecstasy, or wonder. Such moments may have important consequences; after a peak experience we may see ourselves or our world in a different or more positive way. Recall and discuss one of your peak experiences (or, at least, one of your "minipeaks") and also note any consequences or aftereffects.

4. *The peak stimulus.* Some of our peak or minipeak experiences occur in connection with certain stimuli that appeal strongly to our senses. Possible examples are the sight of an orchid or a Van Gogh painting, the taste of chocolate or licorice, the smell of mint or lavender, the touch of velvet or satin, the sound of a favorite singer or composer, or our inner response during a moment of meditation or relaxation. For this exploration each member brings or conveys to the group something that elevates her or his own moods. The group is encouraged to feel or empathize with this person in her or his experience. (Specifically prohibited are all stimuli and activities that are illegal or that are likely to result in loss of employment or other antipeak experiences for the instructor.)

5. *The peak period.* Certain periods of our lives may be traumatic and have far-reaching effects while others may be particularly happy and important in this respect. Write an account of the happiest period of your life and its effect on you. As an option,

---

1. Adapted from the work of Hadley Cantril and also Alden E. Wessman and David F. Ricks.

these accounts may be shared in the larger group, small groups, or in dyads.

6. *The happiness list.* Poets and writers remind us that there are many things available in our daily life to bring us pleasure if we open ourselves to them and allow ourselves to enjoy them. Professor Sol Gordon has written an essay—a recipe really—on how to be happy; he holds that "we should be able to intensely enjoy at least the number of things equal to our age."[2] Make up a happiness list for yourself. Each item on the list should be something that you are able to deeply enjoy. Number the items as you record them, and don't stop until you have as many items as you are years old.

7. *The optimism list.* Psychologists Gary Reker and Paul Wong have measured optimism by asking subjects to list all the desirable events to which they are looking forward at that moment and indicating their degree of confidence that each of these events will occur. A five-point scale is used to measure the degree of confidence, as follows: 1 = not confident at all; 2 = slightly confident; 3 = fairly confident; 4 = very confident; and 5 = extremely confident. An index of personal optimism can be obtained by multiplying the number of anticipated events by the average degree of confidence. Make up an optimism list for yourself, and score it in the way indicated. Also note how many of the events are self-initiated and how many are other-initiated or events over which you have no control. Then, over a period of several days, try to increase your score by thinking of additional events and/or by more actively planning to make good things happen in your life.

8. *The happiness formula.* List five things that are very important to your own happiness and indicate why each is of importance.

9. *The happiness formula (revised).* List in order (most important first) five things that are very important to your own happiness. When you have done this, imagine a life without the thing you have put in fifth place on your list, and try to see how your life could still be happy. Then imagine a life without the things in fifth *and* fourth place, and try to see how your life could still be happy. Continue in this way until you have tried to picture a happy life for yourself without any of these things. Afterward, write an account of your experience with this exercise or share your experience in the larger group, in small groups, or dyads.

10. *The up list.* We talk to ourselves, and the things we say can influence how we feel. Telling ourselves good things, we can raise ourselves up. Telling ourselves bad things, we can bring ourselves down. On a small card, list ten good things about yourself, and carry this card with you for a week. Read the card at least five times each day; these should be times immediately before positive, reinforcing events (coffee breaks, meals, movies, etc.). In addition, whenever you have a negative thought about yourself,

2. Gordon, S. Creative infidelity: On being happy in an unhappy world. *The Humanist,* January/February 1975, pp. 25–26.

stop it, and immediately read your card. At the end of the week write an account of your experience.

11. *The exposé.* If you had a choice between depression and happiness, you would choose happiness, wouldn't you? Or does happiness have some shortcomings? And could depression have some rewards? (George Bernard Shaw claimed that a lifetime of happiness would be impossible to bear, and Shakespeare wrote, "Sweet are the uses of adversity.") Write a brief essay exposing the limitations of happiness and pointing out the rewards of depression. Or as an alternative, form pairs of questioner and questionee. The questioner persistently repeats a set of two questions (pausing after each question for the questionee to reply): "How can happiness be a problem?" "How can depression be a solution?" When the questionee has run out of answers (but don't give up too soon because the answers slowest in coming ʳ ᷉ be the most revealing), exchange roles and continue as befoᵣ᷉. Afterward, share experiences.

To Read Further

Bloomfield, H. H., & Kory, R. B. (1985). *Inner joy: New strategies to put more pleasure and satisfactions in your life.* New York: Jove. (paperback)

Cousins, N. (1989). *Head first: The biology of hope.* New York: E. P. Dutton. (Penguin paperback, 1990)

Gordon, S., & Brecher, H. (1990). *Life is uncertain . . . Eat dessert first! Finding the joy you deserve.* New York: Delacorte.

McGinnis, A. L. (1990). *The power of optimism.* San Francisco: Harper.

Ornstein, R., & Sobel, D. (1989). *Healthy pleasures.* Reading, MA: Addison-Wesley.

Peterson, C. (1991). *Health and optimism.* New York: Macmillan.

Seligman, M. E. P. (1991). *Learned optimism.* New York: Alfred A. Knopf.

Siegel, B. S. (1990). *Love, medicine and miracles.* New York: Perennial Library. (paperback)

Siegel, B. S. (1990). *Peace, love and healing.* New York: Perennial Library. (paperback)

Taylor, S. E. (1989). *Positive illusions: Creative self-deception and the healthy mind.* New York: Basic Books.

Watts, A. W. (1979). *The meaning of happiness.* New York: Harper & Row. (paperback)

Little Joys

Abe Arkoff

When Salman Rushdie was sentenced to death by the Ayatollah Khomeini for writing "The Satanic Verses," he went into hiding. Reminiscing about the life he left behind, he said, "What I miss is ordinary life: walking down the street, browsing in a bookshop, going to a grocery store, going to a movie. I've always been a big movie addict, and I haven't been in a cinema for a year."

"I haven't driven a car for a year," Rushdie continued. "I really love driving, and suddenly I have to sit in the back seat all the time. What I miss is just that, these tiny little things. "

The value of little things was what playwright Thornton Wilder had in mind when he wrote *Our Town*, which proved to be his most famous work. The play was, he said, "an attempt to find a value above all price for the smallest events in our daily life." In this simple but moving drama, he eloquently shows what is extraordinary about the most ordinary and commonplace.

In *Our Town*, Emily, who has died in early adulthood, finds she can return to relive a day of her life. When she returns to relive her twelfth birthday, she finds her experience—from the vantage point of death—too poignant and in too great a contrast to the living who move matter-of-factly through the day. Overcome, she returns to death saying:

> Good-by, good-by, world. Good-by Grover's Corners . . . Mama and Papa. Good-by to clocks ticking . . . and Mama's sunflowers. And food and coffee. And new-ironed dresses and hot baths . . . and sleeping and waking up. Oh, earth, you're too wonderful for anybody to realize you . . . Do any human beings realize life while they live it?— every, every minute?

My favorite essay on joy is a brief paper by Hermann Hesse. Although written almost 100 years ago, it sounds remarkably up-to-date as it laments the speed of "modern life," with the feverish pursuit of entertainment and ironically less and less joy. Hesse reminds the reader of the little joys available in daily rounds if one will only take a moment for them. He concludes his essay, "It is the small joys first of all that are granted to us for recreation, for daily relief and disburdenment, not the great ones."

Some recent research suggests that Hesse's advice is good psychology. Seek out as many as possible of the small joys each day. Studying both college-age and older persons, Professor Ed Diener of the University of Illinois has found that it is frequent little joys rather than an occasional big joy that make for a general sense of well-being. While less intense positive emotions are common, intense positive emotions are infrequent; furthermore, such intense events are often purchased at the price of past unhappy events and can serve to diminish the sensation of future positive events. Diener found happiness to be associated with those persons who frequently experience positive emotions rather than those whose positive experiences are intense. Thus, Diener and Hesse agree that the key to well-being is to fill one's days with little joys.

More evidence concerning the limited value of big joy was found by a research team who compared the levels of happiness in 22 major lottery winners with the levels of a control group similar in other respects. Each group indicated how happy they were at present, had been earlier (for the winners, before winning; for the controls, 6 months earlier), and expected to be in a couple of years. Significant differences between winners and controls in previous, present, or anticipated levels of happiness: none.

Even more striking results were found when both groups were asked how pleasant they currently found seven activities: eating breakfast, reading a magazine, watching television, talking with a friend, hearing a funny joke, getting a compliment, and buying clothes. Compared to controls, the winners found significantly less pleasure in these activities. Although the emotional big high of winning had not brought a significant, lasting increase in happiness, seemingly, by comparison, everyday little highs had paled.

The Chinese philosopher Lin Yutang passionately described the little pleasures that made his own life joyful. Indeed there were many, and in his enthusiasm, he gave a number of them first place. For example, he wrote, "If there is a greater happiness than lying in the sun, I'd like to be told." But then he noted, "If a man will be sensible and . . . count on his fingers how many things give him enjoyment, invariably he will find food is the first one." Still, later, seemingly to settle the matter, he set down the final truth: "If one's bowels move, one is happy, and if they don't move, one is unhappy. That is all there is to it."

There is much in our day we think of as routine that could become little joys if approached in another way. Rushdie noted that he missed things he once thought completely unimportant—even chores—such as shopping for groceries. What once were tasks now were seen as privileges.

George Leonard recommends the Zen strategy of finding joy in the commonplace. What this requires is not a change of activity but rather a change of attitude. Leonard writes, "You might think that the value of Zen practice lies in the unwavering apprehension of the present moment while sitting motionless. But a visit to a Zen retreat quickly reveals that potentially, *everything* is meditation—building a stone wall, eating, walking from one place to another, sweeping a hallway."

Psychologist Frank Dougherty has made an important distinction between the pursuit of relief and the pursuit of delight. Some of us who (perhaps without knowing it) have spent our lives pursuing relief, wonder why we never feel delight, but no amount of relief can produce delight. People whose minds are set on relief work to make sure that everything is taken care of and under control. There will be time for delight, they think, when things settle down, but of course, things never do.

To pursue delight requires a different mindset, and we can pursue delight even though everything isn't in order. We don't let the work waiting on Monday morning interfere with our enjoyment of the picnic this lovely Sunday afternoon.

Sir Alexander Korda recalled talking with Winston Churchill during the war when some bad news arrived. Churchill glanced at his watch and announced he was due back at 10 Downing Street. "It will all look different after a good lunch, a cigar, and a nap," he said. "Besides, Marshall Stalin has sent us some excellent caviar by courier, and it would be a shame not to enjoy it."

Often, the event that produces relief for one person delivers delight to another who approaches it in a very different way. In this connection, one of my students recalled a backpack trip he had been on with a group of others. Each day, the same person was first to reach their destination. One evening, the group was sharing the memories of the day's beautiful vistas, and this person finally spoke and said, "I guess all I really saw today was the top of my shoes."

Years ago, Sol Gordon wrote a brief set of instructions on how to be happy in an unhappy world. It was simply "to be able to enjoy at least the number of things equal to our age." Gordon was 51 years old at the time, and he wrote out the 51 things he enjoyed. The list included bittersweet stories and chocolate, uninterrupted classical music, reading slowly the good novelists, being warm and intimate with people he really cared about, and fantasizing that one of his still unpublished books was number one or number two on the *New York Times* best-sellers list.

Following Gordon's advice, my students and I make up our own lists of little joys when we are on the topic of happiness. I have found that just making up a list and sharing it with others makes one feel good.

As director of a freshman seminar program and coordinator of a program for older persons, I have taught some of the youngest and oldest students on my campus. The older students seem to compose their long lists of joys as easily as the youngest students do their much shorter ones.

My oldest student (and the one most full of fun and joy) was 91 years old when she made out her list and had no trouble in arriving at 91 items. Now 95, she is recovering from open-heart surgery and writes that she is enjoying in anticipation her next trip to Hawaii.[1]

After my students compose their little joy lists, I ask them to go back and put a star or asterisk by each item they have actually enjoyed

1. Since I wrote this, she has made the trip to Hawaii, and we celebrated her 96th birthday together; she is as full of fun and joy as ever.

in the past 30 days. What good is something that can bring joy if one doesn't take time to enjoy it? I enjoy reading my students' lists as much as my own. Most of the items cost very little or nothing at all. One of the most common items, of course, is chocolate. It appears on Sol Gordon's list and, I confess, my own. However, other common items are calorie-free, such as music, reading, nature, movies, a favorite TV program or comic strip.

The most uncommon joy producer that I have seen on any list is "Standing in the barn loft—after feeding hay to about 100 cattle—and listening to them crunch or munch the hay." It was on the list of one of my older students—a 64-year-old man from Tennessee. His whole list was quite special and not only because it didn't mention chocolate even once. Other items on his list included giving a flower to a lovely lady and watching her eyes light up; sitting on the patio and watching the fields and valleys and mountains change with the shadows as the sun moves across the sky; looking at—and feeling proud of—the many afghans and quilts his mother made and gave to him; driving a good, responsive car on a curvy mountain road; and after a hard, tiring day outside, a drink of good straight sour mash whiskey, mixed with a little 7-Up and cranberry juice.

I remember a joyful poem of Robert Louis Stevenson's that went in part: "The world is so full of a number of things, I'm sure we should all be as happy as kings." And so it is, and so we can be. Make up your list of little joys today, and make sure that in 30 days, each has a star by it.

To Apply This Reading to Yourself

1. *Make a list of all the things you are able to deeply enjoy, and include as many items as you are years old. Put a star or asterisk in front of each item you have actually enjoyed in the past 30 days. Then write an account of your thoughts and feelings as you worked on and read over your list.*
2. *Live an ordinary day as you usually would, except be especially aware of everything in the day that brings you joy. Before you go to sleep, write an account of this experience.*
3. *Live an ordinary day as you usually would, except make the most of each joyful moment or each opportunity for one. Before you go to sleep, write an account of this experience.*
4. *How much is your life a pursuit of relief, and how much a pursuit of delight? Discuss this aspect of your life.*

Lessons from the Peak-Experiences

Abraham H. Maslow

What I'm going to talk about tonight is an excursion into the psychology of health, or of the human being at his best. It's a report from the road, of a job not yet done—a kind of commando raid into the unknown in which I have left my scientific flanks very much exposed. This is a warning to those of you who like neatly finished tasks. This is far from finished.

When I started to explore the psychology of health, I picked out the finest, healthiest people, the best specimens of mankind I could find, and studied them to see what they were like. They were *very* different, startlingly different in some ways from the average. The biologist was right who announced that he had found the missing link between the anthropoid apes and civilized man. "It's *us!*"

I learned many lessons from these people. But one in particular is our concern now. I found that these individuals tended to report having had something like mystic experiences, moments of great awe, moments of the most intense happiness or even rapture, ecstasy or bliss (because the word happiness can be too weak to describe this experience).

These moments were of pure, positive happiness when all doubts, all fears, all inhibitions, all tensions, all weaknesses, were left behind. Now self consciousness was lost. All separateness and distance from the world disappeared as they felt *one* with the world, fused with it, really belonging in it and to it, instead of being outside looking in. (One subject said, for instance, "I felt like a member of a family, not like an orphan.")

Perhaps most important of all, however, was the report in these experiences of the feeling that they had really seen the ultimate truth, the essence of things, the secret of life, as if veils had been pulled aside. Alan Watts has described this feeling as, "This is *it!*" as if you had finally gotten there, as if ordinary life was a striving and a straining to get someplace and this was the arrival, this was *Being There!*; the end of straining and of striving, the achievement of the desire and the hope, the fulfillment of the longing and the yearning. Everyone knows how it feels to want something and not know what. These mystic experiences feel like the ultimate satisfaction of vague, unsatisfied yearnings. They are like a sudden stepping into heaven; like the miracle achieved, like perfection finally attained.[1]

But here I had already learned something new. The little that I had ever read about mystic experiences tied them in with religion, with visions of the supernatural. And, like most scientists, I had sniffed at them in disbelief and considered it all nonsense, maybe hallucinations, maybe hysteria—almost surely pathological.

But the people telling me or writing about these experiences were not such people—they were the healthiest people! That was one thing learned! And I may add that it taught me something about the limitations of the small (not the big) orthodox scientist who won't recognize as knowledge, or as reality, any information that doesn't fit into the already existent science. ("I am the master of this college; what I know not is not knowledge.")

These experiences mostly had nothing to do with religion—at least in the ordinary supernaturalistic sense. They came from the great moments of love and sex, from the great esthetic moments (particularly of music), from the bursts of creativeness and the creative furor (the great inspiration), from women giving natural birth to babies—or just from loving them, from moments of fusion with nature (in a forest, on a seashore, mountains, etc.), from certain athletic experiences, e.g., skindiving, from dancing, etc.

The second big lesson learned was that this was a *natural*, not a *supernatural* experience; and I gave up the name "mystic" experience and started calling them peak-experiences. They can be studied scientifically. (I have started to do this.) They are within reach of human knowl-

1. "If a man could pass through paradise in a dream, and have a flower presented to him as a pledge that his soul had really been there, and if he found that flower in his hand when he awoke, ay, what then!" Coleridge.

edge, not eternal mysteries. They are in the world, not *out* of the world. They belong not only to priests but to all mankind. They are no longer questions of faith but are wide open to human inquisitiveness and to human knowledge. Observe also the implication of naturalistic usages for the words "revelation," "heaven," "salvation," etc. The history of the sciences has been one science after another carving a chunk for itself out of the jurisdiction of religion. It seems to be happening again here. Or to put this all another way, peak-experiences can be considered to be *truly* religious experiences in the best and most profound, most universal, and most humanistic sense of that word. It may turn out that pulling religion into the realm of science will have been the most important consequence of this line of work.

The next big lesson learned was that peak-experiences are far more common than I had ever expected: they were *not* confined to healthy people. These peak-experiences occurred also in average and even in psychologically sick people. As a matter of fact, I now suspect they occur in practically everybody although without being recognized or accepted for what they are.

Think for a minute how crazy this is in its implications. It's taken a long time for it to soak in on me. *Practically everybody reports peak-experiences if approached and questioned and encouraged in the right way. Also I've learned that just talking about it, as I'm doing now, seems to release from the depths all sorts of secret memories or peaks never revealed to anyone before, not even to oneself perhaps.* Why are we so shy about them? If something wonderful happens to us, why do we conceal it? Someone pointed out once, "Some people are scared to die; but some are scared to live." Maybe this is it.

There is considerable overlap between the characteristics of peak-experiences and the characteristics of psychological health (more integrated, more alive, more individual, less inhibited, less anxious, etc.) so I have been tempted to call the peak-experience a transient or temporary episode of self-actualization or health. If this *guess* turns out to be correct, it is like saying almost everyone, even the sickest people, can be psychologically healthy part of the time.

Still another lesson that by now I'm very sure of: Peak-experiences come from *many,*

many sources and to every kind of person. My list of sources seems to keep on getting longer and longer as I go on with these explorations. Sometimes I am tempted to think that almost any situation where perfection can be attained, or hope fulfilled, or perfect gratification reached, or where everything has gone smoothly, can produce in some people, at some times, a peak-experience. These can be very humble areas of life or of the workaday world; or the situation may have been repeated a thousand times before without producing a peak-experience.

"If your everyday life seems poor to you," wrote Rilke in his *Letters to a Young Poet,* "do not accuse it; accuse yourself, tell yourself you are not poet enough to summon up its riches, since for the creator there is no poverty and no poor or unimportant place."

For instance, a young mother scurrying around her kitchen and getting breakfast for her husband and young children. The sun was streaming in, the children clean and nicely dressed, were chattering as they ate. The husband was casually playing with the children; but as she looked at them she was suddenly so overwhelmed with their beauty and her great love for them, and her feeling of good fortune, that she went into a peak-experience. (This reminds me of my surprise of getting such reports from women. The surprise taught me how much we had masculinized all this.)

A young man working his way through medical school by drumming in a jazz band reported years later, that in all his drumming he had three peaks when he suddenly felt like a great drummer and his performance was perfect.

A hostess after a dinner party where everything had gone perfectly and it had been a fine evening, said good-bye to her last guest, sat down in a chair, looked around at the mess, and went into a peak of great happiness and exhilaration.

Milder peaks have come after a good dinner with good friends as a man sat smoking a fine cigar, or in a woman after she had done a really good cleaning up in her kitchen and it shone and sparkled and looked perfect.

Thus it is clear that there are many paths to these experiences of rapture. They are not necessarily fancy or occult or arcane or esoteric. They don't necessarily take years of training or study. They are not restricted to far-out people, i.e., to monks, saints, or yogis, Zen Buddhists, orientals, or people in any special state of grace. It is not something that happens in the Far East, in special places, or to specially trained or chosen people. It's available in the midst of life to everyday people in everyday occupations. This is a clear support for the writers on Zen and their concept of "nothing special."

Now another generalization which I'm fairly sure of by now. No matter what the source of the peak-experience, all peak-experiences seem to overlap, to tend to be alike. I can't say they're identical—they're not. But they're much *closer* to being identical than I had ever dreamed. It was a startling thing for me to hear a mother describing her ecstatic feelings during the birth of her one child and using some of the same words and phrases that I had read in the writings of St. Theresa of Avila, or Meister Eckhardt, or in Japanese or Hindu descriptions of *satori* or *samadhi* experiences. (Aldous Huxley makes this same point in his "Perennial Philosophy.")

I haven't done this very carefully yet—these are so far only pilot or preliminary explorations—but I do feel safe in generalizing all peak-experiences to some extent. *The stimuli are very different: the subjective experience tends to be similar.* Or to say it in another way: our *kicks* are the same; we just get them from different paths, perhaps even from rock and roll, drug addiction and alcohol in less strong people. I feel more sure of this after reading in the literatures of mystic experiences, cosmic consciousness, oceanic experiences, esthetic experiences, creative experiences, love experiences, parental experiences, sexual experiences, and insight experiences. They all overlap; they approach similarity and even identity.

One main benefit I've gotten from this discovery, and that we all may get, is that it will help us to understand each other better. If a mathematician and a poet use similar words in describing their peak-experiences from a successful poem and a successful mathematical proof, maybe they're more alike subjectively than we have thought. I can make such parallels between a high school athlete running to a touchdown, a business man describing his feelings over plans for a perfect fig canning factory, a college student catching on to the Adagio movements of Beethoven's Ninth Symphony. I feel men can learn more about women's inner life (and vice versa) if they learn about the things that give them their highest satisfaction and feelings of creativeness. For instance, college women significantly more often than college men report their high moments to come from *being* loved. The men significantly more often get their happiest moments from success, conquest, achievement, winning. This finding conforms both to common sense knowledge and to clinical experience.

If our inner experiences of happiness are very similar no matter what stimulates them and no matter how different the people these experiences happen to (that is, if our insides are more like each other than our outside) then this may furnish us a way of being more sympathetic and understanding with people who are very different from ourselves; athletes and intellectuals, women and men, adults and children, etc. An artist and a housewife are not 1000 miles apart. In some moments they speak a common language, have common experiences, and live in the same world.

Can you bring about these experiences at will? No! Or almost entirely no! In general we are "Surprised by Joy," to use the title of C. S. Lewis's book on just this question. Peaks come unexpectedly, suddenly they *happen* to us. You can't count on them. And, hunting them is a little like hunting happiness. It's best not done directly. It comes as a by-product—an epiphenomenon, for instance, of doing a fine job at a worthy task you can identify with.

Of course we can make it more likely, or less likely, out of our experiences in the past. Some fortunate people can almost always have a peak-experience in sex. Some can count on certain pieces of music, or certain favorite activities like dancing or skindiving. But none of these is ever *guaranteed* to bring on a peak-experience. The most propitious frame of mind for "receiving" them is one of receptivity, almost a kind of passivity, or trust, or surrender, a Taoistic attitude of letting things happen without interfering or butting in. You have to be able to give up pride, will, dominance, being at the wheel, being in charge. You have to be able to relax and let it happen.

I think this will do for you what it did for me—renew my interest in Taoism and the lessons it has to teach. So also for Zen. (On the whole, I can say that my findings conform more with the Zen and Tao philosophies than with any of the religious mysticisms.)

I'm very sure now that the ineffability of such experiences has been overstated. It *is* possible to talk about them, to describe them, and to communicate them. I do it all the time now that I've learned how. "Ineffable" really means "not communicable by rational, logical, abstract, verbal, analytic, sensible language." The peak-experience can be described and communicated fairly well if: (1) you both have had such experiences yourselves, and (2) you are able to talk in poetic or rhapsodic language, to let yourself be archaic in Jung's sense, to think-feel in a metaphorical or primary process way—or what Heinz Werner has called physiognomical language.

It's true the psyche *is* alone, encapsulated—cut off from all else—and for two such isolated psyches to communicate across the great chasm between them seems like a miracle. Well, the miracle happens.

What is the relation between the peak and the peaker is my next question. Already it seems evident to me that there is some kind of dynamic isomorphism at work, some kind of mutual and parallel feedback or reverberation between the characteristics of the perceiver and of the perceived world so that they tend to influence each other. To put it very briefly, the perceiver has to be worthy of the percept. Or better said, they must deserve each other like well-married or badly married couples. Kindness can *really* be perceived only by a kind man. A psychopathic personality will never be able to understand kindness, conscience, morality, or guilt since he himself lacks them entirely. But the person who is good, true, and beautiful is more able to perceive these in the world outside—or the more unified and integrated we are, the more capable we are of perceiving unity in the world.

But there is also an effect in the other direction. The more integrated the world, or the more beautiful or just, the more the world tends to make the perceiver more integrated, or beautiful or just, etc. Seeking out the highest values in the world to look at helps to produce or strengthen them in us. For instance, an experiment we did at Brandeis University proved that in a beautiful room people's faces look more alive and alert and higher in well-being, than they do in an ugly room. Or to put it another way, peak-experiences are more apt to come to nicer people, and they are more likely to happen to a particular person the better world conditions are.

This position needs many more examples to make it clear. I intend to write about this at greater length. It's a very important point.

In the peak-experiences, the "is" and the "ought" merge with each other instead of being different or contradictory. The perception is that what *is*, ought to be just that way. What *is* is just fine. This raises so many difficult questions that I don't want to make too much of it at this point, beyond recording that it *does* happen.

Finally, one finding that contradicts some of the mystics, especially of the East: I found all peak-experiences to be transient experiences—temporary not permanent. Some of the effects or after-effects may be permanent but the high moment itself is not.

PROBLEMS AND PUZZLES

Peak-experiences have been highly therapeutic for some people; and for others, a whole outlook on life has been changed forever by some great moment of insight or inspiration or conversion. This is easy to understand. It's like having been in Heaven for a moment and then remembering it in the dull moments of ordinary life. One person said characteristically, "I know life *can* be beautiful and good, and that life can be worth living; and I try to remember that when I need it during the grim days." One woman after natural childbirth, still breathless with the wonder of it said to her husband, "This has never happened to anyone before!" Another one, recalling the same experience said, "Once I was a queen, the most perfect queen of the earth." A man recalled his experience of awe from being in a wartime convoy at night with no lights. He melted into the whole vast universe and was not separate from all its beauty. A man recalled a burst of exuberance going over into sheer crazy, childish joy as he cavorted in the water like a fish, all alone so that he could yell out his great happiness at being so perfectly physical. And, of course, good and beautiful sex under the right circumstances is *often* reported to have this sort of effect.

It is easy to understand how such beautiful experiences should leave therapeutic effects, ennobling and beautifying effects, on the character, on the life outlook, on the way the world looks, on the way that the husband looks, or the baby. What is difficult to understand is why so often this does *not* happen. Practically everyone can be brought to realize he has been through such experiences. Why is it, then, that human beings are such a feeble lot, so full of jealousy, of fear, of hostility, of sheer misery? *This* is what I can't figure out.

One clue may come from a current investigation some of us are making on "Peakers" and "Non-Peakers"; i.e., the ones who reject or deny or suppress their peak-experiences, or who are afraid of them. It is our hunch that the peaks will do no good when they are rejected in this way.

At first it was our thought that some people simply didn't have peaks. But, as I said above, we found out later that it's much more probable that the non-peakers have them but repress or misinterpret them, or—for whatever reason—reject them and therefore don't use them.

Some of the reasons for such rejection so far found are: (1) a strict Marxian attitude, as with Simone de Beauvoir, who was persuaded that this was a weakness, a sickness (also Arthur Koestler). A Marxist should be "tough." Why Freud rejected his is anybody's guess; perhaps (2) his 19th-century mechanistic-scientific attitude, perhaps (3) his pessimistic character. Among my various subjects I have found both causes at work sometimes. In others I have found (4) a narrowly rationalistic attitude which I considered a defense against being flooded by emotion, by irrationality, by loss of control, by illogical tenderness, by dangerous femininity, or by the fear of insanity. One sees such attitudes more often in engineering, in mathematicians, in analytic philosophers, in bookkeepers and accountants, and generally in obsessional people.

The effects of refusing to recognize peak-experiences must be many. We are now trying to work them out.

One thing I have already learned is that authoritative approval lifts the lid off these experiences for many people. For instance, whenever I lecture to my classes or other groups about these peaks, obviously in an approving way, it always happens that many peak-experiences come into consciousness in my audience, or are "remembered" for the first time; or—as I prefer to think

today—emerge out of chaotic, unorganized preconscious experience to be given a name, to be paid attention to, to stand out as figures against the background. In a word, people then "realize" or "understand" what's been happening to them. Many of you who are now listening to me will find this to be so. It's a very close parallel to the emergence of sexual feelings at puberty. But this time, Daddy says it's all right.

A recent subject has taught me something else that may be relevant here; namely that it is possible to have a peak experience as the woman did in childbirth, without recognizing that this is like other peak-experiences—that they all have the same structure. Perhaps this is a reason for lack of therapeutic transfer of peaks, a reason why sometimes they have no generalized effects. For instance, the woman finally realized that her feelings when her husband had once made her feel needed and important to him were very much like her feelings while giving birth, and also like the great gush of motherliness and love when confronted by an orphaned child. Now she can generalize the experiences and use them throughout life, not just in one isolated corner of it.

This work is also beginning to shed some light on an old puzzle noted by many religious writers—especially by those who have written about conversion, like William James or Begbie, as well as many of the old mystics. They implied often that it was *necessary* to go through a "dark night of the soul," to hit bottom—to experience despair as a prerequisite to the mystic ecstasy. I get the feeling from some of this writing that it is as if human will, pride, and arrogance first have to express themselves to the fullest. After will and pride have been proven to yield only total misery, the person in the depths may *then* be able to surrender, to yield, to become humble, to bow his head and bend his knee; to offer himself on the altar; and to say "not my will, but thine be done." I should stress that this is not *only* a religious phenomenon; something of the same sort can happen to the alcoholic, to the psychotic, to the female in her struggle with the male, or to the youngster in his struggle with his parent.

The trouble with this problem has been, I now think, that it can take *either* a healthy *or* a sick form. For instance, this whole scheme works not only for religious conversion or mystic experience, but also for sexuality. It's very easy to pick out sexual elements in mystical literature and you can see how a sex-denying religious would have to reject anything of the sort, and how a debunker like H. L. Mencken would snicker out loud at the whole business. For *all* people for whom sex and religion (in the "higher" life) didn't mix, this was a dilemma they got hung up on. Well, *this* part of the problem is certainly no problem any longer, at least not for those who think sex (or love-sex at least) is a wonderful and beautiful thing, and who are perfectly willing to think of it as one of the gates to Heaven.

But there are other problems. Pride can easily be a sick thing, but so also can the *lack* of pride be, i.e., masochism. It looks as if human beings must be able *both* to affirm themselves (to be stubborn, stiff necked, vigilant, alert, dominant, aggressive, self-confident, etc.) and *also* to be able to trust, to relax and be receptive and Taoistic, to let things happen without interfering, to be humble and surrender. For instance, we now know that *both* in proper sequence are necessary for creativeness, for good thinking and theorizing, for interpersonal relations, and certainly for sexual relationships. It seems true that females have to be extra good at trusting and yielding and males at asserting and affirming, but both must be able to do both.

We have seen that so far as the peaks are concerned, apparently most of them are *receptive* phenomena. They invade the person and he must be able to *let* them. He can force them, grasp them, or command them. Will power is useless; so is striving and straining. What's necessary is to be able to let go, to let things happen. I can give you some very homely examples to show what I mean. It was Angyal who told me that, in his experience, really obsessional people couldn't "float" in the water. They just couldn't let go or be *non*-controlling. To float you must trust the water. Fight it and down you go. The same is true for urination, defecation, going to sleep, relaxing, etc. All these involve an ability to let go, to let things happen. Will power only interferes. In this same sense it begins to look as if the intrusion of will power may inhibit peak-experiences.

A final word on this point. "Letting go," "trusting," and the like does *not* necessarily mean a "dark night of the soul," or "black despair," or breaking down of pride or being forced to one's knees. Healthy pride goes very nicely with healthy receptivity. It is *un*-healthy pride only that has to be "broken."

This, by the way, is another point of difference between mystic experience and these peak-experiences.

I have elsewhere pointed out an unsolved problem, that peak-experiences make some people more alert, excited, "high," while others relax, grow quiet, and more serene. I don't know what this difference means, or where it comes from. Perhaps the latter means more complete gratification than the former. Perhaps it doesn't. I have run across at least one subject who gets tension headaches from peak-experiences, especially esthetic ones. She reports stiffness, tension, and great excitement in which she gets very talkative. The headache is not unpleasant and she doesn't avoid it but rather goes looking for more. This headache goes together with other more usual reports. For instance, I quote, "the world looks nice and I feel friendlier. I have a feeling of hopefulness (which is not usual for me). These are the moments when I *know* what I want—sure, less doubt; I'm more efficient and make faster decisions, less confusion. I know better what I want—what I like. I feel not only more hopeful but more understanding and compassionate," etc., etc.

The questions I asked were about the moments of rapture, of greater happiness. They, therefore, observed the well-known fact that tragedy, pain, and confrontation with death all may produce the same cognitive or therapeutic effects in people with sufficient courage and strength. So also the fusion of happiness with sadness—of laughter's closeness to tears—have to be investigated. I was told often enough of the tears that came with tremendous happiness (e.g., weeping at the happy wedding) or with the triumph of justice (e.g., tears at the happy ending), or the lump rising in the throat (e.g., at the peak of an especially beautiful dance performance), or the chills, goose flesh, shivering—and in one case—even incipient nausea, at musical peaks. These questions call for intensive and extensive investigation.

The study of peak-experiences inevitably brings up a very difficult problem that must occupy psychology for the next century. This is what some of the old mystics and some theologians called the "Unitive Consciousness" and by other names as well. The problem as the religionists phrased it was how to live a godly life in an ungodly world, how to live under the aspect of eternity, how to keep the vision of perfection in an imperfect world, how to remember truth, goodness, and beauty in the midst of falsehood, evil, and ugliness. In the past, all sorts of people left the world behind in order to achieve this vision, e.g., immured themselves in monasteries, or lived ascetic lives, etc. And many have tried to subdue the flesh, the body, the appetites out of the mistaken belief that these contradicted the eternal, the perfect, the divine, the realm of Being.

But think! Peak-experiences can very meaningfully be assimilated to—or even replace—the immature concepts in which Heaven is like a country club in some specific place, perhaps above the clouds. In peaks, the nature of Being itself is often perceived nakedly and the eternal values then seem to be attributes of reality itself, or to say it another way, Heaven is all around us, always available in principle, ready to step into for a few minutes. It's anywhere—in the kitchen or the factory, or on a basketball court—*anyplace* where perfection can happen, where means become ends or where a job is done right. The Unitive Life is more possible than was ever dreamed of, and one thing is very clear—research will bring it closer and make it more available.

One last word. It must by now be obvious to those who are familiar with the literature of mystical experiences that these peak-experiences are very much like them, and overlap them but are not identical with them. What their true relationship is, I do not know. My best guess is that they are different in degree but not in kind. The total mystical experience, as classically described, is more or less approached by greater or lesser peak-experiences.

To Apply This Reading to Yourself

1. *Discuss one of your peak-experiences or minipeaks. What was it? What caused it? What were its effects?*
2. *Maslow notes that although we cannot bring on peak-experiences at will, we can make it more likely that one will occur. What do you do or could you do to facilitate peak-experiences for yourself?*
3. *Note the distinction Maslow makes between peakers and nonpeakers. Which are you? On what evidence is your answer based?*
4. *Maslow writes that "Heaven is all around us." Is this true for you? Why or why not?*

Unhappiness Is Self-Created

Arnold Lazarus and Allen Fay

The tendency to attribute unhappiness to external sources is widespread. It is one of the most serious psychological mistakes. People say: "His remark upset me!" "Her comments hurt me!" "It made me unhappy when he left the room." In reality, remarks, comments and statements do not hurt or upset people. *They upset themselves over these statements or incidents.* The age-old saying (like most age-old sayings) remains profoundly true: "Sticks and stones may break my bones but words can never hurt me!" Though we utter these ideas as children, we do not take them seriously as adults. If we did, we would then say: "I upset myself over his remark," in place of the psychologically inaccurate version, "His remark upset me!" Similarly, we would say: "I hurt myself over her comments," "I made myself unhappy when he left the room," "I distressed myself over the fact that he ignored me."

As long as we incorrectly blame outside sources for our miseries, it remains impossible to do much about them. However, if we realize that *we upset ourselves* over the things that happen to us, we can work at changing. The first step is to ask: "Exactly how do I manage to upset myself?" We then obtain the clues about how to avoid upsetting ourselves.

For example, a young man was extremely distressed because his girlfriend refused to stop dating other men. "Her behavior really upsets me," he said. "No," we replied, "you are upsetting yourself over her behavior." And then we asked: "How are you managing to upset yourself so deeply? What are you saying to yourself?" It took about 10 minutes to piece together the fact that he was upsetting himself by thinking along the following lines: "I am failing as a man. If I were any good, she would want to go out with me exclusively. There must be a serious deficiency in me. She probably finds other men better-looking, more virile, more interesting, and

more stimulating. I'll probably never find anyone who will regard me as really worthwhile." Once we knew how he was so successfully upsetting himself, we were in a position to show him how to stop making himself so unhappy over his present girlfriend's lack of ardor. We told him to challenge each one of his negative self-statements. "How does failure with one woman [or even ten women] add up to being a failure *as a man!* It means that a relationship didn't work out as you had hoped. It says nothing about you as a man in general. How do you know that there is not some quirk in her that prevents her from developing the degree of attachment you would desire?"

The point is that when we recognize where the locus of control resides—*in our heads and not in the external events*—we are able to start doing something to change the way we perceive events. If you make yourself unhappy when your spouse yells at you, or when your in-laws visit you, or when your neighbor's dog barks, you must first discover exactly how you go about inducing this unhappiness. Then you can decide to do something about it.

HOW TO CHANGE

We are now going to show you how to bring about change by demonstrating the specific approach set forth here. Remember: people wrongly blame external factors for their moods and behaviors! How often have *you* said something like: "He made me angry." "She ruined my day." "Those kids are going to give me a heart attack." "My sister-in-law infuriates me." "His attitude upset me." Our guess is that you, like almost everyone, often attribute your feelings and reactions to external events. We simply have not been taught to say: "I made myself angry over his remark." "I allowed her behavior to get in the way of my own pleasure." Few people realize that by talking and thinking in this accurate manner, they immediately create ways of controlling negative situations. Thus, the person who says, "I upset myself over the fact that my wife came home late," instead of the usual "My wife upset me by coming home late," can ask how he went about upsetting himself. Then he would be able to learn how to stop upsetting himself in the future.

The basic tenet of one school of psycho-therapy—rational emotive therapy—is the age-old observation that we are not disturbed by things—external events—but by the views we take of them—our own perceptions. Much of our thinking derives from this school and we strongly subscribe to their basic tenets. If you accept this philosophy—and it is our aim to convince you it is correct—and wish to change your own reactions, here is what you would need to do:

1. *Talk to your friends about the relationship between external events and people's reactions to those events.* A good way to learn something yourself is to teach others. As you explain to others how we miss the point when we say things like, "The way she put me down depressed me," instead of "I made myself feel depressed over the way she put me down," you will be educating them while helping yourself.

2. *Whenever you catch yourself falsely attributing your own feelings to external events, keep a record of this in a notebook, making a notation as soon as it is possible.* This is going to become an important factor in your growth and change. A typical page in your notebook might look something like this:

Tuesday,   11:30 A.M.   Blamed my depression on the boss's temper.

             3:15 P.M.   Accused Tom of hurting my feelings.

             10:20 P.M.   Told Sally that her mother makes me uptight.

Wednesday, 9:10 A.M.   I said the boss is going to drive me to drink.

             Midnight   Told Sally I couldn't sleep because she had upset me.

Thursday,   3 P.M.   Told Mildred that Tom ruined my morning.

Friday,   6 P.M.   Said I was depressed because the party was canceled.

Sunday,   4:45 P.M.   Said I'm in a bad mood because my team lost the game.

3. *Set aside a definite time to correct the faulty reasoning.* Thus, during lunch hour on Wednesday, the three entries made on Tuesday could be thought through.
   a. "The boss's temper can't depress me. I depress myself over his temper. How do I go about doing that? Well, when he yells and carries on, I think to myself that he might fire me. So I guess it's not his temper that depresses me, but I make myself miserable by thinking that he might fire me. Perhaps I could stop worrying so much about being fired."
   b. "Tom can't hurt my feelings. I let my feelings get hurt by the fact that he invited Debbie to lunch in front of me. I told myself that this means he dislikes me. Actually I think he prefers Debbie's company to mine. That makes sense because they both go in for boats and water skiing and other things that turn me off. Why let my feelings get hurt by that?"
   c. "How do I make myself uptight over Sally's mother? I guess I would like her to approve of me and I make myself upset when she is critical. Actually, why do I want her approval? She's an old-fashioned woman with ideas that just don't jibe with mine. So if I take her for what she is, I don't think she will get to me again."

Note what we are doing here: we are recommending an active process, the systematic use of applied psychology. We are not talking theoretically and abstractly. In our approach you are asked to *do* specific things. You are shown how to identify specific responses you wish to change, how to monitor faulty thoughts, feelings and behaviors, and how to introduce new and corrective responses into your repertoire. Many people waste inordinate amounts of time struggling to change by exploring the deeper recesses of the mind, by delving into their early life, by analyzing their dreams, by reading ponderous tomes, and through philosophical reflections about the meaning of life. Life is too short and that struggle too long.

To Apply This Reading to Yourself

1. *Would you agree with Lazarus and Fay that your own unhappiness is self-created? Why or why not?*
2. *Recall a situation in which you felt upset by something that someone said to you. Write an account of it beginning: "He/she upset me..." Then write another account of the same event beginning: "I upset myself..." As a final step, draw any conclusions or insights you can from your comparison of these two accounts.*
3. *Consider a recurring situation that you find upsetting and pose these questions (suggested by Lazarus and Fay) for yourself. "How do I manage to upset myself? What thoughts do I have and what statements do I make to myself in this situation? What clues can I find that will help me keep from upsetting myself in the future?" Write a brief paper describing the recurring situation and incorporating your answers to these questions.*
4. *Carry out the three-point plan presented by Lazarus and Fay and write an account of what you did and what you learned.*

The Psychology of Optimism

Abe Arkoff

Pollyanna was the memorable child heroine of a book written by Eleanor Porter. Pollyanna was noted for her propensity to play the "Glad Game." She found something to be glad about in every seeming misfortune, and in doing so transformed her own life and helped others to transform theirs.

The dictionary on my work table defines "Pollyanna" as a "foolishly or blindly optimistic person" but Pollyanna's relentless optimism, although blind, served her and others well—it made good things happen. And recent research on optimism generally suggests that the "Glad Game" is still worth playing although not blindly.

Reviewing the evidence, Margaret Matlin and David Stang (1978) conclude that there is a "Pollyanna Principle" evident in our language, memory and thought. Some manifestations of this principle are (1) we understand pleasant information more quickly and accurately than that which is unpleasant; (2) we spend more time thinking pleasant than unpleasant thoughts; and (3) if an event is unpleasant it will tend to fade or even lead to the Glad Game as we come to see it in a different light.

We humans generally are optimistic about our future and more so than reality supports. And generally our optimism is not blind Pollyannaism. Shelley Taylor (1989) writes that our "optimism shows a patterning that corresponds quite well to the objective likelihood of events, to relevant experience with events, and to the degree to which one can actively contribute to bringing events about. Positive events are simply regarded as somewhat more likely and negative events as somewhat less likely to occur than is actually the case" (p. 37).

Research suggests that optimists tend to do better and behave differently than pessimists in stressful situations. Optimists are more likely to remain focused on the problem, try different strategies, and seek the help of others. Pessimists are more likely to disengage themselves from the goal and focus on the emotion that has been aroused (Scheier & Carver, 1985; Scheier, Weintraub, & Carver, 1986).

EXPLANATORY STYLE

Some foods are bad to eat, and some thoughts are bad to think. Pessimistic thoughts—unlike optimistic ones—fall in the bad-for-you category. Pessimists and optimists, according to Martin Seligman (1991), have different explanatory styles—different ways of accounting for the events in their lives. Explanations, says Seligman, can be measured along three dimensions: permanence, pervasiveness, and personalization.

Pessimists, depressed persons, and those who give up easily tend to believe that their bad events have a *permanence:* These events will persist, never go away, always affect their lives. Optimists, nondepressed persons, and those who resist helplessness believe the causes of such events to be temporary. For example, the pessimist fails at a task and says, "I'll never be able to do this." The optimist might say, "I'm a bit tired," leaving the door open to success after a bit of rest. Further example after a bad day in Las Vegas: The pessimist says, "I always am unlucky"; the optimist says, "I wasn't lucky today."

For good events, the situation is just reversed. The pessimist sees these as transient in causation, perhaps due to a mood or special effort or circumstance unlikely to be repeated. The optimist, by contrast, sees good events as having permanent causes, perhaps related to traits or abilities. The pessimist: "I had a lucky day." Or "Things went just right for once." The optimist: "I'm a lucky person." Or "I'm pretty good at this."

The second dimension distinguishing pessimists from optimists concerns *pervasiveness*—whether something is universal or specific. Pessimists find universal explanations for bad events and specific explanations for good ones. When something goes wrong, pessimists take this as evidence that everything is wrong, and when something goes right, it is evidence that only that one thing is right. Optimists reverse this pattern. Optimist: "I'm not good at math." Pessimist: "I'm not good at anything." Optimist: "I'm not attractive to him." Pessimist: "I'm just not attractive." Or for good events, optimist: "I'm smart." "I'm attractive." Pessimist: "I'm smart *at math*." "I was attractive *to him*."

The third explanatory dimension is *personalization*—whether or not the person is responsible. Optimists take the credit but not the blame, while pessimists take the blame but not the credit. Optimists are internalizers for good events—they see themselves as making such events happen—but externalizers for bad events, which are seen as beyond their control. Pessimists reverse this pattern. Pessimist: "It's my fault." Optimist: "It's bad luck." Or for a good event, pessimist: "It was a lucky break." Optimist: "I got a clear shot and made the most of it."

Snyder and Higgins (1988) conclude that although we are taught not to make excuses, some excuse-making may have positive benefits, raising self-esteem and lowering anxiety and depression. In many of our excuses, we don't shift blame outside ourselves but only to a less threatening and less central aspect of self. For example we say, "I got a low score because I didn't study" rather than "I got a low score because I'm stupid." Philosopher J. L. Austin (1970) observes that "Few excuses get us out of it completely; the average excuse, in a poor situation, gets us only out of the fire into the frying pan—but still, of course, any frying pan in a fire" (p. 177).

Seligman notes that there are obvious advantages to teaching persons to see bad events as temporary and specific but some dangers in the externalization of the causes of these events. He writes that he does not wish to advocate any strategy that erodes personal responsibility, and, after all, we will not change for the better if we do not assume this responsibility. However, he does encourage such externalization in the case of depressed persons because these individuals assume too much responsibility for adverse events.

LEARNED OPTIMISM

We can learn optimism. Seligman writes that becoming more optimistic is just a matter of

ABC—that is, using Albert Ellis's ABC system to change self-defeating beliefs or thoughts. (Actually, it involves a bit more of the alphabet: ABCDE.) Ellis (1977) writes that we humans tend to attribute many of our responses to external stimuli, but this is incorrect or at least partly so; rather, our beliefs largely determine what we feel and do in a situation. For example, there is an A (Activating experience or event); perhaps we get fired from a good job. This is followed by C (an emotional or behavioral Consequence); we feel dejected and too immobilized to look for another job. It could be erroneously assumed that A caused C, but actually C stemmed from B—our Belief about A. Our Belief may have been that we desperately need and must have that job, it is awful that we lost it, and we can't stand to be without it. If we had, instead, told ourselves that losing the job was unfortunate but not the end of the world, we would not have been so upset and unable to function.

In the present context, Ellis might say that it is not adverse Activating events A that cause adverse Consequences C, such as depression and other miseries; rather it's our pessimistic Beliefs B or explanations. To go from pessimism to optimism, we monitor our beliefs or explanations to determine those that are pessimistic, and then Dispute (D) these, and replace them with optimistic ones. Distraction D—if we don't mind another D—is also a useful technique to keep ourselves from ruminating or brooding. The result: a new optimistic Effect E or outcome.

Seligman (1991) advises that in disputing beliefs, we scan all possible causes and focus on those that are changeable (for example, we were not well enough prepared), specific (this particular competition was a tough one), and nonpersonal (the judging left something to be desired). Seligman writes, "You may have to push hard at generating alternative beliefs, latching onto possibilities you are not fully convinced are true. Remember that much of pessimistic thinking consists in just the reverse, latching onto the most dire possible belief, not because the evidence supports it, but precisely because it is so dire" (p. 222). Those of us who tend to arrive at pessimistic permanent, pervasive, and personal explanations for adverse events need to become skilled at generating alternatives. Here is Seligman's example of a student (Judy) disputing her beliefs, arriving at alternative explanations, and brightening her despair:

> *Adversity:* I recently started taking night classes after work for a master's degree. I got my first set of exams back and I didn't do nearly as well as I wanted.
>
> *Belief:* What awful grades, Judy. I no doubt did the worst in the class. I'm just stupid. That's all. I might as well face facts. I'm also just too old to be competing with these kids. Even if I stick with it, who is going to hire a forty-year-old woman when they can hire a twenty-three-year-old instead? What was I thinking when I enrolled? It's just too late for me.
>
> *Consequences:* I felt totally dejected and useless. I was embarrassed I even gave it a try, and decided I should withdraw from my courses and be satisfied with the job I have.
>
> *Disputation:* I'm blowing things out of proportion. I hoped to get all As, but I got a B, a B +, and a B-. Those aren't awful grades. I may not have done the best in the class, but I didn't do the worst in the class either. I checked. The guy next to me had two Cs and a D+. The reason I didn't do as well as I hoped isn't because of my age. The fact that I am forty doesn't make me any less intelligent than anyone else in the class. One reason I may not have done as well is because I have a lot of other things going on in my life that take time away from my studies. I have a full-time job. I have a family. I think that given my situation I did a good job on my exams. Now that I took this set of exams I know how much work I need to put into my studies in the future in order to do even better. Now is not the time to worry about who will hire me. Almost everyone who graduates from this program gets a decent job. For now I need to concern myself with learning the material and earning my degree. Then when I graduate I can focus on finding a better job.
>
> *Outcome:* I felt much better about myself and my exams. I'm not going to withdraw from my courses, and I am not going to let my age stand in the way of

getting what I want. I'm still concerned that my age may be a disadvantage, but I will cross that bridge if and when I come to it. (pp. 218–219)

DEFENSIVE PESSIMISM

Despite the advantages of optimism, some of us seem to be relentlessly pessimistic at least in certain areas of our lives. The work of Norem and Cantor (1986) suggests that all pessimism is not alike in its effects. There is a kind of "defensive pessimism" in which persons set unjustifiably low expectations to prepare for potential failure and motivate themselves to avoid that failure. As an example, these investigators point to straight-A students who insist they are going to "bomb" an exam: "Nothing their friends can say reassures them; indeed, reminding them of their past successes seems only to lead to more anxiety or confusion. These persons proceed to rush home, drink gallons of coffee, study furiously throughout the night, and, annoyingly, but not surprisingly, receive the highest score in the class" (p. 1209). Norem and Cantor's work suggests that exhorting defensive pessimists to think positively or optimistically may not be useful or helpful. In fact, when such encouragement was provided by Norem and Cantor, it led to impaired performance.

This pair of investigators followed groups of defensive pessimists and optimists in an honors college from their freshman through their junior year and found that pessimism had some long-term costs. Although the two groups did not differ in grade-point average (GPA) or on measures of life satisfaction and stress in their freshman and sophomore years, by the third year, the defensive pessimists were significantly higher in stress and lower in GPA and life satisfaction; they also showed more physical and psychological symptoms. One hypothesis was that overpreparing can be exhausting and also perhaps somewhat dismaying as one sees that one's all-out efforts and worry are usually unnecessary.

Although the long-term costs may be high, there can be some advantages to a pessimistic approach in some situations. Because pessimists expect the worst and prepare for it, they are not likely to be overconfident and more likely to be ready should things go wrong. Because pessimists are less likely to interpret information in self-protective ways, they are better monitors and perhaps quicker to take the measures required by a situation (Cantor & Norem, 1989). They are more likely to see their dentists every six months, watch their blood pressure, and get their mammograms on schedule.

FLEXIBLE OPTIMISM

Cantor and Norem (1989) emphasized the importance of a flexible response to stress that allows for optimistic or pessimistic strategies, as a situation dictates. Seligman (1991), in agreement, makes a case for "flexible optimism," which he describes as "optimism with its eyes open" (p. 292). He adds, "We must be able to use pessimism's keen sense of reality when we need it, without having to dwell in its dark shadows" (p. 292).

When is it good to use optimism as a strategy? When should optimism be avoided? Seligman says that the fundamental consideration is the cost of failure in the situation under consideration. If the cost is high, optimism is wrong. Examples of the wrong times to be optimistic: a motorist deciding whether his failing brakes will last a little longer or whether he needs to buckle up for just a short ride or whether he can drive home after a stop at a bar. Good times to be optimistic given by Seligman: a shy person deciding to start a conversation, a salesperson deciding on one more call, a passed-over-for-promotion executive deciding to put out some job feelers. In addition to the matter of cost, here are four situations in which to use optimism and three in which to avoid it, according to Seligman:

- If you are in an achievement situation (getting a promotion, selling a product, writing a difficult report, winning a game), use optimism.
- If you are concerned about how you feel (fighting off depression, keeping up your morale), use optimism.
- If the situation is apt to be protracted and your physical health is an issue, use optimism.
- If you want to lead, if you want to inspire others, if you want people to vote for you, use optimism. . . .
- If your goal is to plan for a risky and uncertain future, do not use optimism.
- If your goal is to counsel others whose future is dim, do not use optimism initially.
- If you want to appear sympathetic to the troubles of others, do not begin with optimism, although using it later, once confidence and empathy are established, may help. (pp. 208–209)

References

Cantor, N., & Norem, J. K. (1989). Defensive pessimism and stress and coping. *Social Cognition, 7*(2), 92–112.

Ellis, A. (1977). The basic clinical theory of rational-emotive therapy. In A. Ellis & R. Grieger (Eds.), *Handbook of rational-emotive therapy* (pp. 3–34). New York: Springer.

Matlin, M. W., & Stang, D. J. (1978). *The Pollyanna Principle: Selectivity in language, memory, and thought.* Cambridge, MA: Schenkman.

Norem, J. K., & Cantor, N. (1986). Defensive pessimism: Harnessing anxiety as motivation. *Journal of Personality and Social Psychology, 51*(6), 1208–1217.

Scheier, M. F., & Carver, C. S. (1985). Optimism, coping, and health: Assessment and implications of generalized outcome expectancies. *Health Psychology, 4*(3), 219–247.

Scheier, M. F., Weintraub, J. K., & Carver, C. S. (1986). Coping with stress: Divergent strategies of optimists and pessimists. *Journal of Personality and Social Psychology, 51*(6), 1257–1264.

Seligman, M. E. P. (1991). *Learned optimism.* New York: Alfred A. Knopf.

Snyder, C. R., & Higgins, R. L. (1988). Excuses: Their effective role in the negotiation of reality. *Psychological Bulletin, 104*(1), 23–25.

Taylor, S. E. (1989). *Positive illusions: Creative self-deception and the healthy mind.* New York: Basic Books.

To Apply This Reading to Yourself

1. Discuss your own explanatory style.
2. Are you an optimist? A pessimist? A defensive pessimist? Discuss this aspect of yourself, and include a consideration of how well your attitude serves you.
3. Consider an adversity you have experienced, and indicate the consequences. Did your beliefs or thoughts or the way you interpreted the situation help or hurt you? Discuss this aspect of the situation.
4. Consider an adversity that now confronts you. Are your beliefs or thoughts or your way of interpreting the situation helping or hurting you? Discuss this aspect of the situation.

The Confidence Game

Robert Ornstein and David Sobel

The optimistic beliefs we have about our own health can sometimes be more important than the reality of our situation. For example, we seem to have a deep-rooted need for control. If you are in a stressful situation and have the illusion you can control it, *even if you can't,* your stress reaction will be reduced. Researchers asked people to perform difficult math problems while distracting them with random bursts of loud, nerve-jangling noise. Half the people were told that they could stop the noise by pressing a button (a button which actually had no effect on the noise). The other subjects were given no such illusion of control. Even though no one pressed the button, the people who thought they could control the stressor experienced fewer stress symptoms (sweaty hands, racing hearts, ringing ears, and headaches).

The optimistic belief that we are in control, capable and competent to make changes, is critical to health. Consider a series of experiments conducted at the Stanford Arthritis Center. The project began innocently enough. A self-management course was designed to help arthritis patients cope better with the pain, disability, fear, and depression often associated with this condition. The program consisted of six weekly two-hour sessions attended by patients and their families and led by instructors, many of whom had arthritis themselves. The patients learned a lot of detailed information about the physiology and treatment of arthritis, strengthening and endurance exercises, relaxation techniques, joint protection, nutrition, and the interrelationship of stress, pain, and depression.

Impressively, participants demonstrated significantly greater knowledge, self-management behavior, and less pain. But why? The people who improved were not those who knew more about arthritis or did the therapeutic exercise. Those who improved had a *positive outlook and felt a sense of control* regarding their arthritis. Those who failed to improve, even if they exercised, felt there was nothing they could do about arthritis.

The key difference appeared to be in the patients' perception of their ability to control or change their arthritis symptoms. The critical feature here is *belief* in this ability, not what skills or capacities the patient actually had.

The health benefits associated with confidence are striking. For example, confidence in our own health turns out to be one of the best predictors of future health—even better than the results of extensive laboratory testing or a physician's examination.

People who rate their health poorly die earlier and have more disease than their counterparts who view themselves as healthy. Even people suffering from illness seem to do better when they believe themselves to be healthy than when they believe themselves weak.

In Canada, more than thirty-five hundred senior citizens were asked, at the outset of a seven-year study, "For your age would you say, in general, your health is excellent, good, fair, poor, or bad?" Those who rated their health as poor were almost three times more likely to die during the seven years of the study than those who perceived their health as excellent. The rating system proved more accurate in predicting who would die than the objective health measures of physicians.

Nearly 15 percent of the people rated their health as fair or poor, even though according to the objective health measures it was excellent or good. These "health pessimists" had a slightly greater risk of dying than the "health optimists," who viewed themselves as healthy in spite of negative reports from their doctors. The predictive power of self-rated health was the same regardless of sex, age, environment, or health. Only increasing age appears to have a more powerful influence on death rates than self-rated health.

How can this be? Perhaps we have a very sensitive internal mechanism that detects subtle changes in health before symptoms appear and before a doctor can detect any problem. Or our attitude with respect to our health may influence future health—pessimistic attitudes translating into physiological malfunctioning and optimism into bolstered immunity.

Finding ways to increase the confidence of a "health pessimist" may pay rich dividends. With all the emphasis on medical technology and diagnostic evaluation, let's not forget the most sophisticated diagnostic machine, the human brain. Quickly assessing a person's overall perception of his or her health may help us identify individuals at greater risk. Perhaps by encouraging more positive self-perceptions we may be able to effect physiological processes and improve health.

What you expect is what you get. Or so it seems. Try this: Write down as many as you can of the wonderful experiences you anticipate in the future. Then describe all the difficult and trying things you expect to happen. How many positive experiences did you write down? How many negative?

The way we respond to this surprisingly simple test seems to predict future health and well-being. In one study, a group of elderly subjects considered their future. They listed all the positive things they had to look forward to. Two years later the optimists reported fewer physical symptoms of ill-health and more positive physical and psychological well-being than did the pessimists. They felt less tension, reported fewer colds, took fewer days off from work, and had more energy.

Another way to assess optimism is by the Life Orientation Test (LOT) developed by psychologists Michael Scheier and Charles Carver.

You might want to try filling it out yourself. Mark how much you agree with each of the items, using the following scale: 4 = strongly agree, 3 = agree, 2 = neutral, 1 = disagree, and 0 = strongly disagree.

___4___ 1. In uncertain times, I usually expect the best.

___3___ 2. If something can go wrong for me, it will.*

___2___ 3. I always look on the bright side of things.

___4___ 4. I'm always optimistic about my future.

___3___ 5. I hardly ever expect things to go my way.*

___2___ 6. Things never work out the way I want them to.*

___3___ 7. I'm a believer in the idea that "every cloud has a silver lining."

___2___ 8. I rarely count on good things happening to me.*

In scoring, you'll need to reverse the numbers for the items marked with an asterisk (*). That is, if you strongly agree with the statement "If something can go wrong for me, it will," give yourself a score of 0 instead of 4. Do this for items 2, 5, 6, and 8. Then total up your score.

When college students completed this test 4 weeks before final exams, the higher-scoring optimists (with 20 points and over) reported many fewer health problems. The pessimists complained of more dizziness, fatigue, sore muscles, and coughs.

The effects of a bright outlook on the future are perhaps even more striking for people facing major trauma, such as open-heart surgery. In one study, the attitudes of patients about to undergo a coronary bypass were assessed just before the operation. Those with a more hopeful, positive outlook showed fewer complications during surgery: their electrocardiograms and blood tests revealed less evidence of heart muscle damage. Those patients with a sunny disposition also recovered more quickly. Their lung function returned speedily, they sat up in bed sooner, and they were able to walk around the room earlier than their gloomier counterparts. Six months later, those who expected an improved quality of life—a quick return to work, hobbies, and exercise—tended to get just what they expected.

There is a biology of self-confidence. When it comes to health promotion, a confident attitude may contribute more to health than specific health behaviors. Think about all your good intentions—the plans for new diets, exercise regimens, stress reduction techniques. If asked, most people can recount a litany of failures. What are the consequences of failing at a health behavior change? So much emphasis has been placed on changing lifestyles, adopting the good life, that what is often missed is that the *feelings of success or failure* may be more important to health than the actual behaviors. Success, even in small things, supports a feeling of self-confidence and competence.

One mistake many of us make is trying to change everything at once. Part of the problem is that most of us can't attain our ultimate, often unrealistic, goals immediately; we then don't take the small steps that could move us forward. Recall a previous experience in which you successfully changed. Why did you change? What were the keys to your success?

If feeling confident and successful is perhaps more important than the specific changed behavior, then the focus should be on developing a series of successful experiences in changing something, no matter how small. Set yourself up for success. Choose something that *you* want to change and take a small step that you are confident you can achieve. Make sure that at regular intervals in your life you take up something new—maybe playing a musical instrument, learning to cook a new dish, studying a new language—something you can learn, something that makes you grow, something you like and is yours. It will pay off more than twice. It may be exercising, losing weight, managing stress more effectively, developing a new hobby—anything you really want to do. It all bolsters hope and optimism.

That sense of confidence not only makes it more likely that you will succeed in changing a behavior—from pain control to quitting smoking—but itself may foster health. Successful change in any part of your life, in hobbies or work, can reinforce this vital sense of confidence.

To Apply This Reading to Yourself

1. *Ornstein and Sobel write, "The optimistic beliefs we have about our own health can sometimes be more important than the reality of our situation." Are you a "health optimist" or a "health pessimist"? Discuss this aspect of yourself and its influence on your life.*
2. *Ornstein and Sobel write, "The optimistic belief that we are in control, capable and competent to make changes, is critical to health." Discuss this aspect of yourself and its influence on your life.*
3. *Take the Life Orientation Test presented in the reading, and relate your results to your health and other aspects of your life.*
4. *Ornstein and Sobel write that self-confidence may contribute more to health than do specific health behaviors, but we may lack this confidence because of our failures in trying to change these behaviors. Discuss your own self-confidence and your feelings of success or failure resulting from your own change efforts.*

FULFILLING POTENTIAL

In the beginning—at the moment of conception—we are each a single cell. By the time we each reach adulthood, we have grown into approximately 1 trillion (1,000,000,000,000) cells and become very complicated beings.

Our genes carry the blueprints for our growth, and we develop in accordance with these inherited potentialities. But development is not, of course, a simple matter of unfolding. We are shaped and molded—sometimes even kneaded and pummeled—by environmental forces. And we also take a hand to shape ourselves.

Development is a continuous process, but for purposes of study, it is traditionally divided into a number of stages. We are infants, then children, then adolescents, then adults. Finally we grow old and die. Each stage has distinguishing characteristics, and each presents us with some tasks to accomplish before we move on to the next.

Our development tends to be orderly. But in the process, there are spurts and slowdowns. Sometimes we seem to leap ahead, and sometimes we creep along. Occasionally we rest or stay put or even reverse, giving up some perhaps hard-won gains.

Scientists and humanists have always been intrigued by human potentiality, and some of us may wonder what we could become if we realized all of our promise—if we fulfilled ourselves completely. What would we be if we were everything we could be? This, of course, is a question that can never be fully answered, but it is almost impossible not to pose it. Part Four of this book pursues three concepts that touch on this question and the fulfillment process: defense, growth, and death.

Defense refers to the behavior we employ to protect ourselves from threat or anxiety. Many things we perceive in our environment and also in ourselves arouse anxiety and trigger defensive behavior. The process of growth and change itself is sometimes threatening and puts us on the defensive. And, for whatever reason, when we divert substantial energies to defense, our development and actualization suffer.

Growth, in the somewhat special sense it is used in this book, refers to personal development in a desired direction. Because personal values differ, we will not always agree on what is desirable change or even how desirable it is to change. Some of us may be ambivalent about growth; our urge to explore and try new things may be in strong competition with the desire to maintain what we have (and who we are) and play it safe.

Death refers to the cessation or end of life, but all of life is influenced by the inexorability of death, by the certainty that each of us will die, and the necessity of making the most of the years we have allotted to us. Some of us try to shut out all thought of dying to preserve an illusion of neverendingness, but others believe that until we accept the prospect of death, we cannot sense the wonder and preciousness of life and the urgent necessity for making the most of it and of ourselves.

Defense

Subject was a pretty university freshman, but one who did not pay much attention to her appearance. She was shy, inhibited, and quite tense and anxious throughout the interview. She denied the existence of any emotional problems or conflicts.

This student seemed capable of structuring the world only in intellectual terms. She seemed totally out of touch with her feelings and went to great lengths to repress or deny them. What came across was a marked affective barrenness, almost like that in cases of severe emotional deprivation.

She could not handle the expression of anger and had to deny and repress her rage. At times she turned her rage in on herself, and she described crying occasionally in response to feeling hurt. She also tended to project her rage and felt people were out to hurt her.

She led a constricted and inhibited life with very few friends or acquaintances, most of her time being devoted to academic work. "I don't make friends easily. I'm usually backward and shy." She did not confide in friends or her parents. "I don't feel I should burden others—not that I have many burdens."

She had no relationships with young men and had had only one date in her life. "I am pretty young to go out too much. I see downfalls in it. Some kids go steady and it breaks up and they are usually lost. They have lost the art of making friends and it's difficult for them."

She had a long-time interest in becoming a research chemist. She seemed to be doing well academically and was making progress toward this occupational goal; in fact, she seemed wrapped up in this to the exclusion of all else.

—Condensed case study from an investigation of college students by William A. Westley and Nathan B. Epstein

Many situations pose a threat to our well-being and cause anxiety. And some of us carry a heavy load of anxiety with us into many situations. How do we deal with our anxiety? Can we get on with the tasks of everyday living? Can we even risk growing and become different and more than we are? Or must we turn our energies to controlling our anxiety or defending ourselves against it?

Defense refers to behavior that is employed for protection against threat or anxiety. It is helpful to consider a distinction that is sometimes made between defense behavior and task behavior. *Task behavior* is that involved in the achievement of the work at hand, such as taking a test, giving a speech, or running a race. *Defense behavior* bolsters our self-esteem when our task behavior is unsuccessful. For example, if we study hard and apply ourselves to an important test (task behavior), upon learning that we have failed the test we can either prepare to take it again (more task behavior) or try to shore up our self-esteem by depreciating the test or denying that it was important or that we really cared or tried to do well on it (defense behavior).

Human behavior is complex, and a particular action that appears to be task behavior may, upon closer analysis, seem to be a defensive maneuver or at least partly so. The tests we take and pass may move us along in our careers (task behavior), but our motivations in taking them may also be to allay anxiety and reassure ourselves that we are worthy and able to compete and get ahead in this world. However, some of our actions are so obviously defensive (although perhaps not to us), that others see through us right away and perhaps accuse us of trying to cover up.

In a somewhat broader perspective, it is helpful to contrast defense and growth behavior. *Growth behavior* involves movement toward patterns that are more highly valued; for example, when a person becomes more independent, we may say he or she has grown. In contrast, *defense behavior* (or *safety behavior* as it is sometimes referred to in this context) involves adherence to present, familiar, and less valued patterns of response.

To illustrate, compare a person who stays put in a secure, routine job with one who undertakes a new career that involves risk and challenge. Or compare a person who tries to live life by certain minimum essentials and avoids adding new dimensions (the college woman in the case study presented on the previous page is an example) with one who is not so concerned with the tried and true, the safe and familiar, or the easily manageable. In each instance, the contrast is between the defense, or safety-oriented person versus one who is oriented toward growth.

How much of our lives is devoted to defense and safety? How much is concentrated on task accomplishment and growth? We may have defended ourselves so subtly and so well that it is impossible to distinguish one aspect from another. But some of us will sense that our lives are more constricted and less rich than they could be and that we have been more occupied with defense and safety than with growth.

BEING DEFENSIVE

Ingenious as we are, we human beings find many ways to defend ourselves against anxiety. Sigmund Freud, the founder of psychoanalysis, emphasized the importance of a single mechanism (repression), but later came to believe that this was only one of a number of defenses. Freud's daughter Anna, who continued his work, described 10 defense mechanisms. Over the years the number has grown until one psychologist noted that the list of mechanisms students know depends upon who their teacher is and what textbook they read.

The first reading on this topic, adapted from a textbook written by the editor, describes 13 defense mechanisms. Each of these mechanisms is common, each is important, and probably everyone has made some use of each in everyday life. As the reading indicates, whether the particular use of a mechanism is good or bad depends on both its effect in the situation and its implication for the overall well-being and personal growth of the user.

BEING OPEN

Ingenious as we are, we human beings (with a little help from our friends—or therapists) find ways to overcome our defenses and open ourselves to others. And much of what goes on in friendship and psychotherapy is a process of opening, disclosing, or confiding. By opening ourselves or disclosing ourselves to others, we can come to know ourselves better. But how open should we be? Should we disclose all? Confide all? Become transparent selves?

Be 100 percent honest. That is the message Harry Browne delivers in the second reading, and he reviews the benefits of honesty and the problems of dishonesty to make his case. He writes that lying is an attempt to avoid paying the price, but when we try to get something for nothing, we usually wind up paying extra. To Browne, lying is an attempt to be what we're not; only by being what we are can we have free, uncluttered lives with no deceptions to get in our way.

Too much honesty or, at least, too much openness can destroy a friendship or love relationship. This message, at variance with that of Browne, is presented by Morton Hunt in the last reading. Hunt notes that by unburdening ourselves, we may be overburdening others. Although relationships thrive on disclosure, they can be done in by an overdose. He suggests that if we must confide, we should select someone, perhaps a professional, who is uninvolved and unlikely to be hurt by our revelations. "We must set limits to intimacy," he concludes, "not only for our own good, but for the good of those we love."

To Explore Your Own Defensiveness

1. *Studying defensiveness.* Carry a small notebook with you for one week and record every instance of defensiveness you detect in

yourself. Indicate as fully as you can the cause of the defensiveness as well as the feelings, thoughts, and actions associated with it. At the end of the week, write a report on your observations and try to arrive at some new or deeper insights about yourself.

2. *Hiding oneself (individual pursuit).* When we feel defensive, we may try to hide or cover up or escape in some way. At the top of a sheet of paper write the following: "How do I hide? I hide by . . . " Then complete the incomplete sentence in as many different ways as you can. Don't stop until you have wrung yourself completely dry of answers. Afterward study your answers and try to arrive at some new or deeper insights about yourself.

3. *Hiding oneself (dyad pursuit).* Form pairs with one person playing the role of the questioner, the other the questionee. The questioner asks the questionee, "How do you hide?" After the questionee answers, the questioner says "Thank you" and repeats the question. This pattern is continued until the questionee is wrung dry of answers; then the two exchange roles and continue as before. Afterward, the two analyze their responses together and try to arrive at some new or deeper insights.

4. *Understanding defensiveness.* We sometimes become very irritated, annoyed, or defensive when a particular negative quality is attributed to us. Why are we so upset by some negative attributions but not by others? For example, we may bristle when people think of us as cheap or stingy (or we *think* they think of us in this way) but not get upset if they regard us as selfish and conceited. At the top of a sheet of paper write the following incomplete sentence: "I hate it when people think of me as . . . " Then complete this sentence in as many different ways as you can. Afterward underline the quality that you most hate to have associated with yourself and try to arrive at some new or deeper insights.

5. *Disclosing oneself (secrets).* Divide into small groups. On a card each member writes something about which he or she feels defensive or has disclosed to few people (perhaps no one). The cards are gathered and shuffled. Members in turn pick a card and read the secret aloud as though it were their own, adding how they feel about having this secret, and inviting the reactions of the group.

6. *Disclosing oneself (topics).* Form pairs and select one topic (the same topic for both members). The topic should be something of a challenge for both members, perhaps a subject on which neither has disclosed very much or would not ordinarily discuss in a situation such as the present one. Examples of topics (suggested by the work of Sidney Jourard): the happiest or the unhappiest moments of your life; the important failures or unfulfilled wishes of your life; your main goals and dreams for the future; aspects of your present life that you find most satisfying or those which you find most frustrating; your ethnic, cultural, or familial roots and their effect on you; the most important people in your life and your relationship to them; or your religious views or personal values. Once a pair has chosen its topic, the members take turns in disclosing, alternating teller and listener roles every few min-

utes, Afterward, members share how they experienced or were affected by this process of disclosure.

7. *Justifying defensiveness*. Think of something you are very ashamed of or defensive about. Imagine that others have found out about this something; how would they feel about you? Imagine that you have found out that this was true about someone else; how would you feel about her or him? Without identifying the thing that makes you ashamed or defensive, compare and discuss your answers to the two preceding questions, and see whether you can arrive at some new or deeper insights.

8. *Describing defense mechanisms*. In the larger group or in small groups, each member in turn describes or acts out a defense mechanism without identifying it by name. Other members of the group are then asked to identify the mechanism and also to relate their own experience in using that mechanism.

9. *Portraying defense mechanisms*. Members pair and prepare a number of brief skits, each skit portraying (but not identifying by name) a common defense mechanism. These skits are enacted before the larger group or in small groups. Observers are asked to identify the mechanism being portrayed and to relate their own experience in using that mechanism.

10. *Trusting others*. One obstacle to disclosure is lack of trust; as we learn to trust others, we open ourselves to them. In this exercise, the group is divided into pairs. One member of each pair is blindfolded and led on a silent walk by the other for a 10- to 15-minute period. (Caution: Avoid all hazards, no matter how minimal.) Then the partners exchange roles and proceed as before. Afterward the group reassembles, and members share reactions to their "trust walk."

To Read Further

Browne, H. (1982). *How I found freedom in an unfree world*. New York: Avon. (paperback)

Ekman, P. (1985). *Telling lies: Clues to deceit in the marketplace, politics, and marriage*. New York: W. W. Norton. (Berkley paperback, 1986)

Goleman, D. (1985). *Vital lies, simple truths: The psychology of self-deception and shared illusions*. New York: Simon and Schuster. (Touchstone paperback, 1986)

Jourard, S. M. (1971). *The transparent self* (rev. ed.). New York: D. Van Nostrand. (paperback)

Luft, J. (1969). *Of human interaction: The Johari model*. Palo Alto, CA: National Press. (Mayfield paperback, 1969)

Murphy, G., with Leeds, M. (1975). *Outgrowing self-deception*. New York: Basic Books.

Pennebaker, J. W. (1990). *Opening up: The healing power of confiding in others*. New York: William Morrow.

Snyder, C. R., Higgins, R. L., & Stuckby, R. J. (1983). *Excuses: Masquerades in search of grace*. New York: Wiley.

Some Common Defenses

Abe Arkoff

We are constantly flooded by stimuli arising in our environment and from within ourselves. Of course, we cannot respond to every stimulus. We cannot express every impulse.

We find some of the stimuli in the environment unpleasant, painful, and threatening. If these stimuli are too threatening, we may attempt to defend ourselves against them. Perhaps we avoid them or ignore them or reinterpret them so that we no longer find them so bothersome.

Impulses arising in ourselves also can prove threatening. We may have worrisome thoughts and distressing feelings that we seek to inhibit or modify. We may seek to get a grip on ourselves so that we will not do something we are tempted to do.

Or perhaps we have already done something which has filled us with guilt and remorse. We may seek to atone for it or make some restitution. Or we may attempt to alter the memory of it in some way and see it differently so that we can live with ourselves.

Certain patterns of behavior that are employed for protection against threat or anxiety are called *defenses*. These patterns are sometimes called "defense mechanisms" or "adjustment mechanisms" and they do tend to operate in a machinelike or automatic way.[1,2] Sometimes they are referred to as "ego defense mechanisms" since they serve to defend the ego or the self from threat.

Patterns which have been identified as defenses are sometimes very simple. For example, Menninger and his colleagues[3] include such simple expedients as laughing it off and crying it out as "coping devices of everyday living." However, many defenses are much more complicated.

As individuals, we vary in the patterns of defense that we show. Fairly early in life each of us develops a repertoire of defenses that characterizes our own individual adjustment.[4] Still we may show a preference for certain defenses in certain situations or at certain times.[5]

The following are some defenses or defensive aspects of behavior that seem particularly common or particularly important in the adjustment process.

SUPPRESSION, DENIAL

We cannot respond to every stimulus or express every impulse to which we are subject. For one thing, we do not have enough time or energy to do so. For another, some of our impulses may be unacceptable to us or threatening to our general well-being.

One of the ways that we have of dealing with threatening impulses is to make a deliberate effort to inhibit them. We may, for example, be occupied with a bothersome thought or obsessed with some worry, and we attempt to put it out of mind. We may feel that we are about to break down and cry, but we struggle to hold back our tears because we don't want to give the appearance of weakness. Or, perhaps, we are about to lash out at someone but we count to ten to give ourselves time to cool off.

Behaving in this way—that is, effortfully inhibiting the expression of a threatening impulse—is *suppression*. As the definition implies, suppression is a relatively conscious or voluntary process. The person is aware of the threatening impulse and makes an effort to control or suppress it.

When our suppressive efforts are specifically designed to prevent us from acknowledging an unpleasant reality, they are called *denial*. This is a common form of suppression. Any unpleasant truth may be denied and pushed aside, for example, the seemingly obvious infidelity of a spouse or the established irreversibility of a child's mental deficit. Dying persons may deny their terminal condition; not infrequently denial alternates with acknowledgment so that one day the patient may be preparing to die while on the next day he or she is making plans for the distant future.

Suppressive efforts, of course, are not always successful. Despite attempts to achieve peace of mind, we find ourselves occupied with threatening thoughts and feelings. Despite the struggle for self-control, we indulge in actions which cause us trouble and regret.

Sometimes, suppression works or continues to work only if it is combined with other efforts. We may be able to suppress a particularly bothersome thought only if we keep ourselves busily occupied with other thoughts and activities. And we may be able to suppress a particular action only if we avoid environments which seem to stimulate it; for example, we get along with some people only by keeping out of their way and seeing them as little as possible.

We use suppression a great deal in everyday life. We close our eyes to unpleasant sights. We deafen our ears to criticism. In conversations, we sometimes deliberately choose pleasant topics, and when we hit upon material which provokes anxiety, we change the subject by tacit or explicit agreement. For example, at a party the conversation may get around to the subject of cancer, or heart attacks, or nuclear destruction, and somebody will ask that the subject be changed to something more pleasant.[6]

Suppression is a useful and necessary mechanism. Every society requires its individuals to inhibit or modify their impulses in some way. Some people run into difficulty because they lack the ability to make certain suppressions.

All of us have had troublesome thoughts or worries which have kept us from working effectively. It has been suggested that suppression is a defense that can be perfected and used to give us "mental freedom."[7] Through practice we can learn to remove our attention from one thing and focus it on something else. Appropriate use of suppression occurs when there is a task that must be done and when other matters competing for attention are insoluble or may be postponed. Freed, at least for a while, from these other matters, we can become absorbed in the more urgent activity.

Denial has been held to be a useful strategy when there is truly nothing more that can be done about a difficult situation. Preparing for the worst but hoping for the best seems like good advice. In this regard, Norman Cousins, who overcame two life-threatening illnesses, wrote "You never deny the diagnosis, but do deny the verdict that goes with it."

Of course, not all uses of suppression are beneficial. Some people seem overly inhibited or overly suppressed in one or more areas of living. Suppressions can be detrimental when their effect is to push away a problem that should be faced. Constantly shunted aside, many problems grow less manageable, and the momentary relief that suppression brings can be purchased at considerable cost to future happiness.

REPRESSION

The process of inhibition is not always conscious and deliberate. Sometimes it appears to occur automatically, without the individual's awareness. The automatic inhibition of a threatening impulse is *repression*.

Although automatic, noninsightful inhibitions are classified as repressions while deliberate, insightful ones are called suppressions, actual behavior is seldom so neatly dichotomous. Frequently, there is partial insight or semi-awareness of defense processes. Sometimes, too, an impulse which is usually well repressed becomes bothersome, and one needs to take more deliberate actions to contain it.

Suppression is easily understood, but the concept of repression is more difficult to grasp and accept; indeed, many psychologists have challenged the usefulness or validity of this idea.[8] Dollard and Miller have suggested that repression can be understood as a process in which we prevent ourselves from *thinking* about things that would be painful or threatening just as in some instances we prevent ourselves from *doing* things that might cause pain or embarrassment. They state,

> Repression is somewhat harder to understand than other symptoms because we are not used to considering the stopping of thinking as a response. We cannot point to it and study it in the same way that we can examine overt responses.
>
> Yet to stop talking is obviously a response. Everyone has had the experience of catching himself just in time before blurting out something he would have regretted saying. It is possible to learn either to stop talking about certain limited subjects or to stop talking altogether in some situation. According to our hypothesis, stopping thinking is a similar response. (9, p. 203)

A pattern of behavior may have been so heavily punished in the past or so associated with unhappy experience that the person prevents herself or himself from expressing it in any way. Aggressive behavior, for example, is often severely disciplined and, as a consequence, can be severely repressed. In a similar way, early sex behavior may have been the occasion of considerable unhappiness and punishment, with considerable subsequent repression.

Like attempts at suppression, repressive efforts are not always successful. Heightened anxiety levels and bursts of anxiety are commonly interpreted by clinicians as evidence of failing repression. In the same way, some individuals who suffer from chronically elevated anxiety are thought to have considerable but precarious repressions.

Some sudden changes in behavior are also interpreted as failures in repression (and, as will be seen later, as failing reaction formations). For example, a generally meek individual may show a sudden or violent outburst of anger that may surprise others and herself or himself as well. Or a relatively kind and gentle person may do something that seems very cruel and very much out of character.

Slips of the tongue and pen, lapses in memory, and certain mishaps or accidents have also been attributed to the workings of (and weakenings in) repression. Such occurrences have been held by Freud[10] and others to be evidence of incomplete repressions. Brenner writes:

> A slip of the tongue or a slip of the pen is often the consequence of a failure to repress completely some unconscious thought or wish. In such cases, the speaker or writer expresses what he would have unconsciously liked to say or write, despite his attempt to keep it hidden. Sometimes the hidden meaning is openly expressed in the slip, that is to say, it is clearly intelligible to the listener or reader. On other occasions the result of the lapse is not intelligible and the hidden meaning can only be discovered from the associations of the person who made the slip. (11, p. 146)

We all have probably caught ourselves saying things we did not consciously mean to say. A student who flunked a course wrote to his teacher as follows: "I could register for the *curse* in Summer School if I had to."[12] Perhaps we "forget" to check essential materials out of the library, thereby neatly resolving the conflict between studying or not studying over the weekend. Or maybe we do something "accidentally"

which somebody else may claim was accidentally on purpose.

Like suppression, repression serves us by defending us from threatening impulses. It prevents us from thinking depressing thoughts, from feeling distressing feelings, and from engaging in certain actions which might prove dangerous or painful. It helps us hide our thoughts and feelings and actions from ourselves just as we sometimes more consciously attempt to conceal certain things from others.

Repression can prove detrimental in the long run for a number of reasons. Problems that are kept out of awareness cannot be faced and solved. In addition to the use of this mechanism, we may have to restrict our lives in various ways and use other defenses to prevent the inhibited impulses from finding expression. Energy consumed in the process might otherwise be available for the activities of everyday living. Repression brings some relief from anxiety, but it can also restrict, impoverish, and distort behavior.[13]

Whether repression is good or bad depends upon the uses that are made of it. Hall notes what happens when there is a considerable reliance on this defense:

> Although repression is necessary for normal personality development and is used to some extent by everyone, there are people who depend upon it to the exclusion of other ways of adjusting to threats. These people are said to be repressed. Their contacts with the world are limited and they give the impression of being withdrawn, tense, rigid, and guarded. Their lips are set and their movements are wooden. They use so much of their energy in maintaining their far-flung repressions that they do not have very much left over for pleasurable and productive interactions with the environment and with other people. (14, p. 88)

LYING

Throughout life, we constantly struggle to understand ourselves. The reasons for our behavior are often unknown or unclear. For a particular bit of behavior there may be a dozen plausible reasons.

At the same time we are constantly called upon to explain our actions to others: Why did you do that? How could you do such a thing? Why do you feel that way? Where did you ever get such an idea?

How much of the truth do we know? How much of the truth do we tell others? How much of the truth do we tell ourselves? And how much do we need to lie?

Lying, as a defense, refers to the deliberate use of falsehood to prevent threat to one's well-being. Liars attempt to bring about a false belief that would be to their own benefit. Like suppression, lying is generally thought of as a conscious process; liars know that they are lying; although they attempt to deceive another person, they themselves are not deceived.

The very young child does not make a sharp distinction between reality and fantasy, between truth and untruth. Stone and Church write,

> It is because the preschool child's world is a mélange of what to the adult are fact and fiction, shot through with magical potentialities, that the child may seem to adults uninstructed in his ways to be playing free and easy with the truth. During most of this period, however, the very notion of an untruth is inconceivable to the child. A preschool child will have a very hard time complying with an adult's request that he repeat a statement such as "the snow is black," although he could enjoy *pretending* that snow is black. When, however, the child's own wishes conflict with reality, reality is likely to yield. If the child can make things so merely by thinking or saying them, then his claim that he has performed an assigned task or his denial that he has committed a misdeed is sufficient to do or undo the action in question. The young child can create past history—not to mention a present and a future—by waving the wand of his tongue. But he is not lying, in the sense of thinking one thing and saying another. (15, pp. 158–159)

As children grow older, they become better able to tell the difference between what is true and what is not. Demands are placed upon them to always tell the truth and never lie. But, paradoxically enough, demands are also placed upon them to recognize situations in which they should not tell the truth since certain sorts of lies are a prominent part of life. Woolf[16] writes, "What education really demands and teaches the child is to know when not to lie, when not to tell the truth and when a lie is necessary." He presents the following example:

> A mother told me the following story of her four-year-old son. The family was expecting a young girl and her fiancé to call. The child overheard the comment that while the fiancé was nice, he had an ugly long nose which spoiled his looks. In the evening, when the couple was sitting in the drawing room with the family, the child approached the fiancé with a stick in his hand and said as he touched the young man's nose with it: "This has to be cut off." The little boy behaved with calm and assurance and without the slightest awareness of the embarrassment caused by his unsuitable veracity. He was later enlightened, in rather an awkward manner, about the possible negative consequences of truthfulness in real life. His veracity was described to him as insolence and terrible rudeness, and this new point of view was confirmed by suitable "educational measures." (17, p. 266)

George Washington is reputed to have never told a lie. Probably nobody (except a liar) would claim to have equaled that record. Many of us have never stopped to consider what part falsehood plays in our general adjustment. If we do think about it, we will probably admit to having made some use of lying as a defense against threat.

Even those of us who pride ourselves on our honesty may confess to an occasional benign or white lie, that is, one that we feel is trivial, not harmful, or even for someone else's benefit. Even so, we might have to admit that such a lie was for our own benefit as well, that it served our purposes to tell it.

Much of our lying is accomplished by omission rather than by commission. We may justify omitting the truth by saying that what people don't know won't hurt them. Karpman calls this "implied lying." He writes:

> This is a form of lying which consists of merely maintaining silence, of refraining from telling the truth rather than the actual telling of an untruth. It is more correctly called dissembling or dissimulation. A person may say, "I didn't tell you about this before, but—" and then proceed to confess some past action, the absence of your knowledge of which had led you to form an entirely different impression of his behavior than that which is now disclosed by his retarded admission of this or that reprehensible action. (18, p. 147)

A similar way of lying is by telling a half-truth. This is usually a statement that is not really false in itself, but which is designed to be interpreted or misinterpreted in a way that will be beneficial to the teller. For example, suppose there is an important book that we should be conversant with; we did buy a copy, but we have never opened it. A colleague asks us if we have read it, and we answer that we have a copy of it at home. We hope that he or she will assume that we have read it and let the matter rest there.

Telling the truth, the whole truth, and nothing but the truth is not easy. Honesty is valued by our culture, but so are other qualities with which honesty sometimes conflicts. So, for example, is politeness, and it is sometimes impossible to be both polite and completely honest.

From the standpoint of adjustment it is useful to try to understand the push behind a lie. To what extent is it simply a polite convention? To what extent is it benevolent and designed to help another? To what extent is it defensive and used to get oneself out of a difficult or threatening situation?

RATIONALIZATION

Not all misrepresentations can be considered conscious and deliberate. The reason for a particular bit of behavior may be unknown or unclear. Or there may be a number of possible explanations. In such situations it is perhaps only natural that the person leans toward explanations that are socially and personally acceptable.

Interpreting behavior in an acceptable way in order to prevent a threat to one's sense of well-being is *rationalization*. Unlike lying, which is a conscious process, rationalization is usually considered to operate without the individual's full insight or awareness. Liars attempt to deceive others, but they themselves are not deceived. By contrast, the rationalizer deceives others and herself or himself as well.

It is frequently difficult to classify a bit of behavior as either a lie or a rationalization. Sometimes we seem to half-deceive ourselves. We may not be completely satisfied with the way we have explained things. Are we fooling ourselves? Maybe we are, but, then again, maybe we're not.

How do we know if we are rationalizing? If there are two or four or eight possible reasons, how can we know whether a particular one is real or rationalized? Jourard[19] suggests that we may be rationalizing if our announced aim and the consequences of our behavior do not agree, if

there are other possible explanations for our behavior, and if we refuse to consider them. For example, a father may steadfastly maintain that his severe and arbitrary disciplinary policies are for his child's own good even though there is considerable evidence that the child is suffering because of them.

Consider the numerous opportunities that you have to employ rationalization in the course of a single day. Although you have vaguely decided to go on a diet, you sit down to a large breakfast of fried ham and hot cakes dripping with syrup and melted butter because, as you tell yourself, everyone needs a good breakfast to start the day right. In your first class you decide not to take notes because you never seem to get very much out of them anyway. Between classes you go to the snack bar rather than the reserve room because the book you need will probably be checked out already. The waitress forgets to add the price of dessert to your lunch check, but you decide not to call this to her attention because it wasn't very good anyway.

In the afternoon you get into a bridge game with some other students, and when your partner criticizes you for making a couple of stupid mistakes, you announce that you're glad that you don't take the game as seriously as all that. In the evening you sit down to study for a test on the following day, but you can't concentrate. Well, you tell yourself, it's too late to cram now. If you don't know it now, you never will. Besides it would be better to take it easy this evening, relax, and go into the test with a clear head. So off you go to a movie.

MALINGERING

All or almost all of us have been sick, but our experiences with illness have doubtless varied. It would appear to go without saying that a person would rather be well than sick. On reflection, though, such a preference would seem to depend in part on how ill we're treated when we're well and how well we're treated when we're ill. For some individuals, sicknesses are not completely unrewarding.

One of the ways we have of adjusting to difficult situations and protecting ourselves from threat is by pretending to be ill. Removal of a threat or anxiety by feigning illness is called *ma-*

lingering. Like suppression and lying, this defense is usually thought of as a conscious one; malingerers are not deceived themselves, but they attempt to deceive others.

Samuel Clemens (Mark Twain) vividly described this defense in *The Adventures of Tom Sawyer*. Faced on a Monday morning with the sickening prospect of another week in school, Tom cooked up a sore toe that had "mortified" and an aching tooth. However, he staged an astounding recovery when his Aunt Polly laughed away the former and threatened to extract the latter.[20] In the same way, many of us have pretended to have a headache in order to avoid a situation that may be boring or threatening, or, once we are in the situation, the "headache" conveniently furnishes us with an excuse to leave.

Pretending to be ill may serve to get us the attention, sympathy, or nurturance we might not otherwise receive. Like Tom Sawyer, we can overdo this defense and tax the patience and credulity of those who are exposed to it, but it is difficult to disprove an ache or pain or some other such vaguely defined malady. In fact, malingerers themselves may become half convinced of the validity of their complaints.

ADJUSTMENT BY AILMENT

Sometimes, without any conscious pretense, we may feel ill even though the doctor can find nothing physically wrong. Or perhaps we feel more ill or more incapacitated than we should from a particular ailment. Or we get well more slowly than we should.

The relatively noninsightful use of illness, imaginary or real, as a way of averting anxiety is called *adjustment by ailment*. Unlike malingered conditions which are deliberate pretenses, adjustments by ailment imply no conscious deceit. In this latter defense the individual is unaware of the psychological implications of her or his behavior.

In actual practice, however, it may be difficult to distinguish between malingering and adjustment by ailment. Some situations appear to contain elements of both, and an act of malingering may gradually shade into adjustment by ailment as we slowly convince ourselves that we are indeed as ill as we were pretending to be. For example, we may be searching for an excuse to avoid attending a trying social or professional function. If we were ill, we tell ourselves, we wouldn't have to go. Well, we already feel a little upset. The more we think about it, the more upset we become. Finally, we decide that we really are sick; we thus spare ourselves the pain of going to the function as well as the pain of admitting that we didn't want to go.

In anxious states the body's functioning is upset, and it is easy to imagine illness. An upset cardiovascular system may convince us we have heart disease. An upset digestive tract may lead us to believe we have a stomachache or indigestion. Overwhelmed by problems, we indeed feel tired, worn out, and sick. Describing a trying experience we may say, "I was just sick about it," and mean it both figuratively and literally.

This defense protects us from threat in various ways. We may use an imaginary ailment to take our attention away from an anxiety-provoking problem. We may use the "ailment" as an excuse to avoid an unpleasant situation or once in the situation, to get out of it with no loss of face. Sometimes an imaginary ailment serves to attract the attention and sympathy of others. And occasionally we employ it to punish ourselves and rid ourselves of feelings of guilt.

Simulated ailments may help us to handle difficult situations but, to the extent they are successful in doing so, they make it unnecessary for us to face our real problems and attempt to solve them. With extensive reliance on this defense, we may become chronic "psychological" invalids. Not only psychological problems but also real medical problems may go unattended because of the masking effect of imaginary ones.

FIXATION

In the process of growing up we move through a number of stages: infancy, childhood, adolescence, and adulthood. Each succeeding stage offers new opportunities and carries additional responsibilities. Some individuals move continually forward, enjoying the opportunities and accepting the responsibilities afforded by each stage. Others, caught up in frustrations, conflicts, and anxieties, become arrested at a particular stage. And a few, under the pressure of problems, may move backward into earlier, more manageable stages.

Fixation refers to the continuation of a pattern of behavior that has become immature or inappropriate. Persons who use fixation as a defense respond to threat by adhering to old ways of doing things rather than trying out those which would be more suited to the situation at hand. In the face of threat fixated persons are unable or unwilling to vary their behavior, and the greater the threat the more fixated they may appear.

Individuals vary in the extent and duration of their fixations. Some appear to be fixated in many ways or in a number of areas of adjustment, while others show a very few fixated patterns. Furthermore, fixations may be relatively enduring, or they may be quite temporary.

Persons who have made extensive use of fixation will appear to be generally immature. You may know someone who is chronologically an adult, but who acts more like an adolescent. Or someone who, although not immature in behavior, rigidly adheres to the same habits of living and is relatively closed to new experience.

Fixations can occur at any level of development. Those that date from early development, of course, will appear less age appropriate than those which take place later on. Some of us may have been told: Grow up and act your age! But the charge (or insult) is more serious if we're accused of acting like a baby than if we are said to be behaving like a child.

Most fixations are relatively limited and affect only part of one's life. For example, consider the situation of a young man who has completed college, has a responsible and well-paid position, and participates widely in community activities. But he lives at home, has quite a close relationship with his mother, shows very little interest in young women of his own age, and on the few occasions on which he does date, he feels awkward and uncomfortable. Although he is immature in his heterosexual relationships, he is able to function adequately in a number of other areas of daily life.

An instructor who defined fixation as "arrested development" received the following test response from a student: "Fixation is a rest in development."[21] And this is a positive value of

fixation. One cannot always make steady progress in every area of adjustment. Sometimes, there is a need to combine partial progress with partial fixation. Sappenfield sums this up very nicely:

> Continued fixation at a particular level of adjustment in some areas of behavior may provide the feeling of security that is required as a basis for the individual's progression to a higher level of adjustment in some other area of behavior. The individual may progress in certain respects while remaining fixated in certain respects; after a particular progressive adjustment has been "consolidated," so that he feels secure in this adjustment, he may then progress in other respects. (22, p. 265)

Of course, fixations are a serious matter if they are relatively widespread and enduring or if they affect important areas of functioning. Persons fixated at immature levels do not become adults in the complete psychological sense of this word. They may be unable to fully accept the responsibilities of adult status and unable to fully participate in its rewards.

REGRESSION

In time of threat, we may forge on, stay put, or retreat. Sometimes our retreats involve the abandonment of age-appropriate behaviors and a return to those of an earlier stage of growth. Under these conditions, we appear not so "grown up."

Regression refers to the recovery or reinstatement of behavior that had seemingly been outgrown. Used as a defense, regression implies the presence of a threat that provokes an immature response. Responses that are triggered in such situations tend to be those with a notable past history of success.

It is not uncommon for a child to show some regression upon the birth of a sibling. A considerable amount of the parents' attention may be given over to the new baby, leaving the older child with feelings of deprivation. Although he has been walking for several years, suddenly he may insist that he is unable to do so, that he is too little and must be carried. Baby talk, which has been largely outgrown, crops up again and toilet habits may be abandoned. Such regressions may be interpreted as attempts to regain lost attention or status.

Fixation and regression are somewhat similar; both imply the use of behavior that is relatively immature or inappropriate. In fixation, however, the individual has not progressed beyond a certain level, while in regression there has been advance beyond the level followed by retreat. The young man who never formed age-appropriate relations with young women was said to be fixated. Contrast this example with that of a young woman who tries but finds it impossible to meet the demands of marriage and regresses by returning home to her parents.

Regression is encouraged by the human tendency to selectively repress unpleasant memories while allowing pleasant ones free expression. People frequently long for the good old days. Old graduates at class reunions grow nostalgic for their college days. They talk about the football games, parties, and the night of the raid on the women's dormitory but fail to recall the examinations, term papers, and financial privation.

Like fixations, regressions may be relatively permanent and widespread or considerably more momentary and limited in their effects. All of us make some use of temporary, partial, or limited regressions. In recreation we retreat from the responsibilities and cares of everyday living and regress to play activities, to games and sports and hobbies. At a convention or party we may let down our hair and engage in unadult antics. And almost anyone in extreme provocation may indulge in a childish display of anger, tears, or other feelings.

It has been suggested that healthy, mature, and creative adults have the ability to be childlike when they want to be; that is, they have the ability to voluntarily regress and recapture the qualities of childhood.[23,24,25] They can be completely spontaneous, vigorously emotional, and uncritically enthusiastic; they can engage in great nonsense and wild fantasy. Then they can become controlled, rational, critical, sensical, and realistic again (in short, grown-up).[26]

When regressions are involuntary, they are of more dangerous consequence. Regression may become relatively permanent. It may encompass a number of areas of adjustment. It may involve a retreat to very early patterns of behavior. Adjustments have been noted in which there is a general regression to childish or even infantile levels of functioning. In extreme cases, the regressed individual may be completely unable to take care of herself or himself.

IDENTIFICATION

Our lives are bound up with the lives of others. We share in the lives of the people close to us and these people, in turn, share in our lives. To some extent, their successes are our successes, their failures are our failures, and our successes and failures are theirs.

Identification is a general term which refers to the various ways in which we establish a oneness with other persons, groups, or objects. One is said to "identify" with another person when he or she forms a bond and models her or his behavior after that person. We also identify when we regard others as extensions of ourselves so that, in a sense, what happens to them also happens to us.

Used as a defense, identification implies that we feel threatened and respond by drawing upon the valued qualities of others. We may copy their patterns in order to enhance ourselves. Or we may establish or emphasize a mutual identity, which in some way leads to our own enhancement.

Just as we grow physically by ingesting food, our personality grows by taking in or introjecting the forms of behavior that we are exposed to.[27] Small children model their behavior after their parents, their siblings, and other people with whom they come in contact. Behavior that is seen as having successful consequences and models who are highly rewarding and highly regarded are especially apt to be copied.[28]

Parents identify with their children and share in their children's accomplishments. The father who was unable to complete school may pride himself on his children's education. Their diplomas can mean more to him than his own ever could. A mother whose own career or marriage has been a failure may, because of close identification with her daughter, promote or share in the latter's vocational or marital success.

We identify with groups as well as with other people. One may identify with one's neighborhood or school, gang or club, race or religious designation, and state or country. Sometimes such identifications are painful or embarrassing for us, and we struggle to disidentify ourselves and form new, more acceptable identifications.

Identification can be a very open and conscious process, or it can be a very subtle one into which we have only a limited insight. And we may identify with someone or something only in part or seemingly completely. For example, the enthusiastic fan at a football game is more than a spectator; with ten seconds left and goal to go, he is as poised and ready as any man on the field to get that ball over the goal line.

We pattern ourselves after prestigious and accomplished models, those who are successful in reaching the goals for which we may be struggling. In effecting a model's behavior, we may be able to attain the model's successes. Or, at least, he or she may reward us for our efforts (or punish us less) or love us more (or hate us less).

In establishing a common identity with other persons, we participate in their lives. We vicariously share in their status or achievement and feel more worthy and fulfilled ourselves. Identifying with a prestigious group of people or a powerful or successful organization may bring similar feelings of worth and satisfaction.

Difficulty occurs when models for identification are absent, inadequate, or harmful. A boy whose father is bumbling and ineffectual may take over these qualities for himself. Or, at least, he may be very threatened by his identity with his father. A girl whose mother is antagonistic toward males may introject her mother's attitude. When the parent of the same sex is missing, unsympathetic, or hostile, the child may pattern herself or himself after the parent of the opposite sex and develop behavior more characteristic of that sex.

Sometimes damage is done when a number of important models have conflicting patterns of behavior. A husband and wife, for example, may have important differences in standards and values; their children, through identification with both parents, can take over these incompatible systems and experience considerable conflict. Or an adolescent boy may find that his parents, his teachers, and his age-mates, all of whom he is identified with to some extent, present very different examples.

PROJECTION

A feature of some identifications is the taking in or introjection of something from the external environment. Not everything we take in or everything we become will serve us well or be valued by us. Just as we strive to acquire and accentuate prized patterns of behavior, we struggle to avoid, inhibit, or disassociate ourselves from those we hold in low esteem.

Projection refers to our tendency to attribute our own thoughts, feelings, and actions to others. We tend to regard other people as somewhat like ourselves. If, for example, we feel bored in a particular situation, we imagine others are bored too. If we hold a particular belief very strongly, it may be difficult for us to understand how anyone else could not feel as we do.

Both positive and negative qualities can be projected. It has been suggested that we project acceptable and positively valued characteristics to people we like and with whom we identify. Unacceptable, negatively valued qualities are projected to people we dislike, to people whom we believe we could not possibly be like (but, of course, are).[29]

If we sense good in ourselves, we may tend to see good in others. To the pure, all things are pure, goes an old saying. If we sense bad, we may see other people in the same unfavorable light; for example, we may see ourselves and others too as hostile and self-seeking: "It's all dog-eat-dog" we say, "so I better get in the first bite."

Used as a defense, projection implies that a person has certain thoughts or feelings or actions which are threatening to her or him and which are then repressed and attributed to others. As is indicated, three steps are involved: (1) a sense of some unacceptable motive operating in oneself; (2) a repression of this motive; and (3) an attribution of this motive to others.

Those of us who use projection as a defense may be especially hostile to other people who seem to share our unacceptable impulses.[30] "That's like the pot calling the kettle black," we sometimes say when people criticize others for faults they have themselves. Sometimes projectors have some insight into what they are doing and occasionally suggest that maybe the reason they cannot get along with another person is that this person is too like themselves.

In our own culture, aggressive impulses frequently undergo repression and projection. Those of us who sense unacceptable feelings of hostility in ourselves may attribute these feelings to others, most commonly to the person for whom the hostility was originally felt. We may start off with the thought: I hate you, and I'd like to hurt you. Through projection, we wind up with the thought: You hate me, and you'd like to hurt me.

Sexual urges are also frequently repressed and projected. A young woman who senses a strong but unacceptable sexual motivation in herself may deny this and instead see others as overly interested in sex. A man who is tempted to be unfaithful to his wife may be considerably concerned about his wife's "flirtations." An individual who has disturbing homosexual impulses may react against them and accuse others of making indecent advances.

Most frequently people are the objects of projection, but in some cases animals, natural and supernatural forces, or even inanimate articles may serve as objects. Primitives project human motives onto their gods, sometimes perceiving them as angry and at other times content. Sometimes tennis players will conduct ostentatious investigations of their racket after they have completely missed the ball—as if there were a hole in it big enough for the ball to go through. The person who stumbles on a chair may go back and kick the chair for getting in the way.

Jourard[31] suggests a number of guideposts for establishing whether or not a person is using projection as a defense. He says we may suspect such is the case if bad things are imputed to others with little justification, while these same things are denied in oneself but with some evidence to the contrary.

In projecting threatening qualities we are able to accomplish a number of things. First, we can disclaim responsibility for these qualities. (*I* don't have dirty thoughts, but *they* do.) Second, we can attack these qualities, thereby establishing distance from them. (I can't stand people who have dirty thoughts.) Third, we may feel that we are not so blameworthy since these qualities are widely shared. (So what if I have a dirty thought now and then? Everybody does.) And, fourth, we may gain some vicarious satisfaction from seeing these qualities indulged in by others. (I'd better keep my eye on these people and see what sort of dirty things they're up to.)

Insofar as we project positive qualities, our relationships with others may be facilitated. For example, a young woman who is genuinely friendly may project this feeling and expect that other people are friendly too. Whether the people she comes in contact with are friendly or not, her attitudes and behavior increase the possibility of their being so. To some extent people respond in kind, and just as aggression is frequently met with aggression, one friendly overture may prompt another.

In projecting negative qualities we protect ourselves from seeing ourselves in an unfavorable light. In the long run, however, this negative projection can be seriously detrimental. It prevents us from facing problems and dealing with them effectively. Furthermore, as we project negative qualities onto others and then act in accordance with this projection, relationships with others will suffer. The projection mechanism carried to an extreme is seen in certain paranoid processes.

DISPLACEMENT

Some of our behavior is threatening because of the people toward whom it is directed or because of the particular form it takes. Assuming that we express an impulse only in certain ways and only toward certain people, we may escape anxiety.

In *displacement*, there is a shift of thought, feeling, or action from one person or situation to another. Displacement occurs because the original impulse causes or would cause considerable anxiety. Consequently, there is a shift to a neutral object or to one that is more vulnerable or less dangerous than the original.

Sometimes the new object is similar to the original; the two may stand for each other or be identified with each other in some way, and the new object symbolizes the old one. For example, the little boy who is angry with his mother may trample her flower bed instead of attacking her directly. Or he may take his feelings out on his teacher if she in some way reminds him of his mother and is more vulnerable to attack.

Sometimes, however, the similarity between the new object and the old one is quite subtle and can be understood only by a person with a good deal of psychological training. Occasionally, on the surface at least, there appears to be no relationship. Occasionally, too, displacement seems to be a diffuse process in which the troublesome impulse is channeled to many new objects with little apparent rhyme or reason.

It has already been noted that the aggressive impulse is one that is frequently diverted or displaced. Other processes that commonly undergo displacement are fear, love, and attention.

Fears may be displaced in the same way that aggressive impulses are. People who are constantly worried about little things which appear to constitute no danger may actually be concerned about something more important which has been repressed. A little girl who fears her father, a person with whom she must be in constant association, may displace this fear to animals. A woman who hates her husband and fears that she may do him violence may instead express a fear of knives and other sharp instruments.

The people whom we wish to love and be loved by do not always respond. In this event, we may displace our love and affection to someone else. For example, a boy who is unable to establish a satisfactory relationship with his father may turn his affection to a teacher, a scoutmaster, or some other adult male. Sometimes a person who has been jilted by a lover finds and quickly marries someone else on the rebound. Some forms of narcissism appear to be displacements: constantly rebuffed by others, one may take refuge in oneself.[32]

Sometimes we make doubly sure that upsetting problems stay out of the focus of attention by keeping ourselves busy with other activities. A man who is having difficulty with his home life may displace his attention to his work; in fact, he may throw himself into his job with such vigor that his friends mistakenly attribute his difficulties to overwork. His wife and children in turn may seek relationships and activities elsewhere to keep themselves out of the troubled family sector.

Through the use of displacement we are able to discharge our feelings in acceptable directions. Positive and negative feelings may be separated and applied to separate objects. Positive feelings may be displayed to objects that will accept and respond to these feelings. Negative feelings may be diverted from important and dangerous objects onto those which are unimportant and vulnerable. In this way, we may love some things, hate others, and not be torn by ambivalence.[33,34]

Unfortunately, insofar as displacement involves negative feelings, one relationship may be improved at the cost of another. Although the second object is more vulnerable than the first, it may be an important one nevertheless. For example, the employee who displaces work hostilities to the home environment ensures the safety of his or her job at the expense of vital family relationships.[35]

REACTION FORMATION

When we sense things in ourselves that are very threatening to our self-esteem and general welfare, we may attempt to convince ourselves and others that these things are not so. One way we can accomplish this is by accentuating opposite qualities. We strive to feel, think, and act in ways that are sharply in contrast to the ways we tend to feel, think, and act.

Reaction formation refers to efforts to inhibit, mask, or overcome certain impulses by emphasizing opposite ones. Using such behavior as a defense against threat is very common. Sensing fear, we may attempt to act bravely. Sensing weakness, we may attempt to be tough and hardboiled. Sensing unacceptable dependence, we may make a great show of rebellion. Sensing anxiety-provoking affectionate feelings, we may react by being very cynical and take a cold and jaundiced view of human beings.[36]

To illustrate, a man who is strongly tempted by unacceptable sex needs can react against them by being extremely puritanical. He may prevent any sexual expression in himself and avoid almost all association with the opposite sex. Furthermore, he may criticize others who engage in any sexual activity no matter how mild; sometimes he may even attempt to prevent them from doing so. Whether his activities are ostensibly on his own behalf or seemingly on the behalf of others, they are designed to help him keep his own forbidden impulses in check.

To illustrate further, a woman who senses unacceptable aggressive urges in herself can react against them by being very kind. Such a person will appear to be extremely polite, deferent, and solicitous about the welfare of others. She may be unable to be aggressive even when aggressive actions appear to be quite appropriate. Her behavior is dedicated to keeping her hostile impulses under control.

A reaction formation toward selfish tendencies may be manifested in extreme generosity. Stinginess and avarice may be repressed and replaced by magnanimous actions. In this patterning, persons will feel compelled to give and be generous; they must constantly demonstrate to themselves and others that they are not as self-seeking as they inwardly suspect themselves to be.

Reaction formations are characterized by their extreme and compelling strength. As was noted, reaction formations to sex may be manifested in very puritanical behavior, those to aggression may produce excessively mild and gentle actions, and those counteracting selfishness may compel great generosity. In each case the individual will be unwilling and unable to modify her or his position. The force of the reaction is necessary to prevent the original impulse from breaking out of control into open expression.

Reaction formations may show inconsistencies and imperfections. Sometimes the forbidden behavior and the reaction behavior exist side by side. For example, a person who has reacted strongly against a tendency to be dirty and disorderly may still engage in certain activities or have certain places in which he or she is very messy.

Sometimes, too, a reaction formation will break down, allowing the original impulse free expression. A child who has always been extremely polite and well behaved may be caught in acts of extreme cruelty toward animals. A man who has always seemed extremely mild in his actions may suddenly lash out in some verbal or physical aggression. A woman who has spent a good deal of her life attacking certain patterns of behavior may suddenly be found to be engaging in those very behaviors.

Reaction formation plays an important part in the socialization process. Generosity, kindliness, orderliness, and many other personal qualities that are valued in our society are not natural expressions of the child; they are partly formed in reaction to earlier, diametrically opposite patterns of behavior. The small child, for example, has little concept of cleanliness; it is through constant training that one develops a dislike for dirt, a disgust for filth, and a loathing for bodily wastes.

It is interesting to observe reaction formations in the process of development. One might note, for example, a sudden shift in a child from attraction to dirt to aversion to dirt. A little girl who formerly played in her dress until it was filthy suddenly becomes sensitive to the smallest spot. Any garment that is the slightest bit dirty must be immediately removed. Little by little, her actions may become modulated so that she learns to be clean but not excessively so.

Severe, unmodulated reaction formations distort our lives. We need to be clean, of course, but we should not need to be always immaculate. We should be generous, but we should not feel compelled to give. We need to be kind, but we should be able to vent feelings when the occasion seems to warrant it. In general, we should not be strangers to any of our impulses: Instead of attempting to seal them off, we should learn to know them and express them in the ways we value.

FANTASY

The world in which we live—reality—leaves much to be desired. Our efforts may help to change it. Or we may change our perceptions of it and somehow see it as a more desirable place. Or we may be able to escape it for a while by constructing a private and more satisfying world.

Fantasy refers to imaginary constructions. It includes make-believe play, reveries, and daydreams. Novels, movies, plays, and similar literary and dramatic works might be considered to provide the individual with ready-made fantasy experiences.

As a defense, our fantasy life provides us with an escape from the dangers, threats, and boredom of the real world. In our fantasies we can meet our unmet needs and reach our unreached goals. We can picture ourselves as different sorts of people and the world as a different sort of world.

Freud[37] and others have pointed out the strong element of wish fulfillment in fantasies. Holt notes a number of reasons why, in daydreams, wishes may be expressed in very direct, crude, and primitive ways. He writes,

> The fact that the daydream is private and uncommunicated, that it is a regressive and often not recalled kind of thinking, makes it possible for the fulfillment of wishes to be relatively direct and for the wishes themselves to be unsublimated and close to the hypothetical state of original drives. If someone has annoyed us, we can easily imagine killing him or inflicting on him tortures we would not even consider witnessing in reality, much less carrying them out ourselves. (38, p. 29)

Fantasy is a common pursuit at every age. Children act out their fantasies. Their play is filled with make-believe. They pretend that they are who they would like to be, living in a world in which they would like to live. A little boy, for example, becomes his father, a cowboy, a spaceman, or a ferocious animal. He finds himself on the western plains, high above the earth, or deep in the jungle. In this play he escapes the limitations of being young and weak and small and under the domination of adults.

As we grow older, we increasingly daydream our fantasies rather than act them out. We not only create new experiences, we also relive old ones that have been enjoyable. Sometimes our fantasies are previews of events which are to occur in the future; certainly part of the pleasure of a vacation, a trip, or a party is in its anticipation.

"Conquering hero" and "suffering hero" are two common types of fantasies. In conquering-hero fantasies we imagine we are the master of some situation. We are a famous athlete, a brilliant student, a greater lover, or a fascinating conversationalist. We are applauded, acclaimed, and sought after. In fantasy, we may reenact an old experience, but this time we say and do all the things we failed to say and do during the actual experience.

In conquering hero fantasies, a person may have the experiences that are not forthcoming in real life. For example, a youth who is hungry for heterosexual experience may imagine a relationship with some girl who has caught his eye. He may daydream about asking her for a date and then conjure up the conversations they would have, the dances and parties they would attend, and the affection they would share.

In suffering-hero fantasies, we imagine ourselves to be the victim of some situation. We see ourselves as undergoing great hardship or suffering adversity. We are cold and hungry, unloved and unwanted, or destitute and outcast. We may be wounded, dying, or dead.

In fantasizing ourselves in such pitiful circumstances, we become figures deserving of the sympathy and commiseration of others. At the same time we are worthy of their admiration for carrying on so well in the face of such circumstances. Elements of revenge may also be present because now certain people will be very sorry that they did not treat us better in the past. Suffering-hero daydreams are common in children who are having difficulties with their parents.

When life is uninteresting and frustrating, fantasy permits us to escape into a dream world where exciting things occur and difficult goals are reached. In fantasy we can relive the pleasant experiences of the past (sometimes making them even more pleasant than they really were), and we can live in advance the anticipated pleasures of the future. Creative thinking and fantasy are closely related; representing our needs, activities, and goals in fantasy may be the first step to instituting them in reality.[39,40]

Fantasy becomes detrimental when it becomes a substitute for reality achievements. Compared with the ideal goals available in fantasy, the small rewards possible in the real world may seem hardly worth the effort. Fantasy can rob a person of large amounts of time which otherwise might be applied to real-life pursuits. In some serious conditions the individual has difficulty in distinguishing between the worlds of fantasy and reality.

Reference Notes

1. Kroeber, T. C. The coping functions of the ego mechanism. In R. W. White (Ed.), *The study of lives.* New York: Atherton Press, 1963, pp. 178–198.
2. Murphy, L. B., et al. *The widening world of childhood.* New York: Basic Books, 1962.
3. Menninger, K., Mayman, M., & Pruyser, P. *The vital balance.* New York: Viking Press, 1963.

4. Murphy, L. B., et al. *The widening world of childhood.* New York: Basic Books, 1962.
5. Swanson, G. E. Determinants of the individual's defenses against inner conflict: Review and reformation. In J. C. Glidewell (Ed.), *Parental attitudes and child behavior.* Springfield, IL: Charles C Thomas, 1961, pp. 5–41.
6. Dollard, J., & Miller, N. E. *Personality and psychotherapy.* New York: McGraw-Hill, 1950.
7. Dollard, J., & Miller, N. E. *Personality and psychotherapy.* New York: McGraw-Hill, 1950.
8. MacKinnon, D. W., & Dukes, W. F. Repression. In L. Postman (Ed.), *Psychology in the making.* New York: Alfred A. Knopf, 1962, pp. 662–744.
9. Dollard, J., & Miller, N. E. *Personality and psychotherapy.* New York: McGraw-Hill, 1950.
10. Freud, S. *The psychopathology of everyday life* (1904). In *Basic Writings of Sigmund Freud.* New York: Random House, 1938.
11. Brenner, C. *An elementary textbook of psychoanalysis.* New York: International Universities Press, 1957.
12. Vaughan, W. F. *Personal and social adjustment.* New York: Odyssey Press, 1952.
13. Cameron, N., & Magaret, A. *Behavior pathology.* Boston: Houghton Mifflin, 1951.
14. Hall, C. S. *A primer of Freudian psychology.* Cleveland: World Publishing, 1954.
15. Stone, L. J., & Church, J. *Childhood and adolescence.* New York: Random House, 1957.
16. Woolf, M. The child's moral development. In K. R. Eissler (Ed.), *Searchlights on delinquency.* New York: International Universities Press, 1949, pp. 263–272.
17. Woolf, M. The child's moral development. In K. R. Eissler (Ed.), *Searchlights on delinquency.* New York: International Universities Press, 1949, pp. 263–272.
18. Karpman, B. Lying: A minor inquiry into the ethics of neurotic and psychopathic behavior. *Journal of Criminal Law and Criminology, 40* (1949), 135–157.
19. Jourard, S. M. *Personal adjustment* (2nd ed.). New York: Macmillan, 1963.
20. Twain, Mark (Samuel L. Clemens). *The adventures of Tom Sawyer* (1875). New York: Harper, 1929.
21. Vaughan, W. F. *Personal and social adjustment.* New York: Odyssey Press, 1952.
22. Sappenfield, B. R. *Personality dynamics.* New York: Alfred A. Knopf, 1954.
23. Kris, E. *Psychoanalytic explorations in art.* New York: International Universities Press, 1952.
24. Maslow, A. H. Emotional blocks to creativity. *Journal of Individual Psychology, 14* (1958), 51–56.
25. Shafer, R. Regression in the service of the ego: The relevance of a psychoanalytic concept for personality assessment. In G. Lindzey (Ed.), *Assessment of human motives.* New York: Holt, Rinehart & Winston, 1958, pp. 119–148.
26. Maslow, A. H. Emotional blocks to creativity. *Journal of Individual Psychology, 14* (1958), 51–56.
27. Szasz, T. S. A contribution to the psychology of schizophrenia. *A.M.A. Archives of Neurology and Psychiatry, 77* (1957), 420–436.
28. Bandura, A., & Walters, R. H. *Social learning and personality development.* New York: Holt, Rinehart & Winston, 1963.
29. Zimmer, H. The roles of conflict and internalized demands in projection. *Journal of Abnormal and Social Psychology, 50* (1955), 188–192.
30. Cohen, A. R. Experimental effects of ego-defense preference on interpersonal relations. *Journal of Abnormal and Social Psychology, 52* (1956), 19–27.
31. Jourard, S. M. *Personal adjustment* (2nd ed.). New York: Macmillan, 1963.
32. Symonds, P. M. *The dynamics of human adjustment.* New York: Appleton-Century-Crofts, 1946.
33. Isaacs, S. *Social development in young children.* New York: Harcourt, Brace, 1937.
34. Symonds, P. M. *The dynamics of human adjustment.* New York: Appleton-Century-Crofts, 1946.

35. Sappenfield, B. R. *Personality dynamics.* New York: Alfred A. Knopf, 1954.
36. Sarnoff, I. Reaction formation and cynicism. *Journal of Personality, 28* (1960), 129–143.
37. Freud S. *The interpretation of dreams* (1900). London: Hogarth, 1953.
38. Holt, R. R. The nature of TAT stories as cognitive products: A psychoanalytic approach. In J. Kagan (Ed.), *Contemporary issues in thematic apperceptive methods.* Springfield, Ill.: Charles C Thomas, 1961, pp. 3–43.
39. Hartmann, H. *Ego psychology and the problem of adaption.* New York: International Universities Press, 1958.
40. Varendonck, J. *The psychology of daydreams.* New York: Macmillan, 1921.

To Apply This Reading to Yourself

1. *Discuss the use you have made of suppression and/or repression as a defense.*
2. *Discuss the use you have made of lying and/or rationalization as a defense.*
3. *Discuss the use you have made of malingering and/or adjustment by ailment as a defense.*
4. *Discuss the use you have made of fixation and/or regression as a defense.*
5. *Discuss your defensive use of any of the following: identification, projection, displacement, reaction formation, and fantasy.*

Freedom from Pretense

Harry Browne

We've seen how hiding yourself can cause all kinds of social restrictions to be imposed upon you. In the same way, little acts of dishonesty can be a surprisingly easy way to throw away your freedom.

It's such a small thing to shade the truth a little—but the long-run consequences can create tremendous restrictions on your life.

For example, suppose there's something you want to do, but if a given person knew about it there might be problems. So you tell a simple lie to him to cover your tracks.

Then one day you're with him and another person, and the matter comes up in discussion. It becomes necessary to repeat or confirm the lie you told before. But the other person doesn't understand the inconsistency between what you're saying now and something you've said to him before. So you have to invent an explanation that will satisfy both of them.

Now whenever you're with either of these people, you have to remember the separate fictions involved—to keep the original lie from being exposed. And it can become even more complicated as other people become involved.

So to avoid revealing your actions to someone, you can eventually pay a very complicated and expensive price. If you admit to the second person that you lied to the first, your honesty would be suspect in the future. No matter how you handle it, you pay for dishonesty.

In fact, it's a very easy way to jump into a box. When you've lied about something, your actions are restricted by the need to maintain the fiction you've created. You can no longer react freely and spontaneously to new developments; you always have to keep your guard up to avoid doing anything that might reveal your previous acts.

Ironically, I think dishonesty usually comes about as an attempt to *avoid* prices. A friend, Lynda Raff, once pointed out that lying is an attempt to get something for nothing. It's the hope of being able to do something without the consequences that would naturally follow—the reactions of certain people.

And yet, you usually wind up paying a higher price dealing with the problems required to continue the deception.

The value of honesty is greater to the person being honest. It may be helpful to someone else if you're honest with him, but you're helping *yourself* far more by your honesty.

PROBLEMS Of DISHONESTY

Here are a few of the problems you can bring upon yourself by being dishonest:

1. You have to remain on guard, using precious resources to cover up past acts.
2. You miss opportunities to be accepted for yourself, because you're hiding that self. The people who would like you as you really are will never see you if you keep your real self hidden.
3. Dishonesty toward others can lead easily to dishonesty toward yourself. Lying can become automatic. If you're very concerned with maintaining an image, you can remember past lies more clearly than what really happened. After a while, it may become impossible to remember what was true and what wasn't.
4. This can lead to an anxious feeling that what you've obtained by lying can't be preserved. You can feel that you don't really deserve what you have—and so you can't relax and fully enjoy it.
5. Sooner or later someone is going to become aware of your dishonesty—possibly because he has participated in it. Because he knows you've been dishonest in the past, he can't be sure you're being honest in the present. You'll have fewer alternatives available when your word can't be accepted without question.

BENEFITS OF HONESTY

You can avoid those problems by being honest and gain other advantages, too. Here's a brief summary of the various benefits I find that honesty brings:

1. When you prove that you're willing to be honest—no matter what the short-term consequences—others will accept your word more easily. This can open up many opportunities that wouldn't exist if your listeners had to wonder about each thing you say.

For example, when I was promoting my last book through radio and television appearances, I was often asked, "Why did you write this book?" I always answered, "To make money."

A public-relations man suggested to me that I be less honest. "Don't admit you're selfish," he said. "People don't want to hear that. You should tell them you wrote the book to help people."

I asked him how many times he'd heard an author or politician say that he was "only interested in helping people." He acknowledged that he'd heard it many times—and he also acknowledged that he never believed it when he heard it. And finally he admitted that he doubted that other people believed it either.

He hadn't understood that I was helping myself, not hurting myself, by my statement. If I were willing to admit my selfish intentions (usually the first thing someone would lie about), people could more readily accept other things I said when they knew I wasn't covering up anything.

Honesty allows other people to relax around you. They don't have to be alert to evaluate the truthfulness of each statement. Consequently, there's more chance for your words to make an impact.

2. Honesty allows *you* to relax, too. You can say what you think and mean and would like to say—without having to check first to be sure your statements won't contradict a previous remark.

3. As you reveal yourself honestly, you often find that you didn't really know what others wanted to hear; you only assumed you knew. When you tell the truth, you may be surprised to discover that it projects a more attractive image of yourself than one you might have fabricated.

I've often found that others would reveal their feelings only after I'd revealed mine frankly. When they saw that someone was willing to admit the truth about himself, they felt free to follow suit.

4. When you've been honest with everyone you're involved with, you'll know you've earned whatever you have—and you'll feel much freer to relax and enjoy it. You won't have to fear that the truth might someday be revealed and destroy what you've achieved.

5. You'll be free to share your innermost secrets with others. When you decide that you don't have to fear the judgments of others, you won't be afraid to confide in them. When you can verbalize your emotions and desires honestly, you'll probably understand them better and you'll be able to satisfy them more easily.

PLENTY OF ENCOURAGEMENT

Honesty has many advantages, but somehow dishonesty continues to get a good press and plenty of encouragement. Both fiction and real life are filled with examples of "smart" and even "noble" people telling lies.

I imagine you've seen in movies, books, and newspapers how people lie to get what they want, how they lie to avoid hurting someone's feelings, how they disguise their own desires in a show of self-sacrifice, how politicians and diplomats lie in the service of their countries, how lovers lie to arrange secret meetings, and how "little people" lie to get even with big business.

Perhaps the most common encouragement to lying is the idea that you're doing someone a favor when you lie to him.

But I think that idea is dishonest in itself. When a person lies to protect someone's feelings, he's most likely doing it to keep the person from disliking him. A phony compliment usually isn't meant to make an individual feel better about *himself*; it's meant to make him feel better about the person doing the complimenting.

It doesn't work, though. He probably knows the truth already. If you lie to a person about what he already knows, he'll probably respect you less, not more.

And you also hurt your credibility with anyone else who knows about it. Suppose, for example, that you and I are having lunch with Charley, who's known for his large nose. When Charley asks me, "Do you think my nose is large?" I could answer, "Of course not, Charley."

Later, you might ask me if I really meant my remark. Suppose I answer, "No, but I didn't want to hurt his feelings." That may seem noble, but the next time I say something "nice" to you, you'll have no way of knowing whether I meant it or was just trying to make you feel good. My so-called kindness has hurt my relationship with you.

What's the alternative to lying? Do I have to be brutal and hurt Charley in order to be truthful? No. Too often, the "brutal truth" is only a partial truth. When it seems that honesty has caused problems, the trouble is often *too little* truth rather than too much.

For example, when Charley asks me if his nose is too large, I could say, "It sure is!" Would *that* be the truth? Only part of it. It would be more completely honest to say, "You have a large nose—but it doesn't make any difference to me."

Another example of too little truth is the person who angrily says, "I hate you," and then excuses his venom by saying, "Well, you want me to be honest, don't you?" But *is* he being honest? Usually, such an individual doesn't really hate the person—or he wouldn't be in contact with him to begin with.

It might be more accurate to say, "There are many things I like about you, but I dislike very much what you've just done." Or just "I am very angry right now."

That recognizes the broader context in which the issue at hand is only one small part. It makes quite a difference; honesty makes it much easier to deal with whatever has caused the problem.

So if you sometimes fear saying the truth, check first to see if perhaps the problem is one of too little truth rather than too much.

And recognize that you're sacrificing your own reputation and reducing your alternatives when you lie as a supposed favor to someone else. Any problem he has in facing the truth is *his* problem. It isn't your duty to protect him from himself.

100 PERCENT

An important principle underlies the examples we've seen in this chapter: An individual can be sure of your honesty only if you're honest with *everyone.*

How can he be sure you're not lying to protect his feelings if you've lied to protect someone else's feelings?

If you've said you'd lie only if it's "absolutely necessary," how can he be sure you don't consider *this* situation an "absolute necessity"?

If you say you'd never lie to your close friends, how can he be sure he hasn't done something to be demoted from your close friendship?

If you want to prove your honesty to someone, you can do it only by being honest with everyone. He can relax and accept what you say only if you've demonstrated that you'll be honest even when it's uncomfortable for you to do so.

I once had a lady friend who played the typical games with the phone company—placing collect or person-to-person calls that were never completed, just to get a prearranged message through.

Obviously, the phone company didn't create its facilities to enable people to send free messages. To use those facilities fraudulently is just as dishonest as lying to someone's face.

My friend justified her tactic by saying, "But that doesn't mean I'd lie to *you*! And I resent the inference that I would. You're far more important to me than the phone company."

But that's the point. If she'd lie to the phone company to save 85¢, why wouldn't she lie to me if she thought it would save our relationship—especially since she says I'm more important to her than the phone company?

You can prove your honesty to any one person only by being honest to everyone.

There's a greater difference between being 99 percent honest and 100 percent honest than there is between 70 percent and 90 percent. The first exception to your honesty destroys one of its most important benefits—the absolute trust of others.

TESTING YOURSELF

Most people probably think of themselves as being basically honest, even though they tell a few white lies here and there. In fact, it can be so habitual that it doesn't even register with the person as being dishonest.

The Identity Trap can be compelling.[1] One can be so anxious to put his "best foot forward"

---

[1]The Identity Trap, as the term is used here, is "the belief that you should be someone other than yourself."

that he doesn't even notice that it isn't his own foot.

I find it valuable to test my honesty periodically. To do so, I pick a period of thirty minutes or so when I'm talking on the telephone or in person with others. I observe closely everything I say. Did I speak the absolute truth as I know it—or did I say what I felt I "ought" to say in the circumstances?

Through this test, I sometimes realize that I've lied without being aware of it.

It *is* possible to change that, however. And I've found a little exercise for that purpose. In fact, it follows from the test I just described.

Take an hour when you'll be talking with someone. Instead of checking your statements *after* you say them, think twice about them *before* speaking. Stop your first impulse to speak, and check what you were about to say. Is it the truth? If it isn't, determine what is and say that.

After an hour, you may be exhausted from the concentration. So don't overdo it at first. An hour each day might be enough to start with.

After a few days of this, it becomes more automatic and requires less effort to keep up. So you can increase the amount of time you'll devote to the exercise.

Eventually, you should discover that your first impulses to speak *are* truthful. At that point, the monitoring can be dropped; honesty will become natural.

The way I've described the exercise might make it seem as routine as doing an hour of calisthenics each day. But there's a lot more to it.

During the exercise time, you might face some decisive moments. Suppose you've been exaggerating your affection for your wife, and on the first day you try this she asks if you love her. On the third day, you might be divorced.

You might need to answer a question in a way that contradicts an important lie you've been protecting for a long time. If you're not prepared to accept the consequences of that, there's no point in undertaking the attempt.

It's foolish to start using a new technique before you're fully prepared to handle the consequences. You have to be convinced the benefits are worth the discomfort that will accompany the adjustment period.

As with anything else, you can approach absolute honesty on a gradual basis. But it would help to begin thinking of ways to handle the major adjustments that might be required when you acknowledge major dishonesties of the past. I don't think it's worth doing unless you're prepared to go all the way with it eventually.

If you do decide that honesty will be your policy, the rewards should far outweigh the problems. In fact, you'll probably discover benefits far beyond anything I might suggest.

You might develop valuable new relationships—even out of old ones. You may find that more people will respond favorably to you because your honesty is a refreshing difference. As you deal with others, you'll probably feel a great sense of freedom when all need for pretense evaporates. You'll be able to forget about the contradictions and complications you had to keep track of before.

Let me warn you, however, that the only way to demonstrate your honesty is by simply responding honestly to everything. The most *ineffective* way of demonstrating your honesty is by saying, "I'm being honest with you."

WHAT YOU ARE

When you start reaping the benefits of honesty, all temptation to be dishonest may fade away. You'll want to reveal yourself to others as you are—because you'll know that's the way to attract the kind of people who have the most to offer you.

The real you has a lot more to offer the world than the lost-in-the-crowd façade that so many people try to assume. Who wants one more person whose identity is just like everyone else is trying to be?

I've found that my most useful assets are many of the things I used to try to hide—my selfishness, my laziness, the ease with which I cry when I hear good music or see good drama. Those things have helped me find likeminded people who appreciate the same things. And those are the people I've always wanted to be with—not the ones for whom I'd have to suppress myself.

I've found that suppressing embarrassing things about myself costs me far too much freedom to be worth it. So, if I feared that a given person might discover something I had been trying to hide, I went to him and told it to him myself. The experience never failed to give me a wonderful sense of freedom. I no longer had to worry about it; the price had been paid once and for all, and I didn't have to think about it again.

In the same way, if there is something about myself that makes me self-conscious, I examine it closely. I invariably discover that it's either nothing to be self-conscious about or something that can be easily changed.

INTEGRITY

Honesty is displaying yourself to others as you really are. But, of course, you can't be truthful about something you don't know.

And that's why it's so important to examine yourself, understand yourself, and accept yourself. Only when you know who you are can you honestly represent yourself to others.

The individual who doesn't know himself can't speak with authority about himself. He can't make promises, because he doesn't know himself well enough to foresee his future emotions and actions. He can't express authoritative opinions, because he doesn't really know what he believes.

He uses the word "I" dishonestly. He begins statements with "I think . . . " but he's only repeating what he's heard. He says, "I will . . ." but he doesn't really know what he's going to do.

The word "I" is one of the most important words in the English language. It refers to a unique, individual entity, different from all others in the world. When you use the word, you should be sure you're really expressing the unique, individual entity that is *you*—not simply repeating something that sounded good to you.

To be honest, you must know yourself well. And that involves integrity—which is honesty's twin asset. *Integrity is knowing yourself well enough to be able to mean what you say.*

The person with integrity can use the word "I" with authority. He *knows* what he thinks—for he's thought it out for himself.

AN UNCLUTTERED LIFE

The effort to prevent discovery of facts about yourself can be costly and draining. But it's perhaps the easiest self-destructive habit one can practice.

I've had to work with it—and work with it again. It's so important to me that I don't like to go for very long without rechecking myself to be sure I haven't unthinkingly relapsed into dishonesty. And, unfortunately, sometimes my rechecking reveals that I *have* fallen back.

But my efforts to correct it have been worth the trouble many times over. Discovering myself and displaying that self has brought me countless benefits, valuable friends, a clean, uncluttered life, and a wide expanse of freedom that I didn't even know existed until I tried being totally honest.

Dishonesty is a form of the Identity Trap. When you lie to someone, you're falling for the temptation to think that you'll be more attractive (and get more of what you want) if you appear to be something different from what you are.

Learn to trust your own nature, your own identity. Accept it, live it, reveal it. Don't suppress it; don't attempt to shade it with little lies and half-truths. When you do, you miss so much of life and the happiness that can be yours.

By being only what *you* are, you can awaken each morning to a new day that's an opportunity to seek whatever you want—with no previous deceptions to get in your way.

To Apply This Reading to Yourself

1. *How honest are you? 100 percent? If so, why so? If not, why not? Write a brief paper incorporating your answers to these questions.*
2. *Discuss some problems you have found with being honest and/or dishonest.*
3. *Complete the honesty test and/or exercise described by Browne on page 268 and write up the results.*

4. Browne writes, "Learn to trust your own nature, your own identity. Accept it, live it, reveal it." Are you living in accord with Browne's advice? Why or why not? Write a brief paper giving your answers to these questions.
5. Browne writes, "Discovering myself and displaying that self has brought me countless benefits, valuable friends, a clean, uncluttered life, and a wide expanse of freedom that I didn't even know existed until I tried being totally honest." Would being totally honest enhance your own life in the same way? (Or, if you are already totally honest, has it done so?) Why or why not?

The Limits of Intimacy

Morton M. Hunt

When I was in my teens, I daydreamed of the ideal girl I would some day love. Naturally, she would be beautiful, intelligent and gentle. But the essential thing about her was that she would *understand* me. She would listen to all my innermost thoughts, not only my hopes and fond desires, but my darkest moods and memories, my sorrows and sins.

Somehow, though, I never envisioned myself listening to her in return. I would find her dear because she would understand and accept *me;* it did not occur to me to understand and accept *her.* For the desire for self-revelation is both immature and selfish.

Yet, even in adulthood, many people suppose that they have a right, almost an obligation, to express to the people closest to them their doubts and fears, their ugliest or most pessimistic thoughts. I submit that we have no such right. If anything, the obligation is in the other direction: *not* to indulge in total self-revelation to those we love and who love us. Intimacy between any two loving human beings should have certain limits, for the good of both persons, and when we ignore those limits, we do so selfishly, out of an immature desire to shift our burden onto the other person. But, as a wise rabbi said long ago, "If thy secret oppress thine own heart, how canst thou expect the heart of another to endure it?"

The secret that modern man most often seems to want to confess—to the very person it will hurt worst—concerns sexual infidelity. When a man or woman has an extramarital affair, he or she is likely to be nagged by guilt. Many an adulterer, undetected, almost wishes his wife would find out somehow, so that he might confess and ask forgiveness. Yet when that happens, he frees himself of pain by transferring it to her; he is healed while she suffers.

A marriage counselor told me of a young woman married to a brilliant real-estate developer in his late 30's. Their marriage had been warm and rewarding for some years until one night he told her about a brief, torrid affair he'd had while out of town some months earlier. He said that there had been no emotional significance to it. Having been through it, he felt he'd be able to control such impulses in the future; he said he felt far better for having told her, and believed it would bring them closer than ever before.

He was wrong—as any psychologist could have told him. For since that night their love life, previously sound and happy, has been blighted for her. She finds herself always wondering, "Am I as exciting as that other woman?" She feels suspicious about the women he meets at business, and is in agony whenever he goes out of town. *His* secret has shattered *her* peace of mind.

Why do people make such revelations to those who love them? Was this man's act a genuine effort to become closer to his wife? Her marriage counselor thinks not. The confession was not a mature and loving act. "Let me see how real your love is," he was saying, in effect. "Let's see if you can love me, even if I show you something ugly." Mature love on his part would have made him feel: "This was my wrongdoing, my cross to bear. I have no right to free myself of it at her expense."

The same is true of sexual wishes that we never actually carry out. Lewis Terman, a psychologist, made a famous survey some years ago in which he found that a majority of husbands, and a smaller number of wives, sometimes feel longings for extramarital affairs even when their marriages are happy. Total intimacy would call for them to confide such yearnings to their mates; happily, compassion and caution combine to keep most of their mouths shut.

I say "happily" because the admission of such desires is tantamount to telling one's mate, "You are not enough for me; you leave me wanting something more." Why should anyone expect his mate to receive this news without hurt? Would he like to hear the same thing?

Like the love between a man and a woman, the affection between two friends may be destroyed by too much intimacy. Friendship involves a blessed freedom to be truthful about ourselves, but, like all other freedoms, this one must be exercised with restraint lest it become license. Conscious and unconscious feelings of guilt are aroused when friends know too much about us. These are the beginning of the end.

Consider a woman with whom I had been friendly for years, who once wrote me a long and incredibly revealing letter when I was gathering data for a book on the problems of American women. Writing late at night when she was feeling sorry for herself, she told me that she often bitterly regretted having children.

They had brought her far less joy and far more emotional upset than she'd ever expected, and, while she often loved them, quite often she hated them. A day after I received the letter, she sent a telegram asking me to burn it. Though she and her husband were longtime friends of mine, I have not seen or heard from them since. Friendship, though it flourishes on the nutrients of sharing and intimacy, can be killed altogether by an overdose.

One similarly goes beyond the allowable borders of intimacy when he tells a friend the things he dislikes about him if those things are essential parts of his character. To tell a friend you are angry because of something he has done may be helpful; to tell him his basic faults, rather than accepting them without comment, is a very different matter.

Fundamentally, the desire to pour out our thoughts and to confess our misdeeds to the people closest to us originates in a childish conception of love. As one psychiatrist explains it, "To tell everything—one's past or present misdeeds, one's impermissible wishes—is reminiscent of the way an infant tests and demands parental love. A baby makes a mess—and expects Mommy not to be angry but to clean it up with a forgiving smile. A grown person who tells the worst about himself is symbolically making a mess and asking to be loved despite it."

Still, isn't confession good for the soul? Doesn't the whole practice of psychiatry prove that certain private sorrows and fears, if kept bottled up, will sometimes overwhelm us? Of course—but the crucial question is: If you must confide, to whom should you do so?

In the case of secrets such as I have been discussing, the answer is: Not to the persons you are most intimate with, but to someone detached and uninvolved, unlikely to be wounded by what you reveal. Your minister, rabbi or priest is often an excellent choice as confidant and adviser. And the family doctor or lawyer, though he may lack the prerogatives of spiritual leadership, is often able to perform much the same function for the person who needs to relate his inner torment.

In more severe emotional problems and disorders, it may be necessary to seek a social worker, a psychologist or a psychiatrist. Such people can let us say the worst we have to tell—indeed, can encourage it—without being harmed by it themselves. Moreover, they are trained to help us learn to live with our own feelings.

But self-revelation to an intimate is unwise, if not downright dangerous. We must set limits to intimacy, not only for our own good, but for the good of those we love.

To Apply This Reading to Yourself

1. *Would you agree with Hunt that you should not totally reveal yourself to those you love and are loved by? Why or why not?*
2. *Have you ever had a friendship or love relationship damaged by too much disclosure? Or too little disclosure? Discuss your experience in this regard.*
3. *Do you tend to reveal yourself to others easily or too easily, or with some difficulty or great difficulty? Discuss yourself in this regard.*
4. *Do you have or have you had a confidant—a person to whom you could confide and disclose yourself quite fully? Discuss the effect that the presence or absence of such persons has had on your life.*

Growth

You are almost certainly much better than you think you are. More than you now permit yourself, you can be happier, stronger, braver. You can be more loving and giving; warmer, more open and honest; more responsible and responsive. You can perceive worlds richer and fuller than any you now experience. You have it in you to be more creative, more zestful, more joyous. All these prospects are within you. They are your potential.
—from Growth Games by H. R. Lewis and H. S. Streitfeld

Upon meeting a friend who has been away for some time, we may be startled by how different he or she is. Or perhaps someone we see every day suddenly appears to be changed in some way. Or maybe it is ourselves who seem somehow to have a new dimension. People change. When these changes are for the better, we say that they represent growth.

Growth, in the sense used here, refers to personal development in a desired direction. Of course, people's values differ and we may not agree as to what constitutes desirable change. Generally, an individual is said to show growth when he or she becomes more capable and competent, more productive and creative, more perceptive, insightful, and understanding, or more knowledgeable, prudent, and discerning.

What we consider to be growth for one person may not be the same as growth for another. For example, we may feel a particular individual shows growth when he settles down and becomes more conscientious about his undertakings. We may conclude that another person has grown when she loosens up, becomes more spontaneous, and stops worrying so much.

Some writers have described growth as a process of self-actualization. In growing, we realize more of our potentiality. We become more fulfilled, completed, or perfected. Each of us possesses a set of capacities—a promise of what we can become—and as we grow, we develop these capacities and make good on this promise.

It can be both bothersome and intriguing to consider this notion of potentiality. It is bothersome because we can never really know our own growth capacities until we realize them. A set of test scores may provide a rough estimate of our limits in a certain area, and sometimes in a burst or spurt of development we get some inkling of the persons we might be, but generally this notion is a rather mysterious one.

Still, it is intriguing to consider the ramifications of this concept. Various thinkers in this area suggest that human beings generally develop only a small fraction of their potentiality. What could we accomplish if we somehow developed the unrealized part of ourselves? Who would we be if we were everything we could be?

UNDERSTANDING GROWTH

The first reading, by Abe Arkoff, introduces the concept of personal growth. As the reading notes, our potential for growth is prodigious, and our impulse to grow is strong, but so are the obstacles to growth. Arkoff reviews the growth that occurs during the college years and in psychotherapy, and contrasts the inner (individual) and outer (collective) paths to growth. He concludes, "There are many kinds of growth and many routes—each of us can find our own way."

TAKING RESPONSIBILITY

Most people seen by psychiatrists, writes psychiatrist M. Scott Peck in the second selection, have a neurosis or a character disorder—and so do most of the rest of us to some degree. Neurotics assume too much responsibility; character disorder clients assume too little; and there are those overly responsible about some things and irresponsible about others. Peck notes that resolving a problem often means choosing the lesser of two evils; that's a painful process we may attempt to escape, but we must accept responsibility for our lives if we are to grow.

GETTING UNSTUCK

Free yourself—you need not let the "I'm stuck" syndrome keep you from growing. That's the encouraging advice of Harold Bloomfield and Robert Kory in the last reading. They say that we get stuck because we fear losing what we have or we tell ourselves that "I've always been that way." There are dividends for self-immobilization but with them comes self-destruction. Bloomfield and Kory present some suggestions to help us transform into action our decision to grow.

To Explore Your Own Personal Growth

1. *The growth potential.* Workers in the human potential movement believe that humans have awesome powers but that these powers remain largely untapped. William James, an early and illustrious

American psychologist, estimated that the average person operated at about 10% of capacity. More recently, anthropologist Margaret Mead hypothesized 6%, and, more recently still, human potentialist Herbert Otto suggested an even lower 4%. Otto attributes this shrinkage to the dawning evidence that humans have even greater potential than was formerly believed. Consider your own potential. Do you feel that you have made the most of what you have? Or are you less or much less than you could be? Discuss your answers to these questions and also the evidence or intuitions on which they are based.

2. *The growth spurt.* In the larger group or in small groups, members share their recollections of a personal growth spurt—a time of their lives when they made rapid progress in some area of development or endeavor.

3. *The growth block.* In the larger group or in small groups, members share their recollections of a personal growth block—a time of their lives when they felt blocked, stuck, and unable to make progress in some area of development or endeavor.

4. *The growth battle.* Within each of us there may be impulses to grow that conflict with impulses to stay put. Let the members of the group silently reflect for a few minutes on the growth and antigrowth forces in themselves and also the reasons behind each set of forces. Then a volunteer enacts this conflict before the group by taking both roles (growth and antigrowth) and staging a dialogue between them. The person should vigorously throw herself or himself into each role, bringing it to life with appropriate words, gestures, stances, and movements, and continuing until some insight or resolution is achieved. Afterward other members contribute their observations, insights, and suggestions.

5. *The growth risk.* "Consider the turtle," goes a relatively recent saying, "it never gets anywhere without sticking its neck out." Even more recently Arnold Lazarus and Allen Fay suggest that if we always "look before we leap," we may end up "missing the boat," and sometimes when we "leap before we look," we may "hit the jackpot." They write, "Life itself entails a series of risks each and every moment. The wise individual will obviously avoid dangerous or harmful situations, but the risks to which we are referring do not fall into this category. Taking calculated *psychological* risks (such as accepting a new job, telling someone off, going out on a blind date, asking a favor, expressing an opinion, or offering advice) tends to change an everyday existence into an exciting life." They suggest that we take at least one psychological risk each day—something we have avoided doing that might be growth enhancing, such as requesting a raise, extending an invitation, or disclosing an intimate feeling. If this exercise seems right for you, try it for a week and write up your experience.[1]

6. *The growth garden.* In a moment, close your eyes and imagine yourself to be a garden that is divided into plots, each plot with a

1. For more on this method and other ways to grow, read *I Can If I Want To* by Arnold Lazarus and Allen Fay.

marker indicating what is planted there. Each plot might represent an important relationship (with father, mother, sibling, lover, etc.) or area of living (family, school, work, etc.). What parts of your growth garden seem thriving or well tended? What parts appear to be languishing? Are you satisfied with your growth garden? Why or why not? What can you do—beginning now—to enhance your garden's growth? Write a brief paper or draw a picture that presents your answers to these questions and, as an option, share your paper or picture in the larger group or in small groups.

7. *The growth list.* From the standpoint of growth, some of our personal qualities are "changeworthy." That is, they are negative qualities, weaknesses or liabilities, which are worth changing and need working on if we are to grow. Other qualities are "praiseworthy." These are positive qualities, strengths or assets, that bolster and promote growth. Draw a vertical line down the center of a sheet of paper. At the top of the left half, write "Changeworthy" and below this list all your changeworthy qualities. At the top of the right half, write "Praiseworthy" and list all your praiseworthy qualities. Some of us do not dwell enough on our positive qualities; make sure that your praiseworthy list is at least twice as long as your changeworthy list. Keep listing until the two sides of your sheet are "properly imbalanced" in this way.

8. *The growth plan.* Form small groups, in which each member in turn becomes the focus of the group's attention. When you are the focus, enumerate your personal strengths as you see them and relate anything that may prevent you from fully developing these strengths. Invite the members of the group to respond to you, adding any further strengths they may detect in you and suggesting ways you may overcome development barriers.

9. *The growth letter.* Imagine that your class is having a reunion ten years from now. Since you are such a great, growing group, you have scattered to the four corners of the globe and are too busy to come together in one place. So you each decide to write a letter instead to let each other know how you have grown. Continue your letter from this beginning:

Date_____
(Exactly 10 years from today)

Dear Class:

Since last we met, ten years have gone by. They have been really great, growing years! What I am most pleased to report to you is . . .

When everyone has finished, read your letters to each other.

10. *The growth autobiography.* This exercise presents a way for you to write your future autobiography. In a moment, relax and imagine yourself at the age of eighty. In your mind's eye, see yourself at that age. As your eighty-year-old self, reminisce about your life as you lived it from your high school graduation until your eightieth birthday. What did you do with your life? Write down in chronological order the most important happenings of your adult

years. Then, returning to your present-day self, comment on how growth-filled your life was as you saw it and what you might do right now to increase the growth prospects of your life.

11. *The growth wand.* Imagine that you have a growth wand and that you can touch this wand to each significant person in your life (including yourself) to cause this person to grow in some important way. What persons would you touch with your wand, and how would you have each grow? Write a brief paper giving your answers to these questions and, as an option, share your papers in the larger group or in small groups or dyads.

To Read Further

Branden, N. (1985). *Honoring the self: The psychology of confidence and self-respect.* New York: Bantam. (paperback)

Branden, N. (1988). *How to raise your self-esteem.* New York: Bantam. (paperback)

Burns, D. D. (1980). *Feeling good: The new mood therapy.* New York: William Morrow. (New American Library paperback, 1981)

Burns, D. D. (1990). *The feeling good handbook: Using the new mood therapy in everyday life.* New York: William Morrow. (New American Library paperback, 1990)

Ellis, A. (1988). *How to stubbornly refuse to make yourself miserable about anything—Yes, anything!* New York: Lyle Stuart/Carol Publishing Group. (paperback)

Johnson, D. W. (1986). *Reaching out: Interpersonal effectiveness and self-actualization* (3rd ed.). Englewood Cliffs, NJ: Prentice-Hall. (paperback)

Lazarus, A., & Fay, A. (1988). *I can if I want to.* New York: Warner Books. (paperback)

Ornstein, R., & Sobel, D. (1990). *Healthy pleasures.* Reading, MA: Addison-Wesley.

Viorst, J. (1987). *Necessary losses: The loves, illusions, dependencies, and impossible illusions that all of us have to give up in order to grow.* New York: Fawcett Gold Medal. (paperback)

Watson, D. L., & Tharp, R. G. (1989). *Self-directed behavior: Self-modification for personal adjustment* (5th ed.). Pacific Grove, CA: Brooks/Cole.

The Meaning of Personal Growth

Abe Arkoff

Imagine yourself in this situation: You are an illegitimate, six-year-old child. Your mother is a deaf-mute. You have spent most of your life with your mother in a dark room separated from the rest of your mother's family. What kind of person would you be and become?

Isabelle (a pseudonym) actually spent the first part of her life in the condition just noted. When she was discovered at the age of six, she appeared to be half infant and half wild animal. The professionals who examined her concluded she was feeble-minded and uneducable. Fortunately, they decided to try. A year and a half later Isabelle had blossomed into a "very bright, cheerful, and energetic little girl." At the time of the last report, she was fourteen, doing well, and had just passed the sixth grade (Davis, 1940, 1947).

There appears to be a strong impulse to grow in every person (as indeed there was in Isabelle). We desire to be more than we are. Each of us will have our own idea of what we wish to become. Perhaps more informed and knowledgeable, or more understanding and loving, or more capable and creative, or more joyful and serene.

On the path of growth, sometimes we trudge and sometimes we leap ahead. We occasionally have a growth spurt when we make rapid progress and we have an exhilarating sense of being more than we were. It may be a particular summer or year when everything seems to be going just right or it may involve a particular relationship in which we find an enlarged sense of ourselves.

Just as there is a strong impulse to grow, there are strong impediments to growth. Rarely are they as complete and obvious as in the case of Isabelle. But there are growth blocks or impasses in which we are frustrated and seem unable to progress at all. There are even growth reversals—times when we appear to regress and give up hard-earned gains.

Personal growth, as it is defined here, is simply change in a desired or valued direction. Values, of course, vary from person to person. I may feel I have grown when I have freed myself from dependence on my parents. You may experience personal growth when you change your conception of yourself and begin to respond to the world in a new and freer way. My parents, however, may not agree that my new-found autonomy is growth, and your spouse may be threatened by your new self-definition and put pressure on you to revert to the person you were.

Potentiality refers to inherent capacity for growth. What's possible for us? What can we become? What can keep us from becoming all we wish to become? How can we find a path of growth that's right for us? These are some of the questions we will consider in the material that follows.

THE POTENTIAL FOR GROWTH

A Russian scientist has estimated that with our brain working at only half capacity, we could learn 40 languages with no difficulty (Otto, 1972). Many of us, however, find it something of a struggle to learn more than 1. From this perspective, we certainly seem to be less than we could be.

What has come to be called the "human potential movement" began during the 1960s and was dedicated to helping people make the most of their capacities. An underlying assumption—sometimes called "the human potential hypothesis"—was that most people function at only a small fraction of their potential. A further assumption was that by proceeding in certain ways much more of this potential could be realized.

Nearly a century ago William James, one of the earliest American psychologists, estimated that humans, on the average, functioned at about 10% of their capacity. Later, anthropologist Margaret Mead put this figure at 6%. Human potentialist Herbert Otto's original estimate of average fulfillment was a modest 5%, which he later reduced to 4%. He writes that the estimated percentage has been decreasing because "we are discovering that every human being has more powers, resources, and abilities than we suspected ten years ago, five years ago" (1972, p. 14).

A trio of psychologists—Arthur Combs, Donald Avila, and William Purkey (1978)—maintain that human beings are "overbuilt." They write, "One of the most exciting discoveries of this generation is the idea that human capacity is far greater than anything ever thought possible. The fascinating thing about human beings is *not* their limitations, but their immense capabilities.... From everything we can observe, it seems clear that few of us ever remotely approach the potentialities for effective behavior that lie within us. Most of us use but a small fraction of our capabilities" (pp. 69–70, 71).

Norman Cousins administered his own recovery from a supposedly incurable illness. In looking back on this experience, he wrote that what he had learned was to "never underestimate the capacity of the human mind and body to regenerate—even when the prospects seem most wretched" (1977, p. 5). Later, in looking back on his entire life, he wrote,

> What, then, have I learned? The most important thing I think I have learned is that human capacity is infinite, that no challenge is beyond comprehension and useful response. I have learned that the uniqueness of human beings is represented by the absence of any ceiling over intellectual or moral development. In this sense, the greatest gains achieved by the species are not connected to the discovery of nuclear fission or the means by which humans can be liberated from earth gravity. The greatest gains are related to expanding knowledge about the human brain itself. (1980, p. 10)

One of the most optimistic of the human potentialists is Will Schutz (1979). "As human beings," he writes, "we are without limit" (p. 25). In his opinion, the limits we experience are "limits of belief" but not "limits of the human organism." He points out that there are pragmatic advantages to assuming that one is limitless: "If indeed I am truly limitless, and I assume I am, then I may discover that limitlessness. On the other hand, every limit I assume I have prevents me from discovering whether that limit is in fact real" (p. 26). Claim a limit, Richard Bach says, and it's yours.

Despite these enthusiastic voices, optimism about human potentiality is not widespread.

Psychiatrist Cornelis Bakker (1975) has observed a deep sense of pessimism in some quarters concerning basic personality change. Bakker calls this "the myth of unchangeability." It is a myth to which some persons in mental health subscribe when they see dramatic improvements that somehow do not last. It is a myth held by parents who look at their adult child and see what appears to be almost the same personality that was present at age seven or eight. It is a myth any one of us might tend to embrace as we see ourselves wrestling with seemingly the same basic problems year after year or decade after decade.

Bakker has found "a good deal of evidence" to support the thesis that "people are extremely changeable" (p. 164). He feels there are two reasons why the myth of unchangeability persists. One reason is the long-standing hypothesis in Western culture that each person has a basic essence or soul or personality or character which biases the observer against perceiving change. The second reason is there are a number of stabilizing factors that can keep people the same if they allow this to happen. Some of these stabilizing factors are considered later in the section concerning obstacles to growth.

Support for Bakker's thesis is provided by George Vaillant's study (1977) of a group of Harvard students. Vaillant followed this group from college age to about age 50 and found their lives were "full of surprises" and even "startling change and evolutions" (p. 372). Quite notable was a subset of men in the study who had very serious psychological problems, which they dealt with by themselves to arrive at quite satisfactory patterns of adjustment.

Not all students of human nature are convinced that the myth of unchangeability is fully a myth. One of the most eloquent of these is psychologist Bernie Zilbergeld (1983). From his examination of the evidence, he arrives at conclusions far different from Bakker. Summing up, he writes that "people are very difficult to change" and "there are limits to how much each of us can change." In his opinion, "the limits of human malleability are much closer to the ground than they are to the sky" (p. 247). He adds that we may have to question utopian notions and give up our ideas about what is possible for humans.

However, there is a silver lining to Zilbergeld's dark cloud. Although he believes that human beings are difficult to change, he also concludes that there is not as much need for change as is commonly thought. He makes a strong case that many of the most creative and productive persons—Charles Darwin, Abraham Lincoln, Goethe, William James, August Strindberg, Virginia Woolf, Van Gogh, Einstein, etc.—were laden with personal problems and far from "normal." Zilbergeld believes that people don't need fixing as much as they need to change their unrealistic notions of what life can be. He writes, "Much of what we think of as problems—things that ought to be altered and for which there are solutions—are not so much problems as inescapable limits and predicaments of life" (p. 251).

The Impulse to Grow

A point emphasized by the human potentialists is that we have not only a considerable potential for growth but also a powerful impulse to make the most of this potential. Albert Szent-Gyoergyi, a research biologist who twice was awarded the Nobel Prize, has written that it would be impossible to approach the data he had observed without supposing that there is an "innate drive in living matter to perfect itself" (1974, p. 14). A number of personality theorists have similarly hypothesized an "actualizing tendency" in humans, that is, a drive toward growth, enhancement, and perfection.

Carl Rogers (1975) wrote that each living organism is born with "an inherent tendency to develop all his/her capacities in ways that serve to maintain or enhance the organism. " And, he added, each has an inherent wisdom that allows differentiation between experiences that do or do not further the actualization process.

Abraham Maslow (1970) put it succinctly when he wrote what we *can* be, we *must* be. We must be true to ourselves—to our basic nature. Our capabilities are a promise that begs to be kept. Even if all our basic needs are met, we develop a restlessness, a discontent unless we are keeping that promise. As Maslow wrote, "A musician must make music, an artist must paint, a poet must write, if he is to be ultimately at peace with himself" (p. 46).

The Burden of Growth

Is the impulse to grow a blessing or a burden? Little Linus in a Peanuts comic strip once lamented his own situation, saying "there is no heavier burden than a great potential." Maslow (1972) cautioned his own students: "If you deliberately plan to be less than you are capable of being, then I warn you that you'll be deeply unhappy the rest of your life" (p. 36).

In one of her books, Eda LeShan (1976) eloquently describes her own feelings of guilt for not having made more of her own childhood opportunities for growth:

> Many years ago my husband [psychologist Lawrence LeShan] explained to me the meaning of "ontological guilt." He told me it was the very worst kind. It means feeling guilty because one is not living one's own life, fulfilling one's own potentials. As the years have passed I have come to understand this more deeply, and it accounts for my awful sensitivity about examining my own adolescence; I have too much ontological guilt.
>
> The problem is that no matter how much one learns about human fallibility, compassion and acceptance are still hard to come by. When I became deeply depressed at the prospect of having to write this chapter, I said to Larry, "I can't forgive myself for the fact that I was a coward; that I didn't have the guts to fight harder to become free, when that's what I should have been doing." His answer was, "You have nothing to forgive yourself for. You were a nice person—decent and brave—and you couldn't bear to hurt your parents when you know how much they loved you. You made a sacrifice which you later discovered had cost you too much—but it was done out of tenderness, and you have had the courage to fight for your own growth ever since." (p. 128)

In her notebook, Jungian analyst Florida Scott-Maxwell (1968) writes of our need to "live our strengths." She recalls that a client once told her: "I don't mind your telling me my faults, they're stale, but don't tell me my virtues. When you tell me what I could be, it terrifies me" (p. 22).

In her book *Smart Girls, Gifted Women*, Barbara Kerr (1987) takes gifted women to task for not achieving their full potentiality. She maintains that women "are too well adjusted for their own good. They are great at adjusting resourcefully and congenially to whatever situation is handed to them" (p. 5). Kerr herself was criticized for not accepting the women's own choices, but she stuck to her guns suggesting that self-actualization is more than right—it is a responsibility.

The human potentialists and, indeed, the entire field of psychotherapy have been criticized for tending to make people dissatisfied with themselves. Like some other industries that sell their products by convincing people they are not all they should be or can be—that they don't look right or smell right or are not always free of aches and anxieties—potentialists may create or exacerbate the very conditions or dissatisfactions they seek to correct.

Schutz (1979) takes a view contrary to those who see potential as a burden. He understands his own assumption of "human limitlessness" is frequently resisted since there is an implied demand that one live up to one's potential. He maintains there is no obligation to be everything of which one is capable. "If I wish," he writes, "I can choose to feel inadequate because I have not realized myself fully. But it is not inherent in the assumption of limitlessness that failure to achieve all that is possible must lead to feelings of guilt and depression" (p. 26).

Those who have been stuck on life's path—at impasses, up blind alleys, forever marking time, caught up in maintenance, low-level enterprises, getting by perhaps but not getting anywhere—will know the burden that the potentialists write about. Those who have gotten themselves "unstuck" and suddenly able to make more, maybe much more of their lives will know the exhilaration that comes when one is becoming more and more who one can be.

SUCCESS AND FAILURE IN GROWTH

Not long ago, one of my friends was telling me about an old acquaintance who was going to visit him soon. It was someone with whom he had gone to college but who afterward never seemed to make very much of his life. This acquaintance had never married and had moved from job to job in the same industry but none very much different or better from the other. From the outside, at least, it looked like not very much of a life.

A character in Anne Tyler's novel *Breathing Lessons* is rather taken aback when her daughter asks her, "Mom? Was there a certain conscious point in your life when you decided to settle for being ordinary?" Do any of us prepare ourselves for an "ordinary" life? What would you have answered if someone at your high-school graduation asked if you would be willing "to settle for being ordinary?"

Thinking it over, I wonder how my friend's acquaintance regarded his life. Did he see it as disappointingly ordinary, comfortably ordinary, or not ordinary at all—which is the way Tyler's character responded as she recalled the incident with a friend: "It got to me," she said. . . . "I mean, to *me* I'm not ordinary."

I have never been to a high school or college reunion, but more faithful alumni have told me one of the attractions is learning what one's classmates have done with their lives. How high have they climbed on the ladder of success? What have they accomplished? Who have they married? How much have they changed? (One woman told me she went to see how much hair had gone from the heads of her ex-beaus and how much flesh had gathered on the hips of her old rivals.)

Two better alumni than I, Michael Medved and David Wallechinsky made a study of their high school class 10 years after graduation. They published it as *What Really Happened to the Class of '65?* The class happened to be the one *Time* magazine featured in its cover story "Today's Teenagers," who were said to be then "on the fringe of a golden era." Instead, the 10 years proved to be a sad and turbulent decade that included the second Kennedy assassination, drugs, the draft, and the Vietnam War.

During the decade, some alumni continued to blossom, some were transformed, and others met with tragedy. The alumna who had been voted "the most outstanding woman" of the class got her doctorate and a professorship at Princeton. The young man voted "most reserved" earned a degree in engineering and became a Krishna devotee. The quarterback of the football team, "an athletic ladies' man," became a Hollywood masseur. "The grind" went on to graduate from Stanford, drop out of graduate school at UCLA, and then was under intensive care at a state psychiatric institution. The member of the class voted "most popular"—an all-Western League End and baseball team captain—committed suicide.

Ten years later, Wallechinsky did a second survey on the class of '65, but this time not just his own high school. He traveled all over the country and surveyed a varied sample of his generation of age peers. Out of this came a book *Midterm Report*, which includes a report card on his generation midway in life. How do you judge a whole generation? Wallechinsky's criterion: "Did they leave the world in a better condition than they found it?" After considering what the generation had done for culture, education, freedom, peace and security, technology, environment, and standard of living, he awarded it the midterm grade of B. But as he pointed out, the final grade—which was still to be determined—is the more important one.

Continuing the matter of prefinal grades, Gail Sheehy (1981) reviewed the lives of some of history's greats and found they often seemed to be and thought themselves to be failures at some time in their lives. The career of British statesman and author Benjamin Disraeli was described as "failure, failure, partial success, renewed failure, ultimate and complete triumph" (Sheehy, p. 386). Robert Rhodes James titled his biography of Winston Churchill *Churchill: A Study in Failure* because Churchill's career appeared to have ended in complete failure before it renewed and outdid itself. Golda Meir failed as a wife and was far from a model mother but became the mother figure of Israel.

Meir was a failure as a homebody but a success as a public person, and many of society's or history's greats were notable failures in one or more aspects of their personal lives. Charles Darwin, Lord Byron, Shelly, and Tennyson were all hypochondriacs. Ernest Hemingway, Jack London, Edgar Alan Poe, F. Scott Fitzgerald, John O'Hara, William Faulkner, Edwin Arlington Robinson, Eugene O'Neil, James Joyce, Sinclair Lewis, Jack Kerouac, Raymond Chandler, and Thomas Wolfe were alcoholics. Virginia Wolf, Sylvia Plath, George Eastman, Van Gogh, and also Hemingway and London took their own lives (Zilbergeld, 1983).

The memory of Martin Luther King, Jr., has been said by some to have been tarnished by posthumous revelations of promiscuity and plagiarism, but King was highly critical of himself. In one sermon, he said, "You don't need to go out this morning saying that Martin Luther King is a saint. I want you to know this morning that I am a sinner like all of God's children, but I want to be a good man and I want to hear a voice saying to me one day, 'I take you in and I bless you because you tried.'" Neither we nor those who inspire us will be without failure and flaws, but the weeds in our gardens need not choke out the flowers. Speaking of King, Ellen Goodman (1990) writes, "Here was a man, an ordinary man, with human strengths and weaknesses. But when the time came and much was demanded of him, he found the greatness within himself. . . . and he changed the world we live in" (p. A-16).

Inspiration for Growth

Much of our learning as children is through observation and modeling. We learn by watching others and patterning our behavior after them. We are especially influenced by those who are important in our lives or who are receiving rewards we covet or who have qualities we admire.

The persons we pattern ourselves after are *role models*. These models give us a sense of what's possible for us and who we can become. For example, we can grow up and be like our mother or father and do what she or he does. Some models, however, convey a sense of the limits and fallibilities of human beings. If they somehow haven't amounted to much, maybe we can't or won't either.

The terms *role model* and *hero* or *heroine* are sometimes used interchangeably, but a useful distinction can be made between them. Our role models are those we aspire to be like or who at least have qualities we seek. Heroes and heroines are those who make the world better, but they are not necessarily those we want to be like or even feel we could be like. Hero and heroine, as terms, were once reserved for mythical figures and later for real but larger-than-life personages, but these terms are increasingly used to describe those we greatly admire.

Our first role models and heroes and heroines are likely to be our parents and, a little later, our teachers. When psychologist Frank Farley had 340 University of Wisconsin students rank their top five heroes and heroines, the run-away winners were the students' parents. Moms did best, gathering six times more first-place votes than any other heroine. Dads received twice the first-place votes of any other hero (Stark, 1986).

"What man living today in any part of the world do you admire most?" Stop for a moment and arrive at your answer. When you have it, ask yourself who is the woman you most admire. In national polls that have posed this question over the years, nearly half of the male heroes have been presidents or other American political leaders and similarly nearly half the women have been first ladies or other American political figures. Foreign political leaders and religious leaders were also high in the rankings for both sexes (Smith, 1986).

When *Newsweek*'s Charles Leerhsen (1990) asked adolescents at five very different schools (an Indiana military academy, a Bronx eighth grade, a Dallas girls' school, a Midwestern high school, a South Dakota Indian reservation school) to write down their heroes, he got something of a shock. Most frequently mentioned: basketball star Michael Jordan. A number of commentators on the recent scene have lamented that there is an absence of true heroes. Instead we have cult celebrities: sport figures, rock stars, movie idols (Roche, 1988; Walden, 1986). These figures exalt competition, winning, success, power, prestige but not sacrifice, valor, and commitment to some larger good or purpose.

To my friend sociologist Earl Babbie (1985), a hero is somebody who willingly assumes responsibility for working on a public problem. In his book *You Can Make a Difference*, Babbie points out the extraordinary contributions made by ordinary people to make this world a better place in which to live. Among Babbie's heroes are Candy Lightner, who formed MADD (Mothers Against Drunk Drivers) after her daughter was killed by a drunk driver; Helen Caldicott, whose Physicians for Social Responsibility has become a mainstay of the movement against nuclear weapons; and 11-year-old Trevor Ferrell, who became for awhile a special person on the streets of Philadelphia by initiating and leading a drive to provide food, clothing, and shelter for local street people. Babbie believes each of us can make a difference. We each have hero potential.

Obstacles to Growth

Why don't we make more of ourselves and our lives? Why don't we realize more of our potential? These are important questions, and ones many philosophers and psychologists, and stuck, bewildered souls have pondered.

A Diminished Conception of Ourselves. One reason we don't make more of ourselves is that we may have a diminished view of who we are and what we can become. To some extent, we are who we *think* we are, and some of us may not think we're much. Although research suggests we are more likely to overestimate than underestimate ourselves, two psychologists, Ellen Langer and Carol Dweck (1973) write, "We maintain that there are few, if any, of us who have a truly satisfying self-concept. People occasionally put on a good show and seem to others to be on top of it all, but these very same people often think: 'if they only knew the real me'" (p. 29).

The basic goal of many personal growth programs and psychotherapies is to get the individuals concerned to enhance their self-concept and to accept, love, and prize themselves more. A basic goal of some transpersonal approaches is to inspire persons with awe or reverence for themselves and their place in the universe. As such individuals come to see more in themselves, they attempt and accomplish more, and accomplishing more they further enhance their conception of themselves.

The following true story (recalled by a woman psychologist from her prepsychology days) indicates how important an obstacle a negative self-concept can be, and how a positive self-concept can both instigate and stem from growth:

> I was living out in San Francisco at the time. While coming home from work one day I got involved in an accident and required the attention of a doctor. A friend of mine mentioned the accident to his friend, an eager, but not yet established, young lawyer. The lawyer contacted me, and then proceeded to persuade me that I had a case and that he was the one to handle it.
>
> That was the way I met Hank. The impression I got of him after talking over the phone for the next week or so was that he was enthusiastic, good humored, and sort of charming. When he came over to my house to discuss the case further, I had

to add unattractive to the list of adjectives.

After we concluded our discussion of business matters, we got involved in a friendly and rather personal conversation. Hank had recently come to San Francisco from New York. He was divorced and was eager to tell me about the marvelous changes in his life. It seemed that his ex-wife had constantly told him how ugly he was. I thought that that was both cruel and accurate—but kept the latter thought to myself. Hank explained how inhibited this made him with other people. "I had little confidence in myself and was enormously shy." I said I couldn't believe that he was very shy. He recounted some experiences he had had at parties and with clients to convince me. He was successful in gaining my sympathy.

Then he told me how different he was now. He had traveled across the country with the thought that he just might not be as homely looking as she said—so he took some risks. He gradually improved his opinion of himself. He put this a little differently though: "I slowly started to recognize how wrong she was. Now I know I'm good looking. When I walk into a room people take notice of me and believe it or not (I didn't) the girls are all over me at parties." We talked some more, and then a horn started honking outside. He said it was his new girlfriend picking him up. We went over to the terrace to see if it were she—it was, and she was simply beautiful. For a moment I couldn't believe the whole episode. What was even more bewildering was that I started finding him attractive.

Although Hank's somewhat dramatic tale is not unique, most people with negative self-concepts never bother to test out other hypotheses about themselves, as he did. While at first he accepted his wife's opinion as indisputable truth, he later formulated an alternative positive view, "I am *not* ugly," and set out to confirm it. Now Hank tells people how to respond to him. His new manner has an air of confidence, and the subtle and not so subtle cues are effective. It is not surprising that most people listen. (Langer and Dweck, 1973, pp. 40–42)

A Fixed Conception of Ourselves. A second reason we don't grow as much as we might is that we fix our conception of ourself. We begin to think, "Well, I've always been this way." We each begin to think of ourself as a person who can do this but can't do that. In this situation, growth concedes to "destiny."

To find out where our "I've always been this way" originated, Bloomfield and Kory (1980) recommend that we quiz the significant others of our childhood days. How did they see us? What labels did they apply to us? We may hear from their lips the same labels we have come to apply to ourselves. If we announce we're going to change, how do they respond? Does their response seem to say: "Lots of luck and you'll need it because 'you've always been this way.'" For illustration, here is a case presented by Bloomfield and Kory:

> John, a college student, complains, "I can count the number of dates I've had on one hand and not run out of fingers." He's obviously got a sense of humor, but he is afraid to be himself around women. "I'm shy," he says. "That's my nature." John recalls his mother telling people that he was "the shy one." He never realized that his mother had an emotional investment in keeping him tied to her apron strings. John spent his childhood and adolescence living up to the family label of "the shy one." No doubt he had a tendency to be shy as a little boy, but with their labeling, his parents helped him develop that tendency into a full-blown personality characteristic. The question is whether John is going to continue justifying his fears of women with the rationale: "Shyness is my nature." (p. 167)

A fixed notion of who we are can easily result when we continue to move around in the same old sub-environments that call forth the same old response. We can develop a kind of comfort in leading our familiar life and in being our familiar self. To change and grow might bring welcome hope and pleasurable excitement, but it might also bring unwelcome anxiety. More about this in the material that follows.

The Need for Safety. A third obstacle to growth concerns an unwillingness to leave safe places. Maslow (1968) hypothesized that in addition to growth forces, each person also has safety forces and these two sets work in opposition to each other. Maslow noted that the conflict between these forces could block the individual. He diagrammed this process as follows:

Safety <———< PERSON>———> Growth

Elaborating on these opposing forces, Maslow wrote,

> Every human being has *both* sets of forces within him. One set clings to safety and defensiveness out of fear, tending to regress backward, hanging on to

the past, *afraid* to grow away from the primitive communication with the mother's uterus and breast, *afraid* to take chances, *afraid* to jeopardize what he already has, *afraid* of independence, freedom and separateness. The other set of forces impels him forward toward wholeness of Self and uniqueness of Self, toward full functioning of all his capacities, toward confidence in the face of the external world at the same time that he can accept his deepest, real, unconscious Self. (p. 46)

Maslow noted that both safety and growth have drawbacks and attractions for the individual. The person grows when the drawbacks of safety and the attractions of growth are greater than the attractions of safety and the drawbacks of growth. Parents, teachers, and therapists sometimes are able to step in to change the weight of safety and growth vectors. As our conception of ourselves is enhanced, safety becomes less attractive and necessary and growth becomes more attractive and even irresistible.

When I consider the lives of my mother and father, it is easier for me to think of my mother's life as a success. Both my parents were immigrants, my mother from Latvia, my father from Russia. Both were looking for better lives in a new land, and both made their way to a small Midwestern city where they found each other, married, and raised five children.

Success in life, according to Freud's barebones set of criteria, requires success in loving and working, but I never felt my father found his true work or calling. He was a brilliant and spiritual man who would have been fulfilled as a rabbi or teacher. Instead, for almost all of his adult life, he spent six-and-one-half long days a week in a little store, an occupation for which he exhibited little zest or talent. In his late-middle years, he became for awhile quite depressed—his response, I believe, to his inability to move his life along.

Some years ago, I went back to my home town just to wander again around old boyhood places. My parents were long since dead, and no relatives or close friends remained, but I found a man who had known my father quite well. We had coffee together and talked about the old days. He remembered how my father had been a force in the usually rabbi-less Jewish community and one who took it upon himself to round up 10 mostly reluctant men so that a Friday night sabbath prayer meeting could be held. "But," he added, "one thing about your father, he wasn't willing to take a chance. "

I wondered about that: my father, a man who went AWOL from the Czar's army and came to a far-away land whose language and culture was completely strange to him, who fell in love, married, started a business, had five children, became a pillar of his religious community. He had taken chances, made commitments, achieved. What had happened to him along the way? How had he gotten so mired, so stuck?

In her book *Pathfinders*, Gail Sheehy describes a group of "people of high well being"— those who successfully negotiate the crises of life. She concludes that the "master quality" possessed by pathfinders is their willingness to take risks. In her study of lives she found that a continuing sense of well-being generally required a continual willingness to risk change. Similar findings came out of a longitudinal study of men and women by social scientists at the University of California at San Francisco (Lowenthal, 1980). Although the researcher expected those adults who showed a strong sense of continuity in values and goals would show the greatest sense of well-being, instead it was those who demonstrated change.

The Fear of Growth. A fourth obstacle to growth concerns fear of what growth may bring. A number of students of human nature have noted an absolute fear of growth in some individuals. Why should some of us fear to grow? One reason may be that we fear the unknown. Even if we do not like or are not comfortable with who we are, at least, we are accustomed to ourselves. We hesitate to risk what we have (even though it's not all we want) to get something that may be less or worse.

A second reason we fear growth is that we may see growth as bringing responsibilities we doubt we will be able to meet. If we succeed, more will be expected of us and we may doubt our ability to continually meet these expectations. "The higher you climb, the harder you fall," we tell ourselves, "so maybe it's better not to reach too high. "

There is a third fear of growth that Maslow (1971) called "the Jonah Complex." This complex (named after Jonah who wound up in the whale when he ran from a mission he had been given from on high) refers to our fear of our own greatness. Maslow hypothesized that in the presence of very special individuals (saintly persons, geniuses, beauties, etc.) we may tend to feel uneasy, envious, or inferior and therefore countervalue (or depreciate) them or their qualities. Maslow suggests that if we could bring ourselves "to love more purely the highest values in others," we would become better able to discover and love and make the most of these qualities in ourselves.

SOME ARENAS OF GROWTH

Every arena of life offers opportunity for growth and development. Among the more notable or more scrutinized are college and psychotherapy.

Personal Growth in College[1]

Considerable study has been made of the personal growth that occurs during the college years. This growth is not necessarily due to college itself but might be expected in gifted adults whether or not they continue academic work past high school. However, the college experience can act as a catalyst or facilitator, accelerating changes that would have occurred anyway, but at a slower pace.

Intellect, Knowledge, and Learning. One change noted in college students concerns intellectual ability. Contrary to common belief, all persons do not reach their intellectual ceiling during their teens. The research evidence indicates brighter individuals develop faster and longer than those less gifted. This suggests many students will continue to grow intellectually during their time in college.

The research evidence shows general verbal and quantitative skills do improve during the college years. Seniors are superior to freshmen in speaking and writing. Seniors are also more able to think critically (weigh evidence and distinguish between weak and strong arguments) and make reflective judgments (use reason and evidence to decide controversial issues). Seniors

1. This section is largely based on a review by Pascarella and Terenzini, 1991. Other sources include Arkoff, 1968; Kuh et al., 1988; and Perry, 1981.

also demonstrate more intellectual flexibility (see different sides of complex issues).

The longer students attend college, the more knowledgeable they become. The more courses they take in a particular area of knowledge, the higher their score on tests of knowledge in that area. It's reassuring that not everything disappears after the final exams.

Educational Values. Notable changes in attitudes and values take place as students progress through their undergraduate years. Education is increasingly valued for its own sake rather than as simply an avenue to a vocation or higher standard of living. More value is also placed on the intrinsic rewards promised by a career (challenge, autonomy, adventure, etc.) and less on extrinsic ones (job security, compensation, perquisites, etc.).

Liberal education is increasingly appreciated as students move through college. They become more interested in arts and humanities. There is also more interest in classical music, theater, creative writing, and philosophical and historical issues.

Autonomy and Internality. Autonomy and internality grow during college. Students become more independent of their parents although not necessarily more independent of their peers. A number of my commuter students have told me that as freshmen they relied considerably on their parents and a continuing circle of high-school friends, but as the semesters went by they became increasingly detached from both of these sources of influence.

Students become more internal in their locus of control; that is, they see themselves as more able to influence outcomes and produce results. They feel increasingly in charge of their own lives and responsible for what happens in them. They become more their own persons.

For some students the increased autonomy and responsibility is desired and sought, but for others it is imposed and the necessity for it comes as something of a shock. Freshmen find college provides less structure than high school, and no one keeps after them to do what must be done. Financial assistance may be limited or absent making students largely or wholly responsible for their own support.

Relations to Oneself and Others. With an increase in self-sufficiency comes an increase in self-esteem. As students proceed in college, they develop a surer and more positive image of themselves, and scores on tests measuring anxiety and neuroticism recede. Relationships with others including those of the opposite-sex become more mature.

Some of the increasing and more positive sense of self comes from a growing academic efficacy. Later semesters are generally less difficult than early ones. Early semesters can be bruising as students struggle to learn the ropes or to find purpose or direction. One of my students who is a junior recently told me when he began college, studying was all he did and just to keep his head above water. Now, in addition to his study time, there is job time, exercise time, and leisure time.

Moral and Ethical Reasoning. Research indicates that there is a maturing of moral reasoning or judgment during the college years. Specifically, there is some shifting from what has been called "conventional" judgment to "post-conventional" judgment. Conventional judgments are those made according to the expectations of others and the rules or laws of society. Postconventional judgments are made according to moral principles and override agreements, rules, or laws; these principles are selected by individuals themselves but are assumed to have universal applicability. Postconventional judgments take into account the uniqueness, dignity, and well-being of the individual.

Many students come to college expecting to learn what is right or true. As they progress, they learn there is not always a right answer, that different views can be taken, and it may seem that nothing is certain. Ultimately students see there are things about which they must make up their own minds, and they must make commitments but also be open to new evidence that presents itself (Perry, 1981). As one student put it, "It took me quite a while to figure out that if I was going for something to believe in, it had to come from within me" (Perry, 1981, p. 92).

Authoritarianism and Dogmatism. Along with an increasing interest and exposure to liberal education, students become more liberal in their social and political attitudes. The college experience causes students to mull over previously unchallenged and unexamined ideas in these areas. The greater the exposure to dissimilar thoughts and beliefs, the greater the challenge.

Generally, students become less narrow-minded, less authoritarian and dogmatic. *Authoritarianism* refers to attitudes that are antidemocratic and anti-intellectual and that favor submission to authority; students become more critical of authority and more favorable to democratic and intellectual process. *Dogmatism* refers to belief systems that are closed and not receptive or responsive to change or to nonconforming or conflicting beliefs; students become more open to the consideration of new and different beliefs as they proceed through college.

Prejudice. There is a lessening of prejudice during the college years. *Ethnocentrism*—considering one's own ethnic group as superior to others—diminishes. Students become less likely to resort to stereotypes in evaluating a person of another class or culture or race. They are more likely to consider this person an individual on her or his own merits. Both males and females move away from sex-role stereotypes and become more sensitive to the expanding roles the sexes may play in modern-day society.

Religiosity. There is generally a lessening of religious belief and practice during the college years, and this is more likely and more pronounced at secular institutions. There is some movement away from doctrinaire religious views and a greater tolerance for the religious views of others. Students living away from home show the greatest change; those remaining at home are more insulated from the potentially challenging views of other students and more likely to continue familial religious patterns.

General Change. The college years are both broadening and leavening. Pascarella and Terenzini (1991) note the progress made in college is "away from a personal perspective characterized by constraint, narrowness, exclusiveness, simplicity, and intolerance and toward a perspective with emphasis on greater individual freedom, breadth, inclusiveness, complexity and tolerance" (pp. 559–560). These observers further note an increasing "other-person orientation" and concern for individual rights and human welfare.

Factors Influencing Personal Growth in College. The greater a student's involvements in all aspects of college life, the greater the opportunity for personal growth. It has been estimated that over 70 percent of the learning one does at college is the result of out-of-class experience. New peer relationships, relationships with faculty, and co-curricular activities are of considerable importance in promoting growth along with the acquisition of knowledge.

A sense of belongingness is vital to many students' satisfaction, academic success, and personal growth. This sense is more easily provided by small than large institutions, and small institutions also provide proportionally more opportunities for meaningful involvement. Commuter students who have not distanced themselves from their parents or high-school friends are less challenged to reconsider their beliefs. Also commuter students and part-time students are less likely than residential students to become involved in a wide range of campus activities that provide opportunities for growth; however, some nonresidential students are heavily involved in growth-provoking activities off campus.

Personal Growth in Therapy

I have been a therapist many years, and I have been in therapy myself three times during my life. The first time was in graduate school when each of us students entered counseling as a didactic or educational exercise. The second occasion was in my thirties when I seemed to be stuck and unable to move my personal life along. The third involved my whole family and came at a time when my wife and I were at our wit's end and ready to put our adolescent children out for adoption. Thinking back on this experience, I see how I grew quite a bit in the first, very little in the third (except in humbleness), but greatly in the second—when that particular experience was complete I was in some ways a crucially different human being.

There are so many different kinds of therapy and therapists and so many different reasons for entering therapy that it is difficult to generalize about the amount and kind of growth that occurs. It has been estimated that two out of every three people who undergo therapy benefit from it (Garfield, 1983). (That is somewhat in accord with my story since I entered therapy three times and benefited twice.) For many the gains are modest, but for some it can be the doorway to a fuller, richer life.

Carl Rogers (1961), one of the most eminent of all psychologists and therapists, has described how his clients have grown in therapy. His description seems relevant to the growth many of us experience, whether or not it is within a formal therapeutic relationship. Like Rogers' clients, we seem to be asking these two questions: "Who am I?" "How can I become myself?"

The first change Rogers noted in the persons he helped toward growth was that they became more open to their experience. They became less defensive and more able to put aside their masks. They became more aware of their own feelings and attitudes and could respond to the world around them without distortion or preconception.

A second change that Rogers observed in his clients was a growth of trust in themselves, which relates to and stems from the increased openness:

> ... When a client is open to his experience, he comes to find his organism more trustworthy. He feels less fear of the emotional reactions which he has. There is gradual growth of trust in, and even affections for, the complex, rich, varied assortment of feelings and tendencies which exist in him at the organic level. Consciousness, instead of being the watchman over a dangerous and unpredictable lot of impulses, of which few can be permitted to see the light of day, becomes the comfortable inhabitant of a society of impulses and feelings and thoughts, which are discovered to be very satisfactorily self-governing when not fearfully guarded. (p. 119)

A third change was that individuals in therapy increasingly accepted responsibility for making judgments about what was happening in their lives and for determining the directions their lives were to take. They depended less and less on others for approval or disapproval or for standards to live by or for choices and decisions. To see that one is responsible for one's own life, Rogers wrote, is both frightening and an invigorating realization.

The final change concerned the willingness to be a process rather than a finished, perfected product. Rogers noted that when persons entered therapy, they were likely to want to arrive at some fixed state of being or a place where their problems were fixed once and for all. In therapy, they came to accept they were fluid—not static entities—and capable of dealing with whatever arose in their lives. Rogers' clients replaced their need for fixity with the realization that they were and always would be in a "process of becoming."

PATHWAYS TO GROWTH

All of life is concerned with growth, as is all of this book. It would be impossible and unnecessary here to review every pathway to growth that has been proposed or pursued. But it may be helpful to distinguish between two main paths that have aroused some controversy.

One path to growth is an individual way. Its emphasis is on oneself and involves developing one's own potentiality and making the most of one's life and spirit. It is an essentially inner path, although it may move out like a widening spiral to encompass more than oneself.

A second path is an outer and collective path—one of social activism and change. It involves finding ways to change the institutions of society—for example, the home and school and marriage—to enhance the lives of all people. It involves taking responsibility for the betterment of everyone everywhere and especially those less fortunate than oneself.

Some advocates of the second path have called the first a "narcissistic" one because they view it as a selfish pursuit. To them, it is a kind of self-absorption when the times call for social change and the reconstruction of social agencies. They fear that in frustration, people are "searching within" when they should be "reaching out."

Proponents of the first path vigorously disagree. They feel that personal growth or enhancement is a necessary first step—that one cannot reach out if one's center is hollow. If one wants a better world, the way to begin is to make oneself a better or fuller person. They ask how those who do not and cannot respect and love and help themselves hope to relate to and help others.

Roberts Samples (1977) calls the first path "selfness." This is "the state in which self is celebrated in a nonexploitative mode." It is distinct from selfish, the exploitation of others for the benefit of oneself and also distinct from selfless, the exploitation of oneself for the benefit of others. He writes,

> The search for self, alone and in the quiet of one's own skills of introspection, is never done at the expense of the whole. A person who looks inward is no more a deviant from the whole than is a cloud from rivers and seas when one contemplates the water cycle. When one looks inward, it is difficult to avoid coming back more whole, more intact. Of course, here I exclude that small fringe group who look inward and stay there. When those who come back choose to enter a relationship, a community or a culture, they seldom bring a more despotic, more deficient human back into the action. Such people, with a fuller knowledge of their own strengths and limitations, are richer and closer to being psychically balanced and complete.
>
> It is these balanced humans who can be counted on to exercise the most basic kind of morality. I call it selfness. From this point, growth and being become a celebration of one's own person and the purity of all that is called humanness is then extended outward to the whole community of humankind. The extension of this process one day will hopefully eliminate the social and cultural inequities that currently exist—inequities nourished by leaders and followers whose psychic selves are empty. (p. 2)

There is, it seems, nothing essentially incompatible in the two paths. Service to others is a time-honored avenue to transcendence and so is the deep inner pursuit of oneself. One can grow from the inside out or from the outside in or both ways at once. There are many kinds of growth and many routes—each of us can find our own way.

References

Arkoff, A. (1968). *Adjustment and mental health*. New York: McGraw-Hill.

Astin, A. W. (1977). *Four critical years*. San Francisco: Jossey-Bass.

Babbie, E. (1985). *You can make a difference*. New York: St. Martin's Press.

Bakker, C. B. (1975). Why people don't change. *Psychotherapy: Theory, Research and Practice, 12*(2), 164–172.

Bloomfield, H. H., & Kory, R. B. (1980). *Inner joy.* New York: Wyden.

Combs, A. W., Avila, D. L., & Purkey, W. W. (1978). *Helping relationships: Basic concepts for the helping professions* (2nd ed.). Boston: Allyn and Bacon.

Cousins, N. (1977, May 28). Anatomy of an illness (as perceived by the patient). *Saturday Review,* pp. 4–6, 48–51.

Cousins, N. (1980, September). Capacity and control. *Saturday Review,* p. 10.

Davis, K. (1940). Extreme social isolation of a child. *American Journal of Sociology, 45,* 554–565.

Davis, K. (1947). Final note on a case of extreme isolation. *American Journal of Sociology, 52,* 432–437.

Feldman, K. A., & Newcomb, T. M. (1969a). *The impact of college on students: Vol. 1. An analysis of four decades of research.* San Francisco: Jossey-Bass.

Feldman, K. A., & Newcomb, T. M. (1969b). *The impact of college on students: Vol. 2. Summary tables.* San Francisco: Jossey-Bass.

Fiske, M. (1980). Changing hierarchies of commitment in adulthood. In N. J. Smelser & E. H. Erikson (Eds.), *Themes of work and love in adulthood* (pp. 238–264). Cambridge, MA: Harvard University Press.

Fulghum, R. (1990, Fall/Winter). A bag of possibles and other matters of the mind. *Newsweek,* pp. 88, 90, 92.

Garfield, S. L. (1983). *Clinical psychology: The study of personality and behavior* (2nd ed.). New York: Aldine.

Goodman, E. (1990, November 16). King and all those 'P-words.' *Honolulu Advertiser,* p. A-16.

Henry, M., with Renaud, H. (1972). Examined and unexamined lives. *Research Reporter, 7*(1), 5–8.

Katz, J., & Associates. (1968). *No time for youth: Growth and constraint in college students.* San Francisco: Jossey-Bass.

Kerr, B. (1986). *Smart girls, gifted women.* Columbus: Ohio Psychology Publishing.

Kuh, G. D., Krehbiel, L. E., & MacKay, K. (1988). *Personal development and the college student experience: A review of the literature.* Unpublished manuscript, prepared for the College Outcomes Evaluation Program, New Jersey Department of Higher Education, Trenton, New Jersey. Bloomington, IN: Department of Educational Leadership and Policy Studies, School of Education, Indiana University.

Kushel, G. (1979). *Centering: Six steps toward inner liberation.* New York: Times Books.

Langer, E. J., & Dweck, C. S. (1973). *Personal politics: The psychology of making it.* Englewood Cliffs, NJ: Prentice-Hall.

Leehrsen, C. (1990, February 5). Unite and conquer. *Newsweek,* pp. 50–55.

LeShan, E. J. (1976). *In search of myself and other children.* New York: M. Evans.

Maslow, A. H. (1968). *Toward a psychology of being* (2nd ed.). New York: Van Nostrand Reinhold.

Maslow, A. H. (1970). *Motivation and personality* (2nd ed.). New York: Harper & Row.

Maslow, A. H. (1972). *The farther reaches of human nature.* New York: Viking.

Medved, M., & Wallechinsky, D. (1976). *What really happened to the Class of '65?* New York: Random House.

Otto, H. A. (1972). New light on human potential. In College of Home Economics, Iowa State University (Ed.), *Families of the future* (pp. 14–25). Ames: Iowa State University Press.

Otto, H. A. (1974). *A guide to developing your potential.* North Hollywood, CA: Wilshire Book.

Pascarella, E. T., & Terenzini, P. T. (1991). *How college affects students: Findings and insights from twenty years of research.* San Francisco: Jossey-Bass.

Perry, W. G., Jr. (1981). Cognitive and ethical growth: The making of meaning. In A. W. Chickering (Ed.), *The modern American college* (pp. 76–116). San Francisco: Jossey-Bass.

Roche, G. (1988, November). A world without heroes. *USA Today*, pp. 57–59.

Rogers, C. R. (1961). *On becoming a person* (pp. 107–124). Boston: Houghton Mifflin.

Rogers, C. R. (1975). Client-centered psychotherapy. In A. M. Freedman, H. I. Kaplan, & B. J. Sadock (Eds.), *Comprehensive textbook of psychiatry* (Vol. 2, pp. 1831–1843). Baltimore: Williams & Wilkins.

Samples, B. (1977, May). Selfness: Seeds of a transformation. *AHP Newsletter*, pp. 1–2.

Schutz, W. (1979). *Profound simplicity.* New York: Bantam.

Scott-Maxwell, F. (1968). *The measure of my days.* New York: Knopf.

Sheehy, G. (1981). *Pathfinders.* New York: William Morrow.

Smith, T. W. The polls: The most admired man and woman. *Public Opinion Quarterly, 50*(4), 573–583.

Stark, E. (1986, May). Mom and dad: The great American heroes (survey conducted by Frank Farley). *Psychology Today*, pp. 12–13.

Szent-Gyoergyi, A. (1974). Drive in living matter to perfect itself. *Synthesis, 1*, 14–26.

Vaillant, G. E. (1977). *Adaptation to life.* Boston: Little, Brown.

Walden, D. (1986, January). Where have all our heroes gone? *USA Today*, pp. 20–25.

Wallechinsky, D. (1986). *Midterm report: The class of '65—Chronicles of an American generation.* New York: Viking.

Webster, H., Freedman, M. B., & Heist, P. (1962). Personality changes in college students. In N. Sanford (Ed.), *The American college* (pp. 811–846). New York: Wiley.

Zilbergeld, B. (1983). *The shrinking of America: Myths of psychological change.* Boston: Little, Brown.

To Apply This Reading to Yourself

1. *Do you now believe, or have you ever believed "the myth of unchangeability"? If so, give your reasons, and indicate the effect of this myth on you.*

2. *Do you have any sense of a drive within yourself toward growth, enhancement, or perfection? Discuss this aspect of yourself.*

3. *Have you felt any guilt because of your failure to make more of yourself or a nostalgia for the person you might have become? Discuss this aspect of yourself.*

4. *Would you be willing to settle for an "ordinary life"? Why or why not? If not, what would it take to make your life acceptably "extraordinary"?*

5. *Consider the various areas of your life—home, school, work, recreation, social relationships, community services, spirituality, and so on. In which areas are you growing, and in which are you stuck or failing to grow? Why?*

6. *Discuss your own role models, heroes, or heroines, and indicate their influence on you.*

7. *What obstacles to growth have you found in yourself? What have you done about them?*

8. *Are you a risk-taker or a security-seeker? What are the relative strengths of safety and growth forces in your life? Discuss this aspect of yourself.*

9. *Describe the personality change or personal growth you have noted in yourself during your high school and/or college years.*
10. *If you have been in therapy, discuss the changes or growth that took place in you during and/or after this process.*
11. *Compare yourself to Rogers' clients as they emerge from therapy by discussing these aspects of yourself: (a) openness to experience, (b) trust in yourself, (c) acceptance of responsibility for your own life, and (d) willingness to be a process.*

Responsibility

M. Scott Peck

We cannot solve life's problems except by solving them. This statement may seem idiotically tautological or self-evident, yet it is seemingly beyond the comprehension of much of the human race. This is because we must accept responsibility for a problem before we can solve it. We cannot solve a problem by saying, "It's not my problem." We cannot solve a problem by hoping that someone else will solve it for us. I can solve a problem only when I say "This is *my* problem and it's up to me to solve it." But many, so many, seek to avoid the pain of their problems by saying to themselves: "This problem was caused me by other people, or by social circumstances beyond my control, and therefore it is up to other people or society to solve this problem for me. It is not really my personal problem."

The extent to which people will go psychologically to avoid assuming responsibility for personal problems, while always sad, is sometimes almost ludicrous. A career sergeant in the army, stationed in Okinawa and in serious trouble because of his excessive drinking, was referred for psychiatric evaluation and, if possible, assistance. He denied that he was an alcoholic, or even that his use of alcohol was a personal problem, saying, "There's nothing else to do in the evenings in Okinawa except drink."

"Do you like to read?" I asked.

"Oh yes, I like to read, sure."

"Then why don't you read in the evening instead of drinking?"

"It's too noisy to read in the barracks."

"Well, then, why don't you go to the library?"

"The library is too far away."

"Is the library farther away than the bar you go to?"

"Well, I'm not much of a reader. That's not where my interests lie."

"Do you like to fish?" I then inquired.

"Sure, I love to fish."

"Why not go fishing instead of drinking?"

"Because I have to work all day long."

"Can't you go fishing at night?"

"No, there isn't any night fishing in Okinawa."

"But there is," I said. "I know several organizations that fish at night here. Would you like me to put you in touch with them?"

"Well, I really don't like to fish."

"What I hear you saying," I clarified, "is that there are other things to do in Okinawa except drink, but the thing you like to do most in Okinawa is drink."

"Yeah, I guess so."

"But your drinking is getting you in trouble, so you're faced with a real problem, aren't you?"

"This damn island would drive anyone to drink."

I kept trying for a while, but the sergeant was not the least bit interested in seeing his drinking as a personal problem which he could solve either with or without help, and I regretfully told his commander that he was not amenable to assistance. His drinking continued, and he was separated from the service in mid-career.

A young wife, also in Okinawa, cut her wrist lightly with a razor blade and was brought to the emergency room, where I saw her. I asked her why she had done this to herself.

"To kill myself, of course."

"Why do you want to kill yourself?"

"Because I can't stand it on this dumb island. You have to send me back to the States. I'm going to kill myself if I have to stay here any longer."

"What's is it about living on Okinawa that's so painful for you?" I asked.

She began to cry in a whining sort of way. "I don't have any friends here, and I'm alone all the time."

"That's too bad. How come you haven't been able to make any friends?"

"Because I have to live in a stupid Okinawan housing area, and none of my neighbors speak English."

"Why don't you drive over to the American housing area or to the wives' club during the day so you can make some friends?"

"Because my husband has to drive the car to work."

"Can't you drive him to work, since you're alone and bored all day?" I asked.

"No. It's a stick-shift car, and I don't know how to drive a stick-shift car, only an automatic."

"Why don't you learn how to drive a stick-shift car?"

She glared at me. "On these roads? You must be crazy."

Most people who come to see a psychiatrist are suffering from what is called either a neurosis or a character disorder. Put most simply, these two conditions are disorders of responsibility, and as such they are opposite styles of relating to the world and its problems. The neurotic assumes too much responsibility; the person with a character disorder not enough. When neurotics are in conflict with the world they automatically assume that they are at fault. When those with character disorders are in conflict with the world they automatically assume that the world is at fault. The two individuals just described had character disorders: the sergeant felt that his drinking was Okinawa's fault, not his, and the wife also saw herself as playing no role whatsoever in her own isolation. Almost all of us from time to time seek to avoid—in ways that can be quite subtle—the pain of assuming responsibility for our own problems. For the cure of my own subtle character disorder at the age of thirty I am indebted to Mac Badgely. At the time Mac was the director of the outpatient psychiatric clinic where I was completing my psychiatry residency training. In this clinic my fellow residents and I were assigned new patients on rotation. Perhaps because I was more dedicated to my patients and my own education than most of my fellow residents, I found myself working much longer hours than they. They ordinarily saw patients only once a week. I often saw my patients two or three times a week. As a result I would watch my fellow residents leaving the clinic at four-thirty each afternoon for their homes, while I was scheduled with appointments up to eight or nine o'clock at night, and my heart was filled with resentment. As I became more and more resentful and more and more exhausted I realized that something had to be done. So I went to Dr. Badgely and explained the situation to him. I wondered whether I might be exempted from the rotation of accepting new patients for a few weeks so that I might have time to catch up. Did he think that was feasible? Or could he think of some other solution to the problem? Mac listened to me very intently and receptively, not interrupting once. When I was finished, after a moment's silence, he said to me very sympathetically, "Well, I can see that you do have a problem."

I beamed, feeling understood. "Thank you," I said. "What do you think should be done about it?"

To this Mac replied, "I told you, Scott, you do have a problem."

This was hardly the response I expected. "Yes," I said, slightly annoyed, "I know I have a problem. That's why I came to see you. What do you think I ought to do about it?"

Mac responded: "Scott, apparently you haven't listened to what I said. I have heard you, and I am agreeing, with you. You do have a problem."

"Goddammit," I said, "I know I have a problem. I knew that when I came in here. The question is, what am I going to do about it?"

"Scott," Mac replied, "I want you to listen. Listen closely and I will say it again. I agree with you. You do have a problem. Specifically, you have a problem with time. *Your* time. Not my time. It's not my problem. It's *your* problem with *your* time. You, Scott Peck, have a problem with your time. That's all I'm going to say about it."

I turned and strode out of Mac's office, furious. And I stayed furious. I hated Mac Badgely. For three months I hated him. I felt that he had a severe character disorder. How else could he be so callous? Here I had gone to him humbly asking for just a little bit of help, a little bit of advice, and the bastard wasn't even willing to assume enough responsibility even to try to help me, even to do his job as director of the clinic. If he wasn't supposed to help manage such problems as director of the clinic, what the hell was he supposed to do?

But after three months I somehow came to see that Mac was right, that it was I, not he, who had the character disorder. My time *was* my responsibility. It was up to me and me alone to decide how I wanted to use and order my time. If I wanted to invest my time more heavily than my fellow residents in my work, then that was my choice, and the consequences of that choice were my responsibility. It might be painful for me to watch my fellow residents leave their offices two or three hours before me, and it might be painful to listen to my wife's complaints that I was not devoting myself sufficiently to the family, but these pains were the consequence of a choice that I had made. If I did not want to suffer them, then I was free to choose not to work so hard and to structure my time differently. My working hard was not a burden cast upon me by hardhearted fate or a hardhearted clinic director; it was the way I had chosen to live my life and order my priorities. As it happened, I chose not to change my life style. But with my change in attitude, my resentment of my fellow residents vanished. It simply no longer made any sense to resent them for having chosen a life style different from mine when I was completely free to choose to be like them if I wanted to. To resent them was to resent my own choice to be different from them, a choice that I was happy with.

The difficulty we have in accepting responsibility for our behavior lies in the desire to avoid the pain of the consequences of that behavior. By requesting Mac Badgely to assume responsibility for the structure of my time I was attempting to avoid the pain of working long hours, even though working long hours was an inevitable consequence of my choice to be dedicated to my patients and my training. Yet in so doing I was also unwittingly seeking to increase Mac's authority over me. I was giving him my power, my freedom. I was saying in effect, "Take charge of me. You be the boss!" Whenever we seek to avoid the responsibility for our own behavior, we do so by attempting to give that responsibility to some other individual or organization or entity. But this means we then give away our power to that entity, be it "fate" or "society" or the government or the corporation or our boss. It is for this reason that Erich Fromm so aptly titled his study of Nazism and authoritarianism *Escape from Freedom*. In attempting to avoid the pain of responsibility, millions and even billions daily attempt to escape from freedom.

I have a brilliant but morose acquaintance who, when I allow him to, will speak unceasingly and eloquently of the oppressive forces in our society: racism, sexism, the military–industrial establishment, and the country police who pick on him and his friends because of their long hair. Again and again I have tried to point out to

him that he is not a child. As children, by virtue of our real and extensive dependency, our parents have real and extensive power over us. They are, in fact, largely responsible for our well-being, and we are, in fact, largely at their mercy. When parents are oppressive, as so often they are, we as children are largely powerless to do anything about it; our choices are limited. But as adults, when we are physically healthy, our choices are almost unlimited. That does not mean they are not painful. Frequently our choices lie between the lesser of two evils, but it is still within our power to make these choices. Yes, I agree with my acquaintance, there are indeed oppressive forces at work within the world. We have, however, the freedom to choose every step of the way the manner in which we are going to respond to and deal with these forces. It is his choice to live in an area of the country where the police don't like "long-haired types" and still grow his hair long. He has the freedom to move to the city, or to cut his hair, or even to wage a campaign for the office of police commissioner. But despite his brilliance, he does not acknowledge these freedoms. He chooses to lament his lack of political power instead of accepting and exulting in his immense personal power. He speaks of his love of freedom and of the oppressive forces that thwart it, but every time he speaks of how he is victimized by these forces he actually is giving away his freedom. I hope that some day soon he will stop resenting life simply because some of its choices are painful.

Dr. Hilde Bruch, in the preface to her book *Learning Psychotherapy*, states that basically all patients come to psychiatrists with "one common problem: the sense of helplessness, the fear and inner conviction of being unable to 'cope' and to change things." One of the roots of this "sense of impotence" in the majority of patients is some desire to partially or totally escape the pain of freedom, and, therefore, some failure, partial or total, to accept responsibility for their problems and their lives. They feel impotent because they have, in fact, given their power away. Sooner or later, if they are to be healed, they must learn that the entirety of one's adult life is a series of personal choices, decisions. If they can accept this totally, then they become free people. To the extent that they do not accept this they will forever feel themselves victims.

1. *Discuss the way in which you assume, overassume, or fail to assume responsibility.*
2. *Discuss your sense of power or impotency as you confront your present personal problems.*
3. *Peck writes that life is filled with painful choices, but that we have the power to choose unless we have given this power away. Discuss a painful or difficult choice that presently confronts you, and indicate what you are doing about it.*
4. *Peck writes, "In attempting to avoid the pain of responsibility, millions and even billions daily attempt to escape from freedom." Have you been willing to make painful or difficult choices and abide by the consequences of your choices, or are you among Peck's millions and billions? Discuss this aspect of your life.*

Getting Unstuck: Joyfully Recreating Your Life

Harold H. Bloomfield and Robert B. Kory

I feel trapped. I spend my days wiping runny noses, preparing meals that get cold before they get eaten, doing dishes, clipping super- market coupons, cleaning house. No matter how hard Jim works, we always seem to be scrimping to get by. This isn't what I had in mind when I said "to have and to hold till death do us part." Some days I get the urge to pack up and leave. Other days I feel de- pressed, sort of sorry for myself. Most of the time I'm just bored.

These are the words of a young mother, married to a young aerospace engineer. They live in a quiet residential area, have a small house, two cars, and a future that promises them all the comforts of the suburban American lifestyle.

Jim and Barbara love each other, and their marriage has been stable. Neither raves about their sex life, but neither has sought extramarital sexual contact. Casually appraised, they are ben- eficiaries of the American dream, both college- educated, both products of middle-class families. Nevertheless, Barbara feels she is suffocating; Jim feels too pressured by his work to be of help. Both feel stuck . . . good and stuck.

The "I'm stuck" syndrome, an anhedonic[1] emotional trap if ever there was one, is reaching epidemic proportions. It's widespread among

young marrieds, but the same feelings of depres- sion and resignation are showing up among adults at every stage of life. Perhaps you're feel- ing stuck in your job. If you're older, you may feel cornered by inflation or illness. Many a mother going back to work soon feels stifled by the limited opportunities. Having played out the singles scene, you may be pessimistic about your chances of finding a lasting relationship that will work. Or you may be twenty years into a bad marriage and unable to get out. The common denominator is the feeling of being caught by a situation beyond your control; it leaves you de- pressed about the present and resigned to the future.

If you've been bitten hard by the "I'm stuck" bug, you can marshal any number of reasons to justify your frustrations. You may get angry at the company that doesn't recognize your ability and give you the promotion you feel you deserve. You may complain about the government, which mishandles the economy and allows inflation and taxes to keep rising through the roof. If you're a woman, a black, a Chicano, or a member of any other group that has suffered discrimina- tion, you can blame the system that denied you your opportunities. Spouses make excellent tar- gets to blame for your distress.

The frustrations of the "I'm stuck" syn- drome may be more or less legitimate: you are facing a very difficult and perhaps oppressive sit- uation. But that insight doesn't accomplish very much other than to justify indulging in self-pity. The important questions are: Why do you let difficult situations make you feel powerless? What can you do to start molding your life to suit your desires?

PUTTING IT OFF

Some people get themselves stuck with what may seem to be the best of intentions. They don't want to make trouble for others, or don't want to risk losing what they have in order to create something better. Rather than take con- trol of their lives and accept the risks of growth, they choose to put up with stifling jobs, lingering health problems, collapsing marriages, or de- structive habits. It's an anhedonic trap. The

---

1. *Anhedonic* is a word derived from the Greek *an-* (not) and *hedone* (pleasure) and refers to the inability to experience pleasure. *Anhedonic* means inhibiting plea- sure or interfering with pleasure. For more about anhe- donia and anhedonic things, see another reading by Bloomfield and Kory on pages 462–472 of this book, and also see their book *Inner Joy* from which both of these readings were condensed.—THE EDITOR

longer they procrastinate, the more difficult change becomes, and the more desperate they are likely to feel.

Dianne, a thirty-six-year-old mother of three, spent the last sixteen years trying to convince herself that her marriage could work. When she finally came for help, she was living what Thoreau called a "life of quiet desperation." At her first visit, her eyes were red and inflamed from crying and lack of sleep. She looked drawn, had a bruise on her left arm, and was visibly anxious about seeking assistance without her husband's permission. In an outpouring of feeling pent up for years, she told her story:

Our marriage has been miserable for as long as I can remember. This isn't the first fight or the first affair. He was seeing another woman the first year we were married. When I found out, I was devastated, cried my eyes out until he promised to be faithful. I believed him because I was young, I loved him, and I wanted our marriage to work more than anything else in the world.

I've tried to get him to open up and make our love grow. It never worked. He always kept his feelings inside. There's always been a distance. We haven't had sex for over a year now, but I really don't miss it because it was never any good. Steven wanted to think he was a real macho lover who could drive me wild. I learned to put on a great performance. Maybe he knows, or just got bored with me. I don't think we were real lovers for more than a few months after the honeymoon.

The children came and that gave Steven the excuse he needed to stay out of the house. He earned the money; I raised the children. Sounds corny, doesn't it! But that was our arrangement. He said he couldn't work at home, so he spent several nights a week and most weekends at the office. I actually convinced myself that he was working all those times. Even when I practically knew he was seeing another woman, I wouldn't admit it to myself. Just after our seventh anniversary, a friend of mine told me she saw Steven in a restaurant with a young blonde. I had to confront him. We had a terrible fight that ended with Steven telling me he didn't mean anything and pleading for me to stay. Like a fool, I did.

Two years ago Steven lost his job. He was out of work for six months. Ever since then our rela-tionship has been a quiet hell. We never spend any time together, never even go to the movies or watch TV. Steven is always out or in his den. We still share the same bedroom, but never exchange more than a kiss hello or goodbye. That's more for the children than for us. Steven makes all the decisions about money and never asks me about them anymore. I no longer know how much money we have or even how much he is making.

Last week he came home late. He called to say not to wait up for him. I did anyway. When he came in the door, I could tell right away that he'd had a few drinks. He said he'd stopped at a bar on the way home. Then I noticed a long red hair on his coat. I'd ignored these things before. I don't know what made me ask him about it, but I did. We wound up in a shouting match and a terrible fight. He has never struck me before, but this time he flew into a rage and knocked me down. Said I was an albatross around his neck and he wished he'd never met me. I was shaken, and frightened. I locked myself in our bedroom and cried all night. The children must have heard everything. They got themselves off to school the next morning. Steven is now pleading for me to forgive him again. He admits he's been seeing another woman, and is giving me the same old line.

"Why did you wait so long to do something?" I asked.

"I loved Steven and I was afraid of what might happen. There were the children to think about. I kept hoping things would get better. I told myself maybe Steven would change. If I tried to please him, our relationship would improve."

From the first year of her marriage, Dianne's inner voice was telling her that there were serious problems in her marriage. Year after year she chose to ignore these inner messages and to rely on make-believe. She assuaged her anxiety with the classic self-deception: "Maybe things will get better if I just wait it out." By choosing to ignore her inner voice and hold on to wishful thinking, Dianne created sixteen years of unhappiness. Recognizing her complicity in her misery was a first step toward change.

Dianne eventually convinced Steven to join her in counseling. He professed to want to save the marriage; Dianne took a stand. Either they tried together or it was over. Over the course of ten sessions, Steven's insecurities and Dianne's years of hurt came out in the open. Steven asked for reconciliation, Dianne asked why she should trust him again. The more Dianne learned about her husband, the more doubtful she became about remaining married.

"For the first time," she said privately, "I see how much growing up Steven has to do." She finally summoned the courage to face what she had avoided for so long. "I'll be better off on my own," concluded Dianne. "I've already wasted sixteen years. I can't afford to risk any more."

She filed for divorce and spent the next two years recovering the power she had long put in mothballs. She had three children to care for and no means of support other than alimony. She did not want to remain dependent, but finding work was not easy. For sixteen years she had cultivated the skill of putting things off and turning a blind eye to her real feelings. Many times she had talked about going back to college. Many times she had thought of getting a job. Never had she chosen to listen to those quiet urgings from within. By cultivating the "put-it-off" syndrome, she had dulled her confidence, sensitivity, and will. Once out on her own, she had to learn how to mobilize herself again.

Today Dianne is a single mother with a house and a job of her own. She is working in the public relations department of a large law firm that handles celebrities, including many sports figures and entertainers. After completing her B.A. at age thirty-nine she plans to get her law degree. She is managing to complete her education through a combination of night study, leaves of absence from work, summer school, bank loans, tremendous support from her children, and the fantastic new energy she has discovered surging forth when she chooses to act from her deepest self and go for what she really wants.

The next time you find yourself putting off dealing with a source of unhappiness in your life, ask yourself: Will hoping for improvement really do any good? The answer is no. The longer you put it off, the worse it's likely to get—whatever "it" may be. Gather your courage and choose to get unstuck. Now!

"I'VE ALWAYS BEEN THAT WAY"

Another way many people get themselves stuck is by foreclosing on change with the reassuring rationale, "I've always been that way."

Edith is a forty-two-year-old widow whose husband died of a sudden heart attack two years ago. After a prolonged period of mourning, she is reaching a point where she is ready to love again. Yet she holds herself back. A lovely woman who looks more like she is in her early thirties, she is not lacking in interested men. When her relationship with a man begins to heat up, however, she puts on the brakes. "I'm afraid of sexual involvement, " she says in therapy. "In all my years with Roger, I never had an orgasm. I've always been that way. I can't help it." Sex wasn't so important to Edith when she was married, so the belief that "I'm not orgasmic" wasn't a problem. Now things are different. She is single again, and awakening to new desires. Only after she decided that she has the power to break free from her past was she able to begin rediscovering sexual joy.

John, a college student, complains, "I can count the number of dates I've had on one hand and not run out of fingers." He's obviously got a sense of humor, but he is afraid to be himself around women. "I'm shy," he says. "That's my nature." John recalls his mother telling people that he was "the shy one." He never realized that his mother had an emotional investment in keeping him tied to her apron strings. John spent his childhood and adolescence living up to the family label of "the shy one. " No doubt he had a tendency to be shy as a little boy, but with their labeling, his parents helped him develop that tendency into a full-blown personality characteristic. The question is whether John is going to continue justifying his fears of women with the rationale: "Shyness is my nature." Whenever you resort to a label to explain a negative personality characteristic, you're only making excuses for avoiding the challenge of growth.

Gloria is twenty-six and overweight. She has tried every imaginable diet, managed on several occasions to lose over thirty pounds, but always put the weight back on. She says she wants to shed her excess poundage forever, but in the same breath she reveals why she has always been unsuccessful in her attempts up to now. "I've always had a weight problem, ever since I was a little girl. I must have too many fat cells or a low metabolism or something." Gloria keeps herself stuck with the classic recall to her physiology. What she doesn't see is the hidden payoff. As long as she is fat she has a built-in excuse for feeling lonely and unattractive. Terrified by the prospect of rejection, she avoids it by rejecting herself, then hiding her self-rejection ("I've always been that way"). You may be tall, short, fat, thin, big-bosomed or small-breasted, bushy-headed or bald as a snowball. None of these physiological characteristics is justification for keeping yourself stuck and unhappy. They just aren't that important. Far more significant is your vitality, your friendliness, your self-confidence, your inner joy. These are the qualities you can choose to make outstanding in your life.

Vanessa at twenty-eight has been offered a major promotion at work. A vice-president has asked her to become his administrative assistant. The new job requires that Vanessa polish up on her basic math. Vanessa wants the job, but she is afraid to take it because she has always had difficulty with math. "I barely passed math in high school," she says. "Numbers make me nervous. I can't even balance my checkbook." For sixteen years Vanessa used this "I've always been" to avoid the extra effort required for her to become proficient in basic math. Now she has a choice. She can continue to use her "I've always been that way" as an excuse, or she can decide to focus whatever energy it takes for her to develop her math skills. The first choice is guaranteed to keep her stuck; the second opens broad new possibilities for success. Who knows why she has had difficulty with math in the past? It really doesn't matter, because she has the intelligence to acquire the skills the new job demands. All she needs now is the courage to challenge her "I've always been."

Tim is known for a short temper and frequent angry outbursts. His boss has told him that if he wants to make any kind of progress with the company he will have to learn to control his temper and develop his interpersonal skills. Tim's response has been consistent, "Sure, I have a short temper! I'm Irish." Ever since Tim got into fights on the school playground, his parents indulged his temper with this excuse. Now Tim sits at his desk in a sullen rage; his boss has told him that due to economic pressures on the company, Tim will be out of a job. His boss did not hide the fact that Tim, of all the junior executives, was dismissed because senior management found him hard to work with. This blow was finally enough for Tim to realize he had to make some changes. The alternative was to get stuck not only emotionally, but also economically. Having put all his excuses aside, Tim is now working on developing the emotional skills he needs to be a better manager.

If you want to know where your "I've always been" comes from, have a talk with significant people of your early life (parents, long-time family friends, teachers, grandparents). Ask them how they think you got to be the way you are. You'll hear a list of labels you've learned to apply to yourself. If you tell them you're determined to change, you're likely to meet considerable doubt ("You can't change, you've always been that way"). But why go on living up to labels others have put upon you? Sören Kierkegaard wrote: "When you label me, you negate me." By accepting labels others pinned on you, you negate yourself. You're saying: "I'm a finished product, I can't change." This is an anhedonic choice, because it is a denial of your potential for growth. *No one is ever a finished product!* You are bigger than all the labels you may hang on yourself. Anytime you wish, you can choose to get unstuck by putting your past behind you. All it takes is courage and determination.

THE DIVIDENDS OF SELF-IMMOBILIZATION

Your choice to stay stuck brings rewards. Here are several:

Once again, avoidance of responsibility is a primary payoff.

The choice to remain the way you are is always a choice to live by the dictates of others, so you can say "They're responsible for my unhappiness!" When you choose to exercise your own power, you forfeit this ready-made system for blame. For some people the prospect of assuming full responsibility for their happiness is so onerous that they prefer to suffocate their own creative potential with the weight of others' expectations. This dubious bargain is the essence of being stuck.

Keeping yourself stuck can help you remain self-righteous.

It doesn't matter how stultifying your "shoulds" may be; you can pride yourself on remaining exactly the way you are. You can even look down your nose at others who experiment with new life-styles and violate your sacred rules ("They aren't doing it the right way").

Remaining stuck permits you to indulge in psychological regression.

By following your "shoulds" and living up to your labels, you can take solace in being a "good boy" or "good girl." You can take satisfaction in your obedience. It doesn't matter that mommy and daddy are no longer around to pat you on the back for following their rules. If you refrain from questioning your childhood "shoulds," you can recreate the comfort of having someone else make your important decisions. You avoid having to think for yourself.

Keeping yourself stuck lets you avoid the risk of failure.

If you've been well schooled in the merits of safety, boredom is likely to seem preferable to defeat. You assume that your self-esteem is so fragile that you could never pick yourself up after a fall and try again. For people convinced of their own weakness, avoidance of failure is an alluring reward.

Keeping yourself stuck creates fertile ground for self-delusion.

"Nothing is easier than self-deceit," said Demosthenes. Especially when you stifle your impulse toward growth, we add. By remaining the way you are, you avoid a confrontation with your dreams. You can hold all your options in abeyance while you ponder your possibilities. By planning your first novel but never getting around to writing it, you can keep telling yourself how much potential you have as a writer. By refusing to work on a difficulty in your relationship, you can convince yourself that the relationship is basically sound and will last. Peaceful delusion is the reward.

You create opportunities to substitute complaining for doing.

When a problem doesn't go away, no matter how much you hope things get better, you can complain that you never get any breaks. If you remain in a relationship that's going sour, you can complain about how your lover mistreats you. You're putting up with an unsatisfying job? Berate your boss, the company, and your fate. You were mistreated by your parents? It is so much easier to blame mom and dad than it is to take concrete steps toward becoming the person you want to be. Complaining may not seem to be a reward to you, but some people make a career out of it.

Choosing self-abnegation protects you from fear.

Whenever you take a step in a new direction, as we've often said, you are bound to experience some anxiety. Anxiety is natural when you move into a new job, challenge a failing marriage, go back to school, decide to have children, or venture into any unknown emotional territory. You can't expect to be an explorer of your full potential without encountering a measure of fear. Some people would rather continue believing their lives must inevitably remain flat rather than risk making an adventure of the future.

Reread these reasons why people persist in self-immobilization, and you may have difficulty regarding them as rewards. Under the cool scrutiny of rational analysis, they are obviously self-destructive. Nevertheless, these emotional payoffs constitute the support system for choosing to be less than you could become.

SOME STEPS TOWARD SELF-DIRECTION

Once you have decided to take control, you *have* the power to create your own life according to your personal vision. You *can* establish your own values based on your own experience. To get unstuck, you need to seize this power to break free from your past and transform your intuitions into realities. The decision to take control of your life is a first step. Transforming that decision into action is the real test. Here are some suggestions that you may find useful:

Stop thinking of yourself as fragile.

Behind every anhedonic choice that keeps you stuck is the belief that you (or your life) will fall apart if you challenge the rules. This is a powerful myth! It can keep you absolutely paralyzed! The only way to rid yourself of it is to put your psychological strengths to the test. Few people realize how strong they really are until they stop putting up with the problems in their lives and take some steps toward change. It won't be easy. You may get knocked down a few times, but you won't fall apart. On the contrary, the more you assert your ability to take control over your life, the stronger you'll become. Developing psychological strengths is just like developing physical abilities. The more you exercise, the stronger you become.

Once and for all, you must eliminate the words wish, hope, and maybe from your vocabulary.

These are sedatives you administer to yourself to numb your sensitivity to your emotional realities. Like any narcotic, wishing and hoping weaken your power to take control of your life. In place of wishing and hoping, you have to substitute a new confidence in your willpower.

Substitute *"I will make it happen"* for "I hope things get better."

Substitute *"I am going to do x, y, z, so I'll feel better"* for "I wish things were better."

Substitute *"I will make my marriage work"* for "Maybe my marriage will still work out."

Start considering yourself too important to put up with anxiety about the obstacles in your life.

The best antidote for anxiety is action. Instead of bemoaning your problems or worrying about the long way to a major goal, take the first step. If your job is suffocating you, stop complaining and put together your résumé. Get any assistance you need to make certain it's the best résumé you can possibly write. If you're in a relationship that is faltering, gather up the courage to have a long talk about your future with your lover. Don't put it off until tomorrow. Do it today! Action, even one small step, breaks the illusion that makes personal problems seem insurmountable. You can only solve your problems one step at a time. Taking the first step has the amazing effect of reducing any problem to life size.

If you're feeling ambivalent about your life, try this little experiment.

Imagine you have only one year to live. Now ask yourself whether you're doing what you'd like to be doing given this sudden abbreviation of your life. If the answer is no, better get busy and start making changes. Whether you have one or fifty years ahead, your life is too short to waste. The habit of putting up with a life that you have failed to make your own grows more difficult to break each year. Don't risk looking back on a life of regrets. Dare to challenge yourself now.

Choose one of your bigger dreams and start making it a reality.

One of my clients had always dreamed of exploring the Inca ruins in Peru. She had never been out of the United States and, as a secretary, didn't earn a large income. Nevertheless, this was the dream she chose. I suggested she contact travel agencies, museums, and local universities to explore all possibilities for her trip. The cost of a commercial tour was out of her reach, but she did discover that she could for a modest cost join an archaeological expedition from a local museum. She paid for some of her expenses and joined in the work as a volunteer. The result was the most rewarding vacation of her life. More: by actualizing just one of her dreams, she broke the cycle of defeatism that was keeping her stuck. Now at twenty-seven she is back at school to study archaeology. Fulfilling a dream is an exercise in discovering personal power. It can turn your life around.

Stop feeling you always have to have a plan.

Plans have their place, but planning involves only half of your brain, the verbal, analytic hemisphere. There is a huge silent dimension of your personality, the intuitive dimension, and you're probably not using it. Scientific research on creativity shows indisputably that the creative process depends just as much on the right brain functions (intuition) as on the left brain operations (analysis and language). If you insist on always having a plan, you cut yourself off from your intuitive self and the inner joy it provides. To break planning addiction, indulge in one freedom. Decide to spend a day exploring a park or a neighborhood with curiosity as your sole guide. Enroll in a local university and take a course that strikes your interest. You never know, it may lead you into a new occupation. The next time you feel attracted to someone you don't know, and want to introduce yourself, go ahead. You're likely to make a new friend. By giving yourself freedom to follow your hunches, even in small ways, you develop your sensitivity to your inner voice. You learn to hear the quiet messages that can make your life an adventure.

Once and for all, eradicate your tendency to put things off.

Procrastination is a habit easily broken. First, make a list every morning of everything you have to do that day. Divide the list into areas: telephone calls, letters, housework, reading, writing, appointments, and so on. Make your list early every day so it becomes a habit. Throughout the day, consult your list and cross off what you accomplish. Whatever remains at the end of the day becomes part of the next day's list. If an important item remains for several days, tag it and allot a special time of day to do it. This simple technique can help you end procrastination forever.

Don't be ashamed to ask friends for support when you consider a major change.

You may have legitimate concerns about leaving your job, going back to school, moving to another city, or doing whatever seems necessary to create the life you really want. From some people, you may get very conservative advice: "Don't take risks," "Don't rock the boat," "A boring job is better than no job at all." But you're also likely to get encouragement and help. People will respond to your courage. Doors will open. Try it. You'll be surprised how helpful people are when you ask.

Decide to forego the crutch of old labels you've pinned on yourself to make excuses for remaining the way you are.

Instead of saying "I've always been that way," try a new affirmation: "Until today, I have chosen to be this way. Now I am choosing to change." You have the power to create your life as you wish. For any technique to work, you have to begin with a firm commitment to make it work.

Remember that "should's" have only as much influence over your life as you give them.

If your "should's" have been weighing heavily in many of your important decisions, the time has come to declare your independence. Ask yourself who is making the rules in your life: your parents, a teacher you once had, an aunt or uncle, or you. Take an inventory of the "should's" that are causing you the most trouble. You might even write them down. Then choose to override those "should's" and choose new behaviors. For example, Annette wasn't allowing herself to have orgasms because of all her sexual "should's"—"A woman shouldn't have to tell a man what she wants; it's not romantic," "I should be able to come with intercourse alone, or else there is something wrong with me," "A woman shouldn't be too aggressive during sex." These "should's" are popular misconceptions. When Annette began asking who was making these rules, she began recognizing the absurdity of letting them dominate her. She discovered that she has the power to create an ecstatic sex life if she listens to her needs and gives herself more freedom. You can make the same choice in any area of your life.

Have faith in yourself, your ability to succeed at what you attempt and to get back up if you fail.

William James wrote: "It is only by risking our persons from one hour to the next that we live at all." Often faith in an uncertain result makes the result come true. The greatest rewards of living come when you step out of the bounds of your ordinary existence and extend yourself beyond what you believe are your limits.

Don't let yourself be crippled by the fear of failure.

If you hold back and never depart from your routine because you fear failure, you're letting approval needs get the best of you. The worst part of failure is what others will think. This is a terrible anhedonic trap! It's the basis of all performance anxiety, whether on the tennis court, in bed, in the classroom—wherever someone may watch how well you do. The only way to end performance anxiety is to stop worrying about the audience and do whatever you're doing for the sake of your own enjoyment. This is when you absolutely *must* be selfish! Remember: Pleasure is a sign of optimum functioning. If you follow your own desires to enjoy what you are doing to the maximum, you'll do the very best you can, and that is all you ever need ask of yourself.

Spend more time being a doer, less being a critic.

Many people fool themselves into thinking they are not really stuck by engaging in criticism whenever possible. They have a harsh word for almost everyone, friends, neighbors, movies, books, politicians, doctors, lawyers, the washer repairperson, anyone at all. After criticism comes complaint. What they're really doing is disguising their own unhappiness because they don't know how to create more satisfactions in their own lives. Beware of wasting your own time as a critic and listening to others engage in this usually fruitless activity. When you're caught listening to a critic, ask: "Is any of this going to help either of us right now?" Chances are it won't, so you'll go on to a more satisfying conversation.

Learn to master fatigue.

One of the most common responses to an unpleasant task is a sudden onset of drowsiness. If you're like most people, the first time you experienced this psychosomatic reaction was as a student when you had to do some homework. You sat down full of energy, but twenty minutes into studying, your eyes started to droop. But do you remember how this reaction abates as soon as you start doing something else? Let someone suggest going to a movie and the energy surges. Clearly, your energy level is governed by your attitude. If you get tired trying to complete a difficult or unpleasant task, it's best to take a five-to-ten-minute break. Get up and exercise vigorously or nap in your chair. Either way, you can choose to master this type of fatigue so that you get the difficult task accomplished in minimum time.

Decide once and for all that your happiness or unhappiness is primarily up to you.

There are no guarantees in this world. No matter who you are, living has its ups and downs, wins and losses. Maturity is the ability to derive deep satisfaction from your life whether or not your efforts are yielding full fruit for the moment. Every time you let your happiness depend on others, you surrender a portion of yourself. You reinforce childhood beliefs that someone else will take care of you. Isn't it time to give up these childhood beliefs and discover your own power of inner joy?

To Apply This Reading to Yourself

1. *Describe a "stuck" time in your life, indicating how you got stuck and how you got yourself unstuck.*
2. *Describe a problem or source of unhappiness in your life concerning which you have postponed or avoided action. What do you get by putting it off? How are you hurt by putting it off?*
3. *"I've always been that way." Describe your past and/or current use of this excuse for staying stuck.*
4. *Discuss the dividends that you have received for remaining immobilized or staying stuck during one period of your life (perhaps the present one).*
5. *Review Bloomfield and Kory's "steps toward self-direction." Find two or three steps that you have taken or are taking, and describe their effect on you.*

Death

The confrontation with death—and the reprieve from it—makes everything look so precious, so sacred, so beautiful that I feel more strongly than ever the impulse to love it, to embrace it, and to let myself be overwhelmed by it. My river never looked so beautiful. . . . Death and its ever present possibility makes love, passionate love, more possible. I wonder if we could love passionately, if ecstasy would be possible at all, if we knew we'd never die.
—Abraham Maslow, in a letter written while he was recuperating from a heart attack

. . . there is no such thing as a good death, except for those who have achieved a good life.
—Kenneth L. Woodward

Death can be defined as the cessation or end of life. And some observers say that birth is the beginning of death, that each moment we live we die a little, or at least each moment brings death a little nearer. There are also some who believe that until we face the fact that we will die—until we get a real sense of our own mortality and the preciousness of life—we cannot truly begin to live.

It is difficult for many of us to think or talk about death or to be in its presence. Our language reflects this difficulty. For example, we speak of someone as "nearing the end" instead of "dying," and as "passed away," "gone," or "departed" rather than "dead." We maintain the illusion that somehow a fatally ill member of our family will get better. We resist going to see a friend who is hospitalized and dying. We try to keep some distance from death.

The prospect of our own death is particularly hard to deal with. We human beings are bound up in ourselves. How can we understand that we will one day stop, come to an end, and cease to be? We relish experience. How can we conceive of a time when we will never think or feel or act again? And we are social beings. How can we comprehend being separated from the ones we love—alone, apart, even abandoned?

Early investigators studying death and dying encountered considerable resistance to their work. Death has been something of a taboo topic in our society. For example, psychiatrist Elisabeth Kübler-Ross, who pioneered this area, had difficulty locating dying subjects because hospital personnel denied they had any such patients. In fact, some staff members accused her of having a morbid interest in death, implying that this topic was somehow not suitable for scientific investigation.

Recently there has been a rapidly increasing interest in and candor about death. Publications and programs on this subject have multiplied, and courses on death and dying have been introduced into many high schools and colleges. Much more attention is being given to the care of the terminally ill; there is a growing hospice movement that aims to replace the institutional way of death with a system of care that permits dying persons to complete their lives in comfort and in their own life-style. "Make Today Count," a national organization for persons with life-threatening illness and their families, has chapters throughout the country.

Modern medical technology allows many dying patients to linger on when there is little quality of life but sometimes great pain and crushing financial expense. In response, there has been a widespread movement to permit dying persons to refuse heroic measures that would prolong their lives. There is also a growing and more controversial movement to permit such patients to obtain assistance to hasten their deaths.

Our rate of mortality is 100%. Each of us will die, and death will touch our lives in many ways before our own time comes. The more we bring this subject out into the open, the more we will be able to understand it and accept our own finitude. And the more we will be able to change death as a personal and social event by investing it with meaning and dignity.

ON DEATH AND DYING

Many of life's problems stem from the inability to confront the inevitability of our own deaths. This is the conclusion of J. William Worden, who has made a long-term study of terminal illness. The first reading, an excerpt from a book that Worden wrote with William Proctor, presents a number of exercises to help us understand and raise, if necessary, our own PDA (Personal Death Awareness). According to Worden and Proctor, as we allow ourselves to become more aware of death, we may also find that we are reaching out for life with greater zest.

In the second selection, Abe Arkoff writes that his clinical and hospice experiences convince him that those who face their own mortality and prepare for it, free themselves to live life more fully. He presents his 10-item Dying-Readiness/Freedom-to-Live Test, which is a checklist for persons who would like to free themselves to live by readying themselves to die. To those answering yes to all 10 items on the checklist, he offers his congratulations; to others, he says, "Get busy and put your house in order—not for death's sake but for life's sake."

ON LIVING FOREVER

Death makes life precious because death ends life. But is death the end of everything? Raymond A. Moody, Jr., whose widely read book *Life after Life* is condensed into the last reading, has studied a large number of people who suffered "clinical death" but who then revived. Their "dying" experiences are remarkably similar and suggest the possibility that there may be life after death. The study of death is not just for death's sake because, as Moody notes, "What we learn about death may make an important difference in the way we live our lives."

To Explore Your Own Feelings and Attitudes toward Death and Dying

1. *Trace your growing acquaintance with death.* When we are young, death may be a stranger, but we soon become better acquainted. With the passing years, pets and people we love die, and death increasingly makes itself known. Discuss how your acquaintance with death has grown and how this has affected you and your attitudes toward death and life.
2. *Assess your management of death's intrusions.* Death intrudes itself on our lives. Persons we know and love become ill and die, and we are called on to be with them and to help them in their hour of need. Are we able to help them, or are we so awkward or anxious in the presence of death that our response is less than we would want it to be? Make a list of the times that death has intruded on your life, and indicate how well you managed each intrusion and what you plan to do better.
3. *Chart your "little deaths."* Psychologist Stanley Keleman notes that life is a migration through many little dyings. He writes, "In these little dyings we can learn how to live our big dying." Consider your own life, and chart the salient events in it that in some sense seemed like "little deaths" to you. For each event, note what, if anything, you learned from it that has been or will be helpful in dealing with future little deaths and ultimately in your big death. Share your chart in the larger group or in small groups.
4. *Consider your own death.* At the top of a piece of paper, write "My Own Death." Then write what you expect for yourself after you die. Be careful to note that what you write is not to concern your dying but rather what awaits you when you are dead. Be

brief—one or two paragraphs or one-half page or so. Afterward, share what you have written in the larger group or in small groups.

5. *Symbolize death.* Proceeding in any way you wish, construct or create something that symbolizes or represents death to you. In the larger group or in small groups, share your death symbol, and indicate its significance for you.

6. *Symbolize your life and death.* Form small groups, and darken the room as much as possible. Each person, in turn, is given a wooden match or splint to represent her or his life. When it is your turn, first respond to your match before you light it in terms of your existence before birth; you might begin, "Before I was born . . . " Second, strike your match and as it burns respond to it in terms of your life ("Then I was born . . . "). Third, as or after your match goes out, respond to it in terms of death and anything that may ensue ("Then I died . . . "). Follow this procedure until each person in the group has a turn, and then share feelings and reactions.

7. *Write your own epitaph.*[1] Assume that you have come to the end of your life (whenever that may be) and write a final paragraph—in effect, an epitaph—on this topic: "What I would like to be remembered for." Share your epitaph and your feelings and reactions concerning it in the larger group or in small groups.

8. *Write your own eulogy.*[2] Assume that you have come to the end of your life (whenever that may be), and write a eulogy for yourself to share in the larger group or in small groups. To share, you might hand your eulogy to another person to read; then relax in your chair or lie down on the floor, close your eyes, and imagine yourself in your coffin as you listen. After everyone has been eulogized, share your feelings and reactions.

9. *Discuss suicide.* Suicide is one of the 10 most frequent causes of death in this country for all ages after childhood. It is a serious and complex problem with a number of causes, and it affects not only those who attempt or commit suicide but also those close to them and the larger society as well. There is considerable argument over the moral right of a person to take her or his own life: Discuss the conditions, if any, under which you believe that individuals are justified in doing so.

10. *Debate physician aid in dying.* Have two persons or teams with opposing views debate or discuss this question: "Shall adult patients who are in a medically terminal condition be permitted to request and receive aid from a physician to hasten their dying?"

11. *Seek insights on death and dying.* Make arrangements and go as a group to visit a funeral director at a mortuary or funeral home, or visit a cemetery director at a cemetery or memorial park, or visit a coroner or medical examiner at her or his office or at a morgue. Or invite a hospice worker, oncologist, or someone else

---

1. This exercise is suggested by a report "My students write their epitaphs" by Abraham Blinderman (*The Humanist*, March/April 1978, pp. 4–5).
2. For an instructor's experience with a similar exercise, read "Can a young person write his own obituary?" by Edwin S. Shneidman (*Life-Threatening Behavior*, 1972, 2(4), 262–267).

who works with or has close associations with the terminally ill to visit and talk to your group. Or invite one or more members of "Make Today Count" (an organization for those with life-threatening illness) to come to talk with you.

To Read Further

Humphry, D. (1991). *Final exit: The practicalities of self-deliverance and assisted suicide for the dying.* Eugene, OR: Hemlock Society.

Humphry, D., & Wickett, A. (1990). *The right to die: Understanding euthanasia.* Eugene, OR: Hemlock Society.

Kalish, R. A. (1985). *Death, grief, and caring relationships* (2nd ed.). Monterey, CA: Brooks/Cole.

Kübler-Ross, E. (1969). *On death and dying.* New York: Macmillan. (paperback)

Kübler-Ross, E. (1974). *Questions and answers on death and dying.* New York: Macmillan. (paperback)

Kübler-Ross, E. (Ed.) (1975). *Death: The final stage of growth.* Englewood Cliffs, NJ: Prentice-Hall. (paperback) (Touchstone paperback, 1986)

Kübler-Ross, E. (1991). *On life after death.* Berkeley, CA: Celestial Arts. (paperback)

Levine, S. (1982). *Who dies? An investigation of conscious living and dying.* New York: Anchor. (paperback)

Moody, R. A., Jr. (1975). *Life after life.* Atlanta: Mockingbird. (Bantam paperback 1988)

Moody, R. A., Jr. (1977). *Reflections on life after life.* Atlanta: Mockingbird. (Bantam paperback, 1985)

Moody, R. A., Jr. (1989). *The light beyond.* New York: Bantam. (paperback)

Silverman, W. B., & Cinnamon, K. M. (1991). *When mourning comes: A book of comfort for the grieving.* New York: Aronson.

Staudacher, C. (1987). *Beyond grief: Recovering from the death of a loved one.* Oakland, CA: New Harbinger. (paperback)

What's Your PDA?

J. William Worden
and William Proctor

A friend of mine was at a suburban party where one of the guests, a university professor, began to boast about his openmindedness and willingness to confront any issue, no matter how distasteful.

"If we're going to solve the terrible problems around us," the professor said, "we have to be objective. I've learned to confront any tragedy— the war orphans in Indochina, a widow crying over her husband's dead body in the hospital, the racial hatred that some Americans have for others—and completely eliminate most feelings of emotion, such as fear or revulsion."

As he continued praising his own self-control, my friend, a committed enemy of inflated egos, began to sketch on a blank sheet of paper on a nearby desk. When a lull occurred in the conversation, he turned to the professor and said, "When you face tough problems, you really seem to have learned how to handle yourself."

The professor nodded smugly. "Yes, well, it has taken some work you know—a great deal of stringent, sometimes even painful personal discipline. And I do make wrong decisions sometimes, but not because I lose my head with any unnecessary anxiety or anger. It's a matter of knowing myself, as the Delphic Oracle advised."

My friend nodded solicitously. "Yes, well, how would you react if someone handed you a photograph that looked like this?" He pushed the paper on which he had been sketching, toward the professor. A tombstone was clearly depicted and bore the professor's name, with the inscription, "1940–1993. May He Rest In Peace." From a mound of dirt in front of the marker rose a single flower.

The professor stared at the drawing for a few moments, gulped, and then began to stammer. He crumpled the paper in his fist, and his face flushed in anger. "I think this is thoroughly rude and not at all funny, if it's supposed to be a joke!" he almost shouted through clenched teeth. He stormed to the other side of the room to get himself another drink, and it took several minutes for the others to pacify him.

But my friend's point had been made rather dramatically: The professor may well have been open and detached about dealing with the tragedies of others. But when starkly confronted with his *own* death, he first froze and then lashed out defensively in an effort to avoid dealing with the issue.

Subconsciously, he had eliminated from consideration an entire dimension—perhaps the most important dimension—of his life. The shackles of fear and anxiety about his own limited life span prevented him from even *discussing* his own death, much less considering how understanding his mortality might enhance the quality of his present life.

This professor is like many whose fears of death have put padlocks of denial on important awareness. In the following pages you'll be introduced to some keys that help open these closed inner doors and free you to explore aspects of your personality and relationships that you may have avoided.

As a first step in helping you to break free from some of your own fears, take the following word-association test. Words and phrases which we encounter every day have both a dictionary meaning and a personal meaning. The personal meanings are of special interest in understanding human behavior—your own behavior in this case. There are no right or wrong answers. Just put down the first word that comes to your mind.

BALL—	KEY—
CAR—	DEATH—
DOG—	FRIEND—
WOMAN—	HIGH—
BRICK—	TREE—
RED—	BIRD—
FATHER—	TIME—

I am most interested in your personal response to the word *death*. After you read the word *death*, what was the first thing that came to your mind? I asked a number of people to give their associations to death, and here are some of their responses:

death-life	death-camp
death-evil	death-horrible
death-sorrow	death-grave
death-black	death-sadness
death-destruction	death-loss
death-dying	death-horror
death-knell	death-corpse
death-tomb	death-end

Most of these responses have a negative connotation. How does your answer compare? Some people draw a mental blank when they see the word "death." They can't find an association, or they take a much longer time to respond to the word *death* than they do to more neutral words, like "ball" and "car." In other words, there is a tendency to develop what might be called a "death block." Many regard death as completely bad and evil, something which should be considered only if it's unavoidable.

Because of these negative associations, most people don't want to think about death, especially not their own. Their Personal Death Awareness or "PDA"—their sense of their own mortality—remains at a very low level. Perhaps this is true of you.

To test the level of your own Personal Death Awareness, try another simple exercise. In the space below, draw a line that you think best represents your total life span. The line can be any shape or length that you think is most appropriate.

Some people choose to draw a line from one end of the page to the other—in effect, a line without boundaries which ends only because the edge of the page forces the pencil to stop.

Others draw a line that curves back and forth. Some people find that they can't take their pencils off the paper because they don't want their lines to end, even symbolically:

Some draw a curved line with an apex at the top, indicating, perhaps, that the best portion of their lives is in the middle:

Those who have known hard times or frequent depressions may feel that birth and death are the least painful points in their existence. As a result, they draw an inverted curve:

Now draw another line of any length, this time a straight one with a beginning and an end.

Consider this line to be your total life span. Place a slash mark at any point along the line where you think you are today in your life's chronology. Now, complete the following sentences by filling in the blanks:

I expect to live until age _____
I am currently age _____

When you compare your present age with the age at which you expect to die, how much of your life do you find you've already lived? A third, a half, two-thirds, or more? Now look back at the line with the slash mark. How does your estimate of the time you have left to live on the life-span line compare with your numerical estimate?

Many people who have done this exercise have found that they placed the slash mark at an earlier age than their written guess. When you see your life starkly depicted on a line in front of you, like a racetrack or a road map, the tendency is to give yourself more time to live than you know you probably have.

How did it feel to commit yourself to a definite life span? Some people worry that they may jinx themselves by doing this. Old superstitions rise up and haunt them. Does this concern you?

Did **you** feel any other discomfort? If not, what do you think made you feel relatively comfortable in doing this task? Take a minute and write down your responses below:

I was uncomfortable in estimating my remaining life span because _____
_____
_____
_____

I was comfortable in estimating my remaining life span because _____
_____
_____
_____

By this time you are probably experiencing an increase in your PDA, your Personal Death Awareness. PDA, by the way, does not refer to your awareness of death in general or of someone else's death, but to your awareness of your *own* death. It's a very personal concept.

I usually think of PDA in terms of a four-point scale:

PERSONAL DEATH AWARENESS INDEX

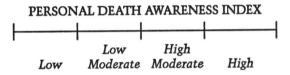

One of the most helpful ways to understand your PDA is to take a moment and recall the number of times today you've thought about your *own*—not someone else's—death or limited span of life. Maybe you thought about your age and evaluated your own progress toward certain life goals. Or perhaps you briefly experienced a fear of dying.

If such a thought didn't occur to you at all, then you're probably in the "low" range today on the index. If these ideas crossed your mind one, two, or three times, then you moved up through the "moderate" range. If you seriously pondered your own death or mortality four or more times, or find it a preoccupation, then you're likely in the "high" range.

Your Personal Death Awareness is a fluctuating phenomenon, moving up and down daily. Some days, you'll be more aware of your own limited life span, and other days you may act and think as though you're going to live forever. I

experience these feelings, and I'm sure you do, too. Because you've been reading this chapter and doing some of these exercises, you probably have a higher PDA now than you did before you began reading.

Most of us usually register quite low on the awareness index because we tend to shy away from thoughts of our own death. Consciously or subconsciously, we deny that someday our lives must end. The more intense our denial, the lower our PDA.

When I first began working with the Omega Project,* I was invited to a small dinner party at the home of some people I had just met. The hostess was a very efficient type who had planned everything perfectly in advance, from the hors d'oeuvres right down to the conversation. As if on cue, she said to me, "And what do you do at Harvard, Dr. Worden?"

"I'm researching death and dying," I replied.

She paled, looked very uncomfortable, and quickly focused her attention on another guest at the table. A discussion of death was definitely not what she wanted for herself or her party. I later learned that this woman was reacting, in part, to a series of recent deaths in her family. These losses had stimulated her PDA to an uncomfortable level; talking about death would have only added to her discomfort.

In addition, many families operate by an unwritten code that Personal Death Awareness must be kept at a low level, and so they avoid any conversation on the subject unless absolutely necessary. A woman said to me recently, "In our family we don't talk about religion, cancer, or death."

An elderly grandfather I know, who had been permanently crippled in an accident, dwelt constantly on his own death. "I don't know why God has kept me alive," he said. "I know I won't be here much longer, and that's the best thing because I'm no good to anybody."

"Don't talk like that, Grandad," his granddaughter replied. "You probably have years to live. You ought to concentrate on finding what God wants you to do rather than on giving up life too early!"

*The Omega Project is a long-term study of terminal illness and suicide at Harvard University and Massachusetts General Hospital—THE EDITOR

We assume the granddaughter was saying this out of love for the old man. Actually, it was to her advantage to speak this way in order to keep her own PDA at a manageable level.

One reason you tend to get upset when a major disaster occurs close to you is that it increases your Personal Death Awareness beyond an acceptable level. You identify with those who have died and become uncomfortable as you're reminded of your own mortality.

I was able to observe this phenomenon firsthand in Boston during the summer of 1973 when a Delta airliner crashed, immediately killing all but one passenger. Our hospital received the dead and injured. Because I was interested in how people cope with anxiety, I spoke with a number of the bystanders watching the incoming ambulances. "This really upsets me!" one woman said. "It's not just that so many people were killed, though I really think that's terrible, you understand. What really gets to me is that I could have been on that plane."

In other words, she was disturbed, not so much by the great loss of life, but by her own mortality. As the implications of death were brought home to her, she experienced a painful increase in her own Personal Death Awareness.

If she had witnessed this same scene on television, this woman might have conditioned herself to maintain a low PDA by ignoring or making impersonal the constant reports of deaths and disasters by the news media.

Doctors and nurses who work with dying patients also devise strategies to keep their own PDA below uncomfortable levels. They rely on in-house humor and often refer to patients as "cases" rather than as persons. In one New York hospital, doctors sometimes refer jokingly to drug addicts and survivors of serious knife or gunshot wounds as "antideath antibodies." Although most medical people are aware of the anxiety beneath their macabre humor, some are completely oblivious to it.

Some colleagues and I did a study of equivocal suicides. We found that the closer the deceased was in age, sex, and professional standing to the attending physician, the less chance there was that the death would be listed as a suicide in hospital records. More likely, the report would say "accidental death." The doctor's identification with the deceased probably raised his own

PDA, and prompted him to unconsciously decide in favor of an accident.

Awareness of death is always tempered by denial. Some denial of death is necessary and important, for without a degree of denial of your own death, you can't function effectively. As François, Duc de La Rochefoucauld said, "Neither the sun nor death can be looked at steadily."

Dr. Avery Weisman, my colleague on the Omega Project, said in a recent book, "The purpose of denial is not simply to avoid danger but to prevent loss of a significant relationship . . . with someone essential to self-esteem. . . . Denial helps to maintain a simplified yet constant relationship with significant others, especially at a moment of crisis."[1]

Despite attempts at denial, *some* awareness of your own mortality, however low, is always there in your consciousness. Are you aware of the pressure of the chair on your buttocks as you sit and read this book? Until I mentioned it, you were probably quite unaware of the pressure. But now that I have mentioned it, your awareness of it has increased. The pressure hasn't changed, of course. You may be squirming more now, but the pressure is the same as it was before.

Similarly, in this book I am encouraging you to consider a pressure which is already there—your own limited life span and the fact that someday you will indeed die. I am purposely asking you to raise your Personal Death Awareness so that you can begin to perceive an entire range of choices about your life and death that you might not have been aware of before.

In Gestalt psychotherapy, there's a technique called "experiencing polarities," which can help people understand themselves better and become more effective persons.[2] If you're very shy, for example, the therapist, through suggested experiments with other people, may help you experience extremely extroverted behavior—the opposite "pole" to your usual shyness. The purpose isn't to make you *become* an extrovert, but rather to give you some experience with a side of your personality you've never tested before. By acting out an extroverted role, you can increase your awareness of what it's like. Perhaps you can acquire enough flexibility so that you don't have to hover around your "shy" behavioral extreme just because it's familiar and safe.

Many people are afraid to try unfamiliar behavior extremes because they're afraid they may get stuck there. I've never known this to happen. More likely, they'll realize they can do and experience things they previously considered impossible.

Just as there are extremes of introversion and extroversion, there are extremes of Personal Death Awareness. You may have willingly experienced only one polarity—the low side of the awareness index. Any high death awareness you've experienced was probably associated with something very unpleasant, such as the death of a friend or loved one, and that makes you resist increasing your death awareness. But I've often found that if a person *willingly* increases his own Personal Death Awareness and looks his mortality squarely in the face, he seldom prefers to return to his previous state of unawareness. The exercises in the book are set up to help you experience a higher PDA.

To understand some of the implications of having a high, low or moderate PDA, look at three people with whom I've worked who fall into each of these categories. Two of these people died from terminal diseases, but their experiences are still relevant to so-called "healthy" people. In a sense all of us are "terminal." It's certain we're all going to die eventually—whether tomorrow in an auto accident, or next year of cancer or a heart attack, or many years from now, quietly, of old age.

1. VERY LOW PERSONAL DEATH AWARENESS

Sam was a fifty-five-year-old man. In the past, he had not been able to stand hospitals, funerals, or wakes. Both he and his wife, Edna, avoided doctors whenever possible. He was admitted to the hospital with gas and back pains, and the attending physician returned a diagnosis of advanced terminal stomach cancer.

Although another member of his family and a close friend had both died of cancer, Sam refused to acknowledge the diagnosis. "The people we know who died of cancer got it after being injured," he rationalized on several occasions. "One of them was struck on the chest by the branch from a tree, and got lung cancer. The

other guy was a printer who worked a lot with ink and spilled it all over himself. That gave him leukemia. But I never had any accident, so how could I have the same thing they had?"

In the next few months he lost forty-five pounds, was in intense pain, and experienced enlarged lymph nodes and a swelling belly. He continued to be puzzled by his illness, and his wife supported his denials of his poor prognosis for recovery. "You'll be up and around in no time," she told him. "Just do what these doctors tell you and get some rest, and I know you'll be all right."

He had always been an aggressive businessman who extolled efficiency and hard work as prime virtues. "I expect I'll be back to work in another month or so," he insisted.

But Sam's condition was hopeless and the medical staff did not expect him to recover. One day before he died, he told a nurse, "I'll be getting better pretty soon. All I need is a good laxative to get this swelling stomach back to normal."

Sam's denial of death created a series of unnecessary problems for himself and his family. For one thing, even when he should have been aware that something was seriously wrong with him, he postponed seeking treatment. Had he taken a realistic look at his own mortality, he might have sought professional help earlier and still be alive today.

Sam also refused to affirm his own religious beliefs. He was a Roman Catholic, yet he did not reach out for the support that his priest and the hospital chaplain were willing to give him. He failed to take advantage of the reservoirs of spiritual knowledge that might have expanded his understanding of his situation.

When he denied his own death, he failed to prepare his wife, Edna, for living alone.

There were no preparations for a funeral and burial. Sam's widow, reluctant to acknowledge that he was dead, refused to spend much time with the funeral director and finally paid much more than she might have. Sam could have settled all these matters for a reasonable cost long before he died.

Sam died without a will. As a result, his funds were tied up in lengthy court proceedings. Edna found herself having to wrestle with details that he could have easily resolved in an hour or two if he had acknowledged his mortality and acted, rather than postponed the decisions about his estate for the tomorrow that never came.

Sam left an emotionally unprepared widow who, even for several months after his burial, spoke of him as though he were away on a business trip. His denial of his limited life span resulted in considerable waste of the last few months of his life and caused a trail of unnecessary expenses and administrative headaches. Sam's life-style—his previous stress on the importance of marital love, efficiency in his daily affairs, and a firm religious faith—was abandoned in his death style of denial.

2. VERY HIGH PERSONAL DEATH AWARENESS

Lisa, a twenty-seven-year-old schoolteacher, found herself constantly preoccupied with thoughts of her own death. Not only did these thoughts cause her a great deal of anxiety, but because of her fear, there were days when she couldn't make it out of bed to go to work.

She had a recurring dream that a huge, black, shapeless force hovered over her. The force would come down on top of her and take her breath away. She would wake up short of breath, and it was difficult for her to get back to sleep.

When she was twenty-five, Lisa had come down with a case of infectious hepatitis—a fairly common liver disease. Although this illness left her with no residual liver damage, she felt that it had. She often returned to her physician for additional liver tests. The tests came out consistently negative, but Lisa refused to believe him. She preferred to see herself as damaged and thought she was going to die in the very near future.

She wanted very much to talk with others about her fear of a shortened life, but found that her friends didn't want to discuss it. This made her feel angry and very much alone. What made it particularly difficult was that for years Lisa had played a "Dear Abby" role with her friends, always being available to listen to their problems. "Now when I need someone to listen to me," she said, "no one is around."

In order to find a sympathetic person who would listen to her and take her seriously, she began psychotherapy. In therapy, she was able to

learn why she had become so preoccupied with her own death.

Lisa's father had died when she was thirteen. For a number of years her father had been an alcoholic, estranged from Lisa and her family. "I can well remember riding on the bus and seeing my father stretched out on the steps of a bar, dead drunk. I really hated him for that. At the same time, I felt sorry for him."

One day Lisa arrived home from school to find the family gathered together in the house making plans for her father's funeral. He had been found dead in a hotel room. The family was so angry with the deceased father for the way he had deserted them that they decided to get the funeral over with as soon as possible. They chose to have no service, to cremate the body, and to spread his ashes. Lisa was the only one who wanted something better for him, but since she was the youngest child in the family, no one paid her any attention. "It wasn't fair. What a crummy way to die. Without a headstone, no one would ever know that he had ever lived." She felt angry and helpless in her frustration.

During therapy, Lisa got in touch with her obsession with and fear of death. She had been afraid that she would end up like her father—with no one caring that she was dead.

Her preoccupation with chronic liver disease was her way of identifying with her father who had damaged his liver with his heavy drinking. She was able to work through her problem and bring her extremely high and debilitating Personal Death Awareness to a more manageable level.

3. MODERATE PERSONAL DEATH AWARENESS

Jack, a thirty-year-old with a terminal kidney ailment, chose to accept his limited life span. The father of six children, he wasn't happy about dying, and he held out hope perhaps even longer than was reasonable. But he didn't fool himself by pretending he was going to live forever.

Jack had had two kidney transplants, one from his father and another from a cadaver. Neither one worked out because of his body's susceptibility to infection. After several months of intermittent hospitalization, he realized he might not pull through. But he wasn't willing to give up hope at that point, especially since his doctors continued to give him some encouragement. He began to sit in the hospital hallway and watch the elevator in the hope that an anonymous donor would appear.

Even though Jack continued to watch and wait, the hoped-for donor never appeared. He even talked about putting an advertisement in the paper for a donor, as one might do for blood donations. He constantly set goals for himself: "A donor will come in this month. Then I'll have the transplant, and by next month I'll be out of here."

Finally, he realized the donor would never arrive. His body's ability to combat infection decreased, and the inevitability of death dawned on him. Jack's first reaction was irritability: he lashed out at his nurses—uncharacteristic behavior for a person as good-natured as he was. He had become a successful salesman through his ability to get along with people, to make them like him under almost any circumstances.

Then his irritation passed, and he assumed a level-headed, realistic attitude toward his limited life span. He and his wife, Ruth, began to discuss their situation frankly. He had given her thirteen yellow roses for their first anniversary, and then a potted plant for each anniversary thereafter. But during his last stay in the hospital, he said, "This year, I want you to have a potted plant. But I think you're going to have to buy it for yourself." With that, they both began to cry. This expression of feeling helped open up communication so that they could make plans for the present and the future.

One day, a nurse walked in on them and found them discussing their marriage, what it had meant to them, and what the future would be like for their six children. During the weeks before he died, Jack brought up every conceivably relevant topic that he felt Ruth should know about. They discussed ways to arrange for mortgage payments to be made so she wouldn't lose the house after he died. Since she had always relied on him for transportation, he insisted that she get herself a driver's license and buy an inexpensive car. He also passed all of his little domestic chores and financial responsibilities to Ruth while he still had several weeks left, so that her transition to head of the household would be easier.

Then came the toughest topic of all: He told her how he wanted to be buried and insisted that he would be unhappy if she spent more than the minimum amount of money on the service, casket, and cemetery plot. "I want the money we save on the funeral to go for the kids," he told her. "Use it for their education."

Although not particularly religious, Jack had always been concerned about the welfare of others and had devoted his spare time to the Boy Scouts and other social service projects. So as his life drew to a close, it was natural for him to want to continue this altruism, to affirm the values of his life in his death. "Ruth, we never talked about this much because I guess I never expected to die," he said. "But I want you to be sure my eyes are donated to people who need them. I lived a little longer because of two kidney transplants, and I want some other people to have the same break I did."

Jack had always been close to his wife and children, perhaps because his own family life had been unsatisfactory. As his death drew nearer, he grew closer to Ruth and the six children.

Jack and Ruth talked seriously about how much they meant to each other and explained to the children exactly what was happening. He told them about the dialysis unit that had been cleansing his blood and keeping him alive between transplants. The oldest child, nine-year-old Sandy, gave a talk to her school class about kidney transplants and dialysis. Although the youngest children had trouble understanding exactly what death meant, all of them talked about it with their parents.

After Jack died, the children finally decided that they would assume responsibility for caring for their father's cemetery plot. One of the boys bought two geraniums for the grave, and the others made regular visits to clear the weeds.

Which of these three people did you most identify with? Probably most of us would say we'd *want* to be like Jack, but *know* we're more like Sam. There seem to be two main reasons why we keep our Personal Death Awareness at a low level. The first and most obvious is that we want to keep our level of anxiety about the threat of non-being, or non-existence, at a low, manageable point. Most people aren't sure what comes after death, but they suspect it's nothingness, and that's not a very pleasant thought.

But there's another reason for keeping the personal awareness level down—the idea that it's futile to think about the inevitable. As Ben Franklin said: "In this world nothing is certain but death and taxes." Or as you might put it, "There's nothing I can do about death, so why think about it? I don't have any choices."

That's where you're wrong. There are many choices open to you. You certainly don't have a choice of *whether* to die or not, but you can exercise quite a few other options.

You can choose:

How you view death.
To recognize you have a limited life span and begin to order your life on that basis.
To let an understanding of your death intensify and improve your present relationships.
What to do with your body when you're finished with it.
How you want to be remembered by friends and family.
Where you would like to die.
To fear death less.
To learn to talk more comfortably about death.
To get the psychological upper hand over a terminal illness.
Not to continue living on artificial, extraordinary support systems.
Whether or not to end your own life.
Whether or not to draw up a will.
Whether or not to carry life insurance.
To develop resources for confronting death.

To help you get more involved in this idea of choices, eight different types of death, based on case studies of people of various ages and backgrounds, are listed below. Look them over and decide which death would be most suitable for you, and also which you would least like to experience.

1. Mary died at age eighty-seven following a brief illness, at home with her family around her. Her relatives loved and cared for her, but she had felt increasingly useless during the last fifteen years of her life.
2. George died at age sixty-nine, working at a job which he enjoyed and from which he refused to retire. He had always wanted to die "in the saddle," and most people felt this is just what happened.
3. Cal died at age fifty-seven in the hospital after a rather painful illness involving several hospitalizations. He was alerted enough in advance of his death so that he could tie up all the loose ends in his estate and prepare his family for his departure.
4. Edgar died in a nursing home at age seventy-two, six months following the death of his spouse of fifty years. The doctors said he died of a broken heart.
5. Henry was walking out of a downtown bank when he got caught in the crossfire of bullets between police and bank robbers. He was fatally shot and died immediately on the street at age forty-eight.
6. Betty died at age thirty-seven when the car in which she was riding was struck by a speeding auto driven by teen-age joyriders. She left a husband of the same age, and two small children.
7. Carrie died at age thirty of an overdose of barbiturates. She had gone through a series of unsuccessful love affairs and found that each one left her more depressed than the one before. Her friends said what she wanted most out of life was to get married, but she had eventually given up hope and foresaw only the bleak prospect of spinsterhood.
8. Keith, a single man, died at age twenty-three when a kidney which he had received through transplantation failed. He had endured many hospitalizations during his protracted illness but still managed to spread cheer among his family, friends, and the hospital staff that attended him.

Glance back over these eight experiences so that you'll have them firmly in mind. Then write down your choices.

The death I would *most* prefer for myself is number _____. The death I would *least* prefer for myself is number _____

The reasons for my choices are: _____
_____
_____
_____
_____
_____

You probably found it easy to pick the types of death that you would *not* want for yourself. But did you have difficulty picking a death you *would* want? If so, you can be sure you have a lot of company. Because death is such a very personal matter, let me suggest that you try to design your own death—a death that would be suitable and appropriate for you, or as Avery Weisman says, "a death that you could live with." You have a style of life which you call your own. What would be your style of death?

To help you in designing a death which might be appropriate for yourself, take a few minutes to compose your own obituary-eulogy. No, don't close the book yet! Many of my students who have taken the time for this exercise have been impressed with its value, especially with the way it makes death personal for them. You can use your own format or the one suggested below. If you use the one below, take your time and fill in the blanks thoughtfully.

OBITUARY-EULOGY

_____ *died today at the*
[Your full name]

age of _____ . *A native of* _____ ,
[Your birthplace]

he/she died _____
[How you might die]

_____ .

He/she is best remembered for _____
_____
_____
_____
_____
_____
_____ .

He/she is survived by _____
_____
_____
_____
_____
_____ .

Details of the funeral and the burial are as follows: _____
_____
_____
_____
_____ .

What was it like for you to compose your own obituary? Did you feel anxious or upset? Did any of the questions make you think about things you had refused or neglected to think about before? Look back at some of the first exercises you did in this chapter. Did you increase or decrease your estimates of your life span in your obituary?

How did you see yourself dying? Was it a so-called "natural" death, a terminal illness, or a quick, violent death, as in an accident or homicide? Perhaps you chose a self-inflicted death like suicide?

Some people find how they want to be remembered a particularly hard question, so they insert something funny. Humor can eliminate the sting, the uncomfortable feelings invoked by a serious issue.

In writing your own obituary one of the most difficult details is listing survivors. It's fairly easy for most people to conceive of living longer than their parents and not living as long as their children. But when it comes to surviving brothers and sisters, that's a much harder matter. Who among your siblings still living do you expect to die before you? Who will outlive you? If you are married, do you anticipate outliving your spouse? The statistics, as you probably know, show that most wives tend to outlive their husbands by several years.

Did you choose a large or small funeral, or any at all? Were you cremated or buried? You may say your final send-off hardly matters because you won't be aware of it. But when most people are honest with themselves, they admit they want a say about their funerals, if only to keep the costs down and preserve their estates.

Now that you've increased your Personal Death Awareness through some hard thinking and by doing several exercises, what feelings are you experiencing? Take a moment to explore your reactions and make a note of them.

Right now I am feeling mostly:

___ anxious	___ happy	___ confused
___ calm	___ amused	___ bored
___ tense	___ frightened	___ interested
___ sick	___ oppressed	___ other
___ angry		

Think of three people you know well with whom you might share these feelings. Write down their names and anticipate how they might respond to your feelings by checking the appropriate columns.

Name	Very helpful	Rather helpful	Not helpful
1. _____	_____	_____	_____
2. _____	_____	_____	_____
3. _____	_____	_____	_____

If you checked the "not helpful" column for any of these people, *why* do you think they would react negatively? Could it be because they keep their own PDA quite low?

In the foregoing exercises and case illustrations we've seen that increasing your own Personal Death Awareness—breaking free from fear and denial—can have several concrete benefits. The most obvious is that you'll be able to make choices about your own death. You only have one chance to die. Don't muff it!

But an awareness of your own mortality can also help you live a more effective life in the here and now:

> You can deal with feelings and not have to hide them.
> You can identify what it is specifically about dying that is causing you anxiety. Once you've pinpointed the cause, you can proceed to do something about it.
> You can take more advantage of opportunities which happen your way. A healthy Personal Death Awareness will prevent you from postponing until tomorrow tasks which can *only* be done today. Tomorrow may be too late.

If you remember that you and your loved ones won't live forever, you can have more significant, less superficial, personal relationships. But if you postpone expressing appreciation and love, death may intervene to make your temporary delay a permanent thing. Or if you harbor longstanding grudges, the grave may prevent them from being resolved. In psychotherapy sessions, I often have to work with people who have profound resentments which they never expressed to their parents. The parents are now dead, but the resentments linger on and have to be worked out in therapy.

I think psychologist Rollo May understood the place of death in life when he wrote, "The confronting of death gives the most positive reality to life itself. It makes the individual existence real, absolute, and concrete. Death is the one fact of my life which is not relative but absolute, and my awareness of this gives my existence and what I do each hour an absolute quality."[3]

People often ask me if working with the dying isn't a depressing experience. It can be a *sad* experience, especially with a person to whom I am particularly close. But on the positive side, working with the dying has increased my awareness of the brevity of life and the importance of living my life now and not postponing things until tomorrow. As you allow yourself to experience a healthy increase in your own Personal Death Awareness, you too may find yourself reaching out for life with a new healthy zest.

Notes

1. Avery D. Weisman, *On Dying and Denying* (New York: Behavioral Publications, 1973), 63, 65.
2. E. and M. Polster, *Gestalt Therapy Integrated* (New York: Brunner/Mazel, 1973).
3. Rollo May, *Existence* (New York: Basic Books, 1958), 49.

To Apply This Reading to Yourself

1. *Discuss your own Personal Death Awareness.*
2. *Complete each of the exercises presented by Worden and Proctor and present your results and any conclusions or insights you formed.*

3. *Discuss the way in which the subject of death was dealt with in the family you grew up in and how you would like to deal with it in the family you have or might establish yourself.*
4. *Discuss any use you have made of denial in dealing with your awareness of death.*
5. *What advantages or disadvantages do you see for yourself in increasing your Personal Death Awareness?*

The Dying-Readiness/Freedom-to-Live Test

Abe Arkoff

In our lives, we move through many turning points. Some are small and taken in stride. Others are large and very affecting. And then one day, we reach a point whose immensity cannot be disputed: death. Death is the ultimate turning point.

Why is the consideration of death and dying so important as we seek to illuminate our lives? Death is a turning point that casts its influence far in advance of its occurrence. How differently we might lead our lives if we knew we would never die. How differently some of us lead our lives as we pretend we never will.

For 10 years (1980–1990), I was a volunteer working with hospice patients and those with life-threatening illnesses. I have also given workshops on preparation for death, which I call "Dying Readiness/Freedom to Live." This, I think, is an apt title because it is my experience that those of us who face our mortality and prepare for it, free ourselves to live more fully. In getting our house in order and readying ourselves for death, we ironically open wider the door to life. Following are some reasons that this is so.

1. The realization that we are mortal makes life precious.

Suppose that there was an account into which $1440 was deposited every day for you to spend. However, at the end of the day, the unspent portion is forfeited because no balance can be carried forward. Furthermore, you are given no idea when the account will be closed. How much of your account would you leave unspent?

We each have an account—a true one, not a fantasy. Each day there is a deposit of 24 hours or 1440 minutes. At the end of the day, all the wasted minutes are forfeited because no time can be carried forward to the next day. Furthermore, you are given no idea when the account

will be closed. How much of this account do you forfeit, waste, and throw away?

The full realization that we are mortal, that we will die one day, and indeed might die at any moment, makes life more precious. Persons who have been very near death but recovered frequently report a new appreciation for life and even the smallest joys of life. Abraham Maslow eloquently expressed this idea in a letter he wrote while recovering from a heart attack, and part of this letter is presented in the epigraph that begins this topic.

When Orville Kelly learned he was incurably ill with cancer, he spearheaded the formation of a self-help group for cancer patients and their close relatives, called "Make Today Count." It now has chapters all over the country and aims "To promote the simple goal of living each day as fully and completely as possible." Kelly (1979) wrote that it took the "specter of death" to make himself aware of the preciousness of life.

2. The full realization that we are mortal makes life purposeful.

Suppose that you knew you were going to live forever, what would you get busy and do right now? There might not be much point in getting a move on if you had until the end of time—which is how long death-denying folks seem to think they have. Elisabeth Kübler-Ross writes, "It is the denial of death that is partially responsible for people living empty, purposeless lives; for when you live as if you would live forever, it becomes too easy to postpone the things that you must do" (p. 164).

Never-ending life has been given considerable attention by writers of imaginative and science fiction. Merritt Abrash reviews this writing in an essay entitled "Is There Life After Immortality?" and concludes there is general agreement that immortality "would not be merely undesirable for various social and philosophical reasons, but a curse upon the so-called beneficiaries" (p. 26). Immortality is seen as destroying life's pleasure, creativity, and significance and as such, ironically, becomes "a fate worse than death."

Suppose that you knew you probably had no more than 6 months of life to live, what would you get busy and do right now? This supposition is not so far-fetched. Quite a number of us will be seated in a doctor's office one day and learn—if our physician is candid—that we probably have little time to live. The question that opened this paragraph is sometimes asked in workshops dealing with death and dying. Many folks respond by saying that with only 6 months to live, they would get busy and do some things they were letting slide or planning to do some indefinite day. Having only 6 months to get things done, filled them with purpose and made them shake a leg and get busy.

Kübler-Ross (1975) writes that when we awaken each morning, it is important to understand that that day may be the last day we have. This understanding or thought might be especially helpful on those days that we have trouble getting a move on. Not forever, not 6 months, just 24 hours. What is it you are going to do today for sure, knowing this is the only day you have for sure?

3. The full realization that we are mortal gives us a useful perspective.

The saying: "I complained that I had no shoes until I met a man who had no feet," suggests that large matters give us some useful perspectives on small ones. There is much in life to fuss and fret about until we separate what is petty or trivial from what is important. One sign of maturity is that we have experienced enough of life so that we are able to tell the difference between the two.

Nothing gives us a better perspective on life than death. In the presence of death, unimportant things indeed seem unimportant, and important things are more easily given their due. "When I thought I might be terminally ill, I thought, my God, how much I love my wife and kids," a man told me, and added, "and I realized how screwed up my values were since I spent so little time with them." Further tests were fortunately negative; he's still alive and living his life more lovingly.

Nobody has written more eloquently or usefully about this matter than Carlos Castenada. In *Journey to Ixtlan*, Castenada describes a conversation concerning death with his mentor, don Juan, who is a Yaqui medicine man:

"Death is our eternal companion," don Juan said with a most serious air. "It is always to our left, at an arm's length. . . . It has always been watching you. It always will until the day it taps you. . . . The thing to do when you're impatient," he proceeded, "is to ask advice from your death. An immense amount of pettiness is dropped if your death makes a gesture to you, or if you catch a glimpse of it, or if you just have the feeling that your companion is there watching you. . . . Death is the only wise adviser that we have. Whenever you feel . . . that everything is going wrong and you're about to be annihilated, turn to death and ask if that is so. Your death will tell you that you're wrong; that nothing matters outside its touch. Your death will tell you, 'I haven't touched you yet.'" (pp. 54–55)

In my own life, I have found don Juan's image of death at arm's length a very powerful one. With death the measure, cataclysms become tremors, whirlwinds whispers, and much pettiness does indeed fall away.

4. The full realization that we are mortal allows us to make the most of the end of our lives.

"To everything there is a season, and a time for every purpose under heaven." These are familiar words from Ecclesiastes, and, indeed, every season of life has its special reasons for being. To have a full life, one would want to live each season fully.

Kübler-Ross titled one of her books *Death: The Final Stage of Growth*. Sometimes, when I talk about dying as an important stage of life, someone will say something like, "No thanks. I would just as soon skip it. I'm hoping to depart suddenly as the result of a massive heart attack at the age of 85."

Every stage of life offers us an opportunity to grow and none more so than the stage called "dying." When I first began to work with terminally ill patients, I thought my visits would be filled with talk of dying and death. Instead, I found my patients more occupied with living and life. Some of them seemed to be living life more fully (if more effortfully) than ever before.

I came to see that dying folks who openly confronted their approaching deaths had freed themselves to live and grow. They were free to regard this part of their lives as a completion to be lived rather than a catastrophe to be denied.

They were free to get their house in order, to catch up on all the things that needed to be done, and to say goodbyes. They were free to realize the preciousness of each remaining day.

I remember visiting a man who had cancer throughout his body. When we began to work together he seemed to be nearing death but managed to hang on and even get a little better. As we sat together, enjoying our cups of hot chocolate, he said to me, "I'm grateful. That may seem strange to hear from a man who has had my troubles the past few years. But my wife and I are closer than we have ever been. I'm still working on my relationship with my sons, but at least I have some time to work on it. I like myself better. I'm a lucky man."

THE DYING-READINESS/ FREEDOM-TO-LIVE TEST

As indicated earlier, my work has led me to believe that those of us who ready ourselves to die also free ourselves to lead our lives more fully than ever before. Typically, in my workshops on dying readiness, I administer my "Dying-Readiness/Freedom-to-Live" Test. I give it item by item, discussing each item as I go, so that the participants may have some basis for their answers.

The 10 items of the test are presented in the material that follows, and each item is briefly delineated. You are invited to take the test now. After you have read each item and delineation, answer by drawing a circle around "Yes" or "No" as is appropriate in your own case. If your answer isn't clearly yes or no, circle the question mark.

Yes ? No   1. I have allowed myself to think deeply about death and my own death and to experience the feelings that this engenders.

Edna St. Vincent Millay wrote a beautiful poem about death that has these lines:

> Childhood is the kingdom where nobody dies.
> Nobody that matters, that is.

Distant relatives die; cats die; but mothers and fathers don't die, and any thought of our own death is far away. But the innocence of childhood is soon lost as we grow and develop an increasing acquaintance with death. We come to know that we too will die. How do we deal with that awesome knowledge?

J. William Worden (1976), a psychologist who has worked with many dying patients and their families, has concluded that many of the problems we face in life stem from our inability to confront the simple fact that we will one day die. He drew up the concept of "personal death awareness" or PDA, for short, which describes the extent to which we are mindful of our mortality, accepting of it, and living our life in accordance with this mindfulness and acceptance.

Although it is possible to be overly preoccupied with death, Worden feels that most of us have PDAs that are too low because we tend to shy away from thoughts of our own mortality; we tend to deny and live in accordance with the denial that our lives will end. His experience is that if we *willingly* increase our PDA and face our mortality, we seldom want to go back to our former state of low awareness.

Worden believes there are two main reasons we keep our PDA at a low level. The first is that we find it anxiety-provoking to think about our own death. Second, we believe it's useless to think about death because there's nothing we can do about it. "That's where you're wrong" Worden writes—and Worden's right. There's a lot we can do about death. There are choices and options open to us, which will become apparent as we proceed with our test.

Your response to this chapter may be a good indication of the level of your PDA. If it makes you quite anxious or you wish it hadn't been included, your PDA may be on the low side. If you ordinarily avoid conversation about death (except to joke) or visiting persons near death or attending funerals, this may be a further indication.

At this point, go back and answer Item 1 if you haven't already. Circle the alternative that best describes your situation. Each of the succeeding items will encourage you to think a little more deeply about your own death and to experience the feelings that this engenders. If in all honesty, you now have to answer Item 1 "no," perhaps by the end of this test you will be a little closer to answering it "yes."

Yes ? No 2. I have made out a will.

Picasso left a huge fortune in art works, real estate, investments, and bank accounts, but he left no will. He predicted that after his death there would be a scramble among his legitimate heirs and illegitimate children and children's children. He said, "It will be worse than anything you can imagine." And it was.

Why don't people make out wills? One important reason is that a will is associated with the idea of our death. As was already indicated, thoughts of our mortality can be anxiety-provoking and whatever provokes anxiety may be pushed aside or avoided.

Some of us find it comforting to assume a kind of immortality for ourselves—or at least a nonmortality—and this is inconsistent with making out a will. Somerset Maugham once wrote that if one were small, one might hope to be overlooked by death. For some, making out a will is like registering to die and signing a will is like signing a death certificate or, at least, a promissory note. By not making out a will or not signing it, we feel we haven't put ourselves in jeopardy.

A second reason for not completing a will is that we assume this is something that can be delayed. Because we don't expect to die soon (if at all), why bother now? We can take care of this when we're old and gray.

A third reason for not making out a will is the assumption that one is not leaving much of value. (But if you die a "wrongful death," you may be worth a lot more dead than alive—and who gets it?) A fourth reason is the wishful thought that somehow things will work out all right and that those who should inherit will inherit; because making out a will is an expense and bother, why not just hope for the best?

Dying without a will may save you some effort and momentary anxiety, but it creates problems for those you leave behind. If you die without leaving a valid will, you are said to have died "intestate." Here is what David Larsen (1980), an attorney specializing in wills, trusts, and estate planning, has to say about intestacy:

> The main problem with intestacy is, of course, that you have no say where your property goes. Your spouse, your children, your adopted children, your parents—all of them may get more, or less, of your property than you might have expected or wanted. That special heirloom may go to a person whom you'd rather not have it. Your funeral and burial wishes may not be carried out. (Will anyone know what they are?) If you and your spouse both die so that your minor children are orphans, the court-appointed "guardian of the person" and "guardian of the property" may be people you'd rather not have watching after your children and their property. The executor of your estate may be some person you wouldn't want. Your executor and the guardian of your children's property may have to post bond, thereby costing your estate money, meaning that your heirs get less. You could end up paying a lot more in death taxes than you need to: the federal government and the [state] can steamroller your estate because you didn't put up any tax-saving defenses. Finally, dying intestate shows a lack of planning, meaning more than likely that your affairs will be a mess when you die. And who's left to straighten out your mess when you're gone? Your family—and at just the time when they are least able, emotionally, to do it. (p. 12)

It seems a bit curious that folks who care for their loved ones and who also care about their own hard-earned or carefully acquired possessions would leave both in limbo upon death. Making out a will shows that you care. It also shows that you weren't afraid to face your own demise. It's an important step in getting your house in order. Before proceeding further, answer Item 2 by circling one of its three alternatives.

Yes ? No 3. I have made known my choice between having and not having my life extended through artificial or heroic measures in the event that there is no reasonable expectation of my recovery from physical or mental disability. (Or I have made out a living will or executed a durable power of attorney.)

Medical science is my shepherd:
  I shall not want.
It leadeth me beside the marvels of
  technology.
It restoreth my brainwaves;
It maintaineth me in a persistent vegetative
  state for its name sake.

Yea, though I walk through the valley of
   the shadow of death,
I shall find no end to life;
For thou art with me;
Thy respirator and heart machine,
   they sustain me.
Thou preparest intravenous feeding for me
In the presence of irreversible disability;
Thou anointest my head with oil;
My cup runneth on and on and on and on
   and on.
Surely coma and unconsciousness shall
   follow me all the days of my continued
   breathing;
And I will dwell in the intensive-care unit
   forever.

—Reverend Robert Fraser

Advances in medicine often make it possible to delay death in terminally ill patients and to keep nonterminal but irreversibly comatose patients indefinitely alive. Sometimes the days that technology adds are of little use or quality, and the additional time is purchased at considerable cost and discomfort. The case against maintaining life at all costs is vividly made in Reverend Robert Fraser's adaptation of the Twenty-third Psalm.

Competent adults have the right to refuse life-sustaining treatment, but what happens if one becomes incompetent to make one's wishes known? In this litigious age, physicians run into few problems if they continue to treat a patient, but there can be considerable danger in stopping treatment. In the absence of specific instructions, it is unlikely that life-support systems would be withdrawn and much less likely in the case of a relatively young patient.

By planning ahead, we can have a say concerning artificial or heroic measures that might be used to prolong our own lives. There are various advance directives that can be employed for this purpose, but the two most important are the living will and the durable power of attorney for health care. Living wills are now recognized by statute in more than half the states, although provisions vary considerably. All states and the District of Columbia have statutes recognizing durable powers of attorney, and in most states, such powers can be worded to create a document covering (and limited to) health care. (Unlike an ordinary power of attorney, which terminates if the principal becomes incapacitated, a *durable* power of attorney continues despite the principal's condition.)

A *living will* (not to be confused with a living trust) is a written, signed, witnessed, and possibly notarized declaration that specifies your wishes concerning the use of life-sustaining procedures in your own case if you become terminally ill and incompetent. A *durable power of attorney for health care* is a written, signed, witnessed, and possibly notarized document in which you (the principal) give another (the agent) the legal authority to make health-care decisions on your behalf if you become terminally ill and incompetent. Because some living wills also provide for a health proxy who, in effect, can serve as an agent, and some durable powers of attorney also specify your health-care wishes, there can be a great deal of overlap in these two approaches. State laws vary, so it is important that a local attorney or some other knowledgeable authority be consulted for assistance as you weigh your options and devise your own plan.

Yes ? No 4. I have planned my own funeral or planned to dispense with a funeral and made these plans known.

Yes ? No 5. I have chosen and made known a plan for the disposal of my body after death.

Although we don't plan our entrance into this world, we have an opportunity to plan our departure. In our plans, we will want to consider our own wishes and also the needs of our survivors and what would be helpful and convenient for them. Careful planning can avoid a situation like this one described by Robert Kavanaugh (1974):

> Not long ago I attended a funeral of incredible ugliness. The minister kept referring to the deceased by the wrong name, totally unaware of frantic cues from the pews, mistaking our winces and near groans for tears of muffled grief. The eulogy by this insensitive last-minute hireling had obviously been canned for any occasion. His suavity hinted he could be speaking to any luncheon club anywhere, except for his rude and impertinent in-

sistence on forcing his religious assumptions on the semireligious friends of a dead nonbeliever.

I wondered then and still wonder what purpose such a funeral was thought to serve. Who needed it? Nearly everyone departed in humiliation and anger, pitying the family too distraught to accept our sympathies. I wondered about that man of God who could be paid to talk so glibly about death without touching a single unifying spark in his saddened congregation beyond anger for himself. I wondered why the family needed this hollow and decrepit ritual and why anyone allowed them to put themselves through such a travesty after six months of watching their daughter die. (pp. 187–188)

Here, in sharp contrast, is a recollection of a member of the Older Women's League:

I'd like to tell you about a memorial service I once attended at a senior center. I didn't know the woman who had died. I was visiting a friend in another city and she invited me to go to the senior center for a memorial service for one of the active members. There was nothing solemn about the occasion—the feeling of the group was warm and friendly. The group leader started by telling about the deceased—some of her special contributions and a couple of amusing anecdotes illustrating her lively character. Another person told a similar story, and soon the conversation was moving along, bringing laughter and an occasional tear. Family members talked of what she had meant to them. One person sang a song, another read a brief poem. A display of pictures and a few clippings were on the wall. The service lasted about 45 minutes, followed by much hugging and then refreshments.

I felt privileged to have heard this re-creation of a remarkable woman's life, told by those who had shared it. The loss was evident, but the group was healing itself and would carry on, with their deceased friend living in their hearts and memories.

What will your funeral or memorial service be like? Or do you want a service at all? Are you leaving this all up to others? In making our own final plans, we help ourselves, in that (1) we can contemplate making a departure appropriate to the wishes of both ourselves and our survivors, (2) we can experience in anticipation this departure just as we preexperience a well-planned trip, and (3) we can gain a sense that we have done what needs to be done and therefore are free to go on to the business of living.

In our final planning, we also help those we leave behind in two ways: (1) We remove the necessity of decision making just at the time when our survivors might be least able to make decisions, guess at what we would have wanted, or resolve differences among themselves. (2) We may ameliorate a common tendency of bereaved persons to overspend on funeral arrangements.

Simplicity is what London schoolmaster Ken James sought in his final arrangements. When he died of cancer, he left an estate of $40,800 but no funds for a funeral. In his will, he wrote, "I specifically forbid a conventional funeral. There must be no ceremony of any kind, religious or otherwise, no floral tributes or mourners or any fuss whatsoever. My ashes are not to be buried or sentimentally scattered, but are to be inconspicuously deposited in any convenient dustbin for refuse collection in the usual way." (That proved to be a bit much for the officials; they had James's ashes buried under a bed of flowers at the crematorium).

For those of us who wish simplicity and economy in our final disposition (but perhaps not quite so simple and economical as Ken James), joining a memorial society is a good option. These societies are cooperative, democratically run, nonprofit organizations that contract with funeral directors on behalf of their members. By practicing simplicity and by bargaining collectively, the members of the society save 50 to 75 percent of usual funeral costs. These memorial societies have low fees to join (rarely over $25), sell no services of their own, and should not be confused with private companies calling themselves societies. For a directory of cooperative societies, contact their national organizations: Continental Association of Funeral and Memorial Societies, 6900 Lost Lake Road, Egg Harbor, WI 54209, or the Memorial Society of Canada, Box 96, Station A, Weston, Ontario M9N 3M6.

Benevolence is what poet Robert Test (1976) seeks in his final disposition. As a last act, he wants to give himself away:

The day will come when my body will lie upon a white sheet neatly tucked under four corners of a mattress located in a hospital busily occupied with the living and the dying. At a certain moment a doctor will determine that my brain has ceased to function and that, for all intents and purposes, my life has stopped.

When that happens, do not attempt to instill artificial life into my body by the use of a machine. And don't call this my deathbed. Let it be called the Bed of Life, and let my body be taken from it to help others lead fuller lives.

Give my sight to the man who has never seen a sunrise, a baby's face or love in the eyes of a woman. Give my heart to a person whose own heart has caused nothing but endless days of pain. Give my blood to the teenager who was pulled from the wreckage of his car, so that he might live to see his grandchildren play. Give my kidneys to one who depends upon a machine to exist from week to week. Take my bones, every muscle, every fiber and nerve in my body and find a way to make a crippled child walk.

Explore every corner of my brain. Take my cells, if necessary, and let them grow so that, someday, a speechless boy will shout at the crack of a bat and a deaf girl will hear the sound of rain against her window.

Burn what is left of me and scatter the ashes to the winds to help the flowers grow.

If you must bury something, let it be my faults, my weaknesses and all prejudice against my fellow man.

Give my sins to the devil. Give my soul to God.

If, by chance, you wish to remember me, do it with a kind deed or a word to someone who needs you. If you do all I have asked, I will live forever.

For those of us who, like Test, would like to give ourselves away, we can do so by completing a Uniform Donor Card, which is a binding legal document in every state through laws based on the Uniform Anatomical Gift Act. This card permits us upon death to make one or more of our body organs available for transplantation or research. For a card or further information, call the nearest organ and tissue bank (look in the phone book yellow pages under "Organ & Tissue Banks"). Some states offer you the opportunity to complete a card when you are applying for or renewing your drivers license. If you wish to donate your body for medical education, call a school of medicine.

For our final disposition, we may choose among a funeral service (held in the presence of the body, with an open or a closed casket), a memorial service (held after the body has been removed for final disposition), a committal ser-

vice (held at gravesite or in the chapel of a crematory), some combination of these services, or no service at all. Ernest Morgan (1984) has listed some options of disposition in approximate order of their cost, least to most expensive:

1. Immediate removal to a medical school, followed by a memorial service.
2. Immediate cremation, followed by a memorial service.
3. Immediate earth burial, followed by a memorial service.
4. A funeral service in the presence of the body, followed by removal to a medical school.
5. A funeral service in the presence of the body, followed by cremation.
6. A funeral service in the presence of the body, followed by earth burial. (p. 44)

Before proceeding, return to Questions 4 and 5, and answer them.

Yes   ?   No   6. I have made out a survivor's guide.

Dear Ann:

I am perplexed by a problem that I have run across three times in the past few years—secretive husbands.

In one case, an older cousin's husband died and the woman had no idea of the state of their finances. He always provided her with plenty of household and pocket money, but became apoplectic when asked about financial matters, even after he became terminally ill. When he died, his widow was unable to find any assets.

In the second case, a successful physician is unwilling to share information about the family finances. His wife (my sister) has no inkling of their financial status. He has a highly successful practice, is chief of staff of the community hospital and a pillar of the medical community, but totally secretive about financial matters. They have recently reconciled after nearly breaking up over this situation. My sister is a successful professional person in her own right and has had to run the household with her own funds, not paying much attention until recently when it became a bone of contention.

The third example is a sister-in-law. Her husband died suddenly last December. She was unable to find any resources except a small stock account and an apartment in London, which was in both names. He never spoke of business matters, even though they appeared to have a solid marriage.

What do you have to say about such peculiar behavior? How can a woman protect herself against a man who is secretive?—Perplexed In The West

Dear Perp:

It is hard to imagine a woman being so ignorant and passive about family finances in this day and age, especially since so many females are knowledgeable and involved in business.

Any wife who reads this and does not know what she can count on if her husband dies before her (and most of them will) should open the subject before another day goes by. If her husband refuses to talk about it, she should tell him he owes her that consideration and if he persists in being uncooperative, she will be forced to see a lawyer. She should not hesitate to make good her threat.

The same goes for men whose wives control the purse strings. They, too, have a right to know what goes on. A marriage in which such information is withheld indicates a serious lack of trust and mutual respect.—Ann Landers

There is often very much that needs to be done when a person dies and the people who need to do it may be in shock or upset and scarcely able to manage. Sometimes it may even be impossible to complete everything that needs doing because vital information is incomplete or unavailable. And yet much of this work could have been easily done long before death by the subject person herself or himself.

The problem noted in the letter written by "Perplexed in the West" is only one of many that can be avoided by filling out a survivor's guide (sometimes called a family guide). This guide is simply a listing of the data necessary to attend to funeral, obituary, legal, financial, and tax matters upon and after your death. You are the best person to gather your own data. You can do in a relatively short period of time what your survivors may be able to do only with difficulty or perhaps not at all.

Survivor's guides take various forms. A typical guide contains the information relative to your death certificate and obituary, desired funeral arrangements, will, safety deposit box, insurance, social security benefits, pensions, annuities, checking accounts, property, and other financial assets and liabilities.

Some funeral homes or mortuaries will provide you with a complimentary survivor's or family guide. To receive a copy of a guide by mail, send $2.00 to the Continental Association of Funeral and Memorial Societies, Inc., 6900 Lost Lake Road, Egg Harbor, WI 54209. Answer Item 6 before continuing on to the next item.

Yes ? No 7. I have made my relationships with "significant others" current by "clearing the past."

We want, of course, to be treated fairly. We want our world to be just. We want what is due to us. We want to get as good as we give. We want others to treat us as nicely as we treat them, and to pay us back for all we've done for them.

Alas, our world is not always just and the people in it who are most important to us—our "significant others"—are not always fair. When we are treated unfairly, unjustly, we may build up a good deal of anger and resentment. The raw deals, the things that others did to us and shouldn't have, the things they didn't do, but should have—these things may fester in our minds and memories.

It is important to distinguish between two kinds of wrongs. There are the wrongs to work on and the wrongs to let go of. It takes some wisdom to know the difference.

Some of us become resentment collectors. We are unable to forgive or forget the wrongs done to us. This kind of collecting accomplishes nothing and can become self-destructive. Our resentment consumes energy and keeps us stuck in the past. Like other persistent negative emotions, resentment can have corresponding physiological reactions that wear down the body and make us ill.

Why do we sometimes choose the heavy burden of resentment rather than the liberation that comes with forgiving? What do we get out of it?

Some persons don't forgive because they confuse forgiveness with condonation. They think that to forgive is to condone or overlook or even give approval to a wrong. By being unforgiving they continue to bear witness to the wrong. They keep the offender on the hook (and perhaps themselves as well). But to forgive does not require one to overlook or approve a wrong. Forgiveness notes there is something to be forgiven and also something to be gained by letting go and moving along.

Some persons don't forgive because no retribution has been made. There appears to have been no punishment, no repayment. To pardon the offender might set a bad example. Or would it present a good model? In any case, what may be more important is the effect of forgiveness on the forgiver and on the relationship of the forgiver to the one forgiven.

If we forgive others, we find it easier to forgive ourselves for what we may have done in the past, whether wittingly or unwittingly. If others don't have to be perfect, we don't have to be perfect either. If others can be forgiven, we can forgive ourselves.

The solution to the burden of resentment is forgiveness. When we forgive, we "clear the past" and write off all outstanding emotional debts. We let go of our resentment and let go of the past. In doing so, we free ourselves to come fully into the present and to make the most of it.

In his wise and helpful book *Forgive & Forget*, Lewis Smedes suggests we look upon our hurts with "magic eyes." Such eyes allow one to see things in a new light so that hurts flowing from the wounds of yesterday may heal.

Smedes asks, "What do you do when you forgive someone who hurts you? What goes on? When is it necessary? What happens afterward? What should you expect it to do for you? *What is forgiving?*" Here are his answers:

The act of forgiving, by itself, is a wonderfully simple act; but it always happens inside a storm of complex emotions. It is the hardest trick in the whole bag of personal relationships.

So let us be honest with each other. Let us talk plainly about the "magic eyes" that are given to those who are ready to be set free from the prison of pain they never deserved.

We forgive in four stages. If we can travel through all four, we achieve the climax of reconciliation.

The first stage is *hurt*: when somebody causes you pain so deep and unfair that you cannot forget it, you are pushed into the first stage of the crisis of forgiving.

The second stage is *hate:* you cannot shake the memory of how much you hurt, and you cannot wish your enemy well. You sometimes want the person who hurt you to suffer as you are suffering.

The third stage is *healing:* you are given the "magic eyes" to see the person who hurt you in a new light. Your memory is healed, you turn back the flow of pain and are free again.

The fourth stage is *the coming together:* you invite the person who hurt you back into your life; if he or she comes honestly, love can move you both toward a new and healed relationship. The fourth stage depends on the person you forgive as much as it depends on you; sometimes he doesn't come back and you have to be healed alone. (p. 18)

I would make two amendments to what Smedes has written. First, I don't think it is necessary to forget wrongs. In fact, not forgetting the hurt of a wrong done to us may keep us from inflicting similar hurt onto others. But it is necessary for us to remember the wrong differently—perhaps with sadness rather than anger or with a generosity that is above revenge and resentment.

Second, with "magic eyes," we may see the person who hurt us in a new light, but these eyes may also help us to see ourselves differently. We may respect ourselves more as generous, forgiving persons than as vengeful, resentful ones, and also find ourselves easier to live with.

When we have done all the necessary emotional work and "cleared the past," our house is in better order. We are ready to die—and we are ready to live our lives without the burden of resentment. Answer Item 7 before continuing on.

Yes ? No 8. I keep my relationships with "significant others" current by manifesting my love.

Immediately following are instructions for an exercise you can administer to yourself.[1] Pause after reading each paragraph, and imagine or simply think about yourself as being in that situation. Answer the questions to yourself. Then go to the next paragraph and continue in the same way until you have completed the exercise.

You are seated in a doctor's office. You are waiting for the doctor to come in with the results of your

1. This visualization is based on Perlin (1982).

medical examination. It has been rather a long wait. Take a little time to imagine how the office looks or just think about how it looks. How does it smell? What thoughts are going through your mind? What do you feel? (Pause)

The doctor comes in and sits down. There are a number of laboratory reports and some x-rays. You wait for the doctor to speak up. Why doesn't the doctor speak up? Finally, the doctor starts to go over the medical findings with you. You begin to realize that the findings are serious, very serious. You must check into the hospital immediately for more tests. What is going through your mind now? What are you feeling? To whom do you want to talk? Or be with? What would you say to them? (Pause)

Some months have gone by. You are at home and in bed. You are aware that you have only a short time to live. Your body is wasted and weak, but your mind is lucid and you can communicate with others. What are you thinking? What are you feeling? With whom do you want to be? What do you want to say to them? (Pause)

You are back in the hospital. There is only a little time left. People have come to see you and be with you, but the nurse has suggested only one or two approach you at a time. Whom do you want to see the most? Imagine or think of them standing there by your bed. What is being said? (Pause)

Now you have died. Your body remains on the hospital bed. Although the medical staff has left, some people have stayed to be with you a little longer. Who are they? If you could speak to them now, what would you say? (Pause)

In one of his newspaper columns, Charles McCabe (1975) wrote movingly about a dear friend who had died the previous week. McCabe deeply regretted that he had never been able to tell this friend how much he loved him. McCabe added, "I do not know how common this affliction is, this inability to express love. I know that it has been with me nearly all my life, and has caused me many moments of regret."

Many of us are like McCabe. After completing the preceding exercise, many persons report that somewhere in the process, they expressed their love and appreciation to a number of significant others—something they had not done recently, very much, or at all. They did not want to die without manifesting their love. But why—if the declaration of love is so important—were they living without manifesting it?

Marshall Hodge points out in his book *Your Fear of Love* that we all fear closeness, although some are much more frightened of it than others. Our fear is based on the fact that caring always involves vulnerability. Hodge writes, "When we open ourselves and permit another person to know that we love him, we risk being hurt. And because we know how it feels to be hurt, this risk is frightening" (p. 7).

Some of us have trouble in expressing our love because we have grown up in cold or undemonstrative families and have never learned how. Some consider love a kind of reward to be administered only when someone performs up to standards. Some are wary of love because it can interfere with independence.

Hodge writes that although love seems to ebb and flow like the ocean, it is not caring itself but rather the *experience* of love and the *expression* that are intermittent. He notes that moments of love are followed by periods of withdrawal. To keep our relationships with others current, we need to continually manifest our love. We need to keep our expression lines open.

It will be helpful to run a check on yourself now. In the space below make a list of all the people in your life whom you love (names, initials, or symbols will do). Then cross out every one to whom you haven't manifested your love in the past half year. (My dictionary says that *to manifest* means to make clearly apparent to sight or understanding; obvious. So just knowing they know that you love them doesn't qualify.)

<u>Persons Whom I Love</u>

Now, based on the preceding exercise and everything else you know about yourself, answer Item 8. Then continue with remaining two items.

Yes ? No 9. I have learned to die my "little deaths" in preparation for my "big death."

Plato, on his death bed, gave this advice to a visiting friend: "Practice dying." Life gives us plenty of opportunity for this practice because life is filled with a number of little deaths. These are the times when we lose not life but something very important to it. Perhaps someone dear to us dies or we are permanently disabled or we lose a relationship or position of many years or we suffer a great financial reversal or we come to the realization that something we have dreamed of and hoped for will never come to pass.

Stanley Keleman (1974) described life as a migration through many little dyings. In each dying, something old is lost, and something new is born. Keleman writes, "Growth, change and maturing occur by deforming the old and forming the new. In these little dyings we can learn how to live our big dying" (p. 26).

Keleman believes that big dying—death itself—is similar to little dying. If we want to know how we will face big death, we can review our little deaths. If we find we haven't died well or learned from our little dyings, we can change the way we live our dying and better prepare ourselves for big death.

How can we manage our little dyings better? An answer lies in the research and writing on mourning, which, according to psychiatrist George Engel, is like healing. If we do our "grief work" properly, we are healed and become healthy. Psychiatrist Will Menninger spoke of troubled people who healed so well they became "weller than well." In effectively managing our little deaths, we can become sturdier than sturdy—more and more able to face and manage big death or the prospect of it.

William Worden (1982) has identified four tasks involved in mourning or in the adaptation to loss. The first task is to accept the reality of the loss. One of the primary responses to loss is denial. We refuse to believe what has happened has happened, we deny that it is irreversible, or we minimize the full meaning of the loss. Our first task requires us to face the facts and realize what has happened, to know that it can't be undone, and to acknowledge its full importance to us.

The second task is to experience the pain of the grief. In grieving, we may feel shock, anger, sadness, guilt, anxiety, loneliness, helplessness, depression, or a combination or alternation of these states. Instead of acknowledging our grief, we may try to deny it, shut it off, and busy ourselves with other matters. Friends and relatives may support our tactics, encouraging us to keep a stiff upper lip and look on the bright side.

Various authorities on mourning believe it is necessary for bereaved persons to go through the pain of grief. If we avoid this pain, the course of mourning is prolonged. Some bereaved persons constrict their lives in an effort to prevent painful memories from arising.

The third task of mourning or adaptation to loss is to adjust to the new reality. We need to pick ourselves up and make a go of it with whatever we have left. This may be enormously difficult—to face life without whoever or whatever it was that made life worth living. But what choices do we have? Judith Viorst (1987) minces no words as she spells out our alternatives when a loved one dies: "To die when they die. To live crippled. Or to forge, out of pain and memory, new adaptations" (p. 295).

Picking ourselves up may mean setting new goals, learning new skills, or playing new roles. Very often it means compromise. But there is also an opportunity for growth and development that otherwise might not have occurred.

A fourth task applies to those situations in which there has been an emotional attachment. Its requirement is that this emotional energy be detached and reinvested in new relationships or enterprises. It is not easy to let go of old attachments. It may, for example, appear disloyal or it may seem that nothing could replace what was lost. And there can be the fear that what was lost once and with so much pain might be lost again.

What little deaths have you suffered? And how have you managed them? What have you learned? Have you learned to accept the reality of your losses? Can you allow yourself to feel the pain of your griefs? Are you able to accommodate your deprivation? Have you invested your emotional energy anew? Consider your responses to these questions, and answer Item 9 before you continue.

Yes ? No   10. I make it a point to appreciate and deeply enjoy the "little joys" of life.

None of us—whether seriously ill or seemingly hale—can count on endless tomorrows. Our lives could end at any moment. Are we fully living our lives, or are we saving our lives to be lived at a later date?

If we don't think of ourselves as mortal, if it's inconceivable to us that we will ever die, then we have forever. What's one day, if we have forever? We can throw it away. What's a little joy, if we have forever? We can keep pursuing big joys, whatever they may be.

One unfortunate notion of life is that it is a staircase. We climb up step by step, and when we get to the top we can be happy. If we are not happy at the top, maybe it isn't the top—maybe it's just a landing—so we need to resume climbing until we get to some place where happiness is.

Hermann Hesse (1988) wrote of the little joys available to us as we make our daily rounds. These are small things to which we may pay little notice but which can give us some moments of delight if we give them their due. A flower, a stretch of sky, a piece of fruit, children's laughter. His advice was that we seek out each day as many as possible of these small joys. He wrote, "It is the small joys first of all that are granted us for recreation, for daily relief and disburdenment, not the great ones."

Happiness, according to Jacques Henri Lartigue, is not an elusive bird that requires work to catch. Instead, happiness is an element—like air—that is everywhere. Lartigue wrote that if "you don't run after it too hard and too long, you'll find it right there, within reach, all the time . . . waiting for you to take it."

When we are ready to die, we are not so focused on large and distant pleasures. We do not primarily pursue the two elusive birds in the distant bush; we attend the one within reach or earshot. We take time to delight in the little joys that present themselves here and now.

Take a moment to recall the little joys you have delighted in today. How about yesterday? What about the day before? Do the memories of little joys come easily to mind, or are you drawing a blank? What about your life as a whole? Are you waiting for some Big Joy to make it all worthwhile? Think about this, and answer Item 10 before you go on.[2]

Take a few moments to review your response to all 10 items of the test. In your own estimation (there is no exact passing score), do your responses indicate you are ready to die? If so, congratulations because then your house is in order, and you are free to live. If your answers indicate you have more work to do, get busy and do it—not for death's sake but for life's sake.

Kenneth Woodward wrote that "there is no such thing as a good death except for those who have achieved a good life." To M. V. Kamath, the art of living and the art of dying are not different; neither can they be separated, for one flows into the other. He writes, "He who has mastered the art of living has already mastered the art of dying; to such, death holds no terrors."

2. For more about little joys, see pages 221–223 of this book.—Editor.

References

Abrash, M. (1985). Is there life after immortality? In C. B. Yoke & D. M. Hassler (Eds.), *Death and the serpent: Immortality in science fiction and fantasy.* Westport, CN: Greenwood Press.

Castenada, C. (1972). *Journey to Ixtlan.* New York: Simon & Schuster.

Hesse, H. (1988). On little joys. In A. Arkoff (Ed.), *Psychology and personal growth* (3rd ed., pp. 270–271). Boston: Allyn and Bacon.

Hodge, M. B. (1967). *Your fear of love.* Garden City, NY: Doubleday/Dolphin.

Kalish, R. A. (1985). *Death, grief, and caring relationships* (2nd ed.). Monterey, CA: Brooks/Cole.

Kavanaugh, R. E. (1974). *Facing Death.* Baltimore, MD: Penguin.

Keleman, S. (1974). *Living your dying.* New York: Random House/Bookworks.

Kelly, O. E. (1979). Making today count. In L. A. Bugen (Ed.), *Death and dying* (pp. 277–283). Dubuque, IA: Wm. C. Brown.

Kübler-Ross, E. (1975). *Death: The final stage of growth.* Englewood Cliffs, NJ: Prentice-Hall.

Landers, A. (July 1, 1986). Share financial data. *The Honolulu Advertiser,* p. D-2.

Larsen, D. C. (1980). *Who gets it when you go?* Honolulu: University Press of Hawaii.

McCabe, C. (1975, September 16). Love untold. *San Francisco Chronicle.*

Morgan, E. (1984). *A manual of death education and simple burial* (10th ed.). Burnsville, NC: Celo Press.

Perlin, S. (1982). Death visualization: A teaching and learning device. *Death Education, 6,* 294–298.

Smedes, L. B. (1986). *Forgive & forget: Healing the hurts we don't deserve.* New York: Pocket Books.

Test, R. (1976, November). The day will come . . . *Reader's Digest,* p. 142.

Viorst, J. (1987). *Necessary losses.* New York: Fawcett Gold Medal.

Worden, J. W. (1982). *Grief counseling and grief therapy.* New York: Springer.

Worden, J. W., & Proctor, W. (1976). *PDA: Personal death awareness.* Englewood Cliffs, NJ: Prentice-Hall.

To Apply This Reading to Yourself

1. *Is your Personal Death Awareness (PDA) at an optimal level? How does your personal awareness of death affect the way you live your life?*

2. *Have you made out a will? Why or why not? Concerning personal items or property with sentimental value or special meaning, who would you like to have inherit these items in the event of your death, why them, and have you ensured that this will be so? Concerning damages that might be paid your estate because of your "wrongful death" (for example, through accident), who would you like to inherit this money, why them, and have you ensured that this will be so?*

3. *Are there any conditions under which you would consider measures to prolong or shorten your life if you were terminally ill or irreversibly comatose? What have you done to ensure that your wishes in this regard are respected?*

4. *What plans for funeral or memorial services or for the disposal of your body after death do you prefer? Why? What have you done to ensure that your wishes in this regard are respected?*

5. *Have you made your relationship with "significant others" current by "clearing the past"? If so, give your proof. If not, why not?*

6. *Do you keep your relationships with "significant others" current by manifesting your love? If so, give your proof. If not, why not?*

7. *How have you dealt with a little death or some great loss in your life? What did you learn from this experience?*

8. *Do you make it a point to appreciate and deeply enjoy the little joys of life? If so, give your proof. If not, why not?*

Life after Life

Raymond A. Moody, Jr.

During the past 12 years I have encountered a large number of persons who were involved in what I shall call "near-death experiences." The first I met in 1965, when I was an undergraduate studying philosophy at the University of Virginia. He was a professor of psychiatry in the School of Medicine, and I was struck by his warmth, kindliness and humor. I learned later that he had been "dead," and heard him give a fantastic account of what happened to him then to a group of interested students. At the time, I was most impressed but, since I had little background from which to judge such experiences, I filed it away, both in my mind and in the form of a tape recording of his talk.

Some years later, after I had received my Ph.D. in philosophy, I was teaching in a university in eastern North Carolina. One day a student asked whether we might discuss immortality. He was interested because his grandmother had "died" during an operation and afterward had recounted an amazing experience, which was almost the same as the one the psychiatry professor had described years before.

As a result, I began to include readings on human survival of biological death in my philosophy courses, being careful not to mention the two death experiences. To my surprise, I found that in almost every class of 30 or so students at least one would come to me afterward and relate a personal "near-death" experience.

In 1972 I returned to college to earn a medical degree. By that time I had collected—and informally studied—a number of these experiences, and a friend talked me into giving a report to a medical society. Other public talks followed. Again I found that after every talk someone would tell me of an experience of his own.

I now know of approximately 150 cases of this phenomenon, falling into three distinct categories.

1. The experiences of persons who were resuscitated after having been thought, adjudged or pronounced clinically dead by their doctors.
2. The experiences of persons who, in the course of accidents, severe injury or illness, came very close to physical death.
3. The experiences of persons who, as they died, told them to other people who were present. Later, these other people reported the content of the death experience to me.[1]

Despite the wide variation in the circumstances surrounding close calls with death and in the types of persons undergoing them, there is a striking similarity among the accounts of the experiences themselves. On the basis of these points of likeness, let me now construct a brief, "ideal" experience which embodies all of the common elements. (I have found no one person who reports every single component of this composite experience. But there is not one component of my model which has appeared in only one account. Each element has shown up in many separate stories.)

A man is dying. As he reaches the point of greatest physical distress, he hears himself pronounced dead by his doctor.

He now begins to hear an uncomfortable noise, a loud ringing or buzzing, and at the same time feels himself moving rapidly through a long, dark tunnel. After this, he suddenly finds himself outside of his own physical body, and sees his own body from a distance, as though he were a spectator. He watches the resuscitation attempt from this unusual vantage point. He notices that he still has a "body," but one of a very different nature and with very different powers from the physical body he has left behind.

Soon others come to meet and help him. He glimpses the spirits of relatives and friends who have died. A loving, warm spirit—a being of light—appears before him. This being asks him a question, non-verbally, to make him evaluate

1. I have found reports of this third type to complement and agree with experiences of the first two types, but have for the most part stuck as closely as possible to firsthand reports.

his life and helps him along by showing him an instantaneous playback of the major events of his life.

At some point he finds himself approaching a sort of barrier or border, apparently representing the limit between earthly life and the next life. Yet, he finds that he must go back to earth, that the time for his death has not yet come. At this point he resists, for by now he is taken up with his experiences in the afterlife and does not want to return. He is overwhelmed by intense feelings of joy, love and peace. Despite his attitude, though, he somehow re-unites with his physical body and lives.

Later he tries to tell others, but he has trouble doing so. He can find no words adequate to describe these unearthly episodes. He also finds that others scoff, so he stops telling them. Still, the experience affects his life profoundly.

STRANGE SENSATIONS

In many cases, various unusual auditory sensations are reported to occur at or near death. Sometimes these are extremely unpleasant. A man who "died" for 20 minutes during an abdominal operation describes "a really bad buzzing noise coming from inside my head. It made me very uncomfortable." Another woman tells how, as she lost consciousness, she heard "a loud ringing. It could be described as a buzzing."

In other cases the auditory effects seem to take a more pleasant musical form. For example, a man who was revived after having been pronounced dead on arrival at a hospital recounts that during his death experience he heard "bells tinkling, a long way off."

Concurrently with the noise, people often have the sensation of being pulled rapidly through a dark space of some kind. I have heard this space described as a cave, a well, a trough, an enclosure, a tunnel, a sewer or a valley, but it is clear that the people involved were all trying to express the same idea.

One man who came very near death drew a parallel from his religious background:

Suddenly, I was in a very dark, very deep valley. It was as though there was a pathway, almost a road, through the valley, and I was going down the path. Later, after I was well, the thought came to me: "Well, now I know what the Bible means by 'the valley of the shadow of death.' "

After his passage through the tunnel, a dying person may find himself looking upon his own physical body from a point outside it, as though he were "another person in the room" or watching figures and events "onstage in a play." A woman recalls:

About a year ago, I was admitted to the hospital with heart trouble, and the next morning, lying in bed, I began to have a very severe pain in my chest. I was quite uncomfortable lying on my back so I turned over, and as I did I quit breathing and my heart stopped beating. I heard the nurses shout, "Code pink! Code pink!" As they were saying this, I could feel myself moving out of my body and sliding down between the mattress and the rail on the side of the bed—it seemed as if I went through the rail—down to the floor. Then, I started rising, slowly. I drifted on up past the light fixture—I saw it from the side and very distinctly—and then I stopped, floating right below the ceiling, looking down. I felt almost as though I were a piece of paper that someone had blown up to the ceiling.

I watched them reviving me from up there. My body was lying down there stretched out on the bed, in plain view, and they were all standing around it. I heard a nurse say, "She's gone!" Another leaned down to give me mouth-to-mouth resuscitation. I was looking at the back of her head while she did this. Just then, I saw them roll this machine in, and they put the shocks on my chest. When they did, I saw my body jump up off the bed and I heard every bone in my body crack. It was the most awful thing!

A 19-year-old informant described an accident that had occurred two years before as he drove a friend home in his car:

I stopped and looked both ways, but I didn't see a thing. I pulled out, and as I did I heard my friend yell at the top of his voice. I saw the headlights of a car speeding toward us. I heard this awful sound—the side of the car being crushed in—and there was just an instant during which I seemed to be going through a darkness, an enclosed space. It was very quick. Then, I was sort of floating about five feet above the street, about five yards away from the car, I'd say, and I heard the echo of the crash dying away. I saw people come crowding around the car, and I saw my friend get out of the car, obviously in shock. I could see my own body in the wreckage among all those people, and could see them trying to get it out. My legs were all twisted, and there was blood all over.

As one may well imagine, unparalleled thoughts and feelings run through the minds of persons who find themselves in this predicament. Many people find the notion of being out of their bodies so unthinkable, even as they are experiencing it, that they do not link it with death for some time. They wonder what is happening to them; why can they suddenly see themselves from a distance, as though they were spectators?

Emotional responses to this strange state vary widely. Most people report, at first, a desperate desire to get back into their bodies, but they do not have the faintest idea about how to proceed. Others recall that they were afraid, almost panicky.

"SPIRITUAL BODY"

Although there are some exceptions, far and away the great majority of the cases I have studied report that they found themselves in another body upon release from the physical one. This new "body," however, is one of the two or three aspects of death experiences in which the inadequacy of language presents the greatest obstacle. Almost everyone who has told me of this body has at some point become frustrated and said, "I can't describe it." Nonetheless, the accounts of this body bear strong resemblances to one another. So, to adopt a term for it which will sum up its properties, and which has been used by a couple of my subjects, I shall call it the "spiritual body."

Dying persons are likely first to become aware of their spiritual bodies in the guise of their limitations. They find, when out of their physical bodies, that although they may try desperately to tell others of their plight, no one seems to hear them. They are also invisible to others and lack solidarity.

People were walking up from all directions to get to the wreck. As they came by, they wouldn't seem to notice me. They would just keep walking with their eyes straight ahead. As they came real close, I would try to get out of their way, but they would walk through me.

Travel in this state, once one gets the hang of it, is apparently exceptionally easy. Physical objects present no barrier, and movement from one place to another can be rapid, almost instantaneous. And yet all who have experienced it are in agreement that the spiritual body is nonetheless *something*, impossible to describe though it may be. Words and phrases which have been used by various subjects include a mist, a cloud, a vapor, an energy pattern. It is agreed that the spiritual body has a form or shape, and even parts analogous to arms, legs, a head.

"Hearing" in the spiritual state can be called so only by analogy, and most say that they do not really hear physical voices or sounds. Rather, they seem to pick up the thoughts of persons around them. As one woman put it:

I could see people all around, and I could understand what they were saying. I didn't hear them audibly as I'm hearing you. It was more like knowing what they were thinking, but only in my mind, not in their actual vocabulary. I would catch it the second before they opened their mouths to speak.

It is not surprising that after a time in this state profound feelings of isolation and loneliness set in. As one man put it, he could see everyone around him in the hospital—yet he could not communicate in any way. "I was desperately alone." These feelings are soon dispelled, however. For, at some point, others come to him to give him aid in the transition he is undergoing.

I had this experience when I was giving birth to a child. The delivery was very difficult, and I lost a lot of blood. The doctor gave me up, and told my relatives that I was dying. However, I was quite alert through the whole thing, and even as I heard him saying this I felt myself coming to. As I did, I realized that all these people were there, almost in multitudes it seems, hovering around the ceiling of the room.

They were all people I had known, but who had passed on before. I recognized my grandmother and a girl I had known when I was in school, and many other relatives and friends. It seems that I mainly saw their faces and felt their presence. They all seemed pleased. It was a very happy occasion, and I felt that they had come to protect or to guide me. It was almost as if I were coming home, and they were there to welcome me. It was a beautiful and glorious moment.

THE BEING OF LIGHT

Perhaps the most incredible common element in the accounts I have studied, and certainly the element which has the greatest effect upon the individual, is the encounter with a very bright light. Typically, at its first appearance this light is dim, but it rapidly gets brighter until it reaches an unearthly brilliance. Not one person has expressed any doubt whatsoever that it was a being. It has, moreover, a very definite personality. The love and the warmth emanating from this being to the dying person are utterly beyond words, and he feels completely surrounded by it and taken up in it.

This description of the being of light is invariable, but the identification of the being varies from individual to individual and seems to be largely a function of the religious background of the person involved. Thus, most Christians identify the light as Christ. A Jewish man and woman identified the light as an "angel." A man who had no religious beliefs or training at all prior to his experience simply identified what he saw as "a being of light."

Shortly after its appearance, the being begins to communicate with the person involved. This communication is of the direct kind, an unimpeded transfer of thoughts. Usually the persons with whom I have talked try to formulate the thought into a question. Among the translations I have heard are: "Are you ready to die?" "What have you done with your life to show me?" and "What have you done with your life that is sufficient?"

All insist that this question is not asked in condemnation, to accuse or threaten them. They still feel total love and acceptance coming from the light, no matter what their answer may be.

Rather, the point of the question seems to be to make them think about their lives, to help them proceed along the path to the truth.

I heard the doctors say that I was dead, and that's when I began to feel as though I were tumbling, actually kind of floating, through this blackness, which was some kind of enclosure. Everything was very black, except that, way off from me, I could see this light. It was a very, very brilliant light, but not too large at first. It grew larger as I came nearer and nearer to it.

It was not a frightening experience. It was more or less a pleasant thing. For immediately, being a Christian, I had connected the light with Christ, who said, "I am the light of the world."

Another report:

It was beautiful and so bright, so radiant, but it didn't hurt my eyes. It's not any kind of light you can describe on earth. I didn't actually see a person in this light, and yet it has a special identity, it definitely does. It is a light of perfect understanding and perfect love.

Another person related:

At first, when the light came, I wasn't sure what was happening, but then it asked if I was ready to die. It was like talking to a person, but a person wasn't there. The light was what was talking to me, but in a voice.

The initial appearance of the being of light and his questions are the prelude to a moment of startling intensity during which the being presents to the person a panoramic review of his life. It is often obvious that the being can see the individual's whole life displayed and that he himself doesn't need information. His only intention is to provoke reflection.

This review can only be described in terms of memory, since that is the closest familiar phenomenon to it, but it has characteristics which set it apart from any normal type of remembering. First of all, the remembrance was extraordinarily rapid. Everything appeared at once, and could be taken in with one mental glance—in an instant of earthly time. Yet, despite its rapidity, my informants agree that the review is incredibly vivid. And, as they witness the display, the being seems to stress the importance of two things in life: learning to love other people and acquiring knowledge.

LEARNING EXPERIENCE

Obviously, all the persons with whom I have talked had to "come back" at some point in their experience. Usually, an interesting change in their attitude has taken place by this time. Remember that the most common feelings reported in the first few moments following death were a desperate desire to get back into the body and an intense regret over one's demise. However, once the dying person reaches a certain depth in his experience, he does not want to come back. This is especially the case for those who have encountered the being of light. As one man put it, most emphatically, "I *never* wanted to leave the presence of this being."

When it comes to the question of the mode of return to physical life, in quite a few instances persons recall being drawn rapidly back through the dark tunnel through which they went during the initial moments of their "death." But few experience the actual re-entry into their bodies. Most report that they simply felt that they "went to sleep" or lapsed into unconsciousness, later to awaken in life.

A person who has been through an experience of this type has no doubt whatsoever as to its reality and its importance. Interviews which I have done are usually sprinkled with remarks to precisely that effect. For example:

It was nothing like a hallucination. I have had hallucinations once, when I was given codeine in the hospital. But that had happened long before the accident which nearly killed me. And this experience was nothing like the hallucinations, nothing like them at all.

The people I have interviewed are functioning, well-balanced personalities. They do not tell their experiences as they would dreams, but rather as real events that actually happened to them. Despite this, they realize that our contemporary society is just not the sort of environment in which reports of this nature would be received with sympathy and understanding. Indeed, many have remarked that they realized from the very beginning others would think they were men-

tally unstable if they were to relate their experiences. So, they have resolved to remain silent on the subject or else to reveal their experiences only to some very close relative.

It has often happened that when, after first interviewing someone in detail about his own experience, I have told him that others have reported exactly the same events and perceptions, he has expressed great feelings of relief.

I am actually happy to know that obviously someone else has been through this, too. Now I know I'm not crazy.

There is remarkable agreement in the "lessons," as it were, which have been brought back from these close encounters with death. Almost everyone has stressed the importance in this life of trying to cultivate love for others, a love of a unique and profound kind. One man who met the being of light felt totally loved and accepted, even while his whole life was displayed in a panorama for the being to see. He felt that the question the being was asking him was whether he was able to love others in the same way. He now feels that it is his mission while on earth to try to learn to do so.

In addition, many others have emphasized the importance of seeking knowledge. During their experiences, it was intimated to them that the acquisition of knowledge continues even in the afterlife. One woman has taken advantage of every educational opportunity she has had since her "death" experience. Another man offers the advice, "No matter how old you are, don't stop learning. For this is a process, I gather, that goes on for eternity."

As one might reasonably expect, this experience has a profound effect upon one's attitude toward physical death, especially for those who hadn't previously expected that anything took place after death. Almost every person expressed to me in some form the thought that he is no longer afraid of death.

I don't have a death wish, or want to die right now. But I am not afraid to die. The reason is that I know where I'm going when I leave here, because I've been there before.

Even those who previously had some traditional conviction about the nature of the afterlife seem to have moved away from it to some degree following their brushes with death. In fact, in all the reports I have gathered, not one person has described pearly gates, golden streets and winged, harp-playing angels, or a hell of flames and demons with pitchforks.

So, in most cases, the reward–punishment model of the afterlife is abandoned and disavowed, even by many who had been accustomed to thinking in those terms. They found, much to their amazement, that even when their most apparently sinful deeds were made manifest before the being of light, that being responded not with anger and rage but rather with understanding, and even with humor. (These sins, of course, were not of a particularly grievous nature.)

Since many persons reported being out of their bodies for extended periods and witnessing events in the physical world during the interlude, the question naturally arises: Can any of these reports be checked out with other witnesses known to be present?

In quite a few instances, the somewhat surprising answer is "yes." Several doctors have told me, for example, that they are utterly baffled about how patients with no medical knowledge could describe in such detail and so correctly the procedure used in resuscitation attempts, since these events took place while the doctors knew the patients involved to be "dead."

Persons have related to me how they amazed their doctors or others with reports of events they had witnessed while out of the body. While she was dying, for example, one girl went out of her body and into another room in the hospital where she found her sister crying and saying, "Oh, Kathy, please don't die, please don't die." The sister was baffled when, later, Kathy told her exactly where she had been and what she had said during this time.

PARALLELS

The various stages of the experience of dying are, to say the very least, unusual. Hence, my surprise has been compounded as, over the years, I have come across quite a number of striking parallels to them, occurring in the literature of several very diverse civilizations, cultures and eras.

In our society the Bible is the most widely read and discussed book dealing with matters relating to the spiritual aspect of man and to life after death. However, the Bible has relatively little to say about the events that transpire upon death, or about the precise nature of the afterdeath world. This is especially true of the Old Testament.

But other sources reveal closer parallels. The philosopher Plato has left us descriptions of occurrences very similar to those experienced in near-death situations. In Book X of *The Republic* perhaps the most striking similarity of all occurs. There Plato recounts the death in battle of a Greek soldier called Er, whose body was laid upon a funeral pyre to be burned. After some time his body revived, and Er described what he saw in his journey to the realms of the afterlife when his soul went out of his body. There were "openings" apparently leading from the earth into the realms beyond. Here souls were stopped and judged by beings, who could see, in some sort of display, all the things that Er had done while in his earthly life. The beings told Er that he must go back to inform men in the physical world of what the other world was like. He woke up and found himself upon the funeral pyre.

Another lengthy description of the various stages through which the soul goes after physical death is contained in the Tibetan Book of the Dead, compiled from the teachings of sages over many centuries and passed down through early generations by word of mouth. It was finally written down, apparently, in the eighth century A.D., but even then was kept secret from outsiders.

First of all, in the Tibetan account, the mind or soul of the dying person departs from the body and he finds himself in a void. He may hear alarming sounds, described as roaring, thundering or whistling noises, like the wind. He is surprised to find himself out of his physical body. He sees and hears his relatives and friends mourning over his body and preparing it for the funeral, and yet when he tries to respond to them they neither hear nor see him.

He notices that he is still in a body—called the "shining" body—which does not consist of material substance. Thus, he can go through rocks, walls and even mountains without encountering resistance. Wherever he wishes to be, he arrives there in only a moment. He may encounter what is called a clear or pure light. The Tibetans counsel the dying one to approach this light with intense faith and humility.

The book also describes the feelings of immense peace and contentment which a person experiences if he "dies well," and also a kind of "Mirror" in which his entire life, all deeds both good and bad, is reflected for both the dying person and the beings judging him to see vividly.

Another interesting parallel occurs in the writings of the Swede Emanuel Swedenborg, who lived from 1688 until 1772. His writings, at first oriented toward physics, mathematics, anatomy and psychology, gained quite a bit of recognition. Late in life he underwent a religious crisis and began to tell of experiences in which he had purportedly been in communication with spiritual entities from beyond.

His later works abound with vivid descriptions of what life after death is like. He claimed that he himself had been through the early events of death, and had had experiences out of his body. Communication takes place between Swedenborg and spirits whom he identifies as "angels," but it is not of an earthly, human kind. It is instead almost a direct transfer of thoughts. "Every man, immediately after death, comes into this universal language."

The dying man may meet other departed spirits whom he knew while in life. His past life may be shown to him in a vision. He remembers every detail of it, and there is no possibility of his lying or concealing anything.

The interior memory is such that there are inscribed in it all the particular things which man has at any time thought, spoken, and done from his earliest infancy to extreme old age. Man has with him the memory of all these things when he comes into another life, and is successively brought into all recollection of them.

Swedenborg describes, too, the "light of the Lord" which permeates the hereafter, a light of ineffable brightness which he has glimpsed himself. It is a light of truth and of understanding.

Is it possible that the near-death experiences I have collected were influenced by works of this kind? Two or three of the persons with whom I have talked knew something about the ideas of Plato. On the other hand, none was aware of the existence of Swedenborg's works or the Tibetan Book of the Dead. Thus, we may well ask ourselves, how is it that the wisdom of the Tibetan sages, the strange insights of Plato and the spiritual revelations of Swedenborg all agree so well, both among themselves and with the narratives of contemporary individuals who have come as close as anyone alive to the state of death?

QUESTIONS

In the years that I have been giving talks on the near-death experience, I have been asked many questions. In general, the same queries seem to come up again and again. Here are my answers.

Q: *Are you just making all this up?*
A: No, I'm not. I very much want to pursue a career in the teaching of psychiatry and the philosophy of medicine, and attempting to perpetrate a hoax would hardly be conducive to that aim.

Q: *How common are such experiences?*
A: I am the first to admit that, because of the limited nature of my sample cases, I am unable to give a statistically significant numerical estimate of the prevalence of this phenomenon. However, the occurrence of such experiences is far more common than anyone who hasn't studied them would guess. To talk about life after death seems somehow atavistic to many who perhaps feel that the idea belongs more to our "superstitious" past than to our "scientific" present. Aware of these attitudes, persons who have had transcendent experiences are usually reluctant to relate them openly.

Q: *How do you know these people aren't lying to you?*
A: It is quite easy for persons who have not listened and watched as others have related near-death experiences to entertain, intellectually, the hypothesis that these stories are lies. However, I have witnessed mature, emotionally stable adults break down and weep while telling me of events that happened up to three decades before. I have de-

tected in their voices sincerity, warmth and feeling which cannot really be conveyed in a written recounting. So to me, in a way that is unfortunately impossible for others to share, the notion that these accounts might be fabrications is utterly untenable.

In addition to the weight of my own opinion, there are some strong considerations which should rule heavily against the fabrication hypothesis. The most obvious is the difficulty of explaining the similarity of so many of the accounts. How is it that many people just happen to come up with the same lie to tell me? Collusion remains a theoretical possibility here. It is certainly conceivable that a nice elderly lady from eastern North Carolina, a medical student from New Jersey, a Georgian veterinarian, and many others several years ago banded together and conspired to carry out an elaborate hoax against me. However, I don't regard this to be a very likely possibility.

Q: *Have you examined any near-death experience that resulted from an attempted suicide?*

A: Yes. These experiences were uniformly characterized as being unpleasant. A man who was despondent about the death of his wife shot himself, "died," and was resuscitated. He states: "I didn't go where [my wife] was. I went to an awful place. I immediately saw what a mistake I had made."

Others who experienced this unpleasant "limbo" state have remarked that they had the feeling this was their penalty for "breaking the rules" by trying to release themselves prematurely from what was, in effect, an "assignment"—to fulfill a certain purpose in life.

Sentiments like these, which by now have been expressed to me in many separate accounts, are embodied in the most ancient theological and moral argument against suicide—one which occurs in various forms in the writings of thinkers as diverse as St. Thomas Aquinas, John Locke and Immanuel Kant. A suicide, in Kant's view, is acting in opposition to the purposes of God and arrives on the other side viewed as a rebel against his creator.

Q: *Are there cases of near-death which do not produce afterlife recollections?*

A. I have talked to a few people who were pronounced dead, resuscitated, and say that they don't remember anything at all about their "deaths." Interestingly enough, I have also talked with several persons who were actually adjudged clinically dead on separate occasions years apart, and reported experiencing nothing on one of the occasions, but having had quite involved experiences on the other.

Q: *Were any of the people you have talked to really dead?*

A: One of the main reasons why this question is so confusing and difficult to answer is that it is partly a semantic question involving the meaning of the word "dead."

All I ultimately want to claim is this: Whatever the point of irretrievable death is said to be, those with whom I have talked have been much closer to it than have the vast majority of their fellow human beings. For this reason alone, I am quite willing to listen to what they have to say.

EXPLANATIONS

Near-death experiences, some say, are only wish-fulfilling dreams, fantasies or hallucinations which are brought into play by different factors—drugs administered at the time of crisis, cerebral anoxia (lack of oxygen) or some other kind of severe bodily stress. Thus, they would explain near-death experiences as delusions. Other alternative explanations include neurological and psychological disorders which may produce hallucinations.

I think several factors weigh against these suggestions. First, consider the great similarity in content and progression we find among the descriptions, despite the fact that what is most generally reported is manifestly not what is commonly imagined, in our cultural milieu, to happen to the dead.

Second, there remains the fact that the persons with whom I have talked are not victims of psychoses or other disorders. They hold jobs and positions of importance and carry them out responsibly. They have stable marriages and are involved with their families and friends. Almost no one with whom I have talked has had more than one uncanny experience in the course of his life. And, most significantly, these informants are people who can distinguish between dreams and waking experiences. Yet they almost invariably assure me in the course of their narratives that their experiences were not dreams, but rather were definitely, emphatically real.

Nonetheless, I have studied several examples of psychologically and neurologically inspired hallucinations. Although certain aspects of the near-death experience are sometimes reproduced, none is as complete, or as real, or in any way as emotionally involving, as the dying experience.

I am not proposing any new explanations of my own. All I want to suggest is this: let us at least leave open the possibility that near-death experiences represent a novel phenomenon for which we may have to devise new modes of explanation and interpretation.

In writing this book I have been acutely conscious that my purpose and perspectives might easily be misunderstood. In particular, I would like to say to scientifically minded readers that I am fully aware that what I have done does not constitute a scientific study. Yet I think that reports of near-death experiences are very significant. What I want to do is find some middle way of interpreting these experiences—a way which neither rejects them on the basis that they do not constitute scientific proof nor sensationalizes them with claims that they "prove" that there is life after death.

I am left, not with conclusions or evidence or proofs, but with something much less definite—feelings, questions, analogies, puzzling facts to be explained. Yet I believe that any light whatever which can be shed on the nature of death is to the good. What we learn about death may make an important difference in the way we live our lives. If experiences of the type which I have discussed *are* real, they have profound implications for what every one of us is doing with his life. For then, it would be true that we cannot fully understand this life until we catch a glimpse of what lies beyond it.

To Apply This Reading to Yourself

1. *What are your own ideas about life after death and how do they influence the way you live your life?*
2. *Would you live your life any differently if you were certain there was life after death than if you were certain there was not? Why?*
3. *Individuals who have suffered "clinical death" but who then revive frequently report a profound difference in the way they view and live their lives. Have you ever had an experience that produced a similar effect? If so, describe it, along with its effect on you and any insights it produced.*
4. *Imagine that at this very moment you suddenly find your life in serious jeopardy—hanging in the balance so to speak. You feel called upon to evaluate or appraise your life. To do so, write a brief paper that might be entitled "What I made of my life." Afterward share your paper in the larger group, in small groups, or in dyads.*

P A R T
five

MAKING
COMMITMENTS

Human beings form commitments, and the commitments we form give pattern to our existence. We are attracted to others, and join our lives to other lives. We become interested in various pursuits and follow them as careers or avocations. The persons and pursuits we join, pledge, and dedicate ourselves to may give us a sense of direction and belonging.

Of course, we vary greatly in the extent and kinds of our commitments. Some of us follow convention and in a usual way complete our education, find a job, fall in love, marry, obtain a home, establish a family, and form ties with a community. Others reject or greatly alter this pattern, moving in our own way and at our own speed to evolve our own unique style.

Many aspects of human life have to do with commitment. Some of the most salient were just suggested and include *loving, pairing, parenting,* and *working.* Part Five considers each of these aspects and focuses some attention on the impact of new and alternate styles.

Loving, a keystone of commitment, has been largely ignored by scientists until rather recently. Some, who have noted the critically short supply of love in the world, have advocated cultivating the ability to love as a sorely needed skill. Certainly the ability to love varies widely from one person to another; some of us are lucky in love or skillful at loving, but many lives include little that could be called "love." The readings on loving will present some ideas concerning its essence and essentials and also its faults and fables.

Pairing is the most common form of pledged relationship. We love to pair, and we pair to love. Sooner or later, almost all of us form a love pair called "marriage," but ideas about intimate pairing and marriage are changing. For one thing, modern marriage is less likely to be a lifetime commitment. Second, the kind of commitment involved in marriage and other intimate relationships is changing. The readings on this topic will contrast the traditional with the newer models of intimate pairing.

Parenting is a popular profession (no certificate or license required). All of us have been parented (in one way or another), and almost every adult is or plans to be a parent. Even so, the profession has lost some of its popularity. More couples these days are delaying parenthood, and more are electing to have only one or two children or none at all. The readings on this topic have been selected to help us consider both the bittersweet and the better side of family life.

When Freud, the founder of psychoanalysis, was asked what a person needed to do well, he answered, "Lieben und arbeiten"—to love and to work. Work is an important part of our life. We work to live, and if we are caught up in our pursuits, we live to work. Our work may help us to grow or keep us from growing. The readings on this topic throw some light on this important matter.

Loving

The cool ocean breeze brushed gently against them. It was midnight, and the beach was deserted. He had been waiting for a moment like this to make his solemn pronouncement. A large wave crested, spraying them lightly with cold ocean water. They laughed and gazed in each other's eyes. The moment was right. He said it: "I love you, honey." It came out as a whisper.

"And I love you, too, dearest."

That night, he gave her the ring he had brought with him, saving it for just the right moment. She accepted. Three months later they were married.

Five years and countless battles later, they were ready to throw in the towel. The marriage was not working at all.

"If you loved me, you would listen to me, and spend time with me, and support me when I get down in the dumps," she said to him, bitterness in her voice.

"But I do love you. If you loved me, you wouldn't be complaining about me all the time, and besides, you'd make love when I get horny, instead of always finding reasons to do something else."

"I can't make love to a man who doesn't have much use for me except as a sex object. The only time you want to spend with me is when we're in bed."

"At least you don't complain then."

A year later they were divorced, both convinced that their love was one-sided.

—Robert Sternberg

When my students and I are on the topic of love, I like to ask three questions: (1) "How many of you have ever told someone you loved them? Let's see a show of hands." Many hands are in the air. (2) "How many of you mean what you say when you say something?" Everybody has a hand up. (3) "Since you mean what you say when you say something, what did you mean when you told someone you loved them?" Silence. More silence. Finally, some students explain what they meant, but the more exact their explanations, the more it appears that each has meant something different. (The most memorable response was that of a woman who recalled her mate approaching her in the kitchen to make up after a spat over the sharing of household duties. He put his arms around her, kissed her, and said, "I love you." She replied, "Does that mean you're going to help with the dishes?")

What does love mean (besides helping with the dishes)? At the dawn of the twentieth century, Henry Finck, who had studied a bit of psychology, concluded, "Love is such a tissue of paradoxes and exists in such an endless variety of forms and shades that you may say almost anything about it that you please, and it is likely to be correct." Very recently—almost at the dawn of the twenty-first century—psychologist Zick Rubin writes that the science of love is still struggling with a definition, and love continues to mean different things to both lovers and scientists.

Whether it's among lovers or scientists, the lack of agreement on love can be a serious matter. Take note of the relationship in the short, short story that prefaces this discussion. What went wrong in that relationship, says love scientist Robert Sternberg, is what commonly goes wrong in many relationships: "Each partner loves the other, but in his or her own way, and not necessarily in the way the other partner loves back and expects to be loved." Sternberg concludes, "At least some of the distress in close relationships might be avoidable if each partner understood what the other meant by love and how the interpretations were related."

LOVE'S ESSENCE AND ESSENTIALS

What is love? What love includes, write Daniel Goldstine, Katherine Larner, Shirley Zuckerman, and Hilary Goldstine in the first reading, is sparkle, disillusionment, and mutual acceptance, and in that order. The first stage—the sparkle—is a heady and fleeting one. In the second stage—disillusionment—appreciation turns to criticism as the partners confront their differences. The third stage is one of *mutual acceptance*, as an accommodation is reached, and each party is provided with support and security to "become most fully himself or herself."

What's love? What's infatuation? How can we tell the two apart? In the second reading, psychologists Elaine Hatfield and G. William Walster claim that love and infatuation are exactly the same—at least while they are in progress. If a relationship continues to bloom, we call it love; if it withers, we conclude that it was merely infatuation.

According to Hatfield and Walster, parents and friends who claim *they* can tell whether *we* are truly in love or not are simply telling us whether they approve or not.

What's love? In the third selection (one of the most read and quoted essays on this topic), psychoanalyst Erich Fromm writes that love is an indivisible attitude, all of a piece, and therefore love for others and self-love are inseparably connected. He writes, "If an individual is able to love productively, he loves himself too; if he can love *only* others, he cannot love at all." Fromm contrasts self-love with selfishness, which he sees as the opposite. Selfish individuals are incapable of loving others or themselves, and their selfishness is an attempt to compensate for their failure to care for and respect themselves. (For another view on the importance of self-love, see Dyer's article on pages 25–30.)

LOVE'S FAULTS AND FABLES

What love isn't is the subject of the fourth reading, by Abe Arkoff. Love may be fabulous, but it's also a field full of fables or myths that can cause mischief and unhappiness. Among the mischievous myths Arkoff punctures are those claiming that love is mysterious, forever (or fleeting), constant, exclusive, and beyond control.

Research suggests that adjustment is easier if lovers share the same culture. Alas, that may not be an option for heterosexual lovers because—as linguist Deborah Tannen notes in the last reading—men and women speak different languages. Male conversation is more likely a negotiation to achieve and maintain status or the upper hand. For women, conversation is more likely a negotiation for closeness and consensus. No wonder that bickering lovers often complain, "You just don't understand." Learning to understand can be vital to keeping love in bloom.

To Explore Your Own Love Ideas, Attitudes, and Abilities

1. *Defining love.* Working separately, write your definition of love on a 3 × 5 card or slip of paper. Form small groups and have a chairperson gather and shuffle the cards and place them face down in the center. Each person in turn picks a card, reads it aloud, and comments on its definition. Finally, try to arrive at one definition acceptable to everyone in your group. As an option, reassemble in the larger group and have the chairpersons report their group definitions.
2. *Loving others.* This may be done in the larger group or in small groups. For a three-minute period, each person silently considers two questions: "How loving am I?" and "How can I be more loving?" When the three minutes are up, share your answers.[1]

1. The second and third exercises are adapted from the work of Herbert A. Otto.

3. *Loving yourself.* This may be done in the larger group or in small groups. For a three-minute period, each person silently considers two questions: "How much do I love myself?" "How can I give myself more love?" When the three minutes are up, share your answers.

4. *Writing a love letter.* Many of us have trouble expressing our love for others. Write a love letter to someone you love or have loved but to whom you have left too much unsaid. (It may be someone alive or dead, present in your life or gone away.) As an option, share your letters in the larger group or in small groups.

5. *Writing yourself a love letter.* Many of us have trouble loving ourselves properly, although Erich Fromm and others have held that if we do not love ourselves, we cannot love anyone. Write yourself a love letter, setting forth all the things you find to love in yourself. As an option, share your letters in the larger group or in small groups.

6. *Compiling love evidence.* Many of us take love for granted. Think of someone you love and make a list of all the ways you tell or show or prove to that person you love her or him. If your list seems a bit short, add some resolutions to your list and your life. As an option, share your lists in the larger group or in small groups.

7. *Compiling self-love evidence.* Many of us take ourselves for granted. How do you tell or show or prove to yourself that you love yourself? What nice things do you habitually say to yourself or do for yourself? Make a list of all the evidence that shows that you treat yourself lovingly. If your list seems a bit short, add some resolutions to your list and your life. As an option, share your lists in the larger group or in small groups.

8. *Sharing love items.* Bring something that has some special significance concerning love in your life. It may be a song, poem, or book, a picture or photograph, a bit of jewelry or anything. In the larger group or in small groups, share the item, and indicate its significance for you.

9. *Playing love games.* We can love, or we can play at love. We know we are playing when our loving seems to take a predictable and somehow unsatisfying course (considered over the long run) or when we seem more occupied with winning or proving something than with loving. Write a brief paper discussing a love game you play or have played, and share your papers in the larger group or in small groups.

10. *Devising a course on love.* To love well is an important skill, but few colleges or universities concern themselves with it. In the curriculum you will find courses on how to speak, write, cook, paint, draft, map, compute, counsel, dance, golf, and on and on but rarely a course on love. Break up into small groups and have each group prepare a course on love that could be taught at your institution. What would be the specific purposes or goals of the course? How would the course be taught and these purposes or goals achieved? What kinds of prerequisites, instructors, methods, examinations, papers, exercises, and practicums would the course

have? After each group has prepared its course, reassemble in the larger group to share (and perhaps prepare a proposal to send to the appropriate curriculum committee?!).[2]

To Read Further

Burns, D. D. (1985). *Intimate connections: The clinically proven program for making close friends and finding a loving partner.* New York: Signet. (paperback)

Buscaglia, L. (1972). *Love.* Thorofare, NJ: Charles B. Slack. (Fawcett Crest paperback, 1985)

Buscaglia, L. (1982). *Living, loving, and learning.* New York: Ballantine. (Columbine paperback, 1985)

Fromm, E. (1956). *The art of loving: An enquiry into the nature of love.* New York: Harper & Row. (HarperCollins paperback, 1989)

Hatfield, E., & Walster, G. W. (1985). *A new look at love.* Lanham, MD: University Press of America. (paperback)

Jampolsky, G. G. (1979). *Love is letting go of fear.* Millbrae, CA: Celestial Arts. (paperback)

Jampolsky, G. G. (1983). *Teach only love: The seven principles of attitudinal healing.* New York: Bantam. (paperback)

Sternberg, R. J., & Barnes, M. L. (Eds.). (1988). *The psychology of love.* New Haven, CT: Yale University Press. (paperback)

Welwood, J. (Ed.). (1985). *Challenge of the heart: Love, sex, and intimacy in changing times.* Boston: Shambhala. (paperback)

---

2. If you would like to read a book that is an outgrowth of a university "Love Class," see *Love* by Leo Buscaglia.

The Three Stages of Love

Daniel Goldstine, Katherine Larner, Shirley Zuckerman, and Hilary Goldstine

STAGE I: THE SPARKLE

Falling in love creates an incontestable high—sweet and bitter-sweet emotions with longing, passion, fondness, uncertainty and wonder.

Such delights aren't savored by every couple, however, because not every couple comes to love each other by way of falling in love. Love between two people can grow little by little, unobtrusively knitting them into a pair. A relationship that unfolds in this deliberate fashion bypasses both the ecstasy and the angst of falling in love.

In fact, some people aren't willing to fall in love at all. It is a risky business that requires people to deliver themselves over to the unknown and live with the awareness that they do not know how love will turn out.

Love unavoidably subjects people to an alarming degree of uncertainty and vulnerability. To fall in love, they must suspend many of the defenses they rely on to shield themselves from pain. The anxiety that falling in love creates can be felt as a nameless, nebulous uneasiness, on the one hand or as pangs of terror on the other.

The anxiety can take a variety of forms. Often a person interprets the uneasiness she feels as fear of rejection. 'What if he doesn't love me back,' she worries. Falling in love requires a person to make herself known to her partner, and people often dread the closeup scrutiny that closeness entails. Carol said retrospectively, "When we were first getting together, I used to tell Jimmy all the time—if he really found out what I was like, it would be all over." To fall in love is to risk having one's shortcomings (intellectual, physical, sexual) discovered and frowned upon by the very person whose censure tells most keenly.

Falling in love jitters can also manifest themselves as a fear of being swallowed up. 'Am I going to be trapped?' 'Will my individuality be blotted out?'

Falling in love can raise a person's anxiety level so high that she backs away from every potentially serious relationship.

While certain kinds of risks and fears are built into falling in love, so are reassurances.

Implicitly and explicitly, being in love provides a person with proof that she is cherished. Her partner's desire to be with her testifies to her significance as does his willingness to set aside old habits and commitments in her favor. The affection and approval he offers are the functional equivalents of a peal of applause—deeply comforting and deeply exhilarating. In fact, being in love tends to act as a self-esteem escalator, which temporarily lifts a person out of self-doubt and enables her to believe that she is the truly lovable person that her partner discerns in her. Often, a couple in love comes to compose a kind of mutual admiration society. Entranced by the desirable qualities they discover in each other, they shrug off what shortcomings they find.

Virtues arouse intense appreciation, and vices appear trivial or irrelevant, a weighting that creates an extraordinarily favorable image of the other. Perceived in these flattering—perhaps fanciful terms, the partner appears to be incapable of doing harm.

Being in love fosters trust; trust fosters intimacy. Susan said, "Always before, I felt I had all kinds of things inside me I could never let out. With Murray I feel as if I can be completely open. I'm not scared with him. Anything that happens is OK, because there's nothing I have to hold in."

Being in Love Makes Pleasers of Us All

As the couple nestles closer together physically and psychically, they develop a growing sense of "usness." Just as both focus on the other's merits and disregard the other's defects, so both experience an overwhelming desire for closeness, which temporarily blots out the fears intimacy might normally arouse in them. Ambivalence about intimacy yields temporarily to the simple childlike wish to be enfolded.

Being in love makes pleasers of us all to some extent, eager to bring happiness to the partner at every opportunity by every possible means. One woman said of her lover, "He's so giving. I feel as if I just want to hold him, be with him; I want to do anything that would make him feel better. Any strength I have I would give to him."

When in love, people give before they're asked. They give spontaneously and ungrudgingly. They experience their own power in terms of their ability to give pleasure to each other, and they give, or at least they appear to give, without keeping score, secure in the trust that "the more I give, the more I will get back."

Being in love inclines people to treat each other with affectionate indulgence, which defuses the impact of whatever differences arise between them. They express their love by giving in to, as well as by giving to each other. Their overall interest in preserving good feeling takes precedence over satisfying narrower interests. For example, rather than spoil the evening, one person relinquishes her preference to see a movie and goes along without complaint to the party her partner wants to attend.

Interactions in being in love often follow a commandeer/accommodate pattern that also minimizes conflict. One person strikes a given note, and the other chimes in to produce a harmony that's gratifying to them both. One partner initiates activity and takes responsibility for making a go of it. The other partner follows the lead, adapting and synchronizing the pace as closely as possible to it. The smooth mesh of the commandeer/accommodate pattern gives both the delightful sensation of being in step together practically as they're in tune together emotionally.

The instinctive teamwork of being in love helps the couple to cope with failure as well as to skirt conflict. When one partner experiences a reverse, the other usually responds in one of several ways. Should one person falter in dealing with the situation, the other will volunteer a rescue if it seems to be within his/her power.

When they are falling in love, people are deeply responsive to each other's needs. They often offer each other unequivocal backing, and display an inexhaustible interest in each other's feelings. The alliance between them is deepened by this interminable talk about what's going on in their lives and how the pair of them should deal with it.

If problems sometimes arise that are too threatening to be discussed, they are apt to be assiduously avoided. When they're falling in love, couples avert their eyes from each other's failures as they disregard each other's faults—to preserve their images of each other and to safeguard their hopes for the relationship.

Matching wits against each other and cutting loose together, the partners can bounce off each other's high spirits.

A person who is falling in love feels good about herself, good about her partner, and good about the relationship—so good that she's tempted to believe that the relationship will realize her fantasies and transform her life.

But under these circumstances, a person's vision of her partner is doubly distorted. Her perception is colored by his selective attention; her desire to seek out and attend to what she finds admirable in the other and to blank out whatever is discreditable.

Both partners strive to be their finest selves and they're apt to be at their most appealing when they're falling in love.

To a certain extent, being in love also cushions individuals from external stress. A reverse at work, a spell of financial trouble, don't pinch as painfully when there's a newfound lover to kiss the hurt and make it well.

But the bleak fact is that this early stage of love is often necessarily fleeting. Often time, satiation dilutes the intense pleasure the partners originally found in being together. Real-world obligations encroach on the relationship. As evidence of each other's shortcomings pile up, and as the relationship begins to exact visible costs, mutual idealization gives way to mutual disillusionment. With the dimming of the sparkle of love, any underlying ambivalence about intimacy begins to reassert itself.

The Most Romantic but Not the Most Enduring Version of Love

Over the long term, conflict will arise between the partners that can't be smoothed away by means of mutual pleasing. Gradually, a couple discovers all the dismal reasons why they shouldn't be together after all.

Someone who's falling in love can take serious chances—financial risks, or birth-control risks, for example—that might have consequences she's not prepared to handle. Falling in love is such a powerful and profoundly pleasurable experience that it can make more mundane activities seem empty by comparison. Preoccupied with the beloved, a person can let her life slip into a muddle of neglected duties.

Furthermore, at this time, a couple's desire for togetherness can be so urgent that it leads them to neglect other relationships. Intent on each other, the couple can become unavailable to the friends and family members who are used to depending on them.

A person who's falling in love necessarily relinquishes some of her prudence and some of her self-control. She may profit greatly from this temporary abandon—this yielding to emotion and this sense of merging with another. Falling in love offers most people the most intense intimacy they have ever experienced with another adult. Furthermore, it means a fresh start, of sorts. To genuinely fall in love is to reach a major juncture in life, a crossroads where old commitments can be reassessed and new alternatives explored. But for best results, this willingness to take risks should be tempered with a little perspective.

This stage of love constitutes the most romantic, but not the most enduring, version of a couple's love. It should be appreciated for what it is—a very special experience, and not mistaken for what it isn't—a paradigm to which all experiences of love should conform. Delightful in and of itself, this stage of love doesn't ensure that a relationship has a potential to endure or flourish.

To have gone through the first stage of love bestows a valuable benefit on a couple's relationship, as well as on them as individuals. In this stage, two people learn how to enjoy themselves together. They discover pleasures they can share and ways to spend time together that make both of them feel good. Needless to say, a couple can't survive on a capacity to have fun together, and likewise, a couple can make do without knowing how to be playful or joyful together. But a relationship that lacks this endowment is the poorer

for it. Evanescent of itself, this stage of love can leave a couple a valuable legacy—the knowledge that they can create pleasure together—that will help them to keep their relationship a source of satisfaction to them both.

STAGE II: DISILLUSIONMENT

In Stage II, a couple must come to grips with the differences which truly divide them.

On discovering ways in which their operating procedures do not mesh, and the features of each other they find neither creditable nor lovable, the question becomes, "What do I do about all those things about him that I don't like, things he can't change?"

It is difficult to be subjected to someone else's flaws and limitations without questioning the wisdom of the commitment to that person. It can also be difficult to keep from using such discreditable discoveries about a person as weapons against him or her. For example, one man told his wife, "It hurt me a lot when you said I was weak. It came from all those times I let you know I felt weak. That bothers me. Why should I want to tell you where I'm at if you're going to use it on me?" Since disillusionment is a painful process all around, Stage II usually entails disenchantment about one's partner.

This Stage also means mutual disapproval, the more painful because it's unexpected. The most concentrated dose of approval people usually get comes when they're falling in love. A major proof of the rightness of a new relationship is the fact that the partner "makes me feel so good." But gradually, the appreciation turns to criticism. It's difficult for most people to maintain their self-esteem in the face of intimate disapproval, and the characteristic Stage II complaint becomes, "You make me feel so bad."

The anxiety and the resentment that mark Stage II often provoke people to behavior they have trouble accepting in themselves. One woman brooded, "I've become a bitch. The more he doesn't listen to me, the more I yell. And I don't like it. I'm always screaming—I'm sick of myself."

Usually a person holds her partner responsible for the unappetizing changes that have been wrought in her. This woman invoked the fact that "I don't get into scenes like that with anybody else" to reassure herself that the fault for them lay with her partner.

The issue of who's at fault obscures the fact that people almost invariably behave badly in Stage II. One of the reasons they do so is because they have realized that their couple relationship is never going to give them the things they truly want. In Stage I, optimism and goodwill sweeten what sacrifices were necessary. The satisfactions a couple didn't obtain from their relationship were deferred ("It doesn't matter, I can go without").

This is more easily said than done over the long term. In Stage II, a couple must come to grips with the fact that "there are so many things that aren't there" in their relationship and that the sacrifices it exacts are not just painful, but are hardening into permanence.

Sometimes what the relationship doesn't offer is passion. Sometimes what's lacking is consideration, or closeness, or security, or room to breathe.

A woman said of her fiancé, "It makes me so angry. I look at him as the man I want to be with for a long time, and there are these things I'm not getting from him. It just makes me so angry. And I think—what I should do is stop caring. He won't give me this, therefore I won't care. I'll make sure I never ask for anything . . ."

Withholding is the other major response to being denied. The withholder says, in effect, "I'm not going to give to you if you're not going to give to me."

Withholding, pushing away, blaming and anxious demanding are all forms of coercion, ways of trying to force a partner to respond to needs not voluntarily. But under pressure to give, the partner often turns stubbornly stingy. One male said of his partner's depressions, "When she's down I get into a 'here we go again' mentality. I get exhausted before we even start. My reaction when I see she's depressed or having a bad time is 'Grow up, Cecile.'"

When the Stage II coin is thrown into the air, for some people it comes down heads, "You don't give me enough"; for some people it comes down tails, "You ask too much." Often a person's sense that enough isn't coming in feeds her resentment about what she's being obliged to put out. She begins to perceive her partner as a burden, a liability.

How people deal with being asked for things they don't want to give can be a major issue. The motivation to refuse can differ from one situation to another. Sometimes a person's "No" means "I don't want to do that." Sometimes it means "I'm scared to do that." Sometimes it means "I want to punish you."

The whole transaction is complicated by the fact that most people feel too guilty to offer a simple straightforward "No." Instead, discomfort leads them to blame. "Why can't you . . ." A refusal comes as rejection. "Get off my back! Leave me alone. Why can't you do something for yourself for a change?" The partner isn't just turned away, she's pushed away.

Maybe We're Not Right for Each Other

In Stage I, each partner believed that she could trust the other to respect her wishes and respond to her needs. In Stage II, it's hard to keep this faith. No longer entirely confident of each other, or of the love between them, the partners take care to protect themselves, resorting to strategies which feel defensive on the inside but look offensive from the outside. The person on the receiving end of such measures often finds her self-esteem, her trust or her sense of autonomy jeopardized by her partner's maneuvers.

Old injuries are dredged up and stock accusations exchanged and the battle escalates. The more wronged each feels, the more ruthless they become.

Each blamer believes herself/himself wholly innocent and believes the other to be completely at fault. Each tries to vindicate herself by forcing the other to admit the truth of her interpretation, but what looked like harsh facts to the one seemed like distortions and aspersions to the other.

The indictments are painful, however, even when their validity is contested. "I keep telling myself—he's angry and he's trying to get me. He doesn't mean what he says." Nevertheless, a system of mutual blame eats away trust. "When I see the hatred and contempt she has for me—I just feel as if it's hopeless." The other's abuse is frightening because it provokes the doubt, "How could he possibly love me if he sees me like that?"

Making up after a fight can be as tricky as avoiding a fight in the first place: One wants to forget about it; the other wants to talk it out; one wants affection for reassurance, the other wants sex.

Both, however, are apt to want a sincere apology. Mutual blame makes both parties balk. Neither wants to admit that her accusations were unjustified and both are too threatened to acknowledge their wrongdoing. So resentment "continues to hang in the air after an unpleasantness."

If "the hostility gets to be too much," a person can withdraw from a system of mutual blame. "I can't take it day after day after day, I'm just not going to expose myself to it anymore." Withdrawal into silence and absence is the result.

Mutual blame is a kind of hand-to-hand combat; mutual withholding is trench warfare. And warmth is one of the principal casualties of both. Neither partner considers the other entitled to support or approval, and neither experiences the other as a source of pleasure.

In the depths of Stage II, a relationship may seem hopeless. Each person usually perceives the problem as the product of the other's unwillingness to change. In fact, both are trapped by their common unwillingness to examine or alter their behavior. Each feels his/her strategies are survival measures, innocent because they're essential.

Often, all that a person can think of to do is leave. At a point in time when many people don't believe in commitments of "forever" proportions, the thought that Stage II usually prompts is—maybe it would be different with somebody else. Maybe "she's bad for me," or maybe "we're not right for each other," and maybe all the misery is a symptom of some fundamental unworkability in a relationship.

In fact, lasting couple relationships don't work any other way. Stage II follows Stage I with the relentlessness of death and taxes, no matter who the participants in the relationships are. Stage II means a certain amount of misery, and the experience of that misery is likely to make victims of us all.

A little perspective may help to take some of the edge off that misery. The troubles a person experiences in Stage II should not be allowed to obscure the bearable or the agreeable aspects of the relationship. There are ups and downs within Stage II, and it's possible, with persistence and goodwill, to reach "a place beyond resentment," a place where concord is not banality, and where harmony is not the simple absence of discord.

STAGE III: MUTUAL ACCEPTANCE

By an effort of will, romance and cruelty can be transformed into a love that is stronger and greater.

A Stage III couple has brought their expectations for their relationship into some kind of equilibrium with their everyday lives. Frustrations and anxieties don't stop, but these no longer trigger doubts about their future as a couple. That's settled. Each knows, and knows the other knows, that they're here to stay. Beth, in her mid-thirties, said of her thirteen-year marriage to George, "Even those times when I'm angry with him, I have confidence. There's a reliability there that it's going to get better and it's going to be good. We've seen too many good times not to live through the bad times."

Changes in behavior and feeling must ultimately be accompanied by further changes in expectations. The person who asks that a relationship fulfill the conventional romantic bill is guaranteed disappointment.

A person can only accept and find satisfaction in a long-term relationship if their expectations for it are realistic. The relationship will continue to be more comfortable in some ways than in others, and at some times than at others. And a couple relationship alone can't ensure a lifetime of happiness: Couple trouble is often merely the visible symptom of problems in other areas of the partners' lives.

For most couples, it's two steps forward, a step back, and a spell of footdragging. People get perspective and lose it again. A Stage III relationship can relapse into a Stage II under the brunt of external stresses, like illness or financial reverses. But the same combination of realism and desire that enabled the couple to achieve an equilibrium in the first place can enable them to restore the balance to their relationship.

In some quarters, aspirations are high for reaching Stage III: Coupled love is the solution that will bring meaning to an unsatisfactory life. In other circles, optimism is low. Betrayed by their hope for a happily-ever-after marriage, some couples have begun to question the whole notion of a commitment to love someone "forever." The cynicism is in many ways a reaction against the romanticism, and in many ways it's a constructive development. Couple problems are discussed far more frankly now than they were twenty years ago. And people are no longer as isolated in their disillusionment. But shared disillusionment may foster the conviction that a lasting couple commitment inevitably contracts into a dim business of obligation and resignation. We believe that an altogether different outcome is possible.

We believe it possible to affirm that love "lasteth till 'tis old." But Stage III is an achievement, almost never a happy accident. Stage I can be a product of good fortune, but Stage III is a product of good work. A couple has to struggle to overcome the disillusionment and the mistrust that relationships often create. They have to believe that "there's a place beyond resentment" and persist in their efforts to reach it despite discouragement over the lack of change or the slow pace of change in their relationship.

But although they are essential, persistence and good intentions are not sufficient to reach Stage III. The essence of Stage III is mutual acceptance, the knowledge that with one's partner there's "no need to hurry, no need to sparkle, no need to be anybody but one's self." The partners trust each other and feel at home with each other. Beth expressed it this way: "Part of the success of our marriage is that the family is a kind of safety valve where you can act out in a way and manner you can't someplace else."

"How Can I Be in Love with a Sixty-Year-Old Woman? But I Am"

Stage III also means mutual accommodation. Beth's husband explained: "Ten years ago, or even five years ago, I would have been less happy with her slumps. It's a pain. It's so visible in her, in the way the house looks, in everything. It's striking. But now I'm better about saying, 'Well, I'll pick it up, I'll do it.' I can wait till her mood goes away without getting too upset. Basically we're more sensitive to each other."

One of the prerequisites for survival of any couple is enduring mutual attraction. Al puzzled over how he maintained such an attraction over the years. "I say to her, 'How can I be in love with a sixty-year-old woman?' But I am. So she excites me and I'm grateful for it and I'm grateful that life has dealt me the cards that I can stay excited." As Al pointed out, "We have always been able to have a good time together, just the two of us."

For their relationship to survive over the long term, a couple must not only share a lively interest in each other, they must also share the inclination to seek each other out for pleasure. This demands, of course, the ability to remain curious about what is familiar, and to recognize the unfamiliar where it steals in. This kind of lasting involvement—mental, physical and emotional—creates a deep mutual knowledge that enlightens both partners.

The Stage III couple has learned to accept themselves as lovable people. And they have also learned to embrace each other as mortal, guilty, but entirely beautiful.

Known and appreciated, a person is free to become most fully himself or herself. She can trust her partner, and the slow accumulation of trust over the years spent together enables the Stage III couple to share an unrivaled intimacy, an intimacy not of illusion, but of achieved, earned knowledge.

A lasting couple relationship requires a balance struck between a couple's individual and joint pursuits, between autonomy and interdependence.

The desire for "security" has taken some hard criticism of late. But men and women who are secure—who love and know they're loved in return—are apt to be far more venturesome and spontaneous than those whose emotional footing is insecure. Beth spoke to the point when she said, "We needed to be married to go ahead and do the rest of our lives. We needed that reassurance from each other. That part of our lives had to be sound. Then we could go out and develop the rest of our lives. I needed that successful relationship to be successful elsewhere."

The security of a Stage III relationship accomplishes an indispensable function for the couple. They have each other to rely on, and the strength they exchange reassures them and reinforces them for their struggle through life. But, best of all, that exchanged strength enriches their experience of life.

To Apply This Reading to Yourself

1. Describe the stages in a love relationship that you have experienced or observed in someone close to you.
2. Describe the first stage ("the sparkle") in a love relationship that you have experienced, and compare it with the observations made in this reading.
3. Describe the second stage ("disillusionment") in a love relationship that you have experienced, and compare it with the observations made in this reading.
4. Describe the third stage ("mutual acceptance") in a love relationship that you have experienced, and compare it with the observations made in this reading.

Love Versus Infatuation

Elaine Hatfield
and G. William Walster

QUESTION: How can I tell if I'm really in love . . . or just infatuated?

In movies, lovers never have any trouble telling whether or not they're in love. Intense passion stalks them, shakes them around, and—struggle as they might—overwhelms them. In real life, we're usually not so certain about our feelings. Judith Viorst had this wry response to the question: What is the difference between infatuation and love?

> Infatuation is when you think that he's as sexy as Robert Redford, as smart as Henry Kissinger, as noble as Ralph Nader, as funny as Woody Allen and as athletic as Jimmy Connors. Love is when you realize that he's as sexy as Woody Allen, as smart as Jimmy Connors, as funny as Ralph Nader, as athletic as Henry Kissinger and nothing like Robert Redford in any category—but you'll take him anyway.[1]

College students at three universities were asked what one thing they most wished they knew about romantic love. A surprisingly frequent question was: "What is the difference between love and infatuation?"

The solution to the love-versus-infatuation riddle seems to be, quite simply, that there is no difference. Psychologists have become increasingly skeptical that passionate love and infatuation differ in any way—*at the time one is experiencing them.* Two sex counselors who interviewed young adults about their romantic and sexual experiences concluded that the difference between passionate love and infatuation is merely semantic. Lovers use the term "romantic love" to describe loving relationships that are still in progress. They use the term "infatuation" to describe once-loving relationships that, for a variety of reasons, were terminated.[2]

It appears, then, that it may be possible to tell infatuation from romantic love only in retrospect. If a relationship flowers, we continue to believe we are experiencing true love; if a relationship dies, we conclude that we were merely infatuated. We need not assume, then, that, at the time we are experiencing the feeling, true love differs in any way from the supposed counterfeit—i.e., infatuation.

QUESTION: If passionate love and infatuation are exactly the same thing, how come my mother—and my friends—keep insisting they can tell the difference?

When deciding whether or not to get involved with someone, you're really faced with two separate questions: Do I love the other person? Is that person right for me?

When our parents and friends grudgingly admit that maybe we are feeling the real thing or vehemently insist that we're not—that we're just "infatuated"—they're not really commenting on our feelings. Actually they're telling us whether or not they approve of our relationship. If they approve of the relationship, they are likely to agree that this may well be love—only time will tell. If they don't approve, they are likely to insist that it's only infatuation—here today, gone tomorrow.

But *you* shouldn't get confused trying to make nonexistent distinctions between the two. It's exciting to come to deeply understand yourself and your emotions. It's important to realize that you love someone and to bask in that feeling, even though you are also painfully aware that the relationship can come to nothing.

QUESTION: How can I tell if the person I love loves me?

Usually lovers don't try to hide their feelings: they tell their beloved, their friends, strangers on the bus, and the guy at the newsstand how they feel. Even if they're too shy to come right out and say they're in love, their behavior usually gives them away.

People indirectly signal that they're in love: eye contact, inclination, how close they stand to each other. Men and women in love also tend to give themselves away in several other ways. First, lovers tend to exaggerate their partners' virtues and minimize their faults—love *is* a little blind. Further, they are deeply involved emotionally; they want to share their emotions and experiences with those they love. Lovers treat their partners tenderly, kindly, and responsibly. And, they are *very* drawn to them sexually.[3]

But some of us often miss these seemingly obvious signals from our partners. Why? Psychologists find that our own feelings about ourselves—whether we basically respect ourselves or have dark misgivings—inevitably color our judgments of how others feel about us. Men and women who have unusually high self-esteem versus unusually low self-esteem react in very different ways to admiration and criticism. High-self-esteem men and women thoroughly relish praise—but they conveniently manage to misperceive, refute, or forget criticism. Low-self-esteem men and women are just the opposite. They are forever on the alert for criticism. They recognize it, accept it, and remember it long, long after.[4]

We are all very adept at protecting our egos. Even if we're wildly interested in someone, we start out by making a few tentative probes to find out where that person stands. We carefully observe how the man or woman we're interested in reacts—and only then do we decide whether or not it's worthwhile to pursue things.

High-self-esteem people are quick to recognize when others are interested in them and quick to decide whether or not to reciprocate. Low-self-esteem people are not. They tend to miss subtle signals of interest. Some, in fact, have such painfully low self-esteem that it warps their judgment.

An example: I once had a college friend who had great misgivings about herself. She worried that she was ugly, that she had bad skin, that her ankles were fat—that, really, it would be hard for any man to like her. She was steadily dating a man who *said* he liked her—but she wasn't sure. "He never wants to be seen with me in public," she complained. "All he wants to do is lie around his apartment, listening to records and making love. He doesn't love me—he just wants cheap sex." And she'd cry. On her birthday, she went

out with him again—and again came home crying. What had happened? He'd taken her to a fraternity dinner-dance and, when he'd dropped her off that night, he'd only given her a light peck goodnight. "He's just trying to ease me out," she moaned. "He doesn't even think I'm sexy any more." (It's not quite clear what he could have done to convince her that he loved her.)

Think about it. Are you set for rejection? Do you tend to interpret the behavior of others in such a way that, no matter what they do, you take it as clear-cut evidence that they don't *really* love you? If so, quit it!

There are, of course, times when your partner may have ambivalent feelings about you. He or she just isn't sure that this is the real thing.

QUESTION: What can I do to inspire feelings of love?

ANSWER: Take it for granted that you're loved.

Probably one of the most effective ways to convince someone who is unsure of his or her feelings for you is to act as if you are more confident of the person's love than you really are. Our ideas about ourselves—and the world—are contagious. When we're feeling good and are convinced that we're irresistible, we somehow manage to convince everyone else as well.

Humorist Dan Greenburg, in *How to Make Yourself Miserable,* observes that one surefire way to destroy a budding relationship is to keep questioning your lover's motivation.

Relationship-Destroying Maneuver Number One: The Great Love Test

This maneuver can be used at any stage of a deep relationship, but it seems particularly well suited to the beginning stages of a romance, so we recommend it as your first major stratagem.

This maneuver, as well as the ones that follow, are, of course, based on the reject-me formula.

Reject-me move #1:

You: *"Do you love me?"*

Mate: *"Yes,* of course *I love you."*

Reject-me move #2:

You: *"Do you really* love *me?"*

Mate: *"Yes, I really love you."*

You: *"You really really love me?"*

Mate: *"Yes, I really really love you."*

You: *"You're sure you love me—you're absolutely sure?"*

Mate: *"Yes, I'm absolutely sure."*
(pause)

You: *"Do you know the meaning of the word love?"*
(pause)

Mate: *"I don't know."*

You: *"Then how can you be so sure you love me?*
(pause)

Mate: *"I don't know. Perhaps I can't."*

Reject-me move #3:

You: *"You can't, eh? I see. Well, since you can't even be sure you love me, I can't really* see much point in our remaining together. Can you?
(pause)

Mate: *"I don't know. Perhaps not."*
(pause)

You: *"You've been leading up to this for a pretty long time, haven't you?"*[5]

Thus, high-self-esteem people have a second, continuing advantage over their low-esteem counterparts. Secure men and women are quick to perceive—and respond to—their lovers' expressions of affection. Insecure men and women aren't. Even when their lovers tell them they love them, they remain skeptical. They ask for reassurance. Or, worse yet, they argue with their lovers: "You don't love me. If you loved me, you wouldn't treat me this way." In the end, they usually win their case.

Reference Notes

1. J. Viorst, What is this thing called love? Reprinted from *Redbook*, February 1975, p. 12.
2. A. Ellis and R. Harper, *Creative Marriage* (New York: Lyle Stuart, 1961).
3. Z. Rubin, Measurement of romantic love. *Journal of Personality and Social Psychology 16* (1970): 265–273.
4. A. Cohen and I. Silverman, Repression-sensitization as a dimension of personality, in B. A. Maher, ed., *Progress in Experimental Personality Research*, Vol. 1 (New York: Academic Press, 1965), pp. 169–220.
5. From *How to Make Yourself Miserable*, by Dan Greenburg and Marcia Jacobs. Copyright © 1966 by Dan Greenburg. Reprinted by permission of Random House, Inc.

To Apply This Reading to Yourself

1. *Describe your own experience with passionate love and infatuation, indicating the extent to which you agree with the views of Hatfield and Walster.*
2. *Have you ever used the term* infatuation *to describe a love of your own or that of someone you knew? Exactly what did you mean by this term? How does your meaning compare with the meaning attached to this term by Hatfield and Walster?*
3. *How has your own level of self-esteem affected your romantic relationships?*
4. *How has your sense of security or insecurity affected your romantic relationships?*

Self-Love

Erich Fromm

While it raises no objection to apply the concept of love to various objects, it is a widespread belief that, while it is virtuous to love others, it is sinful to love oneself. It is assumed that to the degree to which I love myself I do not love others, that self-love is the same as selfishness.[1] This view goes far back in Western thought. Calvin speaks of self-love as "a pest."[2] Freud speaks of self-love in psychiatric terms but, nevertheless, his value judgment is the same as that of Calvin. For him self-love is the same as narcissism, the turning of the libido toward oneself. Narcissism is the earliest stage of human development, and the person who in later life has returned to this narcissistic stage is incapable of love; in the extreme case he is insane. Freud assumes that love is the manifestation of libido, and that the libido is either turned toward others—love; or toward oneself—self-love. Love and self-love are thus mutually exclusive in the sense that the more there is of one, the less there is of the other. If self-love is bad, it follows that unselfishness is virtuous.

These questions arise: Does psychological observation support the thesis that there is a basic contradiction between love for oneself and love for others? Is love for oneself the same phenomenon as selfishness, or are they opposites? Furthermore, is the selfishness of modern man really a *concern for himself* as an individual, with all his intellectual, emotional and sensual potentialities? Has "he" not become an appendage of his socioeconomic role? *Is his selfishness identical with self-love or is it not caused by the very lack of it?*

Before we start the discussion of the psychological aspect of selfishness and self-love, the logical fallacy in the notion that love for others and love for oneself are mutually exclusive should be stressed. If it is a virtue to love my neighbor as a human being, it must be a virtue—and not a vice—to love myself, since I am a human being too. There is no concept of man in which I myself am not included. A doctrine which proclaims such an exclusion proves itself to be intrinsically contradictory. The idea expressed in the Biblical "Love thy neighbor as thyself!" implies that respect for one's own integrity and uniqueness, love for and understanding of one's own self, cannot be separated from respect and love and understanding for another individual. The love for my own self is inseparably connected with the love for any other being.

We have come now to the basic psychological premises on which the conclusions of our argument are built. Generally, these premises are as follows: not only others, but we ourselves are the "object" of our feelings and attitudes; the attitudes toward others and toward ourselves, far from being contradictory, are basically *conjunctive*. With regard to the problem under discussion this means: love of others and love of ourselves are not alternatives. On the contrary, an attitude of love toward themselves will be found in all those who are capable of loving others. *Love*, in principle, *is indivisible as far as the connection between "objects" and one's own self is concerned*. Genuine love is an expression of productiveness and implies care, respect, responsibility and knowledge. It is not an "affect" in the sense of being affected by somebody, but an active striving for the growth and happiness of the loved person, rooted in one's own capacity to love.

1. Paul Tillich, in a review of *The Sane Society*, in *Pastoral Psychology*, September 1955, has suggested that it would be better to drop the ambiguous term "self-love" and to replace it with "natural self-affirmation" or "paradoxical self-acceptance." Much as I can see the merits of this suggestion I cannot agree with him in this point. In the term "self-love" the paradoxical element in self-love is contained more clearly. The fact is expressed that love is an attitude which is the same toward all objects, including myself. It must also not be forgotten that the term "self-love," in the sense in which it is used here, has a history. The Bible speaks of self-love when it commands to "love thy neighbor *as thyself*," and Meister Eckhart speaks of self-love in the very same sense.

2. John Calvin, *Institutes of the Christian Religion*, translated by J. Albau (Philadelphia: Presbyterian Board of Christian Education, 1928), Chap. 7, par. 4, p. 622.

To love somebody is the actualization and concentration of the power to love. The basic affirmation contained in love is directed toward the beloved person as an incarnation of essentially human qualities. Love of one person implies love of man as such. The kind of "division of labor," as William James calls it, by which one loves one's family but is without feeling for the "stranger," is a sign of a basic inability to love. Love of man is not, as is frequently supposed, an abstraction coming after the love for a specific person, but it is its premise, although genetically it is acquired in loving specific individuals.

From this it follows that my own self must be as much an object of my love as another person. *The affirmation of one's own life, happiness, growth, freedom is rooted in one's capacity to love,* i.e., in care, respect, responsibility, and knowledge. If an individual is able to love productively, he loves himself too; if he can love only others, he cannot love at all.

Granted that love for oneself and for others in principle is conjunctive, how do we explain selfishness, which obviously excludes any genuine concern for others? The *selfish* person is interested only in himself, wants everything for himself, feels no pleasure in giving, but only in taking. The world outside is looked at only from the standpoint of what he can get out of it; he lacks interest in the needs of others, and respect for their dignity and integrity. He can see nothing but himself; he judges everyone and everything from its usefulness to him; he is basically unable to love. Does not this prove that concern for others and concern for oneself are unavoidable alternatives? This would be so if selfishness and self-love were identical. But that assumption is the very fallacy which has led to so many mistaken conclusions concerning our problem. *Selfishness and self-love, far from being identical, are actually opposites.* The selfish person does not love himself too much but too little; in fact he hates himself. This lack of fondness and care for himself, which is only one expression of his lack of productiveness, leaves him empty and frustrated. He is necessarily unhappy and anxiously concerned to snatch from life the satisfactions which he blocks himself from attaining. He seems to care too much for himself, but actually he only makes an unsuccessful attempt to cover up and compensate for his failure to care for his real self. Freud holds that the selfish person is narcissistic, as if he had withdrawn his love from others and turned it toward his own person. *It is true that selfish persons are incapable of loving others, but they are not capable of loving themselves either.*

It is easier to understand selfishness by comparing it with greedy concern for others, as we find it, for instance, in an oversolicitous mother. While she consciously believes that she is particularly fond of her child, she has actually a deeply repressed hostility toward the object of her concern. She is overconcerned not because she loves the child too much, but because she has to compensate for her lack of capacity to love him at all.

This story of the nature of selfishness is borne out by psychoanalytic experience with neurotic "unselfishness," a symptom of neurosis observed in not a few people who usually are troubled not by this symptom but by others connected with it, like depression, tiredness, inability to work, failure in love relationships, and so on. Not only is unselfishness not felt as a "symptom"; it is often the one redeeming character trait on which such people pride themselves. The "unselfish" person "does not want anything for himself"; he "lives only for others," is proud that he does not consider himself important. He is puzzled to find that in spite of his unselfishness he is unhappy, and that his relationships to those closest to him are unsatisfactory. Analytic work shows that his unselfishness is not something apart from his other symptoms but one of them, in fact often the most important one; that he is paralyzed in his capacity to love or to enjoy anything; that he is pervaded by hostility toward life and that behind the facade of unselfishness a subtle but not less intense self-centeredness is hidden. This person can be cured only if his unselfishness too is interpreted as a symptom along with the others, so that his lack of productiveness, which is at the root of both his unselfishness *and* his other troubles, can be corrected.

The nature of unselfishness becomes particularly apparent in its effect on others, and most frequently in our culture in the effect the "unselfish" mother has on her children. She believes that by her unselfishness her children will experience what it means to be loved and to learn, in turn, what it means to love. The effect of her unselfishness, however, does not at all correspond to her expectations. The children do not show the happiness of persons who are convinced that they are loved; they are anxious, tense, afraid of the mother's disapproval and anxious to live up to her expectations. Usually, they are affected by their mother's hidden hostility toward life, which they sense rather than recognize clearly, and eventually they become imbued with it themselves. Altogether, the effect of the "unselfish" mother is not too different from that of the selfish one; indeed, it is often worse, because the mother's unselfishness prevents the children from criticizing her. They are put under the obligation not to disappoint her; they are taught, under the mask of virtue, dislike for life. If one has a chance to study the effect of a mother with genuine self-love, one can see that there is nothing more conducive to giving a child the experience of what love, joy and happiness are than being loved by a mother who loves herself.

These ideas on self-love cannot be summarized better than by quoting Meister Eckhart on this topic: "If you love yourself, you love everybody else as you do yourself. As long as you love another person less than you love yourself, you will not really succeed in loving yourself, but if you love all alike, including yourself, you will love them as one person and that person is both God and man. Thus he is a great and righteous person who, loving himself, loves all others equally."[3]

3. Meister Eckhart, *Meister Eckhart*, ed. and trans. by R. D. Blakney (New York: Harper & Row, Publishers, Inc., 1941), p. 204.

To Apply This Reading to Yourself

1. *Do you love yourself deeply? Why or why not? And how do you show your love or lack of love for yourself? Write a brief paper incorporating your answers to these questions.*
2. *Are you capable of loving others deeply? Why or why not? And how do you show your love or lack of love for others? Write a brief paper incorporating your answers to these questions.*
3. *Fromm writes that selfishness and self-love are opposites. Relate your past and present capacities for selfishness and self-love, and draw any insights you can.*
4. *Fromm writes that if we are capable of love, we love ourselves, too, and if we can love only others, then we cannot love at all. Relate your past and present capacities for self-love and love for others, and draw any insights you can.*

Myths About Love

Abe Arkoff

A number of psychologists including David Bricker (1978), Gerald Corey (1986), and Albert Ellis (1978), have noted the many myths about love that exist in our culture. Far from harmless, these misconceptions cause a good deal of mischief and unhappiness. Ellis writes that almost every day he sees a person in therapy with a problem related to one or more of these "superstitions." Following are five of these myths, synthesized from lists formulated by these psychologists.

Myth 1. Love is mysterious.

Some years ago, Wisconsin's Senator Proxmire attacked a National Science Foundation's grant awarded for the study of the reasons that people fall in love. In a press release, the Senator wrote that he objected because in his opinion the reasons for falling in love could not be determined scientifically, that whatever reasons were discovered would not be believed, and, further, that he and 200,000,000 other Americans preferred that the whole matter remain a mystery. Columnist James Reston agreed with the Senator that love would always be a mystery. "But," Reston added, "if the sociologists and psychologists can even get a suggestion of the answer to our pattern of romantic love, marriage, disillusions, divorce—and the children left behind—it (the grant) would be the best investment of federal money since Jefferson made the Louisiana purchase."

As it turns out, the "mystery" of love lends itself quite well to scientific study. Since the 1950s, when scientists began to research various aspects of love, a lot has been discovered. Hatfield and Walster (1985) write, "Taken all together, this information begins to shed some light on what love is, who finds it and who doesn't, and what causes love to flourish . . . or die" (p. 2).

Dozens of studies concerning love are currently presented each year in scientific journals or at conventions, and the *Journal of Social and Personal Relationships* devotes much of its space to this subject. Perhaps the most famous of all love sonnets was written by Elizabeth Barrett Browning in the last century and begins, "How do I love thee? Let me count the ways." Love researcher Rick Zubin (1988)—impressed by the output of his professional colleagues—suggests that if it were written today, it might begin, "How do I love thee? Let me count the articles" (p. viii).

None of this should be taken to mean that psychologists know as much about love as poets. As Zubin, himself admits, "the science of love is still in its infancy." Much is unexplained, but nothing appears inexplicable. Zubin writes, "Psychologists are not about to displace poets or novelists as society's preeminent observers of love, but the researchers are beginning to pierce the veil of love in their own ways. As they pursue this research, psychologists have an opportunity not only to satisfy their own scientific curiosity but also to enrich people's lives" (xi–xii).

Myth 2. Love is forever./Love is fleeting.

"I'll be loving you always, with a love that's true always," is an old song classic, but Corey declares "the notion that love will endure forever is nonsense" (p. 195). And it is dangerous nonsense because it can lull us into a false sense of security and prevent us from continuing the work that every worthwhile relationship requires. People change, and the love they feel for each other may change in quality or depth. Well-tended relationships deepen; commitment and shared experience produce a formidable bond. But people grow, and sometimes they grow irrevocably apart.

Some of us subscribe to an opposite myth— the belief that love is fleeting. We may not even be fully aware that we are influenced by this myth, but if we are the child of a broken marriage or have been around or involved in a number of failed relationships ourselves, we can develop a kind of cynicism or pessimism about love. We may be too quick to declare a struggling relationship dead or too slow to apply the first aid that could move a stuck or unsatisfying relationship to a better place.

Myth 3. Love is constant.

Ellis writes, "Love, even when it is deepseated and intense, tends to be a distinctly intermittent rather than steady, incessant feeling" (p. 157). And he adds that this is especially so in love relationships that endure for a considerable length of time. Marshall Hodge (1967) agrees and notes that love itself does not come and go, but our *experience* of love and our *expression* of love is intermittent" (p. 13).

Corey believes we can only stand so much closeness. There are times when we need to be in the company of others and times when we need to be apart. He has observed that periods of separation from a loved one can be healthy, and the inability to separate or to allow some separation may be a symptom of a deeper problem.

Myth 4. Love is exclusive.

"Forsaking all others" is a phrase out of a traditional set of marriage vows, but Ellis and Corey object and refuse to "forever hold their peace." Ellis leads the attack and points to a great mass of biographical and clinical data indicating that it is possible to love two or more members of the opposite sex deeply, intensely, and at the same time. Corey maintains that genuine love is expansive rather than exclusive. He writes, "If I love you, I encourage you to reach out and develop other relationships. Although our love for each other and our commitment to each other might preclude certain actions on our parts, we are not totally and exclusively wedded to each other. It is a pseudo-love that cements one person to another in such a way that he or she is not given room to grow" (p. 201).

Some couples get wrapped up in themselves and let other friendships drop away. But it is not reasonable to expect one person to meet all our needs. Other people nurture us and encourage our growth in other ways, and when we are experiencing difficulties, these others can help us with support and understanding (Doress & Wegman, 1984).

Despite our love and sexual attraction to our mate, it is normal to also feel an attraction to others. Ellis writes that if we are only sexually attracted to our mate and never interested in anyone else, then we are "a most unusual and very probably, abnormal individual." This does not mean, Ellis adds, that we do something about these interests, only that it is almost impossible not to have them.

There are some aspects of love or of our thoughts and feelings that we may share only with our mate and some perhaps that we never share with her or him. Many couples choose to have sex only with each other; this to them is an essential commitment. Some women find it easier to share their innermost thoughts with a close woman friend or a continuing circle of friends rather than with their husbands; these friends may be able to share perspectives and experiences and respond in ways their husbands would never be able to.

Myth 5. Love is beyond our control.

A personality dimension called "locus of control" describes the measure of influence we believe we have on our lives. Some individuals, called "externals," believe they lack control—that things happen to them. By contrast, others, called "internals," believe they exercise control—that they make things happen. Of course, none of us is purely or completely one or the other. Many of us tend to be externals in some situations and internals in others.

Sometimes, the very language of love suggests that love is an arena over which we can exercise little control. For example, in describing the advent of a romantic relationship, we may say we "fell in love" as if we were the passive victim of overwhelming forces. We may say, "I wish I could get over my feelings for her" or "I wish I cared more for him" as if we were at a loss and unable to do anything about this aspect of our life (Bricker, 1978). Or we attribute our attraction to "chemistry" which is either right or wrong; if it's right, there's nothing that needs to be done, and if it's wrong, there's nothing that can be done (Bricker, 1978).

Many psychologists and other students of human behavior have taken strong exception to this notion of love. Their view is that love is not something that happens to us. Love is something we make happen.

In this view, love is not passive; it is not an affect or feeling that just comes over us. Love is active, and lovers are activators. "Love is as love does," writes M. Scott Peck (1978). "Love is an act of will—namely, both intention and an action" (p. 83). Or to say it another way, when we love, we mean well and we do good.

Peck maintains that what is called "falling in love" is not love at all because it is not an act of will. As he sees it, "falling in love" is a kind of genetic trick to get us to mate and enhance the survival of the species. Falling in love is a temporary and sexually motivated experience in which we are drawn beyond our usual restraints or defenses or boundaries. In this state, we wish to merge with the other. There are accompanying feelings of ecstasy and omnipotence, which, alas, disappear when reality with its everyday problems intrudes. We become individuals again and hardly omnipotent. Peck writes that at this point, we either say goodbye or begin "the work of real loving."

The "work of real loving" is very much within our control. We take responsibility to make things good rather than waiting for good things to happen, and we either find good or make peace with all that occurs. Probably few observers have been as perceptive as Robert Johnson (1985) on the work of real loving:

> Many years ago a wise friend gave me a name for human love. She called it "stirring-the-oatmeal" love. She was right.... Stirring the oatmeal is a humble act—not exciting or thrilling. But it symbolizes a relatedness that brings love down to earth. It represents a willingness to share ordinary human life, to find meaning in simple, unromantic tasks: earning a living, living within a budget, putting out the garbage, feeding the baby in the middle of the night. To "stir the oatmeal" means to find the relatedness, the value, even the beauty, in simple, ordinary things.... The real relatedness between two people is experienced in the small tasks they do together: the quiet conversation when the day's upheavals are at rest, the soft word of understanding, the daily companionship, the encouragement offered in a difficult moment, the small gift when least expected, the spontaneous gesture of love. (p. 18)

References

Bricker, D. (1978). Myths of romantic love. *Rational Living, 13*(1), 31–35.

Corey, G. (1986). *I never knew I had a choice* (3rd ed.). Monterey, CA: Brooks/Cole.

Doress, P. B., & Wegman, P. N. (1984). Working toward mutuality: Our relationships with men. In The Boston Women's Health Book Collective (Ed.), *Our bodies, ourselves,* (2nd ed., pp. 123–140), New York: Simon & Schuster.

Ellis, A. (1978). *Sex without guilt.* North Hollywood, CA: Wilshire.

Hatfield, E., & Walster, G. W. (1985). *A new look at love.* Lanham, MD: University Press of America.

Hodge, M. B. (1967). *Your fear of love.* Garden City, NY: Dolphin (Doubleday).

Johnson, R. (1985). Stirring the oatmeal. In J. Welwood (Ed.), *Challenge of the heart* (pp. 18–20). Boston: Shambhala.

Peck, M. S. (1978). *The road less traveled.* New York: Touchstone/Simon & Schuster.

Zubin, R. (1988). Preface. In R. J. Sternberg & M. L. Barnes (Eds.), *The psychology of love* (pp. vii–xii). New Haven, CT: Yale University Press.

To Apply This Reading to Yourself

1. *Of the love myths in the reading, select one that has affected you, and describe this effect.*
2. *Of the love myths in the reading, select one that you do not agree is completely a myth, and argue your point of view.*

3. Describe a love myth not presented in the reading that has affected you, and describe this effect. (Examples: There is one ideal mate for each of us. You can love another without loving yourself. You must have someone to love in order to be happy.)
4. Describe one or more of your earlier beliefs about love (whether myths or not) that your experience with love has caused you to modify.

You Just Don't Understand

Deborah Tannen

A married couple was in a car when the wife turned to her husband and asked, "Would you like to stop for a drink?"

"No, thanks," he answered truthfully. So they didn't stop.

The result? The wife—who had indeed wanted to stop—became annoyed because she felt her preference had not been considered. The husband, seeing his wife was angry, became frustrated. *Why didn't she just say what she wanted?*

Unfortunately, he failed to see that his wife was asking the question not to get an instant decision, but to begin a negotiation. And the woman didn't realize that when her husband said no, he was just expressing his preference, not making a ruling. When a man and woman interpret the same interchange in such conflicting ways, it's no wonder they can find themselves leveling angry charges of selfishness and obstinacy at each other.

As a specialist in linguistics, I have studied how the conversational styles of men and women differ. We cannot, of course, lump "all men" or "all women" into fixed categories—individuals vary greatly. But research shows that the seemingly senseless misunderstandings that haunt our relationships can at least in part be explained by the different conversational rules by which men and women often play.

Whenever I write or speak about this subject, people tell me how relieved they are to learn that what they had previously ascribed to personal failings is, in fact, very common. Learning about the different (though equally valid) conversational frequencies men and women are tuned to can help banish blame and help us truly talk to one another. Here are some of the most common areas of conflict.

STATUS VS. SUPPORT

Men grow up in a world in which a conversation is often a contest—either to achieve the upper hand or to prevent other people from pushing them around. For many women, however, talking is typically a way to exchange confirmation and support. I saw this firsthand when my husband and I had jobs in different cities. When people made comments like "That must be rough" and "How do you stand it?" I accepted their sympathy.

But my husband would react with irritation. Our situation had advantages, he would explain. As academics, we had long weekends and vacations together.

Everything he said was true, but I didn't understand why he chose to say it. He told me that he felt some of the comments implied: "Yours is not a real marriage. I am superior to you because my wife and I have avoided your misfortune." It had not occurred to me there might be an element of one-upmanship, though I recognized it when it was pointed out.

I now see that my husband was simply approaching the world as many men do: as a place where people try to achieve and maintain status. I, on the other hand, was approaching the world as many women do: as a network of connections, in which people seek consensus.

INDEPENDENCE VS. INTIMACY

Since women often think in terms of closeness and support, they struggle to preserve intimacy. Men, concerned with status, tend to focus on establishing independence. These traits can lead women and men to starkly different views of the same situation.

When Josh's old high-school friend called him at work to say he'd be in town, Josh invited him to stay for the weekend. That evening he told Linda.

Linda was upset. How could Josh make these plans without discussing them with her beforehand? She would never do that to him. "Why don't you tell your friend you have to check with your wife?" she asked.

Josh replied, "I can't say I have to ask my wife for permission!"

To Josh, checking with his wife would mean he was not free to act on his own. It would make him feel like a child or an underling. But Linda actually enjoys telling people, "I have to check with Josh." It makes her feel good to show her life is entwined with her husband's.

ADVICE VS. UNDERSTANDING

Eve had a benign lump removed from her breast. When she confided to her husband, Mark, that she was distressed because the stitches changed the contour of her breast, he answered, "You can always have plastic surgery."

This comment bothered her. "I'm sorry you don't like the way it looks," she protested, "but I am not having any more surgery!"

Mark was hurt and puzzled. "I don't care about a scar," he replied. "It doesn't bother me at all."

"Then why are you telling me to have plastic surgery?" she asked.

"Because *you* were upset about the way it looks."

Eve felt like a heel. Mark had been wonderfully supportive throughout her surgery. How could she snap at him now?

The problem stemmed from a difference in approach. To many men, a complaint is a challenge to come up with a solution. Mark thought he was reassuring Eve by telling her there was something she could *do* about her scar. But often women are looking for emotional support, not solutions.

INFORMATION VS. FEELINGS

A cartoon I once saw shows a husband opening a newspaper and asking his wife, "Is there anything you'd like to say before I start reading?" We know there isn't—but that as soon as the man begins reading, his wife will think of something.

The cartoon is funny because people recognize their own experience in it. What's not funny is that many women are hurt when men don't talk to them at home, and many men are frustrated when they disappoint their partners without knowing why.

Rebecca, who is happily married, told me this is a source of dissatisfaction with her husband, Stuart. When she tells him what she is thinking, he listens silently. When she asks him what is on his mind, he says, "Nothing."

All Rebecca's life she has had practice verbalizing her feelings with friends and relatives. To her, this shows involvement and caring. But to Stuart, like most men, talk is for information. All his life he has had practice in keeping his innermost thoughts to himself.

Yet many such men hold center stage in a social setting, telling jokes and stories. They use conversation to claim attention and to entertain. Women can wind up hurt that their husbands tell relative strangers things they have not told them.

To avoid this kind of misunderstanding, both men and women can make adjustments. A woman may observe a man's desire to read the paper, for example, without seeing it as rejection. And a man can understand a woman's desire to talk without feeling it an intrusion.

ORDERS VS. PROPOSALS

Diana often begins statements with "Let's." She might say, "Let's park over there" or "Let's clean up before lunch." This makes Nathan angry. He has deciphered Diana's "Let's" as a command. Like most men, he resists being told what to do. But to Diana, she is making suggestions, not demands. Like most women, she wants to avoid confrontation and formulates requests as proposals rather than orders. Her style of talking *is* a way of getting others to do what she wants—but by winning agreement first.

With certain men, like Nathan, this tactic backfires. If they perceive someone is trying to get them to do something indirectly, they feel manipulated and respond more resentfully than they would to a straightforward request.

CONFLICT VS. COMPROMISE

In trying to prevent fights, some women refuse to openly oppose the will of others. But at times it's far more effective for a woman to assert herself, even at the risk of conflict.

Dora was frustrated by a series of used automobiles she drove. It was she who commuted to work, but her husband, Hank, who chose the cars. Hank always went for automobiles that were "interesting," but in continual need of repair. After Dora was nearly killed when her brakes failed, they were in the market for yet another car.

Dora wanted to buy a late-model sedan from a friend. Hank fixed his sights on a 15-year-old sports car. Previously, she would have acceded to his wishes. But this time Dora bought the boring but dependable car and steeled herself for Hank's anger. To her amazement, he spoke not a word of remonstrance. When she later told him what she had expected, he scoffed at her fears and said she should have done what she wanted from the start if she felt that strongly about it.

As Dora discovered, a little conflict won't kill you. At the same time, men who habitually oppose others can adjust their style to opt for less confrontation.

When we don't see style differences for what they are, we sometimes draw unfair conclusions ("You're illogical," "You're self-centered," "You don't care about me"). But once we grasp the two characteristic approaches, we stand a better chance of preventing disagreements from spiraling out of control. Learning the other's ways of talking is a leap across the communication gap between men and women, and a giant step toward genuine understanding.

To Apply This Reading to Yourself

1. *Recall the misunderstanding associated with a relationship you have or have had with a member of the opposite sex, and relate this misunderstanding to the findings presented in the reading.*
2. *Recall or observe the conversations between yourself and a significant other of the opposite sex, and relate your findings to those presented in the reading.*
3. *Recall or observe the conversations in a male–female pair you know (perhaps your parents or a brother and sister-in-law or a sister and brother-in-law), and relate your findings to those presented in the reading.*
4. *Recall your own conversations of the past several days, or listen in as you converse tomorrow and the next day. How much of your conversation is designed to achieve or maintain status? How much is to exchange confirmation and support? Relate your findings to those in the reading.*

Pairing

It takes two to tango.
—song title

Two's company and three's a crowd.
—old saying

Now! At Last! The new fall lineup of the very latest plans and styles for satisfactory living together. The list includes a dazzling variety of sizes and shapes, options and accessories, never before made available to the general public, and the cost is surprisingly low. You pay your money and take your choice, and may you live happily ever after. Or at least until next Tuesday.
—preface to Man + Woman: A Consumer's Guide to Contemporary Pairing Patterns Including Marriage by Carlfred B. Broderick

It takes two to tango—and to do many of the other enjoyable and important things of life. Human beings tend to pair.

Two's company and three's a crowd. Two's simple and makes for only one relationship (A and B). When three persons join together, there are three relationships (A with B, B with C, and C with A), and from there it gets increasingly complex. When four people join, there are six relationships, five make for ten, and ten for 45.

One close twosome is the most that many of us can manage at a time. In his book *Intimate Friendships*, James Ramey writes, "We are much more likely to develop a few close relationships or a lot of shallow relationships than to develop a great many close relationships. In fact, many people develop only one primary relationship at a time. . . . A primary relationship requires almost constant availability because it becomes central to the way one's life is organized."

In our lifetime, we are one half of many pairs. In the beginning, there is the mother–child bond, then other bonds including pals, best friends, and confidants; crushes, sweethearts, lovers, and cohabiters; and, sooner or later, almost all of us become part of a pair called "marriage." Marriage is the most popular of all the more-or-less intimate and more-or-less permanent kinds of adult pairings.

From one vantage point, American marriage appears to be in trouble these days. As minimum estimates, one in every three first marriages and one in every two second marriages end in divorce. In some urban areas and other sections of the country, divorce rates are sharply higher than this. To these rates must be added those marriages effectively ended by legal separation and desertion.

Even among those who remain married, the situation seems far from perfect. Lederer and Jackson interviewed 601 couples on the West Coast and in New England for their study *The Mirages of Marriage.* They found that more than three quarters of these couples had frequently and seriously considered divorce, and over half remained married only because divorce was too difficult, painful, or expensive.

Further ammunition for the critics of marriage can be found in the current high infidelity rates. It is not easy to get an accurate reading on adultery, but the Kinsey Institute recently estimated that 37% of American married men have had extramarital relations. For women, the estimate was somewhat lower; 29% were estimated to have had extramarital sex. Some other researchers have made considerably higher estimates.

However, from another vantage point, marriage seems to be in no danger of going out of style. Despite its fragile clasp, wedlock has lost little of its popularity. The United States is one of the most marrying countries in the world: about 90 percent of American adults marry.

Even among people who get divorced, matrimony remains a popular institution. Such people appear not to be escaping marriage but, rather, looking for a better one. Most divorced persons remarry, and if they get divorced again, they remarry again. Today about three out of four divorced women and five out of six divorced men have remarried.

According to some experts, divorce, infidelity and related marital phenomena are not symptoms of terminal disease, but rather signs that marriage is changing to better accommodate present-day conditions. Despite a growing tolerance for other patterns, there is little threat to monogamous wedlock as the principal kind of pairing. After evaluating the field, Carlfred Broderick, in his guide to pairing (see the epigraph to this topic), recommends "the ever-popular traditional marriage." "In fact," he writes, "I've had one for twenty years myself and it's running better today than when it was new."

In the readings that follow, the traditional and a variety of other pairing models are presented. For good measure, there is even honorable mention of singlehood—an "unpair" model for those who feel that two may be one too many.

THE TRADITIONAL MODEL

Two out of every three mothers are in the paid labor force, but according to a very recent poll, a majority say they would consider quitting their jobs if money were not a factor. (Working fathers were not polled.) According to Susan Hayward, a spokesperson for the firm that conducted the survey, "Women seem to have come to the conclusion that they're never going to have it all, and they might die trying. Their attitude is, 'Let's get real, here.'"[1]

In the first reading, Patricia Kroken mounts a spirited defense of the traditional model. Her husband is the breadwinner, and she has chosen to be a full-time homemaker and put her teaching certificate aside. Aware of the pressures her husband faces, she views her home as a sanctuary rather than a prison. Says she, "being a wife and mother has given me as full a life as I could wish for."

THE TWO-CAREER MODEL/THE SHARED-ROLES MODEL

In the second reading, Karen Barrett describes the two-career marriage, which she calls "*the* major social change of this century." Some two-career couples exemplify the shared-roles model in which the partners share equally in household chores and parenting. But in many two-career couples, the wife is left with the major portion (even all) of domestic responsibilities. As Barrett points out, the potential rewards of the two-career model are high, but it also involves a lot of work not only within the couple but also in changing society to better accommodate it.

SOME ALTERNATIVE MODELS

Recent years have found increasing numbers of adults pairing without marriage or in openly gay relationships or living alone. *Cohabitation,* a general term for unmarried, living-together pairs, is being partly supplanted by a more elegant designation, *domesticated partnership* (DP). This latter term is mostly reserved for cohabitants whose relationship is stable and financially interdependent. What's new is that a few local governments and corporations have established policies that give DPs formal recognition and, in the case of the corporations, some benefits provided to married employees.

"Singlehood" and "singleness" are somewhat different concepts. *Singlehood* generally describes those who never pair while *singleness* more broadly refers to all adults who are unpaired; this latter designation includes those who have never paired and those who have been separated, divorced, or widowed. There is less social pressure to marry or to marry early these days, and singlehood or singleness is more of an option than before; still, almost all adults plan to pair or marry.

1. The *Time* poll of 18- to 24 year-olds, reported on page 80 of this book, found that two thirds of the women and nearly half the men were interested in staying at home and raising the children.

Heterosexuals commonly believe that homosexuals do not form long-term relationships, but it is just such relationships that many homosexual men and most homosexual women prefer. The AIDS epidemic has led to a radical alteration of sexual expression in gay males and a considerable increase in monogamous relationships. The stability of cohabiting homosexual pairs compares favorably with that of cohabiting heterosexuals.

In the third reading, Sol Gordon and Craig Snyder discuss cohabitation, singlehood, and gay relationships at greater length. They note that there are a variety of ways to be happy *and unhappy* both within and outside of marriage, but those who elect a less traditional path may have a harder time of it. No prudes, Gordon and Snyder favor a society in which there is true freedom to choose the path that fits best, and so does the editor of this book.

THE MYTHICAL MODEL

We begin to learn marital myths early in life. There are more than a few children's tales that end, "and so they were married and lived happily ever after." I don't remember a single one that ended something like, "and so they were married and lived together for 9.4 years" (which is how long the average American marriage lasts).

These days, it's open season on marital fairy tales. In their book *Husbands and Wives*, psychologists Melvyn Kinder and Connell Cowan explore and explode 15 marital myths, and in his book *Marital Myths*, psychologist Arnold Lazarus turns his guns on 24 of the same. (These author-clinicians might be considered ungrateful because marital misbeliefs cause the dissatisfaction that brings them business.) In the last reading, which is an excerpt from Lazarus's book, he shoots down 7 very important myths, which, he says, "can ruin a marriage (or make a bad one worse)."

To Explore Your Own Pairing Ideas, Attitudes, and Inclinations

1. *Weighing partner qualities (assets).* List all the qualities that you feel would be essential or important in a person with whom you would form a long-term or permanent intimate relationship. Put a star in front of the three qualities that you consider the most essential or important, and write a brief paper explaining why you hold these starred qualities in such high regard. Share your paper in the larger group or in small groups. Small groups may also be asked to winnow to arrive at a single list of three qualities to report back to the larger group.
2. *Weighing partner qualities (liabilities).* List all those qualities that you definitely would not want in a person with whom you would form a long-term or permanent intimate relationship—qualities that would be undesirable or liabilities in such a relationship. Put a star in front of the three qualities that you consider the most undesirable, and write a brief paper explaining why you consider

these starred qualities such liabilities. Share your paper in the larger group or in small groups. Small groups may also be asked to winnow to arrive at a single list of three qualities to report back to the larger group.

3. *Weighing your own qualities (assets)*. List all the desirable or positive qualities that you have that would contribute to the success of a long-term or permanent intimate relationship. Put a star in front of the three qualities that would contribute most, and write a brief paper explaining why they would be such desirable assets. Share your paper in the larger group, in small groups, or in dyads.

4. *Weighing your own qualities (liabilities)*. Consider all your personal qualities that would be undesirable or liabilities in a long-term or permanent intimate personal relationship. Put a star in front of the three qualities that would detract most, and write a brief paper explaining why they would be so undesirable. Share your paper in the larger group, in small groups, or in dyads.

5. *Comparing mate values*. Divide into subgroups composed of all men and all women. Each subgroup meets by itself and arrives at a written list of five qualities that the members agree are important in a mate. Then the whole group reassembles, and subgroups compare their separate lists of qualities and determine reasons for any discrepancies.

6. *Rejecting pairing models*. Review various kinds of pairing models, and pick out one that you feel would be wrong for you. Then write a brief paper explaining why, and share your paper in the larger group or in small groups. In your review of pairing models, consider the following (and any others you wish): traditional (the male is primarily the breadwinner and the female is primarily the homemaker); shared roles (the parties share equally in the breadwinning and homemaking activities); reversed roles (the female is primarily the breadwinner and the male is primarily the homemaker); cohabitation or living together (the parties live together without being formally married and, possibly, without intent to have children or permanency); and singlehood (the person lives alone).

7. *Selecting pairing models*. Review various kinds of pairing models (note those listed in the previous item), and pick out one that you feel would be right for you; then write a brief paper explaining why. Share your paper in the larger group or in small groups.

8. *Boosting and bursting pairing models*. Form groups of five persons. For each group, write the following terms in lowercase letters on slips of paper (one term per slip) and place them in an envelope: (1) traditional model, (2) shared-roles model, (3) reversed-roles model, (4) cohabitation or living-together model, and (5) singlehood model. Then write the same terms again on slips of paper—except this time use all capital letters—and place them in a second envelope. Each person draws a term from each envelope. Begin the boosting with the person who has drawn the traditional model spelled out in capital letters; this person, the booster, carefully concealing real feelings and beliefs, must make an enthusiastic case for this model, indicating (a) its general advantages and

(b) its specific advantages for the booster. The person who has drawn the same term in lowercase letters, the burster, while withholding real feelings and beliefs, must argue vigorously against the model, indicating (a) its general disadvantages and (b) the specific disadvantages it would have for the burster. After the first booster–burster brouhaha, continue in the same way for the remaining models. If a person draws both booster and burster slips for one model, have this person take both sides.

9. *Learning from pairing and unpairing models.* Consider a married, separated, or divorced pair with whom you are well acquainted. How has your knowledge of and/or interaction with this pair affected your ideas, attitudes, and inclinations concerning pairing? Write a brief paper giving your answer to this question, and share your paper in the larger group or in small groups.

10. *Role-playing pairing models.* Have volunteers role-play various situations that throw light on pairing models; for example: (1) role-play a traditional couple, and then for contrast a reversed-role couple, as each assembles itself for dinner; (2) role-play a traditional and then a living-together couple, as each deals with a serious interpersonal crisis; (3) role-play a traditional couple in which one spouse (but not the other) wishes to change the pair's pattern to a shared-roles model; (4) role-play the confrontation between a set of unsympathetic parents and their adult daughter or son who has elected a living-together or singlehood model, or (5) role-play a dual-career couple as they decide how they will divide domestic responsibilities (child care, house cleaning, laundry, shopping, cooking, household accounts, and yard work). Afterward, have everyone comment on and draw insights from the role-playing activities.

To Read Further

Clark, D. (1987). *The new loving someone gay.* Berkley, CA: Celestial Arts.

Goldberg, H. (1983). *The new male-female relationship.* New York: William Morrow. (New American Library paperback 1984)

Harayda, J. (1986). *The joy of being single.* New York: Doubleday.

Kimball, G. (1983). *The fifty-fifty marriage.* Boston: Beacon Press. (paperback)

Kinder, M., & Cowan, C. (1990). *Husbands and wives: Exploding marital myths, deepening love and desire.* New York: Signet. (paperback)

Kirkendall, L. A., & Gravatt, A. E. (1984). *Marriage and the family in the year 2020.* Buffalo, NY: Prometheus Books.

Lazarus, A. A. (1985). *Marital myths: Two dozen mistaken beliefs that can ruin a marriage (or make a bad one worse).* San Luis Obispo, CA: Impact.

Medved, D. (1989). *The case against divorce.* New York: Ivy Books. (paperback)

Scarf, M. (1987). *Intimate partners: Patterns in love and marriage.* New York: Random House. (Ballantine paperback 1988)

Smith, A. D., & Reid, W. J. (1985). *Role-sharing marriage.* New York: Columbia University Press.

I'm a Housewife— And I Have the Right to Be Proud

Patricia Kroken

I delight in being a woman, and even more, I delight in being a married woman, for I feel that marriage is the foundation on which my identity rests. I cannot discuss myself without discussing my husband and our relationship. Rather than feeling stifled, as married women frequently say they do, I am convinced that my marriage has provided me with a framework on which to build a fulfilling life, a framework that has allowed me to expand my consciousness and to enjoy being the person that I am.

My husband and I met as high-school students and were "in like" long before either of us admitted to being in love. In spite of parental protests because of our tender age, we found a relationship that endured the trauma of adolescence and the death of both his parents and that culminated in our marriage.

Bruce was a junior in college and I a sophomore. We had dissimilar fields of study, converging and diverging opinions on nearly everything, little money and a strength in our union that made us feel that as long as we were together, we could weather anything. Ours was a partnership, and we did not discuss our roles as man and woman, husband and wife, for they evolved naturally according to our personalities and the demands made upon us.

Bruce earned the money with his part-time job and I governed its dispensation. I typed his term papers and he proofread mine. We did not see our "weaknesses" as inherent in our respective sex but rather in our individual personalities. Instead of trying to change each other to fit recognized roles, we adapted to each other's flaws and capitalized on our strengths.

When Bruce was graduated we moved quite a distance from the college we'd both been attending so that he could take his first teaching job. I resigned myself to the fact that I would get my degree "someday" when we were living closer to a college. "Someday" wasn't good enough for Bruce. He encouraged me to work as a student teacher at a nearby secondary school, thus fulfilling one of the degree requirements for my major. Later on he endured our five-day separations when I commuted to classes, living at a college during the week and driving home on weekends.

In the midst of my harried education I suffered a ruptured ectopic pregnancy and nearly lost my life. Frantically I threw myself into schoolwork as therapy. When I felt myself totter under the weight of our despair Bruce comforted me; when I felt sorry for myself he chided me; and when I finally was graduated with honors *we* rejoiced—together.

After graduation I turned eagerly to a new job—that of housewife. And my world expanded before me as I grabbed at opportunities my schooling had forced me to neglect for years. I joined a service club and a children's-theater board, took part in two plays, instructed a group of majorettes, began sewing most of our clothing, joined the city band and read insatiably. We were cautiously joyful when I once again became pregnant and wildly joyful when our daughter Christina was born.

Through all this I watched the Women's Liberation Movement flower. I listened to its proponents, read their articles in magazines, agreed and disagreed with them in turn. I examined my life in terms of who I was as a person, ticking off the limitations that had been imposed on me by a child, by a husband and by the rambling old home we had bought. My teaching certificate weighed on my conscience like an albatross around my neck. Why was I sitting at home when I could enjoy the rewards—not to mention the extra income—of the profession I was trained for? Why? Because I had *chosen* to live this way. I could (and can) agree with the movement in theory, but in reality being a wife and mother has given me as full a life as I could wish for.

Granted, housework implies seemingly endless janitorial duties—babies bring mounds of diapers and husbands must be fed and kept in clean shirts—but a woman's life need not end there. A housewife has time on her hands, either the long, empty hours of the complainer or the fleeting, flying minutes of the eternally curious innovator. Time can be either a wife's bane or her boon, and I use mine resourcefully, cramming each minute with the business of living, growing and learning.

I feel that feminists make a grave and perhaps fatal error when they demean the housewife and mother, depicting her life as filled with empty hours and enslavement to squalling brats. Perhaps it is because I view my home as a sanctuary rather than a prison. Yes, I work hard for "room and board," but no one can convince me that my job is inferior to anyone else's because I am not monetarily paid. I see my husband come home exhausted by the pressures of his job; I know he lacks the time to pursue many activities he would like. No, I don't want his so-called "rights."

After six years of marriage Bruce and I still are partners, and we still need each of our special talents. It's my turn to bolster him—my turn to encourage, to push and to comfort. We have given, we have endured, we have loved—we love. I am a woman, and I wouldn't have it any other way!

To Apply This Reading to Yourself

1. In your own case, could marriage serve as the foundation or basis of your identity? Why or why not?
2. What effect, if any, has the feminist movement had on your own sex-role ideas, attitudes, and behavior? Why?
3. Do you feel that the roles of wife and mother, as they are traditionally defined, would be demeaning for you (if you are female) or for your spouse (if you are male)? Why or why not?
4. Would you feel that you had more rights, privileges, and prestige as a breadwinner than as a homemaker? Why or why not?
5. Kroken writes, "I am a woman, and I wouldn't have it any other way!" Are you as enthusiastic about your gender and sex role? Why or why not?
6. Would you find a traditional marriage satisfying and fulfilling for yourself? Why or why not?
7. Describe a traditional marriage with which you are familiar, and note its advantages and disadvantages for the partners.

Two-Career Couples: How They Do It

Karen Barrett

The two-career marriage phenomenon—because of its potential for radically altering the family power structure, the division of household labor, and the way we care for our children—is *the* major social change of this century. Sociologists are ranking it with such critical tides in human history as the domestication of animals and the Industrial Revolution.

Philip Slater, in his 1970 book, *The Pursuit of Loneliness* (Beacon Press), says the word "career" connotes "a demanding, rigorous, pre-ordained life pattern, to whose goals everything else is ruthlessly subordinated.... When a man asks a woman if she wants a career ... he is saying, 'are you willing to suppress half of your being as I am, neglect your family as I do, exploit personal relationships as I do?'"

But within today's two-career couple there is usually a mutually professed commitment to home and family life. Nevertheless, the individuals in a two-career couple each make major investments of time, energy, and ego in their work, and each faces daily challenges, responsibilities, and headaches that are not easily left behind at the end of the workday. Consequently, logistical crises, identity problems, and conflicts with the expectations of parents, of employers, and even of friends, go with the territory. Meanwhile, the societal changes that would genuinely support the two-career family—and make running the home and caring for children while juggling two engrossing jobs less of a marvelous feat—have barely begun.

What has kept the system running is the fact that most wives and mothers don't have careers—not in the sense that husbands and fathers do. Institutions can get by with pretending nothing much has changed, because the majority of married women who have jobs also retain the primary responsibility for household maintenance and child care.

Expectations are of course different from those of an earlier era when married women who worked outside the home made every effort to conform to conventional sex roles within it. But recent surveys show that couples today by and large have modified their attitudes more than their behavior. In a national poll conducted by a cigarette company—the Merit Report—more than half the respondents said that husband and wife should take equal responsibility for preparing meals, but the wife did the cooking in three couples out of four.

WHAT THE EXPERTS SEE

Sociologists Pepper Schwartz and Philip Blumstein describe the problem this way in their recent book, *American Couples* (Morrow): "It is frequently difficult to separate what couples *think* is the nature of their work arrangement from what actually happens in their day-to-day lives.... Husbands of women who work help out more than husbands of homemakers, but their contribution is not impressive." Thousands of interviews brought Schwartz and Blumstein to the sorry conclusion that even when a husband was unemployed, he did much less housework than a wife who worked full-time. And in households where husband and wife both felt strongly that housework should be shared equally, "when they broke it down to time actually spent and chores actually done, the idea of shared responsibility turned out to be a myth." Not only that, the more housework done by the man, the more the couple fought.

American Couples does not distinguish between dual-career and dual-earner couples. (In the latter, the female partner has a job that is clearly subordinated in her own mind to her husband's and to family priorities, even though her wages may be necessary to make ends meet.) However, research done by Lucia Gilbert, a professor of educational psychology at the University of Texas, focused specifically on husbands of women with careers. She found that these men fell into one of three categories with equal frequency: one third were "traditional" husbands, who insisted on traditional mate immunity from home and family chores; another third were "participant fathers," who were proud to take an active role in parenting, but shied away from mundane household tasks; the rest were "real role-sharing husbands."

The real role-sharers, says Gilbert, recognize that a commitment to become equal partners with their wives in home and family responsibilities and to give equal priority to their wives' careers could mean slowing down their own career development. Such men are also more likely than the other husbands to be aware of the barriers to women's career advancement. The role of father is more integral to the real role-sharer's self-concept than to that of the "armchair liberal" participant daddy. The latter was characterized by one dual-career wife as "the guy who brags to me about 'babysitting' his kids as proof of his new-age egalitarian lifestyle; meanwhile the one who is really pulling his weight doesn't talk so loud."

In their book, *The Two-Career Couple* (Addison-Wesley), Francine and Douglas Hall call couples in which one partner is responsible for maintaining home and family while the other pursues a career, "accommodators"; "allies" are couples who have agreed to simplify their lives by arriving at mutually acceptable standards that are easy to meet—living on pizza, perhaps; "adversaries" both have conventional standards for career, home, and relationship and each presses for the other to provide the support structure; "acrobats" are both trying frantically to have and do it all. Needless to say, the first two categories have the least conflict.

REAL-LIFE LOGISTICS

Janet Hunt, a sociology professor at the University of Maryland, worries about her undergraduate students who have "bought the idea that a glamorous dual-career marriage is easy. They say, 'Of course we'll put our children in daycare' as though day care centers existed in the volume that would be necessary to accommodate them all. . . . There was a time when all these wonderful, bright women with limited career options were available to care for your children, but that day has passed."

Very often it's special circumstances that make it possible for couples to continue in the pursuit of two careers without fear of sacrificing

their children's welfare. A couple in Virginia lucked out when his parents retired and moved nearby and they were able, "by offering her more money than she made at her old job at the bank," to induce his mother to take care of their daughter. In Minneapolis, the fact that a husband's career in real estate management could be plied from a home office made it possible for him to take care of their son after school every day while his accountant wife worked standard office hours plus overtime.

Janet Hunt and her husband, Larry (also a sociologist at the University of Maryland), identify themselves as a couple who make it a priority "to being available to our kids on their terms." This has meant sacrificing their social life. Furthermore, Larry's commitment to genuine symmetry in household and family responsibilities has made him unfathomable to many of his male peers. "Men don't always get the credit that is due them when they deliver on egalitarian promises," Janet Hunt says. "They may have gained from being married to strong women and having close relationships with their children, but they have also had to give up some pretty attractive privileges."

To ease the pressures inherent in parenting as a two-career couple, many couples are examining their assumptions about children and their care, and adjusting their expectations concerning what is necessary, what is possible, and who the caregivers will be.

Lucia Gilbert observes that more people of means are receptive to recruiting some qualified person(s) to help rear their children, "not just a baby-sitter to keep them out of harm's way, but someone to share in the parenting function." Take the New York City couple, both lawyers, who opted for full-time child care from the time their son was four months old. Says she, "No one handles every situation the way you would, and that's frustrating and guilt-provoking. 'If you want something done right, do it yourself' is what you keep thinking. But a lot of that is an ego trip; maybe it's better to admit that even if you were there, you wouldn't always have the best answer. Raising a child is not the kind of thing where there's only one right way to go about it. Our mothers may have been perfectionists because it was their one big chance to shine; and still we didn't all turn out perfect."

Likewise, if a couple have high environmental standards for the home—waxed floors, ironed pillowcases, home-cooked meals on china so shiny they can see their reflections in it—they had better be earning enough to pay for a housekeeper. Sounds obvious, yet the research identifies a major source of conflict in couples' desire to have their cake and eat it too—to have the economic returns and personal satisfaction of two careers, without trading off any of the amenities that Mom used to supply.

In the interest of streamlining housekeeping tasks, two-career couples may make choices that appear eccentric. One couple agreed to use paper plates, "because neither of us could see demanding that the other wash the dishes when we each hated it so much." Why not? Life is short. Another couple "held down the number of balls being juggled" when they decided not to have children. "Maybe I'm a perfectionist or maybe I have less energy than average, but what I would have to offer after a full day at work could not be called 'quality time,'" she says. The same couple also rarely complicate their lives with a lot of separate activities. Their social life tends to revolve around a few close mutual friends and "more often than not we stay home, trading dime novels back and forth across the pillow."

Pepper Schwartz warns that not only do couples have to be realistic about what it means when no one person is in charge of the home full-time, but they must also pay attention to a crucial area of responsibility, which they may not readily identify: an "emotional caretaker" function that, according to Schwartz and her research partner, someone has to assume in order to keep the relationship on track. "It's not like housework, where it becomes obvious quickly—because there's no dinner on the table, for example—that the other person needs to step in and take up the slack," says Schwartz. Nor is it as easily remedied by delegating the task to a third party: "You can't just hire a therapist, to take over the emotional nurturing the way you can hire a housekeeper. This is a function that has to be integrated into the couple's daily life. Someone—not necessarily the woman and not necessarily all the time—must put the relationship first a lot of the time."

Traditionally, the wife was the relationship-guardian. Columnist Ellen Goodman, after seeing the film "On Golden Pond," aptly described Katharine Hepburn's character as the "family switchboard"; Henry Fonda could get away with being a self-absorbed old curmudgeon so long as his sensitive, diplomatic mate was there to cajole him into a good humor and interpret him to other family members as a lovable character.

These days, it's not only men who feel the need for an accommodating, supportive person to create for them a comfortable, nurturing environment, a place to relax after a long, hard day. Career women often long for the same support. Two career-oriented highachievers, both coming home craving a "wife," or at least the emotional sustenance she traditionally provided, are headed for frustrating encounters. Sex sometimes gets to be a problem too. There are the obvious things that get in the way—exhaustion, or never being home and awake at the same time—but sexual problems, according to some researchers, most frequently arise from changes in the distribution of power as the woman gains confidence and becomes more likely than before to assert her sexual needs. The good news is that therapists have found that when dual-career couples sought treatment for sexual problems, their level of candor seemed to be higher than that of other couples in that situation.

WHEN PROFESSIONAL CHANGES BRING PERSONAL CONFLICT

Several couples who were interviewed say it's critical that dual-career spouses understand each other's career goals and working conditions. A Houston cardiologist, married to an architect who specializes in health/care facilities, advises: "You have to have a sense of the demands and content of the other's work. I knew that she wasn't someone who just thought it sounded romantic to marry a doctor—her father is a doctor, so she knew exactly what it would mean. Meanwhile, I tried to understand what she would be up against, as far as meeting deadlines and having to travel on consulting jobs."

In the same vein, a Minneapolis real estate manager, whose wife had no career aspirations when they married seven years ago, talks about the difficulties he's had accepting her newfound enthusiasm for accounting: "I have trouble imagining how she could be so into a job that has so many restrictions. I keep thinking how could she prefer punching a clock and sitting all day at a desk to being able to spend more time with our son, or on staying up late with me?"

The plaint of the husband whose wife changed the rules after the marriage was well established is a familiar one. A particularly striking example of a couple adjusting to two-career status in midstream is found in Houston, where a college theater professor and director learned to cope with a wife who decided after 15 years of conventional marriage that she had a calling for the priesthood. "She told me from the outset that she didn't want to be 'just a housewife,'" he recalls. "I have her letters from before we were married to prove it; but I guess I thought she'd get over it." Says she, "As long as I didn't know what it was I wanted to do instead, it wasn't much of an issue."

"When she first came to me twelve years ago and said, 'I really want to become an Episcopal priest,'" he says, "I replied, 'that's wonderful, dear,' in the most patronizing tone. I figured she'd get over that too." Five years of stormy transition followed: she began traveling, campaigning for women's ordination; he was teaching, directing, parenting, counseling students, entertaining—on his own. She applied to a seminary in Massachusetts; when she was accepted, he took a sabbatical and they moved up there with their children, then ages eight and 10. When she completed her studies, they returned to Houston, where she became a deacon and finally a priest with a parish of her own.

The professor continued to find it hard to adjust to his wife's new directions. "As each new demand was made of me, I would say 'no, I don't mind,'" he recalls, "but I could feel my face tightening. I remember lying in bed unable to sleep because my heart was pounding so hard. I guess it was a combination of conceptual adjustment and sheer physical overload. I also remember screaming at her: 'I'm a decent man. I make a decent living. We have a lovely home, wonderful kids. Why can't you be satisfied?'"

Characterizing the first 15 years as "uncomfortable—I stayed really busy with work to avoid dealing with her dissatisfaction"—and the next five as "trying beyond belief," he says the last seven years have been "fabulous—our marriage is more solid than it ever was." A major reason for their survival, he concedes, was her always taking time for the emotional caretaking function. "My instinct for nurturing, for knowing when one of my children needed attention, was always more highly developed than my instinct that it was time to vacuum the rug," she laughs.

Some couples admit to a sense of relief at having been spared the major career sacrifices that are often necessary. For example, an academic couple who managed to land tenure at the same university stress how rare this is. Since in general, upward mobility in their field requires geographic mobility, couples who seek to maximize two professorial careers risk splitting up.

Understanding each other's career goals may not always be enough. It can get very complicated when career goals change for both of you, or if your individual career strategies and work values are in opposition. One couple, an aspiring singer–songwriter whose husband is an unsung filmmaker and video producer, began their marriage on a romantic and egalitarian footing. When they met, she lived just outside Philadelphia and he lived in Los Angeles. They fell in love and they easily negotiated how they would share the bills and the housework, but where would they live? She agreed to move out to Los Angeles with him if he would support her until she found work.

The wife soon decided that the most practical course would be to take some more lessons and get a "regular pay-the-rent job." Working first as a waitress in a jazz club and then as a receptionist at a talent agency, she began slowly to make contacts in the music business. Then her husband thought it was time to pursue his dream of starting an independent film production company, and abandon the "piddling" jobs— videotaping conventions, working as a projectionist—he had been doing to earn money. Without that income and with a run of bad luck, they were brought to a point last winter when they couldn't pay their rent.

He explains: "To me, it's not such a big deal to be broke. You have to take risks to succeed in this society; it's how people make money. It's really hard to imagine how your spouse could fail to share your enthusiasm about a creative opportunity." She was furious. "I'd had one too many snide comments about my 'dumb' office job. He seemed to think he was taking his art more seriously than I took mine; meanwhile, I was the chump, taking the marriage seriously, playing it safe, saying 'maybe next year for my demo tape' while he blew our savings." They separated and are seeing a counselor. Now, she says, "I realize it's not enough to appreciate each other's talents and goals; you have to make sure you have similar philosophies on how to reach those goals."

"Whenever one of us faces a career turning point, there's a potential for crisis in the relationship," observes one woman, an advertising executive who is a relative newcomer to the fast track. "We learned it's terribly hard if you're both undergoing transitions at the same time."

People whose career commitments are in conflict are likely to encounter a vicious cycle. "When my marriage began to get shaky, that's when I felt I could least afford to be slacking off at work," recalls a women whose two-career marriage ended in divorce after two years. "You think, 'if he walks, this job is all I've got' and you aren't up to staying up all night having it out when you know you've got to be bright and alert at your desk the next morning. You put off dealing with him because you don't want to fall apart at work—even though you sense you might be forfeiting your last chance to patch it up—because you know what it takes to keep the job and you don't know how to keep him. Meanwhile, he's got an edge; he's not afraid that emotional turmoil could cost him his job."

DUAL CAREER BLISS

Reflecting the social values of the times, the "scientific" evidence published in the 1950s and 1960s indicated that two-career marriages were miserable. However, the late 1960s saw a turnabout—all the literature became suddenly upbeat, perhaps naïvely so, in support of the newly sanctioned lifestyle.

Now there is general agreement, among those who study the state of the art of marriage, that the potential rewards of two-career coupleship are great. For starters, it offers a higher standard of living. The relationship is strengthened when each partner is economically viable and feels that she or he is achieving a lot at work as well as at home.

Pepper Schwartz (who has been married for two years to an architect and has a small child)

maintains: "There's nothing like a dual-career couple who are functioning well. Each person has a sense of control over her or his own life. No one is feeling helpless, or trapped by the other one's dependency. Each has the other to respect, care for, and feel proud of."

Women who take satisfaction in their work outside the home generally report a higher degree of satisfaction in their marriages than women who do not. And although you might have been tempted to suspect that men prefer the "biscuits in the oven, buns in the bed" model of wife—whatever the hip, egalitarian protest to the contrary—Schwartz and her colleague Blumstein concluded that men respect employed wives more.

Of course, a man may respect the hell out of his career-oriented wife and still not want to keep on living with her. The strains implicit in the daily life of a two-career marriage make it a big-payoff, big-risk game. Schwartz calls attention to the high divorce rate among high-earning women and successful men. It is tempting to believe that this is just because economic dependency is no longer keeping women in unhappy marriages, but her findings show that it is more often the husbands who walk out: "A lot of men end up realizing that they are not so liberated after all about not having a wife to provide traditional female comforts," she says, sighing.

WHERE WE ARE HEADED

The proportion of young adults who expect to have no children is growing, and studies have linked that expectation to the desire to achieve career goals. Employers may make concessions, but as long as there is another category of workers who do not seek such benefits, the "gains" made by parents will only serve to differentiate them from serious careerists, warn Janet and Larry Hunt in a joint article: "What used to be a tracking system that separated elite men from the rest of the work force will become one that assigns different institutional destinies to careerists and parents."

What is becoming incompatible with family life, the Hunts insist, are *careers* as they have been traditionally understood. In opposition to their grim vision of countless pairs of narrow, hard-driving, obsessive careerists, Francine and

Douglas Hall point to the emergence of the "Protean career," in which success is equated as much with emotional satisfaction and an improved overall quality of life as with increased money and prestige. All the indications are that marriages stand a better chance when it is feasible for either or both partners to subscribe to that approach.

Nor does Lucia Gilbert believe that nonparent careerists are going to be a major element of society in the decades to come: "People like that—people with very high power needs and very low relationship needs—are a minority. And what's going to happen to them? They'll die of heart attacks at an early age." However, Gilbert does agree with the Hunts that "we are experiencing a child-care crisis." She points to the fact that the United States is the only Western country that doesn't have a child-care policy.

In fact, this country is behind most of the developed world and much of the Third World when it comes to having an articulated family policy. What it has instead is a set of Madison Avenue myths—and the one where Mom stays home and discusses fabric softeners with her pals is gradually being replaced by the myth of the smoothly running two-career family.

But two-career marriage is a lot of work, and the rewards lie mostly in areas that don't show up in the images of popular culture. In any case, the emphasis has been too much on individual solutions, when real institutional change is needed. Feminine accommodation guilt of the 1950s said women needed to try harder to make marriage work, and there's a contemporary version of this burdensome assumption with respect to dual-career marriage—we keep seeing variations of the phrase, "balancing career and family," applied always to women, not to men. The truth is that men and women must cooperate—not only on the personal front but also in the search for solutions on a larger scale.

To Apply This Reading to Yourself

1. *Would you find a shared-roles marriage satisfying and fulfilling for yourself? Why or why not?*
2. *Describe a two-career marriage that you are familiar with. To what extent is it a shared-roles marriage? What are its advantages and disadvantages for the partners? How satisfied or dissatisfied is each partner?*
3. *List all the two-career marriages you are familiar with, indicating whether the men are traditional husbands, participant fathers, or real role-sharers. Which marriage appears most successful? Which seems least successful? Why?*
4. *List all the two-career marriages you are familiar with, indicating whether the partners are accommodators, allies, adversaries, or acrobats. Which marriage appears most successful? Which seems least successful? Why?*

Cohabitation, Singlehood, and Gay Relationships[1]

Sol Gordon and Craig W. Snyder

In American society, since marriage is the norm for approximately 90 percent of the population, anything other than marriage might be considered an *alternative*. Both within and outside marriage, however, many options exist that are nontraditional. The major alternatives covered in this reading are cohabitation, singlehood, and gay relationships.

COHABITATION

Cohabitation (living together) was first heralded in the 1960s as the choice for people who didn't need marriage—"just a piece of paper"—to legitimize their love for another person. Today, it is fairly common on college campuses for lovers to share an apartment, or a room in a house that is shared with other students. The depth of feeling in the relationship may range from convenience to sexual involvement, to what is perceived as an enduring commitment. Since it first began to make headlines some twenty-five years ago, cohabitation rates have grown more rapidly than almost all other forms of relationship patterns.

The questions that people have before entering into cohabitation usually have to do with: Will this arrangement lead to marriage? Will we be monogamous, or will we be free to see other people? Should I tell my parents and what will they say or do when they find out? If the relationship ends, will the hurt I feel be worth the experience? If I decide a month after we move in

together that it's all a mistake, how will I get out of it?

First, people need to be clear with each other concerning whether living together symbolizes a trial period before marriage, a meaningful way to be loving and intimate, or an economic reprieve from hard times. A college junior from Massachusetts related how she and her lover talked the whole thing over beforehand and agreed that it wouldn't necessarily lead to marriage. He was graduating a year earlier than she was anyway, and wanted to feel free to pursue his career in other cities without worrying about abandoning her. "Underneath it all, I was hoping that he'd want to marry me and would hang around for a year waiting for me to finish school. I never told him that and I was enraged when he left in June to work in another state."

There exist both public and hidden agendas, and it is mainly the hidden variety that leads to troubles. The male above could not be held responsible for her unspoken hopes; he was, on the contrary, upset over her concealing these feelings from him. He commented later that "It made me feel like the bad guy when rationally I knew I had acted in good faith."

When the question comes to monogamy versus a more open relationship, again there is often both a public and a private agenda. The overwhelming majority of couples agrees together that they will not become sexually involved—even for an evening—with anyone else. The facts of people's behavior, however, reveal that during "monogamous" marriages, for instance, as many as half of all husbands and wives experience extramarital sex at some time. When cohabiting, the sex outside the relationship is usually kept secret; when it becomes known, it often ends the relationship in a short time.

For young adults especially, the living together may be with a first love. The pain of jealousy and learning of one's lover's infidelity can be agonizing. Our intention here is not to pass judgment, but instead to raise the issues that people need to consider before becoming involved outside a relationship. These include: Am I having sex with another person because my lover does not satisfy me? Because I need variety? Because I'm too young/impulsive to commit

1. This reading has been condensed from *Personal Issues in Human Sexuality* (2nd ed.) by Sol Gordon and Craig W. Snyder. This book is strongly recommended for those who would like to more fully pursue these or other aspects of human sexuality.

myself to only one person? Because I don't believe in monogamy for myself (though I agreed to it to keep this relationship alive)?

Moving in together represents a risk, and there's no way to know beforehand how it will all turn out. Common sense dictates that it's best if couples explore their feelings extensively together before making any commitments. The real dilemma emerges for those who find themselves involved in a situation that feels disastrous and from which they wish to escape. Sometimes, from fear of hurting the other's feelings, or from fear of loneliness and never again finding someone to love, people prolong unsatisfying relationships. In a sense, the energy in their relationship is invested in moving away from something (loneliness) rather than toward something (love, togetherness).

When these ambivalent feelings (concerning whether or not to leave a relationship) fester, they often produce hostility for the other person, or guilt and/or anger directed against the self. These slowly destroy the fabric of living-together relationships and interfere with day-to-day living (quarrels, sharp words, silences may prevail). In this way, the authentic meaning of the conflicts may not surface, and instead people concern themselves only with the symptoms of a bad relationship (that is, fighting over spilt milk). It's best, although difficult, to open things up and confront what's happening between you.

Living together, of course, may be a wonderful experience. It has the potential to bring partners closer together and allow them to explore the give and take between themselves. There can be opportunities to explore the many feelings that one has concerning loving relationships. Following are a few quotes from people who felt positive about their cohabiting:

We'd been living in separate apartments and it got to the point that mine was always empty— we spent all of our time at Marsha's place. Once we moved in together, it felt so much more relaxing, like some of the questions concerning how we felt about each other weren't so unresolved. Living together just felt like the right thing to do—I've never questioned that.

Mitch and I spent the first three months of our living together trying to adjust to each other's styles of living. At first I felt angry with him, because once we were living together it seemed like he was suddenly doing things he never did before—like stay up half the night, come home from classes in a lousy mood and stay that way all evening. Gradually we started to see that we'd been hiding those things from each other, trying to present only a positive image to each other. Once that painted-on face wore away, our love for each other seemed less contrived, more involved with the real guts of our lives.

Living with Adrienne was good from the start. We had a wonderful sexual attraction for each other and a good life outside of bed, too. Even though we eventually split up and went our separate ways, there wasn't that much animosity— I still look back on that time as one of the best.

Never before in my life had anything felt as good as being loved by, and loving, Frank. Ever since I had entered my teenage years I had been wanting to have someone special to be with and living with him felt like I wasn't so alone anymore. Once we started living together, it was obvious that we wanted it to last, and we were married after about a year. And we're still together.

Nevertheless, for many students, anxiety over the response of parents consumes a great deal of energy, and sometimes helps determine the fate of the relationship itself. Our clinical observations are that the male's parents are more likely to be told than are the female's; apparently the double standard, in which women are criticized more for premarital sexual experiences, influences couples in their decision of whom to tell.

When one or both sets of parents have not been told of the living arrangements, an interesting acrobatic act may ensue. One partner, for example, may never be allowed to answer the phone, or may have to move his or her clothes into the attic and take a nameplate off the mailbox when parents visit. An intricate web of deception and half-truths can grow. The alternative, as experienced by many students, is that parents react very negatively to the news, and family relationships suffer. Parents have been known to sever financial aid, disinherit, and otherwise punish their children in an attempt to force the cohabitation to end. Even after graduation, and among older people, cohabitation may elicit similar negative responses from families.

Despite the most strenuous efforts to prevent it, parents inevitably find out sooner or later (couples who are planning on marriage may hope that this occurs after the wedding). What happens next will probably be easier to bear if you have already established a reasonably good relationship with your parents, and if your parents like and approve your choice of a partner. Even when parents do not object morally to cohabitation, they usually do react angrily to having been deceived. The nature and duration of parents' responses can be roughly predicted from their behavior in stressful or crisis situations that arose in the past. If they have tended to respond with interested, caring support, or angry withdrawal, they may be expected to react similarly to the news of your cohabitation.

One recent graduate of a technical school in the Midwest related to us how she handled her parents' reaction: "I decided just to let them be angry for a while. I knew that I would be if my child had concealed that kind of thing from me. My acceptance of their anger seemed to help them cool off. I've seen friends of mine become defensive with their parents and attack them for not approving, and the situation just lasted that much longer with more bitterness on both sides. I told them I understood that they were upset and told them why I did it; what my plans were. They never really liked the whole idea, but after a while at least we could see each other without there being a lot of tension."

Those who view living together as a possible prelude to marriage usually are curious about the effect this will have on their lives together once married. The majority of formal studies that have been conducted in this area have reported few, if any, differences in the marriages of those who cohabited versus those who did not. This means that in the areas of marital satisfaction, resolution of conflict, egalitarianism, emotional closeness, self-disclosure, and degree of commitment, there have been no differences found between those who cohabit and those who do not (among those who ultimately marry).

A number of people live together for long periods of time without ever marrying; in fact, they express the desire not to. Some of these cases have made headlines. In one instance, the actor Lee Marvin was sued by his ex-lover with whom he had lived for many years, on the grounds that he had promised to take care of her financial needs. This suit gave rise to the concept of *palimony*; it did not, however, spawn a glut of similar cases as was predicted it would. Among the elderly, there is also a significant trend toward living together since marrying at this late stage of life for many would entail the loss of pensions or social security benefits.

Cohabitation, for some couples, undoubtedly helps them learn to live with each other. It also seems true, however, that the same lessons are learned in the first year or two of marriage among those who do not live together beforehand. The key element seems to be the quality of the relationship itself. In other words, a good relationship has a good chance of being successful regardless of whether or not one cohabits, and a bitter, unhappy relationship will probably fail no matter what living arrangements are made (you can't save a relationship by deciding to cohabit any more than you can save a marriage by deciding to have children).

SINGLEHOOD

The concern in this section is with those who choose to remain single, or who are considering this decision, and those who remain involuntarily single for prolonged periods. Remaining single by choice is legitimate when the individual prefers this lifestyle and wishes to preserve his or her autonomy and independence. A fair number of people stay single because it permits them to devote their energies fully to an important cause. Single people sometimes are better able to give priority to their work, or to a vital mission that represents their life's purpose. This is true of people who devote themselves to a variety of religious orders.

It is becoming clear that many single people actively choose not to marry or even to cohabit because it fits the positive image they have of themselves and their preferred lifestyle. As more people delay marriage in favor of higher education or to advance their careers, they discover that the sense of personal freedom is satisfying. There also is less of a societal sanction against singlehood, though this may be less true for people, say, over 45.

Remaining single in no way means that people necessarily forego loving, intimate relationships entirely. Many singles enjoy relationships that last for years with the same person(s), though they never marry or live together (a well-known example of this is Katharine Hepburn and Spencer Tracy). It is just as true, though, that significant numbers of people choose to remain single and in some cases, celibate, without conducting intimate relationships.

Perhaps the central questions that people need to answer for themselves are: Am I leaning toward the single life because I don't want to cope with the hassle, pain, and trauma I fear sexual involvement or marriage will bring? Or, is singlehood my preference because it best meets my needs for autonomy, dedication to my work, or adherence to my moral values? If remaining single is an expression of a fear of sexuality and intimacy, then it may be a wise decision to remain unmarried, at least until the problems are substantially resolved. For some people, this may mean that personal problems keep them apart from a loving relationship for most of their lives. There are also instances, though, where this decision, based on fear and anxiety, provides an immediate solution but is ultimately disappointing. The individuals thus may not create opportunities to work through their apprehensions and reach a level of functioning that would be more satisfying in the long run. Marriage is definitely not for everybody. On the other hand, some people deprive themselves of love and intimacy because of problems that could be alleviated.

The situation is entirely different for those who would like to marry, but who, for various reasons, are not able to obtain an acceptable partner. Society traditionally has not been kind to such people. They have been saddled with derogatory labels such as spinster and old maid; men, while enjoying the relatively innocuous label of bachelor, nevertheless may be suspected of being "latent homosexuals" if they remain single much beyond the age of 40. Although the numbers of single people have been steadily increasing, an undesirable stigma is still attached to the never-married.

A study conducted by Neil G. Bennett, a Yale sociologist, and David E. Bloom, a Harvard economist, estimated that women over age 30 have a 20 percent chance of marrying, and women over 40 have a 2.6 percent chance. A second study by the U.S. Census Bureau predicts the chances to be 66 percent at age 30 and 23 percent at age 40. It's an interesting commentary that these statistics differ so greatly, and are not as routinely computed for men, who are generally thought to have a greater chance of marrying if they want to.

It is disappointing to spend many years alone when one would prefer not to. Those who marry with the belief that this will end forever their struggle against loneliness, however, are often dismayed. Some of the loneliest people are involved in marriages that offer little in the way of companionship or shared interests. In addition, many studies have found that those who are single or divorced often report themselves to be happier than those who are living in miserable marriages. In this perspective, it's apparent that a variety of satisfying and unsatisfying lifestyles exist both within and outside marriage; those who remain single need not be the targets of sad condolences. And feeling sorry for oneself can become more destructive than the fact of being single (some singles, naturally, feel sorry for their married friends!).

GAY RELATIONSHIPS

Despite all the research done on the possible causes of homosexuality, society has still no idea what the causes are (any more than it knows the causes of heterosexuality). Extensive research hasn't led to more and more understanding; in fact, such research adds plausibility to the commonsense notion "the more we know, the less we know." The point is to poke fun at those researchers who "know." Once upon a time, all of us knew: If you had a weak father and a strong mother, the chances of becoming homosexual were magnified. Most professionals in the field only recently discarded this theory. Apparently, researchers started out with the erroneous assumption that all homosexuals were in a state of arrested development. Lately, professionals have taken another look at American families: It appears that many consist of strong mothers and weak (or absent) fathers. In addition, nearly all the research on homosexuals has been done on patients in therapy. This would be analogous to concluding that heterosexuals are disturbed because about 90 percent of people in therapy are heterosexual.

Until the end of the nineteenth century, it was believed that people were either homosexual *or* heterosexual. Freud, however, postulated that all of us were born polymorphous perverse with a potential for bisexuality. Alfred Kinsey fairly well destroyed the either-or notion with his monumental research of the 1940s and 1950s. His work, conducted at the Institute for Sex Research in Indiana, suggests that people's sexual behavior could be categorized as follows:

0—Exclusively heterosexual behavior
1—Largely heterosexual but incidental homosexual behavior
2—Largely heterosexual but more than incidental homosexual behavior
3—Equal amount of heterosexual and homosexual behavior
4—Largely homosexual but more than incidental heterosexual behavior
5—Largely homosexual behavior but incidental heterosexual behavior
6—Exclusively homosexual behavior

Kinsey's studies found that about 4 percent of males and 2 percent of females were probably exclusively homosexual. By the time they reach middle age, about 50 percent of males and 29 percent of females have had an overt erotic experience with a member of their own sex. In addition, 37 percent of all males and 13 percent of females had at least one homosexual experience to the point of orgasm between adolescence and old age. The Institute for Sex Research defined a homosexual as anyone who has had more than six sexual experiences with members of his or her own gender. We don't happen to agree with this definition, but it is estimated that homosexuals constitute about 10 percent of the population of the United States. Though accuracy is uncertain, members of the homosexual community believe that less than 10 percent of the homosexual population has come "out of the closet," that is, publicly identify themselves as being gay.

In our judgment, erotic desire and fantasy, as well as behavior, constitute the main elements in determining a person's sexual orientation. Our definition of a homosexual is "A person who, in his or her adult life, is sexually attracted in both fantasy and behavior mainly to members of the same sex." Some adolescents, of course, are aware of their sexual attraction to members of the same sex, and their sexual orientation as adults is gay, lesbian, or bisexual. Some, however, are confused by ambivalent impulses; thus, adolescent feelings and behavior are not necessarily predictive of adult sexual orientation (for heterosexuals or homosexuals). A person could have many homosexual fantasies and experiences and still not be a homosexual. Masters and Johnson studies reveal that even exclusive heterosexuals acknowledge having homosexual fantasies. The idea that thoughts and even some experiences make one a homosexual could have a devastating impact on a person's life.

Though the causes of homosexuality are hotly debated, leading scholars have reached a consensus that a person's sexual orientation is largely determined by the age of 4 or 5. Many individuals do not become aware of their homosexual orientation until long after this formative period, perhaps in their late teens or twenties (some postmenopausal widowed women become lesbian after their fifties and sixties, with no prior lesbian history). The political and personal ramifications of this are powerful, since it is often alleged that people "choose" to be gay or lesbian or "switch" to homosexuality as a conscious decision after a painful divorce, after being raped, and so on. Choice certainly exists over with whom to engage in sexual activity, but a basic sexual orientation is not subject to such dramatic change. Much of the animosity toward homosexuals seems to be grounded in the belief that they deliberately adopt this orientation as a means of belittling heterosexual family values and flaunt themselves outrageously.

Crusades against homosexual rights ordinances in many cities are based on the popular myths about the seduction and recruitment of children into the homosexual lifestyle. Fear of this is often cited as justification for preventing the hiring of gays or lesbians in public schools. Yet, established research in the field documents that in less than 10 percent of the instances of child molestation, teachers actively seduced children of the same sex. In any case, more than 90 percent of all child molestation in schools involves heterosexual males and is directed at females. Should heterosexual males be barred from teaching in the public schools? Even if sexual identity were not determined by age 5, it would be unrealistic to think that in a school where the teaching staff consists of 90 percent heterosexuals and 10 percent homosexuals, most of the children would flock to the latter. Can heterosexuals be so easily eliminated as role models for children?

It is all right to have your personal opinion about homosexuality. In our view, it's not acceptable to harass or to discriminate just because you are in a position to do so. What consenting adults do in private is no one's business. There is something wrong with people who intrude into other people's private affairs. People who inspire the least respect are those who use the Bible to justify their hatred or bigotry. God's message to all of us is to love thy neighbor as thyself.

This is of great concern in the homosexual community, where the loathing of heterosexuals combines with the self-hatred of many homosexuals to create great tension. Some straights can be heard saying such things as, If a faggot so much as comes near me, I'll kill him. Why does it have to be murder? Can't no thank you suffice? Among homosexuals, the psychological and physical violence from the outside can be overwhelming, and it is very likely this violence that has given rise to large homosexual communities in such cities as San Francisco and New York. Here, living among peers serves both a protective and a social purpose. Homosexuals must fight harder to survive in, say, a Midwestern industrial city than in New York City.

That is an important consideration if you are homosexual. Certainly it will be easier to resolve your own personal struggles if you don't have to cope daily with hostility from people who are threatened by your sexual orientation. It's a trade-off if you elect to remain in the closet; then there is no need to deal with people's reactions, but there is the anxiety that comes with living a life that is unauthentic to you.

Beyond the issue of public versus private identity, the crucial issue for most homosexuals concerns the nature of their intimate relationships. The script for heterosexuals is well defined: marriage. But for gay men and lesbian women, society offers no such covenant. The public image of homosexuals, especially men, is that their relationships are consummated in restrooms and bathhouses, furtively sneaked behind bushes in public parks or in backrooms of gay bars. There is little recognition of enduring love and commitment between homosexuals in the public eye. The book, *The Male Couple,* by McWhirter and Madison gives ample testimony to enduring homosexual relationships. *The Gay Report* by Karla Jay and Allen Young found that the majority of lesbian women were involved in relatively stable relationships.

Ongoing relationships between homosexual partners make many heterosexuals anxious; if they can characterize all sexual activity between gays and lesbians as impersonal and "immoral," they can rigidly maintain their rejection of homosexuals themselves. The notion that loving, caring relationships might develop threatens these attitudes.

For homosexuals themselves, committed, perhaps live-together relationships represent more of an "advertisement" to the outside world of their sexual orientation. It's fair to say that much of the alleged promiscuity among homosexuals is partly a response to the hostility of straights; impersonal sex, or short-term liaisons, are most easily kept secret. Among the gay community, many voices have been raised in protest against the self-damaging nature of multiple sexual partners. Fear of AIDS is credited in part with more conservative sexual behaviors among gays.

The AIDS scare has also served to highlight another dimension of the dilemma: Casual sex undermines many people's desires for loving, intimate relationships. In truth, the degree of promiscuity among homosexuals has been grossly exaggerated by the media. Many gays do not have one-night stands, though they struggle with the same issues of monogamy and fidelity as do the rest of the population. It has been suggested by some antihomosexual factions that AIDS is the plague sent by God to punish homosexuals for their sins. It might just as well be claimed that Legionnaires' disease was sent by God to punish Legionnaires. Hypocrisy often requires such nonsensical comparisons to reveal its true nature.

A great number of homosexuals enter into heterosexual marriages, and many have children. A young woman attending a large California university loved a young man deeply, though she was troubled by their infrequent, unsatisfying sexual relations. When she began making remarks about marriage, her lover informed her of his predominantly homosexual orientation and said that he'd like to marry her anyway. She felt tremendously conflicted over her decision and ultimately chose not to marry him. They remained close friends, however, and several years later he attended this young woman's wedding to another man.

On the other hand, when Ann Landers printed a letter in her column from a woman married to a homosexual male, she received hundreds of letters from women married to homosexual men. The women's letters said, in effect, that they had better marriages than most of their friends who were married to heterosexuals. Of course, a large number of women are very distraught when such news is revealed.

Some homosexuals, in gay, lesbian, and heterosexual relationships, have adopted children or had their own biological children. There is no evidence to suggest that children raised in these homes are influenced in any way to become homosexual themselves, or that they develop problems in greater proportion than other children. Among some segments of society, some opposition to the adoption of children by homosexuals exists. Yet, all people who support the rights of homosexuals to adopt believe that they should meet the same criteria as heterosexual parents must: Would they be good parents? Provide a good home, nutrition, loving support? Would they be stable emotionally, vocationally? There is a short supply of white infants for adoption, but tens of thousands of other children who are disabled, minorities, or over 5 years of age are candidates for adoption. Why eliminate homosexuals as prospective adoptive parents?

Most studies, as well as our personal experience, reveal that most homosexuals do form affectionate, enduring relationships. Some couples are married in homosexual churches and their vows have for them great meaning, though no legal contract is involved. This legal exclusion has many practical implications: Joint income taxes cannot be filed; partners may not be able to be beneficiaries on life insurance policies, or to rent living quarters that prohibit occupancy by unrelated tenants; partners cannot be included on each other's health insurance policies and may be prohibited from visiting an ill lover in the hospital because they are not immediate family.

Homophobia appears to be widespread in our contemporary society, and seems to afflict men in far greater numbers than women. It's best defined as a fear of homosexuals, sometimes reinforced by religious views, or a fear of being a homosexual, or a fear of being seen as effeminate, nonmasculine. Homophobia is a metaphor for a fear of being different in any of countless ways. It can stimulate sadistic behavior toward others when someone else's homosexuality awakens the same impulses that humiliate oneself. It also interferes with friendships and the expression of affection among members of the same sex. Even more profoundly, it emerges as justification for the denial of civil rights and an alienation of segments of society from each other.

Over the past decade, AIDS has cast a pale on the entire gay community, with many thousands of young people already dead and tens of thousands dying still. It's a sad and tragic story that affects all of us—friends, relatives, and human beings. On an autumn day a few years ago, several hundred thousand supporters of gay and lesbian rights marched by the White House in one of the largest demonstrations ever held in the United States. The march was led by 3000 people with AIDS. It was a poignant and courageous demonstration for the rights of all of us.

To Apply This Reading to Yourself

1. *What is your view concerning and/or your experience with cohabitation?*
2. *What advantages and disadvantages are there or would there be for you in singlehood as a lifestyle?*

3. *Gordon and Snyder write, "It's all right to have your personal opinion about homosexuality." What is your personal opinion on this subject, and how have you arrived at it?*
4. *Gordon and Snyder indicate that although it is all right to have your personal opinion about homosexuality, it's not acceptable to harass or discriminate on this basis. What is your view concerning homosexual couples marrying and adopting children? Why?*
5. *If you are an "out of the closet" gay or lesbian, relate your own views and experience to the material presented by Gordon and Snyder.*

Marital Myths

Arnold A. Lazarus

I have been practicing marriage therapy, sex therapy, and psychotherapy for over 30 years. I have treated hundreds of married couples and found a number of myths or mistaken beliefs that result in marital dissatisfaction. In my book *Marital Myths*, I present two dozen mistaken beliefs that can ruin a marriage (or make a bad one worse); here are seven very important ones.[1]

Myth 1. Romantic love makes a good marriage.

The lights dim, the curtain rises, a concealed orchestra quietly plays a languorous melody of love as a man and woman stand clasped in each other's arms watching the sun slowly sinking into an iridescent sea. They exchange vows of passionate and eternal devotion. Their commitment to each other knows no bounds. Their love will transcend such prosaic barriers as cultural dissimilarities, parental objections, money, and social position. Love and romance, the greatest of life's gifts, are theirs. They will be united and the passage of time will only intensify their romance.

This pretty picture inspires a great number of people, young and old, in our society. In search of romantic marriage, they often end up in romantic—or not so romantic—divorce. Men and women who expect to find marriage a continuation of the ecstasy of courtship are in for an enormous disappointment. Romance thrives on barriers, frustrations, separations and delays. Remove these obstacles, replace them with the intimacy and everyday contact of married life, and the ecstatic passions fade. The thrills and chills of romance are doomed in the face of day-to-day proximity. When romance dies, the couple often feels cheated. As soon as the edge wears off,

1. For those who would like to find out about all 24 myths, order a copy of *Marital Myths* from Impact Publishers, Post Office Box 1094, San Luis Obispo, California 93406.

when the carefree rapture is replaced by the uninteresting routine of daily life, these unhappy ex-lovers declare the marriage bankrupt.

People tend to grow weary of each other's company unless they have cultivated common interests and values. Romantic love is passionate and fiery. It soon burns out. Conjugal affection is a slow-burning, heart warming flame that brings security and comfort.

In the early months and years of marriage, partners inevitably discover that their spouses do not have the attributes of their dream heroes and heroines. Most are able to adjust to this reality, but extreme romantics are unable to do so. The male romantic idealist searches fruitlessly for a mate who will provide the tenderness, the security and the solicitude of the ideal mother, as well as the ecstatic sexual joys of a fantasy sweetheart. The romantic woman wants her man to be the ideal father, husband, caretaker, companion, and lover, all rolled into one. Viewed from a clinical perspective, these perceptions are decidedly abnormal. Indeed, the very language of romantic love attests to the psychotic quality of the interaction. She is "crazy" about him; he is "mad" about her. In the throes of this all-consuming passion, otherwise rational and responsible people have been known to cast aside, quite recklessly, all obligations to family, friends and society.

While we balk at the idea of abandoning our romantic idealism, much emotional pain would be spared if more people knew how to replace romantic love with conjugal affection as the basis for a truly successful marriage. The affection that enables a marriage to endure is something finer, deeper, and more rewarding than the romantic love of the story books.

Conjugal caring and affection cannot exist without mutual evidence of several key qualities:

- kindness
- consideration
- communication
- harmonious adjustment to each other's habits
- joint participation in several activities
- consensus on important values and issues

- reciprocity rather than coercion, and
- clear evidence of respect for one another

Married couples must adjust to daily routines of dressing, eating, working, sleeping and similar habits that call for synchronous schedules, and countless activities that become conditioned to each other. The aim is to build up a "common capital" of acts, habits and experiences that result in a profound acceptance of each other, without the false hopes and impossible illusions of the romantic ideal.

Myth 2. Opposites attract and complement each other.

It is not uncommon for an outgoing, vivacious, and extroverted person to attract someone who is more intellectualized, controlled, and introverted. Insecure folks may seek "strong silent types" who can offer stability and security. Steady, highly controlled persons tend to view more spontaneous potential mates as warm, vital, fun-loving creatures, who can offset the serious side of life.

Such opposites are sometimes drawn to each other's different styles of living. As friends and lovers, for a short time, they usually relate well, and do in fact find a complementary relationship which tends to neutralize some of their own inadequacies and liabilities. But if they marry, their different outward styles clash, and bring them face-to-face with the fundamental differences between them. Her flamboyance and flirtatiousness become sore points; his staid and predictable behaviors create ennui. He withdraws and she feels rejected; she frantically attempts to regain her ground, but he feels criticized and withdraws further. Soon a power struggle takes over, and both resort to tactics that undermine the true intimacy they each desire.

That unfortunate sequence is drawn from reports in the psychological literature and from my own clinical observations. Polar opposites may find one another enjoyably different and alluring for a limited time. Long-term relationships usually flourish when similarity rather than dissimilarity prevails.

The popular film and television series, *The Odd Couple*, capitalized on the clashes that arose when a slob lived with an immaculate perfectionist. In a marriage where one partner is extremely fussy and fastidious, clashes are likely if the other is disorganized and sloppy.

Incessant nagging to clean up, stop messing, and be more considerate typically interferes with more important issues and results in mutual antagonism. I have treated innumerable couples in which an obsessive-compulsive housewife drove her husband to drink, or a houseproud obsessional husband demanded such perfectionism that his wife had a "nervous breakdown."

When people with opposing views and dissimilar tastes spend much time together, certain clash-points are inevitable.

- Picture a couple wherein one member is fond of talking, of sharing feelings and ideas, while the other is a very private person who enjoys solitude and wants to be alone.
- Or think of a gregarious person who loves being with other people and seeks out the company of many different types of individuals, married to a loner who basically distrusts and dislikes the vast majority of other people.
- Or take a fiery, passionate, highly-sexed individual married to someone with a low sex drive.
- Consider a miser being attracted to a spendthrift and marrying that person.

How much marital bliss would be likely to ensue in each of the instances mentioned?

The "opposites attract and make good marriage partners" myth probably arose from the fact that *some* differences can be enriching, stimulating, even exciting and fascinating. Only a committed narcissist would desire to marry a clone! But it is a quantum leap from the fact that slight differences can prove beneficial to the notion that polar opposites make good marriage partners.

Myth 3. You should make your spouse into "a better person."

"After Mel and I are married," confides a young fiancee to her friend, "I will make him over into a new man." Perhaps Mel is quite content with his "old self" and has no wish to be remodeled. Even worse, Mel himself may have intentions of transforming his bride into a "new and better" woman.

I have seen dozens of couples locked in mortal combat, one sculpting the other in his or her own image, both living lives of mutual frustration and vexation, for *years*.

The arrogance of those people who insist that their view of the world is the one and only "right way" is exceeded only by those who are also determined to inflict this view on others!

The idea that it is a husband's or wife's right to educate and make over the other person goes hand-in-hand with the notion that "things will get better after we are married." Things that are bad before marriage tend to get *worse* afterwards. A person who is short-tempered, selfish, sexually unresponsive, and personally intrusive but who promises that things will get better "after we are married," should be viewed with extreme skepticism and suspicion by any would-be partner.

Many people have *rescue fantasies*. I call this the "Dick Diver syndrome" (from F. Scott Fitzgerald's *Tender Is The Night*, in which psychiatrist Dick Diver falls in love with his patient Nicole, marries her, and then becomes a mental and physical wreck himself).

Marriages based on the rescue fantasies of one or both partners are invariably exceedingly complex, but the end results are often predictable. To satisfy the rescuer's desire for power, approval, or control, the recipient must continue to be (or appear to be) needy. These relationships seldom stand the strain of readjustment to an equal footing. Frequently, the rescuer turns out to be far more emotionally indigent than the person being rescued. Rescuers invariably feel that they are entitled to eternal gratitude; those who have been rescued resent having to be forevermore beholden.

"We married for the wrong reasons" is a frequent expression of couples where one or the other was intent upon changing—rescuing—his or her partner.

The moral of the story? Get married on the grounds of compatibility and caring, where common interests, attitudes, and feelings may call for slight adjustment but no major changes. And leave rescuing to lifeguards, firefighters, and emergency medical teams.

Myth 4. True lovers automatically know each other's thoughts and feelings.

How often I have heard people claim: "I shouldn't have to explain it to him! If he *truly* loved me, he would know it without being told." "My partner should know what I want. If I have to tell, then it's no good."

This unfortunate myth is especially prevalent in the area of sexual intimacy. "If I have to tell my husband how I like him to behave in bed, it takes away all the pleasure. Besides, if he really loved me, was tuned into me, it would be unnecessary to tell him what to do. He would just know." "When a woman is really in love with a man, she can sense exactly how to please and satisfy him. If she has to be shown how to turn him on, or told what and what not to do, she is not for him—and vice versa."

Poppycock!

One can't experience another person's feelings, regardless of the intensity of one's devotion. People are not like insects that have a complex pattern of responses based on instinct. Human beings have to learn all complex behaviors (and gratifying sexual relations fall into this category!). We are born with some basic drives (e.g., hunger, thirst) and several reflexes (e.g., sucking, swallowing, breathing) but everything else is learned, acquired through instruction, by example, or by trial-and-error.

It certainly is rewarding to be able to predict the way a loved one will respond to a given event—and then to do or not do something, so that the end result is pleasant for both partners. "How did you know that I was wishing for a cassette player?" "It was very kind of you to realize that I would want to visit my aunt in the hospital, and to leave the office party early to bring the car home for me."

If each act of concern or consideration, each gesture of caring, every act of generosity must be explicitly coaxed out of one's partner, the quality of the alliance is undermined.

But the converse is also dangerous. "If you really loved me, or truly cared for me, you would have done *this*, or not done *that*, or thought of doing *the other thing*." Beware of this type of reasoning!

It makes sense for marriage partners to teach one another how best to get along with each other. Say what you mean, mean what you say, and don't expect your spouse to read your mind.

Myth 5. Good spouses should make their partners happy.

One of the most unfortunate errors that many people make is to accept and assume responsibility for other people's feelings. If someone has the mindset that happiness is in the hands of another, the tendency is to sit back, wait, and expect large portions of happiness to be dished up as if it were apple pie. This brings to mind the case of Lionel and Jean.

For fifteen years, Jean ran herself ragged trying to make her beloved husband Lionel happy. She catered to his every whim. But Lionel remained unhappy. He said to me: "I wish that Jean were more stimulating, more exciting, more fun to be around." I inquired how stimulating, exciting, and how much fun it was to be around *him*. "That's beside the point," he said. "The trouble with Jean is that she is too easily satisfied. She's content to sit at home, to read a book, watch TV. I crave excitement." In truth, Lionel was a malcontent. He had a talent for finding fault with virtually everything and everyone (including himself). Yet Jean blamed herself and said if she were a better wife perhaps Lionel would be a happier man. It took years to convince Jean that it is impossible to make anyone happy, least of all Lionel, and that she would be doing herself and her husband a favor if she attended to her own happiness and allowed Lionel to do the same for himself. As Jean stopped taking responsibility for Lionel's happiness, she became more relaxed, more outgoing, and less anxious. When Lionel found that Jean no longer accepted the blame for everything that went wrong in his life, he started occupying his time more productively. He took skiing, tennis, and sailing lessons, joined a book club, and enrolled in an English literature course.

Taking charge of your own gratification and fulfillment increases the likelihood that life in general, and marriage in particular, will be enjoyable and rewarding. If someone else is placing obstacles in your path, some positive and assertive action is warranted. It is not up to your spouse (or anyone else) to make you happy, nor should you permit anyone to undermine whatever fun, joviality or buoyant feelings you can inject into your life.

Myth 6. A happy marriage requires total trust.

Anything taken to excess tends to be unfortunate. If one is too tall, too thin, too clever, too fussy, the implication is that one would be better off with less of that particular attribute. Being *too trusting*, for example, can prove disastrous.

When I was in college, one of my friends was a second-year medical student named Gary, who had been married for about six months. I noticed that Gary's wife spent a lot of time in the company of a particular young man, and I commented to my friend that he was asking for trouble. "Oh come now," he protested, "Mike and I have been pals for years. I have a lot of studying to do, so why should I expect Sue to sit at home and twiddle her thumbs? I asked Mike if he would mind entertaining Sue a few nights a week. This way she gets to see movies, goes to parties, and I don't have to feel guilty while studying." I pointed out that Mike was good looking, well-off financially (he had joined his wealthy father in business), and far too available. Gary insisted that he trusted both Mike and Sue implicitly. Alas, after a very short while, Sue informed Gary that she and Mike had fallen in love, and asked for a divorce.

Shirley had been married to Don for nearly twelve years. She had no reason not to trust him or to suspect that he was involved with another woman. Suddenly, this very astute wife noticed two tell-tale signs. Don, who had hardly ever watched anything but market reports and football on TV began to develop a taste for evening soap operas. A conservative dresser, he came home with three outlandish ties. "To me, this added up to the beginnings of an actual or potential affair. The time to act was *now*, so that I could stop it before it got started, or before it developed into a heavy romance." Shirley's investigations and observations pointed to a petite young receptionist who had recently joined Don's company. Shirley considered confronting the young receptionist, but decided that it would be better to discuss the matter with Don. It appeared that the relationship was still in the stages of an early flirtation. The receptionist finally lost her job, but Shirley's absence of total trust possibly saved the marriage. She and Don then worked with me to upgrade the quality of their relationship.

My third anecdote concerns a conversation that took place in the men's locker room at a country club. As I stepped out of the sauna into the showers, three men were discussing whether or not their wives might be "unfaithful." One of the men was saying that although, in his fifteen years of marriage, he had no cause to doubt his wife's faithfulness, one could never be one hundred per cent sure of anything. Another fellow agreed and added that he was about ninety per cent certain that his wife had not, and would not, have sex with another man, except under the most unusual circumstances—such as being snowbound for three weeks with Robert Redford. The third man said that he was absolutely, one hundred per cent positive that his wife would not have extramarital sex under any circumstances. He referred to her strict religious upbringing, to the fact that she was a prude, basically uninterested in sex, extremely shy and inhibited, and besides, she was far too concerned about public opinion to take such a risk. He added that there was not one chance in ten million that his wife would be capable of "cheating." At this point in the conversation I realized that the last speaker was the husband of one of my patients. His wife was in fact involved in a sexual affair, which was why she came to me for psychotherapy.

Good marriages tend to be based not on total trust, but on a tinge of insecurity. To be absolutely certain of a spouse's fidelity, loyalty, or devotion, is to take the other person too much for granted. Too much certainty breeds a subtle lack of respect. It is more realistic to believe that one's partner is a faithful fallible human being who can succumb to temptation under certain circumstances. Unless one exercises a certain degree of vigilance, it is possible to be usurped or replaced.

The "market value" that one places on one's husband or wife is another important factor. If you regard your spouse as too homely to attract another worthwhile person, your total trust and complete security will not generate very much respect, excitement, or satisfaction. On the other hand, if you consider your spouse quite capable of attracting members of the opposite sex, and liable to respond to these overtures if neglected or mistreated inside the marriage, you will likely increase your own attentiveness and displays of caring and affection.

The "tinge of insecurity" keeps a marriage viable, meaningful, even exciting. It prevents one from taking things for granted, growing fat or sloppy, paying more attention to the job than necessary, or displaying disrespect. What is more, it fosters and maintains the level of love and affectionate caring that makes marriage worth preserving.

Myth 7. Husbands and wives should do everything together.

This "total togetherness" myth is one of the most prevalent. It suggests that the ideal matrimonial union consists of two individuals merging into one entity. To have noteworthy experiences without the other is unthinkable. When discussing this with my clients, these simple diagrams have proved useful:

Some people feel guilty when they do things, or go places without their husbands or wives. "I

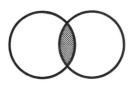

This depicts a poor marriage relationship. There is very little togetherness or common ground.

This depicts an excellent marriage. There is about 75–80 per cent togetherness but also sufficient separateness to permit individual growth and essential privacy.

This represents the romantic ideal where two people merge so completely that they become as one. In practice, were this possible, it would probably result in emotional suffocation.

don't think it's right or proper for a husband to go one way and a wife another. If they want to act like single people, why did they get married?" This statement came from 44-year-old Alf who insisted that his wife should go boating with him. Marie preferred reading a book on the beach while he was out on the boat. She said "I get seasick. I'm not stopping him from going on the boat. Is it asking too much for Alf to do what he enjoys, while I do what I enjoy? After he docks the boat, we can always have a drink on board and then go out for dinner." Alf found this unacceptable. "All the other men go out with their wives. I like doing things as a twosome."

Steve had similar ideas, but in his case, he believed in having family togetherness. Also a boating man, his picture of family solidarity was that of Janet and their two sons on board while he steered his $96,000 vessel around the bay. His wife and their younger son enjoyed swimming, surfing, or merely taking long walks on the beach. So why not go boating with the older boy, while Janet and Billy did their own thing? "That's not my idea of fun or a family outing," Steve explained.

Alf and Steve both used coercion in their marriages. It is not a good idea to bring pressure to bear on one's marriage partner. Most people strongly dislike being pushed and pressured into something they'd rather not do. The inevitable resentments that arise tend to create marital strife and tensions. Alf and Steve did not even offer acceptable trade-offs. They could have said something such as: "It's important enough to me that you do this, that I promise to get tickets for three Broadway plays over the next two months, *and* I will take you out to four fancy restaurants between Labor Day and Christmas."

Cocktail parties had become a bone of contention with a couple I was seeing for marriage therapy. Fred hated them; Kay loved them. Fred declared: "I'd rather stay home, watch television, or read a book. I hate making small talk." Kay said: "I find them a wonderful opportunity to dress up, meet new people, run into old friends, and keep up with the local gossip." She usually managed to cajole her husband into going with her, but at times they almost came to blows. He often tried to sabotage matters by picking a fight just before it was time to get dressed. This is what I advised:

AAL: (To Fred): Tell me honestly, would you object if she went to these parties alone, so you could stay home and relax instead of being dragged there kicking and screaming?

Fred: Would I object? Hell no! I'd love it.

AAL: (Addressing Kay): It seems that you pay a steep price for having him as your escort. Why not go without him?

Kay: How could I do that? What would people think? What would I say if they asked where he is?

AAL: You could say he's out of town, or he's not feeling well, or he had important business to attend to. You could also simply tell them the truth, that he dislikes cocktail parties and that you two have agreed that he doesn't have to accompany you.

Kay took my advice, not only in reference to cocktail parties, but also with regard to shows that she wished to see and which Fred had no interest in seeing (in which case she either went along with another couple, or with one or more friends). The result was a new found freedom for both, fewer conflicts and a closer marriage.

To Apply This Reading to Yourself

1. *Select one of Lazarus's marital myths that you agree is a myth, and present your own reasoning, observations, and experience that have led you to this conclusion.*
2. *Select one of Lazarus's marital myths that you are not fully convinced is a myth, and present your own reasoning, observations, and experience that have led you to your views.*

3. *Discuss your own experience with and conclusions concerning romantic love.*
4. *Are the persons to whom you have been attracted similar to you or opposites! Discuss your experience in this regard.*
5. *Discuss one or more of your relationships in which you and/or your partner worked on the other to make her or him "a better person."*
6. *Discuss one or more of your relationships in which you and/or your partner were expected to know what the other wanted without being told.*
7. *Discuss one or more of your relationships in which you and/or your partner were expected to assume responsibility for the other's happiness.*
8. *Discuss one or more of your relationships in which trust or the absence of trust was a problem.*
9. *Discuss one or more of your relationships in which the degree of togetherness was a problem.*

Parenting

The American family does not exist.
—Newsweek

No longer is there a single culturally dominant family
pattern to which the majority of Americans conform
and most of the rest aspire. Instead, Americans today
have crafted a multiplicity of family and household
arrangements that we inhabit uneasily and
reconstitute frequently in response to changing
personal and occupational circumstances.
—Judith Stacey, Brave New Families

Almost all of us spend almost all of our lives in a family setting. We begin life in families, grow up in them, and then marry to begin families of our own. Our living is family living.

Almost all of us want to have children. Beginning a family soon after marriage is not a foregone conclusion these days, especially for two-career couples. Still, current surveys show that the vast majority of respondents continue to value parenthood, to believe that child-bearing is an integral part of marriage, and to feel some social pressure to have children.

Some of the rewards to be found in parenthood were noted by Sharryl Hawke and David Knox in their studies involving a broad spectrum of parents. In addition to simply enjoying their children, these parents reported a greater sense of fulfillment, as well as greater personal and marital growth. They also valued the love and the link with the past and future that their parenthood fostered.

A contrary view of parenthood emerges from Denise Polit-O'Hara and Judith Berman's review of research concerning marital satisfaction and parenting. This research shows greater marital strain in parents than in nonparents, at least while children are young and at home. The strain is greater in large families and particularly if there are many small children. However, young children—while they tend to lower marital satisfaction—also lower the probability of divorce.

In their book *The Case Against Having Children,* Anna and Arnold Silverman argue that many people become parents for the wrong reasons and would be better off with no children at all. And some authorities have noted that many parents not only have the wrong reasons but also the wrong skills or no skills at all for the complicated task of raising children. It is odd that our society, which regulates so much of life from birth to death (it requires a license to be an obstetrician or a mortician or to practice many other trades that look after us in the intervening interval), imposes no limitations on parenthood. It's a profession that anyone with a certain minimum of equipment and cooperation can enter.

The Case Against Having Parents is not a book but rather a recent avalanche of paperbacks about "toxic" or abusive parents—some incompetent, some bad, and many of them hurt human beings themselves. These books and a number of self-help organizations attempt to provide some understanding, guidance, and support for those who are trying to recover from their childhoods. A number of nationally prominent persons have spoken out or written of their own abuse as children.

The American family no longer exists—no longer is there a dominant pattern. These days, if someone asks you to meet their family, you might not know what to expect. There might be a single parent (divorced or never married), a set of remarried parents and stepfamily, or unmarried heterosexual or gay or lesbian parents. Or possibly a "sandwich-generation" family, with a set of parents caring for their children and also looking after one or more of their dependent parents; a "skip-generation" family, with one or two grandparents raising their grandchildren; or a communal arrangement of multiple adults and children.

What's coming up for the American family in the future? Here's what *U.S. News & World Report* saw several years ago when it looked into its crystal ball:

> On a spring afternoon half a century from today, the Joneses are gathering to sing "Happy Birthday" to Junior. There's Dad and his third wife, Mom and her second husband, Junior's two half brothers from his father's first marriage, his six stepsisters from his mother's spouse's previous unions, 100-year-old Great-Grandpa, all eight of Junior's current "grandparents," assorted aunts, uncles-in-law and stepcousins. While one robot scoops up the gift wrappings and another blows out the candles, Junior makes a wish—that he didn't have so many relatives.

Junior just might not have so many relatives if the visions of some other futurists come true. Electing parenthood may not be so simple a matter in the years to come, and some considerable changes in this area have been predicted for the next half century. Concern for the quality of parenting as well as overpopulation and diminished natural resources are some of the pressures that may result in a tightening of control. Scientific and technological advances also promise some interesting innovations.

Some futurists foresee a time when the decision to reproduce will no longer be a private and simple matter. What follows here is a collage of their ideas about what's to come. More people will decide to remain child-free, and those who want children will need to be screened by experts in genetics, medicine, marriage, and the family. Rigorous training, licensing, and careful monitoring will be provided for parenting, just as they are now provided for any profession of consequence. Reproduction will be accomplished on a quota basis with authorization from an appropriate agency (which would step in to terminate illegal pregnancies). If the genes of a parent were considered defective, donor ova or sperm would be used; fertilization could be performed in vivo or in a laboratory culture dish and the fetus could be carried to term in the mother's uterus or in an artificial womb. It may not be so simple to answer children of the next century when they ask, "Where did I come from?"

Such predictions will amuse some of us and alarm or aggravate others. Some want to preserve the traditional family, and the intrusion of Big Science and Big Government is highly unwelcome. Others believe that government action is needed, not in the next century, but right now in the form of a national family policy. Observer Jerrold Footlick writes that such a policy could include family allowances and full health care scaled to the number of children. The policy could also include pay equity for women, full job protection after maternity leave, compensation for lost wages, and high-quality child care.

In the readings that follow, no more time is spent on the future or the cloudy crystal ball. The first group of selections takes us into our own past and up to the present in a reconsideration of our relationships to our parents. The second set is designed to provoke some thought about the hallmarks of a *good* family.

FAMILIES—THE BITTERSWEET

Some persons remember their early years as an almost idyllic time. One wag wrote that childhood is so beautiful it is a shame to waste it on children. Others have bittersweet or even dismal memories of their childhood years. In his book *Escape from Childhood*, John Holt opines that most young people experience childhood as a prison rather than as a garden. He notes that even in seemingly normal families, it is common for children to be exploited, bullied, and humiliated.

Some writers have felt that the power of parents to influence their children has been somewhat overdrawn, while the power of children to influence parents has not been given its due. In this view, children are neither as innocent nor as powerless as they have been made out to be. George Bach and Ronald Deutsch, for example, note that children are devilishly clever at foiling parental authority, and in their book *Stop! You Are Driving Me Crazy!* describe some of the ways children devise to undo their parents and drive them berserk.

An important task for children when they reach adulthood, as Baba Ram Dass notes in *Be Here Now*, is to get "unstuck" from the past and "get straight" with their parents. He writes, "Even if the parent has died, you must in your heart and mind, reperceive that relationship until it becomes, like every one of your current relationships, one of light. If the person is still alive you may, when you have proceeded far enough, revisit and bring the relationship into the present. For, if you can keep the visit totally in the present, you will be free and finished."

Getting unstuck from our parents' values and devising our own is the subject of the first reading by Howard Halpern. He makes an important distinction between "good enough" parents, who teach us how to make choices, and parental "saints," who impress upon us their own revealed and absolute truths, codes, and rules. If we don't follow these rules, we may receive the message that they still *love* us (because that's one of their rules) but that they don't *like* us (and that's a heavy burden to bear). Halpern suggests some questions that we can ask ourselves to get free of parental injunctions and get in touch with our own wisdom.

Getting unstuck from the dependencies of childhood and the belligerencies of adolescence are the twin concerns of Martin Shepard in the second selection. He writes, "Those stuck in the childhood phase remain overly docile and dependent. Those stuck in adolescence relate to their parents in a perpetually rebellious and ill-tempered way." The solution: grow up, become self-sufficient, and adopt more realistic views of both ourselves and our parents.

Getting unstuck from being a victim of the familial past is the concern of Melinda Blau in the third reading. She profiles the "adult child" movement and notes that parent bashing has become both a national obsession and big business. Blau is heartened by some within the movement who encourage those who were abused as children to take responsibility for their own lives—to move beyond anger and blame to reach forgiveness.

FAMILIES—THE BETTER SIDE

In Blau's article, after a young woman laments her childhood as "dysfunctional," her mother asks, "I'd like to know—how many *functional* families are there?" That's a good question. Except for television's Huxtable family, where love and order prevailed and conflicts were resolved in 30 minutes (minus time for commercials), successful family living takes considerable effort, skill, and a bit of luck.

In the fourth reading, Joyce Maynard (who was 18 at the time of the writing) describes a *functional* family—her own. In her portrait, her parents emerge as individuals whose strengths are warmly appreciated and whose faults and eccentricities are accepted or fondly regarded. Maynard's family is notable for its coherent set of values, rituals, tastes, and—to be fair—pressures. It's not a perfect family but there's more than love; there's friendship.

Social critic Midge Decter says you can't fool Mother Nature, no sir, "A family is a mommy and daddy and their children." All the same, when a random sample of 1200 adults was recently asked to define "family," only 22% agreed that it was "A group of people related by blood, marriage, or adoption." Almost three out of four chose this definition: "A group of people who love and care for each other."

If a family is a group of people who love and care for each other, and if you don't have such a group handy, why not assemble your own? That's what Jane Howard has done and describes in the last reading, thereby silencing the old saying that you can choose your friends but not your relatives. For those of us who lack enough family "by chance" and want to obtain or complete one "by choice," Howard identifies 10 hallmarks of a *good* family. By these 10 criteria, Joyce Maynard's family stacks up pretty well. Does yours?

To Explore Your Parenting and Family Feelings and Attitudes

1. *Childhood sun and shadows.* First complete this sentence: "When I think of my childhood, I like to remember. . . ." Second, complete this sentence: "When I think of my childhood, it hurts to remember. . . ." Then write a brief paper amplifying your two responses and share your paper in the larger group or in small groups.
2. *The home tour.* Prepare a script for an imaginary guided tour through your family home (the one you grew up in or, perhaps, that of the family you have established). In your script, meet your guests on the front walk or at the front door, and describe each room and its most important elements as you walk through it. And, let it be a time when all the members of your family are home and each in a logical or usual room or place. When you get to this place, introduce the member and tell a little about her or him and your relationship with each other. You might begin: "We are now approaching my home. You will notice that . . ." Or "Hello. Come in. This is our living room . . ." Share your completed scripts in the larger group or in small groups.
3. *The family sculpture.* This exercise is based on the work of Virginia Satir and may be done in the larger group or in small groups. One member, the sculptor, picks people from the group to represent members of her or his family. A tableau is created to symbolize something significant about that family, perhaps how its members relate to each other. The sculptor "sculpts" (places and poses) each person to create the desired effect and gives a narration or explanation. Afterward the sculpted persons are encouraged to tell how they felt in the sculpture and how they might feel as members of that family. Then, as time allows, other members create their family and sculptures.
4. *The family commandments.* What "thou shalts" and "thou shalt nots" did your mother or father or both parents model for you or try to teach you? See whether you can list five of these command-

ments, and then write a brief paper describing them and their effect on you. Share your paper in the larger group or in small groups.

5. *The family gift.* In a moment, close your eyes and passively allow an image of a wrapped gift (of any size or shape) form in your mind's eye. Inside is a present symbolic of something special your mother or father or both parents gave to you. Unwrap the gift to see what the present is and read the card that accompanies it. Then open your eyes and write a brief paper concerning this experience, perhaps to share in the larger group or in small groups.

6. *Letters home.* Close as they are, family members frequently fail to tell each other all they would like to say. Select one member of your family (living or dead) with whom important things were unsaid or unheard. Then write a letter to this person, setting forth all the things you would like to say. Afterward, share your letter (and/or your feelings about it) in the larger group or in small groups.

7. *Letters from home.* If you have just completed the previous item and written a letter to a family member, now, for a little while, become that person and as that person write a reply back to yourself. Or you can do this exercise by itself. To do so, pick out a member of your family (living or dead) with whom important things were unsaid or unheard; for a few moments, become that person and as that person, write a letter to yourself. Afterward, share this letter (and/or your feelings about it) in the larger group or in small groups.

8. *Crazy-making.* It is well known that parents have the power to drive their children crazy, but children—far from being innocent and helpless—find ways to undo their parents. Bach and Deutsch point out that children can be very clever at foiling parental authority and keeping parents off balance. Children may use crazy-making tactics to defend themselves against their parents' crazy-making and to punish or disarm parents or to establish their own identity. Did you or one of your siblings sometimes drive a parent "crazy" or nearly so? Write a brief paper giving your answer to this question and share it in the larger group—or in small groups.

9. *The generation gap.* Values are simply the importance we attach to the various things of life. Values vary considerably from person to person and from generation to generation. What one person or generation thinks important and meaningful, another may regard as worthless or even contemptible. Write a brief paper comparing your values with those of your parents and indicating how the congruity or discrepancy in value systems affected you. Then share your papers in the larger group or in small groups.

10. *Parenthood—plus and minus.* Most of us appear to be drawn toward parenthood, but some of us are not, and many see or experience parenthood as a mixed blessing. How do you regard the possibility or actuality (if you are already a parent) of parenthood in your own case? What pluses and minuses do you see in your being a parent? List all the pluses on the left side of a page and all

the minuses on the right. Then balance the two sides, and write up your conclusions, which may be shared in the larger group or in small groups.

11. *Your future family.* Describe your family situation as you expect it will be 10 years from today. What will probably be your marital status? Your parental status? How important and satisfying will this aspect of your life be? Write a brief paper incorporating your answers to these questions, and share your paper in the larger group or in small groups.

12. *The parenthood license.* Many professions and trades require a license or credential of some kind to ensure that the practitioners are qualified, and it has been suggested that parenthood should, too. If you disagree with this suggestion, make a list of the reasons for your disagreement. If you agree, list the reasons for your agreement, and suggest the minimum qualifications that each licensee should have and how the licensing board would evaluate each applicant. As an alternative or supplementary approach, have everyone vote "yes," "no," or "undecided" on the following question: "Every person who seeks to be a parent must qualify for a license." Then break into small groups, each composed of individuals of varying opinion, and argue it out. As a final step, have everyone reassemble so that the small groups can report back and so that another vote can be taken to detect any change of opinion.

To Read Further

Bombardieri, M. (1981). *The baby decision: How to make the most important choice of your life.* New York: Rawson, Wade.

Burgwyn, D. (1982). *Marriage without children.* New York: Harper & Row. (paperback)

Daniels, P., & Weingarten, K. (1982). *Sooner or later: The timing of parenthood in adult lives.* New York: W. W. Norton. (paperback)

Ehrensoft, D. (1987). *Parenting together: Men and women sharing care of their children.* New York: Free Press.

Elvenstar, D. C. (1982). *Children: To have or have not. A guide to making and living with your decision.* New York: Kampmann.

Halpern, H. M. (1976). *Cutting loose: An adult guide to coming to terms with your parents.* New York: Simon and Schuster. (Fireside paperback, 1990)

Hawke, S., & Knox, D. (1977). *One child by choice.* Englewood Cliffs, NJ: Prentice-Hall.

Kirkendall, L. A., & Gravatt, A. E. (Eds.). (1984). *Marriage and the family in the year 2020.* Buffalo, NY: Prometheus.

Paul, J., & Paul, M. (1987). *If you really loved me . . . From conflict to closeness for everyone who is a parent and everyone who has been a child.* Minneapolis, MN: CompCare. (paperback)

Polit-O'Hara, D., & Berman, J. (1984). *Just the right size: A guide to family-size planning.* New York: Praeger.

Pruett, K. D. (1987). *The nurturing father: Journey toward the complete man.* New York: Warner Books.

Rubin, N. (1984). *The mother mirror: How a generation of women is changing motherhood in America.* New York: Putnam.

Stacey, J. (1990). *Brave new families: Stories of domestic upheaval in late twentieth century America.* New York: Basic Books.

Weiss, J. S. (1981). *Your second child: A guide for parents contemplating, expecting or raising a second child.* New York: Summit Books.

Whelan, E. (1980). *A Baby? . . . Maybe: A guide to making the most fateful decision of your life* (rev. ed.). Indianapolis: Bobbs-Merrill. (paperback)

Good Enough Parents and Saints

Howard M. Halpern

Some of us have been blessed by parents who are saints and we still may be trying to recuperate from this blessing.

Parents need not even be religious in order to function as priests, ministers, rabbis or gurus. To be ordained they simply must be in touch with the absolute truth about how people ought to behave. Once so ordained, elevation to sainthood involves just a few more fairly easy steps. They must preach their truths to you and all who will listen. They must show they have suffered very trying life experiences, such as raising you. They should have achieved some position of respect such as housewife, parent, provider, salesman, foreman, teacher, rich man, P.T.A. president, so that they have the necessary stature. And to complete their canonization, they must be able to show how professing these truths has aided the moral development of others, particularly their offspring. Having achieved all this, they need only tilt their head at the right angle for their flashing halo to blind you to perceptions of reality other than theirs.

An important aspect of parenting is imparting values and morality to your offspring. Does this make every parent who does this a saint? Not at all. "Good enough" parents teach you the importance of judgment and making different choices; saints teach you ready-made codes and rules.

Good enough parents teach you to make your decisions flexibly, basing them on your assessment of the whole picture; saints present you with a rigid system of shoulds and should nots.

Good enough parents teach you that it is often difficult to know what is the better, more effective, more moral, more self-actualizing thing to do; saints teach you that there is right and wrong with no in-between. (In fact saints couldn't easily accept the term "good enough parent." You are a good parent or a bad one.)

Good enough parents teach you to differentiate among life's big questions and little questions, to establish a hierarchy of what's important; saints tell you that there are no little questions. Saints can often be as morally outraged about an unmade bed or a fashion color clash as they'd be if you wrote a bad check.

A good enough parent is aware that you are different from him, that you have your own needs and ways of looking at the world that help determine what's best for you; a saint can't see a clear boundary between him and you so he expects you to live by his perceptions and values.

Good enough parents can accept the possibility that their values were largely swallowed whole when they were children, and they attempt to subject their values to rational scrutiny; saints have no awareness that the rules, fears and prejudices they live by are not built into the order of things but, rather, are clearly childhood indoctrinations.

Good enough parents try to indicate the reasoning and life experiences that go into their positions on morality and social protocol; saints often try to connect their injunctions with a greater power such as God, church, gospel, absolutes, historical imperatives, public opinion, etc.

Finally, when good enough parents use ordinary words they do it to communicate information; saints can shape these same words into barbs that provoke guilt and fear. Commonplace terms become commands, belittlements, narrowers of perception, limiters of alternatives, prescriptions for salvation. For this reason, before proceeding further in our discussions it will be useful to take a look at the semantics of sainthood.

GLOSSARY OF SAINTLY WORDS AND TERMS

Always—as in "We Always," "One always" "We always" denotes a rule your parent lives by and you will always live by, with no exceptions, no maybes, no sometimes. This rule is forever.

Variation: "You always" says that stretching from your past and into your distant future, you everlastingly mess things up and do things wrong.

Examples: "One should *always* be courteous."

"I *always* keep the house spotless."

"We must *always* be careful not to let others take advantage of us."

"I *always* put on a cheerful face."

"You *always* try to get out of anything difficult."

Ashamed—as in "You should be ashamed," "I am ashamed"

"You have done something that makes me feel small, wormlike and embarrassed (or would make me feel that way if I had done it) and I hope you feel like you want to disappear into a hole because people are looking at you. In fact, I wish you would disappear into a hole and then maybe people will stop looking at me."

Examples: "You ought to be *ashamed* to go around dressed like that."

"I was so *ashamed* when you didn't say a word to anyone at the party."

"I was so *ashamed* when you made yourself the center of attention at the party."

Bad—as in "That's bad," "You're bad"

Your parent wants you to believe that you are breaking an important social taboo ("that's bad") and you should feel that you are an awful person ("you're bad") for doing it. Freely translated it means, "I don't like what you're doing."

Variation: "He's bad": Don't be like him or I will turn this same angry, disapproving countenance in your direction.

Examples: "It's a *bad thing* to be closer to your friend than your family."

"I never thought a child of mine could be so *bad*."

"He's a *bad* egg and he's having a bad influence on you."

Best—as in "I know best," "Do your best"

"I know best" means that "compared to you or anyone else you invoke, I have a particular insight and knowledge about what should be done that is clearly superior."

"Do your best" means that although

the saint really believes only perfection will do, he is willing to concede to your obvious limitations as long as you always do things as well as you are capable of doing them.

Examples: "Buy the heavier coat. Believe me, I know *best*."

"I don't expect you to be the top in the class as long as you do your *best*."

Dirty—as in "That's dirty," "You're dirty"

"What you are doing or saying makes me feel revolted and nauseated and I can assure you my parents would have felt the same way if I did it, which only goes to prove that there is something in the very nature of such behavior that is filthy and disgusting."

Examples: "Hearing you talk about sex so blatantly makes me feel *dirty*."

"Anyone who picks his nose is a *dirty pig*."

"He's a *dirty old man*."

Foolish—As in "Don't be foolish," "That's foolish"

Any behavior that's just for fun, that "wastes" time or that is frivolous—i.e., behavior other than what your parent wants you to do, but not a serious enough transgression to be labeled sinful, bad or shameful. Similar to "silly," "childish."

Examples: "Going to a hockey game is a *foolish waste* of time."

"Spending that much on a dress is *foolish*."

God—as in "God wants," "God will"

Often used simply to express a belief in a higher power or holy spirit. But sainted parents may also invoke it as the ultimate in elevating and transforming their preferences into the wishes of a divine and omnipotent authority.

Examples: "*God wants* you to have children."

"*God will* punish you if you are mean to your parents."

"*God doesn't like* liars."

"*God knows* when you are doing something wrong."

"Don't be bitter—it is *God's will*."

Good—as in "Be good," "That's a good boy"

This simply means your parent is made happy by that behavior. Do more of it and you will be smiled upon all the time.

Variation: "He's good" stands for someone your parents approve of. Be like him and they'll be happy.

Examples: "*Be good* and stay out of my way."

"Look how *good* and quiet Mary is."

Grateful—as in "You should be grateful" "We should be grateful"

"You should be grateful" means "Don't want too much from life or from me because there are people in the world, like me, that are or were much worse off. So instead of being angry, disappointed or demanding, be thankful for what you have and what I have done for you."

"We should be grateful" means "See how resigned I am? How about you?"

Examples: "So you have a limp. You should be *grateful* you can walk."

"Why do you want to go back to work? You should *be grateful* your husband makes a good living."

"We must *be grateful* she didn't suffer."

Guilty—as in "You should feel guilty"

You have violated a major parental injunction that has been set out for you as social protocol, the word of God, tradition, etc. You should feel self-loathing and remorse. Admit your transgression and repent.

Examples: "You should feel *guilty* for not calling your father when he was sick."

"You should feel *guilty* for letting your children go out without sweaters on a day like this."

"You should feel *guilty* going out with a married man."

Must—as in "You must," "One must"

A strong, no-nonsense command. Similar to "should" but more immediate. The clear implication: "You'd better or else."

Examples: "You *must* always make the bed before leaving the house."

"One *must not* cancel a social engagement."

Never—as in "We never," "I never" or "Never!"

"We never" applies to behavior that is so beyond the pale that it must never even occur to you as a possibility.

"I never" is spoken with smug pride by the parent who is telling you that he has wiped from his repertoire all possibility of this errant behavior.

"Never!" is an ultimate imperative, a no-no reaching to eternity, and violating it chances losing parental love and respect—at least for a while.

Examples: "We *never* talk with food in our mouths."

"I *never* buy in expensive (or cheap) stores."

"*Never* discuss family matters with friends!"

"*Never* marry a black (white, yellow, brown, Jewish, gentile, poor) man!"

One—as in "One doesn't," "One must"

The implication here is that there are rules everyone must live by that are quite impersonal and certainly do not arise from your parents' own beliefs, thoughts, and hang-ups. And it doesn't leave much room for recognition of your individuality, does it?

Examples: "*One* isn't seen in places like that."

"*One* doesn't wear those shoes with that dress."

"*One* doesn't get angry at his parents."

"*One must* have children."

People—as in "What will people say?" "People will talk"

"There's a whole world of others out there, and I am afraid that those others, known or anonymous, will disapprove of me. I want you to be afraid of others disapproving of you because, since we are connected, if they disapprove of you, they disapprove of me."

Variation: "The best people." These are not only the judges of our merit, but you should emulate them as they rate high on your parents' value scale.

Variation: As in "People can't be trusted."

Note the paradox—often parents who are most concerned to have the respect and high regard of others feel that these same others are not to be trusted.

Examples: "If you go away with him for a weekend, you know what *people* will say."

"Only the *best people* go to that hotel."

"Never tell *people* your problems."

Right—as in "Do it right," "That's right"
There is always a prescribed way that you should act and your parents know exactly what it is. Always do right and you will become the kind of person they will be proud of.

Variation: "I am right" usually means "end of argument."

Examples: "Now that is the *right way* to set a table."

"Can't you ever do anything *right!*"

"I know I am *right* so there's no use discussing it."

Should—as in "You should do, think, believe, etc."
It really means "I want you to do it that way." But look how much more mileage a parent can get by presenting it as a "should." It becomes an injunction, a given rule, instead of a personal preference or prejudice.

Examples: "You *should* always love your parents."

"You *should* visit Aunt Helen."

Shouldn't—as in "You shouldn't do that"
Translation: "If you do that I'll be anxious and upset because I wouldn't like it, other people may not like it and if they don't like what you do they won't like me."

Examples: "You *shouldn't* wear your dress so short."

"You *shouldn't* travel alone."

"You *shouldn't* turn down a good paying job."

Sin—as in "It's a sin"
This is worse than doing something "bad" or "wrong" because here you are not only breaking cultural taboos or social protocol but God's own word as perceived and interpreted by your parents. The appropriate reaction is *guilt.*

Examples: "Throwing out food is a *sin.*"

"Going away with a man for a weekend is a *sin.*"

"It's a *sin* to play with yourself."

They—as in "They say"
This is similar to "people" except that it has a more mysterious and global quality as if "they" carry the omniscience of correct social protocol. It really means "This is what I'd like you to believe and do but you may not accept it if it just comes from me. However if I can make you believe that everybody else agrees with me or that I'm just agreeing with everybody else, then maybe what I say will have more weight."

Examples: "*They* are wearing dresses longer this year."

"*They say* if a woman is too easy, men will never respect her."

Today—as in "People don't know how to live today"
This means that morality is going to the dogs. "People (you) are now doing things that I was brought up to know were wrong and therefore they (you) are *bad.*"

Examples: "Young people have no respect for anything *today.*"

"There's no patriotism *today.*"

Tomorrow—as in "You must think of tomorrow"
Sometimes means "plan ahead." But it often translates: 'Don't enjoy yourself today because that's sinful and scares me. So live for the ever-receding future and you can guarantee not living too fully in the here and now. That will make me feel less anxious."

Examples: "If you don't worry about *tomorrow* you'll have plenty to worry about *tomorrow.*"

"Forget about having a good time. What about *tomorrow!*"

Ungrateful—as in "You are ungrateful"
Usually means "After all I've done for

you, you ought to feel terribly guilty if you (1) don't appreciate it; (2) want anything more from me; (3) question my motives."

Examples: "It took me all day to clean and rearrange your room. How can you be so *ungrateful?*"

We—as in "We never" or "We don't"
There's no separation between mommy (or daddy) and you. You are part of them, like an ankle, thumb or jawbone. And "we" must always do what "we" are programmed to do.

Examples: "*We* never leave dishes in the sink."

"*We* mustn't be silly."

"*We* don't talk to strangers."

Wrong—as in "That's wrong," "You're wrong"
This applies to behavior that your parents know to be incorrect, inappropriate, harmful or sinful. They expect you to accept this knowledge as gospel. If you do "wrong" things, or question whether doing the "wrong" thing would lead to dire consequences, you are "bad."

Examples: "It's *wrong* to go out to a party when your child isn't feeling well."

"You're so obviously *wrong* I won't dignify your behavior with a comment."

SHAME AND SCANDAL IN THE FAMILY

Few behavior modification psychologists are as adept in the use of rewards and punishments for shaping behavior as are saints. Starting with the earliest childhood comprehending, saintly semantics structure the range of permissible behavior through the ubiquitous, built-in praise and condemnation. In fact, their rewards and punishments not only set limits on permissible behavior but on conceivable behavior. It is not enough to say that the saint enforces his values by his approval or disapproval, because all parents do that, willingly or unwillingly. When parents are being saintly the threat to their offspring is not that they might make them feel guilty, as when parents are being martyrs, nor is it making them afraid of parental rage, as when parents are being tyrannical. The threat is in their attempt

to make their children feel *shame*. The child thinks he has done something unthinkable, beyond the pale. His punishment for deeply disappointing the parents is not the withdrawal of love, but the withdrawal of their *respect*. The granting and withdrawal of respect are enormously powerful enforcers. We need to feel that our parents value us as worthwhile human beings, and do not simply love us because we are theirs. We need to feel our parents *like* us. Saintly parents communicate that if we don't follow their rules, they may still love us, because, after all, as parents they *should*, but they won't *like* us. And that's heavy.

In addition, the very personality of the saint, the righteousness that is conveyed in his bearing, becomes a very early model for the child to identify with. And the young child may have no way to discover that alternate values and ways of behaving even exist because the people his parents would tend to associate with, the family members and friends that are around most, often share the parents' way of seeing the world.

IT AIN'T NECESSARILY SO

The structure of the parent's values will meet some baffling challenges as the child runs into people who see things differently from the saintly parent. Sometimes this occurs concurrently with the saint's teachings, as when the other parent may not agree with the saint. Sometimes it is another family member, a friend, a friend's parent, a teacher who presents the child with alternative possibilities. What often happens is that the child rejects these possibilities because they carry the threat of the saint's disapproval and disrespect. These new ideas are labeled "bad," "wrong," "sinful," etc., by the child, and thus dismissed. Sometimes he rejects them because they are so alien that his mind simply cannot encompass them. For many people, this early value system remains stable and unquestioned throughout life, with the person accepting the inevitable happy or unhappy consequences of that system.

The saintly injunctions usually do not become challenged until the child, now grown, feels pain and discomfort because the old code is keeping him from satisfying his own goals, constricting his freedom, confusing his sense of what is right for himself, or causing new people that he cares about to reject him for being so judgmental.

Often the constriction of living with injunctions that have become oppressive and suffocating produces physical symptoms, such as headaches, breathing difficulties, exhaustion, muscle spasms. It is illustrated by the old joke about the doctor who tells his patient who doesn't drink, smoke, go out with girls, that he has a headache because his halo is on too tight.

Usually this constriction is accompanied by rage—rage at his own impotence to exchange the injunctions for a mode that enhances his self-realization.

I'VE GOTTA BE ME

If you have a saintly parent, then your suffering, if not converted to helpless self-pity, your rage, if not expended in ineffectual flailing, can spur a reappraisal of the codes and rules that have been nailed to the door of your mind. Each chafing injunction must be viewed through an attribute you may not even know you have, your *wisdom*. You have wisdom through the millions of times you have observed cause and effect in the way people behave. You may have ignored the data that didn't fit into the most entrenched parental dictates, but the data is there, and you must start to trust your own feelings by testing the rules you live by against reason. Here are some questions to help mobilize your wisdom:

Why am I following this injunction?

Does this way of behaving make sense to me now or am I adhering to it simply because that is what I was taught?

What are the *consequences* of continuing to follow this injunction?

What are the consequences if I break with this injunction?

If I break with the old rule, will somebody get hurt? Will I?

If I break with the old rule, will my life go better or worse?

Am I doing this only to rebel, or to get even with my parents for past injuries, or do I feel I really need to make this change to live more fully?

How much parental disapproval will result from this change? Can I bear their disapproval? Can I get them to be more accepting?

To Apply This Reading to Yourself

1. *Would you classify your own father and mother as "good enough parents" or "saints" (as Halpern defines these terms)? Discuss the evidence on which your answer is based.*
2. *Develop a "glossary of saintly words and terms" for the family in which you were raised, or pick out and discuss the terms in Halpern's glossary that apply.*
3. *How was shame used in your own family, and what effects did this use have on you?*
4. *Pick out a parental dictate or injunction that has had an untoward effect on you, and ask and answer the questions Halpern presents in order to mobilize your own wisdom.*

Parents

Martin Shepard

Learning to accept your parents as people in their own right—different and distinct from you—is a task that poses difficulties for quite a large number of people. There should be nothing surprising in all of this. For we all have one very good historical reason—our childhoods.

The infant is born into a world in which he is, literally, *part* of his mother. Without her to comfort, clothe, feed and shelter him, he could not survive. During childhood our little girl and boy still depend greatly on their parents. They have not yet acquired the skills necessary to provide for and sustain themselves. This is a time one learns certain "do's" and "don'ts." You learn how to count and how to read, how to cook and how to sew, how to hammer and how to saw. And you learn *not* to swallow iodine, *not* to put a fork in the electrical outlet, and *not* to cross a street unless you look to make sure there is no traffic approaching.

Typically the child's contract with the parent is one in which he accepts the dependent role in return for the favors/protection/guidance/and support he receives from them. There are, of course, dissatisfactions. He prefers taking things out to play with more than he does putting them away. He wants to do and try things he sees grown-ups doing and resents it when they say "No." He may want to come and go more freely than they are ready to allow. And he'd rather watch television than do his homework or practice the piano.

Adolescence marks the years during which relatively accepting and "sweet" children become adults in their own right. Following the sexual maturation of puberty, adolescents typically reject the dependent contracts that as children they had with their parents. It is a period of much storm and strife, both in the inner life of the adolescents and in their relationships to their parents. Opposition/confrontation/argumentation are a natural part of the process as the adolescent seeks to break away and find his or her own adulthood. If it is accomplished smoothly, and the adolescent truly feels adult, he comes to accept his parents as he would other adults. If they share common interests and *if* the parents accept him as an adult (not only as their child), they remain close. If their interests are not similar and/or if the parents cannot transcend their *roles* as parents, there is a polite distance—as any adult would have with people who are on different wavelengths. This second alternative is a more common outcome of maturation.

What I have described thus far is "normal" maturation. Many individuals, no matter how old they are, never make it, psychologically speaking, past either childhood or adolescence when it comes to relating to their parents. Those stuck in the childhood phase remain overly docile and dependent. Those stuck in adolescence relate to their parents in a perpetually rebellious and ill-tempered way.

Given the cultural roles males and females are assigned (males presumably being "aggressive" and females "passive"), one might expect that women are more likely to become stuck in the childhood state and men in the adolescent one. And—although there are many reversals to this expectation—such is usually the case.

Louise is a good example of such a child/woman. In her childhood and adolescence, her parents were perpetually available to her. They were quick to comfort and pamper her. They always soothed her hurts, took her side, indulged her fancies. She, in turn, pampered their egos by letting them know how exceptional they were, how they were the only people who understood her, how much wisdom and sage advice they had, and how appreciative she was.

At twenty-two she married for the first time. Her husband, Greg, was an insurance salesman and just out of college. He was a decent, responsible, upright young man, who looked forward to supporting Louise and raising a family. But it never worked out that way.

Louise was incapable of accommodating herself to the rigors of a more spartan and independent existence. She consulted her mother daily, both to ask for advice on simple housekeeping chores and for consolation over any minor inconveniences she was having with Greg. She was incapable of sticking to a budget and so, behind Greg's back, ran to her physician father for extra funds to pay her charge-account bills and indulge her passion for clothes, cars (which she insisted on changing yearly), and innumerable redecoration schemes.

When her first and only child was born, her parents hired a maid for her. And Mother came over daily for several months to help out and give advice.

After three years of marriage, Louise left Greg. Marriage didn't conform to her picture of "picket fences and lace curtains." She was interested in playing more and working less. Her parents were sympathetic. They agreed with Louise that Greg was "cheap," "selfish," and that he "always got his way." Besides which, Mother was willing to raise Louise's daughter while Louise went back to school and tried to find a new man.

Now thirty-nine years old and on her fifth husband, Louise lives in another city. But she still phones her family a few times each week.

Sam, who is twenty-eight, is the sort of person who typifies adolescent "stuckness." For he remains continuously close to, yet antagonistic toward, his parents.

While attending a local college, he, like many other students, began smoking marijuana. Not content to do it privately, he naturally let his parents know of his activities. They were frightened, shocked, and strongly disapproving. Sam, rather than dropping the subject, continued to let them know of his usage by smoking at home. Quarrels/insults/door-slamming occurred frequently on both sides.

Dinner conversations to this day are reminiscent of the popular television series *All in the Family*—with Sam typically attacking his father's political and social points of view and Mother acting as a harassed peacemaker.

Four years ago Sam moved out of his parents' home but continued to bring home his laundry for his mother to wash. His attitude was sullen. If his mother inquired about his life he would give her flippant answers or accuse her of trying to hold on to him. Yet he made it a point to inform his parents of many of his activities that he knew they objected to—his dating a woman of another religion, his intention of quitting a promising job, his experimentation with LSD.

Every now and then he would ask his father for a loan or the use of the family car. He felt it was coming to him. On those occasions when his father refused him, he always had some unkind words for the old man.

Two years ago he married. He made it a point to tell his mother not to interfere when she offered to help care for Suzy, Sam's daughter, who was born eight months ago. But whenever Sam and his wife, Brenda, have a party to attend, Sam calls up his mother, expecting her to be always available for babysitting. When she is not, he accuses her of being a hypocrite for having offered to help out earlier.

How can you tell if you are *stuck*, in any respect, regarding your parents? One way is to see if they embarrass you. Perhaps you don't want your parents to meet your friends because you fear they will act in a way that will humiliate you; that they will treat you as their little girl or boy, correct you, or behave "coarsely" in front of your friends.

Such embarrassment is often related to your still feeling yourself a *part* of—an extension of—your parents. You fail to realize that if your parents do react absurdly, it is *they* who will be laughed at, not you. Unless, of course, you take it as personally as a thirteen-year-old who brings her first date over to the house.

Other indications of dependency are the making of routine daily or weekly telephone calls to your parents, wanting their approval constantly, or finding that there is "no other person as good, wise, and kind to me as my mother (or father)."

Signs of rebelliousness are so self-evident, emotionally, to the sufferer, that they need no further elaboration.

There is a certain validity to a child's blaming a parent when things don't work out to his satisfaction. After all, the parent *is* in charge. If a meal doesn't taste good, the child can't very well cook his own. If the family moves and the child must give up his neighborhood friends, that is the parents' responsibility, not his. *But once you pass the age of eighteen*, those conditions no longer hold true. There is no further need to depend upon your parents.

The task of both the *child-stuck* and *adolescent-stuck* person is to get *un-stuck*, by learning to do things on your own and, in doing so, becoming a more self-sufficient human being. You can't have a very good self-concept—can't very well consider yourself any person's equal—if you remain a child-at-heart in relationship to your parents. Whatever *advantages* there are in taking things from your parents by continuing the "child" or "adolescent" integrations are more than offset by the loss of basic self-esteem that results from staying in that role.

The "child" is reluctant to go *through* the adolescent, rebellious, phase. The "adolescent" is reluctant to achieve total self-sufficiency. He wants all of the advantages of both childhood *and* adulthood, but none of the disadvantages of either. "Adolescents" are too embarrassed to admit how much they still *want* their parents, and how much they might even love them.

Both groups ask for their parents' support and approval (albeit in different ways) long after they are capable of managing their own lives. Not only does this interfere with their lives in general (witness Louise and Sam), but it certainly prevents the possibility of their establishing a realistic present-day relationship with their parents.

I've talked frequently in this book[1] about living in the *here and now*, and how emotions, people, and relationships change. One of the things that can certainly be said of people who have trouble dealing with their parents is that they are usually reacting to *memories* of both their parents and themselves—as they all were ten, fifteen, or twenty years ago—and *not* in terms of the realities of all of them now. This is always due to the *holding back* of the maturational process.

We are left, therefore, with many adults who still *blame* their parents for the way they have treated them. As if their parents had *chosen* to make the child's life miserable.

Yet there are very few parents who *intentionally* act cruelly. Every set of parents, if they could choose, would elect to be the world's best parents.

Of course, lack of "intent" does not mean that parents don't occasionally act cruelly. Why shouldn't they? They are primarily *people* before

they are parents. All of us are capable of cruelty. Besides, they had parents who "misunderstood" them, too. Parents, like all people, can be tight-fisted, generous, disappointing, helpful, indifferent, funny, tender, or short-tempered.

When I was twenty-five and a student in medical school, I was still reacting to my parents as an adolescent. I resented having to go visit them each week. I felt they were still trying to control me. When I was questioned by my analyst whether the situation might not be reversed—whether I might not be trying to control *them*—I realized that I made my weekly sojourns to pick up a weekly allotment that they were generous enough to offer me. And that I could possibly manage to get by with a much lower amount. And that I needn't show up weekly to "pay my dues" for their generosity—that they gave it out of kindness and not for my weekly shows of obeisance. With that realization I stopped my mechanical visits, cut down on what I was receiving, and began to relate to them more adultly.

A therapist friend of mine was treating a young man who constantly fought with his mother. He wanted her approval, but she was constantly critical. Mother was an exceptionally irrational woman and never saw how much her son wanted her blessings. He, in turn, could not accept her irrationality.

My friend asked his patient the following question: "If you passed by a mental institution and saw your mother looking through the barred windows on one of the floors, and she was screaming the same things at you, as you passed by, that she now screams at you at home, would it still trouble you?"

"No," said the young man. "I'd discount it, because I'd know she was crazy."

"From now on, then, every time your mother gets on your nerves, I want you to recall that picture of her shouting from that hospital window."

His patient did just that and found his aggravation and frustration subsiding.

A device such as this is, I think, a useful tool for people who find themselves continuously fighting with a non-accepting parent.

A rule to bear in mind that will help you to see your parents more realistically, is:

Grown-ups are merely children in aging skin.

---

1. Martin Shepard is referring to his *The Do-It-Yourself Psychotherapy Book* from which this reading was taken.—The Editor

When you get to feeling overwhelmed by your parents' (or parent substitutes—such as bosses or teachers) "wisdom" or resentful over their "shortcomings," try to see the child that is hiding and acting inside of them.

I have purposely avoided writing a chapter on *being a parent*—on dealing more effectively with *your* children—for a number of reasons. One is that there is no way to be a *parent*. You can only be *yourself*. And if you become a mentally healthy adult (as, I'm sure, all of the readers of this book are trying to become), you will do all right both as *yourself* and as a parent.

As a psychiatrist, I have seen hundreds upon hundreds of people complaining about their parents. If they were given a great deal of material advantages, they would complain that "my parents bought me things as a substitute for love." If they were given few things, the complaint was "my parents were cheapskates and didn't love me enough." If they were given a great deal of freedom by their parents, they would lament that their "parents weren't interested in me or what I did." But if they were closely supervised, it was because "my parents were too strict."

Naturally it helps to be kind, tolerant, and understanding of your children. Remembering your own childhood helps. But sometimes a spanking or some punishment may well be in order.

So there are no suggestions I have to offer you as a parent, except to bear in mind that *whatever you do, it is likely to be wrong in your child's eyes.* But when and if your child grows to maturity—if he or she doesn't get stuck in childlike or adolescent behavior—your child will come to appreciate that you did the best that you could.

And further—it is your *child's* responsibility to grow up, to mature—not yours to do it for him. Just as you must realize that you are no longer part of your parents—that things aren't *their fault*—your child has to learn the same things about you.

The exercises that follow attempt to help you continue your own maturational process vis-à-vis your parents. You may need *repeated* work on the exercises in order to abandon your unrealistic views of both yourself and your parents. For you must, eventually, learn to let go of them, give up your demands that they be different than

they are, forgive them their faults (and all of the things that they "should" have done, did do, and didn't do)—and come to realize that your parents couldn't possibly have been anything other than what they were and what they are.

SHEPARD'S EXERCISES

1. Work with two empty chairs. Put your father in one and tell him all of the negative things you've held back from him—your resentments, frustrations, hatreds. Be as specific as you can. Then, switch seats, be him, and respond to "you." Say how you feel hearing all of these negative things. Keep the dialogue going by changing chairs once more and telling your father what you needed, now need, wanted, and now want from him. Have him respond by saying what he needs and wants from you (past and present). See whether or not you can achieve any greater understanding of one another's positions, as you keep the dialogue going, as opposed to finding yourselves simply *arguing*.

2. Repeat exercise 1, substituting your mother for your father.

3. Pretend you are your father and write a short composition about "The Difficulties I Had In Raising My Child."

4. Repeat exercise 3, but now write as your mother instead of your father.

5. Place your father back in the empty chair. Tell him all of the things you've appreciated or loved about him. Switch seats and, as your father, say what you *feel* about your child's telling you such nice things. Keep the dialogue going.

6. Repeat exercise 5 with your mother.

7. Be your father and tell your child all the things you've loved and appreciated about her (or him). Switch chairs, be yourself, and say how you feel about hearing these things. Be your father again and respond.

8. Repeat exercise 7 with your mother.

9. List all of the secrets concerning your private life that you would never tell your parents. Place each of your parents in an empty chair in front of you and tell each one, in turn, these secrets. Be your parents and react. Again, keep switching chairs and get a dialogue going. See whether you can move

toward mutual understanding rather than conflict and confrontation.

10. If your relationship with either parent is characterized by dependent routines, daily or weekly phone calls or visits (if you are living away from home), take a month's vacation from these activities. Don't call. Don't visit. Politely tell your parents that you simply want to see what it's like to live without such regular contact with them. And stick to your word.

    If you are over twenty-one and still live with your parents spend the next month living elsewhere, giving the same reasons. Move in with a friend or series of friends, into a Y, a hotel room, with a sibling, or with a different relative. Better still, try all of these different arrangements for a few nights each so that you might see what it is like to live in different spaces.

11. If your relationship with either parent is characterized by aloofness or grumpiness, or if you have not had much contact with them in some time, see what it is like to try to get closer.

    Make a date to meet them somewhere and treat them to a dinner. Give them a small gift—a token of your "appreciation" (whether it is felt or not). Ask them details about their lives. Tell them whatever things you appreciate or like about them—and work hard at avoiding unkind words during this experience.

    A day later, write about your experience. Describe what it meant to you and what you learned from it.

    If either of your parents is dead, do the above exercise in fantasy for the one (or ones) you can't bring along in reality.

To Apply This Reading to Yourself

1. *Are you, as Shepard defines this term, a "child-stuck" person? Discuss your experience with (or freedom from) this kind of stuckness.*
2. *Are you, as Shepard defines this term, an "adolescent-stuck" person? Discuss your experience with (or freedom from) this kind of stuckness.*
3. *How much acceptance, understanding, and compassion can you sum up for your parents (or their memory)? Have you learned, as Shepard says you must, "to let go of them, give up your demands that they be different than they are, forgive them their faults (and all the things they 'should' have done, did do, and didn't do)"? Write a brief paper incorporating your answers to these questions.*
4. *Carry out one of the exercises presented by Shepard and write an account of your experience and what you learned from it.*

Adult Children—
Tied to the Past

Melinda Blau

Barbara and her mother are trying to work out their conflicts in a family-therapy session. Recovering from the most recent of many love affairs gone sour, Barbara is convinced her shattered romances reflect an abusive childhood. Her anger is palpable.

"How do you have a good relationship?" she asks the therapist, her eyes narrowing as she leans forward in her chair. "If you grew up in a house where relationships were good, you learned that. I'm 44 years old and I'm reading books like *Toxic Parents* to learn what healthy is about!"

The "toxic parent," 75-year-old Evelyn, seems willing to make peace with her daughter. But Barbara has another agenda: "Without some resolution of the past, I can't go forward," Barbara asserts. "Part of this has to do with my mother . . . obviously. Whether she will take any level of responsibility and make it easier for me is questionable."

Barbara sees herself as the victim. "It's very painful. The way I feel has to do with things done *to me*—not because of who I am as a person. I'm dealing with it on several levels. I'm going to a therapist. I'm also starting to go to ACOA."

The mother looks confused. Her daughter is speaking a foreign language. "AC-what?" she asks.

"Adult Children of Alcoholics and other dysfunctional families," Barbara explains authoritatively. She makes it clear that there was "absolutely no alcohol" in her house—but her childhood was nonetheless "dysfunctional."

The mother inhales deeply and sighs. She asks innocently, "I'd like to know—how many *functional* families are there?"

These two generations are worlds apart. The mother, a child of the Depression, was taught to put others' needs first, to repress her feelings and silently endure life's hard knocks. In contrast, Barbara flaunts her distress; she is low on compassion. A grown woman, she laments, "There is a little girl inside of me who never got the mothering she wanted—and she still wants it."

But that's not all she wants. The therapist, who had warned her client "mother bashing" would not be permitted, says, "Barbara wanted someone to hold her mother still, so she could beat her up."

Blaming parents for what they did or didn't do has become a national obsession—and big business. Like Barbara, increasing numbers of people are now referring to themselves as "Adult Children," a curious metaphor. With self-help groups and a spate of books such as the best-selling and pointedly titled *Toxic Parents* to guide them, plus magazines and TV talk shows eager to air their dirty laundry, Adult Children are definitely front and center on the American scene.

The movement began about 10 years ago with survivors of extreme abuse: children of alcoholics and drug abusers or victims of incest and physical or mental violence, who very early in life learned the unwritten credo—don't feel, don't think, and don't trust. What once was survival for the child became a way of life for the adult. "I lived in constant terror," recalls a 34-year-old incest survivor whose parents were alcoholics. "One time, on the way home from a restaurant, my father was speeding recklessly, shouting, 'I've met my Maker, and I don't care who I take with me!'"

But the scope of the movement has grown enormously. It now includes a cadre of parent-bashing Adult Children eager to tell their parents, It's your fault we love too much or not at all and *never* the right person; that we don't trust ourselves or anyone else; that we are "afflicted and addicted," as a recent *Newsweek* cover story declared; that we are divorced, drunk, desperate and—pardon the jargon—"dysfunctional." These Adult Children are looking for the Answer—and many think their parents are *it*.

If you believe some experts, 90% of us are suffering from the ravages of childhood. And salvation, say the gurus who lead these flocks of Adult Children, lies in the embrace of the recovery movement. You must face the reality of your chaotic childhood and reclaim your life by looking at the pain you've never been allowed to talk about, much less feel.

But therapists are concerned. "The whole new 'wounded child' mythology has given people a language for talking about pain, grieving over it," notes family therapist Jo-Ann Krestan, coauthor of *Too Good For Her Own Good*. "But there's really no such thing as an 'Adult Child.' That's a description of where you came from, not a diagnosis of who you are today."

Certainly, the Adult Child movement will help many people exorcise childhood demons of shame and isolation. It will also help them understand that what happened to them as children wasn't their fault and that as adults they need no longer be victims. They don't have to stay stuck in the problem—they can *do* something.

But as the media and the fluorescent self-help movement continue to encourage Adult Children to stand up and be counted, many experts now ask: Will those same people get stuck in the solution? In therapy, Barbara dumps her sorrows on her mother; other Adult Children assemble to flesh out forgotten images from painful childhoods. But there may be little talk of forgiveness, much about blame, and, sometimes, fantasies of revenge. Will chronic angst simply be transmuted to chronic anger! And if parent bashing *is* the prescription, what are the long-term effects of that "medicine" on succeeding generations? How will the children of these Adult Children view *their* parents?

WHY NOW?

Parent bashing isn't new. Freud sparked the idea around the turn of the century. Convinced that adult problems were reflections of childhood conflicts, Freud unwittingly laid the groundwork upon which modern-day pop-psychology empires have been built, explains psychologist Ronald Taffel, director of family and couples treatment at the Institute for Contemporary Psychotherapy in New York City. In many of the therapies popularized since the '50s—analysis, the child guidance movement, encounter groups—"parents have always been deemed at fault, especially mothers," says Taffel.

Many therapists agree that parent bashing is often a euphemism for mother bashing. Most post-Freudian therapists—reflecting society in general—promoted the basic assumption that mothers, as the family "gatekeepers," were somehow responsible for how children turned out. If the kids had problems, Mother was either too involved or not enough; if Dad was depressed, it was because Mom was emasculating him. If fathers have been blamed for anything, it's that they haven't been there. Even in cases of incest, the mother has often been held responsible—for not stopping it.

In her recent book, *Don't Blame Mother*, psychologist Paula Caplan reports that on reviewing 125 articles published between 1970 and 1982, mothers were blamed for 72 different kinds of problems in their offspring, ranging from bedwetting and learning problems to schizophrenia.

No segment of our population has been more affected by the prevailing winds of psychotherapy than the children raised by these mothers—the 76 million baby boomers, now 26 to 44 years old. "Children of Dr. Spock," they grew up in a permissive, child-oriented era when it was okay to be rebellious, even to tell parents what was wrong with them. Not only was it no longer a stigma to be "in therapy," the implication was that somehow they could perfect themselves.

To be sure, the boomers have tried just about everything: est and self-actualization, aerobics and health foods, Eastern philosophies and Western materialism, therapy and more therapy—but nothing has "worked." As Taffel observes, "Many of them have been through it all. And guess what? The problems are still there. They can't make their marriages work, their kids are troubled and their own personalities haven't changed that much.

The mere fact that adults are labeling themselves "children" implies that there's some resistance to actually growing up and facing adult responsibilities. Landon Jones, the journalist whose *Great Expectations* tracked these whiz kids through 1980, also suspects it's in keeping with the baby boom mentality. "All of their life stages have been prolonged—their childhood and adolescence—and they stayed in college and were single longer," says Jones. "Now they're approaching middle age, when one of the tasks is to come to terms with your parents. But they're not ready to accept who they really are."

In the '80s, disco glitter began to lose its charm; midlife caught up with the boomers and suddenly they found themselves running out of time and bottoming out on sex and substances, the magical elixirs that had once worked so well. Escalating divorce rates, child abuse, wife battering, drug overdoses and the specter of AIDS have cast a pall upon the boomers' adolescent dreams—that promise of infinite happiness and eternal prosperity.

The boomers' parents had lived through the Depression, witnessed the devastation of World War II and learned to live with it all. In contrast, the children of the Me Generation had the time and money to indulge themselves in the pursuit of perfection. When their dreams began to shatter, say the experts, the boomers began to point a finger at their parents. After all, it must be *someone's* fault.

"When you look at the 'recovery movement,' you see a mass audience turning childhood into an illness you recover from," says Taffel. "They even have networks and support systems to keep it going. These obviously serve a useful purpose—but only if parent bashing doesn't become an end in itself."

If the fitness movement belonged to the '80s, then "recovery" may well be the hallmark of the '90s. An influx of alcoholic and addicted boomers caused Alcoholics Anonymous to double its membership between 1977 and 1987. Al-Anon, AA's companion program, now has over 19,000 groups nationwide; and scores of me-too groups, like Cocaine Anonymous and Shopaholics, have been created to accommodate boomers who didn't drink but found other ways to soothe inner discomfort. But none responded to the grassroots call for self-help in greater numbers than the unhappy adults who called themselves Adult Children.

Although ACOA's original focus was on alcohol, the Adult Child movement now reaches out to all kinds of suffering adults. ACOA's growth has been staggering—at last count, from 14 Al-Anon-affiliated ACOA groups in 1981 to over 4,000 meetings nationwide, many of them independent of Al-Anon.

Predictably, big business, always monitoring the pulse of the baby boom generation, has also jumped on—and propelled—the Adult Child bandwagon. Between 1978 and 1984, the number of private residential treatment centers in the country increased 350%, and case loads quadru-pled. Thanks to the marketing genius of the recovery industry, these rehabs, with their promises of "renewal" and "hope," are becoming the spas of the '90s.

And there's no shortage of reading material. A plethora of self-help books describes various "types" of Adult Children and offers a laundry list of characteristics, which are also read aloud at many meetings. But individuals are not so easily quantified.

"I had a man call me and say, 'I'm an Adult Child, and Dr. So-and-So said I'm one of the worst cases he's ever seen.' I cracked up," recalls Marianne Walters, director of The Family Therapy Practice Center in Washington, DC. "I told him I'd see him, but as an Adult Person. I'm concerned about these typologies—not that they don't resonate with some truth. But if you're so self-absorbed and only understand yourself this way, you don't take as much responsibility for your own behavior, for others, or for the world you live in."

What's more, Adult Children expect others to understand "where they're coming from." Howard, a recovering alcoholic familiar with many 12-step recovery programs, observes, "It used to be people took time getting to know one another. Nowadays, you go out on a date and within the first few minutes she tells you her father is an alcoholic, her mother committed suicide, a cousin abused her sexually, and she's bulimic—so you'd better watch her boundaries. Everyone talks in terms of 'fear of intimacy.' Meanwhile, the real message comes through: 'I'm damaged goods—so hands off.' "

STUCK IN BLAME

Many therapists encourage clients to attend programs like AA and Al-Anon as an important adjunct to treatment and a safe place to share feelings. After all, the 12-step structure calls for admitting you're powerless over the problem—whether due to your own behavior or someone else's—and then, with group support, looking honestly at *your own* contribution.

But some Adult Child meetings, which tend to be "younger" than the more established 12-step programs, may encourage just the opposite: blame. There isn't as much guidance from seasoned veterans who've worked through their anger, observes New York City, therapist Nancy Napier, author of *Recreating Your Self.* "So you've got a bunch of people in pain, and the pain just builds up."

Also, AA and Al-Anon have always urged members to keep the focus on themselves. But at ACOA meetings, parents and other caregivers are fair game.

"I went to ACOA meetings for about a year—but week after week people just dumped." Karen, whose mother was alcoholic, is referring to the litany of complaints common to many of these meetings. One of her resentments was that her parents had refused to send her to college: "I carried that around for years." Her brothers were sent to college, her parents went to Europe, but "poor" Karen had to go to a local junior college. "I'd share it at meetings, but I'd leave feeling worse," she says.

Some meetings were also downright frightening, says Karen. She recalls the time an angry woman screamed about her father and threw a chair across the room. "It scared the s—t out of me. I couldn't take it anymore."

"In ACOA groups, people definitely have to get through the anger and denial," says Michael Elkin, a family therapist at a school for disturbed adolescents in Stockbridge, MA. "But that's only the first step in the process—it's where people have to start. Hopefully, they'll move past the blame. However, some people get stuck—they misuse the program."

Family therapist Jo-Ann Krestan also sees some people using "recovery" in much the same way they used drugs or other substances—to avoid their real feelings. "They think if they could only do recovery 'right,' they won't have to feel uncomfortable," she points out. "But if you really begin to look at your own choices, at who you are, it's going to be uncomfortable."

Karen decided to go through the pain. A counselor at an ACOA rehab she attended encouraged her to write letters to each of her parents, telling them everything she was angry about. "When I had to read them aloud and talk about my part, I realized I always blamed *them* when I failed."

Karen, a recovering alcoholic, now takes full responsibility for her choices as an adult. "Sure, there was a lot of anger over my mother's drinking, and for years I blamed my own drinking on

her. It made it easier for me. She did inappropriate things to me as a child, such as making me her confidante and telling me about her sex life, but I was never physically abused. There is no fault, no blame. Millions of people grow up in the same kind of household I did, and they don't all drink. It was easier to blame than to take responsibility for my own lifestyle."

Equally important, Karen now also understands the context of her own mother's life. "This was the early '50s; my father traveled, my mother was young and knew nothing about having a child. She was lonely. There were no support groups then."

CONFRONTING "TOXIC PARENTS"

Had Karen read California therapist Susan Forward's *Toxic Parents*, she might have gained no such insight. Nor would she have been interested in hearing a basic truth about many supposedly "abusive" parents: Most never intended to hurt their children.

Even Dr. Alice Miller, the Swiss psychoanalyst who unwittingly inspired much of the popular focus on the "inner child," stressed that the issue is not culpability. In *Prisoners of Childhood* (later changed to *The Drama of the Gifted Child*), Miller wrote: "Many parents, even with the best intentions, cannot always understand their child, since they, too, have been stamped by their experience with their own parents and have grown up in a different generation."

Therapist Marilyn R. Frankfurt, of the Ackerman Institute for Family Therapy in New York City, agrees that parental attitudes of the earlier, child-centered *Not-Me* Generation are totally foreign to today's Me Generation. "Those earlier mothers," she says, "were told they had to shape their children and make them conform to cultural expectations. But often they had no emotional attention from their own parents. Despite this, they didn't complain. Now they're being held responsible for how their children feel.

"We're imposing ideas on the past generation that don't apply," says Frankfurt. "These Adult Children act as if their parents knew all of this and chose not to act."

But Dr. Forward offers no such compassion in *Toxic Parents*. Relentlessly presenting case after case of manipulative, selfish parents, she tells readers it's not their fault. That's fine, but as Frankfurt points out, "Forward also implies, 'Someone's got to be responsible.' The author even goes so far as to warn readers not to be fooled by comments like, 'We did the best we could,' or, 'You'll never understand what I was going through.' She says that's the parents' problem."

Forward declined several requests to be interviewed for this article, but it's clear she has tapped into a ripe market. Drawing its examples from the extremes—people who were terribly abused—the book seems to appeal to anyone along the continuum of an "unhappy childhood." Replete with check lists to help the reader take "your psychological pulse" and "uncover your self-constricting beliefs, feelings and behaviors," *Toxic Parents* also includes a phone number "for persons interested in her methods."

Offering what appears to be a new twist in exploiting the Adult Child craze—dial-a-therapist—Forward (or an associate) charges $40 for a 25-minute phone consultation or $80 for 50 minutes. First you send in a check, along with the "intake fact sheet" and "confidential background information form," which incorporates a smorgasbord of 60 "problem areas." Assuming your check has cleared, a counselor will call back to set up an appointment.

Though Krestan doesn't support the idea of blaming parents, she does agree with Forward on one point: "Adult Children need to acknowledge what's theirs and what belongs to their parents—and get through the grieving process. Forward's book will certainly help validate those negative shameful experiences that people have had." Krestan adds, however, "You have to get good and God-damned angry, but that doesn't constitute healing. It's not helpful to confront and cut off."

Janet Woititz, author of the 1983 landmark work *Adult Children of Alcoholics* and an unofficial "grandmother" of the Adult Child movement, points out that an understanding of our childhood "gives us insight into who we are and what gets in the way of our achieving healthy relationships in adulthood—but that's all. If we get stuck in blame, it develops a smoke screen so that we don't have to make changes ourselves.

"Books can just offer awareness," she stresses. "Looking at our parents is step one.

Then we have to look at ourselves and what we're doing to the next generation."

BREAKING THE CYCLE

Without doubt, there are abusive parents who willfully brutalize their children, but most are themselves victims. As Michael Elkin puts it, "Toxic parents have toxic kids who become toxic parents and so on. In the end, forgiveness is the only place peace comes from. That doesn't mean overlooking the pain and harm—it means understanding that you have emerged from it."

Psychologist Augustus Napier, director of the Family Workshop in Atlanta and author of *The Fragile Bond*, about intimacy in marriage, is also opposed to "making parents the villains." People have a right to their anger, he stresses, but in some cases, there's a kind of excuse-making going on for the purpose of gaining sympathy. "I help patients express their feelings about the past without having them actually take it out on the parent. My work honors both generations."

Napier tells of a professional in his 30s who was beginning to be abusive to his own son. First, Napier helped the young man look at the past two generations of his family: His abusive father also had been abused by his father (the patient's grandfather), a European immigrant who left home at 11 to become a merchant seaman and was beaten regularly by his shipmates. "There were extremes of abuse, neglect and inhuman treatment in this family—and those forces were transmitted across the generations. But there were no 'villains.'"

"Life is basically unfair. Our families are dealt to us like a deck of cards. So it's to the person's advantage to come to terms with the hand you were given," says Betty Carter, director of the Family Institute of Westchester, NY. "It's understandable that the person is furious about whatever happened—and I empathize and try to get him or her to ventilate the feelings. But anger and blame poison them." Forgiveness is important, adds Carter. "I don't mean an intellectual gloss-over; I mean a forgiveness of the heart that comes out of a very long journey."

Marianne Walters concurs: It comes down to "understanding your parents' lives and then negotiating a new kind of relationship—adult to adult."

As the process of examining the past unfolds, Adult Children begin to see how the forgotten fears and pain of childhood have seeped into their adult lives. A woman whose anxiety-ridden mother forced her to wait up at night until her drunken father came home can now see one reason she's turned into a chronic worrywart. Sometimes, a parent's actions are misinterpreted. Paula Caplan remembers one woman who insisted her mother "never trusted me, never let me out of sight." It turned out that the mother, at age 13, had been molested in an outhouse and as a parent wanted to protect her own child from similar abuse.

"If you continue to blame your parents, you'll feel all right for a while, but it's no way to live. You then use blame to resolve other problems," Taffel observes. When many of his clients get into relationships, he says, they try to solve problems by blaming or disengaging altogether. "We need to try to see what our parents were up against," he suggests. His reason is simple: "Until you can see your parents as human beings you can't see yourself as a human being."

"Blaming is a nonproductive perspective that makes future generations suffer," agrees Dr. Harriet Lerner, author of *The Dance of Intimacy*. "When you have your own kids, you pass it on."

There's also the other side of the equation. Dr. E. Joan Emery, a New York City psychotherapist, reminds us: "The way our parents treated us is the way we will treat our aging parents. We can stop passing the buck if we finally look at the transgenerational picture. And from one generation to the next we can heal some of the wounds."

A MORE FORGIVING FUTURE

The baby boomers are now referred to as the Sandwich Generation—caught between the needs of their children and the needs of their aging parents. Baby boom chronicler Landon Jones suggests parent bashing may be just an evolutionary step toward the Me Generation's finally accepting the burden of middle age. Indeed, there are signs the Adult Child movement is in transition.

On *thirtysomething*, the popular TV series designed to depict real-life dramas, the theme of blaming parents crops up frequently. Marshall Herskovitz, the show's 37-year-old executive producer, points out that the scenarios have evolved from portraying parents very negatively, to a more even-handed, forgiving view of the older generation.

In one early show aired in 1987, "The Parents Are Coming, The Parents Are Coming," Hope, who had never gotten along with her mother, is relentless in refusing to see the older woman as anything but judgmental and intrusive. "Letters poured in from baby boomers, who, without exception, were relieved to see that other people had the same problems with their parents," says Herskovitz. "Parents, on the other hand, wrote about how distressed they were to see parents shown in such an unfavorable light."

In contrast, on a show two years later, Gary, whose father is now dead, blames his mother for taking his father's side. The mother, as well as Gary's live-in girlfriend, tells him it's time to grow up. Herskovitz sees a trend: "Since I was in college people have been blaming their parents. But I see a movement toward actively dealing with these issues. I think it's extremely positive—we're moving from blaming our parents to forgiving them."

If, in fact, "Life imitates art," he may be right. There are other heartening signs as well. Anthony Jones, founder of the National Association of Adult Children of Dysfunctional Families, contends, "People first have to go through periods where they want to throw rocks, but that should be short-lived. After that we need to move away from shame and blame and make people aware of how certain types of family systems pass abuse on as if it's a virus."

The recent publication—and instant popularity—of Dwight Lee Wolter's newest book, *Forgiving Our Parents*, also mirrors a hopeful trend. Wolter, 39, in recovery as an Adult Child for the past five years, said he couldn't have written the book earlier. "But I finally walked around angry at my parents long enough.

"I'm not talking about the fact that my daddy wouldn't let me go to Harvard. Mine is an open-and-shut case of child abuse," says Wolter, referring to an anecdote in his first book: One day when he forgot to walk his dog, to teach young Dwight a lesson, his father shot the dog. "The question no longer is: 'Who is to blame?' or 'How could they do such things?'" Wolter writes. "The question is: 'Who has been hurt and how can we get [him] back on track?'"

And as Adult Children mature, moving from anger and blame toward forgiveness and acceptance, they might also teach society a valuable lesson about being human. In Wolter's words, "As we begin to forgive our parents, we begin to forgive ourselves. And we begin to forgive the world for not being perfect either."

To Apply This Reading to Yourself

1. *What have you needed to forgive your parents for? Have you forgiven them? Why or why not? What have been the effects of this forgiveness or lack of forgiveness?*
2. *What have your parents needed to forgive you for? Have they forgiven you? Why or why not? What have been the effects of this forgiveness or lack of forgiveness?*
3. *Write an unsent letter to your parents explaining what it was like having parents like them.*
4. *Become your parents for a little while, look at yourself through their eyes, and write a letter from them to you explaining what it was like having a child like you.*
5. *Trace the evolution of your relationship and attitudes toward your parents, beginning with your earliest recollection and continuing to the present.*
6. *Make a list of all the things concerning your relationship with your parents that you remember with pleasure.*
7. *Make a list of all the things concerning your relationship with your parents that it hurts to remember.*
8. *"Tied to the past" "Trapped in childhood" "Stuck in blame" Have any of these applied to you? Do any apply now? If so, discuss this aspect of yourself and your life.*

My Parents Are My Friends

Joyce Maynard

On the bus to the airport, just after leaving my parents for a summer away from home, something quite sad happened, and I haven't been able to get it out of my head. The bus stopped in some small town, and a girl about my age got on—clearly, like me, going away for the summer. Her mother was at the bus stop with her—a woman about my mother's age but very tired-looking with her hair tied back and an apron on. The mother helped the girl with her luggage—a couple of shopping bags, cardboard boxes tied with string and a very fancy overnight case—then hugged her goodbye and the girl stood on the steps of the bus with her arms at her sides. Then she took her seat by a window, and the mother moved so that she was standing right next to the window, with just glass between them. She was crying by this time, but trying to smile, and waving. And the girl sat stiff in her seat, looking straight ahead. Finally the bus pulled out, and the mother turned around and left. She was wearing that furry kind of bedroom slippers.

First I just felt so angry at the girl I wanted to shake her, and terribly, terribly sorry for the mother. I tried to imagine what the mother could have done to deserve that, and what the daughter felt like, and how that girl would be with her own kids—which brought me to parents and children generally, and what it was that mine did that worked so well. I missed them, but not in an unhealthy, dependent way; I just like being at home—enough, I think, so that it was important for me to get away last summer, as I did. I'm happy away from home, and not homesick, just as I know they're happy when I'm there and happy when I'm not, and their lives don't begin and end with the children (which, when one's children are 18 and 22, is a pretty dangerous place to have them begin and end).

We've got a pretty good thing going, our family. But we are hardly typical. What worked for us can't be taken as general rules. So—not presuming to suggest that this is how things should be done, but just that this is how we did things—here is a portrait of one good and loving parent–child relationship: my parents' and my own.

First, though, some kind of explanation, because there's a danger that I'll come out of this sounding like an apple polisher—the kind I always hated when I was little. (Pollyanna, I suspected, was too dull to get in trouble. As for Shirley Temple at her sunniest—well, I always rooted for Jane Withers.) I feel dangerously close to becoming Pollyannified myself now. At an age when I should be rebelling, I'm without a cause. I think that's because my parents' standards are so reasonable; it's hard to protest principles that make sense, principles based not on tradition or prejudice or an arbitrary laying down of laws for their own sake. There is a wholeness to our way of life: What we admire in human conduct is of a piece with what we admire in poems and flower gardens. In other words, what my parents passed on to us is not a bunch of unrelated fragments but a coherent set of values, all of which speak for reason, order, symmetry. Our lives are filled with family rituals, family phrases, family tastes.

Family. We didn't have religion, we didn't have a large circle of friends close by or a cozy network of relations. But we had a family style, a distinctive way of doing things. When my sister married, the first thing she asked for was a large schefflera tree. In our family *we have scheffleras.*[1] In our family we dislike coloring books and painting by numbers; we admire Mexican crafts, we love Mozart operas and shortbread cookies . . . . I could fill in all the blanks. Some kids don't even know what, if anything, their family represents.

We could be called opinionated. Certainly we are a hypercritical family—we don't lavish superlatives on things and places and people. I was raised to look closely, not to accept easily. My father and I took long walks together, examining mushrooms and leaves, stopping in mid-

---

1. In case your family didn't have scheffleras (mine had rubber plants) and you don't have an unabridged dictionary handy, scheffleras are shrubby tropical plants with showy foliage.—The Editor

sentence and midstep sometimes to catch a bird-call. We went to museums together and talked about paintings, or sat side by side on the floor listening to music he conducted with a pencil in the air. My mother's training came evenings, after dinner, when she sat on the living-room couch marking papers and I sat next to her, reading her corrections. Not just marked—in commas and circled misspellings, but paragraph-long notes on how a story might be improved. We talked about the scripts of TV commercials and the designs of cereal boxes and the arrangements of people's flower beds—the opinions never let up. I couldn't suspend judgment even when I wanted to; it was as if I went through life with X-ray glasses on, seeing through not just the things I wanted to see through but the things I'd just as soon have believed in, too. I longed to wallow in a sentimental movie with my friends, to join them in the delicious Friday night tears that followed every movie we'd see—but I'd always end up munching popcorn while they wept, and commenting to myself on the stiffness of an actor's speech or the corniness of the sound track.

I was old before my time, a junior sophisticate who could analyze the appeal of Barbi dolls compared to baby dolls long before I stopped playing with either. My sister and I weren't prodigies by any means; we were just raised in a household whose chief sport was conversation. While other families played basketball, we volleyed words and ideas. My parents never said "Don't talk back" (though rudeness was out), because we learned from argument. From Perry Mason and from my father, I learned how to find a loophole in a thought; from my mother, I learned how to present my case persuasively.

The criticism we applied to everything we encountered we applied to ourselves as well. Never "You are bad," but "You could do better." I like to see a job done really well, and if that means ripping out a seam and starting over, or spending all day in the library doing research for a term paper, I'll do it. My parents never let me feel satisfied with an encyclopedia-copied oral report or a hem held up with safety pins. My parents' greatest compliment to us was their high expectations. Not everything we did was wonderful to them just because we did it. They never implied that we were the most wonderful children in the whole world, but they certainly made us feel unique. So why would we want to copy other people instead of showing what *we* saw and felt?

My father taught me to appreciate the morning. Sometimes, when I've stayed up till three A.M. and the alarm inside my head, conditioned by my father's predawn rising, wakes me at seven, I wish ours had been the kind of household where everybody slept till ten and lounged in pajamas all afternoon. My father wouldn't have kept us from sleeping in, of course, but it would have saddened him. We would have missed the birds in full song and the angle of the sun before it's high and scorching and the feel of grass when it's still damp. Getting up early may sound like an unimportant thing, but it's central to everything my family cares about. Discipline, energy, activity, distaste for wastefulness, love of sunshine, and a pretty good balance, I think, between order and freedom. There might be piles of clothes on the chairs in my bedroom sometimes—four outfits tried on and discarded—but I always felt compelled to make my bed. We had something of the same balance in relation to meals. Breakfast, comfortable and free: bathrobes, Ann Landers, *TV Guide,* but dinner at a set time (*always* at six), sit-down, really quite formal, with no reading at the table and considerable thought to the way things looked.

I have friends whose families never eat a meal together. They drift in and out of the kitchen from five to seven, cooking hot dogs and munching potato chips standing up, or sitting down in front of the TV with a bowl of salad, gulped down in the space of a commercial. I've never been much of an eater myself (though my mother is a fine, creative cook), but meals have always meant a lot to me. Even if all I'm eating is an apple, I want to eat it at the table with my family, with places set and the good silver laid out. (Why should guests get silverware while children eat with stainless steel?)

And we never eat in silence, we never need to make polite conversation. Sometimes my mother will tell about a person she met on the street—what he wore, how he walked; she doesn't simply give the facts, she tells a story. My father is a dreamier observer who will tell us that he heard something interesting today, but forgot it, or that someone we know just gave birth to triplets, but he can't remember her name. He doesn't have the knack for minute detail my mother has but—like her—he understands the way people operate, why they do things. Our dinner conversation makes the food taste better. My parents are never boring.

We serve wine with dinner. We all know it's just about the cheapest kind you can buy, but my mother keeps it in a vintage bottle from years back and serves it in chilled crystal, not just for grown-ups. I've always preferred milk, but being offered wine (and having the luxury of refusing it) made me feel trusted. It has to do with the humiliation of childhood and the dignity that every child deserves to feel. (My mother gave us wine because it was part of a pleasant ritual, not to experience drunkenness.)

I remember my first high-school drinking parties—the line outside the bathroom of people looking sick and the limp bodies sprawled in heaps along the floor. For them liquor was *booze*, gulped down in closets and bathrooms at school or late at night in cars. Scotch tasted good because it was forbidden. It never was forbidden to me—and to me, it never tasted very good.

I cannot think of a single rule my parents ever told us to obey. What they gave us were principles—a concern for property, a desire to please them. Somehow, we just *knew*. I wouldn't have wanted to toss my mother's white linen sofa cushions on the floor (and I still remember how it pained me when a friend did once) because I was proud of our house and aware (as I told my friend, in what must have seemed like a hopelessly goody-goody tone) that my mother spent a lot of time making those pillows. Good behavior comes down to a good imagination—being able to see how things will look to another person, being able to tell if something you do will hurt him, being able to predict the consequences. Not that empty phrase, "Put yourself in someone else's shoes," but my favorite childhood game—fun, not Sunday school morality: putting myself in someone else's head.

In our town, the usual punishment for high-school kids is grounding—keeping the villain at home for a few weeks and sometimes even locking him in his room. That accomplishes little except to make him more careful not to get caught next time. What it does is to humiliate. There's no dignity in being locked up or sent to bed at 6:30 or told: "You're my child. As long as you live in my house, you'll do as I say." I've never felt as though I were my parents' possession, and no child should. A child who does will realize that the only way to hurt his parents (and that's what he'll want) is to hurt himself, to break their favorite toy.

I've never felt that my fate was totally out of my hands, that no matter what I did, I could change nothing. (Parents say that so often: "I don't care what you say, I'm not changing my mind.") I always had a fairly early bedtime, but a flexible one. (Households with no bedtimes, where weary children are allowed to drag around until they finally collapse, have always saddened me. They're hard on the parents and, most of all, hard on the kids.) If I really wanted to stay up late to finish a book or watch TV, I could. I made sure I'd get that permission by not asking for it too often.

There's a distinction that has to be made between treating children with the respect adults get and treating children like adults. My parents talked to us in a grown-up way, never baby talk. They let us see fairly grown-up books and movies (censorship—like locks on the liquor cabinet—only make the forbidden thing seem more exciting), and they exposed us to grown-up ideas. But they never made the mistake of turning us into little adults—we were never dragged out to join their cocktail parties or freed from the disciplines (not rules, but structures) of our lives. What my parents did was, quite simply, to treat us as politely as they'd treat an adult. I'm always embarrassed for my friends when their parents scold them in front of me, a guest. It's humiliating to them and, most of all, it's rude. My parents allowed us the dignity that so many children lose when their parents force them to wear clothes they dislike or eat foods they hate. Parents who do that, robbing their children of the adult right to choose, aren't just treating their children like children, they're treating them like babies. A child who announces that he doesn't like green sweaters or fried chicken is asserting himself for the first time. How can he ever have opinions on books and people and politics if he doesn't first have opinions on spinach?

I think it was my parents own good manners in their relationship with me that have given me the good manners I now have in relation to other people. Simple good manners, especially among people of my generation, are so rare. Mine come quite naturally (I am the kind that everybody's grandmother loves) not because my mother ever drilled me on please and thank you, but because, even when she was angry, she was never impolite.

I remember a first-grade friend of mine who didn't know what her parents' first names were. In fact, she didn't know her parents *had* first names. What seems sad is that my friend never really thought of her parents as human beings. Except when they got mad at her, they never showed their feelings, never admitted their weaknesses, as though saying, "I'm sorry" or "I'm sad" would have made them harder to respect.

My parents never presented themselves to me as perfect and infallible, so I never had that awful moment so many children face when they suddenly discover their parents can be wrong—that Superman is really just Clark Kent. The stories they told about their own childhoods weren't simply illustrations of how good they'd been, how hard the times were, and how grateful my sister and I should feel for having shoes with soles on them and schoolrooms with radiators; they were stories about the times my father played hooky and the day my mother cut off the lace from my grandmother's wedding gown.

I knew what my father's job was (so many children know a meaningless title and nothing else). I knew not only that my father was an English professor, but what his office looked like and what books he taught from, and sometimes I'd visit his class. Whenever my mother wrote a magazine article we'd all gather in the living room to hear her read the first draft and discuss the changes she should make. And even when I was very young, she consulted me ("What kinds of games do they play at recess?" "What's the name of a TV show with policemen in it?"). My parents never bought a piece of furniture that any one of us disliked. We didn't command the household, my sister and I, but we had a say in what went on. How can you have a comfortable relationship between parents and children if all the knowledge is on one side? They knew about us; it was only fair that we should know about them.

My father is a liberated man. He doesn't boss our household, nor is he bossed. My parents have no formal contract of dividing up the chores because they really don't need one—my father helps before my mother needs to ask him. Until I left home and encountered men making jokes about "never trusting a woman," and men who laughed at women drivers, I never understood what male chauvinism meant. It was a shock, discovering that not all men were like my father. (Most men with two daughters and no son would be disappointed.) But being insulated in that one area gave me something terribly valuable: complete confidence in myself. I never wished I were a boy or felt that, since I wasn't one, I would have any fewer options in my life.

Long before "recycling" was made an everyday word, we were doing it. A burned-out flashcube was a dollhouse aquarium; an old umbrella frame, trimmed and stuck on a base, became a comically ugly kitchen Christmas tree. My mother and I can't walk down the street on trash-collection day without finding some discarded treasure to bring home. We go to rummage sales for bargain dresses that we transform into evening gowns; we save popsicle sticks and plastic straws and aspirin bottles. We do not like to waste.

My mother's junk collecting has given me a well-trained eye that can look at a cork or a thimble and see the half dozen other things they might become. Her frugality is sometimes extreme, but it has taught me to take no amount of money lightly. I don't ever shop for the simple pleasure of spending money. My pleasure comes from saving it, and from getting something just as nice with a pot of batik dye and fabric or with a needle and thread.

Some people have nightmares about car accidents and forests full of wild animals and escaped convicts and falling from the top of a high building. My recurring nightmare is that our house burns down. I wake up, uncertain for a moment whether it happened or not, and terribly upset, not just because a house is worth a lot of money, and losing it means great expense, but because our house is so much a part of our family, so full of objects we're attached to. We never had a lot of money, but we always lived in style. Every piece of furniture we put in the house, every pillow, every bowl, is something we really care about. It's a house you can feel comfortable in—no slipcovers—but not a tumble-down house. Something happens to a family, I think, when they live in too much decorator-perfection or too much untidiness. There may be dust under the rug at our house, but the surfaces are neat, and when they begin to get messy and disorganized, so do I.

I think of one fine, earnest, committed family whose dining-room table is always cluttered with posters for the latest grape boycott or political campaign. The walls are covered with peace signs and taped-on newspaper clippings no one ever bothered to take down. Our kind of insulated comfort—our "gracious living"—would probably seem irresponsible to them. My feeling is that not until you make a reassuring, comfortable base for security can you go beyond and deal with the discomforts of the outside world. My mother never needed to put a slipcover on the sofa or tell us not to bounce or we'd break the springs—we just knew. Our house is filled with plants and paintings and Mexican pottery and comfortable big pillows and straw baskets full of fruit, and plenty of light. To lose it (and this is why the nightmare comes) would be to lose not just my roof but my foundation.

My parents made some bad mistakes, of course. Their way of doing things was so strong and definite that sometimes it was hard to keep in mind that other ways existed—just because *we* didn't like gladiolas and store-bought birthday cards and Jell-O; just because *we* poured our milk in the cereal bowl before adding the cereal—that didn't mean that plenty of good people didn't have a perfect right to like things done their way. *We:* I use that word too much. My family is too close, perhaps, too much of a club; the delineations—*us* and *them*—are too clear. The critical faculties my parents gave me have made me more demanding than I should be, given me standards that the real, flawed world can't live up to. There are things my parents did and shouldn't have done, and things they should have done and didn't. There was at times a feeling that our house was a factory of the arts, with every moment spent in what the experts call "creative play"—constant painting and writing and acting and dancing. My parents never really pushed, but they raised me to push myself too hard, to be impatient with myself when I wasn't doing something worthwhile.

I wish I'd been sent to church when I was little (if only to have had a religion to rebel against later; as is, I have nothing, plus an ignorance of the Bible that catches me up every time I read a book, almost, or go to a museum). The image of my mother playing any outdoor game besides croquet is impossible to picture. My father was more athletic, but never a player of baseball or a skier and, as a result, neither was I. I grew up dreading gym periods at school, spending more energy thinking up excuses than I would have spent out on the playing field, where teammates knew enough to keep the ball away from me. Only recently have I learned that I'm not so uncoordinated after all, but I'm years behind now, and filled with silly, irrational fears (Will I hit my head? Will I fall? Will it hurt?) that I'm only beginning to overcome.

But I can't imagine feeling bitter toward my parents, as the girl on the bus to the airport with me must have felt—not even to have blinked while her mother waved good-bye. I have friends who are embarrassed to be seen with their parents. Very occasionally I've been tempted to pretend I didn't know mine, too (when my frugal mother returns a single bruised banana to the supermarket; when my father swims with me—in a bathing cap). Mostly I'm proud of them, and sure enough of myself not to worry about what people will think. I look at their faults and their strangeness with amusement and affection—not as odd, but as unique. I could no more hide my family and my upbringing than a friend of mine who's black could hide her blackness. And I want not just to recognize my family—to hold my father's hand when we cross the street and to sit with my mother at the movies—but to tell about it, too, because I can't help boasting—I've come out pretty happy. Saturday mornings, when I'm home, I like to go grocery shopping with my father. He's supposed to carry the shopping list my mother made up, but usually he loses it, so we drift through the aisles exclaiming on the price of lettuce, examining avocados and stocking up on boysenberry yogurt. I gave up drinking whole milk four years ago and haven't touched peanut-butter sandwiches since the days when I carried a lunch box, but he still asks me, every Saturday, "Do you need any milk? How are we fixed for peanut butter?" We look at the magazines together, he picks up some new brand of vitamins he thinks I need. We finish with soup, my father pacing in front of the Campbell's wall muttering, "What fine thing shall I have for lunch today?" and arriving, each time, at the chicken noodle as if it were a new discovery. We drive home at 20 miles an hour as high-school kids, friends of mine, whiz past, honking. Sometimes I'm impatient, but my father hardly notices. He steers the car like a Viking—his back straight, both hands tight on the wheel—slowing down to ten when he spots an interesting bird. Halfway home he'll remember—*mushrooms*, the one thing my mother specially asked for, and we'll turn back. They know us well at the checkout counter.

My mother and I cook together, side by side, my gestures just like hers, only less practiced. I've learned to scoop an egg out with my thumb to get every drop of the white, and then to beat it in the center of the bowl with the dough, already mixed, forming a well around my pool of frothy liquid. We rake leaves—she makes the piles, I jump in them—and we shop, not at big department stores (our town doesn't have any) but at funny, junky little shops we descend upon like hunters in search of treasure. Sometimes we go to an auction and come back with a boxful of handmade lace scraps whose possibilities—cuffs, collars, pockets, bodices—nobody else noticed, or an ancient mimeograph machine neither of us has any use for.

We don't spend all our time together. All three of us (and my older sister, who's married now) lead fairly independent lives. Saying that we love each other doesn't tell all that much— the most hostile children and the most frustrated parents can feel love. More than that, my parents are my friends.

To Apply This Reading to Yourself

1. *Maynard writes her family had a family style, "a distinctive way of doing things." Discuss your family's style or the things about it that are or were distinctive.*
2. *Maynard writes her family had principles that the children "just knew" but not a single rule they were told to obey. Discuss the presence or absence of rules in your family and its effect on you.*
3. *Eating meals together with some formality, graciousness, and conversation was an important ritual in the Maynard family. Compare this with your own family's eating patterns.*
4. *Maynard writes, "What my parents did was, quite simply, to treat us as politely as they'd treat an adult." Compare this with the treatment accorded children in your own family, and note the effect of this treatment on you.*
5. *Maynard writes that her house was very much a part of her family and very important to her. Discuss what your childhood home (or homes) means (or meant) to you.*
6. *Maynard notes some of her parents' mistakes and shortcomings that had an unfortunate effect on her. Discuss your parents' mistakes and shortcomings and their effect on you.*
7. *Maynard writes she is mostly proud of her parents although very occasionally she's tempted to pretend she doesn't know them. Discuss your feelings of pride and shame or embarrassment concerning your own parents.*
8. *Maynard writes that her parents are her friends. Are your parents your friends? Why or why not?*

Good Families—By Chance and By Choice

Jane Howard

Call it a clan, call it a network, call it a tribe, call it a family. Whatever you call it, whoever you are, you need one. You need one because you are human. You didn't come from nowhere. Before you, around you, and presumably after you, too, there are others. Some of these others—in my view around nine—must matter. They must matter a lot to you and if you are very lucky to one another. Their welfare must be nearly as important to you as your own. Even if you live alone, even if your solitude is elected and ebullient, you still cannot do without a clan or a tribe.

The trouble with the families many of us were born to is not that they are meddlesome ogres but that they are too far away. In emergencies we rush across continents and if need be oceans to their sides, as they do to ours. Maybe we even make a habit of seeing them, once or twice a year, for the sheer pleasure of it. But blood ties seldom dictate our addresses. Our blood kin are often too remote to ease us from our Tuesdays to our Wednesdays. For this we must rely on our families of friends. If our relatives are not, do not wish to be, or for whatever reasons cannot be our friends, then by some complex alchemy we must transform our friends into our relatives.

The thing to keep in mind is our need to devise new ways, or revive old ones, to equip ourselves with uncles and other kinfolk. Maybe that's what prompted whoever it was ordered the cake I saw in my neighborhood bakery, labeled "HAPPY BIRTHDAY SURROGATE." I like to think that this cake was decorated not for a judge, but for someone's surrogate mother or surrogate brother: loathsome jargon, but admirable sentiment. If you didn't conceive me or bring me up that doesn't mean you still cannot be—if we both decide you ought to be—a kind of parent to me.

It is never too late, I like to hope, to augment our families in ways nature neglected to do.

New tribes and clans can no more be willed into existence, of course, than any other good thing can. We keep trying, though. To try, with gritted teeth and girded loins, is after all American. That is what the two Helens and I were talking about the day we had lunch in a room way up in a high-rise motel near the Kansas City airport. We had lunch there at the end of a two-day conference on families. The two Helens both were social scientists, but I liked them even so, among other reasons because they both objected to that motel's coffee shop even more than I did. One of the Helens, from Virginia, disliked such fare so much that she had brought along homemade whole wheat bread, sesame butter and honey from her parents' farm in South Dakota, where she had visited before the conference. Her picnic was the best thing that had happened, to me at least, those whole two days.

"If you're voluntarily childless and alone," said the other Helen, who was from Pennsylvania by way of Puerto Rico, "it gets harder and harder with the passage of time. It's stressful. That's why you need support systems." I had been hearing quite a bit of talk about "support systems." The term is not among my favorites, but I can understand its currency. Whatever "support systems" may be, the need for them is clearly urgent, and not just in this country. Are there not thriving "megafamilies" of as many as three hundred people in Scandinavia? Have the Japanese not for years had an honored, enduring—if perhaps by our standards rather rigid—custom of adopting nonrelatives to fill gaps in their families? Should we not applaud and maybe imitate such ingenuity?

And consider our own Unitarians. From Santa Barbara to Boston they have been earnestly dividing their congregations into arbitrary "extended families" whose members all are bound to act like each other's relatives. Kurt Vonnegut, Jr., plays with a similar train of thought in his fictional *Slapstick*. In that book every newborn baby gets assigned a randomly chosen middle name, like Uranium or Daffodil or Raspberry. These middle names are connected with hyphens to numbers between one and twenty, and any two people who have the same middle name are automatically related. This is all to the good, the author thinks, because "human beings need all the relatives they can get—as possible donors or receivers not of love but of common decency." He envisions these extended families as "one of the four greatest inventions by Americans," the others being *Robert's Rules of Order*, the Bill of Rights, and the principles of Alcoholics Anonymous.

This charming notion might even work, if it weren't so arbitrary. Already each of us is born into one family not of our choosing. If we're going to go around devising new ones, we might as well have the luxury of picking their members ourselves. Clever picking might result in new families whose benefits would surpass or at least equal those of the old. The new ones by definition cannot spawn us—as soon as they do that, they stop being new—but there is plenty they can do. I have seen them work wonders. As a member in reasonable standing in six or seven tribes in addition to the one I was born to, I have been trying to figure which earmarks are common to both kinds of families:

(1) Good families have a chief, or a heroine, or a founder—someone around whom others cluster, whose achievements as the Yiddish word has it, let them *kvell*, and whose example spurs them on to like feats. Some blood dynasties produce such figures regularly; others languish for as many as five generations between demigods, wondering with each new pregnancy whether this, at last, might be the messianic baby who will redeem us. Look, is there not something gubernatorial about her footstep, or musical about the way he bangs with his spoon on his cup? All clans, of all kinds, need such a figure now and then. Sometimes clans based on water rather than blood harbor several such personages at one time.

(2) Good families have a switchboard operator—someone like Lilia Economou or my own mother who cannot help but keep track of what all the others are up to, who plays Houston Mission Control to everyone else's Apollo. This role, like the foregoing one, is assumed rather than assigned. Someone always volunteers for it. That person often also has the instincts of an archivist, and feels driven to keep scrapbooks and

photograph albums up to date, so that the clan can see proof of its own continuity.

(3) Good families are much to all their members, but everything to none. Good families are fortresses with many windows and doors to the outer world. The blood clans I feel most drawn to were founded by parents who are nearly as devoted to whatever it is they do outside as they are to each other and their children. Their curiosity and passion are contagious. Everybody, where they live, is busy. Paint is spattered on eyeglasses. Mud lurks under fingernails. Person-to-person calls come in the middle of the night from Tokyo and Brussels. Catchers' mitts, ballet slippers, overdue library books and other signs of extrafamilial concerns are everywhere.

(4) Good families are hospitable. Knowing that hosts need guests as much as guests need hosts, they are generous with honorary memberships for friends, whom they urge to come early and often and to stay late. Such clans exude a vivid sense of surrounding rings of relatives, neighbors, teachers, students and godparents, any of whom at any time might break or slide into the inner circle. Inside that circle a wholesome, tacit emotional feudalism develops: you give me protection, I'll give you fealty. Such treaties begin with, but soon go far beyond, the jolly exchange of pie at Thanksgiving for cake on birthdays. It means you can ask me to supervise your children for the fortnight you will be in the hospital, and that however inconvenient this might be for me, I shall manage to. It means I can phone you on what for me is a dreary, wretched Sunday afternoon and for you is the eve of a deadline, knowing you will tell me to come right over, if only to watch you type.

(5) Good families deal squarely with direness. Pity the tribe that doesn't have, and cherish, at least one flamboyant eccentric. Pity too the one that supposes it can avoid for long the woes to which all flesh is heir. Lunacy, bankruptcy, suicide and other unthinkable fates sooner or later afflict the noblest of clans with an undertow of gloom. Family life is a set of givens, someone once told me, and it takes courage to see certain givens as blessings rather than as curses. Contradictions and inconsistencies are givens, too. So is the war against what the Oregon patriarch Kenneth Babbs calls malarkey. "There's always malarkey lurking, bubbles in the

cesspool, fetid bubbles that pop and smell. But I don't put up with malarkey, between my step-kids and my natural ones or anywhere else in the family."

(6) Good families prize their rituals. Nothing welds a family more than these. Rituals are vital especially for clans without histories, because they evoke a past, imply a future, and hint at continuity. No line in the Seder service at Passover reassures more than the last: "Next year in Jerusalem!" A clan becomes more of a clan each time it gathers to observe a fixed ritual (Christmas, birthdays, Thanksgiving, and so on), grieve at a funeral (anyone may come to most funerals; those who do declare their tribalness), and devises a new rite of its own. Equinox breakfasts and all-white dinners can be at least as welding as Memorial Day parades.

(7) Good families are affectionate. This of course is a matter of style. I know clans whose members greet each other with gingerly handshakes or, in what pass for kisses, with hurried brushes of side jawbones, as if the object were to touch not the lips but the ears. I don't see how such people manage. "The tribe that does not hug," as someone who has been part of many *ad hoc* families recently wrote to me, "is no tribe at all. More and more I realize that everybody, regardless of age, needs to be hugged and comforted in a brotherly or sisterly way now and then. Preferably now."

(8) Good families have a sense of place, which these days is not achieved easily. As Susanne Langer wrote in 1957, "Most people have no home that is a symbol of their childhood, not even a definite memory of one place to serve that purpose ... all the old symbols are gone." Once I asked a roomful of supper guests who, if anyone, felt any strong pull to any certain spot on the face of the earth. Everyone was silent, except for a visitor from Bavaria. The rest of us seemed to know all too well what Walker Percy means in *The Moviegoer* when he tells of the "genie-soul of the place which every place has or else is not a place [and which] wherever you go, you must meet and master or else be met and mastered." All that meeting and mastering saps plenty of strength. It also underscores our need for tribal bases of the sort which soaring real estate taxes and splintering families have made all but obsolete.

So what are we to do, those of us whose habit and pleasure and doom is our tendency, as a Georgia lady put it, to "fly off at every other whipstitch?" Think in terms of movable feasts, for a start. Live here, wherever here may be, as if we were going to belong here for the rest of our lives. Learn to hallow whatever ground we happen to stand on or land on. Like medieval knights who took their tapestries along on Crusades, like modern Afghanis with their yurts, we must pack such totems and icons as we can to make short-term quarters feel like home. Pillows, small rugs, watercolors can dispel much of the chilling anonymity of a sublet apartment or motel room. When we can, we should live in rooms with stoves or fireplaces or anyway candlelight. The ancient saying still is true: Extinguished hearth, extinguished family. Round tables help, too, and as a friend of mine once put it, so do "too many comfortable chairs, with surfaces to put feet on, arranged so as to encourage a maximum of eye contact." Such rooms inspire good talk, of which good clans can never have enough.

(9) Good families, not just the blood kind, find some way to connect with posterity. "To forge a link in the humble chain of being, encircling heirs to ancestors," as Michael Novak has written, "is to walk within a circle of magic as primitive as humans knew in caves." He is talking of course about babies, feeling them leap in wombs, giving them suck. Parenthood, however, is a state which some miss by chance, and others by design, and a vocation to which not all are called. Some of us, like the novelist Richard P. Brickner, "look on as others name their children who in turn name their own lives, devising their own flags from their parents' cloth." What are we who lack children to do? Build houses? Plant trees? Write books or symphonies or laws? Perhaps, but even if we do these things, there still should be children on the sidelines, if not at the center, of our lives. It is a sadly impoverished tribe that does not allow access to, and make much of, some children. Not too much, of course: it has truly been said that never in history have so many educated people devoted so much attention to so few children. Attention, in excess, can turn to fawning, which isn't much better than neglect. Still, if we don't regularly see and talk to and laugh with people who can expect to out-

live us by twenty years or so, we had better get busy and find some.

(10) Good families also honor their elders. The wider the age range, the stronger the tribe. Jean-Paul Sartre and Margaret Mead, to name two spectacularly confident former children, have both remarked on the central importance of grandparents in their own early lives. Grandparents now are in much more abundant supply than they were a generation or two ago when old age was more rare. If actual grandparents are not at hand, no family should have too hard a time finding substitute ones to whom to give unfeigned homage. The Soviet Union's enchantment with day care centers, I have heard, stems at least in part from the state's eagerness to keep children away from their presumably subversive grandparents. Let that be a lesson to clans based on interest as well as to those based on genes.

Some days my handwriting resembles my mother's, slanting hopefully and a bit extravagantly eastward. Other days it looks more like my father's: resolute, vertical, guardedly free of loops. Both my parents will remain in my nerves and muscles and mind until the day I die, and so will their other child, my sister, but they aren't the only ones. If I were to die tomorrow, the obituary would note that I was survived by my father and sister. True, but not true enough. Like most official lists of survivors, this one would be incomplete.

One reason I feel in healthy spirits right now, on a Thursday noon, is that in the time since last Thursday noon I have not only had fruitful blocks of solitude but supped with, talked at length with, laughed with, and been hugged by nine of the people whom I think of as part of my family though not one of them technically is. I have also had three heartening long-distance phone talks, with other such folks. Before long I'll be seeing them, too. Nine in the flesh, three on the phone. A surplus. An embarrassment of riches. A family.

To Apply This Reading to Yourself

1. *Howard writes, "Even if you live alone, even if your solitude is elected and ebullient, you still cannot do without a clan or a tribe." Could you be happy living by yourself or just with your spouse (and possibly children) without meaningful ties to a "by chance" or "by choice" larger family? Why or why not?*
2. *Howard presents 10 criteria of "good families." Use her criteria to evaluate the family in which you grew up or the one you have established.*
3. *Howard presents 10 criteria of "good families." Draw up your own set of criteria, compare it with Howard's, and use it to evaluate the family in which you grew up or the one you have established.*
4. *If in your view, the family in which you grew up or the one you have established falls short of being a "good family," indicate its shortcomings and the effect on you.*
5. *If in your view, the family in which you grew up or the one you have established falls short of being a "good family," indicate what you can do and are doing to make it better.*
6. *If you have insufficient family "by chance," indicate your feelings and plans concerning assembling a family "by choice." Or, if you are assembling a family or have assembled a family "by choice," discuss your experience in doing so.*

Working

I stay at the office so late that I must race home with all the other blind drivers on the expressway to hurry with dinner and sit with a stack of papers to be read or, too tired to think, stare at the TV until past bedtime. My work is a series of fighting crises . . . There is virtually nothing intellectual about my work—I am clearly a paper-pushing puppet in a system which deadens my spirit perceptibly day-by-day.

—Robert Potter, Ph.D., college administrator

My chisel and mallet seek some more-organic form hidden within a block of Hawaiian koa wood. The power saw that cut the block is no respecter of the flowing lines of light and dark that mark the pattern of growth. Sometimes, when my efforts at seeking the lifelines in the wood succeed, the form seems to take on a liveliness reminiscent of the forces that shaped the once tall and supple tree.

Now, as I seek to shape my life in more flexible, natural ways, the schools and offices that claimed so many of my years seem like a buzz saw that cut me into blocks irrespective of the life forms hidden within.

There are so many joys in my new vocation I wonder that I did not find it sooner. Perhaps, my life had to be cut into blocks in order for me to know that was not the form I sought.

—Craig Mosher, Ph.D., woodworker

Much of our adult lives is spent at work. We work because we must—in order to earn a living. We work because we want to—in order to keep busy and fulfill ourselves. And if we are lucky, we find a job that allows us to earn a living in a fulfilling way.

Most of us are able to get some sense of fulfillment or at least contentment from our work. Over the years, many investigations have been made of job satisfaction, and the results indicate that the majority of workers are content. However, the level of satisfaction varies considerably with the people and the jobs studied. Generally speaking, minority-group members and women are less satisfied than white males, and there is less satisfaction among persons whose work is low in pay, security, or prestige, or is unsuited to their interests and abilities.

Work is a very important part of our identity. To a large extent, our job defines who we are. If one asks for information about a person, it frequently is presented in terms of what the person does for a living. "He's a teacher." "She's in real estate." "He works down at the plant."

For adolescents and young adults the search for identity is bound up with the struggle to find a career direction. And when they are unable to hit on a career or pursue the one they have elected, a full-fledged identity crisis may result. Erik Erikson, a prominent theoretician in this area, wrote that "it is primarily the inability to settle on an occupational identity which disturbs young people."

The important part that work plays in the middle years of life is dramatically shown when a career in which a person has heavily invested himself proves to be unfulfilling or is interrupted in some way. Beyond the sheer economic privation that may result is the devastating loss of purpose and identity, as demonstrated in these comments by two unemployed air industry workers. A technician: "Not working for the first time since I was a kid really knocked me for a loop at first. It's the feeling of worthlessness that gets you. A man's got to do something. Can't just stand around. Drives you nuts." A supervisor: "The psychological blow of not being a breadwinner was devastating. I felt like a blemish. A failure. A flop. And when people asked me what I was doing, I just felt like a complete washout."

Other observers have noted the identity crisis that is common at the time of retirement. Suddenly, without the pattern and definition provided by one's work, a person may feel completely adrift. One retiree writes, "With your occupational identity gone, you have to find another existence for yourself." If one has spent most of a lifetime in one line of work, this is not easily done.

For a woman, the work world presents special identity problems. Although considerable gains have been made in some sectors, women as a group are still second-class citizens when it comes to pay and promotions. Many married career women find that their spouses welcome the added income more than the sharing of family responsibilities. Some middle-aged homemakers—children grown and husbands engrossed in their own careers—seek new meaning in a vocation but find the path difficult.

Our world is undergoing rapid change, and the world of work is changing too. The future is very uncertain. With affluent times, there is more freedom to explore careers before making a commitment and also more freedom to change careers in midstream, to combine a career with other pursuits, or to pursue a life-style that integrates vocation and avocation. With the advent of less prosperous times and a scarcity of good jobs, earning a living can be paramount, and we may be less willing or less able to hang loose, explore, and grow.

TAKE YOUR TIME

Some time ago, I was in a large audience of adults—young, middle-aged, old—to whom the speaker addressed this question and asked for a show of hands: "How many of you are still waiting for your life to settle down?" There was considerable laughter, but as I looked around, everyone seemed to have a hand in the air—including me.

I remember another question—one from my childhood—that I was asked many times: "What do you want to do when you grow up?" The question seemed to imply that one might decide on some certain thing to do, do it, and that would be that—as if life could be that simple.

Growing up and settling down. The use of the term "settling down" always amused me. When a person finds a job filled with demands and unknowns, gets married, which as statistics show is a fragile state, has children—a deeply affecting and demanding enterprise, and assumes a mortgage with frightening payments, he or she is said to be "settling down." Compared to all of that, childhood might seem like a breeze.

Life doesn't seem to settle down. We can spend an inordinate amount of time, money, and energy preparing ourselves for our so-called lifetime career, but we may be in for some considerable surprises. A study of 100 men who were followed from high school to their middle 30s found that 30% had already shifted vocational fields completely. A study of college women who were interviewed before graduation and 14 years later, found them to be living lives very different from their original plans.

In the lead article, Emanuel Berger points out that students are under considerable pressure to make early vocational choices, but most cannot or should not do so because they know too little about themselves and occupational demands. As a result of this pressure many students make premature choices that do not pan out and are then experienced as failure. Berger holds that all vocational decisions should be considered to be tentative: Each choice is one to be explored and then confirmed or disconfirmed. More than this, every career remains to some extent exploratory because we may move from one subfield to another within our field or even change careers completely to accord with our personal development.

A case for "wasting time" is made by writer James Michener in the second selection. He maintains that with a few exceptions, we each have until the age of 35 to find a vocation. Something of a slowpoke, he took five years longer than that. He writes that had he committed himself to a career when he was 18 (as he was encouraged to do), any choice would have been wrong. "Stumbling and fumbling" are part of creative vocational exploration, and in the end, the time we "waste" may be the most valuable.

WEIGH YOUR VALUES

An important distinction can be made between the "standard of living" and the "quality of life." To put it in a nutshell, the first relates to how well we eat and the second to how well we fulfill ourselves and grow. If we are fortunate, we find work that provides us with both a comfortable and a fulfilling life.

Having it all (or trying to) doesn't make for a fulfilling life. That's what more and more people are finding out, writes Janice Castro in the third reading, which is condensed from a *Time* cover story. It's goodbye to trendiness and materialism, and hello to "the simple life." What increasing numbers of Americans value these days, reports Castro, is "having time for family and friends, rest and recreation, good deeds, and spirituality." Some but not all of *Time's* readers agreed, as the sampling of letters appended to the reading indicates. Some think that the simple life is more have-to than want-to, some that a few repentant yuppies don't make a trend, and some just can't get off the fast track.

Because our life spans are increasing, maybe we can have all of whatever it is we want, but not all at the same time. In the fourth reading, Ken Dychtwald and Joe Flower note that lives have been linear, straight-line marches: we learned, we worked (at family and career), we died. Lives are now becoming cyclical; pursuits can be repeated, and we have second and third chances at educational careers, and families. No longer is there just one time or one right time to be doing something. The cyclical option is attractive to those who value chance, challenge, and excitement, but not to those who prefer constancy and well-trodden paths.

According to Harold Bloomfield and Robert Kory in the last reading, the successful life includes 100 percent personal growth (or inner development) and 100 percent vocational success (or external achievement). Many of us give up one for the other, but they believe that both are attainable by following their 200 percent success formula. This a formula for doing less but accomplishing more, for *having* what we want while *being* who we want to be rather than sacrificing one for the other.

To Explore Your Own Vocational Values and Directions

1. *Aspirations.* "What do you want to be when you grow up?" How many different answers have you given to that question over the years? Beginning with the very first answer that you can recall, list in chronological order all your vocational aspirations right up to the present. When your list is complete, indicate next to each item why that particular choice might have been appealing at the time.

As a last step, write down any insight your list provides concerning your present aspirations or choices.

2. *Achievements and abilities.* What have you done that you recall with some pride or satisfaction? List in chronological order all your achievements or accomplishments. (You might note such things as making an honor roll, placing in a competition, becoming proficient in something, mastering a handicap or overcoming an obstacle, getting along with a difficult relative, etc.) When your list is complete, indicate next to each item the aptitudes or abilities that this achievement demonstrated (for example, athletic prowess, writing talent, mathematical, mechanical, or musical aptitude, ability to get along with others, persistence, self-discipline, leadership, etc.). As a last step, write down any insight your list provides concerning your present aspirations or choices.

3. *Traits.* What personal qualities have you discovered in yourself over the years? Write this heading on a page: "What I have learned about myself." Then list ten of your salient traits or qualities. (Examples: "I'm ambitious." "I'm very independent." "I like to be by myself." "I like to take care of others." "I'm a fighter." "I like people." "I'm creative." "I get bored easily." "I'm a careful, cautious person.") As a last step, write down any insight your list provides concerning your present aspirations or choices.

4. *Wants, needs.* What do you want or need from your career? Some things that people seek in a career are sufficient money, prestige, security, challenge, advancement, harmonious associates, enjoyable activity, freedom, leisure time, opportunity for creativity, personal growth, etc. List all the things you want or need from your career in order of their importance, most important first, second most important second, and so on. Then consider your present career path. Does it or will it provide for each of your wants or needs? Why or why not in each instance? What do your answers, taken as a whole, suggest about the wisdom of your vocational direction?

5. *Success (the poet's corner).* What does success mean to you? Below is a poem expressing Ralph Waldo Emerson's idea of success. Study the poem and then write a poem or a paragraph of your own, stating your idea of success.

What Is Success?

To laugh often and love much;
To win the respect of intelligent
persons and the affection of children;
To earn the approval of honest critics
and endure the betrayal of false friends;
To appreciate beauty;
To find the best in others;
To give of one's self without the
slightest thought of return;
To have accomplished a task,
whether by a healthy child, a rescued
soul, a garden patch or a redeemed

social condition;
To have played and laughed with
enthusiasm and sung with exaltation;
To know that even one life has
breathed easier because you have lived;
This is to have succeeded.

6. *The good life.* Philosophers and other philosophical folks have tried to define "the good life." What, for you, would be a good life? And how good is your life now? Write two paragraphs, side by side, one to answer the first question and the other to answer the second. Then below them, centered, write one or more paragraphs containing any insights or conclusions prompted by your comparison of your paired paragraphs.

7. *Life without a job.* What if you didn't have to work for a living? Suppose, for example, that you won a state lottery and were provided with an income (after taxes and adjusted for inflation) of $60,000 a year for the next 60 years. What would you do with your life? Why?

8. *Little dream, big dream.* What would be your dream job? This is your opportunity to dream two dreams. First, dream up and write down a job that you would like to have, and might well have some day—a realistic dream. Second, dream up and write down the very best job that you can think of for yourself; make sure that this second dream is a big dream—even a wild dream. As an option, you might form small groups and take turns sharing your two dreams. One suggestion is that if the group decides that someone's big dream is not big or wild enough, that person must expand the dream until the group is satisfied.

9. *Five lives.* If you had five lives, how would you live each one of them? Note that this doesn't mean who you would be if you could be five different people. It means who you would be if you could be five different versions of yourself—you, five times over—each time developing some interest, need, talent, or potentiality to its fullest. Write a description of the five lives that you would choose for yourself and in each case indicate why.[1]

10. *One life* (a follow-up for those who have completed Exploration 9). If we plan our one life well, then no important interest, need, talent, or potentiality will go unfilled. Reflect on the lives you described in the previous exploration and the important aspects of yourself that they encompass. Does your present life provide ample opportunity for the expression of each aspect? If so, how? If not, why not? Answer these questions, and, as a last step, devise and describe a plan that would allow you to roll all five lives into one—a plan that would allow every aspect of yourself ample expression.

1. Explorations 9 and 10 are adapted from *Wishcraft* by Barbara Sher and Annie Gottlieb.

To Read Further

Bolles, R. B. (1981). *The three boxes of life: And how to get out of them.* Berkeley, CA: Ten Speed Press. (paperback)

Bolles, R. B. (1991). *What color is your parachute? A practical manual for job-hunters and career changers* (rev. ed.). Berkeley, CA: Ten Speed Press. (paperback)

Johnson, D. W. (1987). *Human relations and your career* (2nd ed.). Englewood Cliffs, NJ: Prentice-Hall. (paperback)

Saltzman, A. (1991). *Down-shifting: Reinventing success on a slower track.* New York: HarperCollins.

Sher, B., & Gottlieb, A. (1986). *Wishcraft: How to get what you really want.* New York: Ballantine. (paperback)

Sinetar, M. (1989). *Do what you love, the money will follow.* New York: Dell. (paperback)

Terkel, S. (1985). *Working.* New York: Ballantine. (paperback)

Vocational Choices in College

Emanuel M. Berger

The very freedom of our college-bound youth to choose a vocation has become an important problem and task for most of them. More so than in most other countries of the world—and more so than their grandparents before them—young people in our country today have freedom to decide on how they want to work. At the same time that there is greater freedom to choose, there is greater difficulty in choosing because of the much-enlarged number of possibilities to choose from in an increasingly complex occupational world. This situation requires knowing much more about one's self and about possible occupations if one is to make satisfying choices.

In my work as a counseling psychologist, I see many students who are disturbed to various degrees by not knowing what their vocational goals are. According to the students' reports, this lack of vocational goals is responsible for much anxiety, low motivation in college work, poor grades, and—not just occasionally—for their leaving college until they know what they want to accomplish there. This is not a distinctly local situation, certainly, but one that exists for thousands of college people all over the country.

And it is not just the students who are concerned, but also their parents. One large part of parental concern, understandably, is that their children be content in the work they choose. Another part, also understandable from their point of view, has to do with using hard-earned money to finance a college education when their children are so confused or uncertain about vocational goals that it seems doubtful that their eduction will have any practical, vocational value.

These concerns are nourished and aggravated by a general social pressure on students to make a vocational choice before they enter college, or soon thereafter. Other students, parents, relatives, the community in general, and even some teachers, counselors, and advisers in high school and college, are a party to the pressure. In high school, and to an increasing extent in earlier grades, there is likely to be a vocational counselor and prominently displayed occupational information—a general stimulation and prodding of students to make a vocational choice. When they enter college, they are likely to be asked what their vocational choice is, from which it is easy for students to take the implication that they are expected to be able to make one at the outset. Even among some professionals concerned with education and counseling there is a use of language that implies that there is but one grand and lasting choice to be made and that students should be able to make that choice now or very soon. They talk or write of choosing *a* career, of making *a* vocational choice.

Although the high tide of pressure seems to center on students about to begin their college experience, perhaps because this is seen as the beginning of serious professional training, the pressure continues for the more advanced students if they have not been able to make a satisfactory vocational choice.

The pressure is based on an erroneous and misleading assumption, namely, that most college freshmen are able to make a lasting and satisfactory vocational choice as freshmen or soon thereafter. The assumption is erroneous because most college freshmen have not yet learned, and will not learn in a short time, what they need to know about themselves and about occupations in order to make a first, satisfactory vocational choice. The assumption is misleading because it creates the impression that the student's vocational task is merely one of "choosing" a vocation, cafeteria style, rather than a potentially lifelong task of vocational self-discovery which may reasonably include many vocational choices, especially in the process of discovering a satisfactory occupational field. In a sense, the assumption requires that freshmen be omniscient, that they foresee their future experience and development, that they predict what their eventual vocational choice will be before they have had the experience and undergone the development out of which satisfactory choices emerge.

ILL EFFECTS

In response to the pressure to make a definite vocational choice, many students commit themselves prematurely. They tell the world they are going to be engineers or architects or nurses or whatever, before they know whether they can handle the required subjects, before they know whether they have the required talents or special aptitudes, before they know what the training is actually like, before they have any idea of how much they would like the day-to-day work possible in their chosen field. Then, when they discover that their choice was not a good one for some reason or reasons, such as the possibilities just suggested, their tendency is to view the experience as a "failure." They said they were going to become engineers, etc., and they could not do it. And to the extent that people around them share the same assumption, that they should have known better somehow when they made their choice, the feeling of failure will be reinforced. They should not see such experiences as a failure on their part. The fault is in their point of view.

Another unhappy effect of the pressure stems from a sort of corollary of the assumption underlying it. If students don't know as freshmen or shortly thereafter what they want to do vocationally, the thinking goes, then they should not be in college. How many times I have heard students say that they have no idea of a major, no vocational goals, so they plan to leave college and go into the military service or get a job. They express the vague hope that such experience will help them decide on their vocational plans, and this could be the case. But they assume that it is a waste of time and money, from a vocational point of view, to go to college when one doesn't have any definite vocational plans. It is difficult to assess the extent to which these students delay or distort their vocational development when they act on this assumption.

And when students and parents become anxious because the student has not been able to make a definite, satisfactory vocational choice as a freshman or soon thereafter, that anxiety is needless. It is needless because the assumption on which it is based is in error. Most such students have not yet learned enough about themselves or about occupations to be able to make a definite, satisfactory vocational choice. The fault again is in their point of view.

DISCOVERY—NOT "KNOWING"

A healthier and more realistic point of view recognizes that students eventually discover and confirm that a vocational choice they made is satisfactory, following experiences that permit them to do so. They cannot know in advance of such experience that they will be able to handle the academic requirements or be able to find a satisfying way of working in some chosen field. And yet, that is apparently just what our society expects of its young college people.

Even those students who eventually realize an early choice with satisfaction did not really "know," but rather discovered and confirmed that the early choice was a good one.

It then follows that every student who has made a choice at all—with little or much confidence—should consider it a *tentative* one rather than a committed one. Then the task becomes one of discovering, testing, confirming whether or not the choice was a good one in much the way a scientist goes about testing a hypothesis. Students do not have to defend the presumption that they knew all they needed to know about themselves and the field they chose at the time they chose it, before they had any opportunity to confirm their choice by experience. They can avoid a position where they cling unrealistically to a choice mainly because they told the world of their decision as if it were final in response to the social pressure to make a definite vocational choice.

In this perspective, the negative experiences that students have in their efforts to confirm a choice can be seen in a different light. Such efforts can be seen as the "error" part of a trial-and-error process that is necessary and inevitable in any successful solution of a difficult problem. When students discover that they lack the ability, aptitude, or talent that is required to maintain their vocational choice, this is a negative experience in relation to that choice but it has the positive aspect of eliminating an inappropriate choice, thereby narrowing the field of best looking vocational possibilities from which they are trying to make a choice. It brings them closer to a positive choice. Also, students who see their task as one of discovering their vocational choice through experience are more likely to accept the discovery of limitations as part of the process they must go through on their way to a satisfactory choice. But students who have committed themselves to a choice on the assumption that they should be able to choose wisely in advance of confirming experience will tend to see the interfering limitations as "incompetence" and the inappropriate choice as a kind of "failure." Of course, not all students react this way, but many do, and in a sense they are beating themselves into a loss of self-esteem because they were not omniscient enough to choose wisely from the beginning.

A broad academic experience can be helpful to a student who has not yet been able to make a first, tentative choice of vocation. Most liberal arts colleges require students to fulfill requirements in a variety of fields—sciences, social sciences, and humanities. Students have an opportunity to follow up interests they have and discover new interests in subject matter and to see how well they can handle different kinds of college courses. Learning about their abilities, limitations, and interests helps them to narrow down the field of best vocational possibilities for them. The point for those students who cannot see the vocational value of broad academic experience is that military service or a job, though possibly valuable experiences in other ways, are not likely to permit students to learn about their interests, abilities, and limitations in relation to academic subjects. But what they can aspire to educationally and vocationally depends on just that sort of self-knowledge.

While I consider the above to be generally true, it should be recognized here that students' performance in college sometimes improves greatly with increased maturity. Thus, a period in which they work at a job or are in the military service may contribute indirectly to improved academic performance when they return to college. This in turn can permit them to raise their vocational aspirations. It is in view of just this sort of possibility that students might, under certain conditions, help their vocational development by leaving college for a while to work or go into military service.

Choice of a specialty within a field is also a matter of discovery and confirmation. Students who feel pretty sure that they want to be in a certain occupational field are generally misplacing their anxiety if they worry a lot about how they want to specialize. This is something they either confirm or discover, something to be learned from experience rather than known in advance of experience.

ABILITIES AND LIMITATIONS

One of the primary ways in which students need to have learned about themselves to some degree before they can begin to choose a field is with respect to their abilities and limitations at the college level. Generally speaking, students aspire to vocational goals in the belief that they have enough of whatever abilities and talent are required to reach those goals and do well in the field.

But students' conceptions of their abilities as they enter college are likely to be based on high school experience. Although there are some exceptions, most high schools in our country pitch the level of difficulty of subject matter at some medium point so that most students will be able to understand it. Also, the degree of responsibility, initiative, and effort required of students in most high schools in order to "pass" is relatively much less than that required by most colleges.

As a result, many of our high school graduates have little conception of their limitations. They tend to have one or another omnipotent attitude: (1) that they can do well at just about anything in school if they really want to and try hard enough; (2) that they are so bright that they can do well at just about anything in college with only a little effort.

College freshmen who learned little about their academic limitations from their high school experience are likely to get a jolt if they go to a college with relatively high standards. They will fail courses or do poorly as a result of too little effort or lack of sufficient aptitude in certain subjects. They are then forced to face their academic limitations perhaps for the first time. For some students this can be a serious problem. Their conception of what they can do in college and thereby vocationally is contradicted by their college performance. Unfortunately, many quite capable students interpret this as meaning that they are not competent. They confuse limitations with incompetence, and their self-esteem is damaged.

Determining what one's specific limitations are is a tricky and uncertain business at best. In an abstract and ideal way we learn about a limitation by doing our "best," making a maximum effort to achieve something, and then evaluating the outcome of our efforts. But our best efforts in arts or academic subjects at one stage of our development may have very different results five or ten years later when we have become more mature. And, at any particular time in our lives, a "best" effort is limited by our circumstances and our attitudes about what a maximum effort is.

The question is really one of the nature of limitations. With what degree of effort and at what level of difficulty do the limitations occur? In what specific subject matter? What are the implications of the limitations for the individual's choice of vocational field?

Limitations due to level of difficulty may mean that an advanced degree in mathematics is out, but they may still be able to do well enough to become competent engineers. At a somewhat lower level, they may be able to do well enough to teach high school math or go ahead with training in business.

Also, some students have an either-or attitude, which says in effect: "Either I will be among the best in my field or I won't go into it—I refuse to be mediocre." Then, getting a C in some course in a major field or doing slightly above average work is a sign to them that they cannot possibly be "among the best." They are then ready to look elsewhere to some field where they can be "at the top." They do not recognize that no one excels in every subject in a field all the time or in every way—or that there is a very large segment of people in any field who are quite competent and make a modest contribution most of the time, and some of them will eventually make an outstanding contribution despite "not being among the best" when they were doing their academic work. Given a degree of accomplishment sufficient to admit a student to an occupational field, it is the willingness to accept the risk that one's continued efforts may not result in an outstanding contribution that I see as the necessary but not sufficient condition for making an outstanding contribution in one's field.

THE DEVELOPING COLLEGE STUDENT

The task of students who are trying to reach a vocational decision about a field of work is a complex one. They must eventually bring together in a harmonious way their conception of themselves that might in any way be vocationally relevant and their knowledge of occupations. But important changes in their vocational thinking may and do occur during the college years, thus complicating their problem. Students must not only be able to clarify and assess accurately the nature of their abilities, limitations, talents, interests, values, and personal dispositions, they must also be able to cope with changes that may take place in these aspects of themselves at the very same time they are trying to evaluate such aspects in relation to ways of working in some occupational field.

Some of the change can be attributed to students' difficulties with courses basic to a field they chose earlier. Would-be nurses have trouble with chemistry, etc. Naturally, such difficulty leads many students to change their vocational plans. It represents a complication due to a change in students' conceptions of their academic or creative abilities and limitations.

Students also change their vocational thinking as a result of the development of their interests and values. In general, social and aesthetic values and interests develop later in adolescence and it seems that the special stimulation of the college experience spurs their development. Not for all students, certainly, but for many.

There may be changes in students' conceptions of their nonacademic potentialities as a result of experiences they have along with the academic experience or before they complete it. It may be a summer camp experience where the student enjoyed helping young teen-agers, or working on a student newspaper and confirming a commitment to journalism, or being an officer in the service and discovering a potential for management. Many kinds of nonacademic experience can contribute to students' developing sense of themselves as potential teachers, newspapermen, or managers, or whatever.

Another factor is that of the students' knowledge of occupations—the nature of the training, abilities, and personal qualifications required as well as the specific ways of working possible within the occupation. As things are, some students choose engineering because they want to design airplanes or are mechanically minded, only to discover from experience that engineering training emphasizes mathematics and sciences and theories, and that the design of airplanes will have to come much later, after all that, and that one's mechanical skills may not be important in engineering and certainly not a sufficient basis for choosing it. Even at a much later vocational stage, engaging in the work of an occupation, there are those who discover from that experience that they are not suited to the field in some way—not patient enough to do chemical research, more interested in people problems than they are in engineering problems, etc.

Knowledge of occupations, like other kinds of awareness and information, grows with time and experience, is an aspect of the developing person, and another complicating factor in the process of vocational development and choice.

REASONABLE EXPECTATIONS

Considering all of the potential for change in students' vocational thinking, when could we reasonably expect students to be able to make a stable and satisfying vocational decision about a field? There is no simple, general answer to this question although one might say what we could reasonably expect of most students, with qualifications.

We would expect most seniors in college to have matured enough so that their awareness of their abilities, limitations, interests, and values has become stable enough to permit them to make a satisfying choice of an occupational field. Then the matter of how they want to work more specifically within the field can be worked out later as they get more training and experience.

Even then it is not so unusual or necessarily a sign of some special problem if a student majors in one field, graduates from college, and then switches to some quite different field. In my own field of psychology, I can think of at least a dozen acquaintances who switched to graduate work in psychology from undergraduate majors in science, engineering, or mathematics.

Some people manage to make rather radical changes even in their middle years without undue hardship to themselves or others. One acquaintance switched from a career in engineering to one in law in his mid-thirties. And most of us have heard about or read about the lawyer in mid-career who switched successfully to writing or to composing hit musicals or the salesperson who switched in middle age to acting, with success and satisfaction.

THE LONG LOOK

The opportunity or necessity of making further vocational choices does not end with a satisfactory choice of an occupational field. With experience, what people enjoy doing most and do best may come more sharply into focus. They may develop new skills, different aspirations. The physician who has done well in general practice for several years may move with equal or greater satisfaction to specializing in internal medicine or psychiatry, to editing a medical journal, to being a hospital administrator. A lawyer may similarly move from general practice to corporation law, to being a judge, to becoming a congressman.

Not that satisfying development and change will be a general matter for all professionals. Some will be content to continue to work in a certain way most of their lives; others may not be content but may not have the freedom or power to choose other ways of working.

Vocational thinking and choices, if we view them in a broad way that goes beyond the matter of earning one's livelihood, may continue throughout one's lifetime, including the retirement period. Then we may again consider our values, interests, abilities, and limitations in relation to the question of how we can most satisfactorily engage ourselves in our later years. Some retirees are content to putter around the house, go fishing, play golf, etc. Others, needing something more akin to "work," take to community projects or writing or painting or turning out fine carpentry.

The point is that as long as we live, develop, and change, we can and may think about and evaluate ourselves in relation to how we use our energies in the world much in the same way we did when we made our choice of an occupational field.

To Apply This Reading to Yourself

1. *What pressures have you felt, from either others or yourself, to make an early vocational choice? What has your response been?*
2. *Berger writes that college can be a shock for some students because they face their academic limitations for the first time; if they confuse limitation with incompetence, self-esteem suffers. Discuss your own experience in this regard.*
3. *Interview a number of seniors, graduate students, or instructors to determine the number of times each changed academic majors or vocational choices. What insight do your findings give you concerning your own career explorations or decisions?*
4. *Interview a number of persons of retirement age to determine the number of times each changed career directions. What insight do your findings give you concerning your own career explorations or decisions?*

On Wasting Time

James A. Michener

We all worry about wasting time, about the years sliding past, about what we intend to do with our lives. We shouldn't. For there is a divine irrelevance in the universe that defies calculation. Many men and women win through to a sense of greatness in their lives only by first stumbling and fumbling their way into patterns that gratify them and allow them to utilize their endowments to the maximum.

If Swarthmore College in 1925 had employed even a halfway decent guidance counselor, I would have spent my life as an assistant professor of education in some Midwestern university. Because when I reported to college it must have been apparent to everyone that I was destined for some kind of academic career. Nevertheless, I was allowed to take Spanish, which leads to nothing, instead of French or German, which as everyone knows are important languages studied by serious students who wish to gain a Ph.D.

I cannot tell you how often I was penalized for having taken a frivolous language like Spanish instead of a decent, self-respecting tongue like French. In fact, it led to the sacrifice of my academic career.

Still, I continued to putter around with Spanish, eventually finding a deep affinity for it. In the end, I was able to write a book about Spain which will probably live longer than anything else I've done. In other words, I blindly backed into a minor masterpiece. There are thousands of people competent to write about France, and if I had taken that language in college I would have been prepared to add no new ideas to general knowledge. It was Spanish that opened up for me a whole new universe of concepts and ideas.

Actually, I wrote nothing at all until I was 40. This tardy beginning, one might say delinquency, stemmed from the fact that I had spent a good deal of my early time knocking around this country and Europe, trying to find out what I believed in, what values were large enough to enlist my sympathies during what I sensed would be a long and confused life. Had I committed myself at age 18, as I was encouraged to do, I would not even have known the parameters of the problem, and any choice I might have made then would have had to be wrong.

It took me 40 years to find out the facts.

As a consequence, I have never been able to feel anxiety about young people who are fumbling their way toward the enlightenment that will keep them going. I doubt that a young man—unless he wants to be a doctor or a research chemist, in which case a substantial body of specific knowledge must be mastered within a prescribed time—is really capable of wasting time, *regardless* of what he does. I believe you have until age 35 to decide finally on what you are going to do, and that any exploration you pursue in the process will in the end turn out to have been creative.

Indeed, it may well be that the years observers describe as "wasted" will prove to have been the most productive of those insights which will keep you going. The trip to Egypt. The two years spent working as a runner for a bank. The spell you spent on the newspaper in Idaho. Your apprenticeship at a trade. These are the ways in which young persons ought to spend their lives . . . the ways of "waste" that lead to true knowledge.

Two more comments. First, I have recently decided that the constructive work of the world is done by an appallingly small percentage of the general population. The rest simply don't give a damn . . . or they grow tired . . . or they fail to acquire when young the ideas that would vitalize them for the long decades.

I am not saying that such people don't matter. They are among the most precious items on earth. But they cannot be depended upon either to generate necessary new ideas or to put them into operation if someone else generates them. Therefore, those men and women who do have the energy to form new constructs and new ways to implement them must do the work of many. I believe it to be an honorable aspiration to want to be among those creators.

Second, I was about 40 when I retired from the rat race, having satisfied myself that I could handle it if I had to. I saw then that a man could count his life a success if he survived—merely survived—to age 70 without having ended up in jail (because he couldn't adjust to the minimum laws that society requires) or having landed in the booby hatch (because he could not bring his personality into harmony with the personalities of others).

I believe this now without question: income, position, the opinion of one's friends, the judg-ment of one's peers and all the other traditional criteria by which human beings are generally judged are for the birds. The only question is, "Can you hang on through the crap they throw at you and not lose your freedom or your good sense?" I am now $67^3/_4$, and it looks as if I've made it. Whatever happens now is on the house . . . and of no concern to me.

To Apply This Reading to Yourself

1. *Have you worried about wasting time while deciding what to do with your life? Discuss this aspect of your life.*
2. *What "wasted time" has proven to be useful in your own case?*
3. *Have you "wasted" enough, too much, or too little time before making some of your major life decisions (for example, leaving or returning home, going to college, choosing a college major or a career direction, getting married, having children, and so on)? Discuss this aspect of your life.*
4. *Have you been pressured from without or from within to make one or more major commitments prematurely? Discuss this aspect of your life.*

The Simple Life

Janice Castro

These are the humble makings of a revolution in progress: Macaroni and cheese. Timex watches. Volunteer work. Insulated underwear. Savings accounts . . . Domestic beer. Local activism. Sleds. Pajamas. Sentimental movies. Primary colors. Mixed-breed dogs. Bicycles. Cloth diapers. Shopping at Wal-Mart. Small-town ways. Iceberg lettuce. Family reunions. Board games. Hang-it-yourself wallpaper. Push-it-yourself lawn mowers. Silly Putty.

See the pattern? It's as genuine as Grandma's quilt. After a 10-year bender of gaudy dreams and godless consumerism, Americans are starting to trade down. They want to reduce their attachments to status symbols, fast-track careers and great expectations of Having It All. Upscale is out; downscale is in. Yuppies are an ancient civilization. Flaunting money is considered gauche: If you've got it, please keep it to yourself—or give some away!

In place of materialism, many Americans are embracing simpler pleasures and homier values. They've been thinking hard about what really matters in their lives, and they've decided to make some changes. What matters is having time for family and friends, rest and recreation, good deeds and spirituality. For some people that means a radical step: changing one's career, living on less, or packing up and moving to a quieter place. For others it can mean something as subtle as choosing a cheaper brand of running shoes or leaving work a little earlier to watch the kids in a soccer game.

The pursuit of a simpler life with deeper meaning is a major shift in America's private agenda. "This is a rapid and extremely powerful movement," says Ross Goldstein, a San Francisco psychologist and market researcher. "I'm impressed by how deep it goes into the fabric of this country." Says noted theologian Martin Marty of the University of Chicago: "We are all warned against thinking in terms of trends that correspond with decades, but this one is a cinch.

I think that people are going to look back at today as a hinge period in the country's history." Some social observers have already dubbed the 1990s the "We decade."

The mood is palpable. In a TIME/CNN poll of 500 adults, 69% of the people surveyed said they would like to "slow down and live a more relaxed life," in contrast to only 19% who said they would like to "live a more exciting, faster-paced life." A majority of those polled, 61%, agreed that "earning a living today requires so much effort that it's difficult to find time to enjoy life." When asked about their priorities, 89% said it was more important these days to spend time with their families, and 56% felt strongly about finding time for personal interests and hobbies. But only 13% saw importance in keeping up with fashions and trends, and just 7% thought it was worth bothering to shop for status-symbol products.

Marsha Bristow Bostick of Columbus remembers noticing with alarm last summer that her three-year-old daughter Betsy had memorized an awful lot of TV commercials. The toddler announced that she planned to take ballet lessons, followed by bride lessons. That helped inspire her mother, then 37, to quit her $150,000-a-year job as a marketing executive. She and her husband, Brent, a bank officer, decided that Betsy and their infant son Andrew needed more parental attention if they were going to develop the right sort of values. Marsha explained, "I found myself wondering, How wealthy do we need to be? I don't care if I have a great car, or if people are impressed with what I'm doing for a living. We have everything we need."

The movement is pervasive. "This is not something simply happening to the burnouts from Wall Street," says sociologist Stephen Warner of the University of Illinois at Chicago. "There is an American phenomenon going on that crosses all social lines. It's true of immigrant groups too, as well as the underprivileged."

. . .

In scaling down their tastes, most Americans are making a virtue out of necessity. Contrary to perceptions, the past decade was an era of downward mobility for the majority of U.S. families, who kept up their spending by borrowing and relying on two incomes. Only the wealthiest 20% of Americans significantly increased their real income during the Reagan era, and the poor slipped further behind. After adjusting for inflation, the national standard of living has actually fallen since 1973; the real average hourly pay for U.S. workers has gone from $8.55 then to $7.54 today. Says Barry Bosworth, an economist at the Brookings Institution: "Americans are not becoming pessimistic. They are becoming realistic. It is right to think of cutting back."

At the same time, the baby-boom generation, which accounted for much of the spending binge of the 80s, is reaching middle age. Here come 75 million aching backs. A generation of reluctant grown-ups is raising children, caring for aging parents and beginning to think about retirement. Instead of pumping iron, preening and networking, they are worrying about orthodontists, skateboards and college tuitions. The backyard now has more appeal than the boardroom.

So forget those champagne wishes and caviar dreams, the right car, vodka, watch, cuisine and music system. Consumers no longer feel they absolutely must have the latest luxury product. Who would be impressed, anyway? "People don't think being square is synonymous with being a sucker anymore," says Dan Fox, marketing planning director of the Foote, Cone & Bolding ad agency. Besides, they no longer seem to get a kick from spending borrowed money.

. . .

Not everyone believes America has changed its stripes, however. "If the present generation has learned anything, it is that talk is cheap. But are they really doing anything different?" asks Stanford economist Victor Fuchs. "The baby boomers are just growing up and playing out a predictable life-cycle change." Elmer Johnson, a Chicago lawyer and former executive vice president of General Motors, sees "a hardness of heart that has not yet begun to be broken." John Kenneth Galbraith, the eminent liberal economist, dismisses the trend as a bicoastal fad among fast-trackers. Says he, with amused cynicism: "I just think it's pure horse_____ ."

Yet a lot of business people who stake their livelihood on shifts in consumer behavior see thousands of small changes that they believe are adding up to something. At a Brookstone store in Boston, a man exchanges a gift, trading in a $99 executive fountain pen ("I'll never use it") for a car-care kit. Suddenly people want to buy toys that don't take batteries. Sales of dolls are up. The 75-store Sharper Image chain, which made its reputation in the '80s with high-tech gadgets, has been blurring its image to include more low-cost, practical goods. Example: a $19.95 aluminum-can crusher for recyclers.

. . .

In fact, that's another reason for rejecting rampant materialism: its impact on the environment. "Whenever I use something or buy something now, I'm thinking, Where is this going to end up?" says Debbie Worthley, 46, a student adviser at the University of Vermont. "I'm not as interested in buying gadgets as I was a few years ago." Seventh Generation, a two-year-old Colchester, Vt., mail-order firm that specializes in goods for the environmentally conscious, has an essay in its catalog titled "Why You Should Buy Less Stuff." Recycling has taken hold as a voguish and satisfying pursuit. People who used to meet at trendy bars now trade bons mots while sorting their garbage into the appropriate bins at the public dump. Even the smaller luxuries are giving way to environmental vigilance. If last year's popular orange juice was a quart of premium with extra pulp, this year's is canned concentrate, which requires less packaging.

. . .

For many Americans the most startling realization is how much they have given up for their careers. In her new book *Down-Shifting*, author Amy Saltzman maintains that baby boomers have grown increasingly skeptical about the payoff for devoting so much time to the fast track. As their huge generation crowds toward the top of the corporate pyramid, many are getting stalled. At the same time, companies have been slashing the ranks of middle managers.

For Karen Glance, 36, it came down to all those little packets of shampoo. She remembers the morning she opened her bathroom cabinet in St. Paul and counted 150 that had followed her home from hotels in dozens of cities. Says the former apparel executive: "I was a workaholic, a crazy, crazy woman. I was on a plane four times a week. I just wanted to get to the top. All of a sudden, I realized that I was reaching that goal but I wasn't happy. A year would go by and I wouldn't know what had happened."

A few months ago, Glance was shopping in a neighborhood grocery store when she learned that its owner was about to retire. Something fell into place. She looked around the old-fashioned shop, where clerks still climb ladders to retrieve goods from the upper shelves, and she decided on the spot to buy the place. The new proprietor of the Crocus Hill market may never come anywhere near to matching her old $100,000-plus yearly income, but she couldn't care less. Says Glance: "It really comes down to saying, 'Slow down. The value of life might not be in making money.'"

Mostly, though, what people want now is more time around home and hearth. Most parents of small children work outside the home. More than 7 million Americans hold down two or even three jobs to make ends meet. "Nobody seems to have any damn time anymore," says Stuart Winby, a Hewlett-Packard executive. "People can't manage their home, work, and personal life." As a result, many working mothers (and some fathers) are giving up full-time careers to devote more time to homelife. "There is a sense of an enormous trade-off between a fast-track career and family well-being," says economist Sylvia Ann Hewlett, author of the forthcoming *When the Bough Breaks: The Cost of Neglecting Our Children.* "Women can see the damage around them and are making different choices than they did a few years ago."

Some couples are even thinking twice about divorce in light of the problems it can pose for children, the financial damage it does to families and other consequences. The U.S. divorce rate, which reached a high of 5.3 per 1,000 people in 1979, is now 4.7 and may still be falling.

Of all those rejecting the rat race to spend more time with their families, perhaps the most famous is Peter Lynch. While the 47-year-old investment superstar was busy building the Fidelity Magellan mutual fund into a $13 billion behemoth, his youngest daughter got to be seven years old, and he felt he hardly knew her. Last spring he stunned Wall Street when he decided to give up his 14-hour workdays. With a nest egg estimated at $50 million, Lynch could well afford to quit. But many ordinary people evidently felt a connection with what he did, for he received more than 1,000 letters of support for his move. These days, while other investment managers are scanning their market data at dawn, Lynch is making school lunches. Says he: "I loved what I was doing, but I came to a conclusion, and so did some others: What in the hell are we doing this for? I don't know anyone who wished on his deathbed that he had spent more time at the office."

The stay-at-home urge, also known as "cocooning," has produced a boom of its own. Consumers spent more than $9 billion renting videotapes in 1990, up 13% from the previous year and nearly twice the $5 billion they paid to see new releases at theaters. Home entertaining is decidedly back to basics. Remember onion dip? The Mom Rule has re-emerged as America's primary meal-planning guide: if she never heard of it, don't serve it. With a couple of children in tow, mothers and fathers simply don't have time to hunt for goat cheese and sun-dried tomatoes in the supermarket. Marsha Bristow Bostick fondly recalls the leisurely evenings she spent at home before her children were born, "cooking wonderful things with my husband while we sipped white wine." Now? "We're eating SpaghettiO's, fried chicken, lots of terrible-for-you casseroles covered in cheese."

Far from becoming hermits, many Americans are reaching out to strengthen their ties beyond the home. Instead of defining themselves mostly by their possessions and work, more Americans in big cities as well as small towns are getting involved with their communities. "I don't think God puts you on this earth just to make millions of dollars and ignore everyone else," says Chris Amundsen of Minneapolis, a commercial real estate expert who took a 34% pay cut when he became the chief financial officer of a nonprofit housing agency.

Lately, charitable agencies and community groups have seen an upsurge in the willingness of Americans to help the less fortunate. . . . Instead of exchanging Christmas presents, many have started making contributions in the names of their friends. . . . Voluntary efforts range from the spectacular to the simply heartwarming. In Los Angeles real estate broker Eric Broida regularly volunteers at the Union Rescue Mission, where he serves meals to the homeless. "A couple of years ago, I went down one night to help out, and it just felt right," he says. "I felt good. I've been going back ever since."

In their search for more enduring gratification in life, many people are seeking spirituality, if not a born-again commitment to organized religion. "Spirituality is in," says theologian Marty, "so much so that I get embarrassed by it." Says Milton Walsh, a Roman Catholic priest who is pastor of St. Mary's Cathedral in San Francisco: "People want some kind of direction and purpose, the basic 'Who am I? Where am I going?'"

The mood has influenced the career choices of college students and recent graduates. Many are spurning high-powered corporate careers to train for teaching, nursing and other community-service jobs. Joe Holland turned down generous offers after graduating from Harvard Law School a few years ago to move to Harlem to help build up the community. Now the owner of a restaurant and a travel agency, Holland has also founded a shelter for the homeless. "I know that coming to Harlem shut the door to Wall Street," says he. "But I can look at a healthy man, a full-time travel agent, who came through my homeless program two years ago strung out on crack. I have absolutely no regrets."

By some analyses, the 1990s will be an anxious era of dues paying for the excesses of the '80s. That may be true in a public sense, but in private lives, how much fun was the past decade? For most Americans it was a time of struggling to keep up with everyone who seemed to be making it big. Now that the bubble of financial speculation has burst, people should—and do—feel entitled to accept more modest aspirations.

. . .

But the final question is this: Is the simple life just a passing fancy, a stylish flashback of the 1960s? Not so, say people who have studied both eras. Contends Berkeley sociologist Robert Bellah: "It's no longer messianic, the way it was in the '60s, but relatively pragmatic. That may give the present mood a greater staying power." That's good, because the American generation now reaching middle age has a lot of promises to keep—not to mention mortgages to carry, tuition to pay and lawns to mow. No wonder they want to keep it simple.

LETTERS WRITTEN IN RESPONSE TO "THE SIMPLE LIFE"

The soul of our quest for the simple life may lie far deeper than polls reveal. The simple life reflects a need to re-establish control of our lives. It shows that we're capable of accomplishing more than we thought—that we can build a table or a house with our own hands, run a store, plant tomatoes or play with children. We can laugh, wonder and depend on our common sense.

Peter V. Fossel, Editor
Country Journal
Harrisburg, Pa.

How wonderful that people have learned money cannot buy happiness and that they have given up high-paying, high-powered careers to enjoy the simple life. They are lucky they have the choice. The majority of us live the simple life because that is all we can do.

Tina Porod
Marinette, Wis.

How ludicrous to think the behavior of a few repentant yuppies constitutes a pervasive movement in America. It sounds as if these lucky folks are taking a break made possible by their once inflated salaries.

Lois Deming Hedman
Chicago

Who are you kidding? Those yuppies who are scaling down are simply taking early retirement.

Crystal Jarek
Fort Myers, Fla.

Here it is 2 A.M., and I've already delivered two babies tonight, and I'm working on 30 straight hours without sleep. I'm reading this article on the simple life and thinking, Wouldn't it be nice to have a farm somewhere and enjoy the simpler things life has to offer? Maybe tomorrow I'll look into it. Oh! That's my patient shouting. Got to go. It was a nice diversion, anyway.

Richard Levine, M.D.
Wyckoff, N.J.

At 42, I decided to retire from medicine and begin Ph.D. studies in mathematics. I settled in a small college town 10 miles from the nearest interstate. The kids can walk to school; I bike to class. Life can truly be a feast.

Robert Ingle, M.D.
Corvallis, Ore.

To Apply This Reading to Yourself

1. *What "really matters" in your life? What are your priorities? Why?*
2. *How have your priorities changed in the past few years? How do you expect them to change in the future? Why?*
3. *Would you like to "slow down and live a more relaxed life"? Why or why not?*
4. *Has your life been getting better or worse? Do you expect it to get better or worse in the next few years or decade? Why?*
5. *Describe what would be an ideal life for you. Would you call it a "simple" life? Why or why not?*
6. *Describe what would be an ideal life for you, and compare it with the life you now have.*

The Cyclic Life

Ken Dychtwald and Joe Flower

THE END OF THE LINEAR LIFE PLAN

Throughout all of human history, the average length of life was short. In a world where (if they survived the high infant mortality rates) most people did not expect to live longer than 40 or 50 years, it was essential, both for the biological continuation of our species and the maintenance of social order, that certain key personal and social tasks be accomplished by specific ages. Traditionally, important lifestyle activities such as "job preparation," "parenthood," and "retirement" were not only assigned to particular periods of life but were also supposed to occur only once in a lifetime.

Until now, the charting of our lives has been very neat and predictable. Stated simply: first you learned, then you worked (at family and career), and then you died.

Specifically, childhood and youth were the time for learning and play. By your late teens, you were supposed to know "what you wanted to be" for the rest of your life. If you were an unmarried woman over 30, you were on your way to spinsterhood. When you chose a mate, it was "till death do you part." The thirties and forties were the years for childrearing; the fifties and sixties, if you lived that long, were for grandparenthood.

You were expected to pick a career in your late teens or early twenties, and to pursue it without respite throughout most of your adult life; in your job, you were supposed to learn, grow, and "climb the ladder." Once you reached "old age," you could expect the remaining years of life to be characterized by declining health, a gradual lessening of school and professional challenges, and a retirement from the work force prior to death. In general, the older you got, the less you were expected to try new things, meet new people, or experiment with new ways of living. You were definitely not supposed to go back to school, fall in love, begin a new career, or take up a social crusade.

Almost every event and decision of life, big or small—getting a graduate degree, marrying, adopting a child, learning a musical instrument, bicycling across the country, pursuing a new career—was thought to have a particular age at which it was appropriate, and lots of ages when it was not. It's as though the various activities of our lives had a plan against which they were measured. And the path from childhood to old age was linear: it moved in one direction, with little room for hesitations, detours, experimentation, or second chances.

This linear life plan was kept in place by the forces of tradition. If we didn't behave appropriately for our age, our parents, clergy, teachers, neighbors, and even children could be counted on to remind us of our proper roles. We still tell each other to act our ages, as if a commandment to "Act thy age" had been handed down on Sinai along with the other ten.

Just as you might produce shock and disapproval by doing what society considered the wrong things, you could also reap profound criticism by doing perfectly normal things at the wrong age. "Mom, do you really think you should be applying to college at your age?" ... "Look at that silly old man trying to keep up with the young kids on the dance floor." ... "What does that old woman think she's trying to prove by wearing a bikini to the beach?" ... "Isn't it time you retired and made room for the young people?" ... "Why in the world would that older couple want to adopt a child at their age?"

The linear life plan was also imposed by law. Government regulations and institutional rules have prescribed the ages at which we should go to school, begin and end work, adopt a child, or receive our pension.

And, most powerfully, the linear life plan has been perpetuated by our own assumptions. Almost all of us have said, at one time or another, "It's too late for me to try that" or "If I could only have one more chance to do it over again" or "If only I were younger, I would ..."

In many ways, you were judged, and you often judged yourself, by how successful you were in following the linear plan. If you did things in a different order or didn't do some of them at all, your family and friends would undoubtedly have stories of others who had deviated from the path and ended up poor, childless, and socially ostracized.

The linear life plan was based directly on the biological and social requirements of the short length of life in earlier times. If you expected to be old at 50 and dead shortly thereafter, you didn't really have much time to deviate from the normal course of things. If you wanted to be able to have children and parent them until they grew up, you had to get married and start having babies when you were in your twenties. If you hoped to be able to support your family, you had to get started on building your career early, and you couldn't take any time off to reconsider or to change direction. Life's personal and occupational tasks were straightforward, clearly delineated, and heavily influenced by the brevity of life. Run like a 50-yard dash, the shorter life offered few second or third chances.

Underlying this approach to life were two basic assumptions:

1. The various activities of life were to be performed on time, and in sequence.
2. Most of life's periods of growth took place in the first half of life, while the second half was in general characterized by decline.

THE CYCLIC LIFE PLAN

Imagine that you knew you would live not to 50 or 60 but to 80, 90, or more, and that you could be vigorous and independent almost all of those years. If you could be assured of this longevity, would you be in such a hurry to get everything done early in life? Would you feel you had to select your career right out of school, in your early twenties, or would you take a bit of time to reflect on this important life choice and perhaps spend a few years trying different kinds of employment? Would you assume that you would have only one career during your entire lifetime, or would you plan on having several? Would you be in such a rush to get married and start having children in your early twenties, or might you be inclined to slow your pace and wait a while? If

you became divorced in your middle years, would you see this as the end of companionship, or rather as an opportunity to move on to your next loving involvement?

If your chosen career was no longer satisfying, might you consider going back to school to learn an entirely new professional skill? If you knew you would live eight or nine decades, would you retire from all work in your fifties or early sixties, bunching all of your leisure time at the end of life, or would you instead take time off occasionally during your middle years? If there were special activities that you simply didn't have time for when you were younger—such as learning to play a musical instrument, becoming a gourmet cook, or running in marathons—wouldn't you like to know that you could have a second chance at these activities later in life?

If any of these possibilities appeal to you, or if they affirm lifestyle directions you are already pursuing, you are not alone. The Age Wave is lifting the major components of adult life—family, education, work, leisure, and community service—free of their traditional moorings.[1]

We are witnessing the dissolution of the traditional linear life plan. In its place, a much more flexible arrangement, known as the "cyclic life plan," is emerging.

Family. For example, when the average life expectancy was 45 to 55 years, we spent nearly every moment of our adult years raising our children. As a result, we have come to think our family roles as being primarily that of parent. As recently as one century ago, by the time the last child was grown and ready to leave home, one or both of the parents had already passed away. With the coming of the Age Wave, most of us will have more years of adult life *after* the children have grown and have left home than we had when we were raising them. As a result, the role of parenting will fade in the overall architecture of family life, and the importance of mature friendship and companionship will rise as core elements of mid- and late-life marital relationships.

1. The *Age Wave* refers to the coming transformation of this country due to our increasing longevity and the growing number and influence of older persons.

Education. Whereas education has been primarily geared to preparing the young for their lifetime careers, we are now coming to think of learning as an ongoing, lifelong process. As the pace of discovery quickens and our appetite for learning increases, we will find ourselves being retrained and retooled many times throughout our lives. In addition, as our commitment and need for learning expands, our interest in non-vocation–oriented education will increase as well.

Work. We have thought of work as the job we perform essentially nonstop from our early twenties until we either retire or die. We expect to expand and enlarge our abilities in the early years of our careers, reaching a peak in the late forties or early fifties, and then winding down to a halt during the remaining decades. We will soon find ourselves cycling in and out of several different careers throughout our lives, each interspersed with periods of rest, recreation, retraining, and personal reflection. And some older men and women will hit their career stride for the first time at an age when others are retiring.

Leisure. We have thought of leisure as rest from work and as something we could enjoy for extended periods only during early childhood or old age. Now, we are beginning to envision leisure as an ongoing element of our adult years, with regular time taken away from work for recreation and personal growth.

Community service. Volunteerism and community service have long been the exclusive province of social crusaders, the rich, or older people with lots of spare time. Now, elevated life expectancy and the abundance of time it brings will allow all of us an expanded opportunity to invest our skills, knowledge, and accumulated resources in our communities and culture.

In the new social and economic atmosphere, family, education, work, leisure, and community service will blend into and influence one another, and even—as we shall see—masquerade as one another. Men and women will "retire," only to return to the work force a few years later, sometimes for pay, other times not. Our "families" will become an evolving blend of our true blood relatives and the revolving networks of friends who share our needs and interests at the various stages of our lives. We may devote our leisure time to play and recreation, or we may decide to enroll in a master's program in philosophy at the local college.

While there are as yet few role models for this emerging lifestyle, more people than ever have been opting out of the tight linear life plan and adopting elements of a cyclic life.

For example:

- Increasing numbers of men and women are marrying later in life and choosing to delay parenting until after they have successfully launched their careers and settled into marriage. For women, the average age of first marriages has risen to its highest point (23) in the nation's history; for men, it has reached the highest point (26) since 1900. And more women in their thirties and forties are having children today than at any previous time in history. Between 1975 and 1985, there was a 71 percent increase in births to women 35 years and older in comparison to the preceding ten-year period.
- There are unmistakable trends toward increasing divorce and remarriage. Currently, more than 50 percent of all marriages end in divorce, a percentage that reflects a 43 percent increase since 1970. Eighty percent of divorced people remarry, making "serial monogamy" the norm rather than the exception in America.
- Learning is no longer exclusively the province of the young. In recent years, it has become increasingly common for middle-aged or older people to go back to school. In fact, in community colleges, which traditionally have been home to 18- and 19-year-olds fresh out of high school, the average age of evening students has soared to 38.

At the present time, 45 percent of all undergraduate and graduate students in the United States are over 25.

- Today, it's unlikely that the job you choose to pursue in your early twenties will be the one you'll be working at in your sixties. People of all ages take regular sabbaticals for education or leisure or start entirely new careers. The average American now changes jobs every three years, often with time off for regrouping between positions. And, in support of disengaging the traditional work/leisure lockstep, it's estimated that nearly 14 percent of major American corporations now offer some form of paid sabbatical from work.

- Except for a few specified professions (such as airline pilot), mandatory retirement became illegal, by federal statute, in 1987. The results of a number of recent surveys agreed fairly closely that only about 27 percent of Americans want to stop working completely at retirement age, and more than 60 percent hope to keep working either full- or part-time. Changing attitudes and financial necessities will raise this percentage even higher.

- The percentage of out-of-work executives who start totally new careers rather than seeking new positions in the same industry has more than doubled in the last five years. According to a recent *Money Magazine* story about retirement, when ten retirees who had had a high degree of job success were asked, "What's the best thing about your retirement?" eight of them answered, "My new job!"

And because of the incredible pace of technological and cultural change, the Rand Corporation, a future-oriented think tank in Santa Monica, California, predicts that by the year 2020 the average worker will need to be retrained up to 13 times in his or her lifetime.

All around us, millions of ordinary aging Americans have begun to break free of the traditional expectations of age to shape new and rewarding cyclic lives for themselves.

Witness the case of Jacob Landers, interviewed by radio producer Connie Goldman for her "Late Bloomers" series. Now a public-interest lawyer in New York who gives voice and legal force to the elderly, Landers entered law school at 67, on a whim.

He had never thought of being a lawyer before, but the subject popped up one Thanksgiving in the chance comments of his daughter. The idea quickly became a challenge, the kind Landers had never been able to let pass by.

He had already had several careers. He had spent many years in education as a teacher, administrator, professor of education, and consultant on union educational funds. His career changes had been prompted by health problems: each time he "retired" for reasons of health, he would get restless and find something else to do.

On that particular Thanksgiving, Landers's daughter was talking about her struggles in law school. The emotion that arose in Landers was not pity but envy. "She was telling us about her experiences going to law school, about her classes and her friends. I said, 'I wish I could do that!' She said, 'Why don't you?'

"I said, 'How can I? Here I am—I'm already too old for that. Besides, what law school would want to accept an old man in his dotage?' I said the usual things one says when one doesn't want to do something.

"She was very direct. She said, 'Look, if you really want to do it, you can! If I can, you can!'"

By the end of the conversation, Jacob had promised that he would at least find out about it. The next Monday he called a registrar at New York University.

I asked her point-blank whether it was possible. She said, "Why not? You know there's an anti-discrimination law. We can't turn you down solely because you're too old. This Saturday we're going to give an exam. If you want to, you can be a walk-in candidate."

I hustled over to a bookstore to get some of the practice materials. I studied very hard. On Saturday I walked in and took the test. To my surprise, I did very well.

So I went to law school. I made friends among the people who were there. Most of them were very young. They were very kind. In the beginning they tried to baby me, as if to say, "Here's this elderly gentleman, and we have to be nice to him." But after a while they forgot about that. They accepted me. They treated me just the way they treated each other. I was subject to the same congratulations and derision. They argued with me and debated with me.

One of the proudest moments of my life was at graduation in Carnegie Hall. The dean had cautioned the audience not to applaud or do anything else that would disrupt the proceedings. And they didn't. But when my name was announced, *everybody* got up and applauded. I was so proud and so pleased for just that gesture. If I had won all the medals it would not have meant as much to me.

Like any new law graduate, Jacob Landers framed his diploma and prepared to search for a job. Then he received an offer from a foundation concerned with the legal issues of the aging. They had read about him in the newspaper. Landers took the job in order to advance the rights of the elderly.

According to Landers, "Most people have been brainwashed to believe that at a certain age they must turn up their toes and prepare to die. One day you might be in charge of a big organization. You're tremendously efficient and everybody kowtows to you. Everybody thinks you can do things. You retire, and the assumption is that the very next day you become a nonentity. You can't do anything. Society tends to place the elderly in a separate world. Society tends to feel that older people should just operate on the fringes, not in the center."

Today, Landers is a staff attorney at the Brookdale Center on Aging at Manhattan's Hunter College, lobbying for the elderly and taking on cases that involve retirement guidelines, Social Security, and Medicaid. He says of his job, "I feel I am able to do something. I feel a part of a larger society. Within my own sphere I have a certain amount of power."

And how about Detroit newlyweds Louis Gothelf and Reva Schwayder? He is 86, she 85. Both painters, they met and fell in love four years ago on a group painting tour of England. Each had been widowed in the early 1980s after more than 55 years of marriage. Of his first wife, Lou says, "After she died, I just sat in my apartment. When you're in your eighties and you sit alone day after day, it's so lonely. Oh, God, I felt alone."

Both assuming that romance would never touch them again, Reva and Lou were flabbergasted when they felt the pangs of "love at first sight" for each other. "This girl, she had a magnet," Lou proclaims. "As far as we were concerned," adds Reva, "there was no one else on that painting trip."

After experimenting with various live-in arrangements for several years, they finally decided to tie the knot last year, as much to quiet the neighbors as to legalize their affections. When asked how long they hope this new love will last, Lou philosophizes, "I live for today—you never know what's going to happen tomorrow. So I never, never buy green bananas."

Some lifestyle experimenters will use the opportunity of extended life to have a second chance at developing entirely different aspects of themselves. For instance, Bob Phelps, another of Goldman's "Latebloomers," worked as a conservative journalist for 40 years, cultivating the objectivity and detachment of a top metropolitan daily newspaperman, until he retired from the Boston *Globe* in his late fifties.

After retiring, Bob decided to become an actor. Not just a nights-and-weekends community-theater actor, but a pro—going to acting school, taking his résumé around to the agencies, getting small parts, doing commercials, dinner theater, summer stock—in short, making a career.

He explains:

I had had absolutely no experience on the stage in any form. When I made the decision to retire, I remembered back as a young boy sitting on the porch of the house in which I was raised in Erie, Pennsylvania, thinking about what I was going to do after high school. At that point I had two choices in front of me: go to college, or go to the Pasadena Playhouse in California and become an actor. After due deliberation I decided that I was going to go to school. Now I thought, "Why don't I do the other thing now?"

Acting, for Phelps, is much more than a way to while away the hours of retirement. It's a complete personality change.

As an editor, I held my feelings inside, and that was valuable. But in acting you have to follow the impulse. So to be an actor I've had to break down the training of over 40 years. And in doing that, I have learned that I hardly knew what an impulse was. I had submerged my freedom to do things, to say things, to raise an eyebrow. Now I'm trying to get that freedom back. I see things in people I never saw before, and I see them in myself. And I wonder what would have happened in the rest of my life if I had not done this.

For Phelps, long life comes as a liberation: "Since we have only one life, why not live a number of its possibilities instead of just sticking to one?"

And then there's Sarah Conley. At the age of 104, she graduated from De Anza College in Cupertino, California. It took her ten years to complete her associate of arts degree in the college's Older Adult Services program, finishing her last courses while she was a resident of the Sunnyvale Convalescent Hospital. On graduation eve, as the other residents gathered around to celebrate her grand accomplishment, a local television reporter showed up to interview her.

"Are you proud to get a college degree?" he asked.

"Why, yes, wouldn't you be?" Conley answered with a smile.

It is not just older men and women who are taking on new challenges, careers, and relationships. Set free by the Age Wave, younger people are also breaking free of the traditional linear life pattern. Take Laurie Bagley, for instance. Laurie had worked her way through the University of California at Berkeley, obtaining an advanced degree in library science. After a decade in the field, including five years as my researcher on this book, she decided that it might be fun to try an entirely new career. After some reflection, she decided that she would like to become a veterinarian.

At 35, Laurie resigned from her position as director of research at Age Wave, Inc., and went back to the life of a student. "It will take me at least six years before I can hang out my shingle," she says. "I spent the first part of my twenties in the 'poor-student' mode. I had a wonderful decade as a successful professional, and now I'm going to spend my late thirties as a starving student again. But I feel that if I will probably live to be at least 80 and will in all likelihood be working most of my life, it's certainly not too late for me to embark on a new career and lifestyle."

Other people just want a break, and the cyclic lifestyle easily accommodates this strategy. Jeri Flinn was director of public relations for Memorex, the Silicon Valley data-storage giant; her husband, John, had been a reporter for the San Francisco *Examiner* long enough to qualify for a sabbatical. When they had saved enough money, John took the sabbatical and combined it with accumulated vacation time, Jeri quit her job, and they headed off around the world. For a year they journeyed through the Pacific islands, Australia, Asia, and the Middle East. They celebrated John's thirtieth birthday in Katmandu, Jeri's in Edinburgh. When they returned, he got back the job guaranteed him by the Newspaper Guild contract, and she became the manager of financial public relations for Tandem Computer, another large Silicon Valley company. "We worked toward [the trip] for four years," Jeri says. "It was a fulfilling experience. I had never realized how much there was out there to see and experience."

BREAKING FREE

During my travels across America over the past 15 years, I have repeatedly been struck by how many stories I hear of men and women at all stages in their adult lives who have chosen to embark on a path or pursue a dream that was somewhat out of line with what most other people their age were doing, and even with what they themselves had been doing earlier in their lives. Although no one has yet conducted a study of the number of people who are shedding the confines of the linear life plan for the more diverse and flexible choices of the cyclic life plan, I am convinced that this is the wave of the future.

To date, medical science has done remarkably well at adding years to our lives. However, most of us haven't yet figured out the purpose or explored the opportunities of these extra years. And although a few years ago a 62-year-old Congressional freshman, an 83-year-old "wrinkled radical," a 67-year-old law-school student, a 35-year-old "retiree," a 104-year-old college graduate, or a 55-year-old aspiring actor may have seemed the odd circumstance, in the years to come such early lifestyle experimenters will come to be remembered as the true social pioneers—"elderheroes"—of the Age Wave.

Of course, not all of us will live in ways that are wildly at odds with the ways we have lived in the past. Most people will probably still choose to marry and start families in their twenties. For most, career peaks—at least for first careers—will still come between the ages of 30 and 50. Many people will continue to retire from work in their sixties.

What is different about the cyclic life plan is not that most people will choose to do things differently than they have in the past, but that they all have the option to do so.

The dead hand of tradition, the weight of regulations, and the power of our own expectations will no longer force us to do exactly what everyone else our age is doing. In a longer life, there are second and third chances—opportunities to go back and do some of the things we weren't able to do, for whatever reason, earlier in life.

To Apply This Reading to Yourself

1. *How linear or cyclical has your life been, and how linear or cyclical do you want and expect it to be? Discuss this aspect of your life.*
2. *How much change and how much constancy has there been in your life, and how much change and constancy do you want and expect in the future? Discuss this aspect of your life.*
3. *Make up a linear or cyclic life plan for yourself that would provide you with the maximum amount of fulfillment and personal growth.*
4. *Suppose through a stroke of good fortune, you no longer had to work for a living. What would you do? How would your life change? Why?*
5. *Suppose through a stroke of bad fortune, you were no longer assured a long life. What would you want to crowd into it? Why?*
6. *At what things in life might you want a second and even third chance? Why?*

The Successful Life

Harold H. Bloomfield and Robert B. Kory

There is an epidemic in our culture, a social disease that won't go away with a pill or vaccination. It's the belief that ultimate satisfaction is yours when you have finally amassed all the money, power, and glamour you covet. You see the effect of this delusion all around you: a wholesale cultural striving after the material attributes of success at the expense of the inner joy and primary life experiences that make success truly worthwhile. You find millions engaged in the anhedonic[1] struggle for the external trappings of success—money, power, possessions, sex—while family life, health, personal integrity, and the ability to enjoy life suffer steady decline.

What have you already paid, physically and emotionally, for your success? What will the human costs be in the future? Are the satisfactions you have achieved worth the price?

These are difficult questions. No matter where you stand on the ladder of the American dream, your money and power are rarely enough if along the way your marriage falls apart, you begin chewing Maalox like candy, you become so tense that you hardly enjoy a day off, you compromise your values so often that protecting your self-interest becomes the mainstay of your personal ethics, or you often wonder if life has any real meaning beyond your ability to earn a bigger paycheck.

Much has been written in condemnation of what William James called "the American worship of the bitch-goddess Success." We do not subscribe to this view. The problem, as we see it,

is not success, but what people do to themselves in their quest to achieve it. The solution to anhedonic success striving is not to retreat from the challenge of success, but to develop the basic knowledge that enables you to relish every moment of life. This is what we call the *200 percent success profile*—full inner development to complement maximum external achievement.

The issue in this chapter is how your personal vision of success (and your efforts to get there) are affecting your inner life. Human beings are created with a nearly unlimited capacity for growth. We can always extend ourselves to greater heights. No doubt this is basic to the American dream that given an opportunity, perseverance, and hard work, anyone can achieve the better things in life. What has been sadly overlooked is the one-sided application of this effort toward the acquisition of things worth *having* at the expense of the things worth *being*. Now the pendulum is swinging in the opposite direction. The culture is awakening to the need to reach not just for wealth but also for depth; not just for quantity but also for quality of experience; not just for exciting pleasures but also for lasting satisfactions. The challenge is integration, and the issues involved are vital.

DEFINING SUCCESS IN YOUR OWN TERMS

The first thing to understand in assessing your own success profile is that there is no one to compare yourself with but you. Since childhood, parents and society have bombarded you with expectations about what you ought to become and what you ought to achieve. These expectations are not easily set aside. Nevertheless, do remember that you are unique; only you can know what you truly want out of life. The final measure of your personal success as a human being is whether you manage to create a life of abundant satisfactions that you reap from living life on your own terms.

But what about money? The American definition of success hasn't changed much over the last hundred years. What you own (not what you are) is still the primary criterion. Given this heritage, most people are reluctant to consider the

---

1. Anhedonic is a word derived from the Greek *an-* (not) and *hedone* (pleasure) and refers to the inability to experience pleasure. Anhedonic means inhibiting pleasure or interfering with pleasure. For more about anhedonia and anhedonic things, see another reading by Bloomfield and Kory on pages 297–304 of this book and also see their book *Inner Joy* from which both of these readings were condensed.—THE EDITOR.

folly of this one-sided view until they begin to discover its consequences for themselves.

George Bernard Shaw once wrote: "There are two tragedies in life. One is not to get your heart's desire. The other is to get it." Here is the hidden pitfall and primary challenge in shaping your personal vision of success. No matter what your dream, achieving it will rarely live up to all your expectations. There will always be personal costs that you did not expect and parts of yourself that remain unfulfilled. The practical implication of this hard fact of life is that genuine success cannot be defined as the achievement of any particular goal.

Success is not static. It isn't the final reward for a single achievement—becoming president of the company, getting married, making a million dollars, writing a best-seller, having children, or buying a huge house. Real success is dynamic. It is growth. It is discovering opportunities each day to express your talents and abilities to the fullest. It is learning to create your life joyfully even when things may not be working out as planned. It is knowing each day that your work has meaning. It is making your life an adventure and living not just for yourself, but also for a better world.

This definition of success makes some people uncomfortable because it doesn't include any absolute measures. There are no status symbols to prove you have made it or any list of perquisites to prove how powerful you are. The issue of personal success is taken out of the arena where you judge yourself by what others think of you and is placed squarely on your shoulders, what you think of yourself. Once you begin to define success dynamically, the key issues are those of personal values and satisfactions. Are you enjoying your life fully? Enthusiastic about what you are doing? Able to live according to your own values?

Through the interviews with hundreds of men and women caught up in the struggle to succeed, we have identified typical signs of an anhedonic success profile. You may well be caught on a treadmill of self-destructive striving if you:

- feel chronically short of time
- doubt whether your work or life has meaning

- are reluctant to go on vacation for fear of falling behind
- often compromise your values and beliefs
- find it difficult to enjoy leisure because you can't stop thinking about problems at work
- feel vaguely guilty whenever you relax, especially when you're facing a deadline
- spend less and less time with your family as the years go by, even though you resolve to change
- move, walk, and eat rapidly because you don't want to waste even a minute
- tend to be impatient, become upset when you have to stand in line
- avoid delegating responsibility for fear of losing control over your sphere of power
- frequently take work home and work late into the night
- feel all your success is due to speed and hard work rather than insight and creativity
- have developed a hostile attitude toward others, especially those people with whom you may be competing for promotion
- view everything in terms of "how much" and "how many"
- feel you always have to be "on," whether you're at work or at a party
- regularly suffer heartburn, headaches, muscle spasms, and/or anxiety
- frequently feel tense
- worry about your ability to keep your job

A less common but equally destructive success profile also emerged from our survey. It comes not from self-destructive striving, but from the new philosophy of not striving at all. We found it primarily among young people determined not to get into a life-style that they view as akin to a prison sentence. Avoid too much responsibility, postpone commitments, take it easy, be laid back. These are the primary characteristics of the new anhedonic success profile. The run from ambition becomes the flight into purposelessness. Here are other characteristic attitudes and behaviors:

- a fear of traditional commitments, marriage and children appearing only as a potential burden offering little or no joy
- cynicism, the belief that the world is not about to change, so why bother

- lack of personal goals, only a vague vision of the future
- inability to sustain love relationships, difficulty accepting the responsibility of intimacy
- boredom
- the desire to live comfortably by extending the minimum possible effort
- the absence of any desire to make a contribution or make the world a better place
- obsessive concern with personal pleasure
- the absence of ambition

Strive to climb the ladder and win status or wealth—or eschew the clamor for upward mobility and settle into a laid-back life-style. These two choices are the Scylla and Charybdis of the new American dream that promises not only a comfortable life-style but also personal growth. Now that the pendulum of success expectations has swung in both directions the anhedonic consequences of a life at either extreme have become clear. The new challenge is to find your own middle ground where a 200 percent success profile becomes possible.

THE SUPERACHIEVER

The desire to win is so strong in some people that they have cultivated the ability to push themselves at a peak of their capacity for weeks and months at a time. These are the superachievers, who have learned how to gear up for high performance under constant pressure. They can work long into the night when necessary, get very little sleep, and be bright and cheerful the next day. Nothing makes them shine more than a difficult problem that stretches their creative abilities. Their most distinguishing trait is the evident relish they take in almost everything they do. They have an awesome ability to enjoy their lives fully.

Most people who function at this high level can't explain how they manage to push so hard without becoming anhedonic. On occasion they may break stride and slip back into a state where pressure begins to take its toll in fatigue or anxiety. What causes the rhythm to be lost and later regained is usually only vaguely understood. "I take off for the weekend," says one corporation president, explaining what he does to get back in sync when his gears begin to grind. "Sleep," says another superachiever, "I slow way down and catch up on my rest." The remedy for a third is to get up every morning at six thirty and play tennis until eight. "If I stick to that routine for a week, have a sauna, let the problems sit on the back burner for a while, I snap back into shape." Most of the time these personal methods of reattunement work. The anhedonic striving along with the tension and anxiety passes; the old energy and clarity reemerge on their own. In some cases, however, the anhedonic symptoms don't diminish. In fact, they may grow, steadily diminishing performance and exacerbating anxiety.

When a superachiever gets caught in an anhedonic trap and can't get out, panic may set in. The experience can be emotionally devastating enough to prompt the search for help. "I felt like I was cracking up," is how one executive racehorse described his panic when he began suffering tension headaches and losing his sharp concentration. "I was always at the top. I could push myself and love every minute of it; then the sand started shifting under my feet. I began having doubts. I couldn't count on myself anymore." We have worked with many of these superachievers who have lost the inner attunement necessary to sustain their high level of functioning. In the process, we have gained insights into the dynamics of balancing a high-performance life-style with the personal growth necessary for inner joy.

CAUTION: WORKAHOLIC AT WORK

There he is in his office working late again. He called his wife to say he wouldn't be home for dinner; she's used to that. Now it's 9:00 P.M., time to pack up his briefcase. In a few minutes he has collected from his overloaded desk more paperwork than he can possibly do at home before he goes to bed. On the way out the door, the heavy briefcase is reassuring. He is a man of weight; he works hard; the company can't do without him, or at least that is what he would like to believe. Lurking just beneath that self-importance, however, is a desperate fear of failure. He is vaguely aware that he gets too bogged down in needless paperwork and that his thinking is going stale. He occasionally has the feeling of pedaling very hard and getting nowhere. So pervasive is his concern about his job that he only rarely takes time off and when he does, he usually doesn't enjoy it. He is a workaholic.

Some people work long hours because they love their jobs and feel they're making a genuine contribution. Others spend most of their waking hours at work because they have become addicted to their jobs as a means of self-protection from their real feelings. The former are hard workers; the latter are workaholics. The principal difference between the two lies in the ability to stand outside of the job. Both enjoy hard work, but the hard worker can separate himself from it. He doesn't take his problems home, so he is able to derive enormous enjoyment from family and nonwork activities. The workaholic, on the other hand, is truly enjoying himself only at work, so he unconsciously strives never to be far from his work responsibilities. When he tells his wife and children that he is too busy to take a vacation, he would like to think it's true. In truth, he doesn't take vacations because he finds them boring and feels at a loss whenever he is away from the preset routine and pressure of the office. The ability to stand outside the job is crucial to creativity. That's why the workaholic tends toward routines and is excessively preoccupied with the stuff of business (memos, letters, meetings) rather than its substance, creative thinking.

The emotional price of workaholism is usually paid in the home, where neglect often leads to resentment and divorce. "He's married to his work, not to me," said the wife of one workaholic. Children also suffer from this absentee father.

THE NEW DREAMERS

What about the success profile of the new generation weaned from college on the slogans of the sixties and now about to cross that once distant age barrier, the thirty-year mark? No one talks about a generation gap anymore, because the majority of those who once decried the establishment are now well on their way as its inheritors with their three-piece suits, short hair, and attaché cases—as if to say that the upheavals of the sixties have long since been forgotten. Or have they? The newest studies of young pacesetters of the new generation indicate that the generation gap may not be as wide as it once was, but it is still there.

Many men and women in their twenties or early thirties are aware of all that we have said so far about the pitfalls of a success profile built around the accumulation of wealth. They reject this vision of the American dream. Their view of success includes ample time for personal growth and leisure. They are not willing to become coronary candidates just to climb one more rung on the corporate ladder. Nor are they willing to rape the land and pollute the cities to make an extra dollar. They are trying to balance conflicting internal and external pressures to create lives rich in personal satisfactions.

They take a comfortable life as a given, but they don't want to work too hard. They want to see problems of poverty and injustice resolved, but they don't want to sacrifice time needed for personal growth. They would like to have a lot of money (a million dollars would do as a starter) but they're wary of getting locked into any job that makes them just another cog in the corporate machine. More than anything else, they want to be loving and enjoy loving relationships, but they are wary of commitments—marriage and children—that put sustaining love to the test. The new pacesetters mold their personal visions of success out of trade-offs between these conflicting desires. Is this balancing act leading to a new integrated vision of success or to a moral paralysis that hides an underlying selfishness with uplifting talk about personal growth?

OBSTACLES TO TRANSFORMING YOUR SUCCESS PROFILE

Perhaps you have decided that you want to make some changes in your success profile. Between your intention to take hold of your life and the changes you want to make lie the psychological rewards you are reaping for remaining exactly the way you are. These psychological dividends explain why change is often difficult. The rewards cause psychological inertia. Awareness of these resistances is the key to surmounting them. Here are several to consider.

Your current success profile may be providing feelings of self-importance that you're reluctant to challenge.

Nothing is more difficult than letting the hot air out of your own ego. Still, that may be what you must do to find out what really provides satisfaction and where your doors of opportunity actually lie. A false sense of self-importance based on confusion between image and actuality of success is the greatest obstacle to a dynamic success profile. It is so easy to get caught up in memos, heavy briefcases, long hours, and appearances because these are the signs we use to convince ourselves and others that even if we haven't made it yet, we're at least on the way. All too often, that leads to anhedonic striving and a tremendous waste of energy or, in the words of one executive friend, "doing more but accomplishing less."

The look of success is helpful to a point, but far more important are high levels of energy, creativity, and personal enthusiasm. You can't develop these qualities as long as you keep yourself caught on the treadmill of constant striving. Instead, you have to learn how to turn the process around so you can "do less but accomplish more." This requires changing your success profile. Too bad that some people would rather hold on to images than accept the challenge of growth.

Your success profile may be protecting you from a fear of failure that you have yet to conquer.

To avoid the fear, you may be among those who always adopt a defensive posture, rarely speak your mind, never risk disapproval, rarely volunteer to take on difficult tasks, never stick your neck out. You leave risks, and the fast track up the ladder, to others. You may maintain your feeling of security, but only at the price of personal stagnation. Unless you understand the dynamics of success, this may seem preferable to the risk of failure.

The irony is that failure is an integral step to success. No one ever made it to the top without risk, and risk inevitably leads to some failures. The lives of most great men and women are punctuated by failure. Look at them! George Washington was an abysmal failure in the French and Indian wars. During the Revolution he lost battle after battle against the British before finally winning at Yorktown and later becoming the first president. Abraham Lincoln lost his bid to unseat Stephen Douglas as senator for Illinois.

The Duke of Wellington was so inept in his youth that his mother said he was "no better than food for powder." Packed off to the army in disgust, he eventually became a field marshal and victor at Waterloo. Winston Churchill failed at school, failed as a cavalry officer, and failed to win many early elections. As first lord of the admiralty he single-handedly engineered a monstrous failure in the British attempt to seize the Dardanelles, and later failed dismally as chancellor of the exchequer. Yet in 1940, with England almost on her knees, he rose to become a national hero and a legend. To fail is clearly to join distinguished company!

Avoiding risks, hesitating to make changes, holding on to what you are (at the expense of what you could be) are sure paths to boredom and regrets! If this is your carefully considered choice, fine. The tragedy is to hover in a very restricted circle of your potential being without even *considering* all that you have the power to become.

Some people use the success striving as a justification for avoiding problems in love and marriage.

If you and your spouse are having difficulties, it's so much easier to say you have to work late than to come home and deal with the hassles that may await. Work is the classic excuse for avoiding sexual anxieties. When you and your lover both accept the myth that you have no choice but to work late night after night, neither of you has to face what may be going on in your relationship. After all, you're doing it all for the family. This gambit usually leaves you and your lover losing at work *and* at home. The underlying tension in the relationship saps your effectiveness at work and you miss the opportunity to resolve the problem and discover new joys. The longer this goes on, the more difficult it becomes to correct. Eventually, a crisis is likely to erupt. None of this may seem very rewarding, but there's a payoff nonetheless. The couple avoids facing the problems in the relationship for months or years. To some people, avoidance is preferable to growth.

The incessant struggle to succeed can become a means of avoiding issues concerning your own personal satisfaction.

This is another form of the "I'll be happy when..." syndrome. As long as you can convince yourself that your efforts will eventually lead you to nirvana, you don't have to think about the real level of joy you get out of living now, today. The reward is a short-term conservation of your energy. To change your success profile you have to expend some effort. Some people feel they're better off putting all their energies into striving for the top rather than investing in internal changes that may not seem to have an immediate result.

If you study 200-percent successful people, you'll find that they thrive on change, especially change within themselves. They're always looking for opportunities to discover new abilities and untapped sources of creativity. They adapt to failures and learn from their mistakes. Avoiding the issues of personal growth may appear sensible when you're overloaded with work, but that's the shortsighted view of the anhedonic person. In the long term, an investment in your own growth is an investment in your power to succeed.

An anhedonic success profile may also be your insulation against doubts about your personal values.

Are you satisfied with your job? What do you really want out of life? What would you rather be doing? These are value questions, and few personal queries are more difficult. The answers aren't usually clear-cut, and when they are, they often point to a need to make major personal changes. Many people find it easier (and therefore preferable) to avoid asking the big questions in the first place. That way the issue of change is neatly avoided. The price of avoidance is less joy and less vitality, but some people would rather pay that price than face the possibility that they may have been on the wrong track. Better to keep striving and hope that the American dream comes true.

There you have the dividends of holding on to an anhedonic success profile. They all represent the choice to live at a level lower than you could achieve. The alternative is to accept the challenge and the risk of going for 200 percent of life, full inner and outer development. The strategies for change are available. To create success on your own terms you need only your will, the determination to use them.

HOW TO CREATE AN INTEGRATED SUCCESS PROFILE

The ultimate solution to the conflicting pressures of a dynamic life-style is what we've called learning to "do less but accomplish more." You don't have to let yourself get forced into anhedonic choices between work and family, personal ambition and personal growth, achievement and enjoyment. You can have both. The best proof is the lives of the most successful people in business. At the highest levels of the corporate world, you find many people with an integrated success profile. They get a terrific charge out of their work—and also have time to enjoy their family and personal interests. They work hard, but they also make time to relax One striking characteristic is their ability to sustain an inner sense of ease and well-being even during their worst high-pressure days.

One highly successful executive described this possibility very lucidly:

Money was never my primary goal. I wanted to get rich, everyone does. But it wasn't my primary reason for working. The main goal was to do something I could be proud of and have fun in the process. I began by taking over a small bankrupt company, assembled a good team. We turned the business around and then started growing. At each stage we were having a terrific time. The challenge of beating companies ten times our size was exhilarating!

Now I'm at the top, corporate jet, corporate helicopter, limousine. We have our own building in New York. Some people think I work so hard that I can't enjoy the money. Bull! My work is a source of great satisfaction, and I have plenty of time for my family and for vacations. Sure, I do a lot of work at home, but it doesn't drain me to sit beside my pool in California. It's a terrific thing. I don't work harder than other people who are less successful. I've learned to enjoy my work and my life a lot more, that's all. I'm sure that's been the main ingredient of my success.

Another chief executive put it this way:

Success is a game. At first, you work very hard. You're young and just getting a feel for the business world, you don't yet know the real secrets of success, so you strive too hard and make yourself miserable. If you're going to make it to the top, you have to learn somewhere along the line that struggle and striving isn't the key. The guys who get caught at that level never make it all the way.

You have to stand away from the whole thing and see how funny it is. When you do that, you begin to relax. You ease up inside, and that makes for a tremendous increase in your energy and your creative ability. You discover how to maintain detachment under intense pressure. It's hard to maintain detachment under intense pressure. It's a kind of grace. When you stop trying altogether, you finally reach your peak potential. That's when it becomes a pure game. When you hit that moment, you've made it and nothing can stand in your way.

Here are some techniques to help you re-shape your success profile.

Begin by giving yourself full permission to succeed.

Most people are held back by the fear that they don't have what it takes. While they may pay lip service to believing in themselves, they turn right around and complain about all the obstacles that stand in the way: the boss, the company, too much work, too little work, too many "bad breaks." The fact is that many successful people do not have exceptional ability and many have limited education. They didn't score at the top in IQ tests, nor did they go to the best schools or get the best grades. Many come from humble backgrounds and have had bad breaks. The common denominator among all successful and happy people is desire, determination, and confidence. Your chance of success and fulfillment is just as good as anyone else's, and probably much better than you think. Only when you understand this key fact can you plunge ahead with enthusiasm and start functioning at your full potential.

Think of success as a process, not a final destination.

Highly successful people don't set out to achieve one grand goal and, on achieving it, pronounce themselves successful. They view their lives as an adventure and themselves as the heroic players. Perhaps this seems a little grandiose

to you, but it's far better to think of yourself as a hero and play life to the fullest than to minimize your abilities and never give yourself a chance to exercise all your talents. You are the creator of your life; why not create it heroically? It doesn't matter how old you are or where you may be on the success ladder. You have the power to create a life that will exceed your highest expectations. All you have to do is learn how to use it.

Make enjoyment of your work and your life, rather than money, your highest priority.

Not that the desire to be rich is bad. Almost everyone would enjoy being wealthy, and the desire for luxuries is healthy and normal. However, time and time again, studies have shown that people who make satisfaction in their work a top priority are the ones who perform best, receive the fastest promotions, and wind up making the most money. Those who make money the primary goal rarely achieve their economic goals and often wind up chronically unhappy. If you are stuck in a job that you don't enjoy, then you are unlikely to go very far in it even if you are being paid very well, because money is simply not a sufficient motivator. Maximum performance comes from maximum enjoyment. If you make enjoyment of your work and your life your top priority, you will do your best, and very often that will be better than you think you can do. The result will be success, and the money follows just as naturally as morning follows dawn.

Beware of any lingering fears of success.

It may surprise you to hear that many people block their success by fear, but the facts are there to be examined. Success implies change—in responsibility, life-style, relationships, and many other aspects of life—and for most people change is frightening. They're reluctant to surrender the safety of the routine and the familiar. Except in rare individuals, the instinct to resist change, do nothing, and accept the mediocre is measurably stronger than the desire to succeed.

People undermine their success in subtle ways. They choose wrong jobs, submit to employers who use them, behave in ways that undermine their chances of promotion, rely on weakness out of habit, and ignore strengths out of ignorance. To create a success profile of maximum opportunity you have to put an end to any lingering fears of success. You must be determined to discover your strengths and cultivate your talents; you must learn to relish your own growth.

Set attainable goals and learn to enjoy each small step of progress.

One of the most common ways people sabotage themselves is by trying to achieve too much too fast. There is a Wall Street saying that warns against this folly: "Bulls make money, bears make money, hogs never make money." While learning to take risks is important, foolish risks are nothing other than foolish.

Remember that rest is the basis of dynamic activity.

Several thousand years ago the Chinese sage Lao-tzu wrote: "All action begins in rest." In our hedonistic culture we seem to have forgotten this simple wisdom. If you are most people, you push yourself during the day and often at night as well without getting the rest you need. Look inside the typical office. Sagging shoulders, dark circles under the eyes, yawns, and fuzzy thinking are the norm. Without the coffee and cigarette machines, half the people might well fall asleep at their desks.

The importance of getting enough rest cannot be overrated. Consider your own experience. Remember how you feel on those days when you wake up fully refreshed and come to work bristling with energy and mental vitality. Not only do you work more efficiently and creatively, but you enjoy yourself more. If you're tired, even small problems can seem insurmountable. The point is: Feeling fully refreshed doesn't have to be left to chance! You can feel that way every day without cutting back on your busy life-style if you take the time to learn how to master a technique for getting very deep rest in a short period of time. The most dynamic people at the top of corporations often come upon these techniques by instinct. You may have to spend a few hours learning one.

Here are the four steps for a technique that uses positive imagery:

1. Close your eyes and take three or four deep breaths, preferably through the nose. Notice the soothing effects of the air filling your lungs, then flowing out through the nostrils.
2. Gently direct your attention to your toes and feel them relax. Let your attention glide slowly up your body—feet, ankles, calves, knees, thighs, hips, abdomen, back, chest, neck, hands, arms, face—and stop at each part to feel relaxation taking place. Let the warm heaviness of relaxation spread through your body.
3. Now imagine that you are floating in space, or lying in a warm meadow. Create any mental image that you find peaceful and deliciously enjoyable. Let the world slip away and drift naturally in your reveries.
4. After ten minutes, slowly make your way back to awareness of your body and surroundings. Take a few minutes to get oriented before opening your eyes. When you're finally back to reality, you will feel terrific. It's as if you've taken a vacation.

Dr. Herbert Benson at Harvard Medical School developed a technique he calls the relaxation response. Some people find it effective. It too has four steps:

1. Sit comfortably in a quiet room.
2. Close your eyes.
3. Relax your muscles systematically as described in the previous technique, beginning with the toes and working your way slowly up the body.
4. Once you're relaxed, repeat the word *one* or any simple syllable to yourself mentally with each exhalation of breath. After ten minutes, stop and slowly come out of your state of relaxation.

None of these techniques is a substitute for getting a good night's sleep, but most people who have mastered the art of concentrated rest find that they need less sleep. The result is a dramatic increase in the number of days that you wake up feeling great, and a significant improvement in the ability to maintain a high energy level throughout the day.

Don't overschedule.

Most people have a tendency to assume they can accomplish more in a given period than they actually can. The problem arises from planning a project without allowing enough extra time for things to go wrong (as they always do). Deadlines are valuable, because most people are more efficient and creative when they accomplish a task within a given period. However, you would be wise in setting your deadlines to allow an extra 20 percent for things to go wrong. When deadlines are so short that they cause anxiety and a last-minute rush, you and your work suffer unnecessarily.

Insulate yourself as much as possible from interruption.

Nothing is more jarring to the nervous system than repeated interruptions when you're in the midst of concentrating on an important problem. One of the worst mistakes is to get into the habit of taking every phone call no matter what you're doing. A good way to handle the telephone is to concentrate your calls in one time segment, say between nine and ten in the morning or four and five in the afternoon. During that time you take all calls, and call people back who called you. You aren't being rude to refuse a call because you are busy. You are being wise. If you are a victim of the telephone, telephone screening can change your work life.

Organize your work so you can always enjoy calm.

This is not as difficult as it sounds. The key is to be organized, and to have a system for keeping constant tab on your priorities. It helps to have four different files through which all your work flows. They should read "Routine Work," "Urgent," "Think," and "Work at Hand." Everything that comes across your desk should fall into one of the first three folders and remain there until you decide to move it to the position of work at hand. Once you start using this system, your work will take on a natural rhythm that will free you from unnecessary anxieties.

Consciously project ease and enjoyment

For example, when you're at a meeting, sit back and relax. This is far more effective for listening than sitting on the edge of your chair.

When you wish to speak, your movement forward will draw attention and quiet the group. Above all, don't hurry your speech. When you have something important to contribute, there is no rush! Your *words* are going to have an impact on your listeners. Take your time, be brief, and speak clearly. Intersperse pauses after key points. The value of silence is too often ignored. Be sure to enjoy yourself. That way you project maximum power and make others feel most comfortable. It's always a pleasure to listen to someone who is calm, speaks clearly, and projects a natural enthusiasm.

Remind yourself that creative intelligence, not hard work, is the source of your success.

The really valuable work you do in your job may be done in as little as five minutes a week! A brilliant idea. A pivotal decision. A simple solution. A telephone call that closes a big sale. In those five minutes you may accomplish more than in the forty hours you may have been trying to make those five minutes golden. This is not to say that you should strive to be inspired at each and every moment. That's obviously impossible. The point is to avoid getting caught up in working so hard that you lose your perspective and undermine your ability to be inspired.

Become aware of your natural optimum work/play cycles.

Just as you have a unique personality, you have an optimum work cycle that is likely to be different than anyone else's. Some people do their best work in the morning, others have an intense burst of concentration toward the end of the day. There are also people who have concentration bursts for brief intervals throughout the day. We call these periods of maximum alertness "prime time." Once you understand your prime time, you can schedule your activities so that you'll tackle the important and challenging ones at your peak creative periods and relegate mundane activities to your low points. Substantial evidence indicates that your prime time and optimum work cycle are biologically or even genetically determined. Trying to force yourself into an unnatural pattern (such as doing your most difficult work in the morning when you concentrate best in the afternoon) is a big mistake. You will cause needless tension, your work will suffer, and you will cheat yourself out of the most important thing of all—enjoying what you're doing.

Identify the conditions that help you get into a "state of flow."

Almost everyone has had the experience of starting work on a project and getting so immersed that they completely forget time, fatigue, even where they are. Many hours later, when the task is complete, they become aware that they've been functioning at a unique, high level where creative energies pour out effortlessly. Psychologists call this a state of flow. This wonderful and productive state is not arbitrary. You can learn how to create it and then use it at will to accomplish a great deal of work in the shortest time. The key is learning what conditions trigger the inner shift from ordinary functioning to flow. For some people, quiet is necessary. Most people must be well rested. Time of day is almost always a key factor. Flow is much more likely during your prime time than during a low period. Perhaps you need to be working at a particular desk or computer for flow to happen. There could be any number of critical conditions. Once you have learned what they are, you have made a major discovery. Flow is one of the basic means of "doing less and accomplishing more." It is also a natural state of inner joy, even ecstasy.

Don't put up with boredom.

Nothing is more stifling to the human spirit than hour upon hour of work that seems meaningless, unchallenging, unexciting. Many jobs are this way, but you don't have to get stuck in one! All you need is the courage to ask for what you want, presumably a job with more responsibility, more excitement, more challenge, more opportunity for promotion. You can get that job if you let other people know that you have the desire and the determination.

Value your time.

This may seem too obvious to mention. It would be if most people's actions reflected a true regard for their time. They don't. All too often, people fritter away time on unimportant activities; work overtime for an unappreciative boss who is taking advantage of a good nature and gullibility; sacrifice time that would be better spent enjoying their family rather than working late. Creating a new success profile requires absolutely that you seize control of your time.

Above all, you must stop wasting time.

One way, remember, is to ask a simple question periodically throughout the day: "It this the most important thing I should be doing right now?" Don't worry about coming up with an answer. As soon as you ask the question, your inner voice will respond. Listen to what it says!

Spend a few minutes every day reviewing your priorities.

Make a list of everything you want to get done each day, then rank the items in their order of importance. Your order of attack will change throughout the day as new situations come up, but setting up your priorities at the beginning of each day will be a helpful guide.

Learn to make decisions effectively without consuming an inordinate amount of time.

For most people, decision making is the most difficult of tasks. Failure to make decisions can consume endless time and cause endless unnecessary anxiety. Actually, decision making is a simple process. All you need is a systematic approach. Here is an excellent method that almost always leads to the best choice.

Let's assume you face a complex decision involving five possible choices. The first step is to consider each choice carefully to determine the worst that can happen as a result. Make a note of the disaster potential for each option. If any choice could result in a completely unacceptable outcome, that option can probably be ruled out right away. Now go on and review each option again to determine the best that can happen from each. Again, make notes. The best choice will usually be the one where the potential negative outcome is the least and the positive outcome the greatest, the middle course.

Set aside some time each day to enjoy a quiet period alone.

You may want to take a walk, read, or just daydream. Collecting your thoughts in this way helps you keep perspective on yourself and what you are doing. Time alone is a mortar that holds the other parts of your new success profile together. You don't need a long time—fifteen or twenty minutes will do—but this period is very important. Do enjoy it!

Cultivate energy by getting things done.

Again this may seem obvious, but too many people ignore this simple principle. They take on big tasks and let them drag on day after day until they get no sense of accomplishment. They get so bored that they give up or finish halfheartedly. The best way to tackle your day is to break it up into discrete tasks—making phone calls, answering mail, writing letters or reports, making decisions. If you tackle each task as an accomplishment of itself and complete it before going on to anything else, you'll enjoy a burst of energy each time you finish a step. Energy rises with accomplishments. It sags with delay. Create your day so you can bask in many small accomplishments and draw on a continuous flow of energy.

Find time to cultivate friendships.

Many people make the mistake of assuming such a fiercely competitive attitude that they fail to make close friends. Some people don't make friends because they regard friendship at work as a waste of time. Others hold themselves at a distance because they view the workplace as a battleground and themselves as combatants.

Failure to make friends at work is a big mistake for two reasons. First, you're passing up an important opportunity to add a bit more fun to your life. Let's face it, friendship is fun, so why not enjoy it? Second, if you need a payoff beyond simple enjoyment, you might remember that almost no one makes it to the top without allies. With the growing complexity of modern life, teamwork is a basic building block of success, and the importance of teamwork is only likely to

increase in the future. Friends can help you tackle a job that is too big to manage alone, and when the job is done well, there is usually more than enough credit to go around.

Take the time to enrich your intellectual and spiritual sensibilities.

One of the best ways to develop your appreciation of your life is to rekindle your interests in literature, poetry, philosophy, history, or any of the humanities that may once have interested you. The less reason to find to visit a library, museum, art gallery, concert hall, theater, or park, the less human you become in the most important sense. Your life narrows and your satisfactions diminish. Without your even being aware of it, your ability to enjoy and to contribute to the world shrinks measurably day after day.

Let yourself dream.

Many people believe that daydreams are destructive flights from reality. Of course, that's what they can become if they're a substitute for effective performance. They are also essential components of a dynamic success profile. Many successful people readily admit that they daydream. They've discovered that dreams are a primary inspiration toward their goals. You can use daydreams in the same powerful way. The key is to link your fantasies to your personal goals.

Many people do this naturally during sex. Fantasies are often the initial stimulus toward erotic activity. Substantial evidence suggests that sexual satisfaction is directly proportional to the ability to enjoy fantasy and put dreams into practice. So too is the world of work. Your ability to succeed is in large measure proportional to your ability to envision the life you wish to attain, and your capacity to put your fantasy into practice.

The message: Set aside a few minutes each day for your dreams—constructive, creative, dynamic fantasy. Dream about what you want to accomplish, conjure up a vision of the rewards—money, fame, power, love, service or anything you choose. The more you enjoy your visions, the more energy you bring back to your work. Your imagination is a principal source of personal power. Use it wisely, and enjoy.

Finally, it's wise to remember that success is just another game and only a fool takes any game too seriously.

If there is one truth about living, it may be the old saying: "You win some and you lose some." No matter who you are—how talented, privileged, blessed—you can never win all the time. That being the case, your sense of humor is an invaluable asset. The ultimate sign of success may be the ability to laugh; to enjoy the simple pleasure of daily living; to appreciate the beauty of a flower or a sunset even at those times when things aren't working out as planned. Remember Murphy's law: "Whenever something can go wrong, it will." This is funny because it's so true. Things are bound to go wrong sometimes! With perseverance, determination, and desire, they are equally bound to go right once again. The key is to never give up, laugh often, and get as much enjoyment as you can!

To Apply This Reading to Yourself

1. *Define success in your own terms and compare your definition with that given by Bloomfield and Kory.*
2. *What obstacles do you face or have you faced in transforming your success profile? What can you do or have you done about these obstacles?*
3. *Review the techniques presented by Bloomfield and Kory for creating an integrated success profile and discuss five, indicating how each is or could be particularly helpful for you.*
4. *Compose your own "to-apply-this-reading-to-yourself" item and answer it.*